INTRODUCTION

TO THE

BOOK OF ISAIAH

INTRODUCTION

TO THE

BOOK OF ISAIAH

WITH AN APPENDIX CONTAINING THE UNDOUBTED
PORTIONS OF THE TWO CHIEF PROPHETIC
WRITERS IN A TRANSLATION

BY

THE REV. T. K. CHEYNE, M.A., D.D.

ORIEL PROFESSOR OF THE INTERPRETATION OF HOLY SCRIPTURE AT OXFORD,
AND FORMERLY FELLOW OF BALLIOL COLLEGE;
CANON OF ROCHESTER

Wipf & Stock
PUBLISHERS
Eugene, Oregon

Wipf and Stock Publishers
199 W 8th Ave, Suite 3
Eugene, OR 97401

Introduction to the Book of Isaiah
With an appendix containing the undoubted portions
of the two chief prophetic writers in a translation
By Cheyne, T. K.
ISBN: 1-59244-909-3
Publication date 5/2/2005
Previously published by Adam and Charles Black, 1895

ERRATA

Page 16, lines 2 and 3 from bottom, transpose 751 and 741.
Page 73, line 17 from bottom, for "(see on lvi. 3)," read "(see on p. 312)."
Page 79, line 13 from top, for "x. 24-27" read "xiv. 24-27."
Page 100, line 11 from bottom, for "a honorific," read "an honorific."
Page 149, line 11 from top, for "(see p. 65)," read "(see p. 61)."
Page 166, line 4 from bottom, for "v. 20," read "v. 21."

Page 175, note, line 6 from bottom, for " ܙܒ݂ " read " ܒ݂ܙ ."
,, last line, for "v. 213," read "p. 213."
Page 183, line 4 from bottom, for "vv. 14-32," read "vv. 14-22."
Page 193, line 3 from bottom, for " עֲמֵשֶׂה " read " מְעֻשֶׂה ."
Page 198, note, line 2 from bottom, for "(see p. 316)," read "(see pp. 300, 316)."

TO THE READER

ONE may happily assume a general interest in the varied and impressive utterances of the Book of Isaiah, and trust that a fresh attempt to grapple with the problems which they present may be cordially welcomed. Critical workers at any rate will require no excuse for such a re-examination. To many of them the inadequacy of the old point of view and of the traditional methods has long been apparent, and a regeneration of the study of Isaiah an object of keen desire. Already several fragmentary contributions have been made to an expanded criticism, and in 1892 a complete and comprehensive work on the Book of Isaiah from an advanced point of view saw the light—I refer of course to the commentary of Bernhard Duhm. This boldly conceived work cannot fail to instruct even those who are farthest from its conclusions, and will not soon be forgotten. Its appearance could not however absolve me from the obligation of completing the present work. What I have to offer has features almost or altogether peculiar to itself, and in particular is predominantly as analytical as Duhm's able commentary is synthetical. It is moreover the natural development of the imperfect but original criticism which underlies my *Prophecies of Isaiah*, and my article on "Isaiah" in the *Encyclopædia Britannica* (1881). And if its very tardy appearance needs some excuse, this will, I hope, be amply supplied by the circumstances of its composition. A year divided between academical duties at Oxford and ecclesiastical functions at

Rochester may no doubt have moral compensations, but is not happily planned either for teaching or for study, and it is an additional heavy drawback to have my hours of work limited by an infirmity of sight during the darker months. I can only trust that the latter disadvantage may not have resulted in too many minute slips through imperfect revision, and that the former may even propitiate some readers towards me. Pastors and preachers at any rate may perhaps read with less suspicion what might strike them here and there as needlessly unsettling, had it not been partly composed amidst the preoccupations of a difficult and responsible preaching office.

Here I might well lay down my pen. Critical scholars both in England and abroad, for whom in the first place I write, need no further introduction. Out of regard, however, to preachers, whose perplexities I understand, and who form a large proportion of Bible students, I may be allowed to add some straightforward remarks. It appears to me, then, that the attitudes of the critic and the preacher, though different, are not antagonistic, and that, if in Germany the critic, in his aloofness from the people, has sometimes been deficient in religious sympathy, our English preachers and teachers, who are expected to "bring forth out of their store things new and old," have not yet shown nearly sufficient willingness to learn from the critics. The effect of this upon our Biblical critics too often is that they give way to misplaced hesitancy. They are conscious that practical church workers are as a rule sceptical of new ideas, and they are therefore tempted to aim at a type of criticism which, though unavoidably new and so far suspicious, shall yet be different in many respects from that which is practised elsewhere. The loss to truth must be great, and the gain to the Church small and transient. How very much better it would be if we critics could in the first place take up a more courageous attitude towards ecclesiastical prejudice, by setting forth in plain terms a theory of the Bible which would correspond equally to critically ascertained facts, and to the needs of true edification, and in the next could practise ourselves oftener in the art of devout but honest Biblical preaching! By taking the first course, we should, without painful controversy, neutralise some of the injurious results of that wrong doctrine of the Bible which colours so much popular preaching, and more than anything else hinders the spread of critical and historical truth, and by taking the second, we should disarm the objections of those liberal-minded preachers whose theology is more practical than systematic, by showing that to treat the Bible historically can be made directly conducive to "building up" the congregation, and to purifying and deepening its thoughts respecting God and man. For what after all is the Bible? Certainly it is a channel for spiritual messages from above to spiritually susceptible minds; this all evangelical preachers see clearly enough. But it is also a record both of the development of the higher life among the Israelites through a combination of natural and spiritual causes, and of the gradually expanding thoughts of this gifted people on some of the greatest subjects. And considering that out of the old Israel arose—strange as it seems—He who is the Root of the new Israel, and that out of the religious society of the Jews sprang, in part at least, the religious societies of the Christians, and that some at any rate of the greatest and deepest of our religious thoughts can be studied in their growth in the Old and the New Testament, and have there received in some respects a classic form, why should preachers be impatient of a criticism which does but show the stages of this long development, and make credible what without it might well appear a beautiful but scarcely credible fairy tale?

I shall not be surprised if for the present many of my brother-preachers hesitate to follow me. It has been so long repeated that there are two Isaiahs (a strange caricature of the older critical view), or at any rate that the prophecies of the two greater writers of the Book of Isaiah have come down to us in substantially their original form, without later insertions or additions, that when, not merely in articles, but in a volume, a different view is advocated, ordinary students may not unnaturally shake their heads. Still the path of progress ought to have been made a little easier for them by a pioneer, and I may hope that some preachers will assimilate the main results of these researches. Should this be the case, and should such students with due caution let their congregations share in the benefit, I think that I can say from experience that no injury will arise to true edification. Criticism of the Bible does indeed destroy some views of history and prophecy which were accidentally connected with the higher life of the soul, but it only destroys to build up again better. Like Hagar's angel it opens our eyes to unsuspected "wells of water," and he who allows it to revolutionise his view of the Book of Isaiah will not only find his insight into the divine training of the Jewish people greatly deepened, but feel the true Isaiah of Jerusalem and the true Second Isaiah of Babylon becoming more and not less of prophets to himself—more and not less capable of bringing the self-revealing God nearer to him than before.

I have addressed myself specially to preachers, because to them the precedence in the work of popular enlightenment rightly belongs. Some of the most necessary reforms in Bible teaching have been well explained by Dr. Briggs in a paper on "The Sunday School and Modern Biblical Criticism," in the *North American Review* for January 1894.[1] Could the moderate suggestions of this article be adopted for our higher Bible classes, it would partly remove the too

---

[1] See also "Reform in the Teaching of the Old Testament," an article by the present writer in the *Contemporary Review*, August 1889, which has not yet lost its point.

just reproach that education has made giant strides in all branches except that of Bible teaching. Still it is not only to preachers, but to all progressive Bible students that the critic, who is not merely an academical recluse, looks for help in this great national work. He asks them to seek fresh light for themselves that they may enlighten others. And the renewed welcome which such students have given to Professor Driver's valuable *Introduction* justifies the hope that they may now be hungry for fresh critical food. If that welcome implies that they have to some extent mastered his volume, I may expect that they will be interested in these new researches, and that the necessity of a forward movement in Isaiah-criticism will very soon become plain to them.

It must however be confessed that Dr. Driver's book, though conscientious and learned, and in its arrangement highly practical, gives an insufficient picture both of the methods and of the present state of the higher criticism, and therefore hardly forms the best starting-point for advanced students. For them at any rate a more representative and clear-sighted guide is indispensable. This amounts to saying that in this as in other subjects the successful student needs more than one teacher. German students have, or used to have, the laudable custom of passing from one university to another to gain scientific breadth of view. In England let students of the Old Testament at least claim the privilege of learning from more than one Introduction. Now the greatest work of this sort which at present exists is that of Kuenen.[1] Or rather Kuenen's work (unfinished as it is) stands alone in its modest greatness, for there is no other

[1] Vol. I. part I. of Kuenen's *Onderzoek* has been translated into English (Macmillan, 1886). An authorised German version of the entire work was completed in 1894. Prof. Budde has translated Kuenen's principal essays on critical subjects into German, with a sympathetic preface (1894); this volume has been generously noticed by Prof. G. A. Smith (*Expositor*, August 1894).

which initiates the student half as well into the present state of knowledge and the problems which await solution. Let us by all means combine this book with Dr. Driver's, but not make the merits of the latter an excuse for neglecting the former. I know that Kuenen's work may be objected to as unsound in its theology; but I know also that the futility of this objection to the fairest contemporary criticism has been sufficiently shown both in Germany and in England. It was not belief in the supernatural which Kuenen opposed, but a particular class of theories respecting the supernatural. The real struggle was ultimately about a definition. It may easily be true that Kuenen's theology was constructively weak—that he could not set forth a perfectly sound theory of religious truth. But our students will be their own worst enemies if they reject a non-theological work of a great critic because of his limitations as a theologian. I am aware that Kuenen has also been accused of a tendency to "extreme" critical views. But this charge is even more devoid of plausibility than the former. By temper Kuenen was a conservative, and if he moved on it was only step by step, and under the compulsion of evidence. But when he did move on, he did not refuse to admit the legitimate historical consequences. His caution had the complement of courage. Dante's warning to himself,

> And if I am a timid friend to truth,
> I fear lest I may lose my life with those
> Who will hereafter call this time the olden,

might have been spoken by Kuenen. Have we nothing to learn from him here?

The pen fell from the hand of this brave but cautious worker when he was in the act of revising his criticism of the Psalter. A younger scholar of high attainments and aspirations has been removed from our own ranks when he was hoping to revise his conclusions on the writings of the prophets. Alas that Robertson Smith is not here to test, or assist the author in testing, the criticism of this volume! He would not have done it hastily, for no one knew better than he the respect which is due to all patient and original work. And I am sure that one who was in the van of progress when Hexateuch-criticism first began to be fully discussed in England, would not have been in the rear when the turn of the prophetic literature came. But he would certainly not have been more content with my work than with his own. He would have given not merely acute but fruitful suggestions, clearing up difficulties, and applying the comparative method in new directions. Of his own later works I have made all the use that was possible, and derived from them some confirmation of several not uninteresting results. Nor can I help referring in conclusion to a more recent loss—that of Dillmann. This great philologist's services to the study of Isaiah are not unworthy of a disciple of Ewald, and have been acknowledged elsewhere in this volume. Of those living scholars who are working so usefully in the same field, I have for the most part spoken in connection with Dillmann. It is only Hackmann who has escaped notice in that context, owing to his not having treated of the Second Isaiah. If this scholar's future work does not belie the extraordinary promise of his work on Isaiah's view of the future, we may expect from him much valuable help in the new phase of our study which has opened.

It only remains to be added that the reader will sometimes find it convenient or even necessary to refer to pp. 248-372 of my *Founders of Old Testament Criticism* (1893), and to my two more recent translations of, and commentaries on, the Book of Isaiah, viz. *The Prophecies of Isaiah* (third ed. 1884), and a contribution which will soon appear in Prof. Haupt's new English edition of the Old Testament (David Nutt), and which, as it exhibits the results of my criticism to the eye by the use of different colours in the printing, will enable the reader to judge for himself what this criticism comes to, historically and theologically. To the latter work a revised edition of the Hebrew text, with critical notes, is planned as a necessary supplement. In using both it should be remembered that the object of this "Bible-work" is not to record the average opinion of Old Testament scholars of critical tendencies in 1893-1895, but to give Bible students an approximate idea of the meaning and historical significance of the Old Testament writings, so far as the respective editors and translators have been able to recognise it. Meantime all who can use it will be well advised to procure a somewhat similar but less elaborate work, edited by Prof. Kautzsch of Halle (*Die Heilige Schrift des Alten Testaments*, 1894). At once practical and scientific, this book ought to be the inseparable companion of genuine students. Its spirit, as the closing pages of the learned editor's historical appendix show, may be summed up in the motto which I venture to choose for this work,—

PRO VERITATE ET ECCLESIA.

OXFORD, *October* 1894.

*** Owing to the unavoidable delay in the appearance of the *Isaiah* in Prof. Haupt's Old Testament, it has been thought best to append to the present volume a provisional translation of the supposed genuine parts of I. and II. Isaiah. By comparing this translation with the criticism of these parts in the Introduction the reader will succeed in forming an idea of the true character and importance of the two chief writers of our Book of Isaiah. It may be hoped that they will appear to him to be both simpler and grander from a moral and religious point of view than they were before. (*Dec.* 1894.)

ABBREVIATIONS

J, E, P	The Yahwistic, Elohistic, and Priestly Records in the O.T. (see Driver and Kuenen).
AM	Rawlinson's *Ancient Monarchies*.
BW	Haupt's (forthcoming) *Bible-Work*.
RT	,, Revised Edition of the Hebrew Text by different Contributors.
RP	*Records of the Past*.
DB	*Dictionary of the Bible*.
EB	*Encyclopædia Britannica*.
GA	Meyer, *Geschichte des Alterthums*.
GGA	*Göttingische gelehrte Anzeigen*.
JBL	*Journal of Biblical Literature* (Boston, U.S.A.).
JPT	*Jahrbücher für protestantische Theologie*.
JQR	*Jewish Quarterly Review*.
KIB	*Keilinschriftliche Bibliothek* (ed. Schrader).
Ges.-K (or -Kautzsch)	Gesenius-Kautzsch, *Hebräische Grammatik*.
AT Rel.-gesch.	Smend, *Alttestamentliche Religionsgeschichte*.
St. u. Kr.	*Theologische Studien und Kritiken*.
Rev. ég.	*Revue égyptologique*.
Zt. f. Ass.	*Zeitschrift für Assyriologie*.
Th. Tijd.	*Theologisch Tijdschrift*.
TSBA	*Transactions of the Society of Biblical Archæology*.
PSBA	*Proceedings* ,, ,, ,,
Theol. LZ.	*Theologische Literaturzeitung*.
ZATW	*Zeitschrift für die Alttestamentliche Wissenschaft*.
ZEJ	Hackmann, *Die Zukunftserwartung des Jesaia*.
ZWT	*Zeitschrift für wissenschaftliche Theologie*.
CI	Schrader's *Cuneiform Inscriptions and the Old Testament* (E.T.).
HL	Hebrew Lexicon, by Brown, Driver, and Briggs.
BL	Cheyne, Bampton Lectures on the Psalter.
Founders	,, *Founders of Old Testament Criticism*.
PI	,, *The Prophecies of Isaiah*.
ICA	,, *The Book of Isaiah Chronologically Arranged*.
J. of Phil.	*Journal of Philology*.
Ond.	Kuenen, *Historisch-critisch Onderzoek*.
Prol.	Wellhausen, *Prolegomenes*.
Die Kl. Proph.	,, *Die kleinen Propheten*.
Rel. of Sem.	W. R. Smith, *The Religion of the Semites*.
Untersuch.	Winckler, *Alttestamentliche Untersuchungen*.
Klost.	Klostermann.
Ges.	Gesenius.
Del.	Delitzsch.
Bred.	Bredenkamp.
Luc.	Lucian's recension of the Septuagint.
Corr. text	corrected text.
Einl.	*Einleitung*.

PROLOGUE

I.—GROWTH OF THE BOOK OF ISAIAH ; PRINCIPLES OF ITS EDITORS

§ 1. THE Book of Isaiah in the Hebrew Canon seems originally to have stood after Jeremiah and Ezekiel (*Baba batra*, 14*b*)—a significant fact to which we shall return later (p. 238, note 3). In the Septuagint, however, it stands between the δωδεκαπρόφητον and Jeremiah. These variations of editors arise from the fact mentioned in the same Talmudic treatise that in former times each single book of the prophets and the Hagiographa was written in a separate roll (*Baba batra*, 13*b* ; cf. Luke iv. 17). The Book of Isaiah, however, cannot always have been written in one roll. It has obviously been produced by combining two volumes, one of which (chaps. i.-xxxix.) is claimed by the heading in i. 1, and virtually by the historical or biographical appendix, for Isaiah, while the other is anonymous. The motive for this combination was probably twofold. (*a*) The extant literary records of the prophecies of Isaiah made up too small a work to set by the side of Jeremiah and Ezekiel. Had not the Book of Isaiah been considerably enlarged, its place must have been among the so-called minor prophets, like the Book of Hosea, which (see the Talmudic passage referred to already) was placed among the lesser prophets simply on account of its brevity. Such a lot would not have been consonant with the dignified position in the state which tradition assigned to Isaiah. (*b*) To ensure the preservation of anonymous prophecies, it was deemed wise to insert them in the acknowledged works of famous prophetic writers. There is indeed no direct evidence of this. But the curious statement in the Midrash that two passages of Beeri were patched on to Isaiah,[1] seems like a reminiscence of the editorial practice in question; for of course these passages were only assigned to Beeri by conjecture. At any rate, this is the only theory which will satisfactorily account for the existence of the Book of Malachi.[2] Nor can we otherwise explain the position of chaps. xl.-lxvi. at the end of Isaiah. The importance of the great prophecy of restoration (for so these chapters may in a wide sense be styled) was recognised by selecting the (expanded) works of Isaiah as the repository of this treasure.

§ 2. The date of the combination of I. and II. Isaiah will have to be referred to again at the close of the survey of critical results which will follow presently. Meantime the *terminus a quo* and the *terminus ad quem* can be settled. (*a*) As to the former. It is generally admitted by critics that no part of Chaps. xl.-lxvi. can have been written before 546 B.C. Now this book (we will assume it for the present to be rightly called a book) must have circulated for a long while in a separate form, and cannot have been combined with chaps. i.-xxxix. till the new religious community of Jerusalem had been thoroughly organised (*i.e.* later than 432?), an event which was at any rate an imperfect fulfilment of the prophecies of the Second Isaiah. It is no objection to this that it directly traverses a well-known statement in the Talmud.[3] (*b*) As to the latter. No one denies that the combined Isaiah was known in 180-170 B.C. to Sirach (Ecclus. xlviii. 22-25). It is not absolutely necessary to place its origin at a much earlier date for this reason. In Sirach's day the old conception of a prophet as one who spoke to his own age had so completely passed away that the combined Book of Isaiah would, as soon as published, be

---

[1] See p. 42.

[2] It is equally inconceivable that " Malachi " was really the name of the author of the Book, and that it was written by Zechariah. Our " Malachi " must once have been an anonymous appendix of the Book of Zechariah. See Cornill, *Einl.*, p. 202 f.

[3] *Baba batra*, 15*a*: "Hezekiah and his associates wrote (כתבו) Isa., Prov., the Song of Songs, and Koheleth." כתב here seems to mean "to redact." Driver's objection (*Introd.* p. xxxiv.) seems insufficient, nor is his own view quite fair to the Talmudists.

undoubtingly accepted as Isaiah's work.¹ For what could more enhance the glory of the prophet than to believe that "by a great spirit he saw the last things" (Ecclus. xlviii. 24)?

§ 3. But to say that our present Isaiah arose between 432 (?) and 180 B.C. is to open a wide door to criticism. As Geiger well says, " The Bible [of the Jews] is and at all times was a Word full of fresh life, not a dead book. This everlasting Word belonged not to a particular age ; it could not be dependent [for its meaning] on the time when it was written down, and as little, upon this theory, could it be without what seemed to be new truths and discoveries. Hence every period, every school, every individuality introduced into the Bible its own way of regarding the contents of the Bible. In later times this took place in the field of exegesis, but before that, when the Bible had not yet attained an absolutely fixed form, the same result was reached by manipulation of the text. Thus the Bible became the full expression of the higher life of the people. That which seemed deficient in the text of the holy book the national spirit innocently supplied, and, unconscious of any breach of law, impressed its own stamp on the traditional text." ² The editors of Isaiah, including that editor who brought together the two parts of our Book of Isaiah, must have worked in this spirit. The fragmentary remains of the old prophet Isaiah had to be filled up when they were imperfect, and completed by the insertion of fresh passages, inspired by the "holy spirit" of prophecy, relative either to the great national chastisement of the Exile, or to the hopes and fears, the merits and the demerits, of the post-Exilic church-nation. Nor could we be surprised if the same view of the range of prophecy and of the requirements of edification affected the

---

¹ It is of course just possible that the combination of the two volumes was itself not unconnected with the later view of prophecy (see p. 240). Apart from these considerations, there is a curious modern parallel to Sirach's mistake in a work of Gregory of Tours, who was misled into representing a canon of the Synod of Gangra as a Nicene canon simply through the copyist's habit of subjoining the decrees of Gangra to those of Nicæa (*Historia Francorum*, ix. 33, in *ICA*, Introd. p. xxiv.).

² Geiger, *Urschrift und Uebersetzungen der Bibel* (1857), p. 72 f.

contents not only of the first but also of the second half of the Book named after Isaiah. If the author of "Comfort ye, comfort ye my people" was really a prophet, he must (it would be thought) have had a message for generations yet unborn, and the students of his writings, themselves not perhaps without some faint consciousness of inspiration,[1] must have ventured to make his presumed meaning clearer by insertions—we will not say interpolations.[2] And if there were any extant writings which proceeded from the same school as the prophecy of comfort, it would be strange indeed if an editor such as I have described did not append them to the model prophecy.

§ 4. This is not the place to justify the view of the post-Exilic editors and translators which is here assumed. That task belongs rather to an introduction to the Hebrew text of the Old Testament and the ancient versions. One may admit the danger of mistake in points of detail, but the body of evidence is too large to be affected by such mishaps. Indeed, the view itself is professedly admitted with more or less qualification by most critics, and progress in the criticism of Isaiah largely depends on a firmer and more consistent use of it. There is nothing in this latter assertion which need startle the reader. Consistency does not require us to fly in the face of tradition, and assign a pseudepigraphic origin to the Book of Isaiah. A tradition confirmed by portions of Isaiah itself declares the Book to contain records of prophecies of Isaiah, nor is it reasonable to suppose that the scholars of the second temple could throw themselves back so perfectly into the times of Isaiah and Hezekiah as to invent so-called prophecies which, as even M. Vernes admits, can both deeply move and delight us, and that "after the doctors of the fourth century (about)

[1] Since the divine spirit dwelt in the community (Hag. ii. 4, Isa. lxiii. 11), it followed that both those who ruled or taught the community, and those who on its behalf edited the records of revelation, were themselves inspired. Cf. *Job and Solomon*, pp. 43, 118; *BL*, pp. 272, 284; *PI*, ii. 228 f.

[2] "Some of the acts which were virtues in Job's days have assumed a different aspect in ours," remarks Mr. Dillon with reference to the supposed "insertions" in the poem of Job (*Contemp. Review*, July 1893).

had closed the Book of Isaiah (chaps. i.-xxxix.), other writers, of the third century apparently, reopened it to insert a new series of [equally post-Exilic and fictitious] oracles."[1] But if we admit that the Book of Isaiah came into existence after the Exile, and that the object of the editors was not critical accuracy but edification, and that they held a view of prophecy absolutely different from that of Isaiah himself, we can no longer assume that a prophecy is Isaianic unless it contains something flagrantly opposed to this assumption (such as the mention of Cyrus or an Aramaic loan-word), but have simply to consider to what period the circumstances presupposed, the beliefs and ideas, and the literary phenomena (including rhythm) most naturally assign it. And this can be done much better now than at any previous time owing to our fuller knowledge of the history of Old Testament literature and of Israelitish religion. The attempt has been made in this volume; and even if it be not always successful, yet the facts at least have been presented, and due care has been taken to indicate the different degrees of probability belonging to the conclusions.

§ 5. In thus recognising the risk of failure, I express the uncertainty which every true critic must feel who ventures on these seldom trodden paths. At the same time, I am very confident that, granting my point of view, and the reality of the results of the "higher criticism" so well summed up by Kuenen, the principal conclusions of the present volume are secure. The threefold argument mentioned above is in most cases exceedingly strong, and though the phraseological section of it is not on the whole so decisive as in Hexateuch criticism, it is evidently destined to count much more than formerly in Isaianic discussions. Let me now sum up the critical results which have here, rightly or wrongly, been reached, and first with reference to chaps. i.-xxxix.

---

[1] M. Vernes, *Précis de l'histoire juive* (1889), p. 805 f.; similarly Havet and Loeb. The theory is somewhat analogous to that of Mr. E. Johnson's *Antiqua Mater* and *The Rise of Christendom;* only it lacks the learned ingenuity of that perverse scholar. See further Kuenen, *Abhandl.* (ed. Budde), p. 427; Lagarde, *GGA,* 1891, p. 505 f.; König, *Einl.*, p. 299 f.

II.—SYNTHESIS OF CRITICAL RESULTS IN I. ISAIAH

§ 1. The plan of the prophecies in I. Isaiah has caused much perplexity to traditionalistic scholars. Some (e.g. Vitringa) have sought to show that the discourses were grouped according to the affinity of their contents—a theory which neglects the most evident signs of a regard to chronology. Others, like Hengstenburg, have advocated the chronological principle, at any rate for the three main groups taken as wholes, chaps. i.-vi. representing the prophet's discourses under Uzziah and Jotham, chaps. vii. 1-x. 4 his ministry under Ahaz, and chaps. x. 5-xxxv. 10 his warnings and encouragements at the time of Sennacherib's invasion, to which last group chaps. xxxvi.-xxxix. form a historical commentary.[1] This was bold, considering the great varieties of style and ideas in the prophecies, but an early Assyriologist[2] went even further, and tried to show that chaps. i.-xxxix. are a continuous record of the years from 738 to 681 B.C. from the prophetic point of view. It is clear, however, that as I. Isaiah now stands, no single principle of arrangement will account for the phenomena. The criticism of I. Isaiah, like that of the Psalter, shows that several minor collections underlie the existing book, and the present form of the larger sections to which the minor collections have contributed requires the hypothesis of a long-continued editorial activity.[3]

§ 2. Accepting this theory, which will fully justify itself when applied to the facts, what are the most obvious divisions of I. Isaiah? Gesenius long ago gave the right answer.[4] The first volume of Isaiah falls naturally into three books,

---

[1] *Christology of the O. T.*, ii. 2, 3.

[2] The late George Smith, *TSBA*, ii. 328 f.

[3] For earlier studies on the composition of I. and II. Isaiah, see Ewald's *Prophets*, vol. i. ; Cheyne, *PI*,³ ii. 178-191, *EB*, xiii. (1881), art. "Isaiah," *JQR*, July and October 1891, July 1892 ; Cornill, *ZATW*, 1884, pp. 83-105 ; Giesebrecht, *Beiträge zur Jesaiakritik* (1890), pp. 84-103 (on "The genuine Book of Isaiah"); Kuenen's *Onderzoek* or *Introduction;* Dillmann's and Duhm's commentaries ; Hackmann, *ZEJ*, pp. 7-52. For the lucidity and completeness of his synthesis, the palm must certainly be given to Duhm.

[4] *Jesaia* (1821), i. 19-22.

viz. (A) chaps. i.-xii., (B) chaps. xiii.-xxiii., and (C) chaps. xxiv.-xxxv. To these, chaps. xxxvi.-xxxix. form a late appendix, analogous in a high degree to Jer. lii.[1] The reason of this threefold division will appear presently. Turning first to A, we cannot fail to observe the isolation of the first chapter. This work appears to be of composite origin, and it is not certain that *vv.* 2-4 come from the hand of Isaiah. They were not improbably added by the earliest editor to adapt the following summary of prophecies (*vv.* 2-26) to the purpose of a preface to chaps. ii.-xxxiii. (or xxxv.). The summary itself represents discourses delivered during Sennacherib's invasion. Verses 29-31 are possibly or probably part of the close of a separate prophecy of an earlier date, while *vv.* 27-28 are certainly the insertion of a post-Exilic editor. The heading in i. 1 comes of course from the editor of I. Isaiah,[2] whereas that in ii. 1 must have been intended originally for the little group formed by chaps. ii.-iv., though the editor of chaps. ii.-xii. would naturally give it an expanded reference to the whole of that group. Not improbably ii. 2-4 (= Mic. iv. 1-3), together with Mic. iv. 4, once stood after i. 29-31. Post-Exilic editors loved to mitigate threatening by promise. This evidently appeared necessary that the vitality of the prophecies might be maintained. Beyond reasonable doubt the fine prophecy in ii. 2-4 is post-Exilic; *v.* 5 is a linking verse, added when the prophecy was placed where it now stands. ii. 6-22 is probably made up of two independent fragments, (*a*) *vv.* 6-10 and 18-21, and (*b*) *vv.* 11-17, both of which are thoroughly Isaianic, and very early. iii. 1-15 is highly composite; the Isaianic fragments cannot be brought below 735 (accession of Ahaz?). iii. 16-iv. 1

---

[1] Both passages, except the Miktam of Hezekiah in Isaiah, come from Kings. That in Isaiah, however, relates to the life of Isaiah, and professes to contain prophecies by him; that in Jeremiah is purely annalistic. Cornill may, however, be right in conjecturing that Jer. lii. has been substituted for an account of the tragic end of Jeremiah, which originally followed chap. xliv. (= li. in Sept.). In choosing the passage to be substituted, the editor may have been guided by the precedent of Isa. xxxvi.-xxxix. (Cornill, *ZATW*, iv. 105-107; cf. *Einl.*, p. 157).

[2] Note that none of the editors of Isaiah are responsible for the title ישעיה, which stands at the head of the Book in the Hebrew Bible; they always prefer the form וישעיהו.

is mostly late; Isaiah's position has an affinity to his work in the preceding section. iv. 2-6 is undoubtedly post-Exilic. It became traditional to provide the old prophecies with Messianic conclusions.

§ 3. v. 1-7 and 8-24 (v. 25 is editorial) from two contemporary prophecies (735?), and ix. 7-20 with x. 1-4 and v. 26-30 most probably once formed a connected prophecy (735?), which, with the two preceding ones, made up the second prophetic collection.

§ 4. Chap. vi., which is partly biographical, partly prophetic, serves as the prologue to the following group of prophecies. We cannot say that vii. 1-ix. 6 is altogether Isaianic. Isaiah's portion belongs to the early part of the reign of Ahaz, and is considerable; but the editor has had much to do in filling up an imperfect text, and the striking prophecy of the ideal king in ix. 1-6 is not Isaianic, and is even probably post-Exilic.

§ 5. x. 5-xii. 6, to which ix. 7-x. 4 was prefixed for certain special reasons (p. 47) by a later editor, is a carefully composed work of diverse origin. The Isaianic elements, which are confined to portions of chap x., appear to belong partly to 711, partly to 722. The inserted passages give the Isaianic prophecy an eschatological colouring, agreeable to post-Exilic times. Chaps. xi. and xii. contain a series of appendices. Of these the latest is certainly chap. xii. The poverty of the psalm-like passages in this section points to a time when all spontaneity in such writing had died away. xi. 1-8 is doubtless much earlier, but must, I fear, share the fate of ix. 1-6, *i.e.* be recognised as non-Isaianic.

§ 6. We now come to B. This book consists of ten משׂאות, or oracles, mostly on the neighbouring peoples, each provided with a heading which contains the word משׂא (*massā*). It is interspersed with four short passages which have no titles, viz. (*a*) an utterance on Assyria (xiv. 24-27), which is probably the misplaced conclusion of the Isaianic prophecy on the plan of Assyria in x. 5-15; (*b*) a prophecy of disaster for the Assyrians (xvii. 12-14); (*c*) a prophecy on Assyria, professedly addressed to the Ethiopians, with a late appendix (chap. xviii.); and (*d*) a saying on Egypt and Ethiopia, with a contemporary historical proem (chap. xx.). All these are presumably late insertions from another source. Of the משאות it is only the first which directly claims an Isaianic origin. The words in which this assertion is made read very oddly, and were obviously meant to claim the whole collection for Isaiah. Did the original collector mean to do this? Or were not the words added when the collection was incorporated into I. Isaiah? The first collector may merely have meant to put together an anthology of prophecies on other nations, without paying attention to the question of authorship. The four untitled passages, which are doubtless Isaianic, look as if they had been deliberately inserted to make the Isaianic origin of the collection more plausible.[1] The original collector probably drew from various literary sources. Thus four passages seem to have come from a collection of songs of triumph and lamentation, connected together verbally by catch-words, viz. xiv. 4b-21 (note שׂמח, v. 8 ; שבר שבט, v. 5 ; מכה, v. 6 ; הילל? v. 12),[2] xiv. 28-32 (cf. אל־תשמחי כי נשבר שבט מכך, v. 29 ; הליל, זעק, v. 31), xv. 1-xvi. 11 mostly (note the singular prominence of the roots ילל and זעק), and chaps. xxiii., already perhaps brought into its present form (note היליל, vv. 1, 14). Chap. xx. may come from an early biography of Isaiah. Chap. xxi. 1-10, 11-12, and 13-14 apparently come from a collection of short oracles on foreign nations.[3] These three passages too are connected by catch-words, and agree in the enigmatical character of their headings. The former only need detain us here. In xxi. 11 we have the prophet represented as a night-watchman as in v. 8, while the two little oracles in vv. 11-12 and 13-14 are linked by the uncommon root אתה. Chaps. xvii. and xxii. may have existed as independent compositions, or they may have come either from the same or from different anthologies. The one gives a picture in

---

[1] Cf. Hackmann, *ZEJ*, p. 13.
[2] If the points in הֵילֵל represent the mind of the collector. Aquila and Pesh. both take the word for the imperative Hifil (cf. Zech. xi. 2).
[3] Duhm, on account of the enigmatical titles, would also include chap. xxii. and even xxx. 6, 7. I am not, however, convinced. More editors than one could employ enigmatical titles. All that it is safe to say is that chap. xxii. was placed where it now stands because in its title it bore an external resemblance to the oracles in chap. xxi. The supposed title of xxx. 6, 7 does not count (see p. 196, and cf. *RT*).

c

the most sombre tints of the future of northern, the other of southern Israel.

§ 7. The date of the first editor cannot be a very early one. If we are right in assigning to him the combination of the ode in chap. xiv. with the prophecy in chap. xiii. (as well as xiv. 22, 23) he must apparently be placed after 432 on account of his peculiar use of גֵּר (see pp. 75, 312), which accords with the usage of P. The second editor, who inserted the four untitled and plainly Isaianic passages, may be responsible for the supplementary passages in xvi. 4*b*, 5, 12-14 (partly Isaianic?), xvii. 7, 8, xxi. 16, 17 (also possibly Isaianic), and perhaps also for xix. 16-25, in which case his date may be about 275 (the earliest tenable date for the epilogue of the *massā* on Egypt; note the mention of Jewish and Samaritan villages in the district of Arsinoe in the Flinders Petrie papyri [1]). We may observe that whoever inserted chap. xxii. was guilty of a happy inconsistency, for *vv.* 15-18 (25) are really an independent prophecy and originally had their own heading (p. 137). The probable dates of the several passages in this book (putting aside editorial additions) are as follows :—

	B.C.		B.C.
xiii. 2-22 } xiv. 4*b*-21 }	close of Exile.	xx. . . . . xxi. 1-10 .	711 close of Exile.
xv. 1-xvi. 11 (mostly) .	772 ? ?	„ 11-12 }	
xvii. 1-6, 9-11 .	before 734	„ 13-17 }	. . 589 ?
xvii. 12-14 . . .	723 ?	xxii. 1-14 . .	. 701
xviii. 1-6 . . .	702	„ 15-18 . .	704-701
xix. 1-15 . .	528-485	xxiii. (basis) .	. 725 ? ?

§ 8. Passing on to C, we notice at once that the only connection between chaps. xxiv.-xxvii. and chaps. xxviii.-xxxiii. is the eschatological colouring which they have in common; there is no sign of any attempt to link them externally together. But there is no reasonable doubt that they were combined by the same editor who combined A and B, on the same principle which directed the original arrangement of Jeremiah (see Sept.) and Ezekiel, viz. that

---

[1] Pointed out by Wilamowicz and Wellhausen (Wellh., *Isr. u. jüd. Gesch.*, 1894, p. 194).

prophecies referring mainly to the present circumstances of Jerusalem should open, and prophecies referring chiefly to the latter days should conclude the collection, while the centre of the book was occupied by prophecies on foreign nations. The earliest documents are obviously contained in the second of the two combined books. Chaps. xxiv.-xxvii. were prefixed, not only to preserve them, but to indicate that the main interest of the following prophecies was eschatological. The invasion of Sennacherib was in fact to be regarded as typical of the last great attempt to extinguish the people of Yahwè. Chaps. xxxiv.-xxxv. were added to emphasise the same view. And now as to higher critical questions. It used to be thought that both the two groups of prophecies which when combined constitute C possessed unity of date and authorship. This however is not borne out by a minute analysis.

§ 9. These are the component parts of C, with their probable dates—

			B.C.
(a) 1. xxiv.; xxv. 6-8; xxvi. 20, 21; xxvii. 1, 12, 13		An Apocalypse of the latter days.	334 ?
2. xxvii. 7-11 (a fragment)	.	The Low Estate of Jerusalem; its Cause and Remedy.	332 ?
3. xxvi. 1-19	. . .	A Liturgical Meditation	,,
4. xxv. 1-5*a*	. . .	A Song of Thanksgiving	,,
5. xxv. 9-11	. . .	Another Song . .	,,
6. xxvii. 2-5	. . .	A Third Song . .	,,

(b) 1. xxviii.	1- 6 (a fragment).	The Fall of Samaria . .	Before 722 (edited late).
2.	7-22.	Warnings to Jerusalem, suggested by the foregoing passage.	703
3.	23-29.	A Proverbial Poem . .	Exilic or Post-Exilic
4. xxix.	1- 8.	The Fate of Arial . . .	703 (edited late).
5.	9-14.	The Punishment of Unbelief and Formalism.	703
6.	15 (a fragment).	The Egyptian Alliance . .	703

ISAIAH

				B.C.
7.	xxix.	16-24.	The Regeneration of Israel against Doubters	Post-Exilic.
8.	xxx.	1- 7 (fragments).	The Egyptian Alliance . .	703
9.		8-17.	The Impending Ruin of Judah	703
10.		18-26.	The Happy Consequences of Judah's Regeneration	Post-Exilic.
11.		27-33.	Yahwè's Combat with Assyria	Post-Exilic?
12.	xxxi.		The Egyptian Alliance . .	702 (edited late).
13.	xxxii.	1-8c.	The Messianic Age (App. I.) .	Post-Exilic.
14.		9-14.	Warning to the Ladies of Jerusalem (App. II.).	,,
15.		15-20.	Judah's Regeneration (App. III.)	,,
16.	xxxiii.		The Prayer of the Oppressed Church-nation.	,,
17.	xxxiv.-xxxv.		Eschatological Appendix .	450-430??

§ 10. The addition of chaps. xxxiv.-xxxv. serves the same purpose as the prefixing of chaps. xxiv.-xxvii.; *i.e.* it determines the main reference of chaps. xxviii.-xxxiii. for post-Exilic readers. A still later editor, however, whose date very probably comes into the early Greek period (to allow time for the different stages of growth which are traceable in these chapters), and who was interested in the historical background of chaps. xxviii.-xxxiii., appended some narratives, derived ultimately from prophetic biographies (p. 213), which also served as an epilogue to the whole first volume of Isaiah. The collected and expanded [1] works of Isaiah appear to have already acquired a special sanctity, at least if we may follow the Massoretic text of xxxiv. 16, דִּרְשׁוּ מֵעַל־סֵפֶר יהוה. The "book of Yahwè" spoken of seems to be, not necessarily chaps. i.-xxxv., but at any rate chaps. xxxiv.-xxxv., and the meaning of the passage is that "if you took this prophetic roll with you to Edom, you would find that the reference to wild beasts was strictly accurate." [2]

---
[1] I use this word as synonymous with "überarbeitet."
[2] *JQR*, Jan. 1892, p. 332. There are two ways of avoiding this conclusion. One is to emend the text by the help of Sept. (so Wellhausen in Bleek's *Einl.*[4], p. 554, after Knobel and Kuenen); for the objections to this see *RT*. The other is to omit *v.* 16*a* (so *JQR, l.c.*) or *vv.* 16, 17 (so König, *Einl.*, p. 439) as a later insertion. But rhythmical considerations are unfavourable to such a mutilation of the poem.

How exactly this view of prophecy agrees with that of later Judaism! The conjecture seems permissible that the date given above for these two chapters is too early, and that they are products of the Greek period. And in any case the composite work, chaps. xxiv.-xxvii., cannot well be placed before the time of Alexander the Great (pp. 157-159). The final redaction of I. Isaiah must however be placed still later, and, failing any reason to the contrary, may be assigned, like xix. 16-25, to the second half of the third century (say 250-220 B.C.). I need hardly say that this is merely put forward as a reasonable date for an event of which we have no traditional notice. It agrees with the generally accepted view of the date of the (provisional) close of the prophetic canon. To the much later date which Duhm has given (about 150-80 B.C.), I have no longer a theoretic objection. But I see no sufficient reason to make any part of I. Isaiah post-Maccabæan.

We cannot leave this part of our subject without asking, How far may Isaiah himself be regarded as an author? An author in the same sense as II. Isaiah, who was a chamber-prophet and addressed an imagined audience, he certainly was not. Nor can he even have been as much of a literary artist as Ewald supposes. With his intensely dark view of the future of Judah and Israel we cannot imagine him sitting down habitually to give literary finish and arrangement to the free though often rhythmical words in which his prophetic consciousness had found expression. Not even with a more palatable prophetic message could Isaiah have done this, for "his soul (like Milton's) was like a star and dwelt apart." It is only when it was specially important to establish the fact of a prediction that we can imagine him writing down and to some extent developing his original utterance (see xxx. 8-10), probably more for the sake of his disciples than for the mass of the people. For the latter, who were obstinately insensible, and already doomed, it was enough to engrave a few words in large enigmatical characters on a public tablet (viii. 1, 2), but for his disciples, whom he sought to mould, and for whom a future was reserved, he would not refuse to write or dictate in orderly sequence the words which could not "return void." Sometimes this record might extend to some length; the "testimony" and the "direction" spoken of in viii. 16, and the "book" (סֵפֶר) in xxx. 8,[1] not improbably contained the original portions of vii. 1-viii. 18·and xxviii. 1-xxx. 17 respectively. At other times, as in the case of the oracles in chaps. vi., xx., and xiv. 28-32 (if this may be added), the written record might be very short. It is worth noticing that all the passages referred to,[2] except xxviii. 1-xxx. 17, have some historical preface, and it is a reasonable conjecture that passages like chaps. vi., vii. 2, etc., and chap. xx. are fragments of an independent work on the prophetic ministry of Isaiah. Our theory would however be incomplete if we did not also suppose that the disciples themselves took notes of some of Isaiah's prophecies. These faithful custodians (viii. 16) of the greater oracles of Isaiah would hardly be satisfied without some records of even the less important because less prominently predictive discourses, and we may justly assume that they were among the most cultivated residents of the capital of Judah.

III.—SYNTHESIS OF CRITICAL RESULTS IN II. ISAIAH.

§ 1. We now come to the second volume of Isaiah, viz. chaps. xl.-lxvi. This work has not, as was formerly supposed, either unity of authorship or unity of historic background. The first part (chaps. xl.-lv.) does indeed form a literary whole, and belongs probably in the main to one author—the so-called Second Isaiah, a gifted religious teacher, who wrote (1) a cycle of poems on the "Servant of Yahwè" (see pp. 304-310), and (2) the great Prophecy of Restoration. With the latter work he more or less successfully interwove his earlier and in some respects finer composition. The date of the composition thus produced cannot be placed before 546-539 B.C. It is a reflex of the hopes and fears of the

---

[1] In viii. 16 I render, with Duhm, "(I will) bind up the testimony, (I will) seal the direction in (or among) my disciples." In xxx. 8, with the same scholar, I omit אתם על־לי, an insertion suggested by the previous insertion at the end of v. 7 (see p. 196, and cf. *RT*).

[2] On the heading in xiv. 28, see p. 80.

Jewish exiles in Babylon on the news of the successes of Cyrus.

§ 2. The second part (chaps. lvi.-lxvi.) is entirely devoid of unity. It consists of about ten compositions, which, except lxiii. 7-lxiv. 11, all belong to the time of Nehemiah, the religious phenomena of which they accurately reflect. Duhm thinks that they are all by one author whom he calls Trito-Isaiah. Many phenomena, however, seem opposed to this view. But so much at least is correct that all the compositions, except perhaps lvi. 8-lvii. 11a, proceed from the same school (hence their phraseological resemblances), and several of them may possibly come from the same writer. The different writers have none of them any original power. Most of them are considerably influenced by II. Isaiah, whose phraseology and rhythm they seek in a mechanical way to copy. The difference between their model and themselves is however immense. Even in an attempted supplement to the prophecy of restoration (chaps. lx.-lxii.) the writer is totally unable to rise above the ground for long together, and his conception of the "Servant of Yahwè" is widely different from that in II. Isaiah. Still more incapable is the author of lvi. 1-8, who sinks after the very first verse. As to chap. lxiii. 7-lxiv. 11, we are forced to suppose that a still later period than Nehemiah's is here represented: most probably we have before us a fresh movement of the oppression and persecution of the Jews under Artaxerxes Ochus (pp. 156, 358 f.). That there is an affinity between this work and lix. 15b-20 need not be disputed. But the former has also a close resemblance to chap. xxvi., which, as we shall see, partly describes the thoughts and feelings of the Jews in the terrible year 347 B.C. The truth is, that the same causes of despondency and depression went on operating from the time of Nehemiah to the fall of the Persian empire. There must therefore be a family likeness between the productions of different sections of that period, though the deepest woe is expressed by the writers contemporary with the insane cruelties of Artaxerxes Ochus.

§ 3. In giving this date to lxiii. 7-lxiv. 11 we imply that the writings which make up chaps. lvi.-lxvi. do not altogether stand in the order of their composition, and were not all necessarily intended to follow chaps. xl.-lv. It would seem that chaps. lx.-lxii. were written as a supplement to chaps. xl.-lv.; the original order was probably lxi., lxii., lx.[1] The object of the writer was presumably to adapt the Prophecy of the Servant and of Israel's restoration to his own times. At any rate, no other motive can be imagined for the passages inserted in chaps. xl.-lv. (see pp. 298-304) than a consciousness in the writers of a want of correspondence between the exhortations of that work and the circumstances of their own times. The other compositions appear to have been appended to II. Isaiah later, and, last of all, lxiii. 7-lxiv. 11 was added at a time when valued documents were in special danger from barbarous foes.

§ 4. It was therefore a mistake when Friedrich Rückert, in 1831, suggested a division of chaps. xl.-lxvi. into three parts, each consisting of nine chapters, while the two former were marked by a refrain (xlviii. 22, lvii. 21). This view has met with considerable acceptance, and several scholars have attempted on this basis to exhibit a unity, not only of form, but of subject and of time. Even the imperfect criticism of Ewald however detected the impossibility of this view, though this keen critic did not recognise that one of Rückert's refrain-passages is really a late insertion made by the latest editor simply with a view to support a factitious threefold division. It is this editor who is responsible, not only for this and for most of the other inserted passages in chaps. xl.-lv., but for the combination of the expanded Prophecy of Restoration with imitative compositions of the times of Nehemiah and of Ochus. He seems to have conceived the idea of producing one fairly large *megilla*, which could also be divided into three parts, each occupying a small *megilla*. He therefore removed the supplement (chaps. lxi., lxii., lx.) from its original position after chap. lv., and placed it between the two visions of deliverance (lix. 15*b*-20 and chap. lxiii.), at the same time (perhaps) attaching to the first of the visions a statement of the covenant between Yahwè and Israel (lix. 21) which embodies his interpretation

---

[1] Observe that chap. lxii. is mainly concerned with personified Zion or Jerusalem, and closes with a direct address to her (*v.* 12*b*); also that lxii. 1*b* prepares the way for lx. 1, and lxii. 2 for lx. 3.

of xlii. 1 and xlix. 2. The effect of these changes, which also include a certain amount of mosaic-work in our chaps. lxv.-lxvi., was not altogether pleasing; chap. lvi. 1-8 is not the happiest of sequels to the loving address to "every one that thirsteth" (chap. lv.).

§ 5. The final redaction of II. Isaiah as a whole cannot be dated with precision. But from the appended passage, lxvi. 23-24 (which, with l. 10-11, may probably be ascribed to the final editor), we may conjecture that this took place very late in the Persian, or even early in the Greek period. I. Isaiah, as we have seen, was probably completed between 250 and 220, and nothing prevents us from assigning the completion of II. Isaiah and its combination with I. Isaiah to the same period. Still a date as late as 200 is not impossible for the reason mentioned above (p. xvi.).

These latter dates may be disputed. This is a matter of comparative indifference. Very little depends on the date of the last editor of Isaiah; it is the period of the prophecies themselves and of their earlier editors which is historically important. And at present the question which seems to me to deserve most attention is this, Are so many prophetic passages, especially of II. Isaiah, rightly regarded as post-Exilic? If they are, a valuable source of illustration has been opened to the historian of the post-Exilic period. For my part, I think that the hesitation which was partly excusable in 1881 can hardly be still maintained by critical students. The proofs are almost superabundantly strong.

IV.—EVENTS OF THE PERIOD OF II. ISAIAH

§ 1. In the remaining part of this prologue I have to refer to some of my historical presuppositions. It is a commonplace to remark that our historical information respecting the Return of the Jews and the post-Exilic period in general leaves much to be desired. In the first place, it is very uncertain how large a number of Jews were carried away in 596 and 586 to Babylon.[1] We know that Jeru-

---

[1] See especially Stade, *ZATW*, iv. 271-277.

salem was entirely depopulated by Nebuzar-adan (2 Ki. xxv. 11), but its population must already have been decimated both by the deportation under Jehoiachin and by war and famine. Apparently the number of exiles who were led away with Jehoiachin was larger than that of the later Gôla. But the difficulties in reckoning both numbers are insuperable, and in any case a not inconsiderable population must have been left behind,[1] which, according to Kuenen's earlier view, even had its representatives in religious literature (Lam. v. and Isa. xxiv.-xxvii. being regarded by him in 1863 as written in Judah during the Exile). In the next, it is very difficult to obtain from Ezra and Nehemiah a consistent view of the events of the Restoration period. Schrader[2] long ago gave reasons for supposing the foundation of the temple to have been ante-dated by the Chronicler in Ezra iii. 8-13, and his arguments have been accepted as valid by Kuenen, Stade, Marti, Ryssel, and König. This, however, was only the beginning of a series of critical doubts, which culminate in the extreme but ill-supported scepticism of M. Vernes, but are also expressed with no slight acumen by such practised critics as van Hoonacker and Kosters, and in our own country by an eminent archæologist, Sir Henry Howorth.[3] The state of these questions in 1890 was set forth with singular fairness and lucidity by Kuenen in a dissertation read before the Dutch *Akademie der Wissenschaften*, and now included in Budde's German version of Kuenen's essays. In it the writer takes occasion from van Hoonacker's hypothesis (which assigns Ezra's arrival in Judæa to the year 397) to discuss the dates of the return of the exiles, the rebuilding of the temple, and the arrival at Jerusalem, first of Ezra and then of Nehemiah. He agrees (as we knew already from *Ond.*[2], i. 501, 504) with Schrader as to the date of the foundation of the temple, which he

---

[1] Cf. Kuenen, *Religion of Israel*, ii. 176 f. ; *Ond.*[1], ii. 150.
[2] *St. u. Kr.*, 1867, p. 479, etc. ; De Wette's *Einl.* (1869), p. 386.
[3] Van Hoonacker's work is entitled *Zorobabel et le second Temple* (1892). Sir Henry Howorth's series of papers on "The Real Character and Importance of 1 Esdras" appeared in the *Academy* for 1893 (see especially April 15, p. 327). His criticism is unsatisfactory, but cannot here be met otherwise than by a reference to Kosters, *Het Herstel*, etc., p. 19.

refers to the second year of Darius Hystaspis, 519 B.C. But on the other points his results confirm the ordinary chronology, and this in spite of the fact that he subjects the books of Ezra and Nehemiah to a thorough-going criticism. We can hardly regret this; it proves how careful Kuenen was not to take a single step forward without sufficient evidence. But a re-examination soon became necessary; Kuenen's conclusions were not sure enough to satisfy all his colleagues, and in particular he had not sufficiently considered the evidence of the prophets Haggai and Zechariah.

§ 2. Kuenen's successor at Leyden (Prof. Kosters) has lately gone over the whole ground again very minutely.[1] The student who can read Dutch should not fail to get his book (it is not long), after having acquainted himself with the masterly criticism of the Books of Ezra and Nehemiah in Kuenen's *Introduction* (vol. i. part 2). I must briefly describe his conclusions here, because in the main points they appear so inevitable that I have constantly pre-supposed them later on in dealing with chaps. lvi.-lxvi. of Isaiah. Like Kuenen, Kosters holds that the temple was rebuilt in 520-516 B.C. under Darius Hystaspis, but the builders, as he takes great pains to show, were not the Gôla, or (returned) exiles, but that part of the Judahite population which had not been carried away to Babylonia. This view respecting the builders makes it much easier to accept Schrader's conclusion with regard to the date of the commencement of the work. Before the publication of Koster's book, it was almost equally difficult to believe that the temple was not begun before 519, and not to admit that on critical grounds this really was the date. How could the exiles have returned in 536, and yet made no attempt to rebuild the temple till 519? If there was any appreciable amount of truth in the account in Ezra i., it was anxiety for the restoration of the temple-worship which brought about the first return of the exiles. And yet Schrader's arguments were very strong. Driver in 1891 evidently felt the difficulty, though he placed it on a different ground.[2] Thinking

[1] *Het Herstel van Israël in het Perzische Tijdvak.* Leiden, 1894.
[2] *Introd.*, p. 514. Ryle (*Ezra and Nehemiah*, pp. xxxii.-xxxiv.) and Kirkpatrick (*Doctrine of the Prophets*, p. 432 f.) defend the general

it impossible "that this tradition can have arisen without some historical basis," he conjectured "that the ceremony described in Ezra iii. 8-13 was one of a purely *formal* character, such as Haggai could afford to disregard altogether." But it is not only the ceremony of laying the foundation which Haggai and Zechariah ignore, but also the supposed first return of the Gôla ("exiles") from Babylonia. It is the Chronicler who (about 250 B.C.) ascribes the rebuilding of the temple to the Gôla (Ezra i. 3, 5 ; iii. 8-13 ; iv. 1 ; vi. 21, 22), and the sources of the Chronicler, preserved in Ezra v. and vi., know nothing of a return of the Gôla prior to the rebuilding of the sanctuary. Nor is there any trustworthy evidence that it was the Gôla which rebuilt the walls of Jerusalem ; Ezra iv. 6-23 (which probably means to assert the rebuilding of the walls by Ezra and his companions) is in conflict with Neh. i. 1-vii. 5. In 445 Nehemiah, on his arrival from Susa, still found the walls unbuilt, and no Gôla in Jerusalem. Very soon, however, the walls were erected, *i.e.* by the same Judahite population which had already erected the temple. Now the promised glorification of Jerusalem appeared a little more possible. But what could Jerusalem be without more inhabitants ? Israel was still for the most part dispersed ; the chief centre of Jewish life was, not Jerusalem, but Babylon. To remedy this, Nehemiah would not wait for the promised miracle— the "gathering of Israel's outcast ones from the four skirts of the earth" (xi. 12); he simply removed a portion of the country population to the "holy city" (Neh. xi. 1). His other measures related partly to the incomes of the Levites, partly to needed social reforms. During this period his restless and bitter enemies were the half-Jews or Samaritans and their allies. After twelve years he returned to Susa, but only to report matters to his royal master.

§ 3. On Nehemiah's second visit to Jerusalem (432) still greater events took place. It is possible, thinks Kosters, that while at Susa he obtained express permission for the return of a portion of the Gôla, and that this was in defer-

accuracy of Ezra iii. 8-13. But a more methodical examination of the question might lead to quite other results (see König, *Einl.*, pp. 281-283).

ence to Ezra, whom Nehemiah may have visited at Babylon. At any rate, the arrival of Ezra and his caravan falls soon after the return of Nehemiah, and henceforth the activity of Nehemiah himself takes a more distinctly religious turn. Positively he directs his energies to the enforcement of the Sabbath rest; negatively, to the prohibition of mixed marriages. This is to be ascribed altogether to the influence of Ezra, who had not merely the religious concentration which Nehemiah the statesman lacked, but brought with him in the Gôla that higher element which was needed to leaven and so to transform the people of Jerusalem. At first even Ezra failed to achieve the separation of the lower or mixed element. He succeeded however in forming a Kahal (קָהָל) or congregation, which had the consciousness of being the people of God, the true Israel. Then came Ezra's introduction of the lawbook—how soon after, we know not; and by degrees the Kahal absorbed the best elements of Jewish society, not however so completely (as the later literature shows) as to exclude the possibility of opposition and reaction.

§ 4. To us this course of things probably appears natural. But to the Chronicler it appeared incredible that the poor country-folk (דַּלַּת הָאָרֶץ, 2 Ki. xxiv. 14, xxv. 12) should have done so much for their religion. The Gôla, which had become the spiritual aristocracy, was in his eyes the only doer of great deeds, the creator under God of the new Israel. And so the same writer of the third century, who rewrote the early history of Israel, transformed in great measure the annals of the later time. Kosters deserves warm thanks for proving this. The result both illustrates and is illustrated by the conclusions to which we are led by the critical analysis of II. Isaiah.

§ 5. But has Kosters seen the whole of the truth? In the famous cylinder inscription of Cyrus, which came from Babylon and is now in the British Museum, we read (line 11) that Marduk (Merodach) "granted the return of all lands."[1] This seems to be an allusion to the fact that the Persians at once recognised the folly of the Assyrian and

[1] *KIB*, iii. 2, p. 122 f. The rendering in *RP*, n. s., v. 165, seems arbitrary. Cf. Kuenen-Budde, *Abhandlungen*, p. 218, note 1.

Babylonian policy of transporting captive peoples; Cyrus doubtless saw clearly enough that by sending home any Jews who were willing to go, he would materially strengthen his own hold of Palestine. Is it not then likely that some Jewish exiles returned in 536? To this question Wildeboer replies in the affirmative.[1] He thinks that we may assume, though we cannot prove, that some Jewish exiles returned both under Cyrus and (see Zech. vi. 9-15) under Darius. I agree with him, and I have in fact made use of this result in my own treatment of chaps. lvi.-lxvi. of Isaiah, some parts of which seem to have been written before the arrival of Ezra. It appears to me that the earnestness of Haggai and Zechariah (who cannot have stood alone) implies the existence of a higher religious element at Jerusalem long before 432 B.C. Whence came this higher element but from its natural home among the more cultured exiles in Babylonia? Nor is it easy to believe that Babylonian Jews, who certainly came on visits to Jerusalem (Zech. *l.c.*), were never induced by their love of Israel's holy places to fix their abode in the city of the sanctuary. I doubt, however, whether we can come to the help of the Chronicler, and say that in Ezra i. "he did but concentrate on a single point of the history what was really the result of a much longer period" [of migration from Babylonia]. For Kosters has acutely shown that in the document to which Ezra v. 11-17 and vi. 1, 3-5 belong, we can trace the earlier stage of the Chronicler's story, and that its assertion that Cyrus ordered the temple to be rebuilt (presumably by the population of Judæa) and sent back the sacred vessels is simply a pious invention. And we can even explain (see pp. 281 f.) how it was that the writer of this document came to assert this: he translated into facts the prophetic language of Isa. xliv. 28*b* ("he that saith of Jerusalem, Let it be inhabited, and of the temple, Let thy foundations be laid"), and of lii. 11 ("purify yourselves, ye that bear the vessels of Yahwè"). Now, if this writer, under the influence of a literalistic view of prophecy, invented facts, why should we suppose that in his addition to his predecessor's story the Chronicler

---

[1] See his review of Kosters, *Theologische Studiën*, 1894, pp. 277-282.

was less purely imaginative? Can we not more naturally account for his version of the story by assuming that he was shocked at the ascription to Cyrus (for the Judæan builders have no credit given them) of what must, he thought, have been at least equally due to the zeal of the exiles (Ezra i. 5, " all those whose spirit God had stirred up ")?

§ 6. If then we admit the possibility that a few of the exiles did from time to time migrate to Jerusalem from Babylonia, we can only justify this by the considerations mentioned above. And we must distinctly assert that, at any rate in the time of Haggai and Zechariah, such immigrants had no appreciable influence. The latter prophet indeed ignores them altogether when he promises that soon "men from far countries" (רחוקים) shall come and work at the rebuilding of the temple (Zech. vi. 15). We need not be surprised at this phenomenon. Even if Cyrus was willing that the Jewish exiles should return, it does not at all follow that many of the exiles were willing to exchange their comparative prosperity in Babylonia for the hardships of life in Judæa. Could they not help the common cause best by retaining that material wealth which was so deficient in the old country? True, the Second Isaiah had dwelt much on a return to Judah. But he had connected his promises with such a prodigality of miracles that in the gray present pious men in Babylon and Jerusalem could scarcely persuade themselves that "the time to have pity on Zion" had as yet come[1] (Ps. cii. 14 ; cf. Hag. i. 2 ; Zech. i. 12). A revolution in opinion was effected by the faith and energy of Ezra. It is virtually, even if not quite literally, true that the Gôla from Babylon first arrived in Jerusalem with Ezra in or soon after the year 432, and with them the organisation of a righteous people, as the preliminary condition of the fulfilment of the promises, became possible.

[1] Cf. lx. 22 (in the later supplement of Isaiah), "I Yahwè will hasten it *in its time.*"

ISAIAH

Chapter I

THIS discourse evidently stands by itself; it forms no part of a group of prophecies. It appears to possess unity; Ewald even discovers in it " four symmetrical strophes," each beginning with a fresh word of Yahwè. Can we trust this appearance, or must we attempt to analyse the discourse into distinct sections, representing different periods, or parts of periods? The attempt will certainly be difficult, for, in so far as Isaiah was a literary artist, he must have sacrificed historical truth to literary form; the strict reproduction of a changeful popular oratory was inconsistent with the smoothness and regularity essential to a literary style. But does not Ewald greatly exaggerate the artistic character of the written discourses of the prophets? It cannot be right to approach the works of Isaiah with the literary presuppositions urged upon us by Ewald. The attempt at an analysis of his prophecies must be made; whenever the transitions of thought and feeling are specially abrupt, and a change of the historical situation may be suspected. It is of no use to reply by referring to the transitions in Semitic poetry. We are not now concerned with poetry proper, but with prophecy, which has conditions of its own.—Now Koppe, the German editor of Lowth, long ago (1789) divided Isa. i. into three parts, composed at different periods, and injudiciously combined by the collector of the prophecies, viz., (*a*) *vv.* 2-9, (*b*) *vv.* 10-20, (*c*) *vv.* 21-31. We will not now consider Koppe's dates, but, while recognising the correctness of his division, so far as it goes, inquire whether there may not be other breaks in the discourse. Several recent critics are of opinion that there are. Stade[1] begins a new section at *v.* 5; Lagarde,[2] followed by Cornill,[3] at *v.* 4 and *v.* 18; Prof. F. Brown[4] at *v.* 27 and *v.* 29. I cannot myself find a clear break after *v.* 3. " Sons that do corruptly " is naturally suggested by " Sons have I made great " (*v.* 2), and *v.* 4 is the natural exclamation of a bystander (the prophet himself) who is shocked at the ingratitude of Yahwè's sons. But I do admit a break after *v.* 4. If *v.* 5 continued the train of thought in *v.* 4 we should expect the prophet to say (cf. v. 4-6), " Therefore will Yahwè stretch forth his hand against his people and smite it ; " instead of which we read, " On what part will ye be further smitten," and soon afterwards we are told that the land has already been laid waste.—Now let us turn to *v.* 18. It begins, "Come now and let us argue with one another, saith Yahwè." But upon the usual hypothesis Israel's trial has been going on all through the chapter. Obviously there is a complete break here.—Lastly we have to ask, Do *vv.* 27 and 28 form a little section in themselves? Certainly they do. They give in colourless and almost aphoristic style the divine principles of action, and they contain a reference to the "conversion" of Zion which is not fully explained by the context.

Thus we get not three but seven sections, viz., (*a*) *vv.* 2-4, (*b*) *vv.* 5-9, (*c*) *vv.* 10-17, (*d*) *vv.* 18-20, (*e*) *vv.* 21-26, (*f*) *vv.* 27, 28, (*g*) *vv.* 29-31. Now as to the historical situation of the several parts. Can we venture to say that it is the same throughout ? Let us try to look at each section with a fresh eye, and see what period it most clearly indicates. First, in which of the reigns to which Isaiah's words may refer could Judah be said to have been raised up on high among the nations ? The answer cannot be doubtful ; *v.* 2, not less than ii. 6, 7, refers to the prosperous state of Judah on the death first of Uzziah and then of Jotham. But

---

[1] *Gesch.*, p. 586, note 2.   [2] *Semitica*, i. 1-5.
[3] *ZATW*, 1884, pp. 86-88; cf. *Einl.*, p. 152. Against Cornill and Lagarde, see Oort, *Études . . . dédiées à M. le Dr. C. Leemans*, 1885, pp. 113-116.
[4] "The Measurements of Hebrew Poetry," in *JBL*, 1890 (p. 83).

the want of special descriptive features in *vv.* 2-4 suggests that the writer recalls a period which is now long past, and intends this section to serve as an effective preface to the reproductions of actually delivered prophecies which follow. This will account for the rhetorical appeal to heaven and earth, which is unique in Isaiah, and only to be paralleled in a literary prophecy such as Mic. vi. 1 (cf. Deut. xxxii. 1 ; Ps. l. 4).[1]

Section (*b*) places us in the reign of Hezekiah. The desolating inroad spoken of is surely not the invasion of Rezin and Pekah in the reign of Ahaz (Ge., Kn., Di., De.). The aim of these kings was not to make Judah utterly waste and so reduce it to insignificance, but to place a vassal-king on the throne, who would be compelled to help them against Assyria. To reply that the ravages of the allied kings must have been terribly great is to go beyond the historical evidence. The statements in 2 Chron. xxviii. 5-14 are framed with a view to edification ; those of *vv.* 17, 18 may indeed be historical, but do not fully justify Isaiah's language. Moreover in chap. vii. (which expressly refers to the Syro-Ephraimitish invasion) the complete desolation of Judah is referred to as still future. We must therefore identify the invaders with still more terrible foes—the Assyrians. Sargon, as Prof. Sayce has stated so often since 1873,[2] describes himself (Nimrûd inscr., l. 8) as " the subduer of *Yaudu*, whose situation is remote," and the same eminent scholar, reading several Biblical passages in the light of this representation, has persistently affirmed an invasion of Judah by Sargon as well as by Sennacherib. This reading of history (though at first attractive even to the cautious Schrader) appears to be a mistaken one. At the very least, the date of the supposed invasion proposed by Prof. Sayce must be too late. Not 710 but 720 would have to be the date. It is not inconceivable that the title of Sargon, in that boastful passage of the inscription, gives an exaggerated but not wholly untrue impression of Sargon's achievements in Palestine in the year of the battle of Raphia, but later than this we could not put

---

[1] Cf. Lowth's note, but observe that in Isa. and Mic. the appeal, though rhetorical, is sincerely felt.
[2] " Critical Examination of Isaiah xxxvi.-xxxix.," *Theol. Rev.*, 1873.

an invasion, for the context mentions the defeat of Humbanigas, king of Elam, and the captivity of Hamath, which took place in that year. Schrader did, in fact, in 1872, admit an invasion of Judah by Sargon in 720 B.C.[1] Still it was justly pointed out by other scholars, that without some distinct Assyrian confirmation of this view it could not be defended with any confidence, and Winckler has shown that it is not impossible[2] that the *Yaudu* spoken of in the Nimrûd inscription may be identical with the *Ya'di* (יאדי) of N. Syria, which was tributary to Tiglath-Pileser, and has by some been identified with the Yaudu of the el-Amarna tablets.

Being compelled therefore to reject Prof. Sayce's conjecture,[3] we must either fall back on the well-attested invasion of Sennacherib as the occasion of *vv.* 5-9, or maintain with Caspari that this section is an imaginative description of the punishment deserved by Judah. The vivacity of the prophet's language is against the latter alternative, which indeed would never have been thought of but for the difficulty of forming a consistent view of the historical situation implied in the prophecy, on the assumption of its original unity. Sennacherib, then, is the invader, and his very plain statement of facts seems fully to account for *vv.* 5-9 : "And as for Hezekiah the Judahite, who had not submitted to my yoke, 46 of his strong cities, his fortresses, and the smaller towns in their neighbourhood without number . . . I besieged, I captured (cf. 2 Kings xviii. 13). 200,150 men . . . horses, mules, asses, camels, oxen and sheep without number, I carried away from them and reckoned as booty."[4] It will be seen later on that the

[1] *St. u. Kr.*, xlv. 738-739. Similar views were held at one time by Brandes, Kleinert, and Lyon.

[2] *Altorient. Forschungen*, i. (1893), p. 16 f. The difficulties of this theory are hardly insuperable. The variations of Assyrian scribes are incalculable, and even if it is only a N. Syrian country which is meant, Sargon might in this context boast of its "remoteness." Observe, too, that Hamath is mentioned next to Yaudu (*KIB*, ii. 4, 5).

[3] For the arguments in favour of Prof. Sayce's view, see *PI*, i. 68, 69, 203-4 ; ii. 181, 183-5 ; against it, see especially Schrader, *CI*, ii. 100 ; Tiele, *Bab.-ass. Gesch.*, p. 258 ; Winckler, *Untersuch.*, p. 141 ; Köhler, *Bibl. Gesch. A. T.*, iii. 431-432 (with further references).

[4] Prism Inscription, *KIB*, ii. 94 f. Cf. Winckler, *Textbuch*, p. 34 f.;

blockade (not siege) of Jerusalem was one of the last events in the Assyrian campaign of 701. It had not taken place when the prophecy summarised in *vv.* 5-9 was delivered, but it was impending, and those verses express the mingled feelings of a patriot and a prophet under such circumstances. Jerusalem, they tell us, is now the sole remnant of Judah. It is as forlorn and helpless as a watchman's hammock, and as thoroughly cut off from the outside world as a besieged city.

We now turn to (*c*), in which the prophet specialises the charges vaguely suggested in *v.* 4. He addresses himself chiefly to the rulers (קְצִינִים, as iii. 6, 7, xxii. 3), who were judges in time of peace, captains in time of war,[1] and describes them as wasting much energy on useless religious observances, while they utterly neglect their first and more sacred duties, viz., the care of the interests of the poor. Now perhaps we understand what Isaiah meant by forsaking Yahwè, and can admit that *vv.* 2-4 form an excellent introduction to *vv.* 10-17, as well as *vv.* 5-9. To what period does the prophecy reproduced in the latter passage belong? That injustice abounded in the reign of Ahaz is certain (iii. 13-15, v. 7); the old morality, based on the tribal and family relations,[2] was going out, and the new morality, based on a sense of national unity, was not yet fully born. But that judicial crimes were not unknown in Hezekiah's reign is clear from Mic. iii. 9, 10, while the fear of Assyria in B.C. 701 amply accounts for the multiplication of sacrifices and prayer-formulæ (cf. Am. v. 22, 24, taken together with *vv.* 15, 18). Accepting this date, it is easy to believe that *vv.* 5-9 and 10-17 represent discourses which followed close upon one another, and to ascribe the juxtaposition of the two views referring to Sodom (*vv.* 9, 10), not to the mechanical procedure of a compiler in quest of catchwords (Cornill), but to the rhetorical art of the original editor.

Schrader, *CI*, i. 286. We might almost have guessed such a captivity from what Isaiah says of the burned cities and the pitiful remnant (*vv.* 7, 9).

[1] Cf. L. A. Bähler, *De messiaansche heilsverwachting* (1893), pp. 5-7.

[2] Tribal justice among the Bedawis is still excellent (Doughty, *Arabia*, i. 249).

—As to section (*d*), we cannot fail to notice in *v*. 18*b* a point of contact with *v*. 16*a*. We must not, however, with Ewald find a reference in *v*. 18*a* to the opening words of *v*. 2, as if the appeal to heaven and earth and the address to guilty men formed part of the same transactions. Upon Ewald's theory, we ought surely to render (as in *PI*), "Come now, and let us bring our dispute to an end," which, I now see, puts too great a strain upon the phrase. But *vv*. 2-4 do not, as Ewald supposes, introduce a great trial scene, of which *vv*. 18-31 give the conclusion, and heaven and earth are not appealed to as legal witnesses, but to shame those rational creatures who refuse to listen to their Divine Father (cf. Jer. ii. 12). The date of the prophecy is clear. *Vv*. 19 and 20 refer to the slaughter and devastation of the Assyrians (cf. *v*. 7).

Section (*e*) begins with a dirge on the faithless city. The complaint of rampant injustice is renewed (*v*. 23*b* alludes to *v*. 17*b*), and with deep emotion the prophet announces a severe punishment for Jerusalem. Evidently the city was not yet blockaded. But, sternly as he begins, he opens a bright prospect for the future. The good old days when the judges administered true justice, and the counsellors sought the advice of Yahwè's prophets, shall return. That— at the period at which this section was written—was Isaiah's imagination of what we call the Messianic age. The king has passed out of sight, or rather (for, as Dillmann has shown, Isaiah cannot here be thinking of the pre-Davidic period) the right position of the king in time of peace is to be simply the first of the judges and of the counsellors of the state (cf. Mic. iv. 9, where "king" is parallel to "counsellor"). Messianic felicity shall spring out of Messianic judgment, but there is now no personal Messiah to distract the attention from Yahwè. · Section (*f*) contains nothing that is distinctly inconsistent with Sennacherib's period. It is deficient, however, in one respect, which is fatal to a claim to reproduce a prophecy of this or of any other crisis. There is no colour of life in it, no feature drawn from contemporary history. Can Isaiah have written thus?[1] The

[1] *Vv*. 27 and 28 are obelised by Prof. F. Brown, Duhm, and Hackmann; *v*. 28 is rejected by Oort.

phraseology, moreover, is not thoroughly Isaianic. Of the four participial class-names, though three have points of contact with Isaiah (see vi. 10, vii. 3, i. 2, 4), none actually occur in the book of Isaiah, except in prophecies, which on many grounds cannot be Isaiah's (*a.* שֶׁבֶר פֶּשַׁע, lix. 20 ; *b.* פֹּשְׁעִים, xlvi. 8, liii. 12 ; *c.* חֹטְאִים, xiii. 9, xxxiii. 14 ; *d.* עֹזְבֵי יְהוָה, lxv. 11). Add to this that מָדָה (though found in Hos. vii. 13, xiii. 14) does not occur elsewhere in the true Isaiah, xxix. 22, xxxv. 10, not to add li. 11, being late passages. Section (*g*) is evidently a torso ; nothing like this could have been written by Isaiah as the sequel to *v.* 26. Must it not be the close of a lost prophecy against tree-worship? We need not doubt Isaiah's authorship. It has all that prophet's energy, and חָסֹן, which has been doubted, is justified by Am. ii. 9. A more effective close for a prophecy can hardly be imagined. We cannot date it with certainty, but considering that tree-worship (like Canaanitish forms of worship in general) specially prevailed in N. Palestine (see Hos. iv. 13), we may reasonably place the composition of this prophecy before the fall of Samaria (722).

How far is this division of chap. i. into seven sections supported by a study of the rhythm? Budde[1] thinks that such a study justifies us in separating *vv.* 21-31, which are a connected dirge on Jerusalem, written throughout in his so-called Kîna-rhythm. This however involves so much correction of the text that, unless exegesis requires it, we are hardly justified in accepting it. But exegesis is very far from requiring it. Nor can one easily admit that *vv.* 27, 28 and 29-31 show the same rhythm as *vv.* 21-26. In this view I am supported both by Brown[2] and Duhm. Nor is it at all natural to combine the fairly symmetrical tetrastichs of *vv.* 2-17 with the hexastichs of *vv.* 18-20.

I conclude that sections (*b*)-(*e*) reproduce prophecies delivered during Sennacherib's invasion (but before the blockade of Jerusalem), skilfully combined by a disciple of Isaiah,[3] and

---

[1] *ZATW*, 1891, pp. 245-247 ; cf. 1882, p. 33.

[2] See Prof. Francis Brown's inquiry into the metres of chap. i., which are, he finds, partly six-toned, partly five-toned (*JBL*, June 1889).

[3] Yet the phrase יֹאמַר יְֽ in *vv.* 11, 18, and כִּי פִּי יְֽ דִּבֵּר in *v.* 20, may justify the suspicion of a later hand. The former only occurs else-

preceded by an introduction ($a = vv.$ 2-4), specially written by the earliest editor. I am reluctant to deny *vv.* 2-4 to Isaiah himself, but the difficulties in ascribing such a purely literary work to a prophet so "full of power by the spirit of Yahwè" as Isaiah, are too great. I must add that the ill-connected appendix (*vv.* 29-31) cannot in my judgment have been attached even by a disciple of Isaiah. *Vv.* 27, 28 clearly show the hand of a late editor who added this passage to link the great preceding prophecy to an Isaianic fragment which needed a safe corner in the book. The fragment referred to is obviously not the beginning of an oracle; may it once have stood at the end? To me it seems more likely that the original Messianic close of the oracle to which it belonged has been either lost or misplaced. We shall perhaps see better after studying ii. 2-4.

It may be well to compare these views with those of Duhm and Hackmann. The former critic agrees with me in separating *vv.* 29-31, which formed "perhaps the close of a long discourse." He also admits that *vv.* 10-26 were perhaps not "spoken in the same breath as *vv.* 2-9," though it was Isaiah himself who appended them to that passage; and there he stops in his analysis. And he gives the same dates as I have done to *vv.* 2-26 and 29-31; indeed, I owe to him the theory of the early date of *vv.* 29-31. Hackmann however goes backward. He admits indeed that *v.* 26 would form a beautiful close of a prophecy, but doubts whether *vv.* 29-31 are a separate fragment, and labours to show that they have a natural connection with *v.* 26. He agrees with Dillm. in referring the whole of chap. i. to the invasion of Rezin and Pekah.

In conclusion, a word must be said on the heading (i. 1). This of course proceeds, not from Isaiah, but from the editor. We must infer from it that chap. i. (or i. 2-26) was placed where it now stands as a preface either to chaps. ii.-xii., or, more probably, to a still larger book (such as ii.-xxxiii. or xxxv.). In the latter case, the heading in ji. 1 will refer primarily to chaps. ii.-iv., but in a secondary sense to chaps. ii.-xii.

where in xxxiii. 10, and in the parallel passage, Ps. xii. 6, also in chaps. xl.-lxvi.; the latter only in xl. 5, lviii. 14; cf. Mic. iv. 4 (late).

CHAPTERS II.-IV

According to Ewald these chapters form a continuous work, written in the heat of prophetic inspiration by Isaiah himself, and embodying the substance not only of recent, but also of earlier discourses. Ewald grants, therefore, that the prophecy has only a literary unity, and it remains to inquire whether we can, to some extent, analyse it into its original elements. Five sections at any rate, which have little or no coherence, strike one immediately, viz. ii. 2-5, ii. 6-22, iii. 1-15, iii. 16-iv. 1, and iv. 2-6, and we may perhaps be able to pursue the analysis further.

(A) With reference to ii. 2-5, three questions may have to be asked—(1) Is the passage really the work of Isaiah, or in the main taken from the Book of Micah? (2) If in the main taken from Micah, by whom was it inserted where it now stands in Isa. ii., by Isaiah or by an editor? (3) If in the main taken from Micah by an editor, to whom does the original passage in Micah owe its present position—to the prophet Micah or to an editor? In answer to (1), we may assert confidently that the passage is in the main borrowed from the Book of Micah. Observe 1. That Isa. ii. 2-4 is found again in a slightly more original form[1] in Micah iv. 1-3 ; 2. That the passage is unnecessary where it now stands in Isa. ii., there being already a very full Messianic prophecy in iv. 2-6, and that its position is against the established usage, which requires the announcement of judgment to precede that of mercy; 3. That neither the phraseology nor the ideas are distinctively Isaianic (see pp. 11 f., 14); and 4. That Isa. ii. 5 is most easily understood as an imitation of Mic. iv. 5 (see below). With regard to (2) it would be almost too absurd to suppose that Isaiah not

[1] Occasionally one may prefer a reading in Isaiah, but, in general, the form of text in Micah appears to be the more original. See Ryssel, *Untersuchungen üb. d. Textgestalt . . . des B. Micha* (1887), pp. 218-9 ; and cf. Briggs, *Messianic Prophecy* (1886), pp. 181-2, and Duhm's Comm. Elhorst's suggestion (1891) that Mic. iv. 4 should be inserted between Isa. ii. 4 and 5, and Mic. iv. 5 between Isa. ii. 5 and 6, is ingenious, but unnecessary.

only quoted from a younger prophet, but placed his extract in this prominent position, nor would such a theory be consistent with our present knowledge of the composition of the prophetic books. In answer to (3) we may safely ascribe Mic. iv. 1-5 to an editor (or rather editors) of the Book of Micah. For 1. Mic. iv. 1-4 is not a natural antithesis to Mic. iii. 9-12. It is true that iii. 12 *ends* with a reference to הַר הַבַּיִת and iv. 1 relates altogether to הַר בֵּית יהוה, but in spirit the two passages differ widely. The temple is only mentioned in iii. 12, because the rulers of Jerusalem boast of its impregnableness (cf. Jer. vii. 4), but in iv. 1-2 it is the central object in the description, and is glorified by the writer himself. Of Jerusalem itself, however, nothing is told us directly. It is the city of the temple, and therefore also the source of true religious instruction. But no allusion is made to its rebuilding, nor is there any contrast to the picture of the corrupt rulers (iii. 9-11*a*). The two passages, moreover, are merely connected by וְהָיָה. 2. Neither the expressions nor the ideas of Mic. iv. 1-4 favour the authorship of Micah. The two divine titles, "God of Jacob" (*v.* 2) and "Yahwè Çebaoth" (*v.* 4), occur nowhere else in Micah, though it must be admitted that the use of "Jacob" as a synonym for "Israel" is specially frequent in Micah (see i. 5, ii. 7 [12], iii. 1, 8, 9 [v. 6, 7]). The phrases, "many nations," "many peoples," only occur in the disputed portion of the book (see Mic. iv. 11, 13, v. 6, 7), nor could we in any case lay much stress on very common expressions (cf. Isa. xvii. 12). It is much more important, however, to notice that the conversion of the "nations" is not referred to in any other part of the Book of Micah; and yet, if such a revolutionary idea had visited that prophet's mind at the close of his ministry, it would surely have received a fuller development and have modified some passages in the context. 3. The tone and imagery are too idyllic for Micah (and also no doubt for Isaiah). 4. There is a chronological difficulty. According to Jer. xxvi. 18 the prophecy in Mic. iii. 12 was uttered "in the days of Hezekiah," but it cannot be shown that any part of Isa. ii. 6-iv. 1 was altered or written as late as this. Consequently, unless we boldly reject that statement,

CHAPTER II. 2-5

Mic. iv. 1-4 must have been both composed and inserted late.

And how late may we put the passage? The emphasis laid on the forms of morality or religion ("ways," as xlii. 24; 1 Ki. iii. 14; 2 Chr. xvii. 3; Ps. xxv. 4, cxix. 3; and often in Deut.; "paths," as in late poetry, see Ps. xxv. 4, xliv. 19, cxix. 15) belongs to the post-Deuteronomic age. The gathering (נהר *confluere*, elsewhere only Jer. xxxi. 2, li. 44) of "peoples," or, as in Isa., "all the nations," to Mount Zion (Mic. iv. 1 = Isa. ii. 2) forcibly reminds us of Jer. iii. 17 (most probably late); Isa. lx. (cf. lxi. 6*a*); Zech. viii. 20-22,[1] xiv. 16-19; Isa. lxvi. 23, and the teachership of Yahwè of Ps. xciv. 10 (see Baethgen), and xxv. 8, and, I venture to add, Isa. xxx. 20 (all late passages), nor can one forget here the prominence given to the spiritual future of the nations in Isa. xl.-lv. It would appear, moreover, that the idea of the physical elevation of Jerusalem (cf. Del.), found here and in Zech. xiv. 10, was borrowed from Ezekiel (see Ezek. xl. 2, and cf. xvii. 22), and the same origin should probably be assigned to the application of the phrase באחרית הימים to the opening of the Messianic age.[2]

[1] Dillm. sees in Zech. viii. 22 an allusion to Mic. iv. 2, 3. Even if this view be correct, how does it prove a pre-Exilic date for the latter passage? Notice, however, that Zech. viii. 20-22 is more concrete, and therefore presumably more original, than the passage in Micah. "Many peoples and numerous nations" in *v.* 22 is surely suggested by "peoples" and "many cities" in *v.* 20. Cf. also Joel ii. 2 (post-Exilic), עם רב ועצום (same epithets as in Zech.), and Zech. ii. 15 (11).

[2] This phrase, as I have said in *PI*, "occurs only in prophecies, mostly (not always, as Kimchi asserts) referring to the glorious Messianic period, which should ensue upon the 'day' or assize of Jehovah, but is sometimes used quite vaguely of future time." For instances of this latter use, which appeared to me to be *more original* than the other, I referred to Jer. xxiii. 20; Deut. iv. 30, xxxi. 29. If, however, these passages belong to the post-Exilic, or, at any rate, later Exilic period, it becomes possible that, though the contents are not distinctly Messianic, yet the thought of the Messianic age may have been in the mind of the writers. Now it is in a high degree probable that the closing words of Jer. xxiii. 20 (if no more) have been inserted by a post-Exilic editor, and that the passages in Deuteronomy are at any rate not pre-Exilic. We must therefore see if there are any other instances of the vaguer use of this phrase, in which a reference to the Messianic period is not to be supposed. As such, it is perhaps still possible to regard Gen. xlix. 1 and Num. xxiv. 14. To suppose with

From the style, however, no definite conclusion can be drawn. The construction נכון יהיה (*v.* 2) may, but need not be late (see on xxx. 20). It would at this point be tempting to adopt Hitzig's conjecture that the passage (as given in Micah) originally stood at the end of the Book of Joel (which Hitzig regarded as the earliest, but which is more probably one of the latest of extant prophecies). The following parallelisms have been indicated by this acute critic :—

Joel i. 12, ii. 22, . cf. Mic. iv. 4 (imagery),
„ ii. 2, . . . „ iv. 3 (phraseology),
„ iv. 10, . . . „ iv. 3 (thought),
„ iv. 18, . . . „ iv. 2 (thought).

Of these, the third suggests Hitzig's most plausible argument, viz. that the subdued nations would naturally have to reconvert their weapons into agricultural implements. Still it must be admitted that the image in Joel iv. (iii.) 10 is more striking in itself, and that Joel iv. (iii.) 18-21 forms an adequate conclusion of the Book. Ewald, to whom the same idea had also occurred, sensibly remarks (*Proph.*, i. 114), "Much more probably the passage belongs to a lost address of Joel." This view was adopted by the writer in *ICA*, p. 10, but it is wiser to affirm simply that Mic. iv. 1-4 is the work of one of those later *literary* prophets, to whom we owe the Book of Joel and much besides, and from the fraternal spirit which it exhibits towards the "nations" we might even assign it, with xix. 16-25, to an early part of the Greek period.[1] The importance of the prophecy need not on this account be denied.[2]

Two other views have a claim to be mentioned. 1. Of the first there are two forms, each of which must be considered. The older form dates from Koppe, and is still

---

Staerk (*ZATW*, 1891, pp. 247-251) that the expression was "first formed during the Exile," seems to me difficult, considering how natural it is, and also that we have its analogue in the Assyrian (*ina*) *aḥrat ûmi* = "in future days" (*CI*, i. 140).

[1] See *BL*, p. 294. Toy, however, assigns both passages to the fifth century B.C. (*Judaism and Christianity*, pp. 313-314).
[2] Cf. Steinthal, *Bibel und Religionsphilosophie*, pp. 76, 77.

held by Dillm., Driver, and König. I advocated it myself in 1880, in *PI*, i. 15. It is that both Micah and Isaiah quote from some earlier prophet, whom (see above) both Hitzig and Ewald identify with Joel. Now, however, I can recognise that such a mechanical process is much more in the style of later writers (cf. Jer. xlix. 7-22) than of great masters like Isaiah, and that the analogy of chs. xv.-xvi., being precarious, ought not to be appealed to. The very words with which I myself once defended this theory may be held to suggest an argument against it. " Both Isaiah and Micah," I said, "were charged with messages of a predominantly gloomy character. Their hearers, however, were familiar with an old and truly divine word of promise, which seemed to some inconsistent with the terrible judgment which later prophets so earnestly announced. Isaiah and Micah, prophets of a kindred spirit, have both quoted this prophecy to show its essential agreement with their own graver revelation." Certainly such an idealistic description must, as I remarked, have seemed to some persons inconsistent with Isaiah's and Micah's burden of woe. But the natural course for these prophets to have taken was surely not that which is here attributed to them. In their writings they would have left that older prophecy alone, as unsuited to altered circumstances, and in their oral discourses they would have controverted it. On the other hand, mitigations of hard sayings and reconciliations of opposing points of view were natural to editors. Exhortations, too, like that in Isa. ii. 5, easily dropped from the pen of didactic writers. Feeling these difficulties in the earlier form of the theory, Kuenen (*Ond.*^{2}, 1889) modifies it thus. Isa. ii. 2-4 is, he thinks, a prophetic fragment, which received its present position from the compiler of chs. ii.-iv. This compiler only erred in ascribing it to Isaiah ; it is however probably from an older contemporary of Isaiah and Micah. I have no objection at all to the new element thus introduced into the theory, but the other portion seems to me inadmissible (see above). 2. Duhm's theory nearly coincides with that of Kuenen. This critic, however, assigns ii. 2-4 to Isaiah himself, and finds it similar both in form and in contents to xi. 1-8, xxxii. 1-5, xxxii. 15-20. All these passages he places in the old age of Isaiah, who wrote them, not as a prophetic orator, but as an inspired instructor of his faithful disciples. They therefore represent, as Duhm thinks, not Isaiah's public teaching, but his highest and most sublime ideas. These so-called "swan-songs" of Isaiah are, however, most treacherous (as we shall see in the case of xix. 16-25), and it is difficult to see any remarkable affinity between ii. 2-4 and the other passages (of which, moreover, only the first can be Isaiah's). And without laying too great a stress on this argument (seeing that prophecies on an uncommon subject must contain unusual phrases), it is noteworthy that the phraseology of ii. 2-4 is not upon the whole Isaianic; אֱלֹהֵי יַעֲקֹב in particular points away from Isaiah. To defend the antiquity of the passage by tracing an allusion to it in Jer. iii. 17 (which is hardly Jeremianic) is imprudent. Nor can it be admitted that friendliness towards the "nations" is inconsistent with a late date (see above, and cf. *BL*, pp. 204-206).

I conclude, then, that Isa. ii. 2-4 is taken from Mic. iv. 1-3, which, together with *v*. 4, or rather with some (lost) passage for which *v*. 4 is a substitute, is the work of a post-Exilic imitator of the older prophets. Mic. iv. 5 is an unskilful attempt, certainly not by the author of *vv*. 1-3, to mitigate the almost startling idealism of *vv*. 1-3 (4) by a practical hortatory remark. "If each of the (other) nations clings to its religion, let not Judah be less zealous in walking in the purer light of Yahwè's law"; such is its meaning. Isa. ii. 5 forms an exact parallel to it, as we shall see on placing the two passages side by side :—

For all nations walk every one in the name of its god; and, as for us, we will walk in the name of Yahwè, our God, for ever and ever (Mic. iv. 5).

O house of Jacob! come and let us walk in the light of Yahwè (Isa. ii. 5).

Observe (1) The hortatory character of these passages, which is not suggestive of the prophets before Jeremiah; and (2) The absence of metre in Isa. ii. 5, which indicates the hand of a very late editor (cf. *v*. 22). [The phrase בֵּית יַעֲקֹב occurs both in late and in early writings (see introduction

CHAPTER II. 2-5

to chs. xl.-lxvi.). It may have been adopted there to lead on to *v.* 6, where the received text gives it in *l.* 1, or, if we there follow Sept., which gives "the house of Israel" instead of "the house of Jacob" (an unique case in Sept. Isa.), it may have been suggested by אלהי יעקב in *v.* 3. באור יהוה (cf. Ps. cxix. 105) is a poetic equivalent for תורת יהוה; a cognate insertion in xlii. 24 (see *BW*) declares that Israel, before the Exile, would not walk in Yahwè's ways, nor obey his *tôra*. Not impossibly באור יהוה was meant to suggest the interpretation בְּאוֹרְיָה (בְּאוֹרְיָא), the Jewish Aramaic rendering of בתורה; cf. Targ. Isa. ii. 5, xlii. 24.]

But why is the relation between the two passages that of parallelism and not of identity? Why did the editor of this part of Isaiah substitute for Mic. iv. 4 a shorter practical exhortation? No doubt the exhortation preserves the point of the original passage; but why was the change made? Considering that the text of *v.* 6*a* has evidently been in part filled up by the editor, and that his hand is visible elsewhere in chap. ii., we cannot hesitate as to the answer. Verses 2-5 had to be made to fill exactly the place of a passage which, standing on the outside of the collected prophecies, had become illegible.[1] It is also probable that the prophecy which now forms Isa. ii. 2-4 (= Mic. iv. 1-3), with the addition of Mic. iv. 4, originally stood after i. 29-31, which, from the later Jewish point of view, certainly required mitigation quite as much as Mic. iii. 12.[2] At least three editors, therefore, have had to do with this short passage—the editor who placed it in Micah,

---

[1] So Studer, *JPT*, 1877, pp. 718-721. Rowland Williams, in 1866, was very near Studer's theory. He thought that the fragment was older than both Isaiah and Micah. Some early editor, finding it in the temple, or some other prophetic archives, and not knowing its author, but thinking it splendid enough for the greatest of the prophets, inserted it here by conjecture. On the criticism of the passage, cf. Stade, *ZATW*, 1881, pp. 165-7, and 1884, p. 292; Toy, *Judaism and Christianity*, p. 313; Hackmann, *ZEJ*, pp. 126-130.

[2] This approaches the view of Lagarde (*Semitica*, i. 7) that "i. 2-ii. 4 form the overture of [a] passage in which the different themes of the tone-work are successively brought before us by the editor." Cf. Stade, *Gesch.*, p. 608; Bickell, *Zt. f. kath. Theol.* 1886, p. 546.

the editor who attached it to i. 29-31, and the editor who transferred it to its present position, and who substituted the words of Isa. ii. 5 for Mic. iv. 4.

(B) We pass on to ii. 6-22, with its indignant description of Israel's sins and sublimely poetic threatenings of judgment. A "somewhat mutilated and disarranged poem" Prof. F. Brown calls it. It remained for Duhm (supported in part by Winckler)[1] to ascertain more completely the amount of the mutilation, and to remedy, as far as possible, the disarrangement. Probably the passage is made up of two fragments relating to the same subject, and of contemporary origin, but of different metre, viz. (*a*), *vv.* 6-10 and 18-21 ; and (*b*), *vv.* 11-17. The refrain of (*a*) we have in three forms, viz. *v.* 10, *v.* 19, and *v.* 21 (*v.* 21, however, is really a variant of *v.* 19, just as *v.* 20 is a variant of *v.* 18). The refrain of (*b*) also occurs in three forms, viz. *v.* 11 (the end of a lost strophe), *v.* 17 (after which *v.* 11 should be corrected), and v. 15, 16 (inserted from the margin, where some reader had written the passage incorrectly). There is nothing wonderful in Isaiah's having written twice in a similar style on the great judgment which, since "Uzziah's death-year" (vi. 1), had lain upon his soul. The poet still contended with the prophet, and Isaiah wrote quite as much to relieve himself as to impress others ; and hence, probably, it is that, in the second strophe of both fragments, he rises so completely above local and national circumstances, and idealises the national almost into a universal judgment (not Yahwè and Israel, but God and man fill up the painter's canvas).—When were these passages written ? They refer, as the expression "the house of Jacob" (*v.* 6 ; cf. viii. 17, ix. 7) shows, to "both the houses of Israel" (viii. 13), so that, though the description in *vv.* 6-8 may be suggested chiefly by Judah, yet it cannot be wholly inapplicable to the Ephraimitish kingdom. Such a period was enjoyed by Judah under Uzziah (who died about 751), and by N. Israel under Jeroboam II. (who died about 741). Although 2 Kings says nothing of the warlike character of Uzziah

---

[1] *Alttest. Untersuchungen* (1892), p. 176. It is of course an error to suppose that *vv.* 12-21 ("the interpolation," as Winckler calls it) is a late imitation of the preceding passage.

CHAPTERS II. 6-22; III. 1-15

2 Chron. (xxvi. 6-15) fills up the lacuna; I fear we must not confirm this by Tiglath-Pileser's references to Izriyau, or Azriyau, of Yaudi.[1] That external prosperity went hand in hand with idolatry we can easily believe, in spite of the character given to Uzziah by the *compiler* of Kings (on whose "framework" cf. Driver, *Intr.*, p. 175). It is not improbable that the two poems on the judgment in chap. ii. were written immediately after the death of Uzziah, and the view is confirmed by the imagery of *vv.* 19-20, which was very possibly suggested by the famous earthquake (Am. i. 1; cf. Zech. xiv. 5). If this be accepted, the section becomes important for Isaiah's early theology; it is almost like a description of the *dies iræ*. See also on the date of section III.

(C) The third section (iii. 1-15) is highly composite. *V.* 1*a* and *b* may perhaps be genuine, but *c* is not; the prophet would not have used the same phrases in parallel lines in totally different senses. The catalogue in *vv.* 2-3 may have an Isaianic basis, though such long catalogues are not in Isaiah's manner, but the present jumble of social titles is not due to Isaiah. *V.* 3*b* presents a point of contact with *v.* 20, a passage which is not Isaianic (לַחַשׁ, "charm-formula"; cf. לְחָשִׁים, *v.* 20, "charmed things," *i.e.* amulets). *Vv.* 4 and 5, however, have points of contact with genuine passages (see *v.* 12, עֹלֵל and נָגַשׂ), though it must be added that *v.* 5, with its parallel expressions נגש and רהב, reminds us forcibly of xiv. 4*b*, a noble passage which can hardly be dependent on iii. 5. At any rate *v.* 4 is undoubtedly Isaiah's; it is finely expressed, and the sudden appearance of the first pers. sing. in *a* speaks for genuineness. *Vv.* 6 and 7 in their present form betray the editor's hand, but, as in iv. 1, the basis may be Isaiah's. Such a picture as they present was effective in oral prophecy. The two parallels for the ellipsis in יִשָּׂא (*v.* 7) are late (xlii. 11; Job xxi. 12), and מִכְשֵׁלָה (cf. *v.* 8) is only found elsewhere (in a corrupt passage[2]) in Zeph. i. 3 (plur.). But שִׂמְלָה "upper garment," חֹבֵשׁ "one who binds up," or "one who restrains,"

---

[1] Schrader, *CI* on 2 Ki. xv. 1; Tiele, *Bab.-ass. Gesch.*, pp. 230-1; Winckler, *Gesch.*, p. 226. For a more correct view, see Winckler, *Forschungen* (1893), p. 1, etc. [2] See note in Kautzsch's Bible.

and קָצִין "magistrate" or "chieftain," are classical Hebrew (see iv. 1 ; Gen. ix. 23 ; Hos. vi. 1 ; Isa. i. 10, xxii. 3). Duhm begins a fresh fragment of prophecy at *v.* 13, but without need. *V.* 13 comes very naturally after *vv.* 9 and 12, if with Sept. we read עַמּוֹ in *v.* 13*a*, and render, "Yahwè stationeth himself to plead ; he standeth to defend the cause of his people" (cf. Deut. xxxii. 36). *V.* 9 says that the partizanship of the princes of Judah testifies against them, and that they have sinned with shameless publicity. *V.* 12 declares virtually that these sinners are not really Yahwè's people, which is misgoverned and misled ; *v.* 13, that Yahwè is already prepared to defend the cause of his true people (viz. the oppressed poor), and *vv.* 14 and 15 continue and develop this thought. It seems to me probable that *vv.* 10 and 11 take the place of four lines which had become illegible in the editor's time, so that we can show the existence of at least two eight-line strophes,[1] and *vv.* 1-7 may very probably correspond to two more, though the disorder of the text, imperfectly remedied by the editor, may prevent us from exhibiting those strophes in their perfection. Now as to the date. A gloomy account is given (iii. 13-15) of the social condition of Judah, not unlike that in v. 7-8. The grandees having become traders and capitalists were able to increase their estates in defiance of ancient usage, and at the expense of justice. There also seems to be a reference to a change of ruler ; the government appears to have passed into the hands of a capricious young man and his favourite ladies (iii. 12*a* ; cf. Am. iv. 1). It is natural to think of the accession of Ahaz for the date. And this may be the right one for *vv.* 8-9, 12-15, but will hardly be so for *vv.* 1-7. In that passage the accession of such capricious young men as Ahaz to power is regarded as still future. The writer looks forward to a catastrophe like that which took place under Jehoiachin (2 Ki. xxiv. 14-16), when few besides the poorer class were left. He may perhaps expect that the king (Jotham ?) will be carried away captive, and the crown-prince Ahaz left by the Assyrians as vassal-king, with his young companions (cf. 1 Ki. xii.

---

[1] Not counting the final נאֻם (*v.* 15*b*).

8) abetting his tyranny.¹ Isaiah, it seems, did not care to recast the earlier strophes, and when Ahaz in due course succeeded his father, the prophet described him by a term which evidently alludes to iii. 4.² The expected captivity was postponed, and Isaiah was inclined to hope (iii. 13) for a milder lot for the oppressed poor than for their oppressors. Observe that there is not even a distant allusion to the Syro-Ephraimitish invasion. The prophecy was therefore completed, we may presume, in the year of the accession of Ahaz (735).

(D) The fourth section (iii. 16-iv. 1) is marked out as such by the introductory formula, "And Yahwè said," the abruptness of which suggests that an editor has been at work, and that the formula (like that in vii. 10, and perhaps in xxix. 13) has only been inserted to connect two originally distinct passages. Upon a closer inspection we find that the section does not possess complete literary unity, but that the editorial insertions and alterations do not introduce any glaringly discordant elements. The inserted passages are two in number, viz. an inventory of women's dresses and ornaments (*vv.* 18-23), and an elegiac description of the desolation of the city after the loss of its choicest men in battle (*vv.* 25-26). The former passage completely conceals the close connection between *v.* 17 and *v.* 24. It also displays an attention to trifles, which is out of character with Isaiah, who in his descriptions selects representative features (see *e.g.* ix. 4, 5), and abstains from giving exhaustive catalogues (contrast Ezek. xxvii.). What is the origin of this passage? Dr. J. P. Peters (*JBL*, 1892, p. 52) thinks that it has grown out of a popular song; but what a dull song, and how unrhythmical! Surely it is

---

¹ קְצִין עַם does not mean "supreme ruler of the people" (as Hitz., Del., Duhm). Isaiah elsewhere assumes a plurality of קְצִינִים (i. 10, xxii. 3), and the phrase אִישׁ בְּאָחִיו is to be explained like similar phrases in *v.* 5a of a frequently recurring detail. So, too, in the parallel passage in iv. 1 it is not an isolated, but a frequently observed circumstance which is described. Isaiah, therefore, does not, as Duhm represents, necessarily contemplate the expulsion or deposition of the representative of the Davidic dynasty.

² תעלולים "wilfulness," *v.* 4; עוֹלֵל (see *RT*) "a wilful child," *v.* 12.

simply a carelessly made prosaic catalogue, and it grew out of the inveterate editorial habit of supplementing. As for the latter passage, it resembles in tone another inserted piece (xix. 5-10), and it seems to have been introduced to explain the "one man" of iv. 1. In its phraseology we notice the poetic terms פְּתָחִים, גְּבוּרָה, מְתִים (as xiii. 2), אָנוּ וְאָבְלוּ (as xix. 8, late; for אָבַל, cf. xxiv. 4, 7, xxxiii. 9, [1]xvi. 10, all late;—but cf. the use of אָבַל in Am. i. 2, and Isaiah's אֲנִיָּה, xxix. 2). All that remains for Isaiah is, therefore, iii. 16, 17, 24; iv. 1. The passage is an attack on the ladies of Jerusalem, who but too faithfully copy the great ladies spoken of in v. 12 (cf. Am. iv. 1), and who shall be reduced to abject poverty. It closes with a companion-picture to that in vv. 5-7: "There the male population are in search of a ruler; here the women are in search of a husband" (Weir). Such marks of date, therefore, as one can find agree with the chief of those in the preceding section.[1]

(E) The fifth section (iv. 2-6) must for several reasons be assigned altogether to a post-Exilic editor.[2] Notice these four points:—(a) The awkward, incoherent style. After reading iii. 25, 26, one expects to hear that, though the survivors will be few, those few will turn to Yahwè and work the works of righteousness. Instead of this we are told that the abundant products of the land, which Yahwè will grant as pledges of his favour, will bring honour to Israel. In other words, v. 3 ought to have preceded v. 2. It seems as if the writer began meaning to write an ordinary Messianic description and then suddenly remembered vv. 25, 26. But after obtaining a point of contact with those verses, he seems to recall a still earlier passage relative to the "daughters of Zion," and so somewhat awkwardly appends v. 4, which tells us what will have happened

---

[1] The beginning of iv. 1 is imitated in Zech. viii. 23.

[2] In 1884 I followed Stade and Duhm in doubting the Isaianic origin of vv. 5, 6 (*PI*, ii. 138). Stade himself not only obelised those verses, but transposed the three preceding ones, his order being 4, 3, 2 (*ZATW*, 1884, pp. 149-151). Dillmann rejects at any rate vv. 5b and 6. Duhm and Hackmann maintain that the whole passage is late; the former already had doubts of vv. 5 and 6 in 1875 (*Theol. der Propheten*, p. 162).

before the holy remnant comes into existence. Then the writer describes the future glory of Zion, laying special stress on the festival assemblies, with images derived from the story of the Exodus, and finishes with a semi-poetic description of the delightful refuge from heat and rain which Zion, or something else, will furnish. (*b*) The absence of rhythm, and the slight amount of parallelism. (*c*) The presence of the non-Isaianic word בָּרָא[1] (if we should not read רָאָה, with Sept.; see *RT*), and the unclassical form מִסְתּוֹר for סֵתֶר, *v.* 6; I do not add חֻפָּה (Ps. xix. 6; Joel ii. 16), because the last clause of *v.* 5 is an interpolation (Duhm; cf. note in *BW*). Suspicious words are also—(1) פְּלֵיטָה, *v.* 2, elsewhere in Isa. only in x. 20, xv. 9, xxxvii. 31, 32, all on various grounds disputed passages; and (2) יָדִיחַ, *v.* 4. In the three other passages in which this Hifîl occurs the reading is contested; on Ezek. xl. 38 (2 Chr. iv. 6) see Cornill, and on Jer. li. 34, Hitzig. The formulæ with which *v.* 2 and *v.* 3 respectively open are, of course, not necessarily late; still they are special favourites of editors and supplementers. (*d*) The predominantly late ideas and images. *V.* 2, note the allusive way in which the heightened fertility of the soil is referred to; cf. Hos. ii. 23, 24 (21, 22); Am. ix. 13. It became traditionally binding to introduce this feature into Messianic descriptions, and being a weak stylist, the writer contents himself with an allusive reference. " For a pride and a glory " (*i.e.* in the eyes of the " nations "); this too is post-Deuteronomic. Cf. Deut. xxviii. 1, " If thou shalt hearken . . . to observe and do all his commandments, Yahwè thy God will set thee on high above all nations of the earth, and all these blessings shall come on thee; . . . and all peoples of the earth shall see that thou art called by the name of Yahwè, and they

---

[1] בָּרָא is a characteristic word of P in the Hexateuch. It also occurs in J, but in passages in which the hand of the editor may with good reason be suspected—viz. in Gen. vi. 7; Ex. xxxiv. 10; Num. xvi. 30; and, besides, in Am. iv. 13 (more than probably an interpolation); Jer. xxxi. 22 (in a section—chs. xxx. xxxi.—written or rewritten late); Deut. iv. 32 (Exilic, together with the whole section, Deut. i. 6-iv. 40). Cf. Wellh., *Prol.*, 3rd ed., pp. 319, 403, 405; Dillm. on Gen. i. 1; Giesebr., *ZATW*, 1881, p. 247; Cheyne, *PI*, ii. 138; Smend., *AT Rel.-gesch.*, pp. 239-241. See also p. 252 (II. Isaiah).

shall be afraid of thee"; also Isa. lxi. 9. The interpretation of Ewald and Dillmann ("instead of glorying in chariots, or in treasures, or in toilet luxuries, the Israel of the future will glory in the divinely given products of the soil") is forced, and must be rejected (see *PI*). "For the escaped of Israel;" for the late idea here expressed, see on x. 20-23. *V*. 3, the "holiness" of Israel, and especially Jerusalem, is also characteristically post-Deuteronomic (Deut. vii. 6, xxvi. 19, xxviii. 9; Lev. xix, 2, xx. 7; Ezra viii. 28; Isa. xlviii. 2, lii. 1, lxii. 12; Zech. xiv. 20, 21; Joel iv. 17; Dan. viii. 24, xii. 7). "Every one who is registered for life," a singular phrase, reminding us, says Duhm, of lvi. 6*b*, and belonging to a more legal period than Isaiah's; the figure of the "register" was a favourite with later writers[1] (Ex. xxxii. 32; Mal. iii. 16; Ps. lvi. 9, lxix. 29; Dan. xii. 1; Enoch xlvii. 3). *V*. 4, "The bloodshed of Jerusalem." Scarcely an allusion to iii. 14, 15. Rather it implies the view that the Exile was a punishment for the bloodshed with which Manasseh "filled Jerusalem from one end to another," 2 Kings xxi. 16, xxiv. 3, 4; Ezek. vii. 23, xxii. 2-4; Ps. li. 16[2] (cf. Matt. xxiii. 34, 35). *V*. 5, "And upon its convocations." Jerusalem then is already first and foremost a city of religious rites (cf. xxxiii. 20). The "convocations" are the "holy" ones of the later legislation (Ex. xii. 16; Lev. xxiii. 2, 4, 37; Num. xxviii. 25, 26, xxix. 1, 7, 12). To Isaiah such festivals were uncongenial (i. 13), nor does he ever mention them in his genuine prophecies with interest. To the writer of iv. 2-6, they would be glorified in the future by a constant appearance of the glory of Yahwè (cf. xxiv. 23, lx. 1, 2, 19, 20; Ezek. xlii. 1-5). This appearance is described in accordance with Ex. xiii. 21, 22. Now although the main features of the Exodus story may possibly have been known to Isaiah, yet there is no absolutely trustworthy evidence of this (x. 26 being more than doubtful, and the language of *v*. 5 is just such as a writer of the time of Ezra would have used). *V*. 6, the images are conventional ones of the later poetry (see on xxv. 4, xxxii. 2).

---

[1] Cf. Charles, *Book of Enoch*, pp. 131-133.
[2] See Cheyne, *Aids to the Study of Criticism*, pp. 208-210, where it

CHAPTER V

This chapter has much more than an "appearance of independence," which is all that Hitzig concedes to it. It was written (so far as it can be said to have a unity) without any thought of completing the prophecies in ii. 6-iv. 1, and when we look at it more closely, we find that it falls into three parts, representing as many distinct prophecies or groups of prophecies, viz. (A) *vv.* 1-7, (B) *vv.* 8-24 or 25, and (C) *vv.* 25 or 26-30. Metrical observations on the whole confirm this division. *Vv.* 1-7 are in two distinct rhythms or metres, but both of them differ from those which appear to be used afterwards; the division is at *v.* 6c, when Isaiah, in the midst of his threatening prophecy respecting the vineyard, suddenly exchanges the light, dancing popular rhythm for a heavy prophetic parallelism. *Vv.* 8-24 present no continuous regular rhythm, owing partly to the corruption of the text, and partly perhaps to the insertion of some lines from other contexts. Of. *v.* 25 and *vv.* 26-30 it is wisest to say nothing at present. Let us now return to *vv.* 1-7.

The greater part of this passage (A) is in the style of a popular song (cf. xxiii. 16). Isaiah who, like St. Paul, "becomes all things to all men," seeks to attract the careless citizens to his new and unwelcome style of prophecy by appearing in the guise of a minstrel. He sings of his friend and of a vineyard, and it may occur to some that he has been sent out by his friend to invite guests to a banquet (see *v.* 12). If so, the bitter irony of the close will dispel their illusion. He only wishes to press upon the people more forcibly than in chap. iii. a declaration of the coming punishment. This prophecy, therefore, need not be much later than those collected in ii. 6-iv. 1, in one of which indeed the figure of the vineyard has already been used (iii. 14).—(B) which should be taken in connection with Mic. ii., iii., consists of six sections, each of which begins with a "Woe" (הוֹי). Its period is clearly marked. The social conditions presupposed are the same as those in ii. 6-iv. 1.[1] *V.* 14 describes (in the

is shown that, even after the Return, the still existing tendency to acts of bloodshed was considered to require a judgment on the people.

[1] Cf. Robertson Smith, *Prophets*, p. 239.

language of prophetic anticipation) how the people of Jerusalem have "gone down into Sheól," exile being equivalent to death ; then should come *v.* 17, with its eloquent picture of lambs grazing in the midst of ruins. It is more than probable that there are several other incorrectnesses in the text, the sections or strophes being not of equal length. The fifth woe (*v.* 21) in particular is deficient in pictorial power; doubtless the lost conclusion would have corrected this defect. The sixth (*v.* 22) seems quite superfluous after *v.* 11, but we might perhaps recall this judgment, if its true continuation had been preserved, for *v.* 23 apparently comes from some other context.[1] But are the denunciations complete? Giesebrecht[2] suggests that the passage x. 1-4 *a*, which begins with a "Woe," and is analogous in its contents to the six "Woes" in v. 8-24, should be placed (cf. n. 2) as the first denunciation. If the metre of x. 1-4*a* did not agree with that of ix. 7-20 as much as it disagrees with that (or those) of v. 8-24, and if the number of lines in x. 1-4 were not exactly the same as that in the three preceding strophes, I should be strongly inclined towards this view. Possibly there were once more than six "Woes," but we cannot recover the missing ones any more than we can fill up those which are evidently imperfect. It only needs to be added that *vv.* 15, 16 (which split the connection) are a quotation from memory, from ii. 11, 17, which has intruded into the text from the margin.[3]

And now as to (C). Does *v.* 25 properly belong to this part or the preceding one? The right answer was to a great extent given by Ewald, who saw two points very clearly. (1) *V.* 25 cannot be the conclusion of the prophecy in *vv.* 8-24, partly because it is in the historical style, and is therefore inconsistent with *v.* 24,[4] partly because the closing

[1] Giesebrecht, following out a hint of Stade, suggests that v. 23 may once have stood between x. 1 and 2 (*i.e.* according to him, in the first "Woe"). He places v. 22 between *v.* 10 and *v.* 11.
[2] *Beiträge* (1890), p. 15. Similarly Koppe, Studer, F. Brown (*JBL*, 1890, p. 91), and Hackmann, *ZEJ*, p. 54.
[3] So Stade (*Gesch.*, p. 605) and Duhm. Eichhorn also omits *v.* 17.
[4] König (*Einl.*, p. 314) thinks it enough to say that *vv.* 25 and 26-30 are a postscript added by Isaiah, in which it is declared that Judah's punishment as a fact began with the invasion of the allied kings and would be completed with the terrible onslaught of the Assyrians.

words state that the hand of Yahwè is still stretched out, whereas *v.* 24 is evidently intended to describe the final judgment on the people. (2) Although *v.* 25 belongs [in a certain sense] to the same prophecy as *vv.* 26-30, it did not originally come just before this passage, but was separated from it by the prophecy, ix. 7-x. 4. To the latter view Ewald was guided by the observation that v. 25 closes with the very words which form the refrain of that prophecy (ix. 11, 16, 20, x. 4). It fell to me to open the series of commentators who adopted this brilliant conjecture (*ICA*, 1870, pp. 14-16; cf. *PI*, i. 63); Diestel followed in 1872 (in Knobel's *Jes.*, 4th ed.), and in 1882 Robertson Smith (*Prophets*, p. 238). Bredenkamp (pp. 38-40) prefers to combine v. 1-25, ix. 7-x. 4, and v. 26-30 in one long prophecy, a view in which (see below) there is an element of truth, though Isaiah must have meant v. 24 as the close of a prophecy. It was, however, left for Giesebrecht to supply what was wanting to Ewald's theory.[1] He pointed out that ix. 7 must be the beginning of a prophecy, and that the expressions in v. 25 (apart from the closing words) are far too vague for Isaiah, and drawn from the common stock of prophetic and poetic imagery (see Ezek. xiv. 9, 13; Isa. xxix. 6, xiii. 13, lxiii. 19; Mic. i. 3, 4; Nah. i. 5; Joel iii. 16; Hab. iii. 5-10; Ps. xviii. 8; Jer. ix. 21, xvi. 4, xxv. 33; Zeph. i. 17). V. 25 (to הָחוּצָה) is in fact a composition of the editor;[2] it is a paraphrastic development of the refrain (referred to above) with which the verse closes. Its original object was to link v. 1-24 with ix. 7-x. 4 and v. 26-30 (or rather v. 26-29, *v.* 30 being, as Duhm has shown, another editorial insertion). The student will observe that

[1] *Beiträge*, pp. 3-24; similarly Cornill and Hackmann.
[2] It is strange that Dillmann and Duhm should retain *v.* 25 for Isaiah. In order to do this, they have to suppose that it belongs to a strophe, the remainder of which has been lost. Dillmann (like Ewald) thinks that the "trembling" of the mountains may allude to the earthquake under Uzziah. This would be not unplausible (cf. p. 17), but for the indications of a late date mentioned above. Remember, however, that the phenomena of earthquakes were familiar to all the biblical writers. The later writers loved to describe theophanies, and the consequent effect upon universal nature (cf. *BL*, pp. 156, 344). Duhm, with most commentators, interprets the verbs as prophetic. But in ix. 7-x. 4, the perfect and imperfect consec. are used, as it seems to me, of past events, and this is here too the most natural view.

both v. 25a and v. 30 are without the beautiful, well-marked rhythm of the prophecy to which they are attached, and that while v. 25a contains nothing suggestive of Isaiah, v. 30 is evidently modelled on viii. 22, the basis of which is Isaianic. (ונבט לארץ) requires as an antithesis a description of a despairing upward look, such as we actually find in viii. 22, cf. Jer. iv. 23.)

It will be clear from what has been said that from the point of view of the ancient editor, but not from that of Isaiah, v. 1-25a, ix. 7-x. 4, v. 26-30 form one long continuous prophetic composition. It will have to be considered later whether x. 1-4 always stood as the continuation of ix. 7-20, and also why the bulk of the "word" (ix. 7) against Israel was transferred (by another editor?) elsewhere. One question only remains to be answered here, viz., Why were v. 25 and 26-30 left when the greater part of the prophecy had been removed? To this we may reply that v. 25 may have been left, because to place it after ix. 6 would have been absurd, and v. 26-30 because the passage serves to give definiteness to the vague prophecies of captivity and desolation in the preceding prophecies. There was also a special need for a fuller and more solemn close to chap. v. in view of the entirely fresh start taken in chap. vi. See further on ix. 7, etc.

CHAPTER VI

The vision and consecration of the young Isaiah with a statement of his prophetic message. The facts related are said to have occurred "in the death-year of King Uzziah," *i.e.* probably in 740 B.C. This may be accepted, but we cannot suppose that the account of the vision was written down quite so early, for the writer evidently regards the vision as a thing of the past. We need not however assume a long interval between the vision and the account of it, merely on the ground of the gloomy pessimism of *vv.* 9-13. There is no sufficient reason for denying that Isaiah entered on his ministry with the certainty of ill success. Ordinary natures would no doubt be paralysed in their moral and spiritual activity by such a stern revelation. But Isaiah, like his older contemporary Amos, had a God-consciousness which lifted his nature above that of the common herd, and made it possible for him to work with no hope of saving his people.¹ He tried both persuasion and denunciation; for instances of the former, which might easily be overlooked, see i. 5, 6, 16-20; vii. 4-11; xxx. 15; and for those of the latter see the earliest not less than the latest prophecies. And after the crowning proof of the truth of his revelation supplied by the "great refusal" of Ahaz (vii. 12) he may be believed to have written down the account of his vision and message in chap. vi., an account which is in all essentials truthful, though not actually penned till 734 B.C.

If however this is the date of the composition of chap. vi., how is it that nothing is said in it of the "remnant" which "shall turn"? This hope must have been Isaiah's in 735 (the year in which Shear-yashub accompanied his father Isaiah to the place where he was to meet Ahaz), and indeed earlier still, for the child can hardly have been less than four or five years old when he took that famous walk, and was very probably born in the very year of the vision (740). We can hardly help admitting that, even if the last three words of vi. 13 are a late addition, yet Isaiah, when he saw his vision, understood it to be connected with a revelation of a "remnant" that should "turn." To account for the non-mention of the "remnant" in ch. vi., we must suppose that this narrative was originally intended as a prologue to vii. 1-viii. 18 (or ix. 6). The unbelief of Ahaz was typical of that of the nation, and the troubles of the Syrian invasion were like a prelude of the sorer judgments announced in vi. 11-13 (cf. vii. 18-25). [The words which at present close ch. vi. were added for the comfort of post-Exilic readers. They contain the late idea of the "holiness" of the people of Israel (see on iv. 3) expressed in a late phrase ("a holy seed," Ezra ix. 2), and they make a clear exegesis of *v.* 13 impossible.² (Isaiah meant that even the "stump" or "stock" should be burned; this however the gloss directly denies.) They are moreover wanting in Sept., though

¹ A fuller study of Amos has greatly helped the author to his present conclusion.
² See Duhm *ad loc.*, and Hackmann (*ZEJ*, p. 72).

supplied in the text of Lucian, and by a later hand (in smaller characters) in cod. A.]

To place chap. vi. earlier (with Hackmann) requires three assumptions, viz.—(1) That "this people" in *v.* 9 means N. Israel; (2) that the name "Shear-yashub" records what may be called the second part of the revelation connected with Isaiah's vision; and (3) that the word שְׁאָר in that name designates Judah. Accepting these assumptions, the revelation of which Isaiah was conscious would be to this effect, that he was commissioned to announce a twofold judgment to the northern kingdom, consisting of a growing spiritual insensibility and a removal of the people from their land. This view would enable us to understand how Isaiah could still cherish hopes for Judah during the crisis of the Syro-Ephraimitish invasion, and it is confirmed (according to Hackmann) by the confidence with which the destruction of N. Israel is foretold in ix. 7, etc., and xvii. 1-11, a confidence which arose naturally out of the great initial revelation. But are those assumptions really justified? As to (1) it is certain that as used by Isaiah elsewhere the phrase refers to Judah[1] (viii. 6, 12; xxviii. 11, 14; xxix. 13, 14), nor can one easily understand how Isaiah could be commanded to "go and say" something to the men of N. Israel and then remain quietly at Jerusalem[2] (contrast the course taken by Amos). As to (2) we may and should accept it, but the question remains, What was Isaiah's view of the first part of the revelation? As to (3) the supposed sense appears to be against Isaiah's usage. In xvi. 14 the "remnant," and in xvii. 3 the "remnant of Aram" (both times שְׁאָר) mean those who have escaped in the judgment (in the one case in Moab, in the other in Aram). If "this people" means N. Israel, then "the remnant" in the supposed second part of Isaiah's revelation must have meant the survivors of N. Israel. (We shall return to Hackmann's view of the reference of Isaiah's early discourses on vii. 18-25.)

[1] ix. 16 is not Isaianic (see Duhm, and *RT*).
[2] Hackmann, it is true, bids us not be too sure that Isaiah did not go to the N. Israelitish frontier.

Chapters VII.-IX. 6

It is specially necessary here to enter on our criticism with right assumptions. Both Del. and Orelli extend this section of prophecy to the end of chap. xii., and state that it forms a compact whole belonging to the reign of Ahaz. Such an extension however we shall find to be impossible; indeed, by Del.'s own admission elsewhere,[1] x. 9-34, at least in its present form, cannot have been written before the time of Hezekiah. Nor can we venture to say even of vii. 1-ix. 6, either that it forms a literary whole, or that it has come down to us uninjured from Isaiah's hand. "It will be observed that chap. vii. does not claim to be the work of Isaiah. There is also a looseness in the connection, and an occasional feebleness of style, which make even the editorship of Isaiah difficult to realise; notice in particular the break between *v*. 16 and *v*. 17, and the cumbrous style of *vv*. 17-25. The same looseness of connection is apparent in chap. viii. Taken together with the very peculiar introduction to chap. vii. [notice the phrase "in the days of Ahaz"], and the cumbrousness of vii. 17-25, it makes it a very probable conjecture that the whole section, vii. 1-ix. 6, only assumed its present form long after the original utterance of the prophecies" (*PI*, i. 42). This view I still believe to be correct; I must however enter here into more detail than was possible in my commentary.

The most obvious divisions of this section seem to be these—(A) chap. vii.[2]; (B) viii. 1-4; (C) viii. 5-10; (D) viii. 11-18; and (E) viii. 19-ix. 6. I do not say that they are the only ones that we shall find, but they are at any rate sufficient for us to start with. Let us notice in the first place certain features which either all or some of them have in common. For instance (*a*) there are parallelisms in the form of expression between vii. 5 and viii. 6, between vii. 7 and viii. 10, between vii. 10 and viii. 5, and between vii. 14, 16, and viii. 3, 4, nor can עמנו אל in viii. 8 be understood without

[1] Del., *Jesaia*,[4] p. 178.
[2] On the text and interpretation of ch. vii., see Budde's study in the *Études* dedicated to Leemans, pp. 121-126; Lagarde, *Semitica*, i. 9-13.

the prophecy in vii. 14. (*b*) The narrative element so conspicuous in chap. vii. is also present in chap. viii., where however it is confined to introductory formulæ, such as "And Yahwè said unto me," and the like (*not*, unto Isaiah). (*c*) From vii. 1 to viii. 10 we meet with references to Rezin and Pekah, though it is only in vii. 1 that we find "the days of Ahaz" spoken of as past. Several inferences may be drawn from these facts. Thus from (*a*) we cannot help inferring that in some form the prophetic portion of chap. vii., together with introductory narrative formulæ (if no more), must always have preceded chap. viii. From (*b*), that the reference to Isaiah in the third person in vii. 3 is due either to Isaiah's scribe or to a later editor. No doubt similar phenomena occur elsewhere in the prophets (Isa. xx.; Hos. i. 2-4, 6; Am. vii. 12, 14; Jer.; Hag. i., ii. *passim;* Zech. i. 1, vii. 1), but these may be accounted for on a similar hypothesis. From (*c*), that even if touched by a later hand, the prophetic basis of vii. 1-viii. 10 (postponing the analysis of this portion) is contemporary with Rezin and Pekah.

Let us now proceed to investigate A. with a view to ascertain whether it is of composite origin, and if so, whether it contains any non-Isaianic elements, also whether any part of the Isaianic text has been lost. And (1), with regard to *v*. 1, which recurs with a little variation in 2 Ki. xvi. 5, Which of these parallel passages is the original? According to Dillm., it is the passage in Isaiah; לְמִלְחָמָה in Kings is "less correct" than לְ עָלֶיהָ in Isaiah, and יָכְלוּ is easier and therefore later than יָכֹל. He adds that 2 Ki. xvi. 5 "stands very isolated," and that Isa. vii. 2 must have had something before it. But the conclusion seems wrong. 2 Ki. has the important words וַיָּצֻרוּ עַל־אָחָז, which are wanting in Isaiah. The war was waged specially against Ahaz (Isa. vii. 6), and Jerusalem most probably *was* besieged (Isaiah leaves this doubtful[1]), though unsuccessfully, and as for לְ עָלֶיהָ, if the phrase just mentioned be accepted, עָלֶיהָ clearly becomes superfluous. יָכְלוּ, not יָכֹל, is the reading of Sept. Isa. As

[1] נִלְחַם עַל might have a wide sense; cf. Isa. xx. 1, xxxvii. 8. 2 Ki. xvi. 5 asserts that Jerusalem was besieged, but not taken by storm (see Dillm.).

for the "isolation" of 2 Ki. xvi. 5, it is simply the result of condensation; the same remark applies to *v.* 6. The closing words moreover are more natural in 2 Ki. than in Isaiah, where they spoil the subsequent narrative.[1] Isa. vii. 1, therefore, is dependent on 2 Ki. xvi. 5. Hence it is at earliest Exilic, for though 2 Ki. xvi. 1-9 is undoubtedly pre-Exilic, it was hardly written very long before the first deportation in 597 B.C.[2] It is true that *v.* 2 (which comes from Isaiah's age) must always have had something before it. But chap. vii. in its original form doubtless stood at the head of a book of prophecies, and the opening lines would easily become illegible (so, independently, Duhm). What did the lost passage contain? It must have referred to the march of the allied forces against Judah, and may have been longer than our *v.* 1, for the poetical style of *v.* 2 implies emotion in the writer, and emotional excitement can but be understood at the end of a descriptive section of some length. This descriptive section, together with *vv.* 3-14, 16, was probably taken from a book on the prophetic career of Isaiah (cf. on ch. xx.).

(2) *Vv.* 2-8*a*, 9. See above. The author of the book referred to was at any rate contemporary with the facts, and has accurately reproduced the prophecy of Isaiah. The rhythm of the prophecy is no doubt irregular, but the style is throughout so energetic that we should hesitate to ascribe any part of it to a late writer. The mention of Shear-yashub suggests that some lost prophecy of Isaiah, which would be known to Ahaz, referred to the conversion of the "remnant." That *v.* 8*b* is a gloss[3] is generally admitted, (1) because it interrupts Isaiah's argument; (2) because it is inconsistent with *v.* 16; and (3) because there is no prophetic analogy for a prediction of what is to happen in 65 years. The writer of the gloss (who was probably alive

---

[1] So Gesenius. From Dillmann's point of view, the closing words are said proleptically (cf. xx. 1).

[2] See Kuenen, *Ond.*[2], i. 420.

[3] Stade (*Gesch.*, i. 594; cf. ii. 206) rejects in addition *v.* 8*a* and *v.* 9*a*, as due to the editor who worked up this chapter, the whole passage being too oracular, too obscure for Isaiah to have delivered under such circumstances. But we have here, presumably, only a summary of Isaiah's prophecy.

near the time to which he refers[1]) may, however, have been right in his impression that the text as it stood was incomplete. The interpolated words are Isaianic in style (cf. xxi. 16, xvi. 14, xvii. 1); the Sopherim who edited the works of the prophets were familiar with their stylistic peculiarities. חחת in Nif. does not, however, again in Isaiah mean "to be broken" (II. Isaiah has it, see li. 6).

(3) *Vv.* 10-16. At the outset observe the singular phrase, "And Yahwè spake further unto Ahaz." At first sight this may seem parallel to viii. 5. It would be strictly so, if Ahaz were the direct recipient of the revelation, but it is really more parallel to iii. 16, where "Yahwè" is either put carelessly for "Isaiah," or equivalent to "the prophet of Yahwè."[2] Both in iii. 16 and in vii. 10 the lax use of the introductory formula is probably due to an editor, and in both cases the formula is used to link passages which have no very close connection. This is of importance for the right comprehension of *v.* 11 f. The solemn words, "Ask thou a sign of Yahwè thy God," etc., imply that some definite and rather startling announcement has gone before. Such an announcement there would be, if we had a right to retain *v.* 8*b* (altering "65 years" into "a little while" as proposed by Del.). But, as a fact, Isaiah's first declaration (qualified by threatening words at the close of *v.* 9) is merely that the attempt of Rezin will be abortive. A man who trembled like forest trees before the wind would surely need more definite comfort than this! We must therefore suppose that here too something has fallen out of the text or been omitted—a view which is confirmed by the formula prefixed to *v.* 10. Can we conjecture what this lost passage contained? Surely we can. It must have been nearly equivalent to the closing words of *v.* 16, words which describe the event of which Immanuel is the sign. Now, from 2 Ki. xvi.

---

[1] The view (*PI*, i. 45; cf. Dillm.) that the calculation is from 736 to 671 (which may have been the year when Esar-haddon brought foreign colonists to Samaria, Ezra iv. 2) must be abandoned, if Winckler's criticism of Ezra iv. 2 is to be accepted (*Untersuch.*, p. 98). The colonisation will then be that of Assurbanipal. The chronology need not of course be strictly correct.

[2] We need not therefore alter "Yahwè" into "Isaiah" (Houb., *PI*), nor read simply וַיֹּאמֶר here and in *v.* 13 (Budde, Duhm).

7, 8 [1] we know that Ahaz applied for help to Tiglath-pileser, and in *vv.* 17-25 (parts of which at any rate are Isaianic) we meet with clear predictions of an Assyrian invasion. May we not suppose that Isaiah, who on a similar occasion afterwards unveiled the scheme of the politicians (xxix. 15), divined the secret purpose of Ahaz, and laboured hard to dissuade or deter the king from it? "In *vv.* 17-25 his language is deterrent; in the lost passage which should precede *v.* 10 it was probably of a persuasive character."[2] Isaiah may have spoken somewhat thus: "Wherefore shouldest thou seek help afar off? Is there no God in Israel who is mighty to save? Yet a very little while and the fortress shall cease from Ephraim, and the kingdom from Damascus. Dost thou not even yet trust the Divine promise? Then ask thee a sign from Yahwè thy God." Such may have been the distinct and startling announcement which preceded *v.* 10, in accordance with the explanation (*v.* 16*b*) of the unasked sign of Immanuel.

How far, however, can we trust the text of *v.* 11? May not the original text have been manipulated by an editor (Lag., Stade)? But why? One is only staggered at Isaiah's boldness till one remembers the lofty style of the man and his present object. Believing in Yahwè's might with primitive simplicity, he makes one more desperate attempt to stimulate Ahaz to the great spiritual effort called "faith." If Ahaz cannot believe Isaiah, then (Isaiah makes this strange condescension) let him choose his own "sign."[3] It is true, the sign actually given is very far below what might have been expected. But this is because the object of the "sign" is now entirely changed. It is no longer meant to persuade the king, but to save the honour of Yahwè's prophet. It consists simply in the name which mothers will, before long, by a kind of inspiration give to their newly-born babes. Not Ichabod but Immanuel, or any similar name expressing the deliver-

---

[1] See also *CI*, i. 225, and cf., on the political unwisdom of this course, Kittel, *Gesch.*, i. 292. [2] *PI*, i. 45.

[3] Though probably against the meaning of the points, it is best to render "deep unto Sheól," and explain in accordance with Job xi. 7, 8. That Isaiah meant literally to offer a sign from Sheól, I cannot believe (see viii. 19).

ance of Judah, shall be the name commonly borne by the children of that generation. Such names will be to all the people memorials of the invading armies, and pledges of the impending desolation of Syria and Ephraim, and to Ahaz they will also be discouraging memorials of his own unbelief (cf. the "sign" in Ex. iii. 12). In short, there are two kinds of "signs," and it is noteworthy that in the fragments of the biography of Isaiah we have another specimen of each variety (xxxviii. 7, 8; xxxvii. 30). On the whole, we have no good reason to doubt the equal genuineness of vii. 11*b* and vii. 14, 16. *V.* 15 however may safely be rejected as a gloss.[1] Not only does it separate "Immanuel" from its natural explanation in *v.* 16, but it is clearly made up from *v.* 22 and *v.* 16 by an early harmonist among the Sopherim, who inferred from these two passages taken together that Immanuel (*i.e.*, according to him, the Messiah) would have a diet of milk-curd and honey shortly after the time when Syria and N. Israel would be laid waste. The alternative is to reject *v.* 16 (Budde, Kuenen). But this involves rendering לדעתו "that he may know," which is both grammatically and exegetically difficult. Moreover, *v.* 16 is strikingly parallel to viii. 4, though Budde's view that "knowing good and evil" is to be taken in a moral sense, somewhat obscures this.[2]

(4) Thus from *v.* 10 to *v.* 16 the tone of the prophet is friendly to Ahaz. The king is no doubt warned against trying the divine patience too far, but a longsuffering God gives him one more chance of turning into the right path. This theory assumes that לָכֵן in *v.* 14 is not uttered in a threatening tone (as i. 24; v. 13, 24; so Dillm.), but means

---

[1] So Hitz., Reuss, Stade, Duhm. Barth, who retains *v.* 15, rightly sees that, if genuine, it must be meant as encouragement (so Rashi). Is not this every reader's first impression? (Forbes, *The Servant of the Lord*, p. 213.)

[2] Budde's view is adopted by Kuenen, *Ond.*[2] This rend. of לדעתו is that of Aquila, Symm., Pesh., Vulg., and among the moderns of Kay, Bredenkamp, and Guthe, *Zukunftsbild*, pp. 11, 40; also of Luther and A.V. In R.V. the more usual modern rend. (Hitz., Dillm., Del., Orelli, *PI*), "when he knoweth," is preferred; ל "towards the time that." Budde's explanation of the whole clause is very difficult however. Is the idea that privation makes for character a likely one for Isaiah, and would he have expressed it thus?

CHAPTER VII

simply "this being the case" (cf. Gen. iv. 15). At *v.* 17 a new prophecy (or summary of prophecies) begins; we have no right, with Sept., to force a connection with *vv.* 10-16 by prefixing an adversative particle. And if *v.* 17 is substantially accurate, the subject of the following passage is the desolation of the land of Judah by Assyria. But is this verse trustworthy? It is at any rate in too bold a style for Isaiah, and is most naturally ascribed to an editor.[1] Conceivably, then, its statement that the sufferings of the people of Judah are referred to is erroneous. Isaiah has just before spoken of the imminent desolation of the land of the allied kings; *vv.* 18-25 may therefore refer to Syria and N. Israel, with whom the prophet is still concerned in viii. 1-4. Hackmann thinks that they do.[2] Isaiah's present mission was to encourage Ahaz; is it likely that he would at once proceed to discourage the king by so alarming a prediction? Moreover, his initial revelation referred to the fate of the N. kingdom (see p. 28), and it was the subject which chiefly engaged his attention at the beginning of his ministry (ii. 6-22; vi.; ix. 7-20; xvii. 1-11; xxviii. 1-4). This, however, is a very hazardous view, and as regards *vv.* 18-25 is neither chronologically sound (see below) nor in itself natural. In chap. viii. we find a prediction of the fall of Damascus and Samaria followed by a prophecy of an Assyrian invasion of Judah; why should not another such prophecy follow viii. 16? We have already heard of a captivity of Judah in chap. v., and Ahaz must have known of this; depressing the prophecy in vii. 18 etc. may have been, but startling it certainly was not. And if it be true that in this chapter, as often elsewhere, we have a summary of prophecies not all delivered on the same day, we may reasonably hold that some change of circumstances justified the prophet's change of tone (of which indeed a warning had been given in *v.* 9). It is possible that between the utterance of *v.* 16 and that of *v.* 18 the embassy to Tiglath-pileser (already—see above—anticipated by Isaiah) had actually

---

[1] Thus we need not burden Isaiah with an unhistorical view of the origin of the N. Kingdom (cf. Stade, *Gesch.*, i. 347). The concluding words, "the King of Assyria," are clearly due to a scribe. Cf. *v.* 20, viii. 7. [2] *ZEJ*, p. 66.

been despatched.[1] But how the transition from *v.* 16 to *v.* 18 was originally made we know not.

It is easy to recognise the hand of a supplementer in the introductory formulæ of *vv.* 18, 20, 21, 22, 23, and of a glossator in the words "with the king of Assyria" in *v.* 20. Lagarde and Guthe,[2] however, reject *vv.* 18 and 19 altogether on the ground that prophecy always has reference to present circumstances, and that no danger threatened Judah at this period from Egypt. Certainly Bokchoris had too precarious a sway over Egypt to intervene in the affairs of Judah; not till Shabaka's victory over the rival princes in 728 was there anything to hope or fear from Egypt.[3] The difficulty referred to would of course be removed by the acceptance of Hackmann's theory mentioned above. But chronology is opposed to this view. Neither as friends nor as foes could the Egyptians have trodden the soil of N. Israel till after 728. And in itself Hackmann's view has been shown to be improbable; *vv.* 17-25 are parallel to viii. 5-8, which refers to Judah. Is there no better way of removing the difficulty? May we not suppose either that a fragment contemporary with Hezekiah's negotiations with Tirhakah (see on ch. xxx.) has been misplaced, or that the geographical definitions— "at the end of the streams of Egypt," and "in the land of Assyria"—are glosses (Duhm)? The latter view is the simpler, and fully meets the difficulty. The "flies" and the "bees" are both symbols of the same formidable power— Assyria. The mistake of the glossator was probably caused by the false reading בגוים in v. 26, which he rightly enough considered to be a parallel passage. They forgot that those who corresponded to the "flies" (if the flies meant the Egyptians) were by no means renowned for the swiftness of their marches. That the verses are Isaiah's, or at any rate early, may be seen by comparing them with *vv.* 21-25. Note, however, the number of rare words. זְבוּב again only in Eccl. x. 1, and in "Baal-zebub." בַּתּוֹת, ἅπ. λεγ. נָקִיק again

---

[1] Cf. Barth, *Beiträge*, p. 8. [2] *Zukunftsbild*, p. 39.
[3] Knobel and Dillm. suggest that Rezin and Pekah may have planned an Egyptian alliance, and sought to put aside Ahaz in order to smooth the way for an Egyptian army. But why should either Egypt or Syria desire to desolate Judah?

only in Jer. xiii. 4, xvi. 16. נַעֲצוּץ again only in lv. 13. תַּעַר הַשְּׂכִירָה, only here in Isa. As to *vv.* 21-25, the careless and strikingly unrhythmical style proves that in their present form these verses are not Isaianic. Possibly, however, shreds and patches of Isaiah may be imbedded in them.

B. (viii. 1-4). This prophecy forms a small section in itself. It was of course delivered before 732 (see *v.* 4), and since Isaiah regards it as a startling announcement, it probably synchronises with the prophecy of Immanuel. The two names in fact supplement each other. But we must not infer from this that Immanuel is another name (or rather, as Hitz. thinks, the only real name) of Isaiah's newborn child. Isaiah would not have called his wife indiscriminately "the prophetess" (viii. 3) and "the *alma*" (vii. 14); indeed, the latter term was altogether unsuitable for the mother of Shear-yashub. Note that Isaiah here aims to encourage the people, as in vii. 4-16 to encourage the "house of Ahaz."

C. (viii. 5-10). "This people"[1] is as despondent (*i.e.* as unbelieving) on account of Rezin and Pekah as King Ahaz. The same threatenings (cf. vii. 17-25) are therefore uttered. Judah is mentioned by name (*v.* 8), so that Hackmann's theory respecting vii. 17-25 cannot be extended to this passage. In *v.* 7 the explanatory words are a gloss, and *vv.* 9, 10 (on *v.* 8*b*, see below) are a later addition to the prophecy. The latter verses are not only in a different rhythm from *vv.* 6-8, but express ideas entirely different from those in the preceding passage. Are they the work of Isaiah, or of a later supplementer?[2] If they are not by Isaiah, they are a good imitation of his style. Certainly their energy is worthy of Isaiah. Nor is the phraseology

---

[1] The view adopted in *PI* that *v.* 6*a* refers to both N. and S. Israel, *v.* 6*b* to N. Israel alone, *v.* 7 chiefly to N. Israel, and *v.* 8 to S. Israel alone, was dictated by the false reading וּמְשׂוֹשׂ אֶת־ ("and because of the rejoicing with"). "This people" must mean Judah (see *vv.* 11, 12). The view of Ges., Ew., Stade, Kue., and R. Smith (cf. Sept.) that the anti-Assyrian party in Jerusalem favoured the enterprise of Rezin and Pekah, is however inadmissible (see vii. 2, viii. 12). We must therefore read וּמָסוֹס מִפְּנֵי (see *RT*), "and despond because of."

[2] The latter alternative is adopted by Stade (*ZATW*, iv. 260) and Hackmann (*ZEJ*, p. 70).

unlike his. רעו, "be angry," may seem to need a parallel passage, but Sept.'s דְעוּ is probably a better reading, and the rare עֻצוּ is a good old form (Judg. xix. 30). For the threatening imperatives cf. xxix. 9, and for a phrase in *v.* 10*b* cf. vii. 7. The ideas too are not alien to Isaiah. It is too bold to assert that the prophets of the 8th cent. never have a large group of peoples ("all the nations") within their view.[1] The extension of the Assyrian empire would naturally tend to expand the religious ideas of the prophets, and that this was actually the case with Isaiah we see from xiv. 24-27, xvii. 12-14, xviii. 3. It may be admitted that the ideas are such as a post-Exilic writer might well have expressed, and that such late writers were not incapable of imitating Isaiah's style. Also that the parallel passages xxx. 28 ("to sift," etc.), xxxiii. 13, Ps. xlvi. 7, 8, 11, 12,[2] are most probably of a later age than Isaiah's. But though on these grounds *vv.* 9, 10 may conceivably be post-Exilic, why should we prefer this hypothesis to any other? It seems to me equally conceivable that these verses are either (*a*) an Isaianic fragment of somewhat later origin inserted here by the editor, or (*b*) that they were written later by Isaiah as an appendix to the preceding prophecy,[3] as probably xvii. 12-14 were written by him as an appendix to xvii. 1-11. Of these alternatives (*b*) is to be preferred. There are two occasions before Sennacherib's time, on which an Assyrian invasion of Judah may have seemed to Isaiah to be imminent, viz. the siege of Samaria (724-722) and the expedition against Ashdod (711). To the former occasion I refer xvii. 12-14; to the latter xiv. 24-27. Both these passages are rather strikingly parallel to viii. 9-10.

[1] See Stade, *ZATW*, i. 165, 166; iii. 14, etc.; iv. 292, and on the other side Cornill and Nowack, *ZATW*, iv. 88, 278, etc.; Ryssel, *Micha* (on Mic. iv. 1-5); Kuenen, *Ond.*[2], ii. 40; Giesebrecht, *St. u. Kr.*, 1888, p. 260.

[2] The parallelism between Ps. xlvi. and Isa. vii. 9, 10, becomes all the stronger if we hold that עמו אל (*v.* 8 end) coheres with vii. 9, for a refrain which opens with עמו 'צ '״ occurs twice (and should occur thrice) in Ps. xlvi. On this psalm, cf. *BL*, pp. 163-166.

[3] So Giesebrecht (*St. u. Kr.*, 1888, pp. 235-248). Duhm regards the passage as an independent prophecy relative to the Syrian invasions.

CHAPTER VIII. 5-10

Take first the conclusion of xvii. 13, and compare it with viii. 9 (the parallelism is here that of idea), noting also the similarity between xvii. 12-13*a* and viii. 7-8*a*—

But when he rebuketh it, it fleeth far away and is chased
Like chaff of the mountains before the wind, and like whirling dust
before the hurricane.

Take knowledge, ye peoples, and . . . ;
And give ear, all ye of far countries !
Gird yourselves, and break to pieces,
Gird yourselves, and break to pieces !

And then compare xiv. 24 with viii. 10 (the parallelism is here both in the idea and in the phraseology)—

Surely according as I have planned, so shall it be,
And according as I have purposed (so) shall it stand.

Purpose a purpose, and it shall come to nought,
Form a resolve, and it shall not stand,
For with us is God.

May we not conclude that one of these occasions gave rise to Isaiah's insertion ? Observe however that this insertion is not limited to *vv.* 9, 10. Bred. must, I think, be right in holding that עמנו אל (or rather כי עמנו אל)[1] in *v.* 8*b* coheres with *v.* 9. The words contain a declaration of the certainty of Judah's deliverance, whereas the preceding words (according to the common explanation) describe the flooding of the land with the Assyrian soldiery. But Bred. does not seem to me to go far enough. The "outstretched wings" must be those either of a gigantic bird of prey, cf. Hos. viii. 1 "(he shall come) as a vulture against the house of Yahwè" (*i.e.* the land of Israel), or rather (since nothing is said of an assault upon the land) of a great protecting bird (cf. Mal. iii. 20 ; Ps. xvii. 8, xxxvi. 8, etc.). If so, it is plain that *v.* 8*b* does not cohere with *v.* 8*a* ; a passage has fallen out between the two halves of the verse. Now, should

---

[1] Render the corrected text of *v.* 8*b*, "and his outstretched wings shall fill the breadth of the land. For with us is God." See Duhm, and cf. *RT.*

not *v.* 8*b* be united to *vv.* 9, 10, and regarded as part of Isaiah's appendix? The contents are not opposed to this view, but the fragmentary appearance of *v.* 8*b* forbids dogmatism.[1]

D. (viii. 11-18). This section is strictly parallel to the preceding one (*vv.* 5-8), but the prophecy which it contains is of slightly earlier date. In the opening verse Isaiah justifies the language of *vv.* 5-8 by reference to the message which he had received when in an ecstasy. He had said in *v.* 6 that "this people" was to be punished for "desponding because of Rezin and ben Remaliah"; this he did in accordance with an imperious warning not to "walk in the way of this people" (*i.e.* clearly, Judah) by "calling everything conspiracy which this people calleth conspiracy," and by "fearing and accounting dreadful" that which "this people" feareth. The date here proposed would be hazardous, were we to accept the plausible emendation קֹדֶשׁ for קֶשֶׁר. *Vv.* 12, 13, with their warning against the adoption of heathenish sacred objects, would then be parallel to *v.* 19 with its warning against necromancy. But clearly such an oracle as this, if addressed at all to Isaiah, would only have been appropriate at the very opening of his career, if even then. The reading קֶשֶׁר must be retained, and interpreted in harmony with usage and with the prophecy of which (כִּי, *v.* 11) it supplies the justification. How, then, are the noun קֶשֶׁר and the verb קשׁר used? They are used of those leagues which have a destructive object— leagues of subjects against a king (1 Sam. xxii. 8, 13; 2 Sam. xv. 12, 31; 2 Ki. xi. 14; Am. vii. 10), of men banded together for immoral or heathenish ends (Jer. xi. 9; Ezek. xxii. 25), or of the confederated enemies of a single nation (Neh. iv. 2). This last application of the term is suitable here. On the first news of the Syro-Ephraimitish invasion there was a cry, קֶשֶׁר, *i.e.* the enemies of Judah are confederated against it. But Isaiah is warned by a strong impulse from above that this is an abuse of terms. Syria and Israel are but "two stumps of smoking firebrands"; how can such feeble powers be said to have formed a קֶשֶׁר? (*Binding* implies strength; cf. קְשֻׁרִים, Gen. xxx. 42.) The

---

[1] All that is most important in this theory comes from Duhm. This critic also regards "For with us is God" (*vv.* 8, 10) as inserted later.

warning is expressed in general terms, לְכֹל אֲשֶׁר, because the same circumstances may arise again. To Isaiah a קֶשֶׁר only becomes worthy of its name when Yahwè is the chief member of the league, as when he "sends" Assyria "against the people of his wrath" (x. 6). But the true fear of Yahwè, which shows itself equally in obedience to his *tôra* (see i. 10-17) and in perfect reliance on his word of promise (vii. 9), binds him to the side of his people. To correct תַקְדִּישׁוּ (*v.* 13) into תַקְשִׁירוּ, an unique Hifil form, with Duhm and Hackmann introduces a needlessly hard riddle. Those who sanctify Yahwè by fearing him in the right way (the few implied by the "many," cf. *v.* 15) make Yahwè their ally. True; but Judah as a nation had cut itself off from this happy prospect, and Isaiah's hearers or readers would scarcely have understood how there could be a קֶשֶׁר against Rezin and Pekah without the nation which those kings were thought to assail. לְמִקְדָּשׁ ו should be deleted; 'מ is a variant to מוקשׁ (Duhm). But after *v.* 15 and again after *v.* 18 there is a clear break. *Vv.* 16-18 form an epilogue to the various prophetic revelations (in their original form) given from vii. 3 onwards. The prophet's mood is gloomy, but not unrelieved by hope; it was otherwise in v. 1-24. The door of hope may be closed for the "house of Jacob" (= "both houses of Israel," *v.* 14), but Isaiah and his children, with their prophetic names, are "signs" of the "remnant" which "shall turn," appointed by "Yahwè Çebaoth who dwelleth in Zion." Notice the grand roll of the phrase, which is evidently intended as the close of the epilogue.

E. (viii. 19-ix. 6). Here we must at once have recourse to analysis. *V.* 19 seems at first sight to contain an address of the prophet to his disciples (cf. *v.* 16). It may be rendered thus, "And when they say unto you, Consult the ghosts and the familiar spirits that chirp and that moan (give this answer), Should not a people (rather) consult its god? on behalf of the living (should men consult) the dead?" But there is no parallel for such an address in Isaiah (see on xxviii. 23), and the cool, didactic style is, in spite of the two Isaianic epithets, not that of our prophet. A Jewish scholar is reported to have questioned this verse in early times.[1] *Vv.* 20-22 at any rate refer to those who have no true faith in Israel's God. Especially puzzling is *v.* 21, which begins, "And he shall pass through it, hard pressed and famishing." The original opening of this descriptive passage seems to have been lost. Some lines must have fallen out or become illegible, in which the land (of Israel or of Judah?) was spoken of, and some light was thrown on the origin of the calamity described. *V.* 20 will be the editor's attempt to make good this deficiency. First of all, it confirms the indignant rebuke—"Should not a people resort unto its God?"—by an emphatic statement that the תורה and the תעודה (and not the oracles of necromancers) are the only trustworthy guides at the most critical times, after which with great skill the editor works in a fragment of a verse really written by Isaiah (viz. "for whom there is no dawn") by prefixing the somewhat awkward words, "Surely they shall speak according to this word." [This view has been reached independently of Duhm. It assumes that תורה and תעודה (which cannot have quite the same reference as in *v.* 16) mean prophetic revelations in general (cf. Ezek. vii. 26; Am. viii. 11, 12—the latter passage a later insertion).[2] But Duhm is not improbably right in taking these words in the sense which תורה and עדות bear in Ps. xix. 8, viz. Scripture, and more especially the Law.]

Thus the introduction to the grandest of Messianic prophecies has been lost, unless the poor little fragment אשר אין לו שחר (cf. ix. 1) belongs to it.[3] The two next verses supply a fresh problem. Obscure enough in themselves, they are also at first sight inconsistent with *v.* 23 and ix. 1-6. Siegfried (whom I followed in *PI*) sought to mitigate the abrupt transition to *v.* 23 by transposing *vv.* 21

---

[1] Acc. to R. Simeon, Beeri (the father of Hosea) prophesied only two things, and since they were not enough for a book they were incorporated into Isaiah. One of them was Isa. viii. 19. Midr. Wayikra Rabba, par. xv. (Wünsche, *Bibl. Rabb.*, xxvi. 98; Dukes, *Mittheilungen*, p. 93).

[2] Cf. König, *Einl.*, p. 304 foot.

[3] Prof. F. Brown remarks, "The opening lines of the prophecy are lost. It is quite likely that the last four words of *v.* 20 belonged to one of these opening lines" (*JBL*, 1890, p. 101). So, too, Giesebrecht (*St. u. Kr.*, 1888, p. 252).

and 22.[1] According to this view, the unfortunate survivors from the great catastrophe look first downward to the earth and then upward to heaven. Then in a moment the condition of the sufferers is reversed—the mute petition of the upturned eye is granted, the thick darkness disappears, and a brilliant day dawns. This gives a good connection, but the words, "and he shall pass through it," etc., are not naturally placed. The received order of the verses must therefore be retained. But why should we suppose that the Massoretic text is correct? V. 22 is evidently not only incomplete but (at the end) corrupt. The opening of v. 23, though it contains Hofal forms such as Isaiah might have used, is not at all in that prophet's style, and the bulk of the verse is certainly too prosaic for Isaiah. The introductory words are, as Duhm has acutely suggested, a gloss, designed to justify the metaphorical use of the term "a thick veil" (read מוּעָף both in v. 22 and in v. 23), and also, of course, of its synonym "gloom" (חֲשֵׁכָה); while the rest of the verse is an attempt to link ix. 1-6 with viii. 21, 22. But considering with what confidence Isaiah predicted a captivity of Judah in the reign of Ahaz (see chaps. iii. and v.), there would be no absurdity in supposing that the editor who inserted viii. 23 was right in so far as he ascribed the following prophecy to the reign of Ahaz, and only wrong in limiting its reference (apparently) to the district of North Israel depopulated in 734 by Tiglath-pileser.[2] For plainly Isaiah must have imaginatively realised the expected Assyrian oppression both of Israel and of Judah as actually present, and requiring a divine interposition to bring it to an end. And the prophecy of the "king with the four names" might be taken as an eloquent protest against the unworthiness of the reigning king of Judah.

I am disinclined, therefore, to follow Duhm in assigning

[1] *ZWT*, 1872, p. 280.
[2] Dillmann, indeed, thinks that the N.E. parts of Israel are merely mentioned through a poetic tendency to individualise, and represent the whole people of Israel, which in ix. 1 is expressly referred to as "the people" (in opposition to the tribes mentioned in viii. 23), *i.e.* the purified remnant. But the transition from the northern tribes to the whole people needs to be somehow explained. As the passage stands, no connected interpretation seems possible.

viii. 21, 22 and ix. 1-6 to different periods. (He makes the former one of the earliest, the latter one of the very latest prophecies of Isaiah.) It is probable, indeed, that ix. 1-6 (which has a distinct rhythm of its own) originally stood by itself, but Duhm has not, I think, justified bringing it down as late as the invasion of Sennacherib. The words of ix. 1 describe a long-continued period of gloom, whereas that great crisis was bitter but short; and it is more than doubtful whether the glowing anticipations of this prophecy harmonise with the prophecies which were certainly delivered during the period referred to. If ix. 1-6 be the work of Isaiah, it most probably belongs to the reign of Ahaz.

So far I have argued on the assumption that the prophecy ix. 1-6 must at any rate be Isaianic. But what if we have to accept Hackmann's view,[1] that the date of ix. 1-6 is subsequent to the fall of the state and of the Davidic dynasty? True, the style is splendidly vigorous, and breathes a sympathy with the warlike side of the divine nature which is worthy of Isaiah (cf. ii. 6-19; xviii. 1-6; xxviii.-xxxi.). On the other hand, the same may be said of xxx. 27-33, which can be shown to be clearly late. And though it might be hypercritical to infer a late date simply from the ἅπ. λεγ. סְאוֹן, סֹאֵן (v. 4), מִשְׂרָה (v. 6), and the δὶς λεγ. מַאֲכֹלֶת (vv. 4, 18), מַרְבֵּה (v. 5; xxxiii. 23), and סֹבֶל (ix. 3; x. 27 = xiv. 25), yet סְאוֹן (see Ges.) may well awaken suspicion. With regard to מַאֲכֹלֶת, there is an analogous Aramaic form, and Hackmann regards it as an ἅπ. λεγ., emending v. 18. The emendation, however, is improbable (see *RT*); we will therefore lay no stress on מַאֲכֹלֶת, which may after all be good Hebrew (cf. מַכֹּלֶת, 1 Ki. v. 25). But מַרְבֵּה and סֹבֶל (on which cf. p. 265) are more important. As to the first, the author of xxxiii. 23 probably regarded it as Isaianic (he adopts it just as he adopts עַד from v. 5). And as to the second, it may be admitted that the supplementer of x. 5, etc., who tries to be Isaianic in style, regards ix. 1-6 as Isaiah's, and therefore takes סֹבֶל from it (see x. 27). Similarly x. 26 and xiv. 5 also contain allusions to ix. 3, and xxxvii. 32 (end) is copied from ix. 6 (end). In short, a

[1] *ZEJ*, pp. 136, 143-149; similarly Marti, *Kayser's AT. Theol.*, pp. 183 f., 247. Cf. Stade, *Gesch.*, i. 596, n. 2.

number of late writers regarded ix. 1-6 as Isaiah's. But what does this prove? Simply that these writers already had before them a collection of Isaianic prophecies which contained ix. 1-6, not that this passage was either Isaianic or even pre-Exilic.

The difficulties, however, in admitting the Isaianic origin of ix. 1-6, and the companion passage xi. 1-8, are not merely, nor even chiefly, linguistic. They include these six derived from the subject-matter:—(1) The description of the Messianic glory stands in no apparent connection with the present circumstances of Judah, and contains no reference to an accompanying moral regeneration of the people. (2) The divine "king in his glory" so filled the thoughts and imagination of Isaiah that there seems no room for any earthly king. Zion's foundation-stone (xxviii. 16) is not the Davidic family but Yahwè, the God who has revealed himself to Israel. (3) If Isaiah had delivered such prophecies as ix. 1-6, xi. 1-8, why does he never refer to them again? (4) Why do neither Jeremiah nor II. Isaiah, who knew Isaiah so well, refer to these great prophecies?[1] and why does Zechariah (i.-viii.) refer only to Jeremiah's prophecy of the צֶמַח (Zech. iii. 8, vi. 12)? (5) V. 3 refers to Gideon's discomfiture of Midian. But the other references to traditional stories in reputed Isaianic prophecies (including x. 26) turn out to be probably not Isaianic at all (see p. 22). (6) The prophecy ix. 1-6 lacks Isaiah's lucidity. Who is the king? is he a member of the family of Ahaz? and how has he been prepared for his great career? Even those who adhere to the Messianic interpretation of vii. 14-16 find it hard to reply to this question. Does not the prophecy look more like the vision of some pious writer after the Exile, when the Davidic dynasty had long since been overthrown? It will be observed that both ix. 1-6 and xi. 1-8, with its supplements, stand at the end of a prophetic work, where editors (as we shall find again and again) were specially prone to attach late compositions, and that neither passage has any obvious link with the nearest preceding Isaianic prophecy. On the whole, after a hard struggle, the present writer concludes that Hackmann is probably right, though he admits that the

[1] Isa. lxv. 25, which refers to xi. 7 (and 9), is certainly post-Exilic.

46   *ISAIAH*

argument for a post-Exilic date is not quite so strong as in the case of ii. 2-4, xxx. 27-33, and chap. xxxii.[1]

CHAPTERS IX. 7-20 ; X. 1-4

We have seen already that ix. 7-20, together with x. 1-4 and v. 26-30, form a connected prophecy. On rhythmical grounds this view is absolutely necessary (as Bickell and Duhm have shown). Thus we obtain a beautiful poetic oracle in five symmetrical strophes,[2] each of which, except the last, closes with the refrain—

> For all this his anger turneth not away,
> And still is his hand outstretched.

The only difficulty in this view is that the fourth strophe (x. 1-4) refers to the corrupt magistrates of Judah, whereas the preceding strophes (at least after line 3 of str. 1) relate to N. Israel, whose punishments in the past (viz. 1. loss of territory through the Aramæans and Philistines ; 2. a crushing defeat ; 3. anarchy, and the continual strife of factions) are successively described, while over all "there comes booming like a storm-bell the awful refrain"[3] (cf. the prophetic retrospect and threat of punishment in Am. iv. 1-12a). Moved by this apparent incongruity, some critics have proposed to include x. 1-3 (or 4a) among the "Woes" of v. 8-24 (see p. 24). It seems reasonable, however, to infer, from ix. 7 and the opening of v. 8, that the prophet originally had Judah in his mind as well as Israel. If so, the final judgment (which we have in v. 26-30) should refer to both kingdoms, and to prepare the way for

---

[1] Notice that the interpolated passage, Am. v. 8, contains the words "that turneth צלמות into dawn " ; cf. ix. 1b. (The earliest passages with 'צ are. Jer. ii. 6, xiii. 16.)

[2] In str. 2, two, if not four, of the original lines (v. 14, and probably v. 15) became illegible, and have had their places filled up by the editor. See Duhm. All (except Del. and Orelli) agree that v. 14 is not Isaiah's. In strophe 4 Hackmann supposes (*ZEJ*, p. 55, n. 1) that the original first ten lines had become illegible, and that to fill up the gap material from another place (the denunciations of Judah imperfectly preserved in chap. v.) was inserted.

[3] G. A. Smith.

this, a strophe relative to Judah is at any rate useful, even if such a strophe was only added by an afterthought. And since the historical survey (ix. 7-20) is over, how else can the offences of Judah (of which, as usual, representative examples are given) be introduced more fitly than by הוֹי ? Observe that the reference to captivity in x. 4 corresponds to that in a former prophecy (v. 13, 14), and points onward to the terrible close of the last strophe ("carrieth it away safe," etc., v. 30). The non-mention of the name of Assyria is in Isaiah's earlier manner. (In v. 26 we should read גּוֹי.)

As to the date, the historical allusions in ix. 7-20 point to the beginning of the reign of Ahaz; the whole poem or prophecy is therefore about contemporary with v. 1-7, and 8-24. The troublesome reference to the Assyrians in the phrase צָרֵי רְצִין (v. 10) is non-existent. The text is corrupt; we might correct as in *ICA* and *PI*, but since רְצִין is metrically superfluous, it is better to read צָרוֹ (as virtually Duhm), casting out ר' as a gloss.[1] To place it still earlier with Duhm and Hackm. is only possible if by altering the points we convert ix. 7-20 into an elaborate prediction. I still adhere to the view of Ewald (revived by myself in *ICA* in 1870) that the passage is a retrospect, comparing the retrospect of the judgments upon N. Israel in Am. iv. 6-12.[2]

It remains to consider why the poetic oracle which now forms ix. 7-x. 4 was removed from its original position between what is now v. 1-24 (25), and v. 26-29 (30). Probably it was in order to fill up the roll on which stood the compilation which now forms x. 5-xi. 16. Great pains were taken to provide this work with a suitable close, and it may well have seemed important to explain the dark allusions to the punishment of Samaria and Jerusalem (x. 11, 12, 20, xi. 11-13) by the "word upon Israel" (ix. 7). Notice also that הוֹי in x. 1 corresponds to הוֹי in x. 5, and אַפּוֹ in x. 4 to אַפִּי in x. 5, also that שׁלל and בו occur both in x. 2 and in x. 6.

[1] On this and on other points see *RT*.
[2] In support of this view see Kuenen, *Ond*.², ii. 46 (where however the false reading in *v*. 10 leads Kuenen to date the prophecy "shortly after the Syr.-Ephr. war"); Dillmann, *Jes*., p. 95; and especially Giesebrecht, *Beitr*., pp. 15-17.

Chapters X. 5-XII. 6

That this long piece possesses literary unity is undeniable. Of the six divisions recognised by Ewald (viz. *a*, x. 5-15; *b*, x. 16-23; *c*, x. 24-34; *d*, xi. 1-9; *e*, xi. 10-16; *f*, xii. 1-6), *b* is linked with *a*, and *c* with *b* by לָכֵן, "therefore," and many have found an implied connection between *c* and *d* ("the Assyrian cedar falls without hope, but the Davidic oak-tree leaves a stump out of which a sprout shall shoot"). The combination of *d* and *e* and of *e* and *f* is authorised by the reference in xi. 10 and xii. 1 to "that day." Besides, the analogy of ii. 6-iv. 6 and vii. 1-ix. 6, and similar instances elsewhere, suggests that such an important prophecy as x. 5-24 would not have been thought complete without a closing picture of Messianic bliss. Experience warns us, however, not to be too sure that the contents of this prophecy belong entirely to one period, or even that every part of it has come from the hand of Isaiah. Provisionally it may be well to consider the prophecy in two parts, viz., (A), x. 5-34, and (B), xi.-xii.

A. (x. 5-34). Three questions arise, (1) Is this to be regarded as a single prophetic discourse? (2) If not, do the parts belong on the whole to the same or to different periods? And (3) Do any of the parts contain later insertions, due either to Isaiah himself, or to an editor? These questions can only be answered after an examination of the several parts of the section. Let us begin with *a* (*vv.* 5-15), the subject of which is a contrast between the plan of Assyria or its king, and that of Yahwè. On reading it we at once notice three breaks, marked respectively by כִּי יֹאמַר (*v.* 8), וְהָיָה (*v.* 12) and כִּי אָמַר (*v.* 13). The first and third of these phrases we can hardly err in regarding as editorial (like וְאָמַר in lvii. 13), and designed to conceal a gap in the Isaianic material. The connection of thought in *vv.* 5-7 is perfect, but both before and after "for he saith" something must be supplied mentally. In *v.* 7, the subject is still Assyria personified, but that of כִּי יֹאמַר is the reigning king of Assyria. It is, moreover, difficult to see how Sargon's or Sennacherib's first thoughts can have related to the power

CHAPTER X. 5-34

or dignity of his generals. Clearly there was a *lacuna* in the text which lay before the editor. Equally poor is the connection between *v.* 12 and *v.* 13, whereas *vv.* 13, 14 (after כִּי אָמַר) cohere admirably. The probability is that *vv.* 13 and 14 contain another part of the royal speech, of which we have an earlier fragment in *vv.* 8-11, or more certainly (judging from the poverty of the style of *vv.* 10, 11) in *vv.* 8, 9. That these verses should follow directly upon *v.* 9 is of course not to be asserted; *vv.* 10-12, with the opening formula of *v.* 13, may fill the place of an illegible (or of a partly illegible) passage. Of course, we cannot deny that *vv.* 10-12 may contain some Isaianic material. The probability of this is however not very great, so far as *vv.* 10, 11 are concerned. The term אֱלִיל (אֱלִילִים) in the mouth of the Assyrian king is difficult to reconcile with Isaiah's usual accuracy. Surely the prophet knew that the Assyrians were idolaters. Probably the editors knew this too, but accidental slips are more easily attributable to them than to Isaiah. But in *v.* 12 there is only one word which is not Isaianic, viz. בִּצֵּע (used figuratively of the act by which God closes a life, xxxviii. 12, and in the derived sense of "finish" in Zech. 4, 9, and of "fulfil" in Lam. ii. 17—all three late passages). The other words or idioms, and all the ideas, can be paralleled from other works of Isaiah. "His whole work" reminds us that from the first Isaiah has proclaimed a judgment of Yahwè upon "both houses of Israel"; the term "work" is used in the same sense in v. 12, 19, xxviii. 21. For פָּקַד עַל, "to punish," cf. פְּקֻדָּה, x. 3. For פְּרִי, cf. iii. 10. For גֹּדֶל לְבַב, cf. ix. 8. For תִּפְאֶרֶת, cf. xxviii. 1, 4 (but not in the derived sense of "vainglory"). For רוּם, "haughtiness," cf. ii. 11. And for the long drawn out construction after the first עַל, cf. xxviii. 1. Still these parallelisms are not decisive, and the unrhythmical character of the verse, and its position between the two not unrelated portions of a speech of the Assyrian king, are not favourable to an Isaianic origin. And now as to *v.* 15. This, in spite of the Isaianic idiom at the end (cf. xxxi. 3), is still more probably a later insertion. The style is wanting in Isaiah's characteristic quality of compression, and the contents would rather suggest connecting it with *vv.* 10, 11.

On the ἄπ. λεγ. מַשּׂוֹי I lay no stress, but the form of the verse reminds us of xxix. 16, which is also probably an editorial comment.[1]

As to the date of (*a*). Delitzsch in eds. 1-3 placed not only *vv.* 5-15 but the whole "prophecy" in the reign of Tiglath-pileser; so also Orelli (who seems to misunderstand the statements of Schrader in *CI*). Delitzsch however coupled this theory with the opinion that the king whom Isaiah really means in *a* is Sennacherib. Isaiah, he thought, knew how Sennacherib would speak after the fall of the doomed city Samaria. But in ed. 4 Delitzsch abandoned this position. A "trilogy of prophecies on the Messiah," belonging to the same period, might, he saw, be purchased too dearly. "*Vv.* 9-11 require us to assign the composition of this section, at least in its existing form, to the time of Hezekiah rather than to that of Ahaz." This view seems to be correct, so far as *vv.* 5-9 and 13, 14 are concerned.[2] For in this passage the fate of five already conquered Syrian cities is referred to, together with that of Samaria, as a warning to Jerusalem. The cities are grouped in three pairs, and the probable dates of their respective captures are as follow :—

Calno[3]	738	Hamath	720	Samaria	722
Carchemish	717	Arpad	740	Damascus	734

---

[1] All that is most important in this paragraph comes from Duhm.

[2] Similarly for x. 5-34 (but on grounds which are not all valid) *PI.* Other advocates of some part of Sargon's reign for this section are Robertson Smith, Guthe, Kuenen (*Ond.*[2]), Giesebrecht, G. A. Smith, Duff. For a later date (Sennacherib's reign) are Ewald, Schrader, Stade, Duhm, Hackmann. Kuenen, too, originally held this view (*Ond.*[1]), and Driver, in *Isa.*[2], pp. 70, 213, 214 (cf. *Intr.*, p. 200), argues ably for it. I am not however convinced that the king of Assyria in x. 8-9 (11) speaks merely as an impersonation of Assyrian policy. Nor can I see that x. 28-32 is at all less significant for being applied to a time when Isaiah believed that his country was in imminent danger of an invasion. For there was a very short interval between the plan of an Assyrian king and its execution. Dillm. thinks that x. 5-xi. 16 represents addresses of Isaiah from the period between 732 and 716 (or 711).

[3] I assume that Calno = Kullani, the date of the capture of which is fixed by the eponym canon (see George Smith, *Ass. Canon*, p. 50, and cf. Tiele, *Bab.-ass. Gesch.*, p. 230).

CHAPTER X. 5-34

Thus the latest of the captures is that of Carchemish, which was effected by Sargon five years after that of Samaria. Now it so happens that shortly before the siege of Ashdod in 711 Isaiah had good reason to think that his country would be invaded by the Assyrians, for a cuneiform inscription declares (see on ch. xx.) that Philistia, Judah, Edom, and Moab were at that time "speaking treason" with Egypt. Of course the late editor of ch. xxxvi. knew nothing of this. It was much if he knew even the name of Sargon. No one can be surprised therefore that he took ideas and phrases from x. 9-11 in making up a speech for a high officer of Sennacherib (xxxvi. 18-20).

Passing now to (b) we notice a break at v. 20. The passage, vv. 20-23, begins with a formula which may indeed be Isaiah's, but may still more easily be due to an editor—"and it shall come to pass in that day." In vv. 16-19 Assyria's punishment is described under the figures of a pining sickness and a conflagration. It is just possible that the passage contains an Isaianic element, but the editorial additions are at any rate much more manifest. x. 18b is self-evidently not from Isaiah's hand (cf. *PI*, ii. 145), and with it should possibly disappear all the (very ineffective) references to pining away. But how can one be sure that even the more striking description of the fire is Isaiah's, at any rate in its present form? How suspicious are these phrases— יֵקַד יְקֹד כִּיקוֹד (v. 16), בְּיוֹם אֶחָד ("in one battle-day," v. 17; note the context), מִנֶּפֶשׁ וְעַד־בָּשָׂר (v. 18)! Of vv. 20-23 very different opinions have been held. Some have thought that vv. 20, 21 were Isaiah's, but vv. 22, 23 not; others, that v. 20 alone belonged to the prophet; others again that the whole passage is due to the later editor. After having for some time rested in the explanation of Giesebrecht,[1] who belongs to the first class of critics, I now recognise that we cannot analyse this passage, and that the whole of it must be regarded as post-Exilic. And this upon three grounds :—

---

[1] This critic thinks (*Beitr.*, pp. 71-76) that vv. 22 and 23 are a later insertion due to Isaiah himself, whose view of the future of Judah had changed. In the midst of consolation they introduce, he says, a discordant note of threatening. He takes "the remnant" in vv. 20-22 to mean Judah.

1. The whole passage is to a great extent a mosaic of Isaianic expressions and images ; Isaiah himself writes freely, and is not so economical with his phrases. Comp. v. 16a (divine titles) with i. 24, iii. 1, also (figure) with xvii. 4 ; vv. 16b and 17 (figure) with ix. 18, xxx. 27, 30, also (for כבוד) with xvii. 4, viii. 7 ; v. 17 ("his Holy One") with v. 19, 24, etc., also ("thorns and briars") with ix. 18, also ("in one day") with ix. 13 ; v. 18 with xxxvii. 24 end (if Isaiah's) ; vv. 19-22 (for שאר) with xvi. 14, xvii. 3, xxi. 17 (xi. 11 is late) ; v. 20, נִשְׁעָן עַל with xxxi. 1 ; v. 21 with vii. 3, ix. 5 ; vv. 22, 23 with xxviii. 22.[1] And observe (1) that one of these phrases is used in a non-Isaianic sense ; "God Mighty-One" (*el-gibbōr*) is, in v. 21, a title of Yahwè, not (as in ix. 5) of the Messiah. (2) That פְּלֵיטָה, v. 20, occurs elsewhere only in the probably or certainly late passages, iv. 2, xv. 9, xxxvii. 31, 32. And (3) that the triple use of יקד in v. 16 points to a time when the word was in common use (Isaiah has part. Qal once, see xxx. 14, but the root is not common in Bibl. Heb.; in the Targums it takes the place of Heb. שׂרף); it also reminds us of מוֹקֵד in xxxiii. 14.

2. The passage is also in no vital relation to the facts of Isaiah's times. Though meant, partly at least, as an explanation of the name Shear-yashub, it is deficient in historical accuracy. This is clear from the statement in v. 20 that "the remnant of Israel (*i.e.* purified Judah) . . . shall no more lean upon him that smote it." Could Isaiah have written thus ? König (1893) thinks that this was possible, either in the first years of Hezekiah, or, the date which he appears to prefer, during the shameful Assyrian vassalage of Ahaz.[2] But let us be exact in our interpretation of the prophets, and in our reading of history. To "lean upon" means to "seek help from" (xxxi. 1). The only such "leaning" of which history knows in Hezekiah's time is the appeal to Egypt which issued in the fruitless aid of Tirhakah (see 2 Ki. xviii. 21, xix. 9, and cf. Isa. xxx. 1-7, xxxi. 1, נִשְׁעָן עַל) ; and in the time of Ahaz, an appeal to Tiglath-pileser (see 2 Ki. xvi. 7-9). The phrase quoted from

[1] Where however אדני is perhaps a late insertion (Duhm).
[2] *Einl.*, p. 315.

CHAPTER X. 5-34

v. 20 is rather the vague inaccurate language of a late writer who has no living conception of long-past events, and even forgets that, according to the preceding passage, Assyria has been destroyed "both soul and body," and is therefore not there to lean upon. It is probable that the words "shall no more lean," etc., really have a reference to Ahaz, and that they may be illustrated by 2 Chr. xxviii. 16-23, where great pains are taken to show that Ahaz sought help in the wrong quarter, viz. from Tiglath-pileser, who "distressed him and helped him not," and from "the gods of Damascus which had smitten him," but which now "were the ruin of him and of all Israel."

3. It is only as an Exilic or (far more probably) post-Exilic insertion that we can thoroughly understand the passage. I have remarked elsewhere that after the Return the overthrow of Assyria "became typical of the great future overthrow of the assembled hostile nations predicted by the later prophets."[1] The "righteousness" of a "holy," *i.e.* God-devoted people was the great aim of the leaders of the church-nation, but even the judgment of the Babylonian Exile had failed to produce this result.[2] A final judgment in which all Yahwè's enemies, both within and without the community, would be destroyed, was therefore still expected. This anticipation is not indeed found in all the eschatological passages of the post-Exilic prophets. It is wanting, *e.g.* in Joel iv., and also in Hos. ii. 1 (A.V., i. 10), which with the next verse seems to be a late insertion. But it is expressed or implied in several (as I believe) late passages of the Book of Isaiah (i. 27, 28 ; iv. 2-4 ; xxix. 27-33 ; lix. 20), in Zech. xiii. 8, 9, and in Mal. iii. 19-21 (A.V., iv. 1-3). Now let us return to Isa. x. 20-23. We have seen that the phrase "shall no more lean on him that smote it" may have some reference to Ahaz, but this does not exclude a reference to much later times. To what times? Surely to those of the Second Temple. The Temple poets delight to assure us that Israel hopes only in its God (Ps. lxxi. 5,

---

[1] *BL*, p. 165.
[2] See many of the Psalms (*e.g.* Ps. cxxxix. 19-22, l. li. lv. lix.) ; and the Books of Ezra and Nehemiah. Cf. also Isa. xlviii. 10, "Lo, I have refined thee, but without winning silver" (in a late insertion).

xciv. 16-18, cxxi. 1, 2, cxlvi. 3-5). Other writers, it is true, cast a doubt upon Israel's sincerity. Thus in probably late parts of Isa. xlviii. we find it stated that though the Jews make their boast of Yahwè, they do it without "faithfulness and truth" (*v.* 1), and that though they rely (נסמך =נשען) upon the God of Israel (*v.* 2), they are as fickle and backsliding as of old (*v.* 8*b*). Not improbably the writer of Isa. x. 20-23 and the supplementer of chap. xlviii. belong to the same circle. Both seem to imply that hearty trust in God does not characterise Israel in their time, and both impress upon their readers (x. 22, 23 ; xlviii. 19*b*) that destruction impends over the unfaithful.[1] Both moreover seem to be acquainted with the promise in Hos. ii. 1 (Heb.). The author of xlviii. 17-19 says, If Israel had been obedient, the promise of a population as numerous as the grains of sand would have been fulfilled ; the writer of x. 20-23, Israel is by nature so disobedient that, even if it were fulfilled, a judgment like that spoken of in xxviii. 22 (expanded in x. 23) would still be needed.[2] The writer of Zech. xiii. 9 agrees with the latter. He also notices and corrects an omission in Hos. ii. 1-3. Honorific titles, like those in Hos. ii. 1, 3, cannot be conferred on Israel till a fiery judgment has reduced its numbers by two-thirds.

We pass on to *c* (*vv.* 24-34), which, like *b*, contains threatening for Assyria and promise for Judah, but in an inverted order. Here too there is a break ; *vv.* 28-34 are evidently in a different style from *vv.* 24-27. The awkward and unrhythmical style of the latter passage forbids us to ascribe it to Isaiah ; if *vv.* 16-19 do not belong to the prophet, much less do *vv.* 24-27, the late origin of which is clear. The title of Yahwè in the opening line is evidently borrowed from the quotation in *v.* 23. The consolatory address to the people of Zion which follows reminds us

[1] Clearly xlviii. 19*b* was written at a time when the very existence of the nation was threatened, or at any rate not long after such a time.
[2] Observe that in x. 23 the words "in the midst of all the earth" are added. But Isaiah seems to have had no distinct idea of a world-judgment. In ii. 19, 21 ("to overawe the earth") the expressions occur in a poetical context, and xiv. 26 only says that Yahwè's purpose of overthrowing Assyria has an interest for the whole world.

CHAPTER X. 5-34

forcibly of xxx. 19 (late), a much finer passage, and certainly not imitated from, but rather perhaps imitated in x. 24. The next verse in like manner reminds us in the opening words of xxix. 17 (late), so that we may assume that the supplementers of x. 5, etc., ch. xxix., and ch. xxx. belong to the same circle. In v. 26 עוֹרֵר is suggested by 2 Sam. xxiii. 18, and בדרך מצרים (twice, v. 24 and v. 26, but with different shades of meaning) by Am. iv. 10. The distich in v. 27 is like part of xiv. 25 (probably interpolated). The Isaianic element is therefore reduced to these few words—מטה and שבט,[1] v. 24, cf. ix. 3 (?), xxx. 31, 32 (?); כלה, v. 25, cf. xvi. 4 (?), xxi. 16; זעם, ibid., cf. v. 5; שוט, v. 26, cf. xxviii. 15, 18. תבלית, v. 25, is ἅπ. λεγ.; חבל, v. 27, reminds us of xxxii. 7 (late), though also of Mic. ii. 10. The allusions to the Exodus story in vv. 24, 26, and to the discomfiture of Midian in v. 26 (cf. ix. 3) were not impossible for Isaiah, but were much more congenial to a later writer (see p. 22). At the end of v. 27 the text is corrupt (see *BW* and *RT*); indeed, the last three words conceal the opening of a fragment (extending to v. 32 or v. 34) by another writer, doubtless Isaiah. There is a parallel passage in Mic. i. 10-15, which refers, it is true, to another part of Judah (the S.W.), but contains very similar plays (bitter enough in spirit) on the names of towns in danger of capture by the Assyrians. Probably both passages belong to the close of the siege of Samaria (722), when it might well seem more than probable that the Assyrian invasion would extend to Judah (see on xvii. 12-14). The editor of Isa. x. 5, etc. preserved this stray fragment by working it into the composite "Woe" upon Assyria. What Isaiah added after v. 32 we can never know. Mic. i. 10-15 does not say that the invader will be laid low, nor is it certain that Isaiah would have said so.

Lastly, does the Isaianic fragment attached to vv. 24-27 extend beyond v. 32? And if not, do vv. 33 and 34 belong to Isaiah or not? To both questions we must answer, No.[2] There is no proper connection between vv. 24-27 and vv. 33, 34. In a style of simple grandeur the former passage

---

[1] But the figure of the rod seems late (see p. 201, on xxx. 30-32).
[2] I agree with Duhm as against Smend (*AT. Rel.-gesch.*, p. 221).

describes how in rapid marches the Assyrian army advances against Jerusalem, spreading terror everywhere. But how shall we connect with this the picture of a forest which follows? Umbreit ventures on the leap thus,—" So now the splendid army, like fair Lebanon with its lofty cedar forest to look at, has planted itself before Mount Zion, but He who sitteth thereon in unapproachable glory reacheth out his strong right hand, and with the axe of righteousness felleth the proud trees."[1] But can Isaiah have imagined an army planting itself on a sudden like trees? *Vv.* 33 and 34 are full of rhetorical phrases and images which, though not without an Isaianic tinge, are clearly put together with a view to effect. Let us examine them.

The divine titles in *v.* 33, line 1, are borrowed from *vv.* 23, 24 (see above); סְעִף is a denom. from סָעִיף, 'bough' (xvii. 6); מַעֲרָצָה reminds us of ii. 19, 21; lines 3 and 4 suggest ii. 12-17; and the figure itself is akin to that in *vv.* 18, 19. In *v.* 34 נִקַּף may perhaps suggest נֶקֶף, xvii. 6; סִבְכֵי הַיַּעַר occurs again in ix. 17; "Lebanon" (cf. *v.* 18) may remind us of xxxvii. 24 (if Isaiah's). On the other hand, the figure of the hewn-down trees is a favourite with later writers. See xxxii. 19; Zech. xi. 2; Ezek. xxxi. 1-14 (Assyria compared to a cedar in Lebanon). In Zech. *l.c.* moreover we find נָפַל, "to be felled," as here (cf. ירד in xxxii. 19), and in Ezek. *l.c.* פֹּארוֹת, "branches" (cf. פֻּארָה, *v.* 33). Note too that אַדִּיר as a title of Yahwè is not Isaianic, and probably late (see xxxiii. 21, and cf. on Ps. viii. 2), and that the conversion of a simple epithet of Yahwè into a quasi-proper name is late (cf. קָדוֹשׁ, xl. 25; Hab. iii. 3; Job vi. 10). Indeed, where is there anything in Isaiah's works like this, "And Lebanon shall fall by the glorious one"? We shall see better presently why the editor may have expressed himself in this unnatural way. He was no doubt a poor stylist, but there is another excuse besides this to offer.

We are now in a position to answer the three questions with which we started. x. 5-34 is not a single prophetic discourse, nor do the parts on the whole belong to the same period, or even to the same author. Part I. belongs in the

---

[1] *Jes.*, p. 104. I quote from this scholar, because he aimed at continuing the æsthetic work of Herder.

main to Isaiah, and was probably written in 711; it has, however, been filled out by the editor. Part II. shows little, if any, trace of Isaiah's hand, and, as it stands, must be reckoned as post-Exilic; Part III. begins and ends with editorial work, but includes a fine fragment of Isaiah's writing, which belongs probably to the year 722.

B. (chaps. xi.-xii.). This section evidently falls into three parts (viz. *a*, xi. 1-9; *b*, xi. 10-16; *c*, xii. 1-6), each of which we must examine separately. Let us take (*c*) first, the case here being the clearest, and inquire, What is the origin of the two little songs put into the mouth of the delivered "remnant of Yahwè's people"? It is the merit of Ewald that as long ago as 1840, by one of those divinations which are rapid inferences from a number of observed phenomena, he pronounced chap. xii. to be a late addition to Isaiah's work. Words, figures, ideas, indeed the spirit of the whole composition are, he said, un-Isaianic. "It is possible" (so gently Ewald expressed himself) "that a copyist who saw that the words of xi. 15, 16 were fulfilled in the deliverance from Babylon, supplemented the (preceding) oracle with these jubilant words," which, as Ewald remarks elsewhere, fitly close one of the two halves of the collection i.-xxiii., and which correspond to the appendix to the oracle on Tyre in chap. xxiii.[1] The considerations which hindered me from adopting this theory in *ICA* were chiefly these :—(1) Granting that Isaiah was poet as well as prophet (cf. v. 1-6, xxiii. 16, and perhaps Ps. xlvi., xlviii.), and that many of the psalms are of pre-Exilic or even pre-Isaianic origin, why should not Isaiah have given such a lyric finale to his great prophecy of consolation? And (2) might not the non-Isaianic words in chap. xii. be explained by the change of subject, and the parallel passages in admittedly post-Exilic psalms be due to imitation of Isa. xii. on the part of later writers? The question had to be reconsidered however in 1880-1881, and the result was a change of opinion. The activity of later editors seemed so clearly proved[2] that I could no longer regard Ewald's theory as arbitrary. If a psalm of Exilic or post-Exilic origin[3]

---
[1] Ewald, *Proph.*, ii. 239, 240; i. 95.
[2] Cf. *PI*, ii. 228-231.   [3] *Ib.*, i. 22.

could be attributed in one case to Hezekiah, and in another to Jonah, why might not Isaiah be represented as having indited songs (for there are *two* songs) for the later Jewish community? Lagarde's advocacy [1] of the late date of these songs greatly confirmed me in my doubts. His instinct appeared to me to be sound; the songs had all the appearance of hymns of the second temple. But he seemed to me to rest his case too much on the extreme lateness of the "Song of Moses." Could one expect English students to accept a hypothesis so imperfectly grounded? I therefore left the question open for the present,[2] and not till a widely ramifying study of the Psalter and its religion compelled me to do so, did I give my vote decidedly against Isaiah.

I have now to collect the literary evidence bearing on the date of chap xii.

1. Phraseological data. To Isaiah belong such words as שָׂשׂוֹן, *v.* 3 (xxii. 13); נִשְׂגָּב, used of Yahwè, *v.* 4 (as xxxiii. 17, late; but also Nifal perf. in ii. 11, 17); גֵּאוּת, *v.* 5 (ix. 17, xxviii. 1, 3); צָהַל, *v.* 6 (x. 30); קְדוֹשׁ יִשְׂרָאֵל, *v.* 6 (twelve times in admitted works of Isaiah). But on the other side note אָנַף, *v.* 1 (never in prophets, four times in Psalms); יְשׁוּעָה, *vv.* 2, 3 (xxxiii. 2, 6); פַּחַד, *v.* 2 (xix. 16, 17; xxxiii. 14); עֹז, *v.* 2 (xxvi. 1); יָהּ יהוה, *v.* 2 (as xxvi. 4; doubtful reading); שָׁאַב (nowhere in prophets, except Nah. iii. 14; nor in Psalms); מַעְיָן, *v.* 3 (not in prophets, except xli. 18); קָרָא בְּשֵׁם, "to call upon the name (of)," *v.* 4 (xli. 25, lxiv. 6); עֲלִילוֹת,[3] *v.* 4, in a good sense (of God's wonders), five times in Ps.; רנן, *v.* 6 (xxiv. 14, xxvi. 19, xxxv. 2, 6, and eight times in xl.-lxvi.); יוֹשֶׁבֶת צִיּוֹן, *v.* 6 (only here and in Jer. li. 35, post-Exilic). We can afford to pass over technical liturgical terms like הוֹדָה (*vv.* 1, 4), זַמֵּר (*v.* 5), זִמְרָה (*v.* 2), the two former of which occur in Ps. xviii. 50, and the third in Am. v. 23 (of instrumental music).

2. Closer parallelisms. Comp. the introd. formulæ in *vv.* 1, 4 with those in xiv. 3, 4, xxv. 9, xxvi. 1 (all late); also *v.* 2*a* with Ps. lxxxviii. 2; *v.* 2*b* with Ex. xv.

---

[1] *Semitica*, i. 28.
[2] *PI*, ii. 187, note 2; art. "Isaiah," *Ency. Brit.*, 1881.
[3] עֲלִילוֹת, in a bad sense, also twice in Zeph., eight times in Ezek., and once in Ps. (cxli. 4).

CHAPTERS XI.-XII

2,[1] Ps. cxviii. 14 ; *v.* 3 with Ps. xxxvi. 10, lxxxvii. 7 ; *v.* 4*a* with Ps. cv. 1 ; *v.* 4*b* with Ps. cxlviii. 13 ; *v.* 5 with Ex. xv. 1*b*, Ps. xciii. 1 ; *v.* 6 with Ps. xlviii. 2. The songs in chap. xii. are in fact imitative throughout. Isaiah however is not imitative. And even if the rules of liturgical poetry necessitated a certain amount of conventionality, yet a genius like his would have found means to express itself. Certainly the psalms in our Psalter are never as colourless as these songs.

And lastly, (3) it can be shown that all other passages in Isaiah which are clearly liturgical (see chap. xxxiii., and especially parts of chaps. xxv. and xxvi., and lxiii. 7-lxiv. 12) are *late.* Adding this to the preceding considerations must we not conclude that the songs in chap. xii. are also late, and, if late at all, then *very late?* The poet[2] was certainly a very poor artist. Not only is he absolutely unoriginal, but, if the present text is correct, he has omitted to complete the second distich of *v.* 2, and has given a tristich instead of a distich in *v.* 3. Comparing *v.* 2*b* with Ps. cxviii. 14, one is tempted to conjecture that the two songs of Isaiah xii. express the joy of Israel at the rededication of the temple in 165 B.C., which is regarded as the opening of a new era for Israelites, both " far off and near."[3]

Next let us study *b* (xi. 10-16). This is obviously an appendix. Even Riehm,[4] who supposes the whole chapter to be Isaianic, speaks of the "strange contrast" between the two halves of chap. xi. In fact, the prophecy of the Messiah and his reign has a perfectly suitable close in *v.* 9, and the main subject of the appendix (viz. the restoration of the

---

[1] Ex. xv. 2 is evidently older than Isa. xii. 2*b*, but how much older we cannot tell. As a whole, the Song of Moses cannot be pre-Exilic. (Cf. *BL*, p. 31.)

[2] Duhm suggests that two different writers may have contributed to chap. xii. There are at any rate two different songs. But the variation of number in the introductory passages in *vv.* 1, 3, 4, is not important, considering that the community may equally well be addressed as 'thou' and as 'ye.' (In *v.* 4 Sept. has καὶ ἐρεῖς.)

[3] Among recent critics, Stade (*ZATW*, 1883, p. 16), Kuenen (*Ond.*[2], ii. 57), F. Brown (*JBL*, 1890, pp. 128-131), Dillm., Duhm, Hackm. (*ZEJ*, p. 17), and König consider Isa. xii. to be a late appendix (König thinks, Exilic). Driver also (*Isaiah*,[5] p. 230) seems now inclined to admit this.

[4] *Messianic Prophecy*, p. 161.

exiles of Israel and Judah) is quite apart from that of x.
5-34 and xi. 1-9. Did Isaiah add this passage himself?
In support of his authorship one might urge the reference to
Assyria and Egypt and other countries within his ken; also
the presence of Isaianic expressions (some doubtfully attested)
such as (1) שְׁאָר (vii. 3, x. 19-22?-xxviii. 5?); (2) נֵס (v. 26
etc.); (3) דָּרַשׁ אֶל (viii. 19?-xix. 3?); (4) סוּר (x. 27?-xiv.
25); (5) הֵנִיף יָד (cf. xix. 16?); (6) מְסִלָּה (vii. 3). On the
other hand, the ideas and anticipations, and the senses in
which certain good old Hebrew words are used, point to a
date not earlier than the Exile. For instance, (1) *v.* 10
implies the idea of the spiritual primacy of Israel. The
"root of Jesse" (itself a very strange expression after xi. 1*b*),
i.e. the Messianic king, is here represented as the organ of
divine revelation (on the phrase, see below). This agrees
far better with the Chronicler's conception of David (cf. 2
Chron. viii. 14, Neh. xii. 24, 'David the man of God') than
with the picture of the Messiah in ix. 3-6, xi. 2-4. As a
consequence, the foreigners are to flock to Jerusalem, not as
tributaries, but as disciples (cf. p. 11, on ii. 3). Observe
too that the idea of the Messiah as the great Teacher appears
here quite suddenly. Those whom the writer addressed
needed no explanation of it. But would Isaiah's contemporaries
have understood his language? (2) The idea of the
glory of Jerusalem in the latter days (*v.* 10) is characteristically
Exilic or post-Exilic (see iv. 5, xxiv. 23). (3) The
anticipations in *vv.* 11, 12, 15, 16 are more natural to an
Exilic or post-Exilic writer than to Isaiah (see xliii. 5, 6,
xlix. 12, and cf. xlix. 22 with xi. 12). For it cannot be
shown to be conceivable either that Isaiah ever looked
forward to a reversal of the stern doom of captivity which
he had himself pronounced (see on xiii. 2-xiv. 23), or that
the Israelites were so widely dispersed in his time as the
verses referred to assume.[1] On the other hand, at the close
of the Exile and after the disappointments of the Return,

[1] All that Schrader can urge is that non-Israelites certainly (and therefore Israelites possibly) were deported to Elam, Babylonia, and Hamath under Sargon (*CI*, ii. 77). Bredenkamp admits that the language of *vv.* 11, 12 does not suit Isaiah's time, but thinks that the prophet gazed into future centuries.

CHAPTERS XI.-XII

prophecies of a full restoration of Israel were frequent, and the Jewish dispersion, which began to be considerable even before the time of Alexander, attained colossal dimensions after the Greek conquests. This argument will retain its force even if we reject the closing words of *v.* 11 as a very late gloss ("and from Pathros . . . coastlands of the sea"). (4) The description of Ephraim and Judah in *v.* 13 shows an inaccurate conception of past history (cf. on x. 20). Pride, not jealousy, characterised Ephraim (ix. 8, xxviii. 3), and Judah was not capable of seriously "distressing" Ephraim. (5) The difference in spirit between *v.* 15 and *v.* 10 is most intelligible in a late writer, who had before him in the prophecies opposite descriptions of Israel's future.

Let us now pass on to the non-Isaianic features of the phraseology. In *v.* 10 we have נֵס used figuratively for one in whom resides a wondrous attractive force for all nations (contrast v. 26, xviii. 3, xxx. 17, and even xi. 12, where נֵס = "banner," "signal"); דָּרַשׁ אֶל (the phrase referred to above which represents the Messiah as the organ of revelation; it is used of consulting oracles, viii. 19, xix. 3); מְנוּחָה, used of the royal city of Yahwè (cf. lxvi. 1; 1 Chr. xxviii. 2; Ps. cxxxii. 8, 14). In *v.* 11 שְׁאָר עַמּוֹ (cf. xxviii. 5, late), and note that שְׁאָר here means the exiles of Israel and Judah (cf. Jer. xxiii. 3, xxxi. 7; and Mic. ii. 12 (late), where however שְׁאֵרִית is used); אִיֵּי הַיָּם, elsewhere only in xxiv. 15 and Esth. x. 1 (cf. אִיֵּי כִתִּיִּים, Jer. ii. 10; אִיִּים מֶרְחָק, Jer. xxxi. 10; אִיֵּי הַגּוֹיִם, Zeph. ii. 11; Gen. x. 5 (P)); and אִיִּים twelve times in Isa. xl.-lxvi. for the coastlands and islands of the Mediterranean. אִי in xx. 6, xxiii. 2, 6 has a more special reference. In *v.* 12 נִדְחֵי יִשְׂרָאֵל reminds us of lvi. 8; Ps. cxlvii. 2; נָדַח is a favourite verb in later proph. writings (incl. Mic. iv. 6; Zeph. iii. 19). For נְפוּצוֹת (from פּוּץ, König, *Lehrg.* i. 344), cf. xxxiii. 3. כַּנְפוֹת הָאָרֶץ, elsewhere only in Ezek. vii. 2; Job xxxvii. 3, xxxviii. 13; Ezek. vii. 2; cf. Isa. xxiv. 16. The plur. כ׳ occurs once again in another phrase in Deut. xxii. 12. In *v.* 14 מִשְׁלוֹחַ, elsewhere only in Esth. ix. 19, 22. In *v.* 15 עָיָם ἅπ. λεγ. (unless we should read עֹצֶם). One should probably add הֵנִיף יָד, *v.* 15 (cf. xix. 16; Zech. ii. 13), though a phrase in x. 32 comes very near.

We shall now be able to judge better of the arguments for the authorship of Isaiah. Of the six Isaianic expressions mentioned above, (1) and (2) are used in a non-Isaianic sense, and (3) has a non-Isaianic reference; (5) occurs also in xiii. 2 (Exilic); (4) and (6) are ordinary Hebrew words, and (6) in particular occurs, in similar contexts, in xix. 23, xxxv. 8, xlix. 11, lxii. 10, all late passages. As for the names of countries, it would be strange if a late writer could not collect some of them from Isaiah. But observe that the writer includes three names (Pathros, Shinar, and b'nê Ammon) not found in the true Isaiah, and that Pathros and Shinar do not occur in any pre-Exilic prophet; also that the geographical phrase which closes the list of countries is self-evidently not due to Isaiah (cf. *PI*, ii. 147).

On the whole one must admit that both ideas and language point to a late date for xi. 10-16.[1] But the absolutely decisive argument remains, viz. the sudden disappearance, from *v.* 9 onwards, of the beautiful metre of *vv.* 1-8. To *v.* 9 we shall return presently. As to *vv.* 10-16 it is clear that this passage gives expression to the hopes and aspirations of the post-Exilic period. "Assyria" has here, as elsewhere, become a symbolic term for the particular Western Asiatic power which oppressed the Jews in the time of the writer. In the present case, it may possibly mean the empire of the Achæmenidæ (called "Assyria" in Ezra vi. 22, and "Babylon" in Ezra *v.* 13; Neh. xiii. 6). In xix. 23-25, however, it means rather the Greek empire of Syria, and Vitringa and Duhm may possibly be right in so understanding it here. (Edom, Moab, and b'nê Ammon are mentioned together again, conventionally, in the Macc. Book of Daniel, xi. 41.) There was always only too much reason to long for the restoration of exiles (cf. Ps. lxxx., cvi. 47), and imitative writers loved to re-echo, each in his own sense, one of the sweetest promises of the tender-hearted Hosea (xi. 11).

Last of all we come to (*a*), the prophecy of the Messianic king and the redemption of nature (xi. 1-8, 9), which opens with the distich—

[1] So Stade, Guthe, Giesebr., Kuenen, Cornill, Duhm, Hackmann, König (exc. for *v.* 10); cf. my notice of Giesebr.'s *Beitr.* in *Academy*, Feb. 21, 1891. Dillm. too admits that Isaiah's authorship is not self-evident.

And a shoot shall come forth from the stock of Jesse,
And a scion from his roots shall bear fruit.

It has been doubted whether or no גזע in l. 1 implies that the tree has been cut down. The word occurs elsewhere only in Job xiv. 8, where "stock" is clearly correct, and in Isa. xl. 24, where "scion" seems to be the best rendering.[1] The meaning "stem" (Ges.) is not proved for any one of the three passages; we have therefore no choice but to adhere to the rend. "stock" for Isa. xi. 1. The idea is that the Davidic family is to become as obscure as it was of old, when a plain Bethlehemite citizen was its head (cf. Mic. v. 2, and the phrase "the son of Jesse," 1 Sam. xxv. 10 and elsewhere), and that then, quite unexpectedly, some one of its members shall be chosen to become a second David. This was probably the view taken of the passage by the writer of x. 33-34, who may intend to suggest a contrast between the fate of the cedar of Lebanon and the oak of Israel (see vi. 13, with the inserted words). The passage, however, is altogether isolated; even if x. 33-34 were Isaianic, we cannot suppose that the writer of xi. 1 himself drew the contrast which Del. and Kay have imagined. And it is this isolation which makes it difficult to determine the date of the passage with any great confidence, assuming it to be Isaianic. All that we can say is that, if viii. 22-ix. 6 belongs to the reign of Ahaz, it is highly probable that xi. 1-8 (9), which seems to have the same presuppositions, is a work of the same period.[2] The latter passage, however, with its more refined, more spiritual description of the Messiah,[3] was, as most have thought, presumably written some time after the former.

Isaiah's authorship has, however, not been unquestioned. The scepticism of some early critics (see Ges.) has been expressed anew by Hackmann (p. 149), who, as

[1] See Hackmann.
[2] So Guthe (*Zukunftsbild*, p. 39); also Giesebr. and Cornill. Kuenen and Dillm. leave the question open. F. Brown (*JBL*, 1890, p. 104) agrees to this extent—that the position of chap. xi. after x. 5-34 is due to the editor. Duhm boldly assigns xi. 1-8 to Isaiah's extreme old age (cf. on ix. 1-6).
[3] Cf. G. A. Smith, *Exposition*, p. 181.

we have seen, also denies ix. 1-6 to our prophet. His argument is twofold, being derived (*a*) from the phraseology, and (*b*) from the subject-matter. (*a*) חֹטֶר (again only in Prov. xiv. 3), גֶּזַע (again only in xl. 24; Job xiv. 8), and נֵצֶר (again only in xiv. 19, lx. 21; Dan. xi. 7) appear to be late in use, and the two former have their cognates in Aramaic. שַׁעֲשַׁע occurs again only in lxvi. 12; Ps. xciv. 19, cxix. 16, 47, 70. הָדָה and (Hackm. might have added) מְאוּרָה are ἅπ. λεγ.; the former has an Aramaic cognate. שִׁעֲשֵׁעַ occurs again only in lxvi. 12; Ps. xciv. 19, cxix. 16, 47, 70. מִישׁוֹר in a metaphorical sense only in late psalms (xlv. 7, lxvii. 5, and partly xxvi. 12, cxliii. 10) and in Mal. ii. 6. עַנְוֵי אֶרֶץ is not pressed, though Hackm. points out that among the passages adduced by Schwally (*ZATW*, x. 220) for the pre-Exilic use of עָנָו in the sense of "poor," Am. ii. 7 is the only one which can *for the present* be admitted. Now, if the argument from subject-matter strongly favours a late date, the preceding facts may be used to confirm it. Let us however proceed cautiously. Observe, first, that Hackm. omits צִפְעוֹנִי (only found in lix. 5; Prov. xxiii. 32; Jer. viii. 17) and פֶּתֶן (twice in Psalms, twice in Job, once in Deut. xxxii.), feeling no doubt that Isaiah might have used these words. Next that שַׁעֲשֻׁעִים occurs in v. 7. Also, that the Aramaic cognate of הָדָה (ܣܰܕܺܝ) means not *extendere* but *ducere*. As to מִישׁוֹר, the root-meaning is "rectitudo," and unless Isaiah had a singularly limited vocabulary, he may well have used it in an ethical sense. The occurrence of עָנָו is no doubt at first sight suspicious (see p. 194, on xxix. 19). The word is specially used in the Exilic and post-Exilic literature to express humility towards God and ready submission to His will.[1] But this sense will not suit in xi. 4. We might indeed render "the meek of the land" (cf. Num. xiv. 3, pre-Exilic). But considering that in Am. viii. 4 עֲנָוֵי has certainly (see Q'rê and Sept., and cf. parallel adj.) been miswritten for עֲנִיֵּי, and that the parallel word in xi. 4*aa* is דַּלִּים, it is much more natural to correct עַנְוֵי into עֲנִיֵּי (note the parallel adjectives in x. 2, xxvi. 6). As for Am. ii. 7, we must of course correct עֲנָוִים (par. דַּלִּים)

---

[1] Cf. Rahlfs, *עני und ענו in den Psalmen*, 1892; König, *Einl.*, p. 354; Smend, *AT Rel.-gesch.*, p. 446; and Schwally, as above.

into עֲבָיִים. Evidently עָנָו was a rare word before the Exile, and the later writers fetched it out (with the derivative עֲנָוָה) to express a new phase of the Israelitish character. (Zeph. ii. 3 I regard with Wellh. and Schwally as probably post-Exilic.) (b) It is urged by Hackm. that since xi. 1 presupposes a general acquaintance with the fall of the house of David as one of the elements of the prophetic teaching, it must therefore be late. There is some force in this; the allusiveness of the style of xi. 1 creates at least a presumption of a late date (as in the case of ix. 5). Hackmann also thinks that the diffuse description of a state of peace is unlike Isaiah, whose soldier-spirit would have revolted at its soft, world-weary tone. The details in *vv.* 6-8, he says, are fantastic, and imply a study of the late cosmogony in Gen. i. (cf. *vv.* 6, 7 with Gen. i. 30). There seems to be some exaggeration in the form of this argument. For in xi. 4*b* we certainly do find the soldier-spirit. The apparatus of earthly war may have been destroyed (ix. 4), but He who is the God of war as well as of peace will permit his king to resort to sharp measures when evil-doers trouble his realm. The writer of xi. 1-5 has no sympathy with the cry of peace at any cost; he is weary of the unjust wars of tyrants, but can bear to see the true king "striking the tyrant with the rod of his mouth" (*v.* 4). And as to *vv.* 6-8, they are quite in the spirit of the ancient Israelites, who drew no sharp line between men and animals.[1] Nor is there any obvious reason why the idea at the root of Hos. ii. 20 (A.V., 18) should not have been still further developed, or why the notion that green herbs were the food of all animals in primitive times should not have been current in Isaiah's age. We must admit, however, that, though probably not inconsistent with Isaiah's ideas, the description in *vv.* 6-8 implies a brooding over traditional ideas which indicates a more advanced stage of intellectual development, and since (cf. *PI*, i. 77) the details of *vv.* 6-8 must be interpreted realistically, it is more natural (if other things point in the same direction) to refer the description to a period which delighted in such præternaturalistic fancy pictures, *i.e.* to the period which preceded that of the early apocalyptic writing.

[1] These verses will be considered again in dealing with lxv. 17.

To these considerations must be added four out of the six already mentioned on p. 45, for they apply to this as well as to the companion Messianic prophecy, ix. 1-6. And these four points, in addition to the presumptions just now indicated, and a few somewhat striking linguistic phenomena, seem to decide the question against the authorship of Isaiah, though not perhaps as self-evidently as might be desired. Anyhow, this is a seriously important result. Human frailty would gladly have avoided it, for (ix. 1-6 having been also found to be late) it involves the resignation of a dear traditional belief, and compels the rewriting of a chapter in the history of Israelitish religion.

Verse 9 must be considered separately. It is not properly the close of the prophecy xi. 1-8, but is connected more closely with *v.* 10. I would not indeed say that there is any real inconsistency between this verse and *vv.* 1-8. The judicial energy of the heaven-sent ruler must ultimately bring about the extirpation of the race of evil men ; and when this has taken place, it will be perfectly true to say that, just as the wolf and the lion have ceased to do harm, so in human society (in Palestine) those deeds of violence which are only worthy of wild beasts have come to an end. The main reason for connecting *v.* 9 with *v.* 10 is the disappearance of metre after *v.* 8 ; it is of less importance, though still noteworthy, that *v.* 9 comes in very abruptly after *vv.* 6-8, and that it lacks the lucidity of the preceding prophecy. That the verse is of late origin is, or should be, clear enough. Not, indeed, because of the supposed dependence of *v.* 9*a* on lxv. 25*b* and of *v.* 9*b* on Hab. ii. 14. The fact that lxv. 25*a* is a condensed quotation from xi. 6, 7 makes it at least probable that lxv. 25*b* is dependent on xi. 9*a*, and not *vice versâ*. And with regard to *v.* 9*b*, if, with Budde, we hold that Hab. ii. 13, 14 is a very late insertion, one part of which (*v.* 13) is borrowed from Jer. li. 58, it is natural to hold in addition that the other part (*v.* 14) is based upon Isa. xi. 9*b*.[1] I

---

[1] Duhm and Smend think that xi. 9*b* is derived from Hab. ii. 14*b*. But surely the reference to "knowledge" is out of place in the former passage, and the closing idiom seems less original in Hab. But though agreeing so far with Budde (*Stud. u. Krit.*, 1892, p. 390), I cannot see that this proves Isa. xi. 9 to be pre-Exilic. For Jer. li. 58, which is

would rather base the lateness of the verse on the poor style and on the late phrase "my holy mountain"; note also the "unique form of expression" מִכַסִּים, on which see Driver, *Tenses*, § 135. 7 Obs. ["My holy mountain," *v*. 9, as lvi. 7, lvii. 13, lxv. 11 (lxv. 25), lxvi. 20; also Zeph. iii. 11 (late); Ezek. xx. 40; Joel ii. 1, iv. 17; Ob. 16; Ps. ii. 6. "Thy holy mountain," Ps. iii. 5, xv. 1, xliii. 3; Dan. ix. 16. "His holy mountain," Ps. xlviii. 2, xcix. 1. Similar expressions with קָדְשׁ, Ps. xxiv. 3; Dan. ix. 20, xi. 45; Zech. viii. 3; Isa. xxvii. 13. The conclusion seems to me irresistible.]

The result at which we have arrived is this, that later hands are visible, not only in parts of x. 5-34, but in chaps. xi. and xii. There are in fact probably three late appendices, xi. 1-8, xi. 10-16 (*v*. 9 is intended as a link between *vv*. 1-8 and *vv*. 10-16), and chap. xii., and in degree of certainty the late date of chap. xii. stands even above that of xi. 9-16.

CHAPTERS XIII. 2-XIV. 23

We now come to a second collection of prophecies, the origin and development of which has been considered elsewhere. Suffice it to say here that in its earliest form the collection was probably limited to those prophecies which are headed with the (un-Isaianic) word *massā*, " oracle," and that the words which follow *massā bâbhel* in xiii. 1 were added, carelessly enough, by the latest editor, with the view of stamping the whole collection as Isaianic. In arguing therefore against the Isaianic authorship of xiii. 2-xiv. 23, I may be merely arguing against the opinion of a very late student of prophecy. I will put the argument as briefly as is consistent with accuracy. (*a*) It is highly improbable that the return of Jewish exiles entered into the anticipations of Isaiah. During the reign of Ahaz the prophet can see no ray of hope for the majority of his people; a captivity, which is moral and political death, is the just

copied in Hab. ii. 13, is post-Exilic (in Hab. read הָגָה with Wellh. and Budde, after Sept.).

punishment of the national sins (see esp. v. 13-14). Various opinions have been held as to his hopes and fears for the future under Hezekiah. But considering that, in what is probably his latest public address (xxii. 1-14), the prophet sees no forgiveness for the mass of the people, it is unreasonable to suppose that he became afterwards such a thorough-going idealist as the conservative hypothesis assumes. Hosea had indeed, by a swift intuition of love, arrived at the great hope of deliverance from captivity (Hos. xi. 11; Egypt and Assyria are referred to). But it required much thought on the part of the prophets, and a further experience of providential leadings, before this tempting idea could become a fixed element of their teaching. Isaiah at any rate was too much of the type of Amos to accept and develop such an idea, and we have already found good reason for assigning xi. 10-16 to a post-Exilic writer.

(*b*) The prophecy before us speaks of a return from *Babylon*. Now, the only predictions of a Babylonian captivity which occur among the prophecies of Isaiah and his contemporaries are in Isa. xxxix. 5-7, and in Mic. iv. 10. But the former passage, however it be interpreted, comes from a writer who lived long after Isaiah, and the words, "and thou shalt go to Babylon" (if no more), in the latter are now generally regarded (see *e.g.* König, *Einl.*, p. 328) as an interpolation. Is it likely, then, that there exists a prediction of a return from Babylon from the hand of Isaiah? especially if we add (*c*) that the writer of xiii. 2-xiv. 23 does not assume the historical position of Isaiah. For what is the purport of his message? Nothing that would have been at all intelligible to Isaiah's contemporaries. " The Medes are described as already crossing the mountains of the frontier. Soon they will enter on their divinely sanctioned work of destruction, and how terribly will they perform it! The vast Babylonian empire, and more especially its guilty capital, shall be well-nigh depopulated. The foreign merchants shall barely escape by a precipitate flight, or, if they are taken prisoners, shall be savagely murdered, while the ruined palaces of Babylon shall become so awful a desolation that even the wandering Arab shall refuse to lodge there. Yet this is the very moment selected by the Divine compassion for the deliverance of the Israelites. They shall return home with a train of captives and proselytes, and utter a song of triumph over their fallen tyrant."[1] Can Isaiah have written thus? Babylon indeed he knew, but it was a Babylon which had to struggle, not less than Judah, against the superior might of Assyria. Media it is barely possible that he knew,[2] but, if he did, it was a Media which could but ill cope with a highly civilised and organised power. It was long after Isaiah's time that the power of Media became formidable, and the empire which the Medes so largely helped to overthrow was, not Babylonia, but Assyria. If Isaiah could have foreseen such a gathering of the Medes and the subject Iranian peoples as chap. xiii. describes, he would (if he saw truly) have represented the Babylonians, not as their foes, but as their allies.[3] To say that "king of Babylon" in xiv. 4 is equivalent to "king of Assyria"[4] is only possible by a sad misuse of archæology.

I will now endeavour to supplement the above arguments by a summary of relevant exegetical and linguistic facts. Thus, notice (1) the *late* ideas, beliefs, and anticipations which occur both in the prophecy and in the poem. (*a*) The imaginative realisation of the "day of Yahwè," as a world-judgment, with all its awful details (xiii. 6-13 ; cf. Zeph. i. ; Joel ii. ; Zech. xiv. 1, 12, 13 ; Isa. xxiv., xxxiv., lxiii. 1-6). (*b*) The expectation that foreign proselytes will be admitted to the community of Yahwè's worshippers[5] (xiv. 1 ; cf. xliv. 5, lv. 5, lvi. 3, 6, Ps. cxv. 11), with which are connected those of the respectful escort given to the retiring exiles (*v.* 2 ; cf. xlix. 22, lx. 9), and of the enslavement of foreigners (*v.* 2 ; cf. Deut. xv. 6 ; Isa. lx. 10, 14, lxi. 5). (*c*)

[1] *ICA*, p. 134. [2] See on xxi. 1-10.
[3] It is Berosus who tells us that Nabopolassar took part in the siege of Nineveh ; Herodotus, who is dependent on Persian authorities, does not mention this. But Herodotus may be right in assigning the chief part in the siege to the Medes, for from this time onwards they had possession of Assyria (see E. Meyer, *Gesch.*, i. 577 ; Tiele, *Bab.-ass. Gesch.*, p. 410). Winckler, however, distrusts the accounts which have come down to us (*Gesch.*, p. 291).
[4] So George Smith, Sir E. Strachey, and Dean Plumptre. See *PI*, i. 81.
[5] Cf. Kuenen, *Hibbert Lects.*, p. 185.

The adoption of the popular idea of Sheól (xiv. 9, 16), to which, as indeed to the popular beliefs in general, the earlier prophets appear to have sedulously avoided referring. This reminds us of Job, where many non-prophetic ideas and beliefs find expression (see *e.g.* Job iii.), but also of the Exilic prophet Ezekiel (xxxi. 10-18, xxxii. 17-32), and of Isa. xxvi. 14, 19 (the "refaim" or shades). (*d*) The mythological description of the morning star as "son of the dawn" (xiv. 12), with a glance at the belief in the jurisdiction of the stars, or star-deities, over the kingdoms of the earth (same verse; cf. xxiv. 21). (*e*) The reference to the divine mountain in the north (xiv. 13). Cf. Ezek. xxviii. 13, 14, 16, i. 4; Job xxxvii. 22, reading, with Siegfried, ירחה for זהב, which passages show that the Exilic and post-Exilic Jews spoke of the "holy mountain of Elohim," and placed it in the north. Whether the poet knows of a Babylonian mythic mountain or not may be left open. (*f*) The use of the Divine name Shaddai (xiii. 6; see p. 72). (*g*) The belief in demons of the desert (the Arabic *jinn* [1]) shaped like goats (xiii. 21; cf. xxxiv. 14; Lev. xvii. 7; 2 Chr. xi. 15), of whom perhaps Azazel (Lev. xvi. 8, 10, 26) was the chief.

(2) Parallels of imagery, etc., in xiii. 2-xiv. 23, to prophecies commonly admitted to be (*a*) Isaianic, or, at any rate, (*b*) pre-Exilic. The value of these will be considered presently. (*a*) xiii. 2, the "banner" for the nations, cf. v. 26, xi. 10, 12 (very doubtful), xviii. 3; the phrase, "wave the hand," cf. xi. 15 (?); xix. 16 (?);—xiii. 19, comparison to Sodom and Gomorrah, cf. i. 7 (corr. text), 9, proverbial; xiv. 5, 6, the "rod" or "staff," cf. ix. 3, x. 24 (?);—xiv. 8, cutting down the cypresses and cedars, cf. xxxvii. 24 (?);—xiv. 11, music hushed in Sheól, cf. v. 12-14;—xiv. 13, 14, impious speech of the king, cf. xxxvii. 24 (?). Under (*b*) notice the following:—xiii. 3, closing phrase, cf. Zeph. iii. 11 (disputed date);—xiii. 8*b*, cf. Nah. ii. 11;—xiii. 14 (fugitives whom "no man gathereth"), cf. Nah. iii. 18;—xiii. 20-22, cf. Zeph. ii. 13-15;—xiv. 2 (opening), cf. Deut. xxv. 19; Jer. xxxi. 2;—xiv. 3, 4, cf. Hab. ii. 5, 6;—xiv. 8, cf. Hab. ii. 17. Parallels to writings commonly regarded as Exilic and

---

[1] Cf. Robertson Smith, *Rel. of the Semites*, p. 113; Wellh., *Prolegomena*, p. 53; *Skizzen*, iii. 178.

post-Exilic. xiii. 2 ("lift ye up a banner"), cf. xlix. 22, lxii. 10, and the use of the imperative in xl. 3-6 ;—xiii. 5, cf. xlvi. 11 ;—xiii. 6, cf. Joel i. 15 (almost complete verbal agreement) ;—xiii. 7 (images), cf. Ezek. vii. 17, xxi. 12 (7) ;—xiii. 8, cf. xxi. 3 ;—xiii. 10, cf. xxxiv. 4 ;—xiii. 13, cf. xxiv. 19 ; Joel ii. 10, iv. 16 ;—xiii. 14, cf. xlvii. 15 ;—xiii. 16*b*, cf. Zech. xiv. 2 ;—xiii. 19-22, cf. xxxiv. 13-17 ;—xiv. 2 (opening), cf. Deut. xxv. 19, Jer. xxxi. 2 ;—xiv. 3, 4, cf. Isa. xxi. 2 (end). On xiv. 1, 2, cf. also p. 69. To these should be added the nine parallelisms between ch. xiii. and Jer. l.-li.[1] (*a*) *v.* 2, cf. Jer. l. 2, li. 27 (li. 12) ; (*b*) *v.* 3, cf. li. 27 ("to consecrate") ; (*c*) *vv.* 7, 8, cf. Jer. l. 43 ; (*d*) *v.* 14*a*, cf. Jer. l. 6, 17 ; (*e*) *v.* 14*b*, cf. Jer. l. 16 (li. 6); (*f*) *v.* 17, cf. Jer. l. 9, li. 1 ; (*g*) *v.* 17, cf. li. 11, 28 (the Medes); (*h*) *v.* 18, cf. li. 3, l. 14, 29 ; (*i*) *vv.* 19-21, cf. Jer. l. 39-40.

Let us now briefly survey these parallels. The most striking pre-Exilic parallels to phrases in chap. xiii. are those in Zeph. iii. 11 and Deut. xxv. 19 (Jer. xxxi. 2). Conservative scholars are confident that Isa. xiii. 3 is the original of Zeph. *l.c.* עָלִיז occurs in Isa. xxii. 2, xxiii. 7, xxiv. 8, xxxii. 13 ; and גַּאֲוָה in Isa. ix. 8, xvi. 6, xxv. 11. True, but of these passages only xxii. 2 and ix. 8 are undisputed.[2] Nor is it certain that Zeph. iii. 11 is pre-Exilic. The relation between this passage and Isa. xiii. 3 must, therefore, be left undecided. But it is at any rate inconceivable that xiv. 2 should be earlier than Deut. xxv. 19 ; הֵנִיחַ לְמ׳ is a characteristic phrase of the Deuteronomic school (Deut. iii. 20, xii. 10, xxv. 19 ; Josh. i. 13, 15, xxii. 4, xxiii. 1 ; Ex. xxxiii. 14) for the state of the Israelites in Canaan after their wanderings ; so perhaps lxiii. 14 (late). Passing on to the parallels in Exilic and post-Exilic writings, we may at once reject those in ch. xxxiv., in Jer. l.-li., in Joel, and in Zech. xiv., as due to a direct imitation of ch. xiii. Of the remainder, the most important are those in ch. xl., etc., which must be viewed in connection with the identity of historic background in ch. xl., etc., and xiii. 2-xiv. 23, and

---

[1] On Jer. l.-li. see Budde, *JDT*, xxiii. 428-470; and cf. Kuenen, *Ond.*[2], ii. 229-245, and Giesebrecht's commentary.

[2] It was, therefore, uncritical of Del., in 1857, to speak of "the peculiarly Isaianic word עָלִיז" (*Anhang* to Drechsler's *Jes.*, iii. 401).

with the parallelisms of phraseology and of idea. (I do not offer them as proving that either of these works is dependent on the other.)

(3) Parallelisms in the vocabulary; a few less important ones have been omitted. I. Isaianic.—(*a*) גֵּם, xiii. 2, as above (2) *a*; but see also xxxiii. 23, lxii. 10. (*b*) עָלִיז, and (*c*) גַּאֲוָה, *v.* 3; see above. (*d*) הָמוֹן and שָׁאוֹן combined, *v.* 4, as xvii. 12, 13. (*e*) אֱנוֹשׁ, *vv.* 7, 12, "man" (or "men"), as viii. 1; but also xxiv. 6, xxxiii. 8, lvi. 2. (*f*) לְהָבִים (לַהַב), *v.* 8, as xxix. 6, cf. Nah. iii. 3; but also xxx. 30, lxvi. 15. (*g*) גָּאוֹן, *vv.* 11, 19, xiv. 11, as ii. 10, 19, 21; but also iv. 2 (late), xvi. 6, xxiii. 9 (both of doubtful origin), xxiv. 14, and lx. 15 (both late). (*h*) נִגַּשׁ, xiv. 2, 4, as iii. 12, ix. 3 (doubtful); also lx. 17 (admittedly late). (*i*) בְּלִי, xiv. 6, as xxviii. 8; but also in xxxii. 10. (*k*) נֶבֶל, xiv. 11, as *v.* 12. (*l*) זֶרַע מְרֵעִים, *v.* 20, as i. 4. (*m*) שָׁאַר, *v.* 22 (see on x. 19-22, p. 52). I hesitate to add (*n*) הֵנִיף, *v.* 2, x. 15 (*bis*), xi. 15, xix. 16, xxx. 28; (*o*) עָרִיץ, *v.* 11, as xi. 4 (corr. text); but also xxv. 3, 4, 5, xxix. 5, 20, xlix. 25, and Ezek. (4 times); (*p*) נֵצֶר, *v.* 19, as xi. 1, lx. 21, even xi. 1, 4 and x. 15 being at best doubtful.

II. Non-Isaianic, and mostly late in use; we should probably add (*o*) and (*p*) from preceding list.—(*a*) נִשְׁפָּה, xiii. 2, ἅπ. λεγ.; cf. שְׁפִי, xli. 18, xlix. 9 (and six times in Jer.). (*b*) קוֹל הָמוֹן, *v.* 4, as xxxiii. 3 (late). For the interjectional use of קוֹל cf. xl. 3, 6, lii. 8, lxvi. 6. (*c*) דְּמוּת, *v.* 4, as xl. 18; cf. *BL*, p. 474. Nowhere else used prepositionally (Ezek. xxiii. 15 is hardly quite in point); but cf. בִּדְמוּת, Ps. lviii. 5. (*d*) עַם רָב, *v.* 4, as Ezek. xvii. 9, 15, xxvi. 7; Joel ii. 2. (*e*) צְבָא מִלְחָמָה, *v.* 4, as Num. xxxi. 14 (P; see Kuenen, *Hexateuch*, p. 99; Driver, *Intr.*, p. 63); 1 Chr. vii. 4, xii. 37. (*f*) מֵאֶרֶץ מֶרְחָק, *v.* 5, as xlvi. 11 (Isaiah's phrase is מִמֶּרְחָק, x. 3, xvii. 13, xxx. 27?). (*g*) מִקְצֵה הַשָּׁמַיִם, *v.* 5, a Deuteronomic phrase; see Deut. iv. 32, xxx. 4 (Neh. i. 9; Ps. xix. 7). (*h*) שַׁדַּי, *v.* 6. The pre-Exilic prophets and narrators (see *BL*, p. 84) avoid this name. It occurs seven times in P, once in Joel, thirty-one times in Job, twice in the Psalms and in Ezek.; also in Num. xxiv. 4, 16 (post-Exilic?). (*i*) לֵב יִמָּס, *v.* 7,

CHAPTERS XIII. 2-XIV. 23

as xix. 1; cf. Ps. xxii. 15 (poetic and rhetorical). (k) צִירִים, v. 8, as xxi. 3. (l) אַכְזָרִי, v. 9; nowhere else in this book. (m) כְּסִיל, "Orion," v. 10, as Am. v. 8 (late insertion); Job ix. 9, xxxviii. 31. (n) הלל, Hif., "to shine" or "make bright," as Job xxxi. 26, xli. 10. (o) רְשָׁעִים, of non-Israelites, v. 11, xiv. 5, as Hab. i. 13; Isa. xxvi. 10; Ps. ix. 6 (par. to "the nations"); (p) זֵדִים, v. 11; Mal. iii. 15, 19; nowhere again in prophecy (it occurs six times in Ps. cxix., and in Ps. xix. 14, lxxxvi. 14; also in the late narrative passage, Jer. xliii. 2, and in a probably late ethical definition, Prov. xxi. 24). (q) שָׁגֵל, v. 16, Deut. xxviii. 30; Jer. iii. 2; Zech. xiv. 2 (need not be a late word, *BL*, p. 471). (r) עוּר Hif., v. 17, not in prophets before Ezek. xxiii. 22 (see on chs. xl.-lxvi). (s) צְבִי, תִּפְאֶרֶת, and גָּאוֹן, combined, v. 19, as iv. 2 (late). (t) עַד־דּוֹר וָדוֹר, v. 20, as Ps. c. 5. Combinations with דּוֹר are common in the disputed parts of Isaiah (see xxxiv. 10, 17, li. 8, lviii. 12, lx. 15, lxi. 4). (u) יֶהֱל, v. 20. We find אָהֵל (Qal) elsewhere only in Gen. xiii. 12, 18. (v) עֲרָבִי, v. 20, as Jer. iii. 2 (see on xxi. 13). (w) צִיִּים, v. 21, as xix. 13 (late; cf. *BL*, p. 477). (x) אִיִּים, v. 22, as xxxiv. 14; Jer. l. 39. (y) עָנָב, v. 22, as lviii. 13 (nowhere else). It is needless to show further that vv. 21, 22 are thoroughly un-Isaianic. (z) גֵּר, xiv. 1, nearly = proselyte (see on lvi. 3). Nowhere in early prophets. In Jer. (vii. 6) still "sojourner." (aa) רָדָה, v. 2; only once before Deut., Jer., Lam., Ezek. (viz. Num. xxiv. 19, where the text is doubtful). (bb) עָצַב, v. 3, as Ps. cxxxix. 24; 1 Chr. iv. 9. (cc) רֹגֶז, v. 3; five times in Job, once in Hab. iii. (late). The verb is Isaianic. (dd) עָבַד בְּ, v. 3; not prophetic before Ezek. (xxxiv. 27). (ee) מָשָׁל, v. 4, not in Isaiah, but in Mic. ii. 4; Hab. ii. 6. (ff) מַדְהֵבָה, v. 4 (corr. text), ἄπ. λεγ.; cf. רָהַב in Isa. iii. 5. (gg) מָשַׁל, v. 5, in bad sense, as xlix. 7, lii. 5, suggesting that the writer was one of the Jewish exiles. (hh) סָרָה, "cessation," v. 6 (a different sense in i. 5). (ii) מֻרְדָּף, v. 7, ἄπ. λεγ.; the corrected reading מִרְדַּת is also unique. (kk) פָּצַח רִנָּה, v. 7; four times in II. Isaiah, cf. also lii. 9. (ll) רְפָאִים, v. 9, as xxvi. 14, 19; Job xxvi. 5; Ps. lxxxviii. 11. (mm) עָנָה, "to address (some one)," v. 10, as Job iii. 2; Song Sol. ii. 10; Zech. i. 10, iii. 4, iv. 11, 12.

(nn) הָמִיָה, v. 11, ἅπ. λεγ. (oo) יָעַ Hof., v. 11, as Esth. iv. 3 (cf. on chaps. xl.-lxvi.). (pp) מְכַסֶּה, "covering," v. 11, as xxiii. 18; Ezek. xxvii. 7; Lev. ix. 19. (qq) הֵילֵל (so point), v. 12, ἅπ. λεγ. (rr) חָלַשׁ transitively, v. 12, an old and rare word, as Ex. xvii. 13 (cf. xxxii. 18); also Job xiv. 10. Has a word dropped out before עַל? (ss) בָּמֳתִי, v. 14; an old form, see Mic. i. 3 (Am. iv. 13 is late), but also found in lviii. 14 (late). (tt) עֶלְיוֹן, v. 14, as a divine name beyond question characteristically late ; cf. my note on Ps. vii. 18, and *BL*, p. 84. (uu) הִשְׁגִּיחַ, v. 16, as Song Sol. ii. 9 ; Ps. xxxiii. 14 (late, see *BL*, p. 469). (vv) מָעַט, v. 19, ἅπ. λεγ. (ww) מַטְאֲטֵא, v. 21, ἅπ. λεγ. (xx) בַּל, v. 21 ; an emphatic negative, seven times in xxvi. 10-18, six times in xxxiii. 20-24, eight times in 2 Isa. (viz. xl. 24 thrice, xliii. 17, xliv. 8, 9 four times), nine times in Prov., twenty-one times in Ps. ; originally perhaps N. Palestinian (König), for it occurs in Hos. vii. 2, and is certainly Phœn. (yy) בֵּין נֵכֶד, v. 22 (Gen. xxi. 23 ; Job xviii. 19). (zz) מוֹרָשׁ, v. 23 (Job xvii. 11 ; Obad. 17). (aaa) קִפּוֹד, v. 23 (xxxiv. 11 ; Zeph. ii. 14). (bbb) אַגַם, v. 23 (xxxv. 7, xli. 18, xlii. 15 ; Jer. li. 32; twice in Ps., twice in Ex.). (ccc) מֵאמֵא (Bär), with deriv. noun, v. 23, ἅπ. λεγ. A colloquialism with new-Hebrew affinities ; cf. *BL*, p. 471, on דִּדָּה. We can scarcely add בְּרוֹשִׁים, xiv. 8 (xxxvii. 24, probably late) ; for if Isaiah had had occasion to refer to Lebanon would he not have used this word?

These exegetical and linguistic facts evidently do not favour the conservative theory. Note especially among the latter the words בַּל, דְּמוּת (prepositional), הִשְׁגִּיחַ, which were certainly not used by Isaiah. Add to this, that nowhere in the true Isaiah is there such a continuously smooth and regular parallelism as in xiii. 2-22, and that for a parallel to the metre or rhythm of the ode in xiv. 4b-21[1] we must go to the taunt-song on Sennacherib in

---

[1] It is hard to find any regular rhythm or metre in chap. xlvii. It is otherwise with chaps. xiv. and xxxviii., where with comparative ease Budde and Bickell discover their respective rhythms or metres (see Budde, *ZATW*, 1882, pp. 12-14 ; 1892, pp. 32-37 ; Bickell, *Carmina VT*, 1882, pp. 202, 207, but cf. *Zeitschr. f. d. Kunde des Morgenlandes*, viii. 101-102). No theory, however, can induce me with Bickell and (now) Budde to omit עִיִּים, or rather אִיִּים, in v. 21b.

chap. xxxvii., and for a parallel to its five symmetrical strophes to the ode on the fall of Babylon in chap. xlvii. How an advanced critic like Winckler can regard the former poem as Isaiah's song of triumph on the death of Sennacherib[1] is a mystery. Phraseology and ideas are alike opposed to this hasty view, and the parallelisms in xiv. 8, 13, 14 to passages of the taunt-song on Sennacherib in xxxvii. 22*b*-29 simply show that both poems proceed from the same (late) school of poets. It is also most unlikely that Isaiah expected that Sennacherib would be "cast far from his grave." Both prophecy and ode, then, are not earlier than the close of the Exile. Do they both belong to the same writer? To prove beyond contradiction that they do not is impossible. But there are such differences in the imaginative pictures of the judgment in the two works,[2] and there is so much more poetic heat in the ode than in the prophecy, that the conjecture (already offered in *PI*, i. 21) of a twofold authorship is a reasonable one. If we accept this, we must ascribe xiv. 1-4*a*, and *vv.* 22-23 (which stand outside the poem, and are in a very inelegant style) to the editor who inserted the ode.[3] Hitzig has expressed a similar doubt whether the song in chap. xlvii. was not itself inserted by an afterthought.

To facilitate the judgment of the reader, I append the last strophe of the prophecy, the prose introduction to the ode, and the ode itself with the prophetic appendix in a translation. Words marked with †, or verses with ††, have been emended in a greater or less degree (see *RT*).

---

[1] *Altor. Forschungen*, pp. 193-194.
[2] See Bredenkamp, *Jes.*, pp. 94-95; Cobb, "An Examination of Isa. xiii.," *Bibliotheca Sacra*, 1892.
[3] Geiger (*Urschrift*, p. 353) takes a similar view of xiv. 1, 2. He points out that גֵּר is already nearly equivalent to "foreign proselyte." In lvi. 3 (see introd. to lvi. 1-8), the writer, remembering the old sense of גֵּר, thinks it necessary to say בֶּן־נֵכָר. Besides lvi. 3, we may compare lx. 10, 14; Zech. ii. 15, viii. 21 (*all* post-Exilic). Moreover, וְנָחַר עוֹד בְּ, *v*. 1, reminds us forcibly of Zech. i. 17, ii. 16. נִלְוָה, too, suggests Zech. ii. 15, and also Isa. lvi. 3; Esth. ix. 27. In xiv. 22, 23 notice (1) the careless rhythm, (2) the colloquialism (*v*. 23*b*), and (3) נְאֻם יְ", used thrice (parallel to the repetition in the late passage, lii. 3-5).

VI

xiii.
20. It will be uninhabited for ever, | and untenanted age after age;
    The nomad will not pitch tent there; | shepherds will not cause (flocks) to lie down there.
21. Wild cats will lie down there, | . . . .
    And their houses will be full of jackals, | . . . .
    Ostriches will dwell there, | and satyrs will dance there,
22. Hyænas will howl to each other in † its towers, | and wolves in the voluptuous palaces;
    Its time is nearly come, | and its days will not be prolonged.

*

xiv.
1. For Yahwè will have compassion upon Israel, and will yet again choose Israel, and settle them upon their own land, and the (foreign) sojourner will join himself to them, and they will
2. attach themselves to the house of Jacob; and peoples will take them, and bring them to their place, and they of the house of Israel will take them in possession on Yahwè's land for bondmen and for bondmaids, and they will become the captors of
3. their captors, and will subdue their taskmasters. And then, when Yahwè hath given thee rest from thy travail, and from thy disquiet, and from the hard service which men laid upon thee, thou wilt take up this taunt-song upon the king of Babylon, and wilt say—

I

4. How still is the despot become— | how still the †raging!
5. Broken hath Yahwè the staff of the wicked, | the rod of the tyrants,
6. Which smote peoples in passion | with unremitting stroke,
   Which trampled nations in anger | with a trampling that no man checked!
7. Still and at rest is all the earth; | they break into jubilee.
8. The pine-trees, too, rejoice at thy fate, | (and) Lebanon's cedars,
   "Since thou hast lain low," (they cry) "cometh up | no feller against us."

II

9. Sheól beneath is disquieted because of thee, | expecting thine arrival;

It arouseth for thee the shades— | all the bell-wethers of the earth ;
It maketh to stand up from their thrones | all the kings of nations.
10. They all address thee . . . | and say to thee,
"Thou, too, art become strengthless like us, | unto us art thou made like"!
11. Brought down to Sheól is thy pride | (and) the clang of thy harps ;
Beneath thee is spread corruption, | thy coverlet are-worms.

III

12. How art thou fallen from heaven, | O radiant one, son of the dawn !
(How) art thou hewn down to the earth, | prostrater of nations !
13. And thou—thou didst say in thine heart, | "Heaven will I scale,
Above God's stars | will I raise my throne,
I will sit upon the mount of (the divine) assembly, | in the recesses of the north,
14. I will ascend above the cloud-hills, | will match the Most High."
15. Nathless to Sheól art thou brought down— | to the recesses of the pit.

IV

16. They that see thee fix their gaze on thee | and consider thee,—
"Is this the man that disquieted the earth, | that startled the kingdoms,
17. That made the world as the desert, | and broke down its cities,
That sent not home free his prisoners, | all the kings of the nations ?"
18. (As for them,) they all repose in honour, | each one in his house,
19. †† But *thou* art flung down among the slain, | (among) the pierced with the sword,
Going down to the stones of the pit, | as a trampled carcass.

V

[How art thou cut off] from thy grave, | as an abhorred scion,
. . . . | clothed [with shame ††] !

20. [As for thy fathers], thou mayest not be joined | with them in burial,
Because thou hast destroyed thy land, | slain thy people :
Never more be named | the seed of evil-doers !
21. Prepare shambles for his sons, | because of the guilt of their father,
That they arise not, and take the earth in possession, | and fill the face of the world with † ruins.
22. I will arise against thee, saith Yahwè Çebaoth, and will cut off from Babylon record and remnant, scion and seed, saith Yahwè;
23. and I will make it a possession of the bittern, and pools of water, and will sweep it with the besom of destruction, saith Yahwè Çebaoth.

The more precise dating of this work (or, these works) is difficult. Some (*e.g.* Knobel and Driver)[1] infer from the reference to the Medes in xiii. 17 that the date is shortly before B.C. 549 (when Cyrus overthrew the Median empire). But, not to mention that before 549 the Medes would hardly have been hailed so confidently as deliverers by a Jewish prophet, it was the custom both of the Greeks in general and of the Egyptians[2] to speak of the Medes where in strict accuracy they should have said "the Persians," and the first certain mention of Persia in the O.T. itself is in Ezra iv. 5, ix. 9,[3] etc. My own opinion or surmise is nearly the same as Ewald's, viz. that xxi. 1-10 is probably the first of the Babylonian Hebrew prophecies, chap. xiii. the second, and chaps. xl.-lv. the third ; on the date of the ode I cannot venture to speak positively—it may or may not be contemporary with the preceding prophecy. It is painful to reflect that chap. xiii. had an attraction for many early readers, as appears from the fact that it is imitated both in chap. xxxiv. and in Jer. l.-li. Cornill, it is true, thinks that chaps. xxxiv.-xxxv. are by the same author as xiii. 2-xiv. 23;[4] but how unlikely in this case that chaps. xxxiv.-xxxv. should have been left outside the collection opened by chap. xiii. !

[1] *Introd.*, p. 202 ; *Isaiah*, p. 127.
[2] *PI*, i. 85, after Révillout, *Rev. ég.*, 1880-1881.
[3] So Davidson, *Ezekiel*, p. 193.
[4] *ZATW*, 1884, p. 98, note[1]; *Einl.*, p. 145 ; cf. Gesenius, *Jes.*, p. 908.

CHAPTER XIV. 24-27

Granting that this passage is really Isaianic (which can hardly be denied merely on the ground of the worldwide significance attached to the destruction of the Assyrians), it must once have formed the close of a prophecy in which an impending attack of Assyria upon the land of Yahwè was referred to. Can we, with any probability, indicate the prophecy? Surely we can. It is the great "woe" upon Assyria, as Rosenmüller, Gesenius, and Hendewerk[1] long ago saw. Only the place to which this fragment on the oath of Yahwè should be restored is not between x. 27 and x. 28 (Hend.), nor yet after x. 34 (Ros., Ges.), but after x. 14 (or 15), in accordance with the critical analysis of x. 5-34. It is important to notice that the style and rhythm of x. 24-27 closely resemble that of the Isaianic part of x. 5-15, and differ considerably from that of x. 16-26, and even from that of *vv.* 33, 34. The contents are just what is wanted to complete x. 5-15. Did "Assyria" or the Assyrian king "plan (וְדִמָּה) to cut off nations not a few" (x. 7)? Yahwè declares that "as I have planned (דִּמִּיתִי), so shall it be," and his "purpose," which is to destroy proud "Assyria," concerns "all the nations" (xiv. 24-26). Did the king make conquered peoples "a trampling, like the mire of the streets" (x. 6)? Yahwè declares that he "will tread him under foot" (xiv. 25). And if in xiv. 25 we are told that this downtreading shall be on Yahwè's mountains, this has been already not obscurely hinted in x. 12 (if some shreds of this may be claimed for Isaiah). So that, if x. 5-15 was written in 711, the same date must be given to xiv. 24-27. There is no adequate reason for assigning this prophecy to the time of Sennacherib (with Hitzig, Ewald, Kuenen, Driver, and Duhm), much less for combining it with xvii. 12-xviii. 7 (Ewald). Least of all could I follow Stade and view the passage as a cento of Isaianic phrases.[2] In spirit as well as in form it is

---

[1] Ges., *Jes.*, pp. 22, 491; Hend., *Jes.*, i. (1838), pp. 317-319.

[2] *ZATW*, 1883, p. 16; cf. Oort, *Th. Tijd.*, 1886, p. 193; Hackmann, *ZEJ*, p. 107 f. Stade groups it with xvii. 12-14, and ascribes both passages to the editor of Isaiah. It is no doubt singular that neither (*a*) יִשָּׁבַע nor

distinctly Isaianic. There is however one interpolation from the margin pointed out by Duhm, viz. the poorly expressed distich at the close of *v.* 25 (see x. 27), which obscures the division of the prophecy into two four-lined strophes and interrupts the connection.

CHAPTER XIV. 28-32

The preceding prophecy being only a misplaced fragment, this is the first complete oracle in the collection which can claim the authorship of Isaiah. It is a striking composition in four strophes of four lines each, and is assigned by the heading to the death-year of King Ahaz (719). Is this statement correct? Certainly not, if it is based on an interpretation of *v.* 29, according to which the broken rod means Ahaz, and the basilisk Hezekiah. For though the latter identification might pass (cf. 2 Ki. xviii. 8), the former is impossible. That Ahaz should have been able to tyrannise over Philistia is contrary not only to 2 Chr. xxviii. 18, but to all that is known of the character and circumstances of that king. But did the author of the heading interpret *v.* 29 thus? It is true that according to the Targum "root of the serpent" (*naḥash*) = " root of Jesse "[1] (cf. 2 Sam. xvii. 25), but this is rather a subtle attempt to explain how the heading came to speak of Ahaz. Let us assume, however, that the author of the heading (who probably wrote not הַמַּשָּׂא, but הַדָּבָר) had good ground for his assertion, and that his statement is purely chronological (cf. vi. 1, "in the year that King Uzziah died"), and has no illustrative value for the contents of the prophecy, and let us see whether in the death-year of Ahaz, or shortly before, any events took place which really do appear to illustrate the contents. Thanks to Winckler, we can point to such events.

(*b*) הֲרֵי (of the mountains of Canaan) occurs elsewhere in Isaiah except (*a*) in xlv. 23, liv. 9, lxii. 8, and (*b*) in lxv. 9 (xlix. 11 is not in point); cf. Ezek. xxxviii. 21, Zech. xiv. 5.

[1] So Duff, who renders, "For out of the Nahash-root there riseth ever a David-seed" (*O. T. Theol.*, i. 174, 202). On 2 Sam. xvii. 25, see Robertson Smith, who thinks that "Serpent" was Jesse's totemistic stock-name (*Journ. of Phil.*, 1880, p. 99).

CHAPTER XIV. 28-32

The year 720 is marked by general disturbances in Syria and Palestine. Arpad, Simirra, Damascus, and Samaria joined Hamath in revolt, and Hanun, king of Gaza, supported by the Egyptian king Shabaka, again asserted his independence. Both in the north and in the south Sargon put down all his opponents. Hanun in particular fell into the hands of the Assyrians. The prophecy may well have been written on the outbreak of this restless Philistine's revolt; the Assyrian "rod" had in fact smitten Philistia since 734 (the date of Hanun's first revolt). But how had this "rod" been "broken," to use Isaiah's phrase? What great shock had the power of Sargon sustained to justify the exulting hopes of the Philistines? Sargon's own inscriptions do not tell us. From them we only hear of successful campaigns, but according to the Babylonian chronicle the battle (in 721 or 720) between Sargon and the Elamites at Dûr-ilu in N. Babylonia, which Sargon represents as a victory, was really a serious defeat for him. The Elamites were allies of Merodach Baladan who in 722 (the year of Sargon's accession) had become master of Babylon, and had thus robbed Assyria of its most prized possession. Humbanigas their king not only defeated, but even pursued Sargon, and Winckler shows reason for thinking that the Babylonian chronicle here gives the more accurate account.[1]

It now becomes needless to ask what Assyrian kings may be meant[2] by the "serpent" and the "basilisk." The prophet has no other foreign king in his mind but Sargon. The "serpent," the "basilisk," and the "flying dragon" represent successive phases of an increasingly despotic rule

[1] *Untersuch.*, pp. 137-139.
[2] Three views have been held. (*a*) G. Smith, Schrader, Duncker, Barth (*Beitr.*, pp. 18, 19), König, are for Tiglath-pileser and Shalmaneser; (*b*) Bred., Giesebr., and Cornill for Shalmaneser and Sargon; (*c*) W. R. Smith, Driver, and Kuenen (also *PI*) for Sargon and Sennacherib. If we had to choose between these views, I should prefer (*c*). Sargon has been virtually called a "rod" in x. 5, and no Assyrian king's death was a more important event to all the weaker peoples than that of Sargon. And if, as Tiele infers from a mutilated passage of the list of eponyms, Sargon really died by violence, the description of him as a broken rod becomes specially appropriate. For Köhler's bisection of the prophecy (*vv.* 29-30, soon after Hezekiah's accession; vv. 31-32, in 701 B.C.) very little can be said (*Bibl. Gesch.*, iii. 431).

(cf. Jer. viii. 17). For a short time, says the prophet, the oppression may be at an end, but the revolt of the Philistines will be surely avenged. The Assyrian yoke will soon be reimposed, and, partly by famine, partly by slaughter, the Philistine people will become extinct (as Am. i. 8). Already the prophet seems to see the avengers advancing from the north. The last strophe is difficult, and no doubt lines 1 and 2 are incomplete. We should probably on metrical and exegetical grounds complete the passage thus (with Bickell),

And what shall [the king of my people] answer,
[When] the messengers of the nation [shall speak unto him]?
—That Yahwè hath founded Zion,
And therein the afflicted of his people find refuge.

The defeat of Sargon was the signal to the anti-Assyrian party everywhere to form plans for concerted action. Judah however seemed slow to move, and the Philistines sought to rouse Hezekiah from his torpor. Isaiah dissuades him from yielding, as he will dissuade him again when pressed by Taharqa (see on ch. xviii.), and assures him that if he stands firm, and trusts in Yahwè alone, Zion will prove to be an impregnable rock in which the poor and afflicted, who are Yahwè's true people, shall find refuge.[1] Thus Isaiah once more opens a little door of hope. He is aware (cf. vi. 9-13, really an early passage) that his advice will not be long followed, but he will give the king and his counsellors every possible chance of amending their ways, trusting in Yahwè, and becoming the protectors of the poor (cf. xxx. 15a). Like Jeremiah, he will work on for a time as if his hearers were capable of amendment. Hezekiah's revolt from Assyria and the consequent limitation of the promise in v. 32 (see xxviii. 16) are yet in the future.

My former date for this prophecy was 705 B.C. (see p. 81, note 2). Even then Isaiah might conceivably have

[1] So in the main Meinhold (*St. u. Kr.*, 1893, p. 21), who thinks, however, that the promise to the "poor" implies that the rulers who oppress them shall come to ruin (as xxviii. 17-19). This is hardly correct. Isaiah means to open "a little door of hope" even for the rulers (see above). My former explanation of the " poor and afflicted " (*PI*, i. 95, so Dillm.) will not, I think, hold.

spoken thus, Hezekiah not having yet revolted. To this date I should have to return, if the death-year of Ahaz could be shown to be 715 (Wellh., Kamph.); as yet, however, this appears to me improbable (see on ch. xxxvi.). Duhm's denial of the authorship of Isaiah is at any rate unnecessary. A post-Exilic writer might of course have spoken of Zion as the foundation of Yahwè (cf. Ps. lxxxvii. 1), and of the Jerusalemites as "the helpless and the poor," and "the afflicted of his people" (cf. on xxv. 4). But Jer., who lived before the Church-nation existed, speaks of the people of the capital as דַּלִּים (Jer. v. 4), and the expressions of *vv.* 30*a*, 32*b*, do not outpass those of iii. 13-15, x. 2, xxviii. 16, which are certainly Isaiah's. The prophet fully believes that the ideal Zion is indestructible, and, for hortatory reasons, speaks as if the actual Zion were equally safe. He has moreover a genuine compassion for the poor, and at moments rebels against the thought that *delirant reges plectuntur Achivi*.

CHAPTERS XV.-XVI

These chapters appear at first sight to present an insoluble enigma. There is nothing quite like them in the whole of the first part of Isaiah. We cannot therefore be surprised if theories to account for the phenomena are numerous.—The poem or prophecy falls into three parts, (I.) chap. xv., (II.) chap. xvi. 1-6, and (III.) *vv.* 7-12, to which *vv.* 13, 14 are attached as an epilogue. That the epilogue is Isaiah's, has been doubted,[1] either because a ground for the definite prediction which it contains could not be found in the history of Isaiah's times, or because the oracle itself was thought to be post-Exilic, and the epilogue necessarily belonged to the same period, or because the phraseology of the epilogue seemed non-Isaianic. Verses 13 and 14, however, are at any rate worthy of Isaiah, and it long appeared to me that almost every word had his mark upon it (see especially xxxvii. 22, xxi. 16, iii. 5, xvii. 3, 4, x. 25, xxix. 17), the only exception being מֵאָז (*v.* 13). I must

[1] Eichhorn, Bleek, Geiger, Oort, Schwally, Duhm.

confess, however, that I can no longer adhere to this view consistently with the results of critical analysis (see *BW*). And what of the oracle itself? Orelli assures us that "despite all peculiarities . . . an unmistakeable Isaianic colouring runs through the whole (cf. *e.g.* xvi. 3, 6)." But this is incorrect. The only part of the oracle which presents anything like Isaianic "colouring" is the second (xvi. 1-6); elsewhere a few words (שְׁאֵרִית, פְּלֵיטָה, יֶרֶק, דֶּשֶׁא, חָצִיר, חוּצוֹת, הָלַם, אָז of intoxication, כַּרְמֶל) may remind us of Isaiah, but the style is about as unlike Isaiah's as it could be. Let us examine the vocabulary. לֵיל (xv. 1, corr. text; xvi. 3; but cf. לֵיל st. constr. xxx. 29; לַיִל in xxi. 11 is hardly Isaianic). יָרַד בַּבְּכִי (xv. 3; cf. Jer. ix. 17, xiii. 17, xvi. 11; Lam. i. 16, iii. 48). חֲלָצִים (xv. 4). הֵרִיעַ (xv. 4). יָרֵעַ (xv. 4, ἅπ. λεγ.; a rare word designed to produce a paronomasia with יָרִיעוּ). בְּרִיחִים (xv. 5; xliii. 14, nowhere else). יְעֹעֲרוּ (xv. 5; dialectic form for יְעָרְעָרוּ according to Ges.-Kautzsch, § 72, König, *Lehrgeb.*, i. 500). Or read יִרְעָעוּ with Lagarde; see *PI*, ii. 150. לֹא הָיָה (xv. 6; Ezek. xxi. 32). יִתְרָה (xv. 7, ἅπ. λεγ.; copied in Jer. xlviii. 36). פְּקֻדָּה (xv. 7, nowhere else in sense of "store"). עֲרָבִים, xv. 7, (Euphratean) poplars, as xliv. 4; or, as Dillm., "steppes," a second plural[1] of עֲרָבָה. יְלָלָה (xv. 8; Jer. xxv. 36; Zeph. i. 10; Zech. xi. 3). נוֹסָפוֹת (xv. 9). שְׁאֵרִית אֲדָמָה (xv. 9) is ambiguous, and in so far not Isaianic. אֲשִׁישִׁים (xvi. 7, "raisin-cakes"; Hos. iii. 1). הָגָה (xvi. 7, "to moan," xxxviii. 14, lix. 11, cf. Jer. xlviii. 31). נְכָאִים (xvi. 7, cf. lxvi. 2). שְׁדֵמוֹת (xvi. 8, with sing. verb, as Hab. iii. 17). אֻמְלַל (xvi. 8, as xix. 8, xxiv. 4, 7, xxxiii. 9). בַּעֲלֵי גוֹיִם (xvi. 8). שְׂרוּקִים (xvi. 8, but cf. שֹׂרֵק, v. 2). שְׁלֻחוֹת (xvi. 8; ἅπ. λεγ.). נָטַשׁ (xvi. 8; but cf. נְטִישׁוֹת, xviii. 5). רִוָּה (xvi. 9. as xxxiv. 5, 7). הֵידָד (xvi. 9, 10, whence Jer. xlviii. 33; also Jer. xxv. 30, li. 14). רִנָּן (xvi. 10). רֹעַ (xvi. 10). Not all these expressions are important; but the fact of

---

[1] See p. 129, note 1. Dillm. argues, (1) the נחל ע׳ can only be the Wâdy el-Aḥṣa, which runs through the Ghôr es-Ṣâfiya into the Dead Sea; and (2) Jeroboam II. ruled as far as the נַחַל הָעֲרָבָה (Am. vi. 14), which also = W. el-Aḥṣa (Wady of sandy plains). But this is hazardous. Wâdy el-Aḥṣa = a valley with water under the sandy bottom. See W. R. Smith, *OTJC*,[2] p. 147 (with the important references).

a non-Isaianic linguistic colour can hardly be denied.—Next, can we even say that xvi. 1-6 is linguistically altogether Isaianic? It may here, too, be well to meet Orelli with facts. The following phrases are certainly or possibly Isaianic :—הַר בַּת־צִיּוֹן (xvi. 1, as x. 32). נוֹדֵד (v. 2, as x. 31 ; but also xxi. 14). סֵתֶר (v. 4 ; as xxviii. 17). מִפְּנֵי (v. 4, as xxi. 15). שֹׁד (v. 4, as xxii. 4). תָּמַם (v. 4, as xviii. 5). רֹמֵס (v. 4 figuratively ; cf. מִרְמָס, x. 6, xxviii. 18). הוּכַן (v. 5, as xxx. 33 ?). דֹּרֵשׁ מִשְׁפָּט (v. 5, cf. i. 17). מִשְׁפָּט and צֶדֶק (v. 5, as i. 21, cf. ix. 6). גְּאוֹן (v. 6, as ii. 10, etc.). גֵּא (v. 6, = גֵּאֶה, ii. 12). גַּאֲוָה (v. 6, as ix. 8). עֶבְרָה (v. 6, as ix. 18). On the other hand these are non-Isaianic. כַּר (xvi. 1). מְשֻׁלָּח (xvi. 1, as xxvii. 10). הָבִיא עֵצָה (v. 3). פְּלִילָה (v. 3, ἅπ. λεγ.). לִיל (v. 3, see above). סַתֵּר (v. 3). נִדָּחִים (vv. 3, 4, as xi. 12, and xxvii. 13). הֱוֵי (v. 4, הָוָה for הָיָה, as once in Neh., twice in Eccles., both post-Exilic, cf. also הֱוֵא, Job xxxvii. 6. In Gen. xxvii. 29, however, הֱוֵה may be North-Palestinian, and so Dillm. takes it here. But cf. the Aramaizing words in Isa. xxi. 11-14). אָפֵס and כָּלָה (v. 4, as xxix. 20). שֹׁדֵד (v. 4, as xxi. 2, xxxii. 1). חֶסֶד (v. 5). מָהֵר (v. 5, rare). כֵּן (v. 6, "sincere"). בַּדִּים (v. 6, "prating," copied in Jer. xlviii. 30 ; cf. Job xi. 3 ; Isa. xliv. 25 ; Jer. l. 36). In the face of these facts it is hazardous to maintain that any part of this poetic oracle except perhaps the epilogue can be the work of Isaiah.

Let us now [1] give due weight to the general impression produced by the style of the passage, in the larger sense of the term. "No trace here of Isaiah's light and rapid march —of his bold transitions and combinations ; the stream of thought flows tediously and heavily along, and cause and consequence are marked by cumbrous accuracy."[1] The heaviness can no doubt be partly accounted for by the "outflow of sympathetic emotion," but it is precisely this *unrestrained* sympathetic emotion which is unlike Isaiah (contrast i. 2-6, 21, xxii. 4, xxviii. 1-4), and which seems to point to a writer who, even if a prophet, was less thoroughly absorbed than Isaiah in his prophetic mission. (This argument is weighty in any case, but especially if the epilogues of Isa. xix. and xxiii. are late additions, and if the sympathetic frag-

[1] Weir, quoted in *PI*, ii. 302. See especially Hitzig, *Jes.*, p. 180.

ment on the Dedanites, xxi. 13, 14, is non-Isaianic.) Moreover, the very awkward accumulation of the particles כִּי and עַל־כֵּן is without a parallel in any of the elegiac passages in the O.T. This prophetic poem has, no doubt, its own merits ; the writer "can use play of sounds very skilfully, lighting up as with a bright glint the things he would have you couple or contrast" ;[1] he has also, with all his simplicity, a genuine descriptive and (if xvi. 1-6 be really his work) dramatic talent. But he carries paronomasia to an excess—there are sixteen cases of it, and he has neither the energetic and effective style of Isaiah, nor yet that great prophet's deep thoughtfulness. Worse still, he does not even mention once the name of Him whom with his whole nature Isaiah worshipped.[2] In justice to both writers, therefore, we are bound to maintain that they are not the same person, though Isaiah may (we will examine the hypothesis later) have given some touches to the poem.

And now let us look at the epilogue more closely. It runs thus—

This is the word that Yahwè spake concerning Moab aforetime. And now Yahwè speaketh, saying, In three years, as the years of a hireling, shall the glory of Moab be disgraced, with all the great multitude, and the remnant shall be very small and puny.

This epilogue, without the introduction, has by the majority of critics been regarded as Isaiah's. But how is this to be reconciled with the admission that the poetic oracle as a whole cannot be the work of Isaiah, even though it may have been touched here and there by that prophet? Gesenius replies — and his answer has been widely accepted [3]—that Isaiah adopted the oracle of another prophet which had not yet been fulfilled, at the same time expressing his assurance that the fresh afflictions of Moab spoken of (xv. 9) were already close at hand. There

[1] Duff, *Old Test. Theology*, p. 202.
[2] It is true that in xv. 9*b* and xvi. 10*b* Yahwè is the unnamed speaker. The former passage however is a later insertion, and the latter probably corrupt.
[3] *E.g.* by von Baudissin, Dillm., Kuenen, Cornill, Guthe (in Kautzsch's *O.T.*), König, Wildeboer, and (formerly) the present writer. Stade (*Gesch.*, i. 586), however, in 1887 already hinted his doubts of the theory.

are, as is commonly believed, analogies, which justify this theory elsewhere in Isaiah and in other prophets. Thus Isa. ii. 2-4 and Mic. iv. 1-4 have been thought to be quotations from a third prophecy, now lost, and a similar view is often held of Jer. xlix. 7-22 (parts), and Ob. 1. 9*a*; in addition to which the very oracle which we are discussing (or, as some think, another version of it) is certainly used, and very freely used, in Jer. xlviii.; moreover, some good critics hold that Isa. xxi. 11-12 and 13-14 are old prophecies adopted by Isaiah. Provisionally, then, let us suppose that this plausible theory is correct. What evidence is there for the date of the oracle republished and supplemented (*ex hyp.*) by Isaiah? What does this strange poem suggest as to its own origin?

The composition is in form, not a prophecy (exc. in xv. 9*b*, xvi. 12), but a lamentation. (On xvi. 2, see further on.) A professional rhythmic curse few but Renan will venture to call it;[1] even the mention of the "grape-cakes" (xvi. 7), laugh as the Parisian reader may, is natural enough in an address to the Moabites.[2] The poet sympathizes with the latter in a calamity which has recently befallen them. The land of Moab has been invaded by an irresistible foe. The two chief fortresses have succumbed to a night attack, and Moab's "armed men" are scattered in flight. The other details of the invasion are not described, but we may suppose that the "fugitives" referred to in xv. 5 were driven from their homes by the continued victorious march of the invaders. On an earlier occasion we are told that the Israelites in Moab "kept beating down the cities, and on every good piece of land cast every man his stone, and filled it; and stopped all the fountains, and felled all the best trees" (2 Ki. iii. 25). So it must have been now, to account for the language of the poem; for how else can "the waters of Nimrim" have so suddenly "become desolate" (*v.* 6), and what else is the meaning of the phrase, so striking in its reserve, "For the cry hath gone round the border of Moab" (*v.* 8)? The name of this terrible foe is

[1] *Histoire*, ii. 417.
[2] The words are, "Therefore let Moab wail unto Moab, wail entirely; for the grape-cakes of Kir-hareseth moan ye, utterly downcast."

withheld, but we may reasonably conjecture that the N. Israelites are meant. We have in the Moabite inscription (about 900 B.C.) an account of Mesha's reconquest from Israel of almost the same territory of which the Moabites in this prophetic elegy lament the loss. The invasion in Isa. xv. 1-xvi. 12 may therefore conceivably be that of Omri referred to by Mesha (inscr., *l.* 5). But it may also be that of Jeroboam II., who extended his sway as far as the torrent of the Araba (Am. vi. 14; 2 Ki. xiv. 25; cf. Isa. xv. 7). In the time of both kings Edom seems to have been tributary to the kings of Judah, so that, accepting the text of xvi. 1-6 as substantially correct, and as rightly interpreted by the critics, the dramatic exhortation to the fugitives to "send the lambs" from the rocks of Edom by the wilderness route to Jerusalem is perfectly natural. On the whole, it may be best to follow Hitzig, Reuss, Dillm., etc., in preferring the latter invasion,[1] whether we adopt the prevalent critical theory or not. At any rate we must, it would seem, place this composition (or the bulk of it) before the fall of Jerusalem, when the feelings of the Jews towards Moab became permanently embittered (Ezek. xxv. 8-11). Conjectures as to the place of residence of the author have no sure ground to go upon.

But is the prevalent explanation of the origin of Isa. xv.-xvi. in all respects sound? It consists of two parts, a determination of the date of the bulk of the work as pre-Isaianic, and a theory that Isaiah adopted and perhaps partly retouched this composition. But, we may ask, were there such accomplished editors in pre-Exilic times as this theory implies? And even if there were, was Isaiah the man to use up another prophet's material? I do not forget the supposed parallels (mentioned above), but think that a critical examination casts much doubt upon their solidity. That Jer. xlix. 7-22 contains passages taken from an older

[1] Cf. Robertson Smith, *Prophets*, pp. 91, 92. Heilprin's objection that Jeroboam II. would have "begun his work at the wrong end of the country, leaving Dibon and Nebo and Medeba near his border to pray and cry," etc. (*The Historical Poetry of the Anc. Hebrews*, ii. 48), is unimportant. A blow at the capitals was enough; the foe knew this. We need not, however, follow Hitzig and Renan in ascribing the original prophecy to Jonah (cf. 2 Ki. xiv. 25).

prophecy, and that free use is made of chaps. xv.-xvi. in Jer. xlviii., is undeniable, but to whom is this literary borrowing to be ascribed? Even if in each case we are bold enough to ascribe it to Jeremiah,[1] yet Jeremiah is admittedly a prophet of the decadence; his age (as many think),[2] even more than that of Hezekiah, was characterised by learned study of the monuments of the past. As for the parallels quoted from Isaiah, cause enough has, at any rate, been shown for regarding them as very doubtful. The most conservative theory which can be defended is, I think, this—that a post-Exilic editor, finding a small fragment of Isaiah on the imminent doom of Moab (it was perhaps the only legible part of a longer oracle) joined it on to an anonymous prophecy of pre-Exilic origin respecting the same people. We have composite poems due to late editors (see *e.g.* on Ps. xix.); surely we may also have prophecies of a similar origin (see *e.g.* on chaps. ii., x. 5-34, and especially xxi. 11-16). It seems a plausible conjecture that *v.* 13 and part of *v.* 14 ("This is the word . . . speaketh, saying") were inserted by the editor to connect xv. 1-xvi. 12 with the Isaianic fragment in xvi. 14 (מֵאָז, at any rate, is not an Isaianic phrase, nor does it occur in any pre-Exilic prophet). I wish I could prove this conjecture, but the genuine element in the passages referred to above is so small that I cannot lay much stress upon it. *V.* 14 may perhaps be Isaianic, or it may be due to an editor who tried to write like Isaiah. If, however, it is post-Exilic, what did the editor mean by it? or did he write without any historical reference at all?

Let us now consider another difficulty. On looking at xv. 9-xvi. 1 we are struck by the obscurity and incoherence of the passage. Surely the writer of the original elegy would have given some better explanation of נוֹסָפוֹת than אַרְיֵה in xv. 9*b*.

---

[1] See Kuenen, *Ond.*², ii. 221.

[2] (I have to speak here from a point of view which I do not fully share.) M. Berger expresses himself thus, " L'époque d'Ezéchias marque une transformation dans les mœurs littéraires du peuple hébreu. Le royaume d'Israël venait de succomber; il fallait recueillir ses anciennes traditions. Il se produisit un mouvement religieux et littéraire qui a été en croissant jusqu'à la chute de Jérusalem" (*Hist. de l'écriture*, 1892, p. 195).

We notice too that xv. 9 is the only undoubted passage in chaps. xv.-xvi. in which the God of Israel is introduced speaking (in xvi. 10*b* read הַשַׁבַּתִּי with Sept.). Next, one observes in xvi. 1 a want of Isaianic parallelism, and yet some Isaianic words at the end ; then in *v.* 4*a* the suspicious verbal form הֱוִי ; in *v.* 4*b* the imperfect connection produced by כִּי,[1] and in *v.* 5 a resemblance to ix. 6. *V.* 2 clearly implies a wrong view of the poetic situation. The Moabitish fugitives are now in Edom, but the writer of *v.* 2 supposes them to be gathering at the fords of Arnon ; he also supposes the composition to be a *prophecy*[2] (the tense is the future). *V.* 6 is unpoetic, and it is difficult to indicate a natural connection with the preceding verses. The spirit of this verse reminds us of xxv. 11 (a very late passage) more than of chaps. xv. and xvi. 7-11. Lastly, in *v.* 12 there is again a want of parallelism. The style too is remarkable by its poverty. If the meaning of the closing words is that Moab will effect nothing by his litany, should we not have expected something like וְאֵין קֹשֵׁב (1 Ki. xviii. 29) ? And even if the too little heeded suggestion of Ewald be adopted[3] (as in *PI*), still ולא יוכל is below the style of Isaiah.

I venture, therefore, to complete my hypothesis thus. I think that here, as elsewhere, the editor filled up all illegible passages (including that which has now become *v.* 12) as far as he could in an antique style. The most interesting of his insertions is certainly that in xvi. 4*b*-5. This passage contains an ideal sketch of the state of Judah in the Messianic age,[4] which reminds us of a part of an undoubtedly

---

[1] Lagarde and Dillmann correct עֲדִי־. But the phraseology of *vv.* 4*b*-5 sufficiently shows that a different writer comes in here ; why try to smooth the connection ? and why throw away the parallelism of xxix. 20 ?

[2] For this reason Duhm proposes to place xvi. 2 after xv. 9.

[3] The suggestion is to render " When Moab . . . cometh to his sanctuary to pray, and prevaileth not," and to restore the missing apodosis from Jer. xlviii. 13, " then shall Moab be ashamed of Kemosh, and turn unto Yahwè." Baudissin's objection that the idea of a final turning of the nations to Yahwè belongs, not to Isaiah, but to Jer., has no force to those who hold that xvi. 12 is a later insertion.

[4] It is not very probable that xvi. 5 refers to the establishment of a Judahite viceroy in Edom. " In the tent of David " surely ought to

late insertion in chap. xxix. (v. 20, where note כִּי־אָדָם and כָּלָה, as in xvi. 4), itself not wholly devoid of Isaianic affinities. Another interesting insertion is xv. 9b, "for I appoint fresh (woes) for Dimon, for the escaped of Moab a lion,[1] (i.e. an Assyrian invader), and for the remnant of the land." The Sept. paraphrast evidently has the feeling that the text was meant to suggest more than is verbally expressed ; it gives, "for I will bring upon Dimon Arabians, and will take away the seed of Moab, and Ariel (i.e. collectively, Moab's heroes), and the remnant of Adama," where "Ariel" corresponds to "a lion" in the Mas. text, and "Adama" to "the land." How much did the paraphrast guess, and how much did he find in his MS.? Rhythm forbids us to accept his version as a whole, but "Ariel" ("a hero"?) may conceivably be right instead of "a lion," and "Adama" (Sept.'s form of "Adma," Gen. x. 19, etc.) instead of "the land"; Moab may be identified with Adma to show the completeness of the destruction (cf. Isa. i. 10 ; Hos. xi. 8), especially as, according to Gen. xix. 37, the Moabites were descended from a daughter of Lot (observe that אֲדָמָה has no article).

And now as to the date of the fragment of Isaiah (if we may accept the conjecture proposed above) in xvi. 14, which evidently belongs to a time when Moab was in great danger from Assyria. The analogy of the term fixed for the predicted event with that given in xx. 3 suggests 711, when Moab among other peoples "spoke treason" against Sargon, rather than 701, when Moab (unlike its neighbours) made voluntary submission to Sennacherib.

It will be readily understood that, even as regards xv. 1-xvi. 12, one can only offer an historically probable hypothesis. Duhm's view that the original prophecy was written under John Hyrcanus, and edited and provided with an epilogue under

mean in the royal palace at Jerusalem. שׁוֹפֵט is merely a choice word for "king" (Am. ii. 3, cf. Ps. ii. 10).

[1] As to the phrase "a lion," would Isaiah have been likely to use it either of Israel or of Judah ? Only if it be likely that he called the king of Judah a "flying dragon" in xiv. 29. The most obvious meaning is "the Assyrians" (cf. v. 29, Jer. iv. 7), and if xv. 9b is an inserted passage, this was probably the sense given to the phrase, if correctly read, by the inserter.

Alex. Jannæus, seems to me on various grounds [1] inadmissible. I can indeed see a resemblance in spirit between xvi. 6 and xxv. 11 (xxv. 9-11 is also referred by Duhm to the time of Jannæus). But xvi. 6 seems to me a late prosaic insertion. Dogmatism as to the date would, however, be out of place.

Lastly, as to the text. Many passages are copied or imitated in Jer. xlviii. 29-38 (see my *Jeremiah: Pulpit Commentary*, ii. 227-233), which supplies some variant readings. Observe that xv. 8, 9 and xvi. 1-5 are neglected by the interpolator of Jeremiah. Among aids to the student (other than commentaries) see von Baudissin, *Theol. St. u. Kr.*, 1888, pp. 509-521; Oort, *Th. Tijdschr.*, 1887, pp. 51-64; Schwally, *ZATW*, 1888, pp. 207-209; Barth, *Beiträge* (1885), pp. 20-23. Of these Barth is the most conservative, ascribing the whole of these two chapters to Isaiah (so Del. and Orelli); Schwally the most radical, asserting the post-Exilic origin of both chapters in their entirety.

CHAPTER XVII. 1-11.

The heading is obviously inaccurate; the eye of the collector went no further than the first line. Even in the first strophe the fate of N. Israel is referred to, and in the second and third it forms the sole subject of prophecy. There is not much doubt as to the period to which it belongs. Evidently Syria and N. Israel are in alliance (cf. *v.* 10); the time has gone by when " Aram before and Philistia behind devoured Israel with open mouth " (ix. 11). But since there is no allusion either to the campaign of the northern powers against Judah, or to the advance of the Assyrians against Damascus, we may place the composition of the prophecy before the group of events related in 2 Ki. xvi. 5-9. The calm tone of the prophecy favours this view, though it is very possible that a strophe has fallen out between the second and what is now the third, and this may have contained some allusions which would have modified our

---

[1] See Bleeker, *Jeremia's Profetieën tegen de Volkeren* (1894), pp. 142-144.

CHAPTER XVII. 1-11

theory. The reason for this remark is that *vv.* 7-8 can scarcely be Isaiah's work; not improbably they are substituted for a passage which had become illegible, though certainly they did not occupy the full space of a strophe. The verses run thus, when freed from some interpolated words [1]—

> In that day shall mortal man look unto his Maker,
> And his eyes have regard to the Holy One of Israel;
> And he shall not look unto the work of his hands,
> And that which his fingers have made he shall not regard.

Now it is quite true that the phraseology is for the most part Isaianic. שָׂעָה עַל, cf. xxxi. 1. אָדָם, in antith. to Yahwè, cf. ii. 9, 11, etc. קְדוֹשׁ יִשְׂרָאֵל, cf. i. 4, 5, v. 24, xxxi. 1. מַעֲשֵׂה יָדָיו and the parallel words, cf. ii. 8. On the other hand, עשׂה of the Creator (of man or of Israel) occurs again only in late passages, xxvii. 11, xxix. 16 (by implication), li. 13, liv. 5; Job iv. 17, xxxi. 15, xxxii. 22, xxxv. 10; Ps. xcv. 6, cxliv. 2; Hos. viii. 14 (see Wellh.). Supplementers were quite capable (see ch. x.) of producing an Isaianic cento, though seldom of putting brightness into their style. It is certain (1) that the style of *vv.* 7-8 is not bright, and (2) that they interrupt the context; if Isaiah had wished to speak of a conversion, he would have referred to this at the end. It is highly probable therefore that the verses are due to an editor, and to be explained on the analogy of x. 20, xxx. 22 (late passages), *i.e.* that they describe the spiritual condition of Israel after the last great judgment, when there shall be no distinction of North and South, Israel and Judah. Criticism is in fact showing more and more clearly that passages of a comforting tendency were frequently inserted by late writers in prophecies which seemed to them too dispiriting for edification. Verses 1-3 have also most probably been touched by the editor (read עָרֶיהָ עֲדֵי־עַד, *v.* 2).

---

[1] On the interpolation see esp. Stade, *ZATW*, iii. 10-13, and Smend, *ib.* iv. 205, who are scarcely refuted by König, *Hauptprobleme*, p. 70. The phrase "the work of his hands" ought to mean, not the altars, but the images (see ii. 8, 20, xxxi. 7). Neither sun pillars nor ashêras are mentioned by Isaiah, though the author of xxvii. 9, as we shall see, already had xvii. 8 before him.

CHAPTER XVII. 12-14

A splendid piece of unconscious word-painting. "Isaiah on his watch-tower hears, and we seem to hear with him, the ocean-like roar of the advancing Assyrian hosts."[1] It is a storm-piece. Not a word could be added to it, or subtracted from it, without injury to the effect. That Isaiah wrote it has been denied by Stade; his grounds are similar to those on which he assigns xiv. 24-27 to a late imitator of Isaiah. I know not whether he stills holds this view. To most critics, xvii. 12-14 and chap. xviii. appear to be necessarily by the same author. In both passages Judah seems to be in the same peril from an Assyrian invasion, and both passages are on the same artistic model, and present the same qualities of style, though not the same phraseology. If ch. xviii. is by Isaiah, but xvii. 12-14 not, then the later writer has imitated the earlier most magnificently, adopting the same historical situation and the same poetical form, but carefully varying the language and the imagery. On the question of Isaiah's authorship, I cannot but agree with the great majority of critics. Some of the best judges[2] also hold that xvii. 12-14 is the prologue or first part of the prophecy in ch. xviii. This view still strikes me (see *PI*) as improbable. There is no doubt a resemblance between the passages both in subject and in poetical form, but there is no connection either in their imagery or (save in the opening word הוֹי, and even this small parallelism is not complete[3]) in their phraseology. Add to this that the last line of xvii. 12-14 evidently forms the close of a prophecy, and the theory of an original union of the two passages seems to become untenable. Three other theories however are open to us. (*a*) xvii. 12-14 may be a short prophecy complete in itself.[4] (*b*) On the analogy of xiv.

---

[1] *PI*, i. 109.
[2] Ges., Ew., Dillm., Kuenen, and Duhm.
[3] In xvii. 12 הוֹי expresses a mingled feeling of pain and indignation; in xviii. 1 it is simply *heus* (lv. 1, Zech. ii. 10, 11).
[4] So Lowth and virtually Hitzig. The former abstains from dating it. The latter groups it chronologically with xvii. 1-11; the enemies,

24-27 (which also has no heading) it may be the conclusion of a prophecy, the rest of which has either been lost or has found a place elsewhere in the book. (c) It may be an appendix attached by Isaiah himself to the preceding prophecy, just as viii. 9-10 was probably written by Isaiah as an appendix to viii. 5-8.[1] If we accept either (a) or (b) there is no reason why xvii. 12-14 should not be grouped chronologically with ch. xviii. In the light of the analogy of viii. 9-10, however, and of the fact that xvii. 12-14 contains two parallelisms to viii. 7-10 (see p. 39), (c) seems to me somewhat more plausible than either (a) or (b). If we adopt it, the date of xvii. 12-14 will be different from that of ch. xviii. We must suppose that Isaiah attached the former passage to xvii. 1-11 during the anxious time of the siege of Samaria, to reassure those who feared that Judah might share the fate of her northern sister. This was not to happen yet, as Isaiah knew; but for all that, even the prophet may have expected an Assyrian invasion of Judah. It would seem that he saw the foe in prophetic vision "spoiling" and "robbing" (xvii. 14) and pressing on, stage by stage, to the capital (x. 28-32), and that then, full of faith, he uttered the defiant words of viii. 9, 10, and declared the final catastrophe in xvii. 12-14. This view I have ventured to support in *BW*.

CHAPTER XVIII

This prophecy, which has no heading, and must therefore have been inserted late in the collection of "oracles," consists of two strophes (*vv.* 1-3 and 4-6) and a brief appendix (*v.* 7) of disputed origin. It was appropriately placed next to xvii. 12-14 as presenting nearly the same artistic structure and pre-supposing a similar historical situation; indeed, but for the undeniable difference between the imagery and the phraseology of the two passages, we might be tempted to combine them. The theme is the destruction of the Assyrian

he thinks, are not the Assyrians, but Rezin and Pekah. In *PI* the author made it contemporary with, but slightly later than chap. xviii.

[1] So Giesebr., *St. u. Kr.*, 1888, p. 263; *Beitr.*, pp. 84, 92. Cf. Cornill, *Einl.*, p. 134.

army. No proper names are given, but the historical circumstances can be tolerably well traced. The Ethiopian suzerain (or virtual suzerain) of Egypt has just now sent ambassadors to the king of Judah to induce him to join an anti-Assyrian league. Isaiah, who recognises greatness of all kinds (cf. ii. 12-16), expresses himself courteously to the messengers of a noble nation, but bids them return, Yahwè being the all-powerful protector of his people. At the right moment (cf. Ps. lxxv. 3) the luxuriant vine-shoots of Assyria shall be cut away, or, in plainer language, the dead enemies of Judah shall be left for a prey to the jackals and to the vultures. Observe the picturesque and dramatic character of the description. Isaiah seems to have actually seen the ambassadors just before he writes and noted their peculiar physical type ;[1] he also records the impression which the recent victories of the Ethiopian sovereigns have produced. From them, too, or from some ex-ambassadors of his own people, he has heard of the canoes of reed used for Nile voyages (cf. Job ix. 26).

There are two indications of the date. (1) An Assyrian invasion of S. Palestine is expected. (2) Egypt has at present a powerful sovereign who belongs to an Ethiopian dynasty. Taken together, these suggest the year 702 as the probable date. It should be remembered that Shabaka, who (if he be the Sib'e of the Assyrians) had been defeated by Sargon at Raphia in 720, was succeeded soon afterwards by Shabataka. This king seems to have been suzerain of Egypt (but with limited recognition) till 704, when he was displaced by Taharqa (the Assyrian Tarqu, the Hebrew Tirhaqah). Taharqa, who was at first officially styled king of Ethiopia alone,[2] owed his title to his mother, who was of the

---

[1] The bulk of the population of Cush may have been closely akin to the Egyptians, but there were doubtless many Nubians and negroes, who are not clearly distinguished on the Egyptian monuments. Isaiah's description in *v*. 2 suggests the Nubians, who at the present day are tall and well-proportioned, and recall Herodotus's description of the Ethiopians as μέγιστοι καὶ κάλλιστοι ἀνθρώπων (iii. 20, 114). On the people of Cush, see Tomkins, "Remarks on Mr. Flinders Petrie's Collection of Ethnographic Types," *Journal of the Anthropological Institute*, Feb. 1889, pp. 213-216; W. M. Müller, *Asien und Europa nach altägyptischen Denkmälern*, 1893, pp. 112-113.

[2] Meyer, *Gesch. Aeg.*, pp. 348, 350.

CHAPTER XVIII 97

old royal stock, and, according to Petrie,[1] a sister of Shabaka. He also smoothed his course by marrying the widow of Shabaka, whose son Rutamen (the Urdamani of Assyrian inscriptions) reigned jointly with Taharqa, and after Taharqa's final overthrow remained king of Ethiopia. It is of this young and energetic ruler (rather than of Shabataka) that Isaiah is thinking.[2] From chaps xxix.-xxxi. it is certain that Hezekiah hoped at this time for Egyptian aid in his projected rebellion, and sent an embassy to secure Taharqa's co-operation. Later on, in 702, when Sennacherib had taken the field to chastise Phœnicia, Philistia, and Judah, Taharqa (as we may interpret chap. xviii.) himself sent ambassadors to Jerusalem to announce the despatch of Egyptian troops, and to encourage Hezekiah to resist the Assyrians.

The prophecy may however be understood differently. Schrader, who groups it with chap. xx., refers it to the period preceding the rebellion of Azuri king of Ashdod (and so Orelli). Thus he obtains a trilogy of prophecies (chaps. xviii.-xx.) all belonging to the time of Sargon. He forgets however that the prophecies in chs. xviii.-xx., being untitled, must be later additions to the collection of "oracles"; we cannot therefore presume that they are contemporaneous. Certainly the tone adopted towards Ethiopia in ch. xviii. differs widely from that in ch. xx., where Isaiah even foretells a victory of Assyria over Egypt and Ethiopia. Another Assyriologist (Winckler) proposes a much more startling theory. Reminding us of the variety of senses of many Oriental and some Biblical names (and among them Cush), he declares that "Cush" in v. 1 means Kaś, i.e. S. Babylonia, and that chap. xviii. contains Isaiah's warning to Hezekiah, when this king was disposed in 720 to form an alliance with the Chaldæan prince Merodach-Baladan.[3] This is surely very

---
[1] *Memoir on Tanis*, Part II., p. 36.
[2] I therefore retract the date given in *PI*, i. 110.
[3] *Untersuch.*, pp. 150-156. That S. Babylonia is "cut through" by rivers, is undeniable. But so also is the Nile-Delta, to whose people Mr. Hodgkin, the historian, has "not a shadow of a doubt" in referring the description (*Friends' Quarterly Examiner*, Oct. 1881, p. 12). And so also, though in a less degree, is Nubia, as distinguished from Egypt south of the Delta.

far-fetched. It also involves some difficult or questionable exegetical assumptions. Why the sense of the phrases which describe the Ethiopians should be so very uncertain,[1] and why יָם in *v*. 2 should not mean the Nile (cf. xix. 5, Job xli. 23 ; Nah. iii. 8 is corrupt), it is difficult to see. Nor has it yet been shown that the intervention of an Ethiopian suzerain of Egypt in the affairs of Palestine belongs to a second hypothetical Assyrian invasion, and not (as most have hitherto believed) to the historically attested invasion in 701.[2] I accept Winckler's statement that "which is beyond the rivers of Cush" (*v*. 1*b*) cannot be a description of the kingdom of Ethiopia, which did not apparently include the island of Meroe.[3] But this simply confirms Duhm's view (suggested by the prosaic style of the clause, and by the exigencies of rhythm) that all after כנפים is a late gloss.

And now as to the appendix. It is undeniable that *v*. 7 impairs the solemn effect of *vv*. 4-6, and in particular that the description of the Ethiopians, which was appropriate enough in *v*. 2, is superfluous here. The idea seems to be that after the great catastrophe Jerusalem will become the centre of an empire to which the neighbouring peoples will hasten to pay tribute. But was this idea of a Messiah-less Israelitish empire current in Isaiah's age? Of the directly parallel passages (Zeph. iii. 10; Isa. xlv. 14; Ps. xlviii. 30, 32), not one can be shown to belong to the Assyrian period. The phraseology confirms our doubt as to Isaiah's authorship. יוּבַל by itself might pass (cf. Hos. x. 6, xii. 2 ; also יוּבָלוּ, though Isa. xxiii. 7 may be late, but שַׁי יוּבַל must be late, cf. Ps. lxviii. 30, lxxvi. 12 (שַׁי only occurs in these three passages; Isaiah would have used מִנְחָה, cf. Hos. x. 6). The phrase "the place of Yahwè's name" is also startling. In form it is unique, though it reminds us of the late passages lx. 9, Jer. iii. 17, where "to the name" = "to the place of the name"; cf. also Deut. xii. 5 ; 1 Ki. viii. 17 (*BL*, p. 328, note *h*). The idea is also strange, for in *v*. 4 the מָכוֹן of Yahwè is surely in heaven. "Name" in this connection seems to mean "worship," as in lvi. 6 (see introd. to ch. lvi.). And lastly,

---

[1] See Dillmann.   [2] See introd. to chaps. xxxvi.-xxxix.
[3] The capital was moved from Napata (Gebel Barkal) to the more southerly Meroe after Taharqa's time.

the introductory formula "at that time" meets us again and again in passages which on other grounds are probably or certainly to be regarded as late insertions.[1]

CHAPTER XIX

We inquire first, as usual, Is this prophecy a whole? and, if not, are the different parts alike written by Isaiah? The chapter falls into four parts, viz. *vv.* 1-4, *vv.* 5-10, *vv.* 11-17, and *vv.* 18-25. Let us take the last of these first, because it is here that the difficulty of admitting the authorship of Isaiah is most palpable. To the question, Is this Isaiah's work or not? my answer in 1880 was as follows:[2] "So much at least is self-evident, that the appendix must have been written later than the rest of the chapter; the prophecy is, from a literary point of view, complete without it, and the tone of prophecy and appendix is entirely different. Of course Isaiah may have added these verses on a later revision of his works, and indeed we can hardly imagine a more 'swanlike end' for a dying prophet; or some later writer—it may be a disciple of Isaiah's—also in his degree a prophet, may have been their author. We know as a matter of fact that prophecy becomes more minute, more circumstantial, the further we go from the age of Isaiah, so that it would not be an audacious conjecture that a prophet considerably more recent than Isaiah made this addition." In this quotation, however, only two of the leading considerations are mentioned. There are two others to which almost equal importance belongs. (1) There is a strong contrast between *vv.* 1-17 and *vv.* 18-25. (I venture to attach *vv.* 16 and 17 to part I. They complete the tale of threats, and are inconsistent with the sequel. But I do not claim that they are Isaianic. They may perhaps take the place of a passage of the original prophecy which could no longer be read; at any rate they link *vv.* 1-15 to the

---

[1] On *v.* 7 I follow Duhm; the last line had already been obelised as superfluous by Merx (Schenkel, *Bib. Lex.*, i. 68).
[2] *PI*, i. 115.

appendix.) In the former section we have the sternest threatenings mingled with sarcastic references to the impotence both of Egypt's religion and of its boasted wisdom, but in the latter the tone is more sympathetic towards Egypt than anywhere else in the O.T., and the expectation is even expressed of the conversion of Egypt to the one true God. And let us remember in this connection that ii. 2-4 and xxiii. 15-18, which open brighter prospects for the nations, are most probably late. (2) To a Jew of Isaiah's time it was the conversion, not of Egypt, but of Assyria, which was of primary interest. This conversion is no doubt implied at the end of v. 23, but, if Isaiah be the writer, why is it only implied? If Isaiah expected that Yahwè would "make himself known" to Assyria as well as to Egypt, he must have given expression somewhere to this bold intuition, nor could such a prophecy have been easily lost. One may add that even the conversion of the less dangerous neighbour Egypt is not a conceivable idea of Isaiah. A prophetic revelation has ever a natural point of contact with the mind of the recipient. But in the present case, where is this point of contact to be found? (3) The circumstantial description in vv. 18-25 is contrary to the prophetic genius of Isaiah. Vv. 23-25 remind us of xi. 15, 16, which occurs in a late appendix. (4) Vv. 16-17 and 18-25 present no stylistic indications of Isaiah's work. The style is prosaic, and Isaianic expressions like תְּנוּפָה, v. 16, cf. xxx. 32; עֵצָה 'יי, v. 17, cf. xiv. 26; שָׁב וְרָפָא, v. 22, cf. vi. 10, need only indicate the writer's acquaintance with Isaiah. Side by side with these there are non-Isaianic phrases, such as (a) אַדְמַת יְהוּדָה, v. 17, a honorific expansion of the simpler term יְהוּדָה (vii. 6) in the later manner, cf. אדמת ישראל, Ezek. vii. 2, and thirteeen other passages. (b) חָגָּא, v. 17, ἅπ. λεγ., with Aram. ending, for חָגָה. (c) כֹּל אֲשֶׁר, with the imperf., cf. כֹּל with partic., 1 Sam. ii. 13; Gen. iv. 15. (d) כְּנַעַן, v. 18, nowhere else in Isaiah; in xxiii. 11 'כ = Phœnicia. (e) הֶרֶס ἅπ. λεγ.; v.l. חֶרֶס, rare word for "sun" (Job. ix. 7). (f) מַצֵּבָה, v. 19, nowhere in Isaiah, but cf. Hos. iii. 4, x. 1. (g) עָבַד, vv. 21, 23, used in a ritual sense. (h) נֶעְתַּר, nowhere else in the prophets. We may add הֵנִיף יָד (v. 16), for xi. 15 and Zech. ii. 13 are surely *both* late. Lastly, would Isaiah have written מִצְרַיִם fourteen times in ten verses?

These considerations militate against the view that *vv.* 18-25 were written by Isaiah, and the fourth compels us also to deny his authorship of *vv.* 16 and 17. They were to some extent present to my mind in 1880, but seemed then to be counterbalanced by two other arguments. (1) In *v.* 19 (cf. *v.* 21) we read of an altar of sacrifice in the midst of Egypt, and a maççêba to Yahwè on the frontier. But the Deuteronomic law permits only one altar (Deut. xii. 5, etc.), and forbids maççêbas altogether (Deut. xvi. 22 ; cf. Lev. xxvi. 1). It was not unnatural to infer that *v.* 19 was written before the reign of Josiah. And (2) it was difficult to explain how the disputed passage came to be added to the prophecy. I could not see my way to follow Hitzig, and an equally complete and more satisfactory explanation did not occur to me. On both these points I now seem to see more clearly and in some respects differently. First, as to *v.* 19, the argument referred to, even if admitted, only proves that the section is pre-Deuteronomic, not that it is Isaianic. It is most improbable that Isaiah should have spoken of an altar thus respectfully [1] (see i. 11). But we need not admit the argument. The passage may be quite naturally referred to the period when there was a compromise between the prophets and the legalists ; in short, it may quite well be post-Deuteronomic. For though the letter of the law in Deuteronomy is violated, the spirit is not. The reference to the altar may, as I suggested in 1880,[2] when considering the post-Deuteronomic date, be purely symbolical. For this we have a striking analogy in Mal. i. 11, which describes how "in every place among the nations a pure oblation is offered" unto the name of Yahwè, where the symbolical meaning is indicated by the context. Had the writer said "there shall be altars," he would have transgressed the spirit of the law, but he says "an altar." So, too, the maççêba is symbolical. It means a protest against the numerous sky-pointing obelisks which reminded the heathen Egyptian of his sun-god. Had the writer said "there shall be altars, and a maççêba by each altar," he

[1] Cf. Duff, *Old Test. Theol.*, i. 271.   [2] *PI*, i. 120.

would have transgressed the spirit of the law, even though he wrote not with a view to Palestine but to Egypt. In the next place, the addition of the verses can quite well be accounted for without Hitzig's too ingenious theory.

Let us begin by examining the reading of v. 18b—"one shall be called, The city of destruction" (v.l. 1, "of the sun"; v.l. 2, "of righteousness"). The received reading עיר ההרס, old as it is (Aq., Theod., Pesh.), is to be rejected as unsuitable to the context, and as introducing an unaccountable ἅπ. λεγ.[1] Our choice, therefore, lies between the two other readings, עיר החרם (Symm., Vulg., Talm. *Menachoth*, 110a, and some MSS.), and עיר הצדק (Sept., but not ed. Complut.). If we accept the former, we are bound to refer v. 18, together with its context, to the Greek period. For the Hebrew name of Heliopolis, still employed by Ezekiel (xxx. 17), is On; עיר החרם is a translation of the Greek name Ἡλιούπολις; no argument to the contrary can be derived from Jer. xliii. 13.[2] If we accept the latter, the name of the city referred to is purely symbolical, and it becomes slightly less improbable that the basis of this passage may be Isaianic. This reading has been lately defended by Dillm., though he does not conceal his suspicion that v. 18b is a later addition, made in the interests of the temple of Onias, and that הרס and צדק are partisan alterations of the original reading חרם. For my own part, I fail to see (1) how the readings עיר ההרס and החרם can be

[1] I agree with Riehm, *Einl.*, ii. 552, 553. König (*Einl.*, p. 86) still retains ההרס, and supposes the clause to be a Palestinian gloss in condemnation of the temple of Leontopolis, הרס being suggested by חרם. His view is an improbable combination of hints from Del. and from Dillmann. On one point only he is undoubtedly correct; עיר ההרס, if it means anything at all, means "destroyed city," not "city of the destruction of idolatry," much less "city of the lion-goddess," or "city of the cat-goddess," as Herzfeld, *Gesch.*, iii. 562, referring to the statement in Jos., *Ant.*, xiii. 3, that the spot where Onias built his temple was at Leontopolis, and yet had a connection with "Bubastis agria" (on which see Naville and Petrie, *Seventh Memoir of Egypt Fund*, pp. 21, 23, 75).

[2] Should we not there read with Winckler (*Untersuch.*, p. 180), ושבר שמש את־מצבות? בית שמש in בית seems to have arisen out of a dittography of the three last letters of the preceding word. The Sept. translator goes further, and makes the whole verse refer to the obelisks and temples of Heliopolis.

accounted for, if the true reading be עיר הצדק, and (2) how, if v. 18b. be an insertion due to friends of Onias, it can have found its way into Palestinian manuscripts of Isaiah. But assuming עיר החרס to be correct, we can easily explain both the other readings. We know that about 160 B.C. the priest Onias (an unsuccessful claimant of the high priesthood of Jerusalem) through the favour of Ptolemy Philometor built a temple for the Egyptian Jews at Leontopolis (in the nome of Heliopolis), and further that Onias appealed to v. 19 as a prediction of this temple.[1] The Jews of Palestine were at first not unfriendly to this temple, but they became so on finding that it occasioned serious losses to the ancient sanctuary. It is a reasonable conjecture that the Jews of Egypt met this hostility by changing עיר הַחֶרֶם into עִיר הַצֶּדֶק[2] (alluding to the description of Jerusalem in i. 26, and so gaining a distinct prediction, as they would call it, of the Leontopolis temple), while the Jews of Palestine, as a counter blow, changed the original phrase into עִיר הַחֶרֶם (interpreting this, of course, of the sectarian temple). On the whole, therefore, we had better read עיר החרס, and if we identify the site of the city of Onias with Tell el-Yahûdîyeh (about 20 miles from Cairo, on the Suez line), M. Naville will provide us with a confirmation of the reading we adopt. It is certain, he says, that the sacred name of Tell el-Yahûdîyeh in the times of Rameses III. was "the house of Ra (the sun-god), on the north of On."[3] This name would correspond to עיר החרס. Josephus, it is true, only makes Onias refer to v. 19; but we must not rely too much on Josephus's accuracy.

The expressions of the epilogue, however, require a detailed explanation. Upon any hypothesis it calls for an effort to realise their meaning. The charge of imaginativeness cannot therefore be brought by one expositor against another. This is my present view of the writer's meaning. Verses 16 and 17, as we have seen, were inserted to link the original prophecy with the epilogue. The writer

---

[1] Jos., *Ant.*, xiii. 3, 1.
[2] Notice how the Egyptian Jewish translator modifies an expression in v. 25, εὐλογημένος ὁ λαός μου ὁ ἐν Αἰγύπτῳ.
[3] *Seventh Memoir of Egypt Fund,* pp. 12, 21.

endeavours to assume the point of view of his predecessor; but though he succeeds in being stern, he cannot make himself very intelligible. One might infer from v. 17 that the "hard lord" of v. 4 was a Jew. This, however, would be inconsistent with the sequel, and cannot really be the writer's meaning. The "hard lord" is rather, according to his view, Artaxerxes Ochus, whose inhuman conduct in Phœnicia and Egypt produced such a deep impression upon his contemporaries. Only thus can we account for the appending of vv. 18-25, which, as we shall see, contain a reference to the Jewish settlements in Egypt in the early Greek period, to a prophecy which the writer, beyond reasonable doubt, attributed to Isaiah. Verses 16 and 17 therefore are not to be interpreted by any facts of history. V. 16 alludes to the mysterious supernatural act of Yahwè spoken of in xi. 15 (which is taken to be Isaiah's), and which, it is assumed in v. 17, will be performed in the land of Judah, where is the "place of Yahwè's name." It is not vv. 16-17 but the succeeding verses which represent the writer's own ideas respecting the past and the future.

Certainly the identification of the "hard lord" with Artaxerxes Ochus was a perfectly natural one. If an exact fulfilment of v. 4 be required, it cannot be found more plausibly than in the cruel treatment of Egypt by Ochus in 343 B.C. For 65 years Egypt had gallantly struggled to maintain its hardly won independence,[1] and in the third campaign of the bloodthirsty Persian tyrant it had finally to succumb. The conqueror filled the land with Persian garrisons, razed the walls of cities, plundered the temples, lavished insults on the sacred animals. The cup of injuries, out of which Cambyses and Xerxes had already made the Egyptians drink, Ochus filled to the brim. The spirit of the old Egyptian people was broken, and we can well understand that when the young and gracious overthrower of the Persian colonies appeared, he was hailed in the Nile valley as a deliverer. Artaxerxes Ochus, then, is to the author of the epilogue the instrument of Yahwè's vengeance upon Egypt, just as Nebuchadrezzar had been to the prophet

[1] See Judeich, *Kleinasiatische Studien* (1892), p. 179; and cf. Wiedemann, *Gesch. von Alt-Aeg.*, pp. 210, 211.

Ezekiel.[1] But if any one prefers to suppose either that all the three Persian invaders of Egypt together (Cambyses, Xerxes, and Ochus), or the two former alone, were in the mind of this early interpreter of Isaiah, I have no objection. For this view he may, if he will, claim the support of the Sept., which renders *v.* 4 as if more than one despotic ruler was referred to.

We now turn to *vv.* 18-25. This passage can, I think, only be explained by the history of the Greek period. In the division of the conquests of Alexander, Egypt fell to the lot of Ptolemy Lagi, who in 320 added to it Phœnicia and Cœle-Syria with the territory of Judah. The possession of S. Syria was, however, disputed with him by Antigonus, and the people of Judah and Samaria suffered harsh treatment from Ptolemy. Many captives, according to Josephus, were carried from Judah and Samaria into Egypt, who, however, soon learned to think gratefully of their captor. Many of them were entrusted with garrison duties as soldiers, while at Alexandria the Jews received equal rights of citizenship (*isopoliteia*) with the Macedonians. We are also assured that not a few other Jews of their own accord went into Egypt, " invited by the goodness of the soil and by the liberality of Ptolemy,"[2] though whether this was before or after the battle of Ipsus (B.C. 301), which confirmed Ptolemy in the possession of Palestine, we are not informed. Now it was during the rule of the first four Ptolemies[3] that both in the fatherland and in Egypt the universalism of the Jews could have first taken such a definite shape as appears in Isa. xix. 23-25 and in Ps. lxxxvii., and it may (as some think) have been for the accession of that "second Cyrus of Israel," Ptolemy Philadelphus, that Ps. xlv. was originally composed.[4] And if one part of the period referred to supplies a more probable date for Isa. xix. 16-25 than another, it is the latter years of Ptolemy Lagi, who might well be regarded as a "saviour" (*v.* 20), both by the Jewish colonists and by the

---

[1] Ezek., xxix. 2-7.   [2] Jos., *Ant.*, xii. 1.
[3] With the death of Ptolemy IV. Philopator, the first long period of Egyptian rule in Palestine came to an end.
[4] See *BL*, pp. 144, etc., 170, etc.; and cf. Smend, *AT. Rel.-Gesch.*, p. 378. But Ps. xlv. may belong to the Persian age.

native Egyptians. For of course there were Jews in Egypt before the foundation of Alexandria (see Jer. xliv. 1), and there were more than five cities of which, with some approach to accuracy, the statement of *v.* 18*a* might have been made. And what does this verse really mean? It runs thus :—

"In that day there shall be five cities in the land of Egypt, speaking the language of Canaan, and swearing to Yahwè Çebaoth ; one shall be called *Ir ha-ḥeres.*"

To me the meaning appears to be this. At the end of the Persian period there shall be Jewish colonies in some of the cities of Egypt,[1] which shall hold aloft the high ideal of the religion of Yahwè, and one of them shall flourish even in Heliopolis, the sacred city of the Sun-god, the Hebrew name of which shall be *Ir ha-ḥeres.* The expressions used are no doubt loose and inexact, but this is simply because the epilogue is meant to be read as the work of Isaiah, who would naturally see such distant events in *chiaroscuro.* The next verse (relative to the "altar" and "pillar") is not less indistinct, but in the light of the context one may interpret it to mean neither more nor less than this, that the regular worship of Yahwè should be set up in Egypt. Synagogues were of course just as much a "sign" and a "witness" (*v.* 20) as literal altars, and the spiritual sacrifices—recognised as such by the noblest of the post-Exilic Jews[2]—of prayer and obedience were infinitely more acceptable than mere animal sacrifices (זֶבַח and מִנְחָה are mentioned to preserve the illusion of Isaianic authorship; cf. i. 11, 13). Such sanctuaries and such offerings consecrated Egypt, which had formerly been to the Jews a land of captivity, as "Yahwè's land" (cf. Hos. ix. 3). Henceforth, whenever the Egyptian worshippers of Yahwè (Jews and proselytes) cried unto him, he would send Egypt a "saviour," such as the native kings

---

[1] This seems the only possible interpretation (cf. Geiger, *Urschrift,* p. 79), else why this limited number of cities? Also why this reference to the Hebrew language? The writer can hardly have expected the true Egyptian population to learn Hebrew, for which there is no analogy elsewhere (neither Zeph. iii. 9 nor Zech. xiv. 9 being in point). The rare word חרס was chosen to produce the effect of archaism and prophetic obscurity. שפת כנען is another affected expression.

[2] See *BL,* pp. 364-367.

CHAPTER XIX. 16-25

(if these were still remembered)[1] who so bravely resisted Persia, or, more plausibly, Alexander the Great and his general, Ptolemy *Soter*,[2] and the large-hearted and open-handed Ptolemy Philadelphus, who restored the prosperity of Egypt, and opened fresh channels of spiritual influence to the Egyptian Jews.

Up to this point the writer has been virtually describing recent history. He now begins to express his high hopes for the future. In *v.* 21 he anticipates that these great deliverances will incline the Egyptians to turn to the true God, so that at "fireless altars" (Philo) they should worship God with the true sacrifices, and even if (*v.* 22) Yahwè should in the future send Egypt fatherly correction, its people would be always able to obtain "healing" by repentance (וְשָׁבוּ עַד י'); cf. R. Jehuda Hallevi's phrase, מובח תשובה). But a still greater idea visits his prophetic mind. Egypt, Palestine, and Syria[3] had a bond of union in the Greek origin of their sovereigns, but dynastic jealousies hindered perfect friendship and free intercourse between the peoples. These jealousies would be terminated if in the three countries the true religion could take firm root. Then there would "arise a highway from Egypt to Syria; Syria (would) come into Egypt, and Egypt into Syria, and the Egyptians (would) serve (Yahwè) with the Syrians" (*v.* 23). Israel, whose religion had been adopted by its neighbours, would then cease to be the battle-ground of the Ptolemies and the Seleucidæ, and would become the link between two friendly peoples—the third and most important because most richly blessed member of a triple alliance. And if in *v.* 25 we may read בְּרָכָה (with Sept., Duhm), we may perhaps find in the words a suggestion that just as Israel had been a source of blessing to Egypt and Assyria, so the three allied peoples

---

[1] The demotic chronicle, written to flatter the Ptolemies, cruelly disparages those kings (Wiedemann, *Gesch. Aeg.*, 1880, p. 67 f.).

[2] On referring to Vitringa, I see that he offers a similar view. Bishop Pearson well illustrates the title Soter (*Expos. of Creed*, 1676, p. 72).

[3] Cf. on xi. 16. In the Ptolemæan period Syria bore the name Asharu in hieroglyphic inscriptions (see Brugsch, *Gesch.*, p. 218). For further elucidation of the use of Asshur for Syria, see my note on Ps. lxxxiii. 9, and cf. *BL*, p. 110; Stade, *ZATW*, 1882, pp. 291-293.

should radiate spiritual light to the "four corners of the earth." The epilogue is therefore the work of an Egyptian Jew, who wrote perhaps about B.C. 275.

This view the author ventured to express briefly in 1891.[1] It differs from the kindred theories of Hitzig and Duhm in allowing a larger measure of vague anticipation, and in not conflicting with the most defensible view of the closing of the prophetic canon. According to these critics, the epilogue is written in the interests of Onias, who, as we have seen, about 160 B.C., conceived and carried out the bold idea of competing with the high priest of Jerusalem on Egyptian soil. Hitzig even supposes that the interpolated epilogue comes from the hand of Onias himself. He adds that the "sun-city" is mentioned in *v.* 18, because Leontopolis, where Onias built his temple, was in the nome of Heliopolis, and infers from *vv.* 23-25 (rendering, with versions, "and the Egyptians shall serve the Assyrians") that the writer expects that the three countries mentioned will be formed into one empire, in which the Syrian Greeks shall be supreme, and which shall be blessed for the sake of Israel. The successes of Judas Maccabæus might, it is urged, encourage the formation of these hopes, and in his brilliant early work (*Begriff der Kritik*, etc., p. 166) Hitzig regarded *vv.* 24-25 as a *vatic. ex eventu* suggested by the marriage of Alexander Balas with the daughter of Ptolemy Philometor (B.C. 150), at which Jonathan was present (1 Macc. x. 51-66). Hitzig also conjectures (*Jes.*, p. 219) that *vv.* 16-17 allude to the defeat of the Ætolian mercenary Scopas, and his expulsion from Palestine by Antiochus the Great.[2]

Thus Hitzig in the later form of his theory becomes more sober in the admission of circumstantial pseudo-prophecy. Verses 21-25 are, he thinks, purely imaginative. Duhm, however, approximates to Hitzig's early view; he explains *v.* 24 by the same event to which that sharp-sighted scholar pointed long ago. He also discovers one more reference to history in *v.* 20, where "a saviour" is, according to him, a collective term for the Jewish generals of Philometor, among whom were sons of the priest Onias

---

[1] See *BL*, pp. 131, 170, 184.   [2] See *BL*, p. 114.

(Jos., *c. Ap.*, ii. 5). He rejects Hitzig's view of *vv.* 16-17, however, as unnecessary, and in *v.* 18 prefers the reading עיר הדרס, which (following old Iken and Michaelis) he renders "Leontopolis." Nor does he venture to ascribe the epilogue to Onias himself. I have already stated the two main reasons why I do not accept either of these theories, and now urge in addition (1) that it seems highly improbable that a passage interpolated by an Egyptian Jew in the interests of Onias should have made its way into Palestinian manuscripts of the Book of Isaiah ; and (2) that a comparatively early date enables us the better to understand the mention of Hebrew as the language of the Jewries of Egypt.[1]

But however we explain the details, the general theory of the late post-Exilic origin of the epilogue will have to be admitted. It is one of those things which, as Kuenen says, may be disputed, but are not therefore disputable. The more we study the history of the religious ideas of the O. T., the clearer will the date of this wonderful passage become to us. "A grander universalism," as the conservative Bredenkamp remarks, "is not conceivable in antiquity. Observe that Egypt and Assyria are placed before Israel, and then consider how much blood and how many tears clung for an Israelite to the names of Assyria and Egypt." As the evidence now stands, this cannot be explained historically in the age of Isaiah.[2] Just as we infer from the reference to Cyrus in xliv. 28, xlv. 1, that the prophecy containing it proceeds from the age of that conqueror, so we may infer from the fraternal feeling towards Egypt and Assyria (Syria) in xix. 23-25 that the epilogue was written when hopes of

[1] A Hebrew-Greek dialect or jargon could never have been styled the "language of Canaan."

[2] Among the older scholars, Vitringa and Lowth fully recognise the reference of *vv.* 18-25 to the Greek period, but of course do not doubt the authorship of Isaiah. Gesenius refers *vv.* 18-20 to a writer contemporary with Jeremiah ; he considers them to be a defence of those who (against Jeremiah's advice) fled into Egypt ; Renan, too, separates *vv.* 18-20*a* from the rest. Grätz assigns the epilogue to the author or one of the authors of the latter part of Zechariah. Kuenen (*Ond.*[2]) inclines with hesitation to the traditional view. Stade and Cornill are also for Isaiah. Geiger (*Urschrift*, pp. 77-80) and Merx (Schenkel's *Bib. Lex.*) agree with Hitzig. Vatke (*Einl.*, p. 622) assigns the section to the reign of Ptolemy Philadelphus. For Duhm's view, see above.

the union and fusion of Israelitish and non-Israelitish elements first became natural for the Jews, *i.e.* in the early Greek period.[1] And if it be asked why such a strongly contrasting passage was attached to the original prophecy, we may answer, just because it is such a strong contrast was it added. The object of the writer was not only to express noble thoughts, but to modify the narrow though fervent Jewish spirit of the preceding work, and to counteract the depressing effect of its gloomy vaticinations.

We have next to investigate the origin of *vv.* 1-15. By most critics this has been held to form a connected passage, and to be the work of Isaiah. Eichhorn, however, denied the authorship of Isaiah,[2] and Ewald, who accepted it (both for prophecy and for epilogue), found a general prolixity and an occasional peculiarity of expression which distinguished this from the other works of that prophet. The author in 1880 left it "an open question whether a disciple of Isaiah had not given the prophecy its present form, working, of course, on the basis of Isaiah's notes."[3] It now remains to consider whether this view is justified, or whether either the traditional or the extreme negative view is preferable, and to discuss the question of date. But, before doing so, I must take leave to deny that *vv.* 1-15 do really form a connected passage. The connection is greatly improved by the omission of *vv.* 5-10. These verses contain a prophecy of the drying up of the Nile (not merely the neglect of irrigation), the death of vegetation, and the fall of industries, which interrupts the picture of the political ruin of Egypt and the infatuation of those who should have averted it. It is a description to which Ewald's word "prolix" (used by him of the whole chapter) fully applies. The details are merely such as would occur to a feeble rhetorician, and such the author of *vv.* 1-4 and 11-17 was not. The phraseology, too, has a distinctive character of its own. Of Isaianic features (which are not wanting in *vv.* 1-4 and 11-17) we can only mention one, יְאֹר, *v.* 5, for "the Nile" (as xviii. 2).

---

[1] It is a mistake to suppose that fierce hatred of the nations pervades the whole of the later literature. There are occasional gleams of a kindlier feeling. See *BL*, pp. 292-297.
[2] So Duhm and Smend.   [3] *PI*, i. 114.

CHAPTER XIX. 1-15

On the other hand, peculiar expressions abound. Notice *e.g.* in *v.* 5, נִשְּׂתוּ (Nifal, as prob. Jer. xviii. 14, of נשׁת ; cf. Qal, xli. 17, Jer. li. 30, both late); in *v.* 6, הָאְזְנִיחוּ (read rather אָזְנִיחוּ, with Ges.—an Aram. form),[1] יְאֹרִים (as vii. 18, xxxiii. 21, xxxvii. 25, late), קָמֵל (elsewhere only xxxiii. 9,[2] late); in *v.* 7, עָרוֹת (of uncertain meaning; Sept. ἄχι), פֶּה, the "brim" of a river (on the analogy of "lip" = shore, Gen. xli. 3), מְזָרֵע ἅπ. λεγ., אֵינֶנּוּ (a frequent formula in Job); in *v.* 8, אָנוּ וְאָבְלוּ (see on iii. 26, p. 20), דָּיָג (nowhere else in K'thib ; cf. דָּוּג, Jer. xvi. 16 ; Ezek. xlvii. 10), חַכָּה (as Hab. i. 15 ; Job xl. 25), מִכְמֹרֶת (as Hab. i. 15, 16), אֻמְלָל (see on xvi. 8) ; in *v.* 9, פִּשְׁתִּים (not proph. before Ezek.), שְׂרִיקוֹת and חוֹרִי ἅπ. λεγ.; in *v.* 10, שָׁתֹת (cf. שָׁתוֹת, Ps. xi. 3), if we should rather read שֹׁתֶיהָ "they that weave it," Aramaicè; and עֹשֵׂי שֶׂכֶר, an unique phrase ('שׂ again only in Prov. xi. 18) ; אַגְמֵי נָפֶשׁ, also unique, cf. Aram. אֲגַם "to be troubled"[3] (Targ., Ps. cxix. 28), and the Mishnic phrase אֲגִמַת נָפֶשׁ (*Moed Qaton*, 14*b*). To these may be added מָצוֹר (*v.* 6), which occurs elsewhere only in xxxvii. 25 (= 2 Ki. xix. 24) and Mic. vii. 12, also perhaps in lix. 19. All these passages must, I believe, be post-Exilic. On the whole, the unity of authorship of *vv.* 1-17 may with good reason be denied, and phraseology points to a post-Exilic date, at any rate for *vv.* 5-10 (see further on). Of course we need not deny that *vv.* 5-10 have a certain fitness where they now stand ;[4] the editor did not act at random when he inserted this melancholy description in the prophecy of the ruin of Egypt. The only plausible argument against this date is that *v.* 5 closely resembles Job xiv. 11, and has generally been thought to be the original of that passage. This may be urged by believers in the pre-Exilic date of Job, to show that Isa. xix. 1-15 is probably pre-Exilic. It is, however, a weak argument, (1) because the speeches in Job are very much more probably post-Exilic, and (2) because Job xiv. 11 is very possibly an interpolation (Studer, Bickell).

---

[1] Cf. אגאלתי, lxiii. 3 (according to the ordinary explanation) ; and see Qimchi, *Miklot*, 64*b*, ap. König, *Lehrgeb.* i. 293.

[2] Cornill, however, finds it also in Ezek. vii. 11 (corrupt).

[3] That Aram. אגם has an Assyrian connection does not prove it to be also classical Hebrew, Assyrian being more closely related to Aramaic than to Hebrew.

[4] See Ezek. xxix. 11, and cf. Robertson Smith, *Prophets*, p. 335.

Next, as to the authorship and date of *vv.* 1-4 and 11-15. Here are some phenomena which may be taken as favourable to the authorship of Isaiah. In *v.* 4 we have the Isaianic phrase, "the Lord Yahwè Çebaoth" (i. 24, iii. 1). For הִנֵּה in *v.* 1, cf. xvii. 1 (but also xxiv. 1). The description of civil warfare in *v.* 2 is like those in iii. 5, ix. 18, 19. For אלילים, *vv.* 1, 3, cf. ii. 8, 18, etc.; for סכסך, *v.* 2, cf. ix. 10; for בלל=בלע, *v.* 3, cf. iii. 12; and for "Zoan," *vv.* 11, 13, cf. xxx. 4. For the description in *v.* 13*b*, cf. iii. 12*b*; for *v.* 14*a*, cf. xxix. 10; for *v.* 14*b* (figure), cf. xxviii. 7, 8; and for the symbolism in *v.* 15, cf. ix. 13. Lastly, if viii. 19 and xxiii. 8, 9, were Isaiah's, we might compare with the one xix. 3, and with the other xix. 12 (end). And here are the adverse phenomena—(1) There is little arrangement of the contents. (2) The references to contemporary history are scanty, and on the whole vague. (3) The statement that Yahwè will come to Egypt is almost unique in prophecy; cf. Jer. xlix, 38. Joel, when describing the judgments upon the neighbouring peoples, says that "Yahwè will roar from Zion, and utter his voice from Jerusalem" (Joel iv. 16). Moreover, the opening figure in *v.* 1 is rather poetic than prophetic (cf. Ps. xviii. 10, 11, civ. 3). Nah. i. 3*b* contains something like it, but Nah. i. is certainly post-Exilic (see Gunkel, *ZATW*, 1893, p. 223, etc.). (4) The description of magic in *v.* 3 is conventional (cf. viii. 19, late), in spite of the new and vigorous expression אטים, "mutterers (of spells)." (5) Observe the tasteless repetition of מצרים (six times in *vv.* 1-4; four times in *vv.* 12-15). (6) אך, *v.* 11 (cf. xvi. 7; Deut. xvi. 15), occurs nowhere in the acknowledged Isaiah. (7) The structure of *v.* 12 is a favourite one since Jeremiah's time (cf. Jer. ii. 28; Deut. xxxii. 37, 38; Isa. xlvii. 12, 13). (8) *V.* 15 is in style as feeble as it is affected. On the form נף (*v.* 13) I lay no stress. We find it again in a genuine and an inserted part of Jeremiah (ii. 16, xlvi. 14, 19); also in Ezek. (xxx. 13, 16): Hosea, according to our text of Hos. ix. 6, has מף. The original form may have been מנף; the vocalisation cannot be determined. Cf. old Egyptian, *men-nefer;* Coptic *manûfi;* old Arabic, *minf.*

That the prophecy as it stands cannot be Isaiah's work

CHAPTER XIX. 1-15

should be evident. Is it, however, possible to rescue at least a basis for the great prophet? The author till 1892 thought that it was, and ventures to state what, as it appeared to him, would be the probable date of the prophecy (*vv.* 1-4 and 11-15) on that hypothesis. "Is there any 'hard lord' known to history who either actually ruled over Egypt, or might have been expected to become its ruler, in the time of Hezekiah? We might think first of some Ethiopian ruler of Egypt, such as Pianchi or Taharqa (Tirhakah).[1] It does not, however, appear that either of these kings would be fairly described as a 'hard lord.' Gentle rulers they were not, according to our ideas; no ancient Egyptian king could have been this. But they were not strange to the culture of Egypt, and it was a boon to Egypt to subject the petty kings in some degree to a central authority. Pianchi, moreover, is too early (B.C. 775?), and a literalist might object that Taharqa's accession to the throne of Egypt in 689 was not preceded by that internecine strife of the local dynasts which may seem to be described in *v.* 2. We must, therefore, look out for some more terrible ruler, and ask, What event was there between 715 and 686 which might, from a prophet's point of view, be ascribed with justice to the advent of the wrathful Yahwè?— The answer is, that the crushing defeat of Shabaka at Raphia in 720 was such an event, and that a less keen observer than Isaiah might easily surmise that the feuds of the petty princes would thereupon assume a new bitterness and intensity. Sargon, therefore, who might most truly be styled a 'fierce king,' is most probably the despot referred to, if the basis of the prophecy is Isaianic.[2] He did not, indeed, actually invade and conquer Egypt; this was left for Esarhaddon (672) and Assurbanipal (662). But Isaiah, as we see from xx. 4, expected in 711 that he would."

"This view, however, can only be maintained if we give up Isaiah's authorship of *vv.* 16, 17. If we retain these

[1] Pianchi has been proposed by Mariette, de Rougé, and (formerly) Stade; see *Rev. archéol.*, n.s., viii. 127. Cornill (*Einl.*) prefers Taharqa. For Pianchi's great inscription, see *RP*, ii. 79-104; cf. Brugsch, *Gesch.*, pp. 682-707 (the stele itself is in the Gizeh Museum).
[2] So Hitzig and Schrader.

verses as Isaiah's, it will be safest to group the whole prophecy (*vv.* 1-17) with chapter xviii., and date it in 702 B.C. The writer of chapter xviii. is convinced that Sennacherib has designs upon Jerusalem, and will besiege it.[1] But the Assyrian's profane purpose will be frustrated (cf. xxix. 4, 5); the dead bodies of his warriors will lie unburied on the mountains of Judah. And what effect will this produce upon Egypt? One of joy? No. Egypt will be aware that this judgment comes from Yahwè, and that it has no claim on the gratitude of Yahwè's people (cf. Ezek. xxix. 6, 7), so that when unexplained disasters befall Egypt, it will be clear to all (see xix. 1, 17) that the evil is from Yahwè."

I must confess, however, that I can now find no sure traces of an Isaianic substratum. Isaianic phrases are easily accounted for by imitation, and since the collection to which chapter xix. belongs includes some late works, the hypothesis of a post-Exilic origin is not *a priori* improbable. We may (as in the case of Zech. ix. x.) expect hints for dating the prophecy from some of those writers who think that Isaiah foretold the events of a much later time, *e.g.* from Sayce, Delitzsch, Vitringa, Luzzatto. By Sayce the prophecy is connected with the Egyptian campaigns of Esarhaddon and Assurbanipal.[2] The indomitable Taharqa had encouraged Baalu, king of Tyre, to revolt from Assyria. Thereupon Esarhaddon came with a large army, part of which blockaded Tyre, while with the main body of the host the Assyrian king marched against Egypt. Memphis ("Noph," Isa. xix. 13) fell, and the conquerors penetrated unopposed as far south as Thebes. The petty princes of Egypt submitted to Esarhaddon, who recognised twenty of them as tributary kings (672). On his return Esarhaddon carved on the rocks of Nahr-el-Kelb, near Beirût, a long inscription, in which he styled himself "king of the kings of Musur and Pathros" (*i.e.* Lower and Upper Egypt) "and Cush" (*i.e.* Nubia), and erected at the place where stands the *tell* at Senjirli in

---

[1] Dillm. writes, "Soon *after* the overthrow of Sennacherib the soaring hopes of the prophet can best be understood." Similarly König. But it is very doubtful whether the criticism of Isa. xxxvi., xxxvii. will permit this view.

[2] See *The Times of Isaiah* (1889), pp. 39, 65.

N.W. Syria, the magnificent stele now at Berlin. To the sculptures on this monolith we shall have to return (see on xxxvii. 29). Suffice it here to quote a few lines from the inscription. " Tarqu, king of Musur and Cush, the enemy (?) of the great gods, from the city of Ischupri even to the city of Memphis, his royal city, a fifteen days' march, I slew a great multitude of his soldiers. Five times made I a deadly attack on him with the point of my spear. Memphis, his royal city, did I lay siege to ; I took it with battering-rams, I laid it waste, I burned it with fire." The wives and children of Taharqa, we are also told, were sent with the captives to Assyria, and "kings, satraps, governors," were appointed anew over all Egypt.[1] The changes and chances of the great Ethiopian's career were, however, not yet ended. In 669 Esarhaddon fell dangerously ill, and Taharqa, who had retired to Ethiopia, reasserted his claims to the Egyptian throne. For a short time he attained his end, but Assurbanipal, to whom in 668 his aged father had transferred the crown, quickly re-established the Assyrian authority, and when Taharqa once more invaded Egypt successfully, again with equal vigour and cruelty put down the revolt. The entire population of Thebes was carried into captivity (Nah. iii. 8-10), and for the third time the twenty tributary kings were re-established. This was in 662.

Of these local dynasts the most powerful was Psamtik, the new king of Sais. His equally able father Nekau (Necho) had already set him the example of throwing off the Assyrian yoke, which example, as soon as opportunity offered, Psamtik promptly followed. After a long struggle he succeeded in putting down the other princes, and united the whole country under his sway in 656 (or 651). He was one of the great rulers of Egypt. What the land was like when he succeeded his father might have been described (with some exaggeration) in the words of *vv.* 5-10 ; what he made it was a strong and prosperous land, covered with monuments of refined artistic taste, though dangerously dependent on the

[1] See Schrader's report in the official *Mittheilungen* of the Berlin Academy (Heft xi., 1893) ; D. H. Müller, *Contemp. Review*, April 1894, p. 596.

aid of Greek mercenaries. It is this king whom Del. identifies with the "fierce king." But his historical justification of this view is too much based on Herodotus, and even more emphatically than in the cases of Pianchi and Taharqa, we must deny that this great patriotic king deserves the title assigned to him. If, therefore, we have to choose between these rival hypotheses Sayce's is the one to be preferred. Let us, then, collect the points which favour the view that the Assyrian invasions of Egypt are referred to. They are three in number :—(1) The picture of Yahwè riding upon a swift thunder cloud (*v.* 1), which reminds us of Nah. i. 3*b* (Nahum may, perhaps, be dated in 650). (2) The reference to the petty kings of Egypt (*v.* 2), who were never thoroughly subjugated before Psamtik I. (3) The mention of Zoan (Tanis) and Noph (Memphis) as leading cities (*vv.* 11, 13). These cities were, in fact, together with Thebes, royal residences of the Ethiopian kings. To find a definite reference in *v.* 2 to Esarhaddon's twenty "satrapies or kingdoms" (so Sayce) seems arbitrary.

There is one strong objection, however, to both these hypotheses. It is drawn from the stylistic poverty of the composition. Surely such imitativeness and want of originality points to a later period than the seventh century. How exuberant in vigour is the Book of Nahum! Indeed, even Mic. vi. 1-vii. 6 (which many refer to this period) rises far above the standard of this prophecy. We must, therefore, pass over the seventh century, nor can we pause till we reach the latter half of the sixth, or even some part of the fifth. For though Nebuchadrezzar's expected invasion called forth Hebrew prophecies, the writers of these prophecies betray in their style an excitement which in xix. 1., etc. is altogether wanting. Whoever the "hard lord" is, the author of the latter work sees no danger from him to Judah. It appears, moreover, that the feeble and imitative style of xix. 1, etc. is characteristic of the literary period which may be said to begin about 536 B.C. We are now ready for fresh suggestions. Vitringa and Luzzatto see in the main part of ch. xix. a prediction of the troublous period which begins with the dodecarchy (Herod.) and ends with the invasion of Cambyses. That this king was a "fierce king" history only too unequivocally declares, and if from the moment of Cyrus's death the Egyptians themselves looked forward to a Persian invasion, we can easily believe that this prospect was equally visible to a Jewish writer. In fact, the Second Isaiah had already promised " Egypt, Cush, and Seba " to Cyrus as a compensation for his clemency to Israel (xliii. 3). It is best not to be too precise, but it is at any rate probable that xix. 1, etc. was written sometime between 528 (final defeat of Psamtik III. by Cambyses) and 485 (reconquest of Egypt by Xerxes). The older prophecies against Egypt (including that in xx. 4) were still unfulfilled, and an imitative prophet might, even without an immediate prospect of its fulfilment, repeat the old threatenings. Joel in fact did this very briefly in Joel iv. 19, and a nameless prophet, also post-Exilic, composed the ill-arranged prophecy against Egypt in Jer. xlvi.[1] (see Schwally, *ZATW*, 1888, p. 177, etc., and Giesebrecht's *Jeremia*). And considering that "fierceness" was not a common characteristic of the Persian kings,[2] it is most natural to explain xix. 4 as referring chiefly to the mad fury of Cambyses. The vagueness of the historical references may be due to the author's wish to pass off his prophecy as Isaiah's, whom, as we have seen, he imitates. This date (528-485) is fully consistent with the prominence given in v. 1 to the fall of Egyptian idolatry (cf. Ex. xii. 12, Num. xxxiii. 4, both in P; Jer. xliii. 12, xlvi. 25; Ezek. xxx. 13). The inserted passage xix. 5-10 was at any rate written before 485.

It was admitted just now that Vitringa may have limited the historical reference of the prophecy too much, and that the date may possibly be as late as the beginning of the invasion of Xerxes. But why stop short here? it may be asked. If, as we have seen, the author of the epilogue identified the "hard lord" of v. 4 with Artax. Ochus (or at any rate with him and with the two preceding Persian

---

[1] Jer. xlvi. agrees with Isa. xix. in the prominence which it gives to Memphis (vv. 14, 19). The other names in v. 14 are simply suggested by Jer. xliv. 1. Thebes is mentioned in v. 25, not for its own sake, but for its still universally honoured god, Amen (Amon). There is, therefore, no objection, on the ground of names of places, to the date given. Assurbanipal had done his best to ruin Thebes (p. 115).

[2] Cf. Wiedemann, *Gesch. Aegyptens* (1890), p. 211.

invaders conjointly), may not his opinion have been correct? The present work had been partly written[1] when Duhm published his view that the whole prophecy (*vv.* 1-15), as it stands, has reference to the war of independence waged by the last native dynasty (the 30th) against Artaxerxes II. and III. It became necessary to examine the question more seriously with the aid of Judeich's very full and critical narrative of this period. The result, however, was not favourable to Duhm's hypothesis, and on once more revising my work I am still unable to alter my conclusion. On the one hand I agree with Duhm that the doings of Ochus may or even must have had some record in Hebrew literature, but on the other I see no sufficient reason for assuming such a record here. The details of Ochus's Egyptian campaign handed down to us do not really account for the description in *v.* 2, nor does the part played by Tanis and Memphis really illustrate the vague statements in *vv.* 11 and 13. Tanis, moreover, had very much sunk in importance since Taharqa's time. That the last Pharaoh (Nectanebo II.) was already in the Greek period considered an arch-magician is true.[2] But how he obtained this reputation Egyptologists cannot say.[3] Certainly Duhm's explanation of *v.* 3 is, to say the least, unnecessary. A check to the prosperity of Egypt would at any time have increased the popularity of magic arts, which, in fact, were cultivated in remote antiquity. Nor could it be said that Egypt was "drained" of the "spirit" of counsel and might (*vv.* 3, 14) in its struggle with Artaxerxes II. and III. There is reason to doubt the accuracy of Diodorus when he represents Ochus as having made an easy conquest of Egypt. The Delta contained very solid temples built or restored during the 30th dynasty, nor is it probable that Nectanebo II. gave up at once in despair, and fled with his treasures to Ethiopia. The language of an inscription at Saft-el-Henneh " points to

[1] See art. in *ZATW*, 1893, pp. 125-128.
[2] See Maspero, *Contes populaires de l'Egypte ancienne*, Introd., p. xxxvi. As a builder and a patron of art Nectanebo II. holds a high rank (see Wiedemann, *Gesch.*).
[3] See Budge, *Alexander the Great* (from the Syriac), Introd., p. xxxviii.

a long reign, at the end of which Nectanebo may have become a vassal or tributary of the great king."[1]

In truth, all the details of the prophecy except one (*v.* 4) are so conventional that they can be explained of any of the periods of actual or impending invasion from the eighth century onwards. Stylistic and other evidence points, no doubt, to the long Persian period, but nothing compels us to descend so far as Artax. Ochus. And there is this strong reason why we should not do so, viz., that this king, so able and so unscrupulous, was only less terrible in Phœnicia and Judæa than in Egypt. After hearing of his vengeance on Sidon (see on chs. xxiv.-xxvii.), and being aware that the Jews had only too much cause to dread the like, a Jewish prophet could not, I think, have written thus coldly and indifferently of his final campaign against Egypt. I am much indebted to Duhm, however, for help in the re-examination of the stylistic evidence, and for stimulus to consider the question of a post-Exilic date.

CHAPTER XX

The oracle in this chapter is preceded by a historical introduction (*vv.* 1-3) in which "Isaiah ben Amoz" is spoken of in the third person. Is this introduction Isaiah's work? Comparing the form of expression in vi. 1 and xiv. 28, which are ancient if not Isaianic passages, we should expect a much simpler apodosis than the trailing "at that time," etc. If, however (with Duhm), we regard *v.* 2 as a late insertion, and take the apodosis from *v.* 3 (". . . Yahwè said"), we get rid of three troublesome things : (1) the late phrase דְּבֶּר בְּיַד, Hag. i. 1, 3 ; Jer. xxxvii. 2 ; 1 Ki. xii. 15 ; Ex. ix. 35 ; Lev. x. 11 ; (2) the expression, found nowhere else in Isaianic passages, *Yeshayâhû ben Amoç*, i. 1, ii. 1, xiii. 1, xxxvii. 2, 21, xxxviii. 1; and (3) an extremely awkward synchronism.[2] Thus lightened, the introduction, which is

---

[1] Naville, *Memoir on Goshen* (1887), p. 5.

[2] In *vv.* 1, 2 it appears to be stated that, in the year of the successful assault upon Ashdod, Isaiah was commanded to go about in the garb of a captive. But from *v.* 3 (where "three years" certainly belongs to the

indispensable to the following oracle, may come from Isaiah or from an early biographer. The oracle can be dated with certainty. We have two cuneiform texts[1] relative to the siege of Ashdod, according to one of which (the Khorsabad text, now at Paris) the date would be 711 B.C., and according to the other (a fragmentary cylinder text now in London), 713 B.C. In reality the latter date belongs to the outbreak of the revolt of the Ashdodites, the former to its issue[2] in the siege and capture of Ashdod by Sargon or (as the Hebrew text more precisely states) his Tartan or general. The oracle on the capture of this Philistine city should of course be compared with the earlier one on the fate of the Philistine nation in xiv. 28-32 (dated 720). Isaiah's tone towards his own people has changed in the interval; he now speaks more in the style of the genuine parts of chaps. xxviii. - xxxi. Evidently it is Hezekiah who is in fault; he has begun to listen to the "crooked" counsels of politicians (cf. xxx. 12). The proof of this is supplied by the fragmentary cylinder text. We read here, "The inhabitants of Philistia, Judah, Edom, and Moab, who dwell by the sea [cf. ישב האי הזה, xx. 6], and had to bring tribute and presents for Assur my lord, who thought on hostilities, and willed (?) that which was evil, who, to make him hostile to me, brought their presents of homage to Pir'û (Pharaoh) king of Egypt, a prince who could not deliver them, and requested of him an alliance —I, Sargon, the legitimate prince . . . crossed the Tigris and the Euphrates,"[3] etc. Does chap. xxxix. refer to this period? The question must be considered later.

The story of the siege of Ashdod is given most fully in the other inscription. Azuri, whose rebellion has been already referred to (on ch. xviii.), was deposed by Sargon,

first part of the verse) we learn that Isaiah's strange symbolic procedure had been going on for three years previous to the fall of Ashdod. Omit v. 2, and the synchronising events are the assault upon Ashdod and the prophecy which closed Isaiah's three years' adoption of the captive dress.

[1] Winckler, *Keilinschriftl. Textbuch*, pp. 30-31 (cf. Peiser, *KIB*, vol. ii. 65).

[2] So *PI*, i. 124, where, however, two sieges of Ashdod, one by the Tartan, the other by Sargon himself, are unnecessarily supposed; and so Winckler, *Untersuch.*, p. 143 (for another view see Schrader, *CI*).

[3] Winckler, *Textbuch, l.c.*

who appointed Azuri's brother Akhimit in his place. The ruling class, however, were anti-Assyrian and put down Akhimit, setting up an adventurer named Yaman or Yatnan on the unstable throne. Then, Sargon says, substituting himself for his general, " In the rage of my heart my whole army I gathered not, neither did I summon my camp. With my soldiers (alone)—those who do not recede from the place whither I direct (them)—I went to Ashdod."[1] Yaman, we are told, fled to Melucha (N.W. Arabia?), while Ashdod, Gath (Gimtu), and Asdudimmu (= אַשְׁדּוֹד הַיָּם, the port of Ashdod) fell into the cruel hands of the Assyrians. We are not expressly told, but we have a right to presume that the Tartan with his small force returned after this success to Assyria. In other words, there was no invasion of Judah (as Sayce supposes). Hezekiah escaped the penalty of his meditated infidelity. The king of Judah, however, received the object-lesson of an Assyrian captivity in his neighbourhood. The inhabitants of the conquered Philistine towns were carried captive, and their places filled by new colonists. Sargon himself held judgment in Assyria on the upstart Yaman, whom the king of Melucha could not venture to protect. Winckler acutely conjectures [2] that the name Yaman (or Yavan) really means "the Ionian." The ill-fated man may, conceivably enough, have come from Cyprus, the Assyrian name of which (commonly read Yatnan) may have meant " the land of the Ionians."

CHAPTER XXI. 1-10

In some respects this little prophecy stands alone. It refers to a fall of Babylon, and yet there are points in which it is so unlike the deutero-Isaianic period that we are led to consider whether it may not refer to some other event than the capture of Babylon by Cyrus in 539. Dillmann's

[1] Peiser, *KIB*, vol. ii. 64-67.
[2] *Sargon*, p. xxx., note 2. So Hommel, *Gesch.*, p. 703 ; Sayce, *Pal. Fund Statement*, Jan. 1893, p. 32. This conjecture, however, finds no place in Winckler's more recent works.

limits prevented him from giving enough space to this question; I venture, therefore, to return to it, especially as Winckler has very nearly adopted a hypothesis which, in 1880, had some attractions for myself. It was an Assyriologist —the late George Smith—who first suggested[1] that some Assyrian siege of Babylon might be referred to ; he thought of the siege of Sargon (710). Probably he had made no deep critical study of the subject, and argued that, if Isa. i.-lxvi. is all one writer's work, and chap. xx. referred to Sargon's capture of Ashdod in 711, xxi. 1-10 was most naturally explained of the siege of Babylon in 710. But it was reserved for Kleinert to furnish a critical and exegetical justification of this view.[2] This, in the main, I adopted in *PI*, i. 125-127, admitting, however, that "a fuller knowledge of the circumstances of the Jews might conceivably enable us to reconcile the prophecy with a date at the close of the Exile." The chief points to which the Berlin scholar drew attention were these. (1) There is a strange tone of depression in *v.* 2*a* (?), 3, 4. The king of Babylon, from 720 to 710, was Merodach Baladan, whose negotiations with Hezekiah are not obscurely indicated in ch. xxxix. Isaiah as a prophet was of course no friend of Babylon, but, knowing that Hezekiah endured the Assyrian yoke with reluctance, may well have trembled as a man for the fate of his own people. [If we put the negotiations with Merodach Baladan in 711-710, Isaiah would have had special grounds for patriotic anxiety, for in 711 Judah had been "speaking treason" against Assyria ; see on chap. xx.] (2) The form of expression used throughout most of the part which describes the " vision " (viz. *vv.* 2*a* and 6-9 ; *v.* 5 on this point is indefinite) may be held to imply that the seer is away from Babylon. (3) There are striking points of contact with the ideas and phraseology of the usually admitted works of Isaiah. Comp. *v.* 1 with xxx. 6 ; *v.* 2 with xxxiii. 1 ; *v.* 5 with xxii. 13 ; *v.* 6 with viii. 11, xviii. 4, xxi. 16, xxxi. 4 ; *vv.* 7, 9 (רָכָב) with xxii. 6 ; *v.* 10 ("threshing" . . . "I have heard") with xxviii. 28 and 22. (4) The pregnancy and picturesqueness of

---

[1] *TSBA*, vol. ii. (1873), p. 329.
[2] *Th. St. u. Kr.*, 1877, pp. 174-179.

CHAPTER XXI. 1-10

the style seemed also to suggest a great genius like Isaiah. (5) The opening words of *v.* 10 seemed to point to a recent invasion like that plausibly ascribed (but see p. 3 f.) to Sargon.

But were there no exegetical data which seemed to oppose Kleinert's view? I could not deny that there were some. There was (1) the mention of Elam and Media together as "going up" against Babylon. This is at once intelligible if Cyrus is referred to, for Ansan, of which Cyrus was king by birth, was situated in Elam (see *RP*, n.s., v. 147), while the authorship of Isaiah seems opposed by the fact that in the days of Sargon a king of Elam was a close ally of Merodach Baladan.[1] Yes; but on the other hand Elam is prominently mentioned in the description of an Assyrian army in the next chapter (xxii. 6). Merodach Baladan's ally was not king of the whole of Elam, for a part of that large region had been already incorporated into the empire of Sargon in 721, while from 810 B.C. onwards the Assyrian kings (including Sargon) record their conquests in Media.[2] (2) There was also the declaration in *v.* 2*b*, "all the sighing thereof do I make to cease." It would appear from this that when the prophet wrote Babylon was an oppressor. True; but was the reading אנחתה correct? Was it not both difficult in itself and inconsistent (however interpreted) with the writer's evident depression elsewhere? And (3) these were the words addressed in *v.* 10 to the Jewish people, "O my threshing, and my child of the floor." These words were clearly not predictive, but described sufferings which were still acutely felt. We had therefore to ask, Had any event taken place in the history of Judah shortly before 710 which could account for this language? In reply I pointed to Sargon's (supposed) invasion of Judah in 711, and ventured to give this interpretation of *v.* 10, "O Israel, who hast lately suffered so much from the cruel Assyrian invaders, how gladly would I have brought thee more cheering tidings! Yet I can but wait upon my office. That which I have heard from Yahwè Çebaoth, the God of Israel, have I announced

---

[1] *RP*, vii. 41, 45.
[2] See *KIB*, i. 191, 53, etc.; *RP*, vii. 27-29.

unto you." "The prophet," I remarked, " implies (cf. v. 12) that there is more trouble in store for his country from Assyria; but he suggests the only trustworthy ground of comfort."

I have long seen, however, that this explanation of v. 10 is untenable, and recognised the improbability that Isaiah should not have referred directly to Merodach Baladan's negotiations if they were really the occasion of the prophecy (cf. xiv. 32, xviii. 2). I have learned, moreover, that Sargon approached Babylon, not as an enemy, but as its deliverer[1] from the Chaldæan upstart Merodach Baladan. ⌠ Sennacherib's siege of Babylon (689) corresponds much more fully to the prophecy before us; the vivid account of it in that king's "Bavian inscription" thoroughly justifies the terror expressed by the prophet in xxi. 3, 4, on the hypothesis that he is looking forward to this event (which, since the battle of Halulu in 691, was to be expected). The historical objection to this hypothesis (the attractiveness of which I admitted in *PI*) is that the Elamites were then in alliance with the king of Babylon, and the same objection is fatal to Winckler's recent conjecture,[2] that the event anticipated is the capture of Babylon by Assurbanipal in 648. Manasseh, king of Judah, may no doubt have been forced by the anti-Assyrian party to join Baalu, king of Tyre, and the other kings of Palestine, in a league with Samas-sum-ukin, king of Babylon, against his brother Assurbanipal, and if this was so, a Jewish prophet might naturally feel anxious, in view of the consequences of an Assyrian victory, for his own people. But how can we get over the words, "Go up, O Elam; besiege, O Media"? Winckler changes צוּרִי, "besiege," into עִירִי, "march on" (cf. Sept.'s οἱ πρέσβεις = צִירֵי); but who will follow him?

We have therefore to turn back and ask, Is there really any insuperable exegetical difficulty in grouping this with

[1] Cf. Winckler, *Gesch.*, p. 126.
[2] *Untersuch.*, pp. 120-125. It is remarkable that according to Winckler's theory the prophet Nahum should have expressed a diametrically opposite conviction as to the issue of the war against Assurbanipal. Also that with strange carelessness Winckler should have represented Ewald and Dillm. as placing xxi. 1-10 in the *beginning* of the Exile.

other prophecies in Isaiah and Jeremiah on the fall of Babylon, which must be of Exilic origin? Let us take in order the three more important points urged by Kleinert. The first is, that the impending fall of Babylon gives the prophet a sensation, not of pleasure, but of pain (contrast v. 3 with xiii. 6). How is this? Had not Jeremiah predicted the end of the Captivity? He had; but it is conceivable that, when the promised boon began to draw near, those to whom it was offered might humanely shrink from its terrible cost in human lives. The Second Isaiah tells us of a class of despondent Israelites who doubted God's "righteousness" (xl. 27, xlvi. 12, xlix. 14). We now come face to face with one of another class, who believes, but not so as to forget that Babylonians are his fellow-men, for the Israelites have already begun to speak of mankind as a "people" (xlii. 5). He speaks, therefore, as if he had a double consciousness. As a man, he is distressed at the terrors of the storming of "Israel's second native city" (Ewald); as a servant of Yahwè, he loyally accepts the divine *fiat*. He is at present only in the initial stage of the prophetic ecstacy, when human thoughts and feelings are not entirely put aside, and has, as it were, to summon his prophetic consciousness to his aid. Hence the singular expression in v. 6. Just as Zechariah distinguishes between himself and the "angel that talked with him" (*i.e.* his prophetic spirit)[1] so this writer as a man would become a prophet, "stations" a "watcher" or seer, *i.e.* by an effort of the will places himself under the influence of the prophetic impulse.

Next, as to the second objection. It is true that the seer speaks as if at a distance from Babylon. But this again is to be explained by the ecstatic phenomena. It is as if a spiritual force had lifted him up like Ezekiel (Ezek. viii. 3), and brought him to Jerusalem. Comp. perhaps lii. 8, if the "watchmen" spoken of are the prophets of the Jews in Babylon (see Dillm.).

And now as to the third point. The Isaianic colouring may well be accounted for by the imitative skill of the later prophetic writers. And we must not suffer it to blind us to certain features of style and expression which point away

[1] See Marti, *St. u. Kr.*, 1892, p. 236, etc.

from Isaiah's authorship. (*a*) Where else does Isaiah adopt such an indirect mode of conveying a message on the fate of a nation? (*b*) Where else is the grammatical sense of an Isaianic prophecy so often doubtful? (*c*) What a strange phenomenon is this twofold consciousness, the only parallel to which occurs in the late prophet Zechariah![1] (*d*) There are two striking points of contact with post-Isaianic writers. Comp. *v*. 3 with Nah. ii. 11 (חַלְחָלָה); *vv*. 6, 8 with Hab. ii. 1 (וָאֲצַפֶּה ... עַל־מִשְׁמַרְתִּי). (*d*) Also the ἅπαξ λεγόμενα צָפִית (*v*. 5), מְדֻשָּׁה (*v*. 10); the rare words מִצְפֶּה (*v*. 8), elsewhere only as a proper name, and (2 Chr. xx. 24) in the sense of "high place," and חַלְחָלָה, *v*. 3, as Nah. ii. 11; Ezek. xxx. 4, 9; and the distinctively late words אֲנָחָה *v*. 2 (cf. on xxiv. 7, אָנַח in Nifal), as Jer. xlv. 3; Isa. xxxv. 10, li. 11; Lam. i. 22; Job iii. 4, 24, xxiii. 2; Ps. vi. 7, xxxi. 11, xxxviii. 10, cii. 6, and פַּלָּצוּת, *v*. 4, as Ezek. vii. 18; Job xxi. 6; Ps. lv. 6. Note, too, חָזוּת "vision," *v*. 2, as xxix. 11 (late), and its combination as *acc. obj.* with הִגַּד, and מִצְפֶּה, *v*. 6, as Mic. vii. 4 (reign of Manasseh, at earliest) as a term for a prophet. Also other non-Isaianic elements are נִבְהַל (*v*. 3), בָּעֵת (*v*. 4), תָּמִיד

---

[1] *V*. 5, צָפֹה הַצָּפִית (not צִפָּה). This may mean (*a*) "they spread the carpets" (*i.e.* the coverings of the cushions for the guests); cf. Rawlinson, *AM*, ii. 570. Reclining at meals was apparently not usual among the Assyrians (any more than among the Egyptians or the Homeric Greeks). In the famous garden-scene (British Museum Assyrian sculptures) Assurbanipal reclines on a rich couch (gazing at the suspended head of Merodach Baladan's grandson), but this is exceptional luxury. Even his favourite queen is seated on a chair of state. Another monument represents four guests seated at a table (Bonomi, *Nineveh and its Palaces*, p. 191; Ragozin, *Story of Assyria*, pp. 403-4). Reclining was however general among more luxurious peoples, such as the Syrians and N. Israelites (in Amos's time; see Am. iii. 12, vi. 4, and cf. Hoffmann, *ZATW*, 1883, p. 102, and the engraving in Cesnola, *Cyprus, its Cities, etc.*, p. 149), the Persians (Esth. i. 6, vii. 8), and probably the Babylonians, on whose luxuriousness see Isa. xlvii. 8; Jer. li. 39. Or (*b*) less probably, "they spread the table-cloths" (see Cesnola, *l.c.*). These renderings are supported by the Jewish Aramaic צִיפָא, צִיפְתָא, (1) covering, (2) mat (see Levy, *Neuhebr. WB*); צִפָּה in classical Hebrew means to overlay with. A third possible rendering is, "they light the lamps." Cf. *Bereshith rabba*, 81 (near end), where the version is supported by R. Abba bar Kahana's statement, that a lamp is in many places called צִפִיָא. Whichever rendering we adopt, the late date of the prophecy naturally follows.

CHAPTER XXI. 1-10

(v. 8), and the gerundial idiom לַחֲלוֹף (v. 1); also the fuller feminine ending ־ָתָה in אַנְחָתָה,[1] v. 2, the use of which is almost confined to lyric poetry (this suggests, what the "subjective" character of the prophecy confirms, that the writer lived at a time when prophetic writing, so far as it was original, tended to become lyric).[2]

A word more on אנחתה, the genuineness of which has been doubted by both Kleinert and Duhm. On our present theory there seems no reason to suspect it. It is just the word and just the form which a "subjective" prophetic writer would have chosen. Notice that הַשּׁוֹדֵד has gone before, and compare Ps. xii. 6, מִשֹּׁד עֲנִיִּים מֵאַנְקַת אֶבְיוֹנִים, עַתָּה אָקוּם, and for the pathetic ending ־ָתָה, cf. אֵימָתָה וָפַחַד, Ex. xv. 16. "All the sad sighing" is the short for "the sighing of all the nations" oppressed by the Babylonian "robber" and "waster"; cf. xiv. 4-7, where "all the earth" rejoices that the tyranny is at an end (שבת). The writer shares the discontent of his captive people, but loathes the horrors of a siege. Cities being commonly stormed by night (cf. xv. 1), "the evening of my desire," he says, "becomes to me a source of terror" (v. 4). The parallelism traced by Duncker and Renan between the picture in this prophecy and the narrative of Cyrus's capture of Babylon in Herod., i. 191 (cf. Xen., *Cyrop.*, vii. 5) is purely accidental, and one of its most striking features arises from a false rendering of צָפֹה הַצָּפִית in v. 5. The language of Renan [3] implies that the Hebrew prophets of the close of the Exile were virtually historians. But if xxi. 1-10 implies a literally correct view of historical events, and if the details of Herodotus are accurate, it would seem that the "prophecy" rather refers to the siege of Babylon by Darius Hystaspis in 521, for it is this siege which Herodotus really describes, tradition having transferred the event to the reign of Cyrus.[4]

---

[1] See *RT*.
[2] One might add, and at a time when the lyric poetry of psalms tended to become prophetic (cf. Ps. ii. 7-9, xii. 6, xxii. 27, xlvi. 11, l. 7-13, 16-21).
[3] *Histoire*, iii. 459, note 1; so Eichhorn and Koppe. Lowth (whose *Isaiah* Koppe edited) virtually agrees, following Vitringa, on the critical question, so far as is consistent with the old orthodoxy.
[4] Sayce, *Fresh Light from the Ancient Monuments*, p. 182.

As a matter of fact Cyrus did not have to besiege Babylon at all; as the inscriptions show, its defenders voluntarily opened their gates to the general of Cyrus.

There is therefore no sufficient reason to doubt that xxi. 1-10 relates to the conquest of Babylon by Cyrus (see on ch. xiii.). Very possibly, as Ewald remarks, it is the earliest of the group of Exilic prophecies on Babylon (*nach der allerfrischesten Empfindung*); it was not yet possible to write in a "calm, exhaustive, and circumstantial manner." xiii. 17 (quoted by Kuenen) supplies no argument to the contrary; the writer represents the "rousing" of the Medes as future, but his quiet tone proves that they have already been heard of as on the march. Kuenen's argument against Kleinert is effective, but too short. [Driver, in *Isaiah*,[2] pp. 216-219, seems to understate the case against Isaiah, but "allows that it now seems to him doubtful" whether Isaiah's authorship can be maintained. On his former view (*Isaiah*,[1] p. 96), see *Founders*, pp. 298-299. In *Introd.*[5] he fully adopts the theory that the prophecy dates from the close of the Exile.]

CHAPTER XXI. 11-12 AND 13-17

Did Isaiah ever profess (but only profess) to address prophecies to foreign nations? He did, if these two prophecies are his. But are they really Isaiah's? How short—how obscure they are! The former in particular one might take for a Delphian oracle, and declare, with Archbishop Magee, that "for all practical purposes, for any use it could have been to the Jews, or to any one since their time, it might as well, apparently, have been unspoken."[1] Pardonably, therefore, has it been supposed that a sense of unsatisfied curiosity prompted the editorial heading in xxi. 11, *mâssa dûmâ*.[2] There are also linguistic peculiarities in

[1] See his noble sermon on "Foretelling and Forthtelling" in *Growth in Grace* (1891).

[2] Assuming this to mean "oracle of silence" (so Ewald, Dillmann). More probably, however, "Dumah" is the symbolic name of Edom (=a stillness as of Sheól, Ps. xciv. 17, cxv. 17), if we should not rather correct "Dumah" into "Edom" (see Sept.).

CHAPTER XXI. 11-12, 13-17

these verses which compel us to question the judgment of most critics, and to deny the antiquity both of *vv.* 11-12, and of *vv.* 13-15. Among these we need not include עֲרָב,[1] *v.* 13, nor perhaps בְּבַד, *v.* 15 (but see xxx. 27, late), but אֲתָא and אֲתָא) בָּעָה and בְּעָא, often in Dan., are Aram. for בּוֹא and שָׁאַל) arouse suspicion. The former occurs also seven times in Isa. xl.-lxvi., three times in Job, once in Proverbs (i. 27), once in a late psalm (lxviii. 32), twice in Deut. xxxiii. (*vv.* 2, 21), twice in Jer. (iii. 22, xii. 9), and once in a late passage of Micah (iv. 8 ; see Wellh.). The latter, in Nifal, in Obad. 6. תִּבְעָיוּן, בְּעָיוּ, אֵתָיוּ (all in *v.* 12) and הֵתָיוּ (*v.* 14) are peculiar, because such forms are very rare in Isaiah (xvii. 12, xxxi. 3, if the closing words are genuine; cf. xxxiii. 7). On the other hand, *vv.* 16-17 may be Isaianic, with the same degree of probability as xvi. 14. One fails to understand how a late editor should have made this addition, Duhm's ascription of the epilogue to the time of Alexander Jannæus being extremely rash (cf. p. 92). The complex genitival combination (in which גבורי and קשת should be transposed) reminds us of xxviii. 1. Comp. also xvii. 3, 4, and especially xvi. 14.

It has been suggested by Ewald, with whom Dillmann agrees, that, as (acc. to him) in the case of xv. 1-xvi. 12, Isaiah may have here adopted and supplemented an already extant oracle of another prophet.[2] It may be objected (1) that no hint is given of this (contrast xvi. 14) in the supposed Isaianic epilogue, beginning " For thus hath the Lord said unto me," *v.* 16. This, however, is not a fatal objection. It is already (according to this hypothesis) Isaiah who speaks in *v.* 15, which Ewald takes to be explanatory of *vv.*

[1] First, because the pointing may be incorrect (versions read בְּעֶרֶב ; so *PI*). And secondly, because, though we next meet with עֲרָב in Jer. xxv. 24, Ezek. xxvii. 21, etc. (cf. עֲרָבִי Jer. iii. 2, Isa. xiii. 20), yet Isaiah may have known the word in the sense of Arabia, for Sennacherib expressly mentions the Arabians (Urbi = Aribi = עֲרָב) whom Hezekiah had hired for the defence of Jerusalem (Prism inscription, *KIB*, ii. 94, 95 ; *CI*, i. 283, 286). Or, if this be thought hazardous, still עֲרָב as a geographical name must first of all have been a " nomen appellativum," and meant " desert-steppe," and this is the sense which Dillm. gives to ערב, ערבים in Isa. xxi. 13, xv. 7.

[2] König even conjectures that these two prophecies are by the author of xv. 1-xvi. 12 (*Einl.*, p. 313).

13, 14; a remark like that in xvi. 13 would not therefore have been altogether accurate. (2) The Aramaisms may be urged against this theory, and, as I think, with justice. At any rate, those who have abandoned similar views with regard to chaps. ii. and xv.-xvi., cannot consistently adopt this theory. Verses 16-17 may indeed be a small fragment (perhaps the only part which remained legible) of a prophecy of Isaiah. But it is reasonable to hold that this was attached after the Exile to two small oracles of unknown authorship (*vv.* 11-12 and 13-15), for which the editor desired to find a home. Now, when can these oracles have been written? Are they pre-Exilic, late-Exilic, or post-Exilic? The relevant historical facts are briefly these. Kausmalaka and Malik-rammu, kings of Edom, paid tribute, the one to Tiglath-Pileser III., the other to Sennacherib. Sargon accuses Edom (as well as Judah) of plotting sedition. Tiglath-Pileser III. received tribute from Zabibiye and Samsiye, queens of Aribi or N. Arabia, and Sargon, Sennacherib, Esarhaddon, and Assurbanipal are all recorded to have warred against Arabian tribes. We also learn that when Samas-sum-ukin, king of Babylon, rebelled against Assurbanipal (see p. 124), he received the support of Melucha [1] (N.W. Arabia) as well as Phœnicia and Palestine. From the Babylonian period few notices have reached us. According to Jer. xxvii. 3, the king of Edom was among the princes who (in 593) joined Zedekiah, king of Judah, in rebelling against Nebuchadrezzar, and from Jer. xlix. 7, 8, 28 (if Jeremiah's), we may infer that the chastising hand of this king was much dreaded both by Edom and by the tribes of Dedan and Kedar.

Which of these pre-Exilic periods shall we select? We may safely put aside the age of the Assyrian kings before Assurbanipal. Winckler, who assigns *vv.* 1-10 to the time of this king, not unnaturally refers the two following oracles to the same period,[2] when a Hebrew prophet had good reason to be interested in the fate of Babylon and its allies (see above). An earlier date is no doubt improbable. But the Aramaic colouring is more favourable to a still later one—

---

[1] Winckler, *Gesch.*, pp. 55, 265.   [2] *Untersuch.*, pp. 37, 122.

the period of Nebuchadrezzar, whom, as Jeremiah shows, Edom and (it would seem) the Arabian tribes had reason to dread. On this hypothesis, we may date the two oracles in the year 589, when Nebuchadrezzar moved into Syria and despatched his troops against the populations of Palestine. It may be objected that in 588 Edom purchased by its malignant conduct the undying hatred of the Jews. That is true, but cannot destroy the fact that, shortly before, Judah and Edom were allies. Nor can it be said that *vv.* 11-12 reveal any sympathy with Edom ; there is no hatred visible, but no cordiality (Edomitish incursions had put hearty friendship out of the question).[1] And my contention is simply this, that a late Exilic[2] or post-Exilic is less probable than a pre-Exilic date, because of that equilibrium of feeling in the prophet which, if it prevents cordiality, not less forbids positive hostility (see on chap. xxxiv.). I would not, however, presume to dogmatise. It is not quite inconceivable that the two oracles may be fragments. In this case, we might conjecture that in their original form the oracle in xv. 1-xvi. 12 and those in xxi. 11-15 belonged to the same period, if not to the same author. The oracle in xxi. 11, 12, as it stands, is not sympathetic, but the recovery of a lost passage might lead us to modify this judgment ; the oracle in *vv.* 12, 13 does appear sympathetic, and is so far parallel to the elegy on Moab in xv.-xvi.

And now as to the (possibly) Isaianic portion, *vv.* 16-17. Observe that the " sons of Kedar " here take the place of the Dedanites (*v.* 13). The Kidrai are often mentioned with the people of Aribi in the Assyrian inscriptions.[3] The oracle may stand in connection with the conquest and transplantation to Samaria of various Arabian tribes by Sargon in 715 B.C. (*KIB*, ii. 43). Note, however, that the earliest Old Testament reference to Kedar, the date of which is certain, is in Jer. ii. 10.

[1] In 2 Ki. xxiv. 2 read " Edom " for " Aram " (Grätz, Klostermann, Buhl).
[2] So Eichhorn, Duhm, and virtually Vitringa and Lowth.
[3] Cf. *CI*, ii. 107 ; Del., *Paradies*, p. 299 ; Winckler, *Gesch.*, p. 288.

CHAPTER XXII. 1-14

Is this prophecy a whole? or does it consist of two independent passages fused together? *Vv.* 1-2*a* contain expostulation; *vv.* 2*b*-4 are like a small elegy,[1] in which the inevitable future is mourned over as if it were past; *v.* 5 is (in accordance with the analogy of parallel passages, such as ii. 12, xxxiv. 8) a prediction of calamity. Verses 6-14, on the other hand, contain a stern denunciation, based on a retrospect of past events. Hence one naturally asks whether the latter passage, or at least some part of it, may not have been transferred thither from a different context. Duhm has lately answered this question in the affirmative. He assigns *vv.* 1-7 to the beginning of the Sennacherib period, when Hezekiah had just asserted his independence of Assyria, and considers *vv.* 8-14 to be a portion of a later prophecy, delivered in view of a possible siege of Jerusalem. It seems difficult, however, to separate *vv.* 6-7 from *vv.* 8-14, and *v.* 13 certainly implies the same circumstances as *v.* 1. My own conclusion (see *BW*), offered with a full consciousness of the difficulty of these problems, is that something has dropped out of the text between *v.* 5 and *v.* 6, *v.* 6 and *v.* 7, and *v.* 7 and *v.* 8, and that the whole of the retrospect and denunciation in *vv.* 6-14 (except the prosaic interpolation *vv.* 9*b*-11*a*) is derived from another nearly contemporaneous prophecy, which, among other things, described the preparations of Hezekiah for a siege. I believe the occasion of both the prophetic passages which make up xxii. 1-14 to be the removal of the Assyrian blockade.[2] The same irreligious trust in mere outward means of defence which characterised the citizens on the approach of the Assyrians was still predominant at Jerusalem. Hence, as I said long ago, in *v.* 12 Isaiah describes a state of things which began in the past, but reaches into the present. "The Lord, Yahwè Çebaoth," called and still calls upon the citizens to repent, but instead of obeying the call they rushed (and again rush) to the

[1] Budde thinks that *vv.* 3, 4, in which he recognises "elegiac rhythm," are a later insertion (*ZATW*, 1882, p. 33).
[2] So independently Hackmann, *ZEJ*, pp. 96, 108.

housetops (*v.* 1) to gaze at the retiring Assyrians, and to the banquet-table to drown their apprehensions of a possible return of their enemies in sensuous luxury,—" behold, joy and gladness, killing oxen and slaughtering sheep, eating flesh and drinking wine, eating and drinking, for to-morrow (say they) we may die " (*v.* 13). I agree with Duhm that *vv.* 9*b*-11*a* were most probably inserted by a learned student of Isaiah (cf. 2 Chron. xxxii. 2-5, 30), who had the post-Exilic passion for completeness, but did not perceive that his enumeration of details drew the attention away from the main point.[1] In the passage which has dropped out between *v.* 5 and *v.* 6 I conjecture that some other peoples represented in the Assyrian army were mentioned. The Elamites were by no means loyal subjects of the Assyrians, and are never referred to in the inscriptions as serving in an Assyrian army. It is not likely that Elam and Kir were sent by themselves to blockade Jerusalem.[2] If, however, the text is right as it stands, there is no choice but to suppose an interpolation. For if it is in itself a startling statement that Elam furnished warriors to an Assyrian army, it is more than startling to be told that Elam and its neighbours were entrusted with such a duty as the blockade of Jerusalem.[3]

Here a reference is due to the objections of Hackmann.[4] This able critic coincides with me (against Duhm) in assigning the whole of the section to one period (the retirement of the Assyrians from before Jerusalem), but disagrees with Duhm (and therefore with me) on the question of disintegration. This arises chiefly from a difference in our exegesis, but partly also from a difference in our view of the rhythm of the section. The situation, as deduced from the exegetical data of xxii. 1-14 as a whole, seems to him clear ; to me it seems obscure. He is right (see above) in admitting a connection between *v.* 7 and *v.* 8 ; Duhm is, I

[1] A few rare words occur. תחתן, 1 Ki. vi. 6, Ezek. (5 times) ; but cf. use of עליון, vii. 3. בצר, "to fortify," Jer. li. 53. מקנה ἅπ. λεγ. ; מקוה, Gen. i. 10, Ex. vii. 19, Lev. xi. 36 (*not* 1 Ki. x. 28, 2 Chron. i. 16, corrupt places). שער, Cant. vii. 14, Lev. (twice), Neh. (twice, of a gate).
[2] I retract my former view of *v.* 5*b* in spite of what Winckler has said in *Untersuch.*, pp. 177-9.
[3] See Friedr. Del., *Paradies*, p. 237, quoted in *PI*, i. 132.
[4] *ZEJ*, p. 94.

believe, mistaken in beginning a new fragment at v. 8. But Hackmann can scarcely be right in maintaining the unbroken connection of vv. 1-7. V. 5 is predictive, v. 6 historically descriptive. V. 5 says, Yahwè has decreed the destruction of Jerusalem, and already I see ("in the spirit") the wall being undermined and hear cries of lamentation. V. 6 describes the arrival of the enemy, and the measures tardily taken by the citizens for their own protection. Indeed, Hackmann himself admits that a new "thought-section" begins with v. 5b (he should, I think, have said with v. 6a). With regard to the rhythm or metre, that this is not always visible owing to the imperfections of the text may be admitted. But the rhythm of vv. 1-5 is surely clear enough (in v. 5 בְּגֵי חִזָּיוֹן belongs to b, as Duhm points out); and so, too, is that of vv. 11b-14.

The date here given differs from that proposed in *PI*, where I explained this as well as the "Arial" prophecy (chap. xxix.) with reference to a supposed invasion of Sargon. This explanation is still given by Sayce (*Times of Isaiah*, p. 60), and Dillmann admits that it would remove all the difficulties of the prophecy more easily than any other, if it could be historically justified. Not the least of these difficulties, as I maintained, was the severe tone of the prophecy. If it belonged, as had been generally supposed, to the invasion of Sennacherib, it was no easy matter to account for it, "as the tone of Isaiah at that great crisis was one of consolation and promise."[1] Cornill said in 1884 that he could not explain "this fundamental contradiction."[2] It appeared to me that the acceptance of Sargon's statement that he was the "subduer of Judah" in the sense once ascribed to the phrase by Schrader, and still given to it by Sayce, removed this difficulty. "The circumstances of the prophet were very probably different in the two invasions. In the latter one there was probably a union of feeling and purpose between the king and the prophet; the preaching, too, of the latter had probably produced some effect on the better minds." It seemed to me that it must have been otherwise in the time of Sargon (cf. on chap. i. in *PI*). Hence "finding the prophecy of Ariel ineffectual as a means of moral quickening, Isaiah may have deliberately chosen

---
[1] *PI*, i. 132.   [2] *ZATW*, 1884, p. 97.

this harder and sharper tone under the double pressure of calamity and opposition." Nor did it seem to me that this view was inconsistent with the reference to Elam in v. 6. For the Annals of Sargon show that a district or province of Elam was annexed by that king as early as 721.[1]

The absence, however, of any decisive proof of an invasion of Sargon compelled me to revert to the old view that it was the blockade of Jerusalem by Sennacherib's general which was referred to—the blockade which is so accurately described in the Prism inscription.[2] We shall have occasion to refer to this later (see on chaps. xxxvi.-xxxix.). It was the blockade which, joined to the other calamities of the invasion, induced Hezekiah to send a heavy tribute to Lachish, or to promise to send it after Sennacherib to Nineveh. This is the point of time to which I venture to refer Isa. xxii. 1-14. Oppressive as the exactions of the Assyrian king may be, Hezekiah has yielded to them, and orders have been sent from Lachish for the withdrawal of the blockading force. The last Assyrian warriors are disappearing from view, and in the rebound from despair to hope the citizens of Jerusalem give expression to the wildest joy. But all the while they know (this feature is derived from the second of the two prophetic fragments), and the prophet knows, that Assyrian good faith is not to be implicitly trusted, "to-morrow we may die" (v. 13). And Isaiah, indignant at their impenitence, assures them that they *will* die, that their sin is indeed a sin unto death (v. 14), for the captivity which awaits them is death to all nationalities which have not the one solid religious basis. Such is Isaiah's lofty prophetic passion. It is not inconsistent with the deepest patriotic sorrow. Isaiah (at least in the first fragment) sits apart, and weeps " for the destruction of the maiden his people" (v. 4), which cannot long be averted.

For the benefit of those who may still stand nearly where I stood myself in 1880 as a critic of Isaiah, I venture to add that the view just given of xxii. 1-14 greatly lightens the difficulty pointed out in *PI*. As long as the city needs his sympathy, and observes at any rate the outward forms of

[1] *KIB*, ii. 94, 95 ; *CI*, i. 283, 286.   [2] Cf. v. 13, 14.

piety (cf. i. 12-15), Isaiah is compelled to blend comfort with threatening, and to paint a fair prospect of better times. But now that this small and imperfect deliverance (so far below what he had hoped for, see chap. xxix.) becomes the occasion of irreligious mirth, Isaiah's passionate love expresses itself in a single mighty threatening word, which may perchance bring the people to a better mind. Thus the change in his tone is simply the effect of bitter disappointment; it may perhaps be only temporary. The answer to the question whether, as a fact, he did change his tone again, depends on our view of the date of chaps. xxxiii. and xxxvii. 22-32 (if these sections are Isaianic). Of course, however, there is a still simpler explanation of the "fundamental contradiction" (p. 134), viz. to deny its existence, on the ground of a critical analysis of chaps. xxviii.-xxxi.

CHAPTER XXII. 15-25

An invective against the "vizier" of the day (Shebna), followed by a promise of his office to a worthier man (Eliakim), to which another appendix is attached, announcing this second vizier's fall. According to Delitzsch, "the prophet wrote down *vv.* 15-25 at one sitting, after the fate of both dignitaries, revealed to him at two different times, had found its fulfilment." This is obviously the result of critical prejudice. Once admit that other hands have touched Isaiah's work, and we need not reject Hitzig's very natural conjecture that *vv.* 24 and 25 are a later prosaic addition. But, if so, who made this addition? Isaiah, after Eliakim had failed to justify the trust reposed in him? The difficulty in this view is that *vv.* 19-23 are themselves an appendix which corrects *vv.* 15-18 in a very material point. As a matter of fact, Shebna's overthrow was not accompanied by the punishment of captivity; he simply fell from one office to another (xxxvi. 3). *V.* 19 therefore simply states that Shebna shall be driven from his present post. Now, we can hardly believe that Isaiah supplemented and partly corrected his original prophecy twice over. Did he even do this once? Is he really the author of *vv.* 19-23? In *PI*, i. 138, I have spoken of the "strong language, almost Messianic in its tone, with which Isaiah hails in spirit the elevation of his disciple Eliakim." Certainly the enthusiasm in these verses is remarkable. But v. 23 at any rate is very awkwardly expressed, and hardly worthy of the great prophet. And the whole passage (vv. 19-25) is full of uncommon words, such as כְּתֹנֶת, אַבְנֵט, מֶמְשָׁלָה [1] (cf. xxxix. 2), אָב (official title, Gen. xlv. 8), בֵּית יְהוּדָה (again in the disputed passage, xxxvii. 31), צֶאֱצָאִים (only in Job and in late parts of Isaiah), צְפָעוֹת, אַגָּנוֹת. On the whole, Duhm is most probably right in assigning vv. 19-25 to two later hands.

The question still remains, What is the date of vv. 15-18? We need not doubt that the prophecy does relate (as the misplaced words in v. 15[2] represent) to Shebna, and that he was the predecessor of Eliakim in the prefectship of the palace. His name suggests that he was Syrian, and we may reasonably suppose that he was a leader of those "crooked" politicians (xxx. 12) who looked for salvation to an Egyptian alliance. Isaiah's invective against him may therefore synchronise with the prophecies against that alliance (cf. v. 18 with xxviii. 17-19, xxx. 12-14), and must at any rate have preceded the prophecy in vv. 1-14, unless indeed the circumstances described in xxxvi. 2-xxxvii. 7 (in which passage Eliakim appears as "over the palace" and Shebna as the "secretary") belong to a perfidious reappearance of the Assyrians before Jerusalem after Hezekiah had bought them off. The latter is the view of G. Rawlinson and G. A. Smith (see on chap. xxxiii.). Isaiah's mood, according to these scholars, changed after the deliverance of Jerusalem. In spite of his strong expressions in vv. 1-14, he came to believe that a change of viziers would avert the threatened destruction of the state. I cannot, however, see any cogent reason for this view, even on the assumption that vv. 15-23 (25) are altogether Isaiah's work. The prospect held out in vv. 1-14 is a black, yawning

[1] מ׳ occurs in twelve certainly Exilic and post-Exilic passages, and in Isa. xxii. 21, Mic. iv. 8. The latter passage being (with vv. 6-7) a late insertion (see Kuenen, Ond.², § 74), the case for the late date of Isa. xxii. 21 (and its context) becomes very strong. Cf. Giesebr., ZATW, i. 243.

[2] עַל־שבנא וגו׳, "concerning Shebna who was over the palace."

gulf, into which the whole nation descends; in *vv.* 15-23 (25) the removal of Shebna (and his fellows) by a deserved captivity, and then a peaceful reform initiated by a worthy vizier. This picture closely resembles that in i. 24-26, which, as we have seen, belongs to the time before the siege of Jerusalem, before that black abyss opened before Isaiah's visionary eyes, into which the entire guilty nation was to descend. But, as it seems to me, the critical analysis puts this improbable theory out of the question.

CHAPTER XXIII

Evidently this chapter is composite.[1] *Vv.* 1-14 form a prophetic elegy in three strophes, each of which may originally have had seven lines, like the strophes of the odes in chaps. xiv., xlvii. (*V.* 5 is evidently a prosaic gloss.) Then follows, ill-connected with the elegy by the loose formula "In that day," a passage (*vv.* 15-18) altogether in prose, except the little dance-song professedly quoted in *v.* 16. The appendix ends in bathos, which we would not willingly impute to the poet of the elegy. Thus, the chapter consists of two parts, one artistic, the other inartistic. These two parts have no points of contact in language, imagery, or subject-matter, and it cannot be called arbitrary to hold that *vv.* 15-18 are a later addition.—We have now to ask when the appendix was added. In reply, one may think first of all (supposing *vv.* 1-14, or the main part of it, to be Isaianic) of the closing years of the ministry of Jeremiah, who expects a seventy years' captivity of "these nations," as well as of Israel (Jer. xxv. 11), and extends the promise of restoration to the neighbours of Israel, on condition that they accept the religion of Yahwè (Jer. xii. 14-17). But it is still more natural to think of the restoration period, when the poverty of the Jews was extreme (Hag. i.; ii. 17; Zech. iii. 12), and when the bitterness of disappointment for a time so sadly lowered the tone of Jewish idealism. When *vv.* 15-18 were

---

[1] So *ICA*, p. 56, following Eichhorn and Ewald.

written, the Jews were strangers to the catholicity of Ps. lxxxvii. 4 [1] (early Greek period ?). It was now not so much the conversion as the destruction or subjugation of the peoples which was their central hope (Hag. ii. 22 ; cf. Isa. lx. 11, 12, lxi. 5, late). It angered them to see the Tyrians, who had fallen behind under Babylon, once more at the height of prosperity (cf. Hag. ii. 7, 8). They were obliged indeed to traffic with them (Ezra iii. 7 ; Neh. xiii. 16), but none the less disliked and despised them, somewhat as fanatical Moslems dislike and despise the Western races to-day. Hence the writer of the appendix takes from Nahum (iii. 5, 6) and Ezekiel (xvi. 37, xxiii. 10, etc.) the disparaging figure of the harlot, and applies it to Tyre (contrast v. 12, and see Ges.) ; he consoles himself for Tyre's prosperity by picturing the Tyrians pouring their treasures at the feet of Yahwè's people (cf. xviii. 7, late). Observe, too, that like another supplementer of prophecy (see xix. 19), he does not scruple to transgress the letter of a Deuteronomic precept (cf. v. 18a with Deut. xxiii. 18).—As to the phraseology. There are no distinctively Isaianic expressions. סְחֹרָה, v. 18, is suggested by vv. 2, 3, 8 (סחר) occurs nowhere else in the generally accepted prophecies ; but cf. xlv. 14, xlvii. 15). On the other hand, note מְקַץ (and cf. the parallel passage Ezek. xxix. 13) ; יֵחָסֵן (the only example of the verb) ; מְכַסֶּה (late, see on xiv. 11) ; עָתִיק ἅπ. λεγ. ; also the combination of the literal and the figurative expression for " gains " in v. 18, and the lengthy phrase at the end of v. 17 with אֲדָמָה in the non-Isaianic sense of " earth " (see on xxiv. 21b).

A greater problem remains,—Was the prophetic ode in vv. 1-14 really written by Isaiah ? Certainly not, if v. 13 (the phraseology of which is altogether un-Isaianic) comes from the same hand as the rest of the poem. But can we venture to affirm that it does ? The meaning of vv. 1-12 is on the whole clear and the connection natural, but the meaning of v. 13 is not clear, nor does the verse fit into the context. Fairly translated, it runs as follows :—

Behold the land of Chaldæa ; yonder people is no more ;
Assyria hath appointed it (viz. the land) for desert-beasts ;

---

[1] See Bl., pp. 118-119, 296.

They have set up its (viz. yonder people's) siege towers; they have razed the palaces thereof (viz. of the land); He (Assyria) hath made it (the land) a ruin.

Certainly, this does not make sense. Let us, then, suppose an interpolation, and cast out זה העם לא היה אשור[1] as a gloss = "this is the people, it was not Assyria (which destroyed Tyre)." How will the verse do then?

Behold the land of Chaldæa; he hath appointed it for desert-beasts;
They have set up his (= their) siege-towers; they have razed the palaces thereof;
He hath made it a ruin.

Taking *v.* 13 with *v.* 11, we might now suppose the poet to mean that the destroyer of Canaan's fortresses will be the land or people (cf. xviii. 1, 2; Ezek. xiv. 13) of Chaldæa. And no doubt this is the sense, but how awkwardly it is expressed, and how ill the passage fits into the context! Why does the writer use such an ambiguous phrase as "the land of Chaldæa," when his meaning is, not that the land of Chaldæa, but that the land of Canaan or Phœnicia was destroyed? Surely, "Behold, the king (or, the host) of Chaldæa," is what we should naturally expect. Shall we then try another conjecture, and change כשדים into כנען (or, against usage, כנענים)?[2] Thus emended, the verse may give the tidings spoken of in *v.* 1; it may even be "a sarcastic cry from the Cyprian colonists, who, as Menander in Josephus (*Ant.*, ix. 14, 2) tells us, had lately revolted from the parent state" (cf. *v.* 12 end).[3] I doubt, however, whether

[1] That אַשּׁוּר goes with הָיָה is also the view of Targ. and Pesh.
[2] Cheyne, *Notes and Criticisms on the Hebrew Text of Isaiah* (1868), p. 25. "Thou shalt have no rest" will in this case mean that the citizens of Citium refuse hospitality to their former lords. But another interpretation is more probable. We know that Sargon received tribute from the kings of Cyprus, for the stele on which their names are engraved is preserved at Berlin. The prophet may have looked forward to the partial conquest thus commemorated.
[3] כנענים, not כנען, is Ewald's conjecture (1837), adopted by Schrader (de Wette's *Einl.*[8], 1869), by myself in *ICA* (1870), by Orelli (1887), and by Del. (1889). Dillmann, too, finds it plausible (1890). The grounds on which in *PI* (1880) I reverted to כשדים were Assyriological. E. Meier and Duhm prefer to read פְּתָיִים (cf. *v.* 12), supplying the reason

CHAPTER XXIII

this is a very plausible supposition. It seems much better to admit that *v.* 13 as it stands is not by the writer of the original poem.

Isaiah's work *v.* 13 certainly cannot be, on phraseological grounds. The particle הֵן is not found again in a certainly Isaianic passage (xxxii. 1 and xxxiii. 7 being both probably late), and occurs, at least, fifteen times (Nægelsbach reckons twenty-one times) in chs. xl.-lxvi., and thirty-two times, according to Budde, in Job. It is, however, a good old Hebrew word (found seven times in J), and we may admit that Isaiah may possibly have closed a prophetic ode by a passage beginning הֵן אֶרֶץ כַּ[נַעַן], though "Canaan" for "Phœnicia" is an unique usage. But the rest of the verse, even in its shortened form, must be post-Isaianic. To begin with, a clear parallel for יָסַד "to appoint" is wanting. צִיִּים is post-Exilic in use (see *BL*, p. 477, on Ps. lxxii. 9). בַחִין or בַחוּן[1] and the form עֹרֵר ("to overthrow") are ἅπ. λεγ.; while מַפֵּלָה only occurs again in xxv. 2, late (but cf. מַפָּלָה, xvii. 1). The style may be vigorous, but similar short word-groups occur in xxi. 1-5, xxxii. 14, which are not Isaianic. Notice, too, the unpleasing change of number. If we assume *vv.* 1-14, in some form or other, to be Isaianic, we must suppose that the editor's copy of the poem became illegible at this point, and that he "restored" the passage in accordance with his own interpretation of the prophecy (viz. that Nebuchadrezzar's siege in 586-573 is intended).[2] In doing so, he may have used up any still legible words or letters. The general purport of the passage may have been suggested by Ezek. xxvi. 8-12; the short word-groups of *v.* 13 are like abbreviations of Ezekiel's more elaborate sentences. And we may admit that, except in the mention of Chaldæa, and perhaps in the completeness which he ascribes to the destruction of Tyre, the editor may have hit the meaning of the poet. For surely we do require some direct reference to the effect of the command in *v.* 11.

for the statement made in *v.* 12. König's reference to myself (*Einl.*, p. 320) needs correction.

[1] Cf. בַּחַן, xxxii. 14 (late), also ἅπ. λεγ.

[2] If the editor thought that Tyre was stormed and destroyed by the Chaldæans, he was of course mistaken (Ezek. xxix. 18). Cf. Pietschmann, *Gesch. der Phönizier*, p. 306; Meyer, *GA*, i. 595.

We saw just now that *v.* 13 as it stands is not by the author of the original poem, and that it was written after 573. Consequently, the original poem is pre-Jeremianic, and we may now consider the claims of Isaiah to the complete or partial authorship of the poem (excluding *v.* 13). (1) Let us first examine the ideas of this prophetic elegy. We cannot expect to find many; the few that exist cannot be called un-Isaianic. National faults, according to Isaiah, bring national punishments, and "all ships of Tarshish" are included in ii. 16 among the symbols of a proud and irreligious civilisation. It is the idea that the proudest human things must be brought low, which the prophet sees about to be realised in the case of Tyre, and which, being also a poet, he expresses in a strikingly artistic contrast between what Tyre has been and what she is about to become; and in the course of the poem he suggests rather than directly asserts that Tyre has brought ruin upon herself by her moral faults. So far as the ideas go, therefore, the poem may conceivably be Isaiah's work.—(2) Phraseology. Points of contact with Isaiah are not wanting. *V.* 1, הֵילִילוּ, cf. xiv. 31. *V.* 2, יֹשְׁבֵי אִי, cf. xx. 6 (where, however, אִי seems to mean all Palestine; here it means the Phœnician coast). *V.* 4, גִּדֵּל וְרוֹמֵם, cf. i. 2. *V.* 8, יָעַץ, cf. xiv. 24, 27. *V.* 11, נָטָה יָדוֹ, cf. v. 25, etc. *V.* 12, בְּתוּלַת בַּת, cf. i. 8. Note also מָעוּז, בַּחוּרִים, עָלָיו, מֵרָחוֹק, גָּאוֹן, צְבִי, הֶקֶל. But, on the other hand, there are these not less striking non-Isaianic features. לָמוֹ (*v.* 1) is suspicious; the form occurs again in xxx. 5, but the text there is probably wrong (see *RT*). See "linguistic phenomena of chs. xl.-lxvi." דָּמַם "to be silent" (*v.* 2), here only in Isaiah, but cf. on xxx. 18. מִלֵּא Piel, here only in Isa., xxxiii. 5, and lxv. 11, 20 being late. שִׁחוֹר (*v.* 3), the most easterly of the arms of the Nile (Josh. xiii. 3; 1 Chr. xiii. 5), but here (as Jer. ii. 18) the Nile itself. כִּנְעָנֶיהָ (*v.* 8), from כִּנְעָנִים = כְּנַעֲנִים "merchants,"[1] Job xl. 30; Prov. xxxi. 24 (sing.);

[1] There is no parallel for this in pre-Exilic literature. In Hos. xii. 8 read, with Wellh., "he dealeth like Canaan," *i.e.* like the travelling Phœnician traders, who in Zeph. i. 11 are actually called עַם כְּנַעַן. The first example of the applied use of 'כ is in Ezekiel's phrase אֶרֶץ כְּנַעַן (xvi. 29 ?- xvii. 4) for "land of traffic" = Chaldæa, because Babylon, in the time of its imperial glory, became a greater commercial centre than Tyre.

Zech. xiv. 21 (sing.), all most probably late. מְזִח "dike" (v. 10), it is barely possible, may be an Egyptian loan-word (Lag.). בְּנַעַן "Phœnicia" (v. 11); nowhere else in O.T. in this sense. מָעֻזְנֶיהָ (v. 11), probably a corruption from מעוזה (see critical note on Ps. lx. 7). מָעֻזִּים elsewhere only in Dan. xi. 19, 38, 39; יָבַל, v. 7 (elsewhere only xviii. 7). Notice also the unclassical peculiarities of v. 5 (cf. xxiv. 9a), and of the gloss in v. 3. On סחר, vv. 2, 3, 8 (see above, on appendix), I of course lay no stress.

On the whole, we must conclude either that the poem is by a later writer who knew Isaiah's writings well, but was no mere imitator, or that it was really written by Isaiah, but was retouched with no sparing hand by a post-Exilic editor,[1] who has in several places taken suggestions from Ezek. xxvi.-xxvii.[2] The former alternative attracted Ewald, who (cf. on ch. xxxiii.) made the author a younger disciple of Isaiah. The latter, which has been adopted by Dillmann, seems to me more plausible. The fate of Tyre can hardly have interested Isaiah less than that of Damascus and Philistia; he would hardly have left it to be described by a younger disciple. This point, however, is not one which is susceptible of a rigorous decision. At any rate, it is clear that, if the original elegy is as old as the age of Isaiah, it has been very imperfectly handed down, and it is not surprising that some good critics should regard chap. xxiii. as altogether late (see p. 145).

On what occasion may such an Isaianic prophecy or poem have been written? In other words, which of the Assyrian kings may Isaiah have expected to be Tyre's conqueror? At first I supposed the reference to be to Shalmaneser IV.,[3] whose two attempts upon Tyre are mentioned in a passage of Menander's history (Jos., Ant., ix. 14, 2). The first of these attempts was altogether successful; the second, begun in 725-24, was terminated, as one may infer from Menander, in 720-19, but not in a manner gratifying to Assyrian pride. The latter

---

[1] To this editor we must impute the unpleasing repetition of וְכָבֵּי in v. 9. V. 5, however, which is unusually poor in style, is probably a late marginal note (see Duhm and Dillmann).

[2] So at v. 13 (see above); also at v. 2a (cf. Ezek. xxvii. 35), and at v. 3 (cf. Ezek. xxvii. 33).

[3] See ICA, pp. 55-56, 238-239.

is alone referred to in the Assyrian inscriptions—allusively. Shalmaneser must have died during the blockade; it was Sargon who brought the operations to a close. Probably, however, he had to content himself with a payment of tribute and a recognition of his suzerainty by the Tyrians. This is the natural inference from the words of Menander (Jos., *l.c.*), and from the modest claim of Sargon in the cylinder inscription (l. 21) that he "pacified" Kuë (Cilicia) and Tyre.[1] This comparative defeat was however more than counterbalanced by the victory over the Egyptians at Raphia in 720. Now, the events of these five years supply an adequate occasion for the original prophecy of Isaiah (which of course did not include *v.* 13 as it now stands). It is perfectly true that Sennacherib made a successful campaign against Luli king of Sidon (as Sennacherib represents) and also (as Menander calls him) king of Tyre in 702,[2] and Isaiah might possibly have referred to this, in spite of the fact that the inscriptions do not mention Tyre among the subjugated cities. But why should we prefer the second occasion to the first? Surely *v.* 7 (which one may reasonably hold to be Isaianic) expresses the prophet's feelings when the idea of an Assyrian conquest of Tyre first suggested itself to his mind. One reason, and one only, induced the present writer to adopt the second hypothesis in *PI*, viz. that he wished to explain the reference to Chaldæa in *v.* 13 without assuming an interpolation. "Behold, the land of Chaldæa; this people is no more," appeared to him to refer to Sennacherib's devastation of Babylonia in 703, an event which Isaiah might well have

---

[1] So Winckler, Peiser, and Schrader (glossary to *CI*). There is a doubt, however, as to the meaning of *ušapšiḫu*, which Schrader (*CI*, i. 157, ii. 101) renders "delivered from their oppression." In 1870 Sayce rendered, "(he) destroyed" (*ICA*, p. 239), and in 1878 Schrader himself rendered, "(he) subjugated" (*Keilinschr. und Gesch.-forschung*, p. 238).

[2] See Schrader, *CI*, i. 284; *RP* (new series), vi. 88, and cf. Tiele, *Bab.-ass. Gesch.*, pp. 237, 289, 314. Meyer (*GA*, i. 467) and Winckler (*Gesch.*, pp. 234, 334) think this to be the campaign referred to by Menander (Jos. *l.c.*). True, Niese's revised text of Josephus gives not ἐπὶ τούτους πέμψας (*text. rec.*), but ἐπὶ τούτου Σελάμψας (= Shalmaneser); see Schrader, *Zur Geographie des ass. Reiches* (Berlin Academy), p. 20. But this, it is urged, may be an error of Josephus. Tiele's view, however, still seems to me more probable.

regarded as foreshadowing the fate of Phœnicia. But he recognises now that a warning like this would not (in so lucid a context) have been expressed so enigmatically.

Other solutions of the critical problem. According to Hitzig, Movers, Bleek, Cornill, chap. xxiii. belongs entirely to the age, if not to the authorship of Jeremiah. With this critically difficult, but, at first sight, plausible view, Eichhorn, Vatke, and König agree, so far as concerns *vv.* 1-14, but they refer *vv.* 15-18 to the Persian period. Kuenen, "after long hesitation," claims *vv.* 1-14 for Isaiah, but regards *vv.* 15-18 as post-Exilic. Stade, *Gesch.*, ii. 208, refers the whole chapter to the age of Alexander. It was left for Duhm to treat *vv.* 1-14 as an elegy on the destruction of *Sidon* by Artaxerxes Ochus in 349 (see on chs. xxiv.-xxvii.). The elegy, he thinks, was altered by an editor (who also wrote the appendix) as well as he could, into a poem on the capture of Tyre by Alexander in 332. This view obliges Duhm to alter "Tyre" in *v.* 8 into "Sidon"; it appears to me the outcome of an unnecessary despair.

CHAPTERS XXIV.-XXVII

This singular production, which at first repels but at length fascinates the student, has no heading, and claims no famous prophet of old time as its author. That it should be Isaiah's, is philologically and psychologically impossible; both language and ideas are opposed to such a hypothesis. How is it, then, that such a scholar as Delitzsch can say (in his first three editions) that, with all its peculiarities, the whole is fundamentally and in a hundred details so Isaianic that it is arbitrary to deny Isaiah's authorship because of those peculiarities? It is clear that Delitzsch must have had some plausible grounds for this statement. Let us search for these in xxv. 6-8, 10, 11, and xxvii. 9-13, passages which may be presumed to make somewhat for his view, since Ewald too regarded them as Isaianic.[1] If it should appear upon the whole very improbable that even these passages are Isaiah's,

[1] *Die Lehre der Bibel von Gott*, iii. 444 note.

we shall have dealt a severe blow not only to Delitzsch's (original) theory that chaps. xxiv.-xxvii. are altogether Isaianic, but to Ewald's that the bulk of the prophecy is late, though fragments of Isaiah's work are embedded in it. Let us begin with the former passage. How vigorous and (in *vv.* 6-8) how picturesque it is! But except the word מַסֵּכָה, *v.* 7 (cf. xxviii. 20), and the concluding formula (cf. i. 20, xxi. 17), there is nothing specially Isaianic in the diction (בָּלַע, *v.* 7, = " to swallow up," but in iii. 12 " to confound "). On the other hand, note the ἅπ. λεγ. שְׂמָרִים, שְׁמָרִים, מָחָה (11.), אֲרָבָה, מַדְמֵנָה, מַתְבֵּן, לוֹט, besides the novel use of the part. מְזֻקָּק. The ideas, moreover, as we shall see, are un-Isaianic. Let us pass now to the latter passage. Isaianic features of the vocabulary are—סָעִיף "branch" (xvii. 6) in *v.* 10, שִׁבֹּלֶת and לֶקֶט (xvii. 5) in *v.* 12. Some critics will add—עִיר בְּצוּרָה (xxxvii. 26) in *v.* 10, חָבַט (xxviii. 27 of fennel) in *v.* 12, and the reference to the *ashêrîm* and the *ḥammânîm* (xvii. 8) in *v.* 9, but all these are highly doubtful phenomena. And though the "trumpet" in *v.* 13 may remind us of xviii. 3, and the picture in *vv.* 10-11 of *v.* 17, the attentive student will notice that the parallelism is by no means complete ; *vv.* 10, 11 are more closely akin to xxxii. 13, 14 (in a disputed section). Add to this that the description of the exiles as "outcasts" in *v.* 13 and the mention of Assyria and Egypt as the lands of exile suggest comparison with xi. 11, 12, which can hardly be Isaianic. Other phenomena are distinctly unfavourable to an early date. Notice in *v.* 10 בָּדָד (not common anywhere), נָוֶה (cf. xxxii. 18, xxxiii. 20, xxxiv. 13, xxxv. 7, lxv. 10 ; also, however, in Hos. ix. 13), מְשֻׁלָּח "driven away," of the city, metonymically (as xvi. 2, 'ק' מ) ; in *v.* 11 הֵאִיר "to set on fire" (cf. Mal. i. 10),[1] and בִּינוֹת, parallel to חָכְמוֹת, תְּבוּנוֹת, and other late abstract fem. plurs. of the gnomic style (cf. Stade, *Lehrb.* § 313*b*) ; in *v.* 12 שִׁבֹּלֶת, if rendered "stream" (cf. Ps. lxix. 3, 16), and לְאַחַד אֶחָד (cf. Eccles. vii. 27) ; in *v.* 13 the pathetic epithet אֹבְדִים (cf. Deut. xxvi. 5, Ezek. xxxiv. 4, 16, Ps. cxix. 176), the Exilic and post-Exilic phrase הַר הַקֹּדֶשׁ (cf. Ezek. xxviii.

---

[1] *HL* compares also Ps. xviii. 29, but here הֵאִיר rather = " to make to shine." Note that אוּר " fire " is probably late in use (see p. 204).

14; Zech. viii. 3; Dan. ix. 20, xi. 4). Nor must we overlook the un-Isaianic meditative tone of *v.* 9.

We may therefore with some confidence reject both the theories mentioned above, a course for which fresh reasons will soon suggest themselves. A third theory is that of Bredenkamp, viz. that the bulk of the prophecy is Isaiah's, but that some passages may have been inserted later, viz. xxv. 1-5, 9, 12; xxvi. 8-13, 20, 21; xxvii. 2-6. There is no doubt a certain plausibility in this theory. These passages, being partly lyric, partly meditative, are specially unlike Isaiah. And when we look into the phraseology, our first impression is confirmed. Of the Isaianic parallels which a conservative critic might adduce, the greater part occurs in much disputed prophecies. Thus, in xxv. 2 we have גַּל and קִרְיָה בְּצוּרָה (xxxvii. 26); in *v.* 3 עַז "fierce" (xix. 4), and עָרִיץ (xxix. 5, 20, and perhaps also xi. 4); in *v.* 4 רוּחַ "angry blast" (xxx. 28, xxxiii. 11); in *v.* 5 צָיוֹן (xxxii. 2); cf. also the imagery of xxv. 4, 5 with that of iv. 6, xxxii. 2; and that of xxvii. 6 with that of xxxvii. 31. Those in little disputed prophecies are very few. In xxv. 1 we have פֶּלֶא (ix. 5), מֵרָחוֹק (xxii. 11), and מִפְלָה (xvii. 1, pointed differently); in *v.* 4 אֶבְיוֹן of the Jewish people (xiv. 30, but the usage is characteristically post-Exilic); in xxvii. 4 שָׁמִיר שָׁיִת (cf. v. 6, ix. 17, but the asyndeton is un-Isaianic, cf. xxxii. 13, late). It is also true that the song in xxvii. 2-5 reminds us of that in v. 1-6. But we cannot venture to make these portions of the work later than the rest, simply because there are fewer Isaianic words. For striking Isaianic expressions are by no means common anywhere. The composition before us has indeed points of contact with Isaiah, but this is sufficiently accounted for by the literary culture of the writer or writers.

That we have to do with a work of a late and imitative literary period is confirmed by the existence of points of contact with other writers besides Isaiah. Here is a list of parallel passages. Compare xxiv. 1 with Nah. ii. 11;— *v.* 2 with Hos. iv. 9, Ezek. vii. 12, 13;—*v.* 4 with xxxiii. 9 (late), Hos. iv. 3, Joel i. 10;—*v.* 5 with Gen. ix. 5, 6, 16 (P);—*v.* 6 with Jer. xxiii. 10, Zech. v. 3; —*v.* 7 with Joel. i. 10, 12, 18;—*v.* 8 with v. 12, 14

(Isaiah);—*v.* 10 with xxiii. 1*b* (late);—*v.* 1·1 with xvi. 7-10 (late);—*v.* 13 with xvii. 6 (Isaiah);—*vv.* 14-16 with xlii. 10-12;—*v.* 16 with Hab. i. 4, 13, ii. 4 ("the righteous" = Israel), Ps. cxviii. 15, etc.;—*vv.* 17, 18 with Jer. xlviii. 43, 44;—*v.* 18 with Gen. vii. 11, viii. 2 (P);— *vv.* 19, 20 with xiii. 13 (late), i. 8 (Isaiah), Am. v. 2;—*v.* 21*b* with xxiii. 17 (end);—*v.* 23 with xxx. 26, lx. 19, Zech. xiv. 6, 7, 9 (all late passages).—On xxv. 1-5 see above, but cf. also *v.* 1 with Ex. xv. 2, Ps. cxviii. 28 (both late).—In ch. xxvi., comp. *v.* 1 with lx. 18, xxxiii. 21 (late); —*v.* 2 with Ps. cxviii. 19, 20;—*v.* 4 with xii. 2;—*v.* 7 (image) with Prov. ii. 9, v. 6, 21;—*v.* 9*b* (idiom) with xxiii. 5 (late);—*v.* 10 ("right things") with xxx. 10 (Isaiah), cf. lix. 14;—*v.* 13*a* with lxiii. 19;—*v.* 13*b* (idiom) with Ps. lvi. 5, 11;[1]—*v.* 14 with Ps. lxxxviii. 11;—*v.* 18 with lxvi. 7, 8;—*v.* 21 with Mic. i. 3.—On xxvii. 2-4, 12, 13, see above, and cf. *v.* 7 ("his smiter") with x. 20 (late).

In comparing the above parallels we may, it is true, be occasionally uncertain which is the original passage, and which the copy, but in many cases the conjecture is a reasonable one that the writers of both belong to the same period, and that that period is a late one. I have next to point to a number of unique or otherwise singular words, verbal forms, or phrases, supplementing the partial lists already given.[2] (1) The following are ἅπ. λεγ. שְׁאִיָּה (xxiv. 12), אָרִים (xxiv. 15?), רָזִי (xxiv. 16), פָּרַר, הִתְרֹעֲעָ, הִתְפּוֹרֵר, הִתְמוֹטֵט (xxiv. 19), אֲסֵפָה (xxiv. 22), אֹמֶן (xxv. 1), זָמִיר (xxv. 5), הֻשַּׁר (Hofal, xxvi. 1), צָקוּן (xxvi. 16? Dillm.), הָבָה (xxvi. 20), עֲקַלָּתוֹן (xxvii. 1), פָּמֵט (xxvii. 4), סַאסְאָה "scaring away" (xxvii. 8; cf. on שָׁאָא, xiv. 23), גֵּר (xxvii. 9; cf. גֵּירָא, Dan. v. 5). (2) Late uses of particles, etc. On the five following, see p. 257 f. (on chaps. xl.-lxvi.); לָמוֹ for לָהֶם, xxiv. 14, 16; בְּמוֹ Q're, xxv. 10; אַף, xxvi. 8, 9, 11; בַּל, xxvi. 10, 11, 14, 18; עֲדֵי, xxvi. 4; זוּלַת with suff., xxvi. 13. Note also זֶה as relative pron., xxv. 9, as in Ex. xiii. 8, Psalms (4), Prov. xxiii. 22, Job xv. 17, xix. 19 (Aram.); and כְּמוֹ in two successive verses, xxvi. 17,

---

[1] See *BL*, pp. 332-333.
[2] Here as elsewhere I include words found in what I hold to be glosses (see *BW*).

18. (3) Words or phrases late in use, and old words in late senses. xxiv. 1, עָוָה *pervertere, conturbare,* again only Lam. iii. 9 ;—*v.* 4, מָרוֹם of high social positions, as Eccles. x. 6 ;— *v.* 5, בְּרִית in religious sense, as eight times in II. Isaiah ; —*v.* 7, נֶאֱנַח, as Ezek. (4), Ex. ii. 23 (P), Lam. i. 8, 21, (part.) 4, 11, Joel i. 18, Prov. xxix. 2 (doubtful date); cf. אֲנָחָה, xxi. 2, xxxv. 10 (verb common in Aram.) ;—*v.* 10, תֹּהוּ, see on chaps. xl.-lxvi. (p. 253) ;—*v.* 11, צְוָחָה (Jer. xiv. 2, xlvi. 12, Ps. cxliv. 14 ; verb in xlii. 11 ; cf. Aram. צְוַח); עָרֵב, again only Judg. xix. 9 ;—*v.* 16, כָּנָף "an end (of the earth)" as xi. 14 (see p. 65) ;—צַדִּיק, *v.* 16 = Israel, cf. Ps. cxviii. 15, 20, etc. ;—*vv.* 18, 21, מָרוֹם "heaven," and *v.* 18, מוֹסָד (pl. c. masc.), see on chaps. xl.-lxvi. (p. 264) ;—*v.* 22, מַסְגֵּר "prison" (xlii. 7, Ps. cxlii. 8) ;—*v.* 23, לְבָנָה and חַמָּה, rare poet. words, also in xxx. 26 (late). In xxvi. 1, חֵל used as in Lam. ii. 8 ;—*v.* 3, יֵצֶר ("mind," new Heb. sense) ;—*v.* 4, עוֹלָמִים (plur., as in xlv. 17 *bis,* li. 9, four times in Psalms, once in Daniel and Ecclesiastes, also 1 Ki. viii. 12 = 2 Chron. vi. 1, 2 ; cf. עָלְמִין in Aram. parts of Daniel) ;[1] —*v.* 6, פַּעַם "foot," as xxxvii. 25, Ps. lvii. 7, lviii. 11, Cant. vii. 2 ;—*v.* 7, מֵישָׁרִים, as xxxiii. 15, xlv. 19, Proverbs (5), Psalms (7), and פֶּלֶס, as Prov. iv. 26, v. 6, 21 ;—in *v.* 10 רָשָׁע of non-Israelites ; see on xiii. 11 ;—in *v.* 12 שָׁפַת, rare, not used elsewhere in poetry or elevated prophecy (see *BL,* p. 469, on Ps. xxii. 16) ;—in *v.* 18 נָפַל "to be born" (nowhere else), and in *v.* 19 its causative, also הֵקִיץ of rising again, as Dan. xii. 2, and אוֹרוֹת "lights" (cf. אוֹרָה, Esth. viii. 16, Ps. cxxxix. 12, and in new Heb.; אוֹרִים Ps. cxxxvi. 7).—In xxvii. 1 לִוְיָתָן, twice in Job, twice in late Psalms ; בָּרִחַ "fugitive," as Job xxvi. 13, cf. Isa. xliii. 14 ; —in *v.* 6 הַבָּאִים (with ellipsis of הַיָּמִים ; see Eccles. ii. 16 ; accus. of time) ; שֹׁרֵשׁ Hif. "to strike root," as Job v. 3, Ps. lxxx. 10 ; cf. Poel, xl. 24 ;—in *v.* 8 הָגָה "to separate," as Prov. xxv. 4 (or read הֹגָה, from יָגָה, also late in use). For *vv.* 9-13 see above. Add the neglect of *waw* consecutive.

To this evidence from the vocabulary we must add that from the artificial character of the style. Note especially the singularity of many phrases (beginning with מרום

---

[1] Is the prevalence of the plur. form a sign of the enlarged later Jewish conception of time ? See, however, *BL,* p. 475.

עִם־הָאָרֶץ, xxiv. 4), the sixteen paronomasias [1] (see esp. xxiv. 1, 3, 4, 6, 16-19; xxv. 6, 10; xxvi. 3; xxvii. 7), the numerous rhymes (xxiv. 1, 8, 16; xxv. 1, 6, 7; xxvi. 2, 13, 20, 21; xxvii. 3, 5), the antitheses (xxiv. 4, 8, 19; xxvii. 7), the emphatic doubling of words (xxiv. 16; xxv. 1; xxvi. 3, 5, 15; xxvii. 5), characteristic also of II. Isaiah, which indicate a consciousness of poverty in the writer (or writers), and point to an age much later than that of the true Isaiah, and later even than that of the noble literary prophet whom we call the Second Isaiah.

This conclusion is confirmed by a study (I.) of the forms of representation, (II.) of the ideas, and (III.) of the social and religious circumstances described in the prophecy. I. The picture brought before us, though not uniformly the same, is chiefly that of a great world-judgment and of its happy consequences for those who escape, especially for faithful Israel. And of what does this remind us? Surely of Ezek. xxxviii., Joel iii. 9-21, and Zech. xiv. In other words, the prophecy is eschatological. True, the writer describes events as an eye-witness, but these events are but the first stage in a great final judgment which will usher in what may be called, in a large sense, the Messianic age. The principal images are of the class which we may call apocalyptic; they, or images analogous to them, may be found in the imaginative descriptions which abound in the later prophecies and in apocalypses. Take, for instance, (a) the physical convulsion of the world (xxiv. 1, 18-20). This we find in Ezek. xxxviii. 19, 20; Hag. ii. 6, 7, 21; Joel iii. 16; Zech. xiv. 4, 5. (b) The going up of all nations to Mount Zion for the divine coronation feast (xxv. 6). Observe that the idea of the feast is found in Ps. xxii. 27 in an eschatological connection; cf. Mark xiv.

[1] Mr. Barnes, on the other hand, remarks that paronomasias are not deficient in the acknowledged parts of Isaiah, and points out a series of them in a single chapter (ch. x.). As a general truth this may be admitted. Such simple rhetorical devices, as Ley has abundantly shown, were inherited from the primitive period of poetry and oratory. But any list of Isaianic paronomasias will have to be carefully scrutinised; one cannot easily believe that the paronomasia in x. 18b comes from Isaiah, and this impression is confirmed by critical analysis. The result of a scrutiny will probably be that the number of instances dwindles, and that on the whole Isaiah uses paronomasia with a tact and naturalness which we do not find in chaps. xxiv.-xxvii.

25 (Lord's Supper). (c) The awakening of the dead by a special divine application of one of the simplest and most universal natural phenomena (xxvi. 19). The image is suggested by Ezek. xxxvii. 9 (where, however, the natural phenomenon selected as the symbol of the divine act is, not the moistening of the dew, but the blowing of the wind, and where the language is more distinctly allegorical); it is the basis of the חְיִדוֹת, which form the "prayer for the dew" still said in the synagogues on the first day of Passover. (d) The committal of the "host of the (heavenly) height" and the "kings of the earth" to prison (xxiv. 21, 22; cf. Enoch xviii. 13-16; Jude 6; Rev. xx. 2, 3). (e) The enigmatical designations of the three oppressive world-empires (xxvii. 1). The choice of the symbols (cf. li. 9;[1] Ps. lxviii. 31) is dictated by the dragon-myths of Egypt and Babylonia, but we may compare the equally enigmatical symbols in Dan. vii. (f) The mighty sword of God (xxvii. 1). The conception is no doubt ancient (cf. Gen. iii. 24), but it is specially prominent in late eschatological descriptions; cf. xxxiv. 5, lxvi. 17; Zech. xiii. 7; Enoch xc. 19, 34; xci. 12; Rev. i. 16; ii. 12, etc. (g) The trumpet which is blown to recall the Jewish exiles (xxvii. 13). The form of the phrase suggests that "*the* trumpet" has become a technical term.[2] In xviii. 3, on the other hand, it is a natural poetic figure.

II. The ideas and ideals of the prophecy are equally conclusive as to the extreme lateness of the date. (a) The view that mankind at large had broken a divine law (xxiv. 5) is late (*BL*, p. 306). "Host of heaven" (see *d*, above) can only be explained by that belief in the angelic patrons of the "nations" which assisted the later Jews to reconcile the oppression of Israel with the sovereignty of Yahwè. The earliest reference to this belief may be in Deut. xxxii. 8 (at earliest Exilic). It finds expression too in Pss. lviii. and lxxxii.[3] (post-Exilic); cf. also Sir. xvii. 17, and the Targ. on

---

[1] See Cheyne, *PI*, ii. 31; *BW, ad loc.*
[2] Both the "dew" and the "trumpet" were fixed elements of the later eschatology. *Cf.* Wünsche, *Neue Beiträge aus Talmud*, p. 312 (on Matt. xiv. 31).
[3] See Cheyne, *Book of Psalms; BL*, pp. 120, 337; Smend, *AT Rel.-gesch.*, p. 395. The conception is coloured by the prevalent bitterness towards the "nations" (cf. Cheyne, *Job and Solomon*, pp. 81, 82). In

Judges v. 13. (c) The visible enthronement of Israel's king on Mount Zion is still in the future (xxiv. 23, xxvi. 13), an idea of frequent occurrence in the post-Exilic psalms and prophecies (see *BL*, pp. 341-342). (d) and (e) The promise of the abolition of death in xxv. 8a (if this is not a later insertion), and the hope of the resurrection of individual Israelites, presupposed in xxvi. 19 [1] (however we read and render the passage), go beyond the Exilic conceptions, and become the more intelligible the later we place this composition in the Persian period.

This, indeed, is an obvious truth, whether with many critics we seek to explain Jewish doctrinal developments without supposing the least foreign influence, or whether (as seems more in accordance with the principles of comparative theology) we admit that Persian ideas could not help influencing Jewish minds both directly and (still more) indirectly. Not even Darmesteter denies that the doctrine of the resurrection, the defeat of the evil power, and the renovation of the world formed an essential part of the Mazdeism of the Achæmenidæ.[2]

(f) The admission of "all peoples" to religious privileges the Greek period gentler feelings arise; hence the "princes" of the "nations" are, in Dan. x. 13, 20, 21, not represented as hostile to Yahwè.

[1] In *ICA* (p. 127) and *BL* (p. 403) I rendered this difficult passage as a prayer, "Let thy dead men (Jehovah!) revive; let my dead bodies arise!" "It is not a sudden revelation of a new truth . . .; rather the Church, among some of whose members the Resurrection-hope is already current, bases a sublimely bold prayer upon this hope." But Duhm's study of the rhythmical movement of this section has convinced me that יחי and נבלתי are interpolated, and it becomes necessary to render in the future, "Thy dead men (Israel!) shall arise," and to continue, reading הקיצו ורננו, "and the inhabitants of the dust shall awake and shout for joy." In this case, the pre-existence of a sure hope of a (limited) resurrection is still more indubitable.

[2] Cf. Cheyne, *BL*, pp. 402-404; "Ancient Beliefs in Immortality," *Nineteenth Century*, Dec. 1891, pp. 965-966. The writer has, however, not undervalued the surmises of a barely possible resurrection to be found in pre-Exilic literature, and which to some extent correspond to similar suggestions in Assyrio-Babylonian inscriptions (*BL*, p. 383). Darmesteter's words are, "Le Mazdéisme achéménide croyait déjà à la défaite d'Ahriman, et connaissait le dogme de la résurrection et la durée limitée du monde fixée à 1200 ans" (*Le Zendavesta*, iii. 1893, p. lxxiii.). The relation of early Iranian to Babylonian beliefs does not greatly concern us; the "dogma of the resurrection" was, as all agree, specially Iranian.

(xxv. 6). This is one of the characteristic ideas of II. Isaiah, and, though sometimes with qualifications, of the later writers in general (see *e.g.* lvi. 6, 7 ; lxvi. 23 ; Ps. xxii. 28 ; Zech. xiv. 16-19). (*g*) The conception, at once so high and so low, of the relation of Israel to God (xxvii. 11). So high, for Israel has been specially "made" and "formed" by Yahwè ; this part of the conception is Deutero-Isaianic (see xliii. 1, xliv. 2). But so low, for Israel's "foolish" lapse into bad religious practices can be atoned for in the most mechanical way, "when he maketh all altar-stones like pounded chalk-stones, so that ashéras and sun-pillars rise up no more" (xxvii. 9). The great pre-Exilic prophets would not have endorsed these easy terms, nor would the Second Isaiah. Only a late writer could have done so. (*h*) The ideal of national life is a prolonged act of worship (xxvii. 13 ; cf. Ps. xxiii. 6). Surely this ideal grew up in a non-political age.

III. The social state described is one in which priests constitute the most important class. "And it shall be, like people, like priest," we are told (xxiv. 2). Nor can this argument be parried by referring to Hos. iv. 9, where the same words occur. For there the proverbial saying, "like people, like priest," stands in a purely religious context, and it therefore stands alone, whereas here it is followed by "like slave, like master," *i.e.* forms part of a catalogue of social relations. In Joel the priests are equally prominent, and there too we meet with the elders (Joel i. 14, ii. 16 ; cf. Isa. xxiv. 23).

It still remains to determine (if possible) to which part of the Persian age the prophecy belongs. Dillmann, who in the main follows Ewald, prefers the first part. The description in xxiv. 4-13 he interprets of the troubles of the warlike reigns of Cambyses and Darius Hystaspis.[1] The "city of desolation" (xxiv. 10, cf. xxv. 2, xxvi. 5, xxvii.

[1] Ewald had already admitted that the capture of Babylon by Darius might be referred to, but preferred on the whole to assign the prophecy to the time when Cambyses was preparing to invade Egypt. At any rate, on Ewald's view, the destroyed city referred to is Babylon, and he might well have illustrated the references by Ps. cxxxvii., which, as he plausibly held, anticipates the fall of Babylon, and was written very soon indeed after the Return.

10) is Babylon, which was still one of the royal residences ; and Dillm. refers to Zech. i. 12, etc., ii. 10 (*A.V.*, 6), as showing that fresh judgments upon the tyrant-city were looked for as late as the second year of Darius (520 B.C.). The language of xxvi. 13-19 suits, he thinks, only the first sixty or seventy years of the Persian rule, and from xxvii. 1, 9 he infers that the circumstances of the pre-Exilic period did not yet belong to a distant past. This view is plausible ; but we have to consider whether the exegesis which it implies is correct. That הארץ throughout this composition means, not "the land" (of Judah), as Oort in many passages explains, but "the earth," may be granted (see *v.* 13). But that "the city" in xxiv. 10, 12, xxv. 2, xxvi. 5, 6, xxvii. 10, is Babylon, is by no means self-evident ; one might more naturally think of Shushan or Susa. Yet surely the writer of *vv.* 7-12 describes as an eye-witness ; Judah suffers from the great political convulsion as much as other countries, and the phrase "the city of desolation" (*tōhū*) in xxiv. 10, which may perhaps be understood collectively (cf. Sept.), refers to cities not so far off as Babylon and Susa. Next, as to xxvi. 13-19, which forms part of a prayerful, meditative retrospect of the Jewish Church-nation. It may be admitted that the early condition of the restored exiles was far from prosperous, but there is no part of the period between 536 and 476 (or 466) which will at all adequately explain the sombre colouring of a great part of ch. xxvi., much less the extraordinary statements of ch. xxiv. Nor can it be said that xxvii. 1, 9 implies that pre-Exilic memories have not yet grown pale. To *v.* 9 we will return later. As to *v.* 1, the three monsters spoken of need not be Egypt, Assyria, and Babylonia ; the second and third may be either Babylonia and Persia, or even less probably Persia and Greece. Let me now add one more decisive argument, viz. that in xxiv. 5 there is an allusion to Gen. ix. 3-6, 15, 16, and in xxiv. 18 to Gen. vii. 11, both which passages belong to P, so that chaps. xxiv.-xxvii. must be later than the reformation of Ezra and Nehemiah (444 or, better, 432), when the priestly lawbook first became "canonical." We must therefore look further down the course of events for the historical setting of these chapters.

The difficulty is to find a period which will equally well explain all the different allusions in the prophecy. Let us then revert to a critical method which we have often employed already, and see whether this composition really possesses literary unity. Upon a close examination, are we not irresistibly led to the conclusion that it is not really a single work (composed of twelve strophes, as Dr. Briggs believes,[1] in the same " hexameter movement "), but a mosaic of passages in different styles by several writers, who, though contemporaries, did not all write in the same part of their period? These passages appear to have been combined with less editorial skill than usual, and we must begin our further inquiry by rearranging them. The first in order contains xxiv. 1-23, xxv. 6-8, xxvi. 20, 21, xxvii. 1, 12, 13. This, from its peculiar style and imagery, we might call the apocalypse. It describes events which have happened, are happening, and, according to the writer, are about to happen, beginning with the desolation of the Persian empire by war, and closing with the final judgment on the powers which have oppressed Israel, with the setting up of the divine throne in the holy city, and with a great coronation feast to "all peoples." It is one of the merits of Ewald to have at once noticed the close connection between xxiv. 23 and xxv. 6, to which Duhm added the observation that xxvi. 20-21 is in a different movement from the bulk of the same chapter, and forms the necessary conclusion of "the apocalypse," while xxvii. 1, 12, 13, which are in the same movement, and relate to the same apocalyptic facts, at any rate belong together, and form a fitting supplement to xxvi. 20-21. Now, looking at this "apocalypse" by itself, can we date it? Probably we can. We require a period of long-continued desolating wars over a large region, including the satrapy of Syria and Palestine. Such a period began in the reign of Artaxerxes II. (Mnemon). The brave and repeated attempts of the Egyptians to regain their independence could not but involve much distress to the neighbouring country Judah. The frequent passage of large Persian armies was itself a calamity for the Jews, and

[1] *Messianic Prophecy*, p. 295. Dr. Briggs, however, notices the contrast between the late vocabulary and the artistic elegance.

once, if not twice, the Jews appear to have been concerned in a revolt against Persia. Cruelly was their rebellion punished by the able but unscrupulous Artaxerxes Ochus. Another monument of the same dark period is that sombre composition, lxiii. 7-lxiv. 11, in connection with which we shall have to describe the circumstances of the Jews at this time with greater fulness. Suffice it to say here that, in the words of Nöldeke, "much blood appears to have been shed in Judæa," and that Prof. W. R. Smith is probably right in transferring the defilement of the temple mentioned by Josephus (*Ant.*, xi. 7, 1) to this period, and seeing in the historian's account a patriotic understatement of the facts. The apocalypse was, we must believe, written under the influence of the despondency which these calamities produced. The phrase "the city (or, collectively, cities) of desolation" (xxiv. 10) alludes to the fate of Sidon and Jerusalem. That the former city was destroyed is a historically attested fact; that the latter was hardly less completely ruined is a probable supposition of the brilliant English scholar referred to already, which explains, not only lxiv. 9, 10 (10, 11), but some words in the great composite prophecy before us—

"For the fenced city is solitary, an abode whose inmates have been scattered, and deserted like the wilderness; there the calf feedeth, and there lieth down, and consumeth the branches thereof. When its twigs are dry, they are broken off, women come and set them ablaze; for it is not a people of discernment, therefore hath its maker no compassion upon it, and its fashioner showeth it no indulgence" (xxvii. 10, 11).

This passage, in short, describes the state of Jerusalem in, or soon after, 347 B.C. The rest of the Jewish territory must have suffered only less terribly. It was peopled by the unhappy remnant which had escaped banishment or death, and which from time to time expressed its mingled feelings, partly in liturgical and apocalyptic compositions, partly perhaps in pessimistic soliloquies like Ecclesiastes. The remaining twenty years of the Persian period are not likely to have brought the Jews much relief, though Jerusalem cannot long have remained deserted. They may well have gone on complaining (like a prophetic writer of the close of the Exile, xxi. 2) that the "robber" still went on "robbing."

CHAPTERS XXIV.-XXVII

Suddenly, however, a gleam of hope appeared. Alexander of Macedon had set out on his march eastward, and the Jewish exiles of the "coastlands" of Asia Minor (cf. Joel iii. 6; Ob. 20*b*?) burst into rapturous songs (xxiv. 14-16) :—

Those (yonder) cry aloud in ringing tones; for Yahwè's majesty they shout from the sea,—"Therefore in the coastlands give honour to Yahwè, in the coastlands of the sea to the name of Yahwè, Israel's God." From the earth's border we have heard songs of praise, "Glory (is come) for the righteous" (*i.e.* for Israel).

But there is no pause in the oppression of Israel; the weakness of the central power seems but to multiply the number and insolence of the tyrants (xxiv. 17). Meantime the writer comforts himself with eschatological pictures, and bids his fellow-believers retire into seclusion till the miseries of these last days are over. For soon shall the utmost imaginings of faith be surpassed, nor shall any single Israelite in the Diaspora be forgotten. (Thus the circumstances of the Jews in 347 and 334 are combined in a comprehensive picture.)

The second passage comprises only xxvii. 7-11; clearly therefore it is a fragment. It describes the judgment which, by means of the Persian king, lately passed over Jerusalem, and by an effective exaggeration represents it as still felt as sorely as at the first. Yet full twenty years have passed since the cruelties of Ochus, and now the prophetic writer can ask, Was Israel punished as severely as within these last few days his punisher (Persia personified) has been? Since that heavy blow which almost slew Israel, the "smiter" has himself been smitten: the field of Issus has been won by Alexander. Will this great change in the political world be profitable to Israel? Only if Israel reconciles itself with its God. Its sore calamity in 347 was the consequence of its own lack of "discernment"—of its lapse into illegal religious practices. Let Israel become more consistent and its guilt will be put away. No doubt, the words of xxvii. 9 sound to us very strangely. But we may learn from other late passages, as well as from II. Zechariah, that the Jews of the Persian age were by no means as correct religiously as might be supposed, and the gloss on xvii. 8 suggests that after the Return even ashéras and sun-pillars were not entirely unknown. (Others may prefer to conjecture that the language of xvii. 8, xxvii. 9*b* is deliberately archaistic.)

The third section (xxvi. 1-19) is longer and more important. It is a liturgical poem, intended, not (as the introduction wrongly states) for eye-witnesses of the glorious coming "day," but for those who are still only on the confines of full deliverance. Jerusalem has indeed been spared by the army of Alexander while far prouder cities have been laid in the dust. But the effects of the cruelties of Ochus cannot be all at once wiped away. The fortifications have not yet been raised afresh (xxvi. 1). And only by a life-giving "dew" from the world of "lights" can those who have suffered for the truth be restored to their brethren's side. The poem is a highly artificial one in four strophes, each consisting of seven lines in the same long movement.[1] The first strophe is full of joy and hope. The three following ones are chiefly retrospective and melancholy. But each opens with a line in a strong idealistic tone, describing either a principle of the divine action, or the experience of a happier past, and the last closes with a confident prophecy of a Jewish resurrection.

The fourth, fifth, and sixth passages are lyric; the first comprises xxv. 1-5*a* (originally perhaps in syllabic metre);[2] the second in xxv. 9-11; the third in xxvii. 2-5. Like the retrospect they may probably be assigned to 332 B.C., the eventful year which intervenes between that which is marked by the defeat of Darius at Issus, and that which saw the foundation of a new centre of commerce and of intellect at Alexandria. Alexander's capture of Tyre must have profoundly impressed the Jewish world, and imitative students of prophecy must have been stirred up to express their joy at this great fulfilment of "ancient purposes" (xxv. 1). Tyre appeared to most observers to be impregnable. Indeed it was not till Alexander joined the island of Tyre to the mainland by a causeway that she fell. But two late Jewish prophets had already again foretold her end, one with much

---

[1] So Duhm. In *vv.* 1-10 there is even a close approximation to syllabic metre (see Bickell).
[2] See Bickell.

bitterness (Joel iii. 4-8), the other (Zech. ix. 2-4) with dignified reserve. From the latter, which was doubtless written at this period, and probably just before the siege of Tyre began, I quote these words—

Tyre built herself a stronghold, and heaped up silver as the dust and gold as the mire of the streets. Behold Yahwè will dispossess her, and smite her bulwark into the sea, and she shall be devoured with fire.

Not less complete, though less startling, was the overthrow of Gaza, after which, according to Josephus, Alexander turned northward and paid a friendly visit to Jerusalem. That the story is a legend is certain, but it is not improbable that other parts of Palestine (at any rate Peræa) suffered from the invaders.[1] Did Moab experience such a humiliation at this time as would account for the song in xxv. 9-11? The bare possibility cannot be denied.[2] Still, as the Moabites had so long ceased to be dangerous to Israel, I am loth to ascribe literal accuracy to the bitter expressions of the poet. Why should not "Moab" be an imaginative type of all the proud enemies of Israel (cf. Neh. xiii. 1 ; Ezra ix. 1)?

The theory which I have offered is not at first sight a natural one, but obviously natural solutions of apocalyptic puzzles are not to be had. There are far worse puzzles, however, than those in chaps. xxiv.-xxvii., and the present solution seems to me to satisfy all the conditions of the problem. Still it is quite intelligible that the reference to Moab (xxv. 10), to ashéras and sun-pillars (xxvii. 9), and to Assyria and Egypt (xxvii. 13), have seemed to earlier critics to prove the pre-Exilic origin of at least some parts of the composition. (1) Incursions of the Moabites took place in Jehoiakim's reign (2 Ki. xxiv. 2), and are probably referred to in Zeph. ii. 8 ; moreover several other prophets (Jer. xlviii. 26 ; Ezek. xxv. 8) denounce Moab's insolent rejoicing at the calamities of

---

[1] The foundation of Pella, Dium, and Gerasa is ascribed to Alexander.
[2] See Smend, *ZATW*, iv. 218. Prof. W. R. Smith finds an allusion to some Moabitish outrage upon the Jews in Ps. lxxxiii. 7, "Moab and the Hagarenes." But the mention of Moab, like that of Amalek, is probably archaistic. In Joel iv. the Moabites are not mentioned among the peoples to whom stern retribution is due.

the Jews. (2) Both Micah (?) and Jeremiah denounce the ashéras (Mic. v. 13; Jer. xvii. 2), while the Deuteronomic law forbids both ashéras and maççêbôth or sacred stones, a term which probably included hammânîm or sun-pillars. (3) The mention of Assyria and Egypt in xxvii. 13 (which is no later addition, as Geiger and Oort supposed) is no doubt parallel to xi. 11-16. But can that passage much longer be defended as Isaianic? Of the two former difficulties explanations have already been offered. (1) Moab is a type. (2) The Jews after the Return were by no means as strictly orthodox in their religious practice as we have supposed. With reference to the third, it hardly need be remarked that Assyria can (see p. 62, on xi. 16) be used by a late writer as a symbolic term (cf. Zech. x. 10, 11).

To conclude. In no part of Isaiah is the necessity of an advanced critical point of view more obvious than here. The complications of the problems were at first but imperfectly realised. Now that we see them better, the solutions which satisfied the earlier critics become impossible. It was unfortunate that from excess of caution both Prof. *Driver* (*Isaiah*,[1] 1888) and Prof. *Ryle* (*Canon*, 1891) revived the already untenable pre-Exilic theory, while Mr. W. E. *Barnes* (who has done good service in other fields) in 1891 actually put forth a learned *Examination of the Objections brought against the Genuineness of Isa.* xxiv.-xxvii., and Dr. C. H. H. *Wright* (art. " Isaiah," Smith's *D.B.*[2]) in 1893 found " nothing really opposed to the Isaianic authorship." Professor Driver, however, has maintained more recently that there are features in this composition in which it is in advance even of II. Isaiah, and now places it between 536 and 440 B.C., while Prof. *Kirkpatrick* (*Doctrine of the Prophets*, 1892, p. 475, etc.) places it in the 4th century.

With regard to continental critics *Kuenen* has well said that there is a growing *consensus* in favour of placing the prophecy in the Persian period. It is enough here to refer to the more important names. Kuenen himself decided (*Ond.*[2], ii. 99) for the 4th century. *Vatke*, after deciding in 1835 for the Maccabæan period (*Bibl. Theol.*, p. 550), came in his posthumous *Einleitung* (1886) very near the most critical view. The data point, he says, to the time of the revolt of Phœnicia from Persia, when, in 349, Sidon was taken and destroyed by Artax. Ochus, and when the inhabitants of Jericho were carried into exile, and Jerusalem itself (he infers this from the prophecy) was laid waste (p. 623).[1] *Hilgenfeld* supplies a needful corrective to the one-sidedness of Vatke's view (*Zt. f. wiss. Theol.*, 1866, pp. 398-448). The latter overlooked certain data which are inconsistent with an ascription of chaps. xxiv.-xxvii. as a whole to the time of Ochus, but his own view—that the period is that of the wars of Alexander (= "the righteous one," xxiv. 16), and that the destroyed city is (only) Tyre— compels him to do violence to certain passages which Vatke can quite well explain. *Smend* is also more than half inclined to adopt the same date as Hilgenfeld, but he is embarrassed by the supposed necessity of finding a single city in all the passages where a city is referred to, and of placing that city in the land of Moab (*ZATW*, 1884, pp. 161-224). *Stade*, too, (*Gesch.*, p. 586), places it early in the Greek period. None of these critics saw the necessity of analysing the supposed "prophecy." This was reserved for *Duhm*, who, however, disturbs well-grounded views of the history of the canon by bringing down the date of the "apocalypse" to the time of the siege of Jerusalem and the devastation of Judah by Antiochus Sidetes, soon after the accession of John Hyrcanus (135), and the beginning of the Parthian campaign of Antiochus, in which the Jews were compelled to take part (about 129). In xxvi. 1-19 he sees a reference to the destruction of Samaria by John Hyrcanus (between 113 and 105), and to the same period he assigns xxv. 1-5, where the "city of the nations" (*v.* 3) is Rome. xxv. 9-11 he assigns to the time of Alexander Jannæus who captured Medaba (Jos., *Ant.*, xiii. 9, 1), but forgets that Moabitis was by this time probably occupied by the Nabatæans. Lastly, *Oort*, mainly on the ground that by the time of Nehemiah the land of Moab must have become Nabatæan, pleads for a date in the 5th cent., but prior to the governorship of Nehemiah (*Theol. Tijdschr.*, 1886, pp. 166-194). If this argument were sound it would still only affect the date

[1] In *JQR*, July 1892, p. 569, the author expressed a general concurrence with Vatke's view.

of the song in xxv. 9-11 ; the evidence for the later date of the other portions of this "prophecy" would retain its full force.

CHAPTERS XXVIII.-XXXIII

These chapters were undoubtedly meant by their editor to form an independent book. A real or apparent unity is therefore to be expected. Nor can it be denied that either Isaiah or another has done his best to produce a semblance of unity. The discourses put together agree in their recurring moods and ideas, and are linked together (with the exception of that in chap. xxxii.) by the introductory particle הוֹי (xxviii. 1, xxix. 1, 15, xxx. 1, xxxi. 1, xxxiii. 1). There are also in all of them phenomena which point (or seem to point) to the authorship of Isaiah, and to the existence of an impending danger from Assyria. Hence Hitzig inferred that chaps. xxviii.-xxxiii. formed a cycle of prophecies of the same period (viz. the year of the invasion of Sennacherib and the preceding year); xxviii. 1-6 was, he thought, a pathetic retrospect of the fall of Samaria, intended as a warning to the over-confident politicians of Jerusalem. He might have added that in xxx. 8 (which no one can deny to be Isaianic) Isaiah is directed to write down his preaching on the Egyptian alliance (*i.e.* perhaps not merely xxx. 1-7, but a larger complex of prophecies) in a "book."[1] His hypothesis, however, presented too many difficulties to be generally received. More discernment was shown by Ewald, who referred at any rate chap. xxxiii. to a disciple of Isaiah who wrote in a later year of the reign of Hezekiah, while of chaps. xxviii.-xxxii. he asserted that it was an "oration complete in itself," produced by Isaiah in all its parts at nearly the same time. It is true he qualified this assertion by distinguishing between xxviii. 1-xxx. 7 and xxx. 8-xxxii. 8. Only the former part, he thought, represented the discourse actually delivered in public, the latter having been written by Isaiah in retirement, in obedience to the divine command (xxx. 8), as a supplement to his public preaching. He also admitted a brief pause in the prophet's "oration"

[1] Cf. Dillmann.

CHAPTER XXXIII

before xxix. 1, after which Isaiah began again from an entirely different point of view. This theory, however, appeared to the present writer to be too violent a rebound from the disintegration theories of Koppe. He therefore adopted a modification of Ewald's view as to chap. xxxiii., but referred chap. xxviii. to an earlier period than chaps. xxix.-xxxii., and admitted that chaps. xxx. and xxxi. contained some passages which can only have been written during an Assyrian invasion.[1] In this view of the close connection of chaps. xxix.-xxxii., the writer went with the prevailing current of critical opinion.[2] In preparing his critical work on the Psalter, however, he perceived that this theory was too much akin to that of Hitzig, and needed correction. After a minute examination of chap. xxxii. he arrived at the same results as Stade, Guthe, and Kuenen; *i.e.* xxxii. 1-8 and 9-20, as well as chap. xxxiii., had to be separated from the rest of the collective prophecy as late appendices.[3] Since the appearance of Duhm's book, he has been led to apply a more searching criticism to chaps. xxviii.-xxxi., but the difficulty of the inquiry is such that in the interests of the student he asks leave to desert the natural order, and examine first the three passages which excited his own earliest suspicions.

Of the passages in question, which we will call collectively A, the third (*c*), viz. chap. xxxiii., may be examined first.[4] It is a poem of varied contents in 16 four-lined stanzas,[5] and shows how Israel's extremity is God's opportunity, and how glorious a future awaits Zion so soon as the unrighteous ones without and within the city shall have been destroyed. It is predominantly an encouraging prophecy (not to say apocalypse); the threatening "woe" (הוֹי)

---

[1] *PI*, ii. 181, where, however, the invader is erroneously supposed to be Sargon.
[2] See Robertson Smith, Guthe, Orelli, Bredenkamp.
[3] See *BL*, pp. 237-249; and cf. Stade, *ZATW*, iv. 256-271. Kuenen, it is true, does not agree with Stade and Guthe that the appendices are post-Exilic; he inclines (but with hesitation) to place them in the reign of Josiah or somewhat later (*Ond.*[2], II. pp. 86, 88).
[4] Its doubtfulness was already admitted by Ewald.
[5] See Duhm, and cf. Bickell's remark, *Beiträge zur sem. Metrik.* (1894), p. 11.

with which it opens is addressed, not to the infatuated rulers of Judah, but to the unjust invader. We may treat the composition from three points of view—from that of history, from that of language, and from that of religious ideas. From the former point of view the question before us assumes this form : Can the work have been produced, whether by Isaiah or by another, in the period of Isaiah, or, more definitely still, in the only possible part of that period, viz. the year of Sennacherib's invasion, 701 B.C. ? The reader will remember the historical situation presupposed in xxii. 1-14. We saw how, on the raising of the blockade of Jerusalem, the citizens gave themselves up to a wild revelry which provoked the sternest of Isaiah's rebukes, and we asked the question, Did the threat of punishment bring the people to a better mind, and did Isaiah (who was no fatalist, and owned the principle expressed in Jer. xviii. 7-9) thereupon change his tone and his message ? To this question we may now answer that he must have done so, if chaps. xxxiii. and xxxvii. 22-32 were written by him in 701 (subsequently to xxii. 1-14). For this view implies that the peremptory sentence of xxii. 14 is virtually cancelled in these two prophecies, in the former of which Isaiah identifies himself so completely with the community which he but lately denounced, that he can pass abruptly from the language of prophecy to that of liturgical petition (xxxiii. 1, 2). It is certainly difficult to realise this, but we know that in xxii. 15-25 (if this is all Isaiah's) the prophet had foretold the happy results of a change of grand vizier, and history shows (according to the ordinary view) that, on the accession to office of Eliakim (xxxvii. 2), Isaiah became the real director both of the conscience and of the policy of the nation. Now if the prophet believed that sins could be so completely forgiven that no moral or physical trace of an evil past was left (i. 18, 19), may he not possibly have inferred from the penitence which he saw around him that the scarlet sins of his people had become white as snow, and that, though the Assyrians had perfidiously renewed their hostilities [1] (after accepting Hezekiah's tribute), it was

[1] Note that, on this hypothesis, the siege or blockade of Jerusalem is placed before the events described in chaps. xxxvi. and xxxvii.

CHAPTER XXXIII

only that the divinely guaranteed security of the reformed state might become manifest?[1] And on this hypothesis can we not understand the joyous words of xxxiii. 5, 6?—

> Inviolable is Yahwè, for he dwelleth on high,—
> He hath filled Zion with justice and righteousness,
> With a wealth of deliverance, with wisdom and knowledge;
> The fear of Yahwè—that is its treasure.

There is no doubt some plausibility in this way of imagining the history. In those early times the moral power of such extraordinary personages as Elijah and Isaiah must, under favouring circumstances, have been immense. It is probable that the reforms with which Hezekiah's name is connected, so far, at least, as they may be historical,[2] belong to this and not to an earlier period of his reign— that they are in fact a monument of the effect produced by the teaching of facts and of Isaiah. Still it would be passing strange if the author of xxii. 1-14 attached much importance to such a mechanical reformation. As a matter of fact, only twenty years later a complete reaction set in. Had Isaiah, who (on the traditional view of xxii. 15-25) foresaw the fall of Eliakim, not even a slight presentiment of this? And is it certain, or even probable, that the order of events in the Assyrian crisis was that supposed in this theory? By no means, as we shall see later. It may indeed reasonably be supposed that the writer of chap. xxxiii. himself held this mistaken view[3] (see *vv*. 1, 7, 8). But if he did, it is clear that he was not contemporary with the Assyrian invasion. And considering (1) that the source from which he derived his notion was presumably 2 Ki. xviii. 13-xix. 37; (2) that the compilation of this narrative (without the poem on Sennacherib) is on good critical grounds to be referred to the Exile, or to the period

---

[1] Cf. Ewald's remarks on the excitement produced at Jerusalem by Sennacherib's "perfidy," and the activity of the *prophets* of Yahwè, who pointed to the treasure of spiritual forces laid up in the true church (*wahre Gemeinde*); *Gesch*. iii. 681.
[2] See W. R. Smith, *Prophets*, p. 359; Stade, *Gesch*., i. 623; Smend, *AT Rel.-gesch*., p. 268.
[3] Stade, however, denies this (*ZATW*, 1884, p. 260).

166   *ISAIAH*

immediately preceding it ; (3) that chap. xxxiii. was evidently written, not in Babylonia, but in Palestine ; and (4) that it shows an imaginative brooding over past history which would be out of place in the anxious closing time of Jewish independence, the 33rd chapter of Isaiah is, from a historical point of view, almost certainly a post-Exilic work.

This result can, I think, be made a certainty by arguments from the language and ideas of the prophecy. A preliminary caution must, however, be given. Christian readers often approach the study of this work with a wish to find in it the highest experiences of the prince of prophets. But let them ask themselves, Why should every striking passage in the Book of Isaiah be at once attributed to that prophet ? And are they certain that they do not exaggerate the literary merits of the prophecy ? Is not the style, when we examine it, in a high degree artificial, and does not the enthusiasm of the writer quickly tire ? Constantly the thread of thought is broken. In little detached word-groups the prophecy or meditation "trips" along. The imagery and vocabulary are both in many respects un-Isaianic. The paronomasias are only less striking than those in chaps. xxiv.-xxvii. There is also the same liturgical tendency which we found in those chapters, and, as a natural result, a large number of parallels to passages in the Psalms.

And now as to the *linguistic forms*, etc. Let us first collect those phenomena which may be taken to be Isaianic, on the ground of their occurrence in commonly acknowledged works of Isaiah (excluding xxxii. 9-20 ; see pp. 177-180) ; some of them, however (indicated by a note of interrogation), are strongly disputed by the present writer.[1] We will begin with a grammatical form and with an idiom, both found once in Isaiah, יִרְבָּיֻן, *v.* 7 (see on xxi. 12, p. 129), and רֹחֲבֵי יָדַיִם, *v.* 20 (xxii. 18). The following words should also be noticed :—הוֹי, *v.* 1, as xxviii. 1, etc. נִשְׂגָּב, *v.* 5 ; cf. ii. 11, 17 (but also xii. 4, late). מָרוֹם, used of the divine dwelling-place (*v.* 5 ; cf. xxxvii. 23 ?—and see note on Ps.

---

[1] Some of the words quoted are, as I hold, not used elsewhere by Isaiah, viz. מָרוֹם, מִלֵּא, אָבַל and אִמְלַל, קָמֵל, אַרְאֶלָּם, שַׁאֲנָן, יְאֹרִים, אַדִּיר. Among these, however, מִלֵּא (a common form) and שַׁאֲנָן (Am. vi. 1) are unimportant.

CHAPTER XXXIII

vii. 8). מִלֵּא, v. 5, as xxiii. 2 ?; cf. lxv. 11, 20. אֶרְאֶלָּם, "their heroes" (?), v. 7; cf. xxix. 1.[1] אֱנוֹשׁ, v. 8; cf. viii. 1. אָבַל and אֻמְלַל, v. 9; cf. xix. 8 ?—also xvi. 8, xxiv. 4, 7, late. קָמֵל, v. 9, as xix. 6. יְיָ אָמַר, v. 10, as i. 11, 18; but see p. 250. חָשַׁשׁ, v. 11; cf. v. 24.[2] חָנֵף, v. 14; cf. ix. 16, x. 6. עָצַם, v. 15; cf. Piel, xxix. 10. מְצָדָה, v. 16; cf. מְצֻדָה, xxix. 7. מֶרְחַקִּים, v. 17; cf. viii. 9, x. 3, xvii. 13, xxx. 27. מוֹעֵד, v. 20; cf. i. 14.[3] שַׁאֲנָן, v. 20; cf. xxxvii. 29 ? יְאֹרִים, v. 21, as vii. 18 ?—xix. 6 ?—xxxvii. 25 ? אַדִּיר, v. 21, as x. 34 ? הֹרָן and נֵס parallel, v. 22, as xxx. 17. עַד, "booty," v. 23, as ix. 5 ? מַרְבֶּה, "abundance," as ix. 6 ?

But how much larger is the list of non-Isaianic words and senses of words, even omitting the more disputable instances. Take these particles. אַף, "also," v. 2; rhetorical or poetical; as xxvi. 8, 9, 11, xxxv. 2 (see introd. to chaps. xl.-lxvi.). בַּל, vv. 20-24 (6 times); only in late parts of Isaiah, see on xiv. 21, p. 74. כִּי אִם, "but," v. 21; but Sept. only reads כִּי, see Dillm. מְקוֹם, "instead of," v. 21, as Hos. ii. 1; see Dillm. And then note the following:—שׁוֹדֵד and בּוֹגֵד, v. 1; as xxi. 2, cf. xxiv. 16. רֻמַּת, v. 3, ἅπ. λεγ., but cf. Ps. cxlix. 6. חָסִיל and שָׁקַק, v. 4; cf. Joel i. 4, ii. 9. מַשַּׁק, גֵּבִים, v. 4, ἅπ. λεγ. אָסַף, v. 4, not in same sense as xxxii. 10, Mic. vii. 1. אֱמוּנָה, "stability," v. 6. חֹסֶן, v. 6; cf. the verb in xxiii. 18. עִתִּים, v. 6; elsewhere only in very late books, including Job xxiv. 1;[4] same sense here as in Ps. xxxi. 16. יְשׁוּעֹת, v. 6, as xxvi. 18; 9 times in Psalms. הֵן, v. 7 (nowhere in the strictly prophetic works of the true Isaiah; see on xxiii. 13, p. 141). מַר, used adverbially, as מָרָה in Ezek. xxvii. 30 (but see xxii. 4). אֲרוֹמֵם, v. 10; in Hithp. again only Dan. xi. 36. מִשְׂרְפוֹת, v. 12; once in Jeremiah, twice in Joshua. שִׂיד, v. 12; again only in Am. ii. 1, Deut. xxvii.

---

[1] "Possibly not without a reference to Ariel, the name of Jerusalem" (Del.). Should we not rather print אֶרְאֶלָּם or אַרְאֵלָּם, and render "the heroes"? We may still suppose a reference to xxix. 1. If chap. xxxiii. is late, the writer may well have interpreted "Ariel" or "Arial" in a way which was not meant by Isaiah, i.e. as meaning "hero" (God's lion), whether "hero-city" or "hero-warrior."

[2] Found nowhere else, except (by conj.) in lxiv. 1 (RT).

[3] In i. 14, however, Isaiah disparages the כְּסִילִים; the parallelism is therefore in language, not in thought.

[4] Ezek. xii. 27 is the earliest instance; in Ps. ix. 10, x. 1, xxxi. 16 we have עִתּוֹת.

2, 4. קוֹץ, *v.* 12; as xxxii. 13 (good Heb.). כָּסָח, *v.* 12; again only in Ps. lxxx. 16 (Aramaism), רְעָדָה, *v.* 14; again only in Ps. ii. 11, xlviii. 7, Job iv. 14 (וָעַד) and רַעַד are still rarer). גּוּר with acc., *v.* 14 (cf. Ps. v. 5, cxx. 5); in xi. 6, xvi. 4, גּוּר occurs with preps., also in the parallel passage, Ps. xv. 1. מוֹקֵד, *v.* 14, as Ps. cii. 4, and probably Lev. vi. 2 (Dillm.); cf. יְקוֹד, x. 16 (late). The root is more common in Aramaic. הָלַךְ with acc., *v.* 15; cf. the parallel passage, Ps. xv. 2. צְדָקוֹת, "righteous acts" (of men), *v.* 15; so lxiv. 5, Ezek. (thrice), Jer. li. 10, Dan. ix. 18). Elsewhere 'צ is used of God; Judg. v. 11 (*bis*), 1 Sam. xii. 7, Mic. vi. 5, Isa. xlv. 24, Ps. xi. 7, ciii. 6, Dan. ix. 16. מֵישָׁרִים, *v.* 15; cf. xxvi. 7 (see introd.); the writer of xi. 4 uses מִישׁוֹר. בֶּצַע, *v.* 15; see on lvi. 11, lvii. 17. מַעֲשַׁקּוֹת, *v.* 15; again only Prov. xxviii. 16. מְרוֹמִים, *v.* 16, of heaven, as Job xvi. 19, xxv. 2, xxxi. 2. מִשְׂגָּב, *v.* 16; as xxv. 12, Jer. xlviii. 1; also Ps. xlviii. 4 (and eleven other psalm-passages). מֵימָיו, *v.* 16, a not uncommon form, found also in the parallel poem, Ps. xlvi. (*v.* 4). הָגָה, "to muse," *v.* 18. אֵימָה, *v.* 18; good Hebrew, but nowhere else in prophecy, except in the late passage, Jer. l. 38, for "idols." סֹפֵר and שֹׁקֵל, *v.* 18, used technically. נוֹעָז, *v.* 19, ἅπ. λεγ. עִמְקֵי, *v.* 19, again only in Ezek. iii. 5, 6. נִלְעָג, *v.* 19, ἅπ. λεγ. בָּוָה, *v.* 20; cf. xxvii. 10, p. 146. עָץ, *v.* 20; ἅπ. λεγ. נָסַע, *v.* 20; rare in prophecy. אֳנִי, *v.* 21; 6 times in 1 Ki.; nowhere else, שַׁיִט, *v.* 21, ἅπ. λεγ.; see Dillm. on xxviii. 15, but cf. מָשׁוֹט, Ezek. xxvii. 6, 29. צִי, *v.* 21; once in Numbers, once in Ezekiel. כֵּן, "the foot of the mast," *v.* 23. נֵס, "sail," *v.* 23, as Ezek. xxvii. 7. שָׁכֵן, *v.* 24. On עַד, "booty," *v.* 23, see above.[1]

Many of these linguistic parallels are highly suggestive. They need, however, to be illustrated by parallels of thought. Though only one word in *v.* 2 is illustrated above by the language of the Psalms, yet the force of this parallelism is much enhanced by the fact that the ideas of the verse are altogether those of the psalmists. *V.* 10 is parallel to Ps. xii. 6, and *vv.* 15 and 16 to Pss. xv. and xxiv. 1-6,[2] and

[1] In the above I have included words belonging to a part of *v.* 20 and to *v.* 23, which are excrescences on the original poem (Duhm; *BW*).

[2] Cf. *BL*, pp. 237, 429. The parallelism of thought remains, even if with Duhm and *RT* we omit from מֹאֵס to בְּרָע as an interpolation.

several passages remind us of parts of Pss. xlvi.-xlviii. (the post-Exilic date of which is certain); comp. *e.g. v.* 21 with Ps. xlvi. 5, *v.* 22 ("our king") with Ps. xlvii. 7, *v.* 21 with Ps. xlviii. 8 (see Del.), and notice the free application of the phrase "reckon up her towers" (Ps. xlviii. 13) in xxxiii. 18. Other interesting parallels, both of language and of thought, could easily be added. Thus, xxxiii. 20*b* seems like a designed contrast to Jer. x. 20. In fact, the commentaries will show how many points of contact with other writings this prophecy contains (see *e.g.* on *vv.* 9-13).

I must now turn, however, to the *argument from religious ideas*. Notice (1) that this chapter is really a prayer or meditation of a "righteous people" (cf. xxvi. 2). There are, no doubt, "sinners in Zion," but they are only mentioned, as it were, parenthetically, and no attempt is made either to bring them to repentance or to terrify them by warnings. Not that believers imagine themselves guiltless in the eyes of Yahwè, but their sins are (we must suppose) either "hidden sins" (Ps. xix. 12), known only to Yahwè, or the sins of Israel's "youth" (Ps. xxv. 7). Upon the whole, it may be said that Yahwè "hath filled Zion with justice and righteousness" (*v.* 5), though a believing people still looks forward to the time when, by an outward sign, it shall know that its "iniquity has been forgiven" (*v.* 24). Now, have we any reason to think that this is a correct picture of the religion of Judah in the year 701-686 B.C.? Surely not. Notice (2) the writer's enthusiasm for the religious services. In chap. i. the prayers and solemn days of the people are said to be Yahwè's abomination, but chap. xxxiii. breathes a happy confidence that the prayers (*v.* 2) and the festival assemblies (*v.* 20, if the opening words are not a gloss) are his delight. The writer himself is intimately acquainted with the Psalms, nor (as I have shown elsewhere) can we blunt the point of this argument by throwing back some of our Psalms (or a substantial basis thereof) to the age of the pre-Exilic prophets. Notice (3) the sensuous conception of the divine presence in Zion implied in *v.* 14. The "everlasting burnings" are so called, not with regard to the eternity of the punishment (cf. lxvi. 24), but because the fire of Yahwè's love and wrath must be, like himself, eternal (so *PI*), and must permanently abide[1] on Zion for its defence (hence "who can tarry"); cf. iv. 5. See also on xxxi. 9. Notice (4) the vagueness of the Messianic belief of the writer. To the ideal king himself only a passing reference is made (*v.* 17). Of his family we learn nothing; of his functions nothing; of the extent of his kingdom almost nothing. He is a shadow-king; the one absorbing reality is "our king, Yahwè," *v.* 22 (a characteristically late phrase; cf. xli. 21, xliii. 15, Ps. v. 3, xliv. 5). Now, can we believe that Isaiah (if he wrote ix. 6, 7, xi. 1-5) would have so neglected the king of the glorious coming age? Is it not irresistibly borne in upon us that the Messianic features of the prophecy are only adopted from earlier writers? Will any other theory equally well explain the vague and enigmatical character of the references? And may we not compare the mention of "a king" in xxxii. 1 and the vague reference to the extension of the borders of the land in xxvi. 15 (where רִחַקְתְּ is parallel to מֶרְחַקִּים in xxxiii. 17)?[2] And notice (5) how indistinct and in part how un-Isaianic a view is given of Jerusalem's enemies! True, the expressions of *vv.* 7, 8 may be taken to refer to Sennacherib's invasion. But they lack the vivid reality of a contemporary prophecy; their seven short clauses are like mere marginal notes on 2 Kings xviii. 13-17. The language will apply quite as well to the Babylonians (see Hab. i. 6-10, 13), or, as an imaginative anticipation, either to the Scythians (? cf. Zephaniah) or to that combination of enemies which was expected to invade Israel in the latter days (cf. Ezek. xxxviii. 9-12). Even so much as this cannot be said of the opening "woe" on the unjust invader,[3] which contrasts strikingly with Isaiah's "woe unto Assyria" in x. 5, and is much more applicable to the Babylonians (cf. xxi. 2) or to the Persians (cf. xxiv. 16).

[1] This inference from מִי יָגוּר I owe to Duhm.
[2] In two other late passages (Zech. ix. 9, 10, Mic. vii. 11, 12) more distinct language is used.
[3] Ewald (see *Gesch.*, iii. 681), followed by G. A. Smith and many others, accounts for this "woe" by the historical circumstances, assuming that Sennacherib accepted Hezekiah's tribute and yet continued hostilities, which is contrary to all that we know of Assyrian usage, and seems a not sufficiently critical reading of history.

Is any corroboration required for the above twofold argument from internal evidence? Then let me refer to the eloquent exposition which the religious ideas of chap. xxxiii. have received from Dr. Duff,[1] who at present believes in its Isaianic basis. Surely it is not the age of Isaiah to which those ideas belong, but that of the Church of the Second Temple. But it is time to bring this discussion to an end. That chap. xxxiii. in its present form is not from the hand of Isaiah is abundantly clear. The only question is whether it may not contain some fragments of that great prophet's work. In *PI* I even ventured to conjecture that these fragments were considerable enough to be described as the basis of the composition. This was pardonable but excessive conservatism. In the abstract it is possible that the writer of chap. xxxiii. did work up fragments of Isaiah. But we have no special reason for supposing that he did, still less for supposing that they were the "basis" of the extant prophecy. Both Isaiah and Jeremiah were so much studied in later times that it was perfectly possible for able writers to assume somewhat of their style; or rather, *sympathetic* as well as able writers could not help writing, at any rate for a short time, in their spirit and in their manner.

A very definite conclusion as to the period of chap. xxxiii. is of course only possible to those who are in agreement with advanced O.T. criticism. On the ground of the vocabulary alone, one could not venture to claim chap. xxxiii. as post-Exilic,—it might conceivably belong to the last century of the kingdom of Judah. But when consistent students of criticism take these five points into consideration, viz. (1) that imitative and reproductive prophecy is characteristically post-Exilic; (2) that chap. xxxiii. is full of the spirit, and sometimes even agrees in phraseology with the Psalms, and that no part of the Psalter has yet been shown to have a pre-Exilic basis; (3) that abrupt transitions like those in this chapter are characteristic of late works; (4) that the references to the attacks of the "peoples" upon Jerusalem can be perfectly well explained by the later eschatology; and (5) that the liturgical tone of the composition suggests a period when not only the germ

[1] *Old Test. Theol.*, i. 258, 281-283.

of a church, but a church itself existed in high spiritual vitality, they will find that a post-Exilic date for chap. xxxiii. is very much more defensible than any other (not excepting Kuenen's).[1] And then, taking up the results of other parts of the critical inquiry, they will feel that they have a very strong case indeed for placing this striking composition side by side with the other church meditations in the Book of Isaiah, viz. xii., xxv.-xxvi., lxiii. 7-lxiv. 12. It shows us in fact how some educated Jews cheered the dark years of the second half of the Persian period (possibly, though not necessarily, in the reign of Artaxerxes Ochus). These pious men had two special consolations or recreations; first, they dwelt in imagination in the glorious future which the deepening gloom did but bring nearer, and next, they enriched the extant prophetic records with insertions and appendices, expressive of their own hopes and aspirations. That chap. xxxiii. gives expression to such hopes we have sufficiently seen. That it is also intended as an appendix to the group of prophecies on the Assyrian invasion is clear, not only from the introductory יהוה, but from the parallelism between $v.$ 2 ("every morning") and xxviii. 19, and between $v.$ 3 and xxx. 27. The writer of course regarded these prophecies as having a still unexhausted validity.[2] It should be added that there are also points of contact between this and the two preceding appendices; cf. $v.$ 2 ("us," "we," "our") and xxxii. 15 ("upon us"); $vv.$ 5, 6 and xxxii. 15-17; $v.$ 20 (בְּרָה and שַׁאֲנָן) and xxxii. 18.

To these two sections (a and b) xxxii. 1-8 and 9-20 we must now turn our attention. Notice at the outset how abruptly each of them begins. Does it look as if Isaiah wrote xxxii. 1 to follow xxxi. 9, or xxxii. 9 to follow xxxii. 8? It is true there is no direct historical reference in either passage which is inconsistent with the date (704-702) to which we shall refer the bulk of the preceding group of

---

[1] Kuenen's date (reign of Josiah) is evidently a provisional compromise. It is impossible to crowd the closing years of the pre-Exilic period with so many literary works. Nor was there at that time a church such as is implied by chap. xxxiii.

[2] The overthrow of Sennacherib having become typical of the great future judgment (cf. Pss. xlvi., xlviii.), which helps to account for the late composition on Sennacherib in xxxvii. 22-29.

CHAPTER XXXII. 1-8

prophecies, and in xxxii. 9-20 we have not only a description of the impending desolation of Judah (xxxii. 13, 14) which can be taken as a supplement to passages in chaps. xxviii.-xxx., but also a statement as to time (xxxii. 10) which is closely parallel to that in xxix. 1. And yet there are very grave doubts whether either of them comes from Isaiah or from his age. Let us examine the grounds for these doubts, first of all with reference to xxxii. 1-8. According to Prof. G. A. Smith, this passage "belongs to a class of prophecies which we may call Isaiah's 'escapes.' Like St. Paul, Isaiah, when he had finished some exposition of God's dealings with His people or argument with the sinners among them, bursts upon an unencumbered vision of the future, and, with roused conscience and voice resonant from long debate, takes his loftiest flights of eloquence."[1] "In Isaiah's book," he adds, "we have several of these visions, and each bears a character of its own according to the sort of sinners from whom the prophet shook himself loose to describe it, and the kind of indignation that filled his heart at the time." But one of the difficulties which some students feel consists precisely in this, that the points of contact with the actual life of Jerusalem, which xxxii. 1-9 presents, are only such as an imitator could produce ($v.$ 3, cf. xxix. 10, xxx. 10, 11; $v.$ 4, cf. xxx. 2 (?); $v.$ 6, "error against Yahwè," cf. xxix. 15, xxx. 11).

Another difficulty arises from the colourless statement respecting "a king" in xxxii. 1 (cf. xxxiii. 17). I will not indeed assert that a really concrete description would prove Isaiah's authorship (see Zech. ix. 9, 10, late), but at any rate such a meagre reference to a king in a description which no one regards as earlier than xi. 1-5 seems inconsistent with the traditional theory. Did Isaiah exhaust himself in xi. 1-5 ? and if Hezekiah is the "king" intended, why is this not more clearly indicated? We may, of course, be told that Isaiah hopes against hope, and cannot bring himself to ascribe to Hezekiah those high regal qualities which he has described before, and that he has become convinced that the "princes" would never consent to be set aside by the son of Ahaz, and would claim to be the supreme heads of the state.

---
[1] *Exposition of Isaiah* i.-xxxix., p. 248.

This, it may be urged, will account for the greater prominence of the "princes," whose character is described in the words, "and each one (of them) shall be as a hiding-place from the wind," etc. (*v.* 2). But even *v.* 2 seems not sufficiently concrete for Isaiah (contrast i. 17), and why are the "princes" dropped so soon? Of course an answer may be forthcoming. Worthy rulers need to be supported by a people which recognises true moral standards, and this requires a systematic moral training, such as the writer proceeds to sketch in outline. But how forced is all this exegetical supplementing! Is there no simpler and more truly critical theory? If on other grounds the theory is acceptable, must we not infer from *v.* 1 that the writer lived at a time when political life was extinct,[1] and when those who most admired the ancient prophecies devoted themselves to imitating them with more or less success?

Let us now consider the objection based on the style. Even Ewald (who does not dispute Isaiah's authorship) remarks that the writer "stoops to the necessities of the hearers (?), becoming at times simply didactic," and that "the description is continued until the verses required to make a strophe have been supplied"—in other words, the style is lacking in spontaneity. Add to this that the forced paronomasia in *v.* 7 is without a parallel in the true Isaiah. The phraseology, too, should lead us to be cautious in admitting the authorship of that prophet. In these eight verses there are no less than eighteen or nineteen words which either do not occur at all, or at least not in the same sense, in the generally acknowledged prophecies of Isaiah. These words are in *v.* 1 הֵן (see above, p. 167);—שׂרר (Prov. viii. 16, Es. i. 22, Num. xvi. 13, Hithp., *bis*);—in *v.* 2 מַחֲבֵא *ἅπ.* λεγ. ;—צָיוֹן (xxv. 5);—פְּלָגִים (xxx. 25, doubtful);—in *v.* 3 קשׁב (here only in Qal);—in *v.* 4 נִמְהָר ("headlong," as Hab. i. 6, Job v. 13; in xxxv. 4, with "heart" as here, but = "trembling") ;—עִלֵּג *ἅπ.* λεγ. ;—צַח (here only metaphorically; in xviii. 4 of clear heat) ;—in *vv.* 5, 6, נָבָל (ethically, as Prov. xvii. 7, 21 ; but cf. נְבָלָה Isa. ix. 16);—in *vv.* 5, 8 נָדִיב ("a noble," as thrice in Job, five times in Prov., and eight times in Psalms, also 'כ as adj., twice in *v.* 8 ;—in *vv.*

---
[1] Cf. Guthe, *Zukunftsbild*, p. 44.

CHAPTER XXXII. 1-8

5, 7 בֵּילַי, כֵּלַי, ἅπ. λεγ. ;—in v. 5 שׁוֹעַ (as Job xxxiv. 19) ;—in v. 6 הֹנֶף ἅπ. λεγ. (but cf. חָנֵף ix. 16, x. 6, xxxiii. 14?) ;—תּוֹעָה "error," again only in Neh. iv. 2 (in another sense), but cf. הֹעֵי־רוּחַ xxix. 24 (late) ;—מַשְׁקֶה ;—הָסַר (in Hifil) ;—in v. 7 זִמָּה ;—אָמְרֵי. The accumulation of new words may indeed be said to be a consequence of the novel subject, viz., the substitution of a new for a conventional morality, and the revision of the meaning of ethical terms. This is partly correct, but will hardly account for such a word as תּוֹעָה.[1] And how came Isaiah to introduce this novel subject? Can the author of chaps. xxviii.-xxxi. have suddenly cooled down and become so reflective and didactic that we could mistake him for one of the sages whose work is summed up in the various parts of the Book of Proverbs?[2] I admit that ethical sayings may perhaps already have been coined in the time of Isaiah, and that according to most critics this prophet actually uses gnomic words in xxix. 24, and frames a parabolic similitude in xxviii. 23-29, and also that in xi. 2 (cf. 1 Ki. iii. 28), if that is Isaianic, we find a "spirit of wisdom" (*hokma*) placed first among regal gifts, and that in xxxi. 2 Yahwè himself is called "wise." But this partly uncertain evidence scarcely accounts for the didactic language of xxxii. 5-8. The only reasonable view is that these verses (with which compare Prov. xxi. 24) belong to an advanced stage of the national development, when ethical terminology had become a subject of study, and the idea of a moral (as opposed to a merely ceremonial) reformation had sunk deeply into the minds of the faithful.

I know that Duhm is content with relegating *vv.* 6-8 to the post-Exilic period; *vv.* 1-5 he wishes to keep for Isaiah. But his arguments for this separation are few and forced. The most plausible one is that נָבָל in *v.* 5 means the arrogant or presumptuous man, but in *v.* 6 the free-

---

[1] Ges.'s note on תּוֹעָה is worth quoting. "Properly error, falling away from the true religion, implying criminality like that of heresy, which meaning (heresy) the corresponding verb ܠܳܥܳܐ has in Syriac. One might almost render 'heresy,' but for the modernness of the expression." There may be a trace of germinant scepticism in a very late appendix of Proverbs (Cheyne, *Job and Solomon*, pp. 149-151).

[2] For a very strange view of Dean Plumptre, see *Expositor*, second series, v. 213.

thinker. But I see no reason why נָבָל in *v.* 5 should not have a mixed ethical and religious significance (like לֵץ). A certain difference in tone between *vv.* 1-5 and *vv.* 6-8 may be admitted. But we cannot bisect *vv.* 1-8 on this account alone.[1] Many of the later writers are equally unable to maintain the same tone long, and *v.* 5 (with which *v.* 6 is connected by כִּי) is the link-verse between *vv.* 1-4 and 6-8. To the passage as a whole there is very nearly a counterpart in xxix. 16-24, where note that the "tyrant" is described as being also a "scoffer" (*v.* 20), as he virtually is in xxxii. 5, 6, and comp. *v.* 6 with xxix. 24, and *v.* 7 with xxix. 21. The chief differences are that there is nothing in xxxii. 1-8 corresponding to xxviii. 16, 17 (but cf. *v.* 17 with xxxii. 15, 16), and nothing in xxviii. 16-24 answering to xxxii. 1, 2. The latter verse in particular, which begins so awkwardly with וְהָיָה אִישׁ, and is so conventional in its imagery, should, I think, have excited Duhm's suspicions.[2]

On the whole, we may reasonably conjecture that xxix. 16-24 and xxxii. 1-8 are by the same post-Exilic writer. The object of both insertions is to induce the much-tried Jews in the 5th century to "cast all their care upon" Yahwè, and the means adopted is a description of the happy future on the other side of the great judgment. Such a picture seemed especially needed to prevent the great prophecy in chaps. xxviii.-xxxi. from closing with words of terror (see xxxi. 8).

And what of the second appendix? Those who regard chaps. xxviii.-xxxiii. as entirely Isaianic, must at any rate admit that xxxii. 9-20 is misplaced. The natural position of an address to the women on the coming trouble is (cf. iii. 16, 17) either before xxxii. 1-8, or after chap. xxxiii. But must we not admit that xxxii. 9-20 is most extraordinary in a collection of prophecies of this period? Verses 13 and 14 (in which both land and people are threatened with a long desolation) belong more properly to such a context as vii. 18-25 (cf. Mic. iii. 12). Surely this passage has no right to be connected with chaps. xxviii.-

---

[1] There is the same rhythmic form throughout *vv.* 1-8.
[2] The parallel passages, iv. 6, xxv. 4, are rightly obelised by this critic.

xxxi., which give so different a picture of the coming judgment. But can it be Isaiah's work?[1] (1) Let us take a general view of the style. Does not the rhetorical indefiniteness suggest a want of contact with real life? Take *e.g.* verses 13 and 14. How vague they are! To account for this Prof. G. A. Smith supposes that they were designed to produce an effective contrast to the carelessness of the women.[2] But if this be accepted, Isaiah is liable to be accused of a want of earnestness. There is no apparent reason why the women should not be warned in definite terms of the judgment which hangs over the state. Verses 15-20, which refer to the future regeneration, are equally indefinite, full, as Prof. G. A. Smith remarks, of "suffused" rather than distinct meanings. This, however, is much less surprising than the vagueness of verses 10 and 11. If Isaiah had wished to address himself to the women, he would surely have spared no pains to awaken their consciences. In iii. 16 he did attempt to do this; he condescended to depict, in the style of a Hogarth, the outward signs of their heartless luxury. Amos, too, with the same object, used very telling language (Am. iv. 1), whereas this writer dismisses the women with a general reproof of their careless security. One cannot help asking whether he really has any women before him at all. Can he be more than a student who tries to write like Isaiah but fails to catch the perfect style of the master?

(2) Notice that in *v.* 15 the expected national regeneration is traced to the "outpouring" of a spiritual influence. This feature does not accord with the older prophetic teaching, which makes reformation a spontaneous moral act (see i. 16, 17, xxviii. 22; Jer. iv. 4, 14, vii. 3, etc.). It is not a sufficient answer to refer to xxviii. 6, since (even if that be Isaiah's, which is most doubtful) nothing is said there of *moral* regeneration. Does not our passage presuppose characteristic Exilic and post-Exilic ideas? Exhortations like "Wash you, make you clean," had been proved to have but a slight effect; nothing but an "outpouring" of the life-giving Spirit on the whole nation could produce that moral

---

[1] Koppe long ago referred this section to the time of Nebuchadrezzar.

[2] *Exposition*, i. p. 268.

revolution which Jeremiah in his earliest period still connected with the labours of an individual. "Until the spirit be poured out upon us from heaven"; surely we are listening to none of the primitive prophets, but to one of the ablest disciples of that great prophet of the Spirit, Ezekiel (see Ezek. xxxvi. 26, xxxvii. 14, xxxix. 29, and cf. Isa. xliv. 3; Joel ii. 28). (3) There is no mention of the sins which have made a destructive punishment necessary. It is no doubt implied in *v.* 16 that judgment and righteousness have been wanting, but would not Isaiah have stated this (v. 7)? (4) The writer speaks in the name of the community (*v.* 15, "upon us"; cf. xxxiii. 2). On all these grounds we should expect the passage to be post-Exilic. How far does the diction confirm this?

To answer this question, let us collect the linguistic and phraseological phenomena which point away from Isaiah. Observe in *v.* 10 the application of the accus. of time ; also the use of בְּלִי before a finite verb (cf. xiv. 6 ; Job xli. 18, both late ; but also Hos. viii. 7, ix. 16 Kt.). In *v.* 11 the *enall. generis* in חֶרְדוּ. Also the four abnormal verbal forms in ־ָה. Are they really lengthened imperatives, 2nd s. masc. (anomalous alike in gender, number, and pausal form)? If not, are they corruptions of the 2nd pl. fem. imperative? Or do they represent the mincing feminine pronunciation of the same form (cf. Dillm.)? Also עָרָה, here only in Qal. In *v.* 12 עַל־שָׂדַיִם with plur. masc. part. Also סָפַד = ספק "to strike." In *vv.* 13, 14 מָשׂוֹשׂ (three times in chap. xxiv.; four times in chaps. lx.-lxvi.). In *v.* 13 the asyndeton קוֹץ שָׁמִיר : cf. שָׁמִיר שָׁיִת, xxvii. 4 (late). Also תַּעֲלֶה 2nd s. fem., the subject being the two nouns taken together as forming a neuter concept (cf. xxvii. 4). In *v.* 14 עֹפֶל (cf. Mic. iv. 8, of doubtful date); בַּחַן ἅπ. λεγ., cf. בַּחוּן, xxiii. 13 (late); and the awkward בְּעַד "(serve) as." In *v.* 17 מַעֲשֶׂה and עֲבֹדָה in sense of "fruit." In *v.* 18 נְוֵה, as xxvii. 10, etc. (see p. 146); מִבְטָחִים, again only in Jer. ii. 37 (the sing. twice in Jeremiah, once in Ezekiel, not elsewhere in prophecy). In *v.* 19 בָּרָד (if genuine) ἅπ. λεγ.; יָרַד, of forest trees, as Zech. xi. 2 (late); שִׁפְלָה ἅπ. λεγ., cf. שֵׁפֶל, Eccles. x. 6, Ps. cxxxvi. 23.

To these may be added some points of contact with

chap. xxxiii. (certainly late), and some with probably late passages woven into chaps. xxviii.-xxxi. The latter, however, will be given together with points of contact with the Isaianic stock of that section (the Isaianic passages referred to being in italics), because it may beyond doubt be assumed that xxxii. 9-20 was written to accompany chaps. xxviii.-xxxi. And last of all may be added verbal parallelisms to passages, two of which are Isaianic, the third probably not. Notice then in *vv.* 9, 11, 18 שַׁאֲנָן, cf. xxxiii. 20; in *v.* 10 אֹסֶף, cf. xxxiii. 4; in *v.* 13 קוֹץ, cf. xxxiii. 12; in *v.* 15 מָרוֹם = " heaven," cf. xxxiii. 5*a*; in *v.* 16 "judgment" and "righteousness," cf. xxxiii. 5*b* (also Isaianic); in *v.* 18 נָוֶה, cf. xxxiii. 20. Next comp. *v.* 9 with xxviii. 23; *v.* 10*a* with *xxix.* 1*b*; *v.* 15 with xxix. 17; *vv.* 14, 17 (עַד־עוֹלָם) with *xxx.* 8 (but also ix. 6); *v.* 17 with *xxx.* 15; *v.* 19 with *xxviii.* 2, *xxx.* 30 (the figure of hail), and with *xxix.* 4 (שׁפל); *v.* 20 ("happy are ye") with xxx. 18, and the whole verse with xxx. 23-25. And lastly, in *v.* 13 עַמִּי suggests *xxii.* 4, קִרְיָה עַלִּיזָה *xxii.* 2, and in *v.* 19 יַעַר "forest" (= proud warriors or princes) x. 34.

The above was mostly written before Duhm's work appeared. On one point I think that this acute critic may have seen further than his predecessors; *vv.* 15-20 (except *v.* 19 and the last two words of *v.* 18, on which see *RT*) may have been removed hither from some other context, עַד in *v.* 15 being an editorial link.[1] But I cannot admit that either section of *vv.* 9-20 comes from the earliest period of Isaiah, or that this passage is pre-Exilic at all. The arguments adduced above have not been met, and it is difficult not to believe that the phrase "days to a year" in *v.* 10 was not written by some one who knew the phrase "add year to year" in xxix. 1. To Duhm's arguments for the

---

[1] The effect of this עַד is to limit the meaning of עַד־עוֹלָם in a way that can hardly have been meant by the author of *v.* 14. Observe that the first of the two distichs in *v.* 15 is imperfect. *V.* 15 should run thus :—

. . . . there shall be poured out
A spirit upon us from the (heavenly) height,
And the wild pasture country shall become garden land,
And the garden land shall be counted for forest.

original separateness of *vv.* 9-14 and *vv.* 15-20 this fresh one may be added—that the writer of the former passage stands apart from the sinners and rebukes them, but the writer of the latter identifies himself with his people ("upon us") even in its moral weakness. Observe too that xxxii. 9-20 may once have been the only appendix to chaps. xxviii.-xxxi., following the analogy of iii. 16-iv. 6. The passage has phraseological points of contact with chaps. xxviii.-xxxi. (see above), but not with xxxii. 1-8. It is tempting but unnecessary to bring the date down as low as the oppression of the Jews by Artaxerxes Ochus.

B. (chaps. xxviii.-xxxi.). We have seen that, just as the great collective prophecies, ii. 5-iv. 1 and x. 5-xi. 8, have been completed by a post-Exilic appendix (or, in the case of the latter, appendices), so the equally important prophetic composition xxviii. 1-xxxi. 9 has received no less than three appendices from post-Exilic writers, in one of which two hands are visible. It is time now to turn our attention to the body of this great prophetic work and ask, as in the case of x. 5-34, (1) Is this to be regarded as a single prophetic discourse? (2) If not, do the parts belong on the whole to the same or to different periods? and (3) Do any of the parts contain later insertions, due either to Isaiah himself or to an editor? We will begin with the first of the discourses introduced by הוֹי, viz. chap. xxviii. It is evidently not a continuous oration, but falls into four parts, (*a*) *vv.* 1-6, (*b*) *vv.* 7-13, (*c*) *vv.* 14-22, and (*d*) *vv.* 23-29.

Chap. xxviii. (*a*) *vv.* 1-6. Subject, the imminent fall of Samaria. "Isaiah sees the city of Omri on her hill which crowned the fat, or olive-planted vale, drooping. Either the garlands, as some take it, on the heads of the drinkers, or perhaps only the beauty and splendour, of which flowers are a natural type, and the majesty which the site of the city embodied, fade away. The conqueror, like a flood, sweeps in, and devours without asking which (fruit) is ripe."[1] In other words, the whole of the people of N. Israel shall be carried into exile (cf. the figure in v. 14). The prophet would not, of course, deny that a remnant of the poorest class might be left (cf. xvii. 6), but these would

[1] Rowland Williams, *Hebrew Prophets*, i. 369.

be too few and forlorn to represent the nation. Then suddenly comes a strange contrast. "In that day" great shall be the glory of "the remnant of Yahwè's people" (*vv.* 5, 6). Their boast shall be of their God, who shall recognise them for his people by granting them a spirit of justice and warlike heroism. It is Judah[1] which is meant by the "remnant" (for, as we have seen, the N. Israelites who escape destruction will be too few to be reckoned as a community), and which, according to the writer, will at the time of the fall of Samaria already have become converted to the religion of the prophet, while its leaders have been endowed with supernatural ability to put down all opposition both without and within the nation. Now this description of the condition and prospects of Judah is entirely opposed to that given by Isaiah in xxviii. 7, 22, xxix. 1-4, 9-15, xxx. 1-17, xxxi. 1-4, but is not unlike the descriptions in iv. 2, 3, x. 20, 21, xxxiii. 5, 6, 23, all of which, as we have seen, are late; and the reference to the "spirit" of judgment and of might reminds us not only of xi. 2, 3, but of lv. 3, where the promises once attached to the Davidic royalty are transferred to the people (*i.e.* in *v.* 6, not the Messiah, but the "remnant," or at any rate its leading class is endowed with the Messianic "spirit"). Now, is it not *primâ facie* improbable that Isaiah should have written *vv.* 5, 6? Especially when we consider that the style as well as the ideas points away from Isaiah. Thus, the phrasing of *v.* 5 resembles partly iv. 2, partly xxviii. 1. The latter passage is Isaianic, the former not. But in both the expressions צְבִי and תִּפְאֶרֶת (= תִּפְאָרָה) are more felicitously used than in xxviii. 5. It is natural to say that the fertility of the soil is a glory to Israel, natural too to speak of Samaria as the glory of Ephraim. But it is not natural to describe Yahwè in the same terms as the city of the drunken nobles of Samaria; only a late supplementer could do this. Note also שְׁאָר עַמּוֹ. The phrase occurs nowhere again in xxix.-xxxi., nor indeed anywhere in the true Isaiah. It is found, however, in xi. 11, 16, and at least reminds us of שְׁאָר יִשְׂרָאֵל in x. 20 (cf. 21), and of הַנִּשְׁאָר בְּצִיּוֹן in iv. 3. All these are late

[1] So rightly Ges., Hitz., Giesebr., and Duhm, against Del. and Dillm. (who hold the view rejected above).

passages. In v. 6, "spirit of judgment" invites comparison with iv. 4 (late), though the phrase there has a different meaning. The only word indeed which by itself suggests lateness is צְפִירָה, "crown," found elsewhere only in Ezek. vii. 7, 10.[1] But we may fairly say that the style in general is that of a declining literature, and that all the arguments together make the authorship of Isaiah extremely doubtful. If we find other more extended passages which display still more conspicuously the same characteristics, the last shadow of doubt will be dissipated, and we shall have to recognise vv. 5, 6 as a post-Exilic insertion, designed (like xvii. 7, 8) to brighten a painfully dark picture.[2]

The date of vv. 1-4 cannot now be doubtful. We have no occasion to suppose with Hitzig[3] that vv. 1-4 are an elegiac retrospect of the fall of Samaria (which had taken place, according to the critic, eight years previously), or with Wellh.,[4] that they refer to Jerusalem as morally a second Samaria, taking the phrase "the drunkards of Ephraim" as an ironical description of the rulers of Jerusalem (cf. vv. 7, 8). Neither theory would have been offered but for the supposed necessity of giving the same date to chaps. xxviii.-xxxii. as a whole. No unsophisticated reader finds vv. 1-4 elegiac, and Hitzig's denial that "in that day" (v. 5) refers to the (future) day of the destruction of Samaria is only legitimate if vv. 5 and 6 are referred, not to Isaiah, but to a later writer. As for Wellh.'s view, it is but the resource of despair. " Ye rulers of Samaria " would have been a possible and effective rhetorical expression in an address plainly intended for the leading men of Jerusalem (cf. i. 10), but no one would have understood Isaiah if he had really meant by his phrase what this great critic imagines. If, however, we

[1] Most give it in Ezekiel the sense of "fate." But see Cornill's text and translation.
[2] So Geiger (*Urschrift*, 1857, p. 92), Duhm, Hackmann. Giesebrecht (whose view formerly satisfied me) holds in his *Beiträge* that vv. 5, 6 are a correction of Isaiah's earlier prophecies of ruin for both kingdoms, made by the prophet himself. Meinhold, that the "remnant" in v. 5 means the holy remnant of iv. 3 (regarded by him as Isaiah's) the separation of which remnant from the ungodly mass of Judah is described, he thinks, in vv. 7-22 (*St. u. Kr.*, 1893, p. 45).
[3] *Jes.*, pp. 830, 833.
[4] *Israel and Judah*, p. 102; *Skizzen und Vorarbeiten*, i. 62.

admit that chaps. xxviii.-xxxii. have only the semblance of unity, and were neither composed entirely at the same time, nor presuppose uniformly the same or even nearly the same historical situation and prophetic anticipations, we shall have no difficulty in following our natural instinct and assigning *vv.* 1-4 to the year preceding the fall of Samaria, *i.e.* 723 B.C.

(*b*) *vv.* 7-13 and (*c*) *vv.* 14-22. Two preliminary questions have to be answered. (1) Is *b* a continuation of *a*? and (2) is *c* a continuation of *b*? The first question may be answered in the negative. Putting aside the opening words וְגַם אֵלֶּה, there is nothing in *vv.* 7-13 which suggests that Samaria's fate lay even in the background of the prophet's mind. Moreover, if our explanation of xvii. 12-14 is correct, Isaiah's addresses to his countrymen during the anxious period of the siege of Samaria were, on the whole, of a reassuring character. It is probable indeed that he expected Sargon to cross the frontier into Judah, but he appears also to have announced with impassioned fervour the final overthrow of the proud "spoilers." Now we can hardly assert that this is what is meant by the threatening language of *vv.* 11 and 13. No; the historical situation of *b* and *c* is the same, and the period referred to must be that which immediately preceded the invasion of Palestine by Sennacherib. This will be plain if we compare the following parallel passages in xxviii. 7-22 and the Isaianic basis of chaps. xxix.-xxxi.; xxviii. 9, xxx. 9;— xxviii. 11, xxix. 5, 7, 8;—xxviii. 12, xxx. 15;—xxviii. 13, 19, 20, xxix. 2-4, xxx. 16, 17;—xxviii. 14, xxx. 10, 12;— xxviii. 15, 18 (phrase), xxx. 32 (?);—xxviii. 16, xxix. 1, 2, xxxi. 4, 5;—xxviii. 16*b*, xxx. 15;—xxviii. 17, xxx. 1, 12, 13, xxxi. 2;—xxviii. 21, xxix. 14. The consequence is that וְגַם אֵלֶּה in *v.* 7 must be due either to a late editor, or to Isaiah himself, who (see xxx. 8) may have been the first editor of some at least of the prophecies of the Assyrian crisis; in other words, *b* is not a continuation of *a*. But though, as we have seen, *vv.* 7-13 and *vv.* 14-32 belong to the same period, and though in *v.* 19*b* we have a phraseological allusion to *v.* 9*a*, it does not follow that *v.* 14 was originally written to follow *v.* 13. The mocking rulers spoken of in *v.* 14 may have been among the revellers referred to in *vv.* 7-10, but they have left the "tables" and are once more cool and collected when Isaiah addresses to them this new and weighty remonstrance. Nothing more is said of "stammering lips" and "reeling with wine," and the scoffing of which we hear in *vv.* 14, 22 is doubtless more intelligent than before. Comparing *v.* 22*a* with v. 18, 19,[1] we may assume that this worse mockery had reference to the apparent failure of Isaiah's oft-repeated threat of captivity. I conclude, therefore, with Duhm that *c* is not a continuation of *b*.

(*d*) *vv.* 23-29. It is on every ground impossible that this passage should have been written as the sequel of *vv.* 14-22. First of all, because (like v. 1-6*a*) it is in the style of a popular song, though with a more obviously didactic aim than the song of the vineyard. Such a composition would naturally introduce, and not follow, a prophetic discourse. And next, because the purport of the passage is altogether inconsistent with that of *vv.* 14-22. For what is this parabolic enigma in two stanzas which the prophet sings to us? It is homely enough in form, and we must not look too far away for the meaning. The first stanza reminds us that, according to the divine ordinances of husbandry, ploughing does not continue all through the year, and that, when the hard soil has been broken up, the seeds of many a useful plant will be scattered. The second bids us observe with what variety of treatment the seed-vessels of the different plants are made to yield their precious contents, and how carefully the husbandman avoids crushing the grain which is to produce the chief food of man. Not less simple is the truth which the singer would suggest. "Ploughers ploughed upon my back," says another poet, "and made long their furrows," but "they prevailed not against me"

---

[1] "And now, behave not as scorners, lest your bands become tight."
"Ha! they that draw guilt (to themselves) with cords of ungodliness,
And sin as with traces of a wain;
That say, Let his work hasten, let it speed, that we may see it,
And let the purpose of Israel's Holy One draw nigh and come, that we may perceive it."

(Ps. cxxix. 3, 2). The "ploughers," in psalm and enigma alike, are the oppressors of the Israelites, who can only carry on their destructive work so long and so far as an all-wise God permits. And the same persons are also the threshers. "O my threshed people, my child of the floor," says a prophet in xxi. 10, addressing the Jews of the Exile. Assyria or Babylon may thresh the people of Yahwè, but not to such a degree as to imperil its individuality. Death and destruction may be the lot of other nations, for the threshing instrument employed has many iron points (see Isa. li. 15), but for Israel there is "a future and a hope" (Jer. xxix. 11). All this has been arranged by him who is not only אֵל גִּבּוֹר but פֶּלֶא יוֹעֵץ.

How, I ask, could this instruction be intended for the scoffing politicians of *v*. 14? Not the gentleness but the severity of Yahwè is the prophet's constant message to the rulers at this period. If *vv*. 23-29 are really Isaiah's work, we must suppose them to be addressed to an inner circle of friends, who have already learned from him that at least a remnant of Israel will be preserved. This would be all the easier to suppose if *vv*. 5, 6 could be taken as a correction of earlier prophecies against Judah, which to the prophet himself in the Sennacherib crisis appeared too unqualifiedly stern. Such a correction would of course be intended, not for the politicians and their adherents, nor yet for the vacillating multitude, but for those who were in any considerable degree influenced by the prophet.[1] And we have (as has been generally supposed) an address of Isaiah to his disciples, as distinguished from the people at large, in viii. 19. Unfortunately the supports of this theory are unsound. Both xxviii. 5, 6 and viii. 19 are of post-Exilic origin, and the idea illustrated by the parable is one which is characteristic of the late Exilic and post-Exilic period (x. 24, 25, xxvii.

---

[1] So Guthe (*Zukunftsbild*, p. 28) and Giesebr. (*Beitr.*, pp. 69-71). The latter critic thinks that xxviii. 23-29 originally followed *vv*. 1-6, from which Isaiah himself separated the passage when he inserted *vv*. 7-22. Meinhold's attempt to make *vv*. 23-29 a "message of terror" for the rulers of Judah in 723 (in that this passage assumes an awful judgment on unbelievers) is unsatisfactory; he sees rightly, however, that the comfort in the passage is meant for the "remnant" (*St. u. Kr.*, 1893, p. 44).

7, Ps. ciii. 9, cxix. 71), though we find a trace of it already in Jer. x. 24. Now, considering that *vv.* 5 and 6 were inserted after the Exile to soften the hard words which open chap. xxviii., may we not give a similar account of *vv.* 23-29? The words which precede this passage (*v.* 22) are as gloomy as any in Isaiah, and (from a late editor's point of view) needed softening as much as *vv.* 1-4. The announcement of an inexorable and all-embracing judgment was well fitted to crush those tender spirits for whom the prophecies were edited. Feeling this, a post-Exilic editor, who had had occasion to quote *v.* 22 (with unimportant alterations), followed up his quotation with a consoling exhortation addressed to the penitent church-nation which might be taken as a motto for the parable before us :—

Fear not, O my people that dwellest in Zion, because of Assyria, if he smite thee with the rod, and lift up his staff upon thee, like Egypt (of old). For yet a very little while, and the indignation will be over, and mine anger will turn to their destruction (x. 24, 25).

Is it not a reasonable opinion that *vv.* 23-29 are a work of the post-Exilic age, and were placed where they now stand by a post-Exilic editor?[1]

The tone and teaching of the passage, as we have seen, favour this view. Can we say this of the phraseology? Not very positively, so far as *vv.* 24-28 are concerned ; rare words were to be expected in this portion of the song. But תּוּשִׁיָּה in *v.* 29 is not less suspicious than לָקַח in xxix. 14. The word occurs elsewhere only in Proverbs and Job, Mic. vi. 9 being corrupt ; in Prov. viii. 14 it is coupled (as here) with עֵצָה. Now, it is not likely that Isaiah (who was heart and soul a prophet) imitated proverbial writers ; xxix. 24, xxxii. 6, 7, and xxxiii. 11, which used to be argued as proofs, are most probably post-Exilic. Nor is the direct imitation of Gen. iv. 23 in *v.* 23 quite in Isaiah's manner. The very same passage is imitated in xxxii. 9, but by a later writer (that the supplementer is here imitating xxviii. 23 as an Isaianic passage is not probable ; comp. his נָשִׁים with נְשֵׁי לֶמֶךְ in Gen. *l.c.*). *Vv.* 23 and 29 therefore

[1] Hackmann agrees with me that the present position of *vv.* 23-29 is due to a late editor, but thinks the passage may possibly be Isaiah's work, though not of the same period as *vv.* 7-22 (*ZEJ*, p. 40).

produce upon us the impression of lateness, nor is this neutralised by the occurrence of (a) הִפְלִא, (b) הִגְדִּיל, and (c) עֵצָה, all generally regarded as Isaianic words (see a. xxix. 14, b. ix. 2, c. xi. 2, xiv. 26, but remember that b and c may nevertheless be late). Had there been absolutely no points of contact with Isaiah (note especially a), we might have been surprised; the late parts of x. 5-34 are not deficient in them. Some may even find an allusion in הִפְלִא עֵצָה (v. 29) to the פֶּלֶא יוֹעֵץ of ix. 5; a kindred writer certainly quotes from the same verse in x. 21. Although probably late, the Messianic prophecy in ix. 1-6 may conceivably enough be earlier than the passage before us. Lastly, as to the imagery of the parable. That Isaiah might have used it, we cannot question; but if vv. 23-29 be late, they complete a chain of late passages in chaps. xxviii.-xxxii. which display a special interest in agriculture (cf. xxix. 23, 24, xxxii. 20). V. 26 explains and justifies this interest. Yahwè himself teaches the husbandman; i.e. he taught the first husbandman the rules of his art. Ben Sira too recommends agriculture on the ground that the Most High ordained it (Ecclus. vii. 15; cf. Gen. ii. 15).

But why does the editor put his exhortation in the form of a parabolic song? To correct or counteract the song of the vineyard in v. 1-6. Another late writer still more distinctly attempts this in the song of the "pleasant vineyard" (xxvii. 2-5). The divine culture of Israel is not all in vain. Affliction will produce the appointed fruit, and then, as another late passage tells us, woe not to Arial but to the "nations that war against" it (xxix. 7).

Chap. xxix. 1-14. Does this little section form a whole? All critics agree that there is a break after v. 8, but most suppose that there is at least a connection of ideas between vv. 1-8 and 9-14, v. 9 describing the stupid amazement which the so-called "riddle" of Arial[1] has produced in the prophet's audience. It is not at all certain, however,

---

[1] "Arial" (aryal) is probably the original form of the name; the l is simply formative. "Ariēl" (Sept. 'Αριήλ) implies the theory that the word is compounded with El ("God's lion"). The interpolator, however, in v. 8 substitutes "Zion," as if he supposed אריאל to mean "mount of God" (cf. the spelling in Ezek. xliii. 15 Heb.).

that הוֹי אֲרִיאֵל was meant by the prophet as a "riddle." If Isaiah's object was to shake the rulers out of their false security (cf. xxviii. 18-22), it is most unlikely that he would suggest two interpretations of the name Arial ("sacrificial hearth"), one of which could not but confirm his hearers' preconceived prejudices. Surely it is better to pay any price to avoid this improbable supposition. The price required, is not, however, as it appears to me, a high one. V. 4b is plainly a gloss on v. 4a. The following verse (almost entirely) and vv. 7, 8 (which are a very poor specimen of Hebrew writing) must be denied to Isaiah. But v. 6, which continues the prophecy of judgment in vv. 1-4a, cannot be dispensed with. It states that "Yahwè himself will appear in a mighty storm to 'visit,' i.e. to punish, Jerusalem. Hitherto Jerusalem has indeed been reduced to great straits, but only by earthly enemies ; now 'suddenly, full suddenly,' a superhuman foe will deal irremediable ruin to his own 'Altar-hearth' city. This stern announcement was too painful for men of a later age, who had done their best to make Jerusalem a fit dwelling-place for Yahwè. The editor therefore inserted promises of the destruction of the enemies, which involved a different interpretation of v. 6 ('visited' in mercy)."[1] It is also possible that v. 7 may contain some Isaianic phrases—the remnant of a lost passage respecting the siege of Jerusalem.[2]

---

[1] וְהָיָה with asyndetic imperf. favours the view here taken (see translation below), and rhythm requires it. פָּקַד here in a bad sense (Nifal, as Prov. xix. 23). לִפְתַע פִּתְאֹם, as (in reverse order) xxx. 13, where it also occurs in a description of judgment upon Jerusalem.

[2] Duhm retains v. 7 (admitting the correctness of b) ; Stade (ZATW, iv. 260) rejects it, but without questioning v. 8. The former critic, however, takes v. 6 as a prophecy of mercy ; Isaiah's message is twofold. He is on safer ground when he detaches the last three words of v. 5, and prefixes them to our sixth verse. Hackmann too defends v. 7, but by a forced exegesis (so also v. 5). I append some of the un-Isaianic phenomena. הָמוֹן, used four times (twice in v. 5, once in v. 7 and in v. 8) ; וְהָיָה, five times (vv. 4b-8). In v. 5, זָרָיִךְ, "thy foreign enemies" (a pregnant sense not found elsewhere) ; עָרִיצִים (see on v. 20). In v. 7, צֹבֶיהָ, ungrammatical. In v. 8, an entire phrase taken from v. 7, except in one point (see p. 187, note 1). Note also the parallelism between the figure in v. 7 and that in Job xx. 8,—a parallelism which extends to the phraseology (cf. Job xxxiii. 15). For the idea, cf. also Obad. 16, end.

Let us see how *vv*. 1-8 appear after the analytic process. The result is in more than one aspect highly instructive. The inserted passages are in italics, and being less rhythmical than the rest are printed as prose:—

1. Ha! Arial, Arial, city against which David encamped!
   Add year to year; let the feasts (again) run their course;
   [Here probably a passage has been lost.]
2. Then will I distress Arial, so that there will be moaning and bemoaning,
   And it will become unto me a true Arial;
3. I will encamp like David [so Sept.] against thee,
   And close thee in with intrenchments, and set up forts against thee;
4. And being humbled thou wilt speak from the ground,
   And thy speech will come submissively from the dust.

5. *And then shall the horde of thine enemies become as small dust, and the horde of the tyrants as flitting chaff.*

6. And then—suddenly, full suddenly, it shall receive doom from Yahwè Çebaoth
   With thunder and with earthquake and a great noise, with whirlwind and hurricane and flame of devouring fire.

7. *And like as a dream, a vision of the night, (so) shall it be with the horde of all the nations that fight against Arial and all . . . and its ramparts, and of them that distress it.* 8. *Yea, as when a hungry man dreameth, and behold! he eateth; but he waketh, and his desire is (still) unsatisfied; and as when a thirsty man dreameth, and behold! he drinketh; but he waketh, and behold! he is faint, and his desire is (still) eager; so shall it be with the horde of all the nations that fight against Mount Zion.*

Surely the portion in common type reveals to us the true Isaiah—the recipient of that stern message which meets us in his earliest revelation, and which could only be endured by one who had been admitted to so clear a vision of Yahwè's awful majesty. And the other verses are the work of a far inferior writer and a theologian of a different type. Rhythm and parallelism come easily to Isaiah; there are but slight traces of them in the passages assigned here to a later writer. And whereas Isaiah can bear to contemplate a sore judgment upon Jerusalem, the author of *vv*. 5, 7, 8, has before him a future day when all nations should gather together against the "holy city," and be cut off.

I can myself see no critical alternative but to accept the

analysis, unless, indeed, with Eichhorn, we reject the whole passage on the ground of its striking inconsistency. This course however implies a failure to enter into the later Jewish attitude towards prophecy. The later Jewish readers could afford to be less exacting than we are. To them Isaiah's prophecies retained a large measure of validity ; the meaning of a scripture was not to be limited to the fleeting circumstances of its origin. Knowing this, the charitable editor sought to mitigate Isaiah's threats as he had already done in chap. xxviii., and as he will do again in the sequel.

Arial then is not the catchword of a paradox ; some other meaning than that mentioned above must evidently be sought for *v.* 9. And surely a comparison of vi. 10, xiii. 8, Hab. i. 5 enables us to find one. It is this—that the rulers are culpably insensible to the divine teaching in prophecy and history. It is therefore a fragment of a new prophecy that we have before us in *vv.* 9-14, and the prosaic style of *vv.* 11-12 warns us that the passage, if Isaianic in origin, has at any rate been recast. After *v.* 12 we have *apparently* the introduction to a new prophecy (" And the Lord said "). The formula however may be deceitful. It shows probably, not that *vv.* 13-14 come from a different context (cf. iii. 16), but that the editor knows that *vv.* 11-12 as they stand are not a sufficient link between *vv.* 9-10 and *v.* 14. At any rate, it need not be doubted that *vv.* 1-14 entirely belong to the same great crisis as the following sections. One may infer from *v.* 1 that Sennacherib had not yet started for Palestine. The date will therefore probably be 703.

xxix. 15-24. The opening words contain the first reference to negotiations with Egypt. Let us take them in connection with xxx. 1-7 and xxxi. 1-3. The date of all these passages, and whatever else must be grouped with them, may now conveniently be determined. We have already met with several indications that Isaiah is under the oppressive sense of near danger from Assyria. Soon will the "scourge" pass along, and those who now hold their heads high in Jerusalem "will be for it to trample upon" ; a "final and decisive" judgment is coming upon the land (xxviii. 18, 22). Precisely how soon Jerusalem will be besieged, Isaiah knows not (see on xxix. 1, *BW*); but the humiliation of David's city is certain ; as by a terrible storm shall it be overthrown. The politicians indeed have a clever way of averting the danger ; " in darkness is their doing," but Isaiah sees through them (xxix. 15). Briefly their policy is — close alliance with Egypt and revolt from Assyria. Soon an embassy is actually despatched from Jerusalem to Egypt. Isaiah at once warns his people of the combined folly and wickedness of the step. Egypt will, he thinks, only prove once more its proverbial incapacity (xxx. 3, 7, xxxi. 3 ; cf. xxxvi. 6). And this time without blame, for Egypt's real foe is Yahwè. She will beyond doubt be overthrown, and will involve Judah in her ruin, or, as xxxi. 4 may originally have said, the lion of Assyria will carry off Judah as he carried away Israel. Now let us ask, When did Judah consider herself in such sore danger from Assyria, and when do we hear of her applying to Egypt for help? The first occasion subsequent to 722 was that which is described by Isaiah himself in chap. xx. The prophet's account is confirmed by Sargon, who tells us that (in 711) Judah like its neighbours had been " plotting rebellion " with the Pharaoh, " a prince who could not deliver them."[1] Now in xxx. 5, 7, Isaiah's language respecting Egypt is precisely parallel to these depreciatory words of Sargon. We might therefore plausibly assign chaps. xxix.-xxxi. to this period, as I have myself done elsewhere.[2] And we might further support this theory by the supposed mention of the double journey of the ambassadors of Judah to Zoar and to Hanes (xxx. 4), implying that they carried their suit for an alliance to the princes of these two districts, who, after the defeat of the Egyptians at Raphia in 720, had reasserted their independence.[3] This would, however, be a mistake. First, because the anxiety and excitement of the prophet in chaps. xxix.-xxxi. presuppose a greater political crisis than (at least for Judah) that of 711 actually was ; next, because

[1] The prince of Sais had assumed the title of Pharaoh.
[2] *PI*, ii. 181. In this case the Pharaoh referred to will be Shabaka (so Winckler, *Untersuch.*, p. 145).
[3] Maspero, *Hist. Anc.*⁴, p. 425.

in 711 Egypt made no attempt to interpose in Palestine (see xxxi. 3); and lastly, because the obscure words of xxx. 4— " For though his princes are in Zoan, and his messengers go as far as Hanes "—refer to the vassal-princes and messengers of the Ethiopian suzerain of Egypt, and describe the extent of his virtual dominion or influence.[1] We must fall back, then, on the next occasion of danger from Assyria. This was in 704-701 B.C. The displacement of Shabataka by his more energetic kinsman Taharqa (Heb. Tirhakah) in 704—for though till 689 he was officially styled only king of Cush, he probably became in 704 virtual suzerain of Egypt (see p. 96)—revived the dormant hopes of the kings and chieftains of Palestine, and led to a coalition of all who hated the crushing yoke of Assyria. Isaiah did not, however, all at once realise the full strength and capacity of Taharqa. The unhappy story of Ashdod (chap. xx.) may have seemed to him reason enough for his contemptuous description of Egypt in xxx. 5, 7. Later on he saw differently, and spoke most respectfully of the power and achievements of the Ethiopian lords of Egypt, even though he dissuades Hezekiah from an Ethiopian alliance (see on chap. xviii.). From the evidence before us I conclude that chap. xviii. was composed subsequently to chaps. xxix.-xxxi., and that these latter (in so far as they are Isaiah's work) represent prophecies delivered at intervals between 704 and 701 (but before the battle of Altaku).

"In so far as they are Isaiah's work." For who can venture to say that either xxix. 16 or xxx. 18 reads at all naturally as a continuation of the preceding verse? Remembering the late insertions in another great prophecy against Assyria (x. 5-34) as well as in ch. xxviii., we cannot

---

[1] "Zoan (now Sân, a dreary fishing village near Lake Menzaleh) and Hanes (now Henassieh, 12 miles west of Beni Sûef) were in times of political confusion the seats of independent kingdoms. Of Taharqa the prophet says that he ruled directly as far as Hanes, and indirectly even as far north as Zoan. The sense will be much the same if, with Brugsch and Naville, we look for Hanes in the Delta (see Naville, Memoir on *Ahnas el Medineh*, 1894, p. 3). For the suzerain would of course send messengers to his vassals, though these messengers would use a gentler style than those who bore the royal commands to immediately subject districts (cf. Nah. ii. 13)." *BW.*

help suspecting that here too an editor has been at work, correcting and adapting Isaiah for the men of his own time. It is no doubt in this part of chaps. xxix.-xxxi. that the case for the supplementer is the clearest. But we have already seen much reason to question the integrity of xxix. 1-14, and we shall find later on that the Isaianic origin of xxxi. 5-9 labours under grave suspicions. Let us first consider the phenomena of xxix. 16-24. In *v.* 15 we had to do with the politicians, who were absorbed in their deliberations and in the maintenance of a secrecy which seemed to Isaiah irreligious. In the rest of the chapter we expect to hear how Yahwè will bring to nought their counsel, and before all the world subject them to the deepest contumely. But no! it is of Israel's approaching regeneration that we are told, and this is apparently intended for an entirely different class of persons, viz. the oppressed and miserable, who are no doubt despondent and slow of perception, but whose blindness is not (as, according to vi. 10, it should be) incurable. Other persons, too, are mentioned, viz. the irreligious tyrants, who by their cruelty and injustice lead the poor to murmur against God's providence. But nothing in the whole description reminds us of Isaiah's present work, which is simply to unmask the politicians and to declare the terrible punishment of "this people" (xxviii. 11, xxix. 13). The judgment which the writer of *vv.* 16-24 foresees is not one upon the whole people of Judah (save the few who form the "remnant") but upon the minority of tyrants who are carefully distinguished from "Jacob" and· "Israel." Take the whole passage out of its present surroundings, and who would doubt that it was a post-Exilic work, addressed to those oppressed but pious Jews for whom Ps. xciv. and other kindred psalms were composed? The following conspectus of phenomena seems to me to settle the point finally. (Cf. on xxx. 18-26.)

Notice first a few points of contact with the true Isaiah. *V.* 18, דִּבְרֵי סֵפֶר; cf. *v.* 11. *V.* 19 (עֲנָוִים is *not* Isaianic; see on xi. 4). אֶבְיוֹנֵי אָדָם; cf. xiv. 30. קְדוֹשׁ יִשְׂרָאֵל, i. 4. etc. *V.* 20, לֵץ, cf. xxviii. 14, 22. *V.* 22, בֵּית יַעֲקֹב, as viii, 17; "Jacob" as in ii. 6, ix. 7 (see p. 252). *V.* 23, עָמְשֵׂה of the divine judgment, as v. 12, xxviii. 21; הִקְדִּישׁ and הֶעֱרִיץ, as viii. 12, 13. Of these words or phrases three are only important (see on *vv.* 18, 20, 23) as showing that *vv.* 16-24 are not an altogether independent work, but were designed as a supplement to xxviii. 1-xxix. 15. The rest of the evidence simply proves that the writer had some knowledge of the prince of prophets. On the other hand, there is a strongly marked affinity to the later literature. The impatient colloquial exclamation הפככם (*v.* 16), *i.e.* How you turn things upside down!—reminds us of the disputes in "Malachi" rather than of the imperious rebukes of Isaiah. The figure in the same verse suggests Jer. xviii. 1-10 and Isa. xlv. 9, lxiv. 7 (xlv. 9 also illustrates the force of the argument). In *v.* 17 we have first עוֹד מעט מוער, a phrase also found in x. 25 (late), and then a slightly modified quotation[1] from xxxii. 15 (late). In *v.* 18 note allusion to xxxii. 3, xlii. 18. " The deaf and the blind are the obstinate and blinded freethinkers, who shall leave the darkness in which they sat, and turn to the light of the law (cf. ii. 5). סֵפֶר, the 'book' κατ᾽ ἐξ., is the law-book (cf. Ps. xl. 8)" (Ges.), or perhaps rather the prophetic scripture, סֵפֶר יהוה, xxxiv. 16 (cf. xxix. 11). In *v.* 19 עֲנָוִים and אֶבְיוֹנִים are favourite designations of the community of faithful Jews in the hymn-book of the Second Temple,[2] and the beatitude, spiritual as well as physical, here ascribed to the עֲנָוִים reminds us of the close of Pss. xxii. and cix. Isaiah's expectations for them (see on xiv. 32) were certainly not suffused with this glow of feeling. The "joy in Yahwè" and "exultation in Israel's Holy One" remind us of Ps. v. 12, ix. 3, xxxiii. 21, cxlix. 2. For עָנָו comp. xxxii. 7, lxi. 1 (both late), and for אֶבְיוֹן xxv. 4, xxxii. 7, xli. 17 (all late). In *v.* 20 the structure of the sentence reminds us forcibly of xvi. 4 (late?); observe too that אָפֵם occurs only in these two passages and in Gen. xlvii. 15, 16;

---

[1] For "wild pasture country" (מרבר) "Lebanon" is substituted, probably because the writer took כרמל in xxxii. 15*b* (which, if we follow K'thib, has no article) for the ridge of Mt. Carmel. The sense is that Lebanon, which now bears vines only on its slopes, shall then brighten its summit with the greenery of vineyards, while the land which already produces vines and other noble trees shall become so thickly set with them as to resemble a forest.

[2] Cf. *BL*, pp. 467-468; Loeb, *La littérature des Pauvres dans la Bible* (1892); Rahlfs, עָנִי *und* עָנָו *in den Psalmen* (1892).

CHAPTER XXIX. 15-24

Ps. lxxvii. 9. Note also עָרִיץ and לֵץ. The former is the external, the latter the internal foe of righteous and afflicted Israel; as in so many of the psalms, the heathen Gentiles and the heathenish or free-thinking Jews are combined. It is true, לֵץ is not a word of the psalmists. It occurs in Ps. i. 1; otherwise almost exclusively in Prov. But it is synonymous in Prov. xxi. 24 with זֵד, which occurs in three psalms (six times in Ps. cxix.), and the class of men which it designates —that of hardened despisers of all religious restraints, and disturbers of the peace of society—plays a prominent part alike in the Psalms and in the Proverbs, and evidently belongs to a time of reaction against an organised legal religion.

These facts tend to show that the passage cannot have been written by Isaiah. To this it may be replied, that in xxviii. 18 Isaiah calls the rulers of Jerusalem אַנְשֵׁי לָצוֹן, and that the same persons might be described by him as לֵצִים. But the reply is invalid. The former phrase is applied to the rulers because they scoffed at the non-fulfilment of Isaiah's prophecies of judgment,[1] whereas לֵצִים in xxix. 20 has evidently a different meaning, viz. that which it bears in Proverbs (see above). The לֵצִים are here further described as עָרִיצִים and שֹׁקְדֵי אָוֶן. For the former synonym we may refer again to Prov. xxi. 24, where זֵד=לֵץ; זֵד, as Ps. lxxxi. 14 shows, is itself synonymous with עָרִיץ (on the usage of עָרִיץ see also p. 72, on xiii. 11). For the latter cf. two of the renderings of לֵץ in Sept. Proverbs, viz. ἀκόλαστος and λοιμός (λ. also in Sept. Ps. i. 1).

V. 21 might no doubt have been written by Isaiah (cf. i. 17, iii. 14, 15, v. 23, x. 1, 2), but injustice was certainly not confined to the prophet's time (see esp. xxxii. 7, late), and תֹהוּ occurs eleven times in late parts of Isaiah. In *v.* 22 אֲשֶׁר פָּדָה אֶת־אַבְרָהָם is presumably not Isaianic (*PI* after Wellh.; Dillm.). פָּדָה is suspicious (see p. 7, on i. 27), and Abraham is not referred to by the prophets before

---

[1] Barth (*Beitr.*, p. 23), following Rashi, Ibn Ezra, and Luzzatto, renders מֹשְׁלֵי וגו' "parabolic writers of this people"; Isaiah, he thinks, in *vv.* 23-29 counteracts the false "parables" by a true one. This view would help to account for Isaiah's use of proverbial terms in parts of chs. xxviii.-xxix.; these false מֹשְׁלִים might be well described as לֵצִים. But the context permits no other rendering of 'מ but "rulers."

Ezek. xxxiii. 24 (Mic. vii. 20 and Jer. xxxiii. 26 being post-Exilic[1]). But there is no reason why these words should be excised alone. The verse as a whole fits in well with the context, which is late. Note the ἄπ. λεγ. חָוַר. In v. 23, the phrase " count holy the Holy One " is parallel to one in v. 16 (late); " Jacob's Holy One " is unique. V. 24, יָדְעוּ בִינָה, as Job. xxxviii. 4. תֹּעֵי רוּחַ, " the erring in spirit," cf. תּוֹעָה, " error " (concerning Yahwè), xxxii. 6. רוֹגְנִים. The verb occurs in Deut. i. 27 (which is copied in Ps. cvi. 25). לֶקַח, " traditional knowledge," belongs (like the תּוּשִׁיָה of xxviii. 29) to the Wisdom-literature. It occurs six times in Proverbs, once in Job (xi. 4), and once in the Song of Moses (Deut. xxxii. 2).

Chap. xxx. (*a*) *vv*. 1-7. Here we are still in the clear atmosphere of prophetic oratory; Isaiah insists, but insists in vain, on the futility of an alliance with Egypt. The unity of subject, however, does not exclude a break of literary continuity. According to Del. *vv*. 6, 7 are a distinct oracle, which the prophet is commanded in *v*. 8 to commit to writing. It is not likely, however, that so solemn a " command " would have been given for so small an object. If a single short passage on the Egyptian alliance was worth preserving, much more so was the entire cycle of prophecies. In other words, in *vv*. 1-5 and 6-7 we have probably two parallel oracles,[2] descriptive of the journey of the ambassadors, and asserting its inutility. The latter would appear to be imperfect; the title is of course due, not to Isaiah (Del.), but to some late reader, who probably placed it in the margin, and to whom may also be due the glosses in *v*. 7, which obscure both sense and rhythm (see *RT*).

(*b*) *vv*. 8-17. To all appearance the close of a prophetic collection formed by Isaiah himself (cf. *v*. 8 with viii. 16), for *vv*. 18-26, as we shall see, are a late composition, and *vv*. 27-33, which describe the fate of Assyria, even if Isaiah's, have no place in the " woes " of chaps. xxviii.-xxxi.

[1] See Wellhausen, *Die kl. Proph.*, p. 146; Giesebr. *Jer.*, pp. 183, 188; *Beiträge*, p. 217.

[2] The view of Kuenen (*Ond.*[2], ii. 60), that *v*. 6*b* is a continuation of *v*. 5, is difficult. But so also is Duhm's theory that *vv*. 6, 7 originally stood, with the *heading* " Oracle (called) ' deserts of the Negeb,' " in the collection of " oracles " on foreign nations (cf. Hackmann, *ZEJ*, p. 12).

If this inference from *v.* 8 is correct, we must suppose that chap. xxxi. (so far as it is Isaiah's) has been moved from its original position. It is remarkable that, though this section was apparently not written for Isaiah's ordinary public (*v.* 8), yet in *v.* 12 the presence of his hearers is dramatically assumed.

(*c*) *vv.* 18-26. This passage must be taken in connection with the other parallel portions of chaps. xxviii.-xxxi., and especially with xxix. 16-24.[1] It is obviously not addressed to the "rebellious people" spoken of just now by Isaiah (xxx. 9), but to a penitent and believing community, the chief grief of which is that Yahwé appears to have withdrawn himself (*v.* 20), and which therefore needs cheering promises rather than reproaches and threatenings. It is true, the fulfilment of these promises lies on the other side of a day of terror—when, after the sore distresses of a siege (*v.* 20), culminating in the forcible entrance of the besieging host, the warriors of Jerusalem shall by a divine impulse "drive back war to the gate" (xxviii. 6), and there shall be a "great slaughter," and the "towers" (cf. ii. 15), *i.e.* the proud, self-confident enemies without, together with the irreligious oppressors within, shall "fall" (xxx. 25), not however altogether nor chiefly by earthly means (xxxi. 8). The promises which will "in that day" be fulfilled should be compared with those in xxix. 16-24, which they supplement. Special stress is laid in them on the transformation of nature [2] which the change in Israel's fortunes will require, and the new success which will attend the labours of husbandry (cf. iv. 2, xxxii. 20). But greater than all these physical blessings will be the spiritual ones. Israel will be under the direct tuition of Yahwè himself (*v.* 20). No danger henceforth of the revival of idolatry. There shall be a final destruction of all those private idolatrous objects [3] which have drawn aside the people from

---

[1] לכן in *v.* 18 seems to mean, "Such being the fair prospects of Israel," alluding to xxix. 16-24.

[2] See *BL*, p. 405.

[3] Kittel, who regards ch. xxx. as entirely Isaianic, candidly states that *v.* 22 has no reference to a reformation of Hezekiah. The prophet means, "not publicly acknowledged sacred objects, but domestic images

pure religion (*v.* 22). To all these points parallels in the later literature at once offer themselves (Ezekiel, Joel, Zechariah). Notice especially the late idea of the teachership of Yahwè;[1] it implies the cessation of the old prophetic teachers, to whom of old Yahwè had given directions (תּוֹרָה) for the good of the people. The late writer of xxxiii. 17 says, "Thine eyes shall see the king (the Messiah) in his beauty." But *this* writer is bolder: "Thine eyes shall see thy Teacher," he says (*v.* 20). There is no real difference however. "There shall Yahwè be for us in majesty," says that other writer (xxxiii. 21),—Yahwè, who, according to the writers of this school, would in the latter day become visible among his people (so xxiv. 23). Cf. also Ps. xvi., where we have in combination a protest against private idolatry (*v.* 4), an assertion of the teachership of Yahwè (*v.* 7), and perhaps, too, of the present enjoyment by the people of the vision of Yahwè (*v.* 11).

The smaller phenomena point in the same direction. The following are Isaianic. *V.* 18, לחכּה, as viii. 17 (but cf. also lxiv. 3, Ps. xxxiii. 20). רום "to lift oneself up," as Ps. xxi. 14, lvii. 6, 12, cviii. 6. חוֹכֵי לוֹ, stat. constr. as v. 11. *V.* 19, בָּכוֹ; cf. שָׂחוֹ, xxii. 13. *V.* 22, פְּסִילִים, as x. 22 (? Isaiah's), cf. Hos. xi. 2. *V.* 23, בַּר, as xiv. 30 (conj.), but see also Ps. xxxvii. 20, lxv. 14. *V.* 25, גִּבְעָה נִשָּׂאָה, as ii. 14. מִגְדָּל, cf. ii. 15. *V.* 26, חבשׁ (figure), cf. i. 6, iii. 7. רפא (figure), cf. vi. 10. But how much more important are these non-Isaianic! *V.* 18, חוֹכֵי, ἅπ. λεγ. in Qal; and cf. the whole clause with Ps. ii. 12. *V.* 19*a*: Note (1) Construction; עָם must be voc. (see Dillm.), and yet we can hardly dispense with אַתָּה before it. (2) Artificial parallelism; the very names have acquired a pathetic significance (cf. x. 24, late). *V.* 19*b*, for idea, cf. the Psalms *passim*, and contrast i. 15. שְׁמָעָה, nom. act., cf. xlvii. 9, lv. 2. *V.* 20*a*, לחם צר וגו׳, almost same phrase as in 1 Ki. xxii. 27. כנף (Nifal), ἅπ. λεγ. והיו וגו׳: note the expression of duration by means of the substantive verb and a participle.

---

which have still been preserved" (*Gesch.*, ii. 301). On the traces of post-Exilic idolatry, see section on inserted passages (ch. xlviii.), p. 316.

[1] *BL*, pp. 343-348, 352 (cf. p. 249).

Each of the other passages in the Book of Isaiah which present this construction (ii. 2, ix. 15 ? xiv. 2, lix. 2) is post-Exilic. The construction is not indeed necessarily late,[1] but is, at any rate (in the earlier period), not in use among the prophets. *V*. 21, forms rare in prophecy (Ezek. xxi. 21). *V*. 22, טַמֵּא, only here in Book of Isaiah. צִפּוּי, again only in Ex. xxxviii. 17, 19, Num. xvii. 3, 4. אֲפֻדָּה, as Ex. xxviii. 8, xxxix. 5. מַסֵּכָה " a molten image," as Ex. xxxii. 4, 8, etc. תְּזָרֵם, alluding to Ex. xxxii. 20. דָּוָה (fem.), here only in prophets. *V*. 23, מִקְנֶה, nowhere else in Isaiah. נִרְחָב, only here. דָּשֵׁן, as Ps. xxii. 30, xcii. 15. *V*. 24, בְּלִיל, only here, and in Job vi. 5, xxiv. 6. חָמִיץ, ἅπ. λεγ. רַחַת, ἅπ. λεγ. מִזְרֶה, as Jer. xv. 7 (nowhere else). *V*. 25, פְּלָגִים (again in xxxii. 2 ; elsewhere only poetic). יִבְלֵי־מָיִם, again only in xliv. 4. הֶרֶג, see on xxvii. 7. *V*. 26, לְבָנָה and חַמָּה, see on xxiv. 23.

(*d*) *vv*. 27-33. A highly poetic oracle which, being a message of comfort, can have formed no part of the " book " referred to in *v*. 8. If it be really Isaiah's work, it must belong to a later period than the preceding discourses, *i.e.* to the invasion of Sennacherib. Upon this hypothesis, the passage would be supplementary to i. 24, 25, which describes the judgment upon the enemies of Yahwè within the nation, just as xxx. 27-33 describes the judgment upon foes without. But the doubts expressed first by Guthe[2] and Smend,[3] and afterwards in a more developed form by Hackmann,[4] seem to me fully justified. The bitterness expressed towards Assyria, and the want of reserve in the description of its punishment, do not remind us of Isaiah, and there are other phenomena which point to the authorship of a much later prophet. That מִמֶּרְחָק is Isaianic (x. 3, xvii. 13) I admit, but the phrase " Yahwè's name " (*v*. 27) is found nowhere in the undoubted parts of Isaiah (xviii. 7 being late), and is here synonymous (cf. lix. 19, Ps. cii. 16) with "the glory of Yahwè," a favourite phrase of the later writers, of whom indeed the whole description reminds us (cf. lxiii. 19-lxiv. 1 ; Hab. iii. ; Ps.

---

[1] Cf. Driver, *Tenses*, § 135 (5).
[2] *Zukunftsbild*, p. 47.
[3] *AT Rel.-gesch.*, p. 282.
[4] *ZEJ*, pp. 42, 43.

xcvii. 3-5). כְּבֶד מַשָּׂאָה needs a parallel. *V.* 28*a* (down to יֵרָצֶה) is based on viii. 8*a.* " To sift (lit. swing) peoples in the sieve of vanity." This condensed figurative expression (in which note נָפָה, ἅπ. λεγ.) reminds us of xxix. 5*a* (probably late). Isaiah might however have used it, but where is the parallel in classical prophecy for its combination with the very dissimilar figure in the next line?[1] *V.* 29. To whom addressed? To the rulers of Judah? But they are "a rebellious people" (xxx. 9). To believers? But the parallel passages on which this view may be based (viii. 19, xxviii. 23, xxx. 18-26, xxxiii. 17-20) are all late. "The song," surely not a "wild war-song" (Duhm), but, as the context suggests, a religious festival-song (cf. Ps. cxxxvii. 4). הִתְקַדֶּשׁ, again in lxvi. 17, and in Ezek. xxxviii. 23, but nowhere else in the prophets. For the night celebration, cf. Ex. xii. 42 (P ; late). *V.* 29*b* is parallel to Ps. xlii. 5 (late), and suggests to Vitringa the description of the procession of those who brought up the first fruits. This sympathetic interest in festival processions would be strange in Isaiah ; it reminds us of xxxiii. 20 (certainly late). צוּר יִשְׂרָאֵל, a poetic phrase, only found elsewhere in 2 Sam. xxiii. 3. צוּר for "God" is itself Isaianic (xvii. 10), but, apart from xvii. 10, only occurs in late writings, *e.g.* Deut. xxxii. (seven times), 1 Sam. ii. 2, Hab. i. 12, Isa. xliv. 8 (cf. the prop. names compounded with צוּר in Num. i.-x., which belongs to P). *V.* 30. The verse is full of striking poetic phrases, but perhaps too stilted for Isaiah. It seems suggested by xxix. 6 (whence the phrase "the flame of devouring fire" is taken), and perhaps by Ps. xxix. 4, 7. The first two lines are specially strange. הוֹד קוֹלוֹ is like הוֹד נַחְרוֹ, Job xxxix. 20 ; indeed, הוֹד is chiefly poetic and post-Exilic. נֶפֶץ and the verbal form נָחַת occur here only. זֶעֶף nowhere again in prophets, except Mic. vii. 9 (late). *Vv.* 31-33 seem to be disfigured by glosses (see *RT*), but even after these have been removed this passage presents much difficulty if regarded as Isaianic. מוּסָדָה (*v.* 32) the fem. of מוּסָד (xxviii. 16), occurs nowhere else ; מַעֲבָר, only twice (Genesis ; 1 Samuel). The whole of the opening phrase is most extra-

---

[1] See the just remarks of Rahlfs, '*Anî und 'Anaw in den Psalmen*, p. 45 n., already referred to by Hackmann.

ordinary, and especially מַטֵּה מוּסָדָה "rod of destiny."[1] If genuine, this must surely be a late phrase; such an abstract expression is not Isaianic. Change it, if you will, to מַטֶּה מוּסָרָה (or מוסרה 'מ); but does the phrase become more classic? Contrast the vivid מַטֵּה שְׁכְמוֹ of ix. 3! And then comes that enigmatical phrase מִלְחֲמוֹת תְּנוּפָה. Is this an abridgement of מ' תְּנוּפַת יַד יי' (cf. xix. 16, late)? Or may we find an allusion to a technical phrase of the ritual, and render "battles of wave-offerings" (Lev. vii. 30), *i.e.* battles in which the human antagonists of Yahwè are irresistibly "waved (lit. swung) to and fro," as a preliminary to their being sacrificed? This may seem to suit *v.* 33, where some scholars think that the destruction of the Assyrian is described as if a colossal human sacrifice. If we accept this view, the authorship of Isaiah cannot, I think, reasonably be maintained (see i. 11). For my own part, I much prefer the simpler view of the phrase referred to (note לְהֶנְפָה in *v.* 28). But even then remember that תְּנוּפָה is not Isaianic.

Nor are the only difficulties of *vv.* 31-33 in the phraseology. The picture of Yahwè dealing incessant blows to personified Assyria (or to the Assyrians), while Israel "sounds the loud timbrel," shows a want of sobriety which is unlike Isaiah, and reveals the hand of a literary student. The image of Yahwè ceaselessly striking with the rod is no doubt partly derived from xxviii. 18*b*-19, but it has also an affinity with x. 24-26. There we read that, just as Assyria smote Israel with the "staff" and the "rod," so Yahwè will "stir up a scourge" and "lift up a rod" upon Assyria, and that in both cases this is "in the manner of Egypt." This not only illustrates the image of Yahwè as a striker, but explains the mention of the musical accompaniment. For when Yahwè "smote" Egypt for the last time at the *Yam-suf,* the narrative of E tells us that after the safe passage of Israel through the sea, Miriam "took a timbrel in her hand, and all the people went after her with timbrels and with dances" (Ex. xv. 20). This suggests that x. 24-26 may be the earlier of the two passages. The writer of xxx. 27-33, however, improves upon his model, and represents the

[1] Cf. יסד, Hab. i. 12. So in *v.* 33 allusion may be made to the pre-ordainment of the Topheth.

timbrels and lyres as being used during the destruction of Assyria, which reminds us of the vindictive pleasure expressed in lxvi. 24, Ps. lix. 11, and similar passages, but goes beyond Isaiah's awful but carefully moderated statement in xviii. 6. *V.* 31. Note first of all these words,—אֶתְמוּל (nowhere else in prophecy; Mic. ii. 8 is corrupt);[1] תָּפְתֶּה, ἅπ. λεγ. (if the text is correct);[2] מְדֻרָה (only in Ezek. xxiv. 9 with וֹ). Next, the awful figure. The carcases of the whole Assyrian host are to be burned as being specially subject to the divine wrath (cf. Lev. xx. 14, xxi. 9; Josh. vii. 15) on a colossal-pyre;[3] this at least is the most natural view, if we excise גם־הוּא למלך (or הגם) as a gloss. The picture is no doubt grand, but hardly Isaianic. It is in xxxiii. 12 that we read of "nations" becoming "as burnings of lime," and it is the Exilic prophet Ezekiel who foretells a raining of fire and brimstone upon the enemies of Israel (Ezek. xxxviii. 22). How conspicuous is the classic moderation in Isaiah's picture of the destroyed vines in xviii. 6 as compared with the awful figure of the grape-treading in the late passage, lxiii. 1-6!

On the whole, xxx. 27-33 is almost certainly not Isaianic; in all probability it is of post-Exilic origin. It differs, however, in style from other supplementary insertions, and there is this peculiarity in its contents—that whereas in *vv.* 18-26 there are but faint echoes of the past tribulation, in *vv.* 27-33 the "great slaughter" (*v.* 25) obscures the thought of Israel's future happiness. The two passages are hardly quite contemporary, at any rate not by the same hand. The latter need not have been long anterior to lix. 15*b*-21 and lxiii. 1-6 (where "Edom" takes the place here given to "Assyria," both names being of course typical).[4] We shall hear more of the fall of "Assyria" in the equally doubtful passage, xxxi. 8, 9.

Chap. xxxi. A supplementary "woe" which has possibly been transferred hither from another place (see p. 197). It is addressed, like xxx. 1-7, to the ambassadors "who go

---

[1] See Robertson Smith, *Prophets*, p. 427.
[2] See *RT*, where מְפֻתָּה עָנֶם is read.
[3] Another view is given in *BW*, derived from Robertson Smith, *Rel. of Sem.*[2], p. 372.
[4] See p. 53, on x. 16-23.

down to Egypt" without the true prophetic sanction, but gives a fuller account of the evil consequences of this irreligious act. In xxx. 7 we heard that the help of Egypt should be in vain; in xxxi. 3, 4 we are informed that the "evil-doers" in Judah and their Egyptian allies shall both come to ruin, and that not merely Assyria but Yahwè himself shall attack Jerusalem.[1] Thus far all seems clear, and in accordance with xxix. 1-4a, 6. That the figure of the lion growling over its prey, applied in v. 29 to Assyria, is here applied to Yahwè, need not surprise us (x. 5). But at v. 5 the scene is abruptly shifted. "Like flying birds (?), Yahwè will protect his city. Repent then, ye Israelites. For ye know that in that day men's idols will be useless. Yea, Assyria will fall by no human warrior's sword, or panic-stricken will take to flight. Thus saith the God who hath a fire in Zion." This may not be very consecutive, but so much at least is clear—that it accords with a passage which we have recognised as a later addition to the "woe" upon Ariel, viz. xxix. 7, 8. To the self-confident politicians it can have had no meaning; or if it had, the meaning can only have served to lull them to sleep.

On looking closer at the passage (*vv.* 5-9), we see first, that it is composite, and next, that it is altogether late. In *v.* 5 how evidently inappropriate is the figure! "Like flying (or fluttering) birds" should, one sees, be followed by "so shall the inhabitants of Jerusalem fly (or, flutter in anxiety)"; cf. xvi. 2. Probably the figure is due to Isaiah, and the following words were introduced later in lieu of words to the above effect which to the editor had become illegible. Note פָּסוֹחַ; the verb פסח is of obscure meaning, and is only found again in Ex. xii. 13, 23, 27. The prosaic sixth and seventh verses probably come from the margin. *V.* 6 reminds us in form of ii. 6, 22 (late), which are also unrhythmical (compared with their contexts); *v.* 7, of ii. 20 (late). The writer of these verses, fired with a holy zeal, and regarding the prophecy as yet to be fulfilled, urges his (post-Exilic) contemporaries to repent, supporting his appeal by a reference to ii. 20. Note בְּנֵי יִשְׂרָאֵל, *v.* 6, of the people of Judah, as in xxvii. 12 (late); in xvii. 3 this

---

[1] צבא על nowhere means "to fight for"; cf. xxix. 7, 8, Zech. xiv. 12.

phrase is used of the N. Israelites, and in xvii. 9 (late) of the ancient undivided people. *V.* 8*a* is rhythmical and, in spite of the repetition of חֶרֶב, might be Isaiah's, if it were only suitable in a "woe" on Judah (אִישׁ and אָדָם coupled, as in ii. 11, 17; compound phrase, as Am. vi. 13). Observe, however, that the other prophetic passages in which the "sword" of Yahwè is mentioned are later than Isaiah's age (see *PI* on xxvii. 1). *Vv.* 8*b* and 9*a* may be a quotation from some poem (Duhm); they hardly seem to be connected with *v.* 9*b*. Otherwise, the writer must have grown weary of the high style and of consistency of expression. Whose sword is it from which "he will flee"? and how is *v.* 9*a* to be rendered? In *v.* 9*b* note first, אוּר, "fire"; elsewhere only in xliv. 16, xlvii. 14, l. 11, Ezek. v. 2 (where, however, we should probably read בָּאֵשׁ with Cornill). אֲשֶׁר־אוּר לוֹ may imply a popular post-Exilic derivation of "Ariel." Does the writer mean that after the Assyrians have been slain (*v.* 8*a*) their dead bodies will be burned with a divine fire? If so, his imagery resembles that of xxx. 32, 33; cf. also xxxiii. 14. תַּנּוּר, "furnace," "oven," seems to allude to Gen. xv. 17. One may presume that the original "woe" came down to post-Exilic times in a mutilated form, and was supplemented by a late writer, into whose work a marginal gloss intruded.

CHAPTERS XXXIV.-XXXV

This is a first appendix to the prophetic volume, which is composed of i. 1-xxxiii. 24. It consists of two anonymous prophecies—one relating to the final judgment upon the nations (especially Edom), the other to the return of Jewish exiles, and the glorious condition of their land in the coming age. That these are by the same author, and were written about the same time, is highly probable. True, they have no external connection (the "desert" in xxxv. 1 not being that of Edom), but there is a connection of subject. They have also the same poetical form (see *BW*), and there is plainly a reference in xxxv. 4*b* to xxxiv. 8, and in xxxv. 7 to xxxiv. 13

(note the form הָצִיר and the phrase בְנֵה תַנִּים). May we, following Gesenius,[1] go further, and ascribe these chapters to the author of xiii. 2-xiv. 23 ? Scarcely. There are indeed some ideas common to both compositions, but in literary merit chaps. xxxiv.-xxxv. are far inferior to the parallel prophecy, and the characteristic faults of the latter reappear, much exaggerated, in the former. Still less can we assume with Ewald[2] and (in 1875) Duhm that the author of chaps. xxxiv.-xxxv. (call this *b*) also wrote Jer. l.-li. (*c*)—a work which, from a literary point of view, is as much inferior to chaps. xxxiv.-xxxv. as these chapters are to xiii. 2-xiv. 23 (*a*). The truth appears to be that (*c*) is the least original of a group of highly imitative works, among which we find (*a*), together with other writings, imitated by (*b*), and both (*a*) and (*b*) by (*c*). The literary problems relative to (*c*) cannot, however, here be discussed ; suffice it to note that the chief parallelisms between (*b*) and (*c*) are these: xxxiv. 6, 7, cf. Jer. l. 27, li. 40 ; xxxiv. 4, cf. Jer. l. 39, and that an author so given to copying as the writer of Jer. l.-li. is not likely to have been himself copied by another.[3]

We proceed therefore to ask, What are the leading ideas common to (*a*) and (*b*) ? These are (1) the imminence of a destructive judgment upon the sinful nations of the world, one of which, specially guilty towards Israel, here represents the rest, and (2) the return home of Jewish exiles. That at any rate the former of these ideas is presented in both writings in a strikingly similar way, is apparent at a glance ; comp. xxxiv. 2-4 with xiii. 5, 9-13, and xxxiv. 11-15 with xiii. 19-22, and it must also be clear that either the passages in chap. xxxiv. are dependent on those in chap. xiii., or *vice versâ*. Which of these alternatives shall we adopt? or, in other words, which group of passages presents the conception of the world-judgment in its most original and intelligible form, and with least rhetorical exaggeration in

---

[1] *Jes.*, p. 908. So Duhm, *Theol. der Proph.* (1875), p. 302 ; Cornill, *Einl.*, p. 145.

[2] *Hist.*, iv. 47 ; *Prophets*, v. 3.

[3] See Budde's masterly inquiry in *Jahrb. f. d. Theol.*, xxiii. 428-470 and 529-562 (especially pp. 435-450); Cheyne, *Exposition of Jer.* in Pulpit Comm., ii. 268-270 (phraseological parallels); Giesebrecht, *Jer. (Handkommentar)*, 1894.

the imagery? Surely the group in chap. xiii. One cannot indeed admire either the tone or the taste of the descriptions in chap. xiii., but there is nothing in them to equal the repulsiveness of passages like xxxiv. 3, 7, 9, 14 (where note the ugly non-Jewish myth of Lilith). Add to this that there is no *obvious* reason why Edom should be destroyed that Jewish exiles may return home. The writer of chaps. xxxiv.-xxxv. may, of course, have had one, but it is far easier to conjecture that Edom was substituted in the latter prophetic picture for Babylon, than that Babylon has displaced Edom in the former.

But we have still to notice certain literary parallelisms and linguistic facts which on the whole point strongly to a late date. I. Parallelisms. (*a*) Pre-Exilic. Compare xxxiv. 8, 13 with Hos. ix. 7, 6; xxxiv. 11 with Am. vii. 7-9; xxxiv. 6, 11 with Zeph. i. 7, 8, ii. 14; xxxiv. 3, 5 with Jer. xxv. 33, 27; xxxiv. 6 with Jer xlvi. 10; xxxiv. 5, 6 with Deut. xxxii. 41-43. I can find no noteworthy parallels in the true Isaiah. (*b*) Exilic and post-Exilic. Cf. xxxiv. 5 with Job iv. 18, xxi. 22, xxv. 2; xxxiv. 6 with Ezek. xxxix. 17-19. Also xxxiv. 1 with Isa. xxxiii. 13; xxxiv. 9, 10, with xxxiii. 12, 14; xxxv. 2, with xxxiii. 9; xxxv. 4, 5, with xxxii. 4, 3 (but note different sense); xxxv. 1 with xxxii. 15; xxxv. 6 with xxxiii. 23 (פִּסֵּחַ). Also xxxiv. 6 with lxiii. 3; xxxiv. 8 with lxiii. 4 (notice too "Bozrah" in both prophecies). Also xxxiv. 5 with xxvii. 1, lxvi. 16; xxxv. 2 with xl. 5, 9, lx. 1; xxxv. 3-5 with xl. 1, 2, 9, xlii. 7, 16; xxxv. 6, 7 with xliii. 19, 20, xlviii. 21, xlix. 10, 11; xxxv. 8 with xl. 3, 4, xlix. 11, lxii. 10; xxxv. 10 with lxi. 7, li. 3. Also especially xxxv. 3 with Job iv. 3, 4.[1]

II. Words and verbal forms. xxxiv. 2, קֶצֶף and חֵמָה for the anger of Yahwè, as (*a*) liv. 8, lx. 10, (*b*) xxvii. 4 and 9, passages of II. Isa.—xxxiv. 8, xxxv. 4, נָקָם for the divine vengeance, as 4 times in II. Isa. (see p. 265).—xxxiv. 1, קִרְבוּ, as xlviii. 16, lvii. 3. צֶאֱצָאִים, once in Isaiah, 5 times in II. Isa.; also in xxii. 24 (late), and four times in Job (late).—

---

[1] We cannot add xxxv. 10 and li. 11, though they agree so nearly, because li. 11 is but an intrusive marginal note suggested by גְּאוּלִים in *v.* 10.

xxxiv. 2, צָבָא ; see on xiii. 4. הֶחָרִים, as xxxvii. 11, Mic. iv. 13,[1] Jer. xxv. 9 (?), l. 21, 26, li. 3 (all probably late passages). Nowhere else in the prophets (in xi. 15 read בַ—).
—xxxiv. 4, מָקַק (Nifal), as thrice in Ezek., Lev. xxvi. 39 (*bis*), Zech. xiv. 12, Ps. xxxviii. 6 (but cf. מֵק, Isa. iii. 24, v. 24).— xxxiv. 5 (7), רִוָּה, Piel intensive, only here (cf. Pesh. John ii. 7). חֵרֶם, as xliii. 28.—xxxiv. 6, דֻּשַּׁן, Hothpaal (nowhere else).—xxxiv. 7, יָרַד = "to be hewn down," of animals, as Hag. ii. 22. רְאֵם, as Num. xxiii. 22 ; Deut. xxxiii. 17 ; Job xxxix. 9, 10 ; Psalms (thrice) ; not a prophetic word. דֻּשַּׁן (Pual). Verb only found in late or in doubted passages. Ex. xxvii. 3, Num. iv. 13, Deut. xxxi. 20, Ps. xxiii. 5 belong to the former ; Ps. xx. 4, Prov. xi. 25, xiii. 4, xv. 30, xxviii. 25, to the latter.—xxxiv. 8, שִׁלּוּמִים (Hos. ix. 7, Mic. vii. 3 have the singular).—xxxiv. 10, מִדּוֹר לָדוֹר and לְנֶצַח נְצָחִים, nowhere else. אֵין עֹבֵר, as lx. 15.—xxxiv. 11, קָאַת and קִפֹּד, as Zeph. ii. 14. יַנְשׁוּף and עֹרֵב, nowhere else in prophets. תֹּהוּ, see on xxiv. 10. בֹּהוּ, elsewhere only Gen. i. 2, Jer. iv. 23.— xxxiv. 12, חֹרִים, once only in pre-Exilic literature, viz. 1 Ki. xxi. 8 (*v*. 11 contains a gloss ; and Jer. xxvii. 20, xxxix. 6 are late). מְלוּכָה, as lxii. 3 (Isa. and, as I think, II. Isa. only use מַמְלָכָה). אֶפֶס, as in chaps. xl.-lxvi.—xxxiv. 13-15. For the names of plants and animals, see parallel passages (Hos. ix. 6, Isa. xiii. 21, 22), noting especially אִיִּים, צִיִּים, שָׂעִיר.—xxxiv. 13, בְּנוֹת יַעֲנָה, as xxvii. 10, etc. (see p. 146). חָצִיר, miswritten for חָצֵר (as also in xxxv. 7), does not count.— xxxiv. 14, פֶּגַשׁ, as in Hos. xiii. 8, Jer. xli. 6 (nowhere else in prophets). קָרָא = קָרָה, as xli. 2 (probably), li. 19. הִרְגִּיעַ, "to rest," as Deut. xxviii. 65. לִילִית, ἅπ. λεγ. (of Babylonian origin). מָנוֹחַ, once only in early literature (Gen. viii. 9; J).— xxxiv. 15 ; קִנֵּן, as Jer. xlviii. 28, Ezek. xxxi. 6, Ps. civ. 17. מִלֵּט, "to lay eggs" (cf. הִמְלִיט, lxvi. 7). דָּגַר, elsewhere only Jer. xvii. 11 (also Targ. and Rabb. Heb).—xxxiv. 16, דָּרַשׁ מֵעַי (?). עָדַר Nif., as Zeph. iii. 5, Isa. xl. 26, lix. 15.—xxxiv. 17, לְדוֹר וָדוֹר, often in Psalms ; cf. on xiii. 20, p. 73.—xxxv. שׂוֹשׂ, as seven times in latest parts of Isaiah. חֲבַצֶּלֶת, as Song ii. 1.—xxxv. 2, אַף, see p. 167 (xxxiii. 2). Note st. constr. before וְ, as xxxiii. 6, li. 21 (see Ges.-Kautzsch, § 130,

---

[1] See Kuenen, *Ond.*², § 74 (ii. 377), and cf. Stade, *ZATW*, 1881,). 168.

2).—xxxv. 2, 6, רנן ; see p. 58 (xii. 6).—xxxv. 4, נִמְהֲרֵי־לֵב, as xxxii. 4 (but in different sense).—xxxv. 5, פָּקַח (Nifal), as (Qal) xlii. 7, 20 (cf. derivative in lxi. 1), xxxvii. 17, Jer. xxxii. 19, Zech. xii. 4 (all late passages ; on Jer. *l.c.*, see Stade, *ZATW*, 1885, p. 175 ; König, *Einl.*, p. 339).—xxxv. 6, דָּלַג (Piel), as Song ii. 8, Ps. xviii. 30 (Zeph. i. 9, Qal).— xxxv. 7, שָׁרָב and מַבּוּעַ (plur. c.), borrowed from xlix. 10 (the two phraseological points of contact establish the indebtedness). See introduction to chapters xl.-lxvi. (p. 269), צִמָּאוֹן, as Deut. viii. 13, Ps. cvii. 33. תַּנִּים, as xiii. 22, xliii. 20. רָבַץ (?), as lxv. 10, Jer. l. 6, Prov. xxiv. 15.— xxxv. 8, מַסְלוּל, *ἅπ. λεγ.* [לָמוֹ ; read לְעַמּוֹ.] אֱוִיל (plural), as xix. 11 (post-Isaianic), Hos. ix. 7, Jer. iv. 22, and 19 times in Proverbs, twice in Job, and in Ps. cvii. 17.—xxxv. 9, פָּרִיץ, not before Exile, except Jer. vii. 11 [חַיּוֹת פ' is a strange expression for a good writer]. בַּל ; see on xiv. 21, xxxiii. 20. גְּאוּלִים, as li. 10, lxii. 12, lxiii. 4 (?), Ps. cvii. 2. —xxxv. 10, פְּדוּיִים. The verb פדה is not characteristically Isaianic (see on i. 27); here (see *BW*) parallel with גאל as in Hos. xiii. 14. יָגוֹן, four times in Jeremiah and in Psalms, once in Ezekiel and in Esther. Nowhere in the early prophets, but twice in Genesis (J). אֲנָחָה, see on xxi. 2 (p. 126).

The preceding evidence is suggestive. How few and unimportant are the points of contact with pre-Exilic literature ! And how close is the affinity of these chapters, both in ideas and in language, with the post-Exilic writings ! The writer was indeed not· ignorant of the early books, but he was only at home in the later ! Even such a late book as Job has been, at least in its outward form, absorbed by him (see parallelisms, I. (*b*), end). Among the later prophetic compositions, chaps. xiii. and lxiii. 1-6 have exerted most influence on ch. xxxiv., and chaps. xl.-lxii. 1-12 on ch. xxxv. If we ask why the imagery used of Babylon in ch. xiii. has been transferred to Edom in ch. xxxiv., and why the picture of the judgment in the latter chapter is so much more glaring, the answer is at hand. It is owing to the influence of that strange vision of deliverance, ch. lxiii. 1-6. The autho of this passage felt (and the writer of ch. xxxiv. shared hi. feeling) that the old prophecies of judgment on Israel's enemies had not been adequately fulfilled,[1] the present enemies of Israel being not less bitter than Edom of old. And not less imperfect, as the writers of chaps. lviii.-lxii. (and with them the author of ch. xxxv.) believed, was the fulfilment of the glorious promises of the second Isaiah. A large part of the Jewish nation was still in exile, and even at home oppression had brought the faithful worshippers of Yahwè to the brink of ruin. Hence the strange-sounding prophecies of building and of conquest in lviii. 12, 14; hence, too, the renewed promise of the restoration of the exiles in ch. xxxv. Both groups of prophecies (chaps. lviii.-lxii. and xxxiv.-xxxv.), it is important to notice, were written in Judah; there is nothing to indicate that the writers are at a distance from Palestine (and from Edom), nor is there any trace in ch. xxxv. of the passionate home-sickness of an exile. The author of chaps. xxxiv., xxxv. must of course be put later than his fellow-scribes. When he wrote, the prospects of Palestine were still of the gloomiest. One of his consolations was helping to adapt the collection of Isaiah's prophecies to his own times. For there can hardly be a doubt that the author of chaps. xxxiv. and xxxv. intended them not only as a supplement to chaps. xxxii. and xxxiii. (note the points of contact between these groups of prophecies), but to the whole "vision of Isaiah ben Amoz." And those who feel the beauty of xxxv. 1, 2, 11 will be disposed to accept chap. xxxv. as such.

These, then, are the reasons for not assigning chs. xxxiv.-xxxv. either with Driver to the beginning, or with Dillmann to the end of the Exile. (1) The writer borrows ideas and phrases from post-Exilic and very late Exilic writings; (2) he lives in Palestine, and only regrets that the restoration of Israel is still so incomplete; (3) the nation whose hostility he now feels most keenly is neither the Babylonian nor the Persian, but the Idumæan (see below). To these arguments we may add that in xxxiv. 16a[2] the writer appeals to his readers as students of Scripture;

[1] So another writer felt that the prophecies of the destruction of Babylon had yet to be accomplished (cf. Zech. i. 12, etc.; ii. 6), and Jer. l.-li. is the result. The parallelism will be complete if the argument in the next paragraph is accepted.

[2] On the text, which is disputed, see *RT* and *JQR*, iv. 332.

cf. xxix. 11, 12, 18, and especially Dan. ix. 2, where סֵפֶר, סְפָרִים = prophetic Scripture (Scriptures). Chap. xxxiv. shares, that is, in the new sanctity which now attaches to the enlarged collection of Isaianic prophecies. Nor can it be urged on the other side that " Lilith " (xxxiv. 14) points to an Exilic date, *lilît* being mentioned among the "evil *utuk*," or demons, in the Assyria-Babylonian hymns.[1] All that the name by itself shows is, that ch. xxxiv. is not of pre-Exilic origin. The growing extension of the Lilith - myth strengthened by Persian elements in post-Exilic times,[2] and the fact that the other names of demons in pre-Christian Jewish literature (*e.g.* Azazel, Aluka, Asmodeus) occur in certainly post-Exilic writings, make it safest to assume that the writer who so naïvely and naturally refers to Lilith lived considerably after 536 B.C.

I have now to return to a point as yet only touched upon, and ask, Was there any special reason for singling out Edom as the arch-foe of Israel at some particular point of the post-Exilic period apart from the great trespass of that people in "the day of Jerusalem" (Ps. cxxxvii. 7 ; Obad. 11-14)? Very possibly there was. We know from 1 Macc. v. 65, 66, and from Jerome's Comment. on Obad. 1, that in the Maccabæan and still later times a large district in the south of Palestine (including Hebron) was reckoned as Idumæan ; we know, too, that during the Exile the Edomites already had the hope of occupying the "mountains of Israel," which were "laid desolate" (Ezek. xxxv. 10, 12). From the fact that the restored Jewish exiles had no difficulty in establishing themselves in Jerusalem and its neighbourhood, it is clear that this part of the ancient Judah was let alone by the Edomites, but there is every reason to believe that the south of Judah (always less purely Israelitish than the north) received Edomitish colonists during the Exile,[3] and it is probable that fresh bands of Edomites

[1] Sayce, *Hibbert Lects.*, p. 502, cf. 145 ; Hommel, *Die sem. Völker*, i. 367.
[2] On the Persian elements, see esp. Bacher in Grätz's *Mt.-schrift*, 1870, p. 188, who connects Lilith with the Persian paris or peris (female evil spirits). In *Baba batra*, 73a, Ahriman is called the son of Lilith.
[3] The husbandmen who must have remained, even after Gedaliah's

poured in during the fifth century. The cause of this fresh immigration seems to be hinted in the opening verses of "Malachi." When the author of this work lived a terrible calamity was impending over the Edomites. Combining Mal. i. 1-5 [1] with certain notices in Diodorus Siculus (xix. 94-99), we gather that the Nabatæans from Arabia had, some time before 312, made themselves masters of the old Idumæa, and that a Jewish prophet who foretold this regarded it as a punishment for Edomitish "wickedness." What was the "wickedness" referred to? Almost certainly a fresh occupation of Judahite soil. The earliest offence of this kind was no doubt no longer recent. But the occupation of S. Judah by the Edomites, not less than that of the land of Edom by the Nabatæans, must have been a gradual process. The closing stage of the former process may have been some time between "Malachi's" writing and 400, and the closing stage of the latter will have synchronised with it. May not the bitter descriptions in lxiii. 1-6 and ch. xxxiv. belong to the period mentioned? Still I confess that the strange phrase "book of Yahwè" (xxxiv. 16) somewhat favours a still later date, and that the expression "seek ye out" seems to breathe the very spirit of the Scribes. At any rate, the date is later than most critics have supposed. "Bozrah" (xxxiv. 6, lxiii. 1) and "land of Edom" (xxxiv. 6) must be regarded as conventional expressions, like "Mount Seir" in the Wisdom of Ben Sira (Ecclus. l. 26), and "Idumæa" in the late classical writers.

murder, in S. Judah, being of somewhat mixed blood, may probably enough have become fused with Edomites. At any rate, we cannot safely argue from Neh. xi. 25 that the restored exiles re-established themselves in Hebron, for the list of cities to which this passage belongs appears to be pre-Exilic (so Smend).

[1] I have long taken this view of Mal. *l.c.* (*PI*,[3] i. 194); *Jeremiah* (Pulpit Comm., 1883-85), ii. 248, after Grätz, *Mt.-schrift*, 1875, pp. 60-66, who however brings down the Edomitish occupation of S. Judah to the time of Antiochus Epiphanes. For this I see no sufficient reason. The occupation must have been gradual. At least two different stages of displacement may be recorded in the three parts of Obadiah (*vv.* 1-7, 8-14, and 15-21), the last of which, if "Sephared" in *v.* 20 is correct, may refer to the deportation of Jews by Artax. Ochus (cf. *Founders*, p. 312). Wellhausen agrees as to Mal. *l.c.*, *Die kl. Proph.* (1892), p. 205, followed by Buhl (*Gesch. der Edomiter*, 1893, p. 79).

CHAPTERS XXXVI.-XXXIX

These chapters form a second appendix to the early Book of Isaiah. Not improbably they were inserted with the special object of illustrating and supplementing chaps. xxviii.-xxxiii., which (see p. 172) were intended by the editor to be referred to the period of Sennacherib's invasion. It is no objection to this theory that the events related in chaps. xxxviii.-xxxix. belong probably to the time of Sargon; the editor of chaps. i.-xxxix. must have had a different opinion. His own date, as the position of chaps. xxxvi.-xxxix. sufficiently shows, is post-Exilic, and he was dependent for his information on a historical compilation (our Books of Kings), which must in the main be referred to a writer influenced by Deuteronomy (D^2) who lived after, and not before, 588.[1] He could not therefore have helped supposing that the narratives which he borrowed from that work all referred (as his authority—see 2 Ki. xx. 6—suggests that they did) to the period of Sennacherib. The form in which this editor presents the narratives agrees in most essential points with that given to them in 2 Ki. xviii. 13-xx. 19.[2] On minor variations no great stress can be laid, both the parallel texts having such a long history behind them. The fact, however, that the writer of Isaiah shows a marked tendency to abbreviate (see especially xxxvi. 2, cf. 2 Ki. xviii. 17 [3]) confirms the view that Isaiah is dependent on Kings and not Kings on Isaiah, and it should at any rate be noticed that, as the texts now stand, the readings of Kings often look more original than those of Isaiah. Of really important peculiarities of Isaiah there are four: (*a*) the absence of 2 Ki. xviii. 14-16; (*b*) the shorter form of

---

[1] See Kittel, *Gesch. der Hebräer*, ii. 179; König, *Einl.*, p. 268.

[2] For a complete list of the variations, see Kuenen, *Ond.*², ii. 79-81 (Germ. ed., ii. 76-78). Comp. the relation of Jer. lii. to 2 Ki. xxiv. 18-xxv.

[3] Stade attributes the mention of "the Tartan and the Rab-saris" in Kings to a later interpolator. It is true that "the Rab-shakeh" figures alone in the sequel, and that in 2 Ki. xviii. 18, Sept. gives πρὸς αὐτόν (= אליו, Isa. xxxvi. 3), but the context in Isaiah is so full of abbreviations that Stade's view seems less natural.

the miracle in xxxviii. 7, 8 as compared with 2 Ki. xx. 8-11; (c) the unsuitable place given in xxxviii. 21, 22 to a shorter form of 2 Ki. xx. 7, 8; (d) the presence (see xxxviii. 9-20) of a song which is ascribed to Hezekiah. With regard to (a), it is easy to understand the omission of the passage in Isaiah, for its statements are nowhere alluded to in the sequel,[1] and were naturally painful to Jewish readers; on the other hand, there is no reason (unless the form "Hizkiyah" for "Hizkiyahu" be considered one) for considering it a later insertion in Kings. As to *b* and *c*, we shall see presently that the "sign" in 2 Ki. xx. 8-11 is a later writer's addition to the original narrative. The editor of Isaiah xxxvi.-xxxix. felt the contradiction between *v.* 7 and the following "sign"; he removed it by (wrongly) cancelling *v.* 7. Another late writer, who supposed this omission to be accidental, supplied the missing passage freely paraphrased, in the margin, and added (in a shorter form) a question of Hezekiah which had been interpolated in 2 Ki. xx. 8 as a consequence of an attempt to make the "sign" still more wonderful. Originally *vv.* 21, 22 must have been placed as a marginal note near *v.* 6, but the subsequent insertion of the song involved their transference to the end of the chapter. The reasons for holding that the "Miktam of Hezekiah" is a very late composition, will be given presently.

The dramatic character of the style of these narratives marks them off from those among which they stand in 2 Kings, and favours the supposition (in itself a natural one) that they come from prophetic biographies, like those from which the Elijah and Elisha narratives are most probably taken. It will be remembered that we have given a similar account of two earlier narratives in the Book of Isaiah itself (vii. 2-14, 16 and ch. xx.), which contain trustworthy information respecting Isaiah placed in a historical framework. We must not, however, at once assume either that the narratives before us are the work of a single hand, or that they are throughout as trustworthy as the two earlier narratives

[1] This arises from the fact that the passage is derived from a different and more ancient document (probably the Annals). The observation is Kuenen's, *Ond.* (ed. 1), i. 269; (ed. 2), i. 415.

referred to, and least of all, with Del., that they are (apart from some "expansions") the work of Isaiah, whom the Chronicler, writing about 200 B.C., represents (2 Chron. xxvi. 22) as the historian of Uzziah. Let us first of all consider the question of unity of authorship. The analogy of many other narratives should lead us to be cautious in assuming that only one hand has been at work; and when we have once recognised this, the evidences of a composite origin become exceedingly strong. Stade, to whom criticism is indebted for the first clear exposition of the case, rightly begins by calling attention to the threefold threat to Sennacherib.[1] The three passages are:—

a. Behold, I will inspire him with a spirit (of craven fear), and when he heareth a rumour, he shall return to his own land; and I will cause him to fall by the sword in his own land (xxxvii. 7).

b. So I will put my ring into thy nose, and my bridle into thy lips, and cause thee to return by the way by which thou hast come (xxxvii. 29).

c. By the way that he came, by the same shall he return, and into this city he shall not come, saith Yahwè (xxxvii. 34).

It is surely most improbable that one and the same narrative would have made Isaiah repeat himself in this way. Such a prophecy as (*a*) ought, of course, to be followed by an account of its fulfilment. We should have expected to be told that, on hearing of Tirhakah's approach, Sennacherib made some move or other, and the prophecy would suggest that this move was a hurried departure to Assyria. Instead of this, we are told apparently that Sennacherib sent a second embassy to Hezekiah, repeating in part the very same words which had been used before. What a strange want of resource! and what a strange lack of oratorical originality! But let us open our eyes, and we shall see that there are still traces of that very account of the fulfilment of the prophecy which we desiderated. It is related in *vv.* 37-38 that Sennacherib "moved camp, and departed,— returned and dwelt at Nineveh." That these verses were intended to follow *v.* 36 (the account of the pestilence) is

[1] *ZATW*, vi. 174.

hardly credible; v. 36 is self-evidently the climax of a description. Is it not in accordance with similar phenomena elsewhere to suppose that the narrative to which vv. 1-9a belong has been interrupted by the insertion of a passage from another document? Thus we get two distinct narratives of the conduct of Isaiah and Hezekiah during Sennacherib's invasion, the one comprising xxxvi. 1-xxxvii. 9a, 37, 38, the other xxxvii. 9b-36, and we can hardly doubt that chaps. xxxviii.-xxxix. (in some form) were originally connected with one of them. To prove this, we must not indeed lay stress either on the correspondence between the prophecy of fifteen years in xxxviii. 5 and the chronological statement in xxxvi. 1, or on the parallelism between xxxviii. 6b and xxxvii. 35, for that statement is probably due[1] to the editor of Kings, who also inserted in a fuller form (for which see 2 Ki. xx. 6) the words of xxxviii. 6. But the character of the fresh narratives is just that of the preceding ones. Isaiah is still the central figure, and in both the story does but enhance the supernatural greatness of Yahwè's prophet. Such a variation as this, that in xxxviii. 4, xxxix. 3 Isaiah is represented as going to Hezekiah, but in xxxvii. 6, 7, 21 as sending his oracle to Hezekiah by messengers, is clearly unimportant. In a private matter the prophet would naturally go himself, and not use the agency of messengers. Probably Duhm is right in ascribing chaps. xxxviii.-xxxix. to the author of the second of the preceding narratives, which also contains a prayer of Isaiah. The view of Wellhausen,[2] that these chapters (= 2 Ki. xx.) are a late appendix, arises from his not having analysed chap. xxxviii., and his failure to notice that an affinity to D^2, the chief author of Kings, is common to chap. xxxviii. and to the second narrative.[3] We

[1] Duhm.
[2] *Die Composition des Hexateuchs*, etc. (1889), p. 293. Kuenen, *Ond.*[2], i. 414, expresses himself more cautiously.
[3] Points of contact with the Deuteronomistic author of Kings (D^2). (1) In chaps. xxxviii.-xxxix. Cf. v. 2 (הסב פנים), 1 Ki. viii. 14; v. 3 (לב שלם), 1 Ki. viii. 61, xi. 4, xv. 3, 14 ("that which is good in thine eyes"), cf. 2 Ki. xviii. 3 ("that which was right in Yahwè's eyes"; in Hezekiah's character); xxxix. 8b, cf. 2 Ki. xxii. 20 (Hezekiah and Josiah are both to close their life in peace). I do not include the point of contact between xxxvi. 7 (first narrative) and 2 Ki. xviii. 4, 5a,

may now inquire—(I.) What additions (if any), common to Isaiah and to Kings, have been made to the *original* narratives; and (II.) To what date do these narratives, and their combination, and any subsequent additions, respectively belong?

I. That such an interesting group of narratives should contain some glosses and editorial insertions is in accordance with analogy. And we have only to read carefully to find some. 1. Let us take chaps. xxxvi.-xxxvii. The chief insertions appear to be eight in number.

a. In the fourteenth year of King Hezekiah (xxxvi. 1).

b. And if ye say (so 2 Kings; Isaiah, thou sayest) unto me, We trust in Yahwè our God, is not that he, whose high places and whose altars Hezekiah hath taken away, and hath said to Judah and to Jerusalem, Ye shall worship before this altar (2 Kings adds, in Jerusalem)? (xxxvi. 7).

c. Beware lest Hezekiah entice you, saying, Yahwè will rescue us! Did the gods of the nations rescue each one his land from the hand of the king of Assyria? Where are the gods of Hamath and of Arpad? Where are the gods of Sepharvaim? and where are the gods of the land of Samaria? have they indeed delivered Samaria out of my hand? (xxxvi. 18-20, corrected text; see *RT*).

d. To reproach the living God (xxxvii. 4).

e. Wherewith the minions of the king of Assyria have reviled me (xxxvii. 6).

f. Besieging Libnah, for he (the Rab-shakeh) had heard that he had moved camp from Lachish (xxxvii. 8).

g. (The taunt-song upon Sennacherib, with the accompanying "sign," xxxvii. 22-29, 30-32.)

h. By the way that he came, by the same shall he return, and into this city he shall not come, saith Yahwè (xxxvii. 34).

With regard to *a*. The decipherment of the Assyrian inscription has revealed a great difficulty in the chronological

because this passage probably does not belong, at any rate entirely, to Deut.[2], but either is or contains an interpolation (see Stade). My conclusion therefore is simply this, that the author of the second narrative also wrote chaps. xxxviii.-xxxix., and that he had the main part of Kings before him. (2) In the second narrative. Cf. xxxvii. 20 (appeal to the world to recognise the only God), 1 Ki. viii. 60.

CHAPTERS XXXVI.-XXXIX   217

statement of xxxvi. 1. It appears from the monuments that the fall of Samaria took place in 722 B.C., and Sennacherib's great western campaign in 701. According to 2 Ki. xviii. 10 the former event occurred in the sixth year of Hezekiah; if this is correct, Sennacherib's invasion belongs to the same king's twenty-seventh year. Yet in Isa. xxxvi. 1 (= 2 Ki. xviii. 13) we are told that in King Hezekiah's fourteenth year Sennacherib "came up against all the fenced cities of Judah and took them." What is the key to this difficulty? Shall we, with Sir H. Rawlinson,[1] change "fourteenth" into "twenty-seventh"? or suppose, with Oppert,[2] that chaps. xxxviii.-xxxix. originally stood before chaps. xxxvi.-xxxvii., and that at that time the opening words of xxxvi. 1 preceded the account of Hezekiah's illness? The first proposal leaves the illness of Hezekiah, the second the invasion of Sennacherib undated. And both are against the traditional text, which evidently makes the illness of Hezekiah synchronise with the invasion (xxxviii. 6; cf. p. 215). Shall we then, with the great Irish Assyriologist, Dr. Hincks,[3] assume that accounts of two invasions, one by Sargon in 711, the other by Sennacherib in 701, have been fused together? Ingenious as this theory is, it can no longer be seriously maintained, as Sargon appears never to have invaded Judah. Nor can it be rendered probable, though the attempt has again and again been made, to show that Sennacherib twice sought to chastise Hezekiah. (To this I will refer later.) Wellhausen and Kamphausen, therefore, after a full chronological discussion, decide to give up the date in 2 Ki. xviii. 10, and maintain that in *v.* 13 (Isa. xxxvi. 1),[4] while Dillmann prefers to abandon the statement in *v.* 13.

[1] Rawlinson, *Herodotus*,[1] i. 479. Bredenkamp, for chronological reasons of his own, proposes "twenty-fourth."
[2] *Salomon et ses successeurs* (1877), p. 31. So Delitzsch[3] and Orelli.
[3] *Journ. of Sacred Lit.*, Oct. 1858, p. 136; Brandes, *Abhandlungen zur Gesch. des Orients* (1874), p. 81, etc.; Sayce, *Theol. Rev.*, 1873, p. 18; Schrader, *St. u. Kr.*, 1872, p. 738; *PI*, i. 202-204. Schrader, however, long ago, and the author more recently, have altered their opinion.
[4] Wellhausen, *Jahrb. f. deutsche Theol.* (1875), p. 630; Kamphausen, *Die Chronologie der hebr. Könige* (1883), p. 28. So Stade, *Gesch.*, i. 606 f. Cf. Driver, *Isaiah*,[2] p. 14.

The note of time in that passage proceeds, says Dillmann, from "the (later) prophetic document" which the compiler of Kings adopted here as his basis, and into which he inserted a fragment from the Annals. And then in the fewest of words Dillmann throws out a hint of what is probably the true solution. In the prophetic document referred to, v. 13 began with some vague formula, like "in the days of King Hezekiah" (Dillm.), or, more simply still, "at that time." As Duhm remarks, it is not likely that any story in a prophetic biography would open in the manner of xxxvi. 1 ; the original reading was either "in the days of King Hezekiah" (Dillm.) or simply "at that time." The number 14 is based not upon historical facts, but upon an exegetical inference, *i.e.* upon a combination of xxxviii. 5 with the misunderstood formulæ in xxxviii. 1, xxxix. 1 ("in those days," "at that time"). Of course, if the illness of Hezekiah synchronised with the invasion, and Isaiah promised the king fifteen more years, the date of the invasion was fixed. In a word, the compiler of Kings had lost touch with the writers of the Isaiah legends, who certainly did not feel themselves bound by chronology (note the wrong order in which the "second narrator" places his three stories).

b. V. 7 interrupts the very pointed address to Hezekiah by a little controversy with the Jews, in which Hezekiah i spoken of in the third person, and a premature use is mad of religious considerations (see *v.* 10). Cf. 2 Ki. xviii. 4, 5ⱻ itself probably more or less an interpolation.

c. Vv. 18-20. "The Assyrian is inconsistent. In hi first speech he had stated himself to be the obedient instru ment of Yahwè (*v.* 10) ; here he represents the wars of th Assyrians as inspired by a religious hostility to th 'gods of the nations,'"[1] among whom he includes Yahw An inconsistency of which no one with such a dramatic styl as the writer of the narrative would have been guilty. Th author of *vv.* 18-20 clearly has before him the composit passage x. 9-11 (p. 49). By this insertion a very fir speech is spoiled.

d. and *e.* hang together with *c. ; d.* in particular weaker

[1] *PI*, i. 213.

the speech (notice that "Yahwè, thy God," precedes) and is copied from xxxvii. 17. גְּדָף occurs again in *v.* 23.

f. This notice is very confusing; clearly it was introduced by the editor to harmonise his first authority, which spoke of Sennacherib as at Lachish (cf. xxxvi. 2), with his second, which placed the king at Libnah, where he wrote his letter to Hezekiah. The two places were doubtless near together, but if Sennacherib came from the north, he would arrive first at Libnah. Like the editors of the evangelic traditions, our editor thought it best to combine both accounts, in however uncritical a way.

g. This passage consists of a poetic oracle on Sennacherib, and a prophecy in plainer language addressed to Hezekiah. That it is an insertion cannot be shown beyond contradiction, and will always appear improbable to those who hold that it is the work of Isaiah. It will be admitted, however, that, apart from other considerations, the form of xxxvii. 21-22*a* is favourable to the view that *vv.* 22*b*-32 are an addition to the narrative. The editor, no doubt, means us to regard זה הדבר אשר־דבר יהוה עליו (*v.* 22*a*) as the continuation of אשר התפללת אלי . . . אשור (*v.* 21). But how harsh this is! We may, of course, soften the grammatical harshness by inserting שמעתי at the end of *v.* 21 with 2 Ki. xx.[1] But the stiffness remains in part, and it is much more natural to regard *v.* 22*a* as the heading (slightly modified) of the following poem in a collection of sacred songs (or of prophetic addresses). Possibly the last editor altered על־סנחריב (not אל) into עליו when he gave the poem its present position. He may also have changed ישעיהו into יהוה, just as, according to some critics, another scribe did in vii. 10. Nor is it impossible that he added the prophecy in *vv.* 30-32, which is in a different rhythm from the poem, and addressed not to Sennacherib but (like *v.* 21*b*) to Hezekiah. If so, the case will be like that of the prophecy (xiv. 22, 23) appended to another great taunt-song.

h. If xxxvii. 33, 35, 36 belongs to the second narrative, and *vv.* 37, 38 to the first, it is clear that *v.* 34, which agrees with *vv.* 7, 37, 38, but contradicts *v.* 36, must be a later

---

[1] So even Stade, the most important critic of these chapters, *ZATW*, 1886, p. 177 f.

insertion, designed to link the different parts of the story together. The alternative, as Duhm points out, is to suppose that *v.* 34 formed the original close of the second narrative, and that *vv.* 35, 36 were added later. But considering that *v.* 34*a* is a virtual quotation from *v.* 29*b* (*i.e.* from the inserted song), and that *v.* 34*b* is a needless repetition of a part of *v.* 33*a*, the former view is more probable. נאם יהוה (*v.* 34*b*) seems appended to justify the repetition.

2. And which are the chief insertions (if any) in chaps. xxxviii.-xxxix.? A simple inspection of chap. xxxviii. is enough to show that several hands have contributed to produce this extraordinary medley. *Vv.* 1-5, together with 2 Ki. xx. 7 (omitted in Isaiah), form a coherent and complete narrative. (*a*) The earliest addition,[1] born of the later Jewish craving for extraordinary "signs" (1 Cor. i. 22), consists of *vv.* 7, 8, the form of which is to be preferred to that in 2 Ki. xx. 8-11. Hezekiah has already recovered; how can he ask for a sign that he will be healed? There is no *sufficient* answer to this argument. (*b*) The next addition, already accounted for on p. 213, is *vv.* 21, 22. According to Bishop Lowth, the editor in Isaiah observed that 2 Ki. xx. 7, 8 "was wanted to complete the narration, and therefore added it at the end of the chapter." This view might be admitted (cf. Job xxxi. 38-40) if there were not such a glaring contradiction between 2 Ki. xx. 7 and 8, which compels us to suppose that the omission of these verses in Isaiah was designed. (*c*) To the editor in Kings is due the next insertion (*v.* 6, from מכּף onwards). The words are, "And from the grasp of the king of Assyria will I rescue thee and this city, and I will shield this city"; 2 Ki. adds, and doubtless correctly, "for mine own sake and for my servant David's sake." The passage implies that an Assyrian army is encamped before Jerusalem, and that Hezekiah is reduced to the last extremity. This may have been the view of the editors in Kings and Isaiah, but is inconsistent with th

---

[1] See Stade, *ZATW*, 1886, pp. 183-185. Thus there are thre stages in the development of the narrative. In the first, there was n sign; in the second, the sign was described simply; in the third (2 K xx. 7, 8), the wonderfulness of the sign was increased by the permissio given to Hezekiah to choose whether the shadow should go forward c backward ten degrees.

sequel which represents Hezekiah as exhibiting his treasures with childlike ostentation to foreign ambassadors. The expressions of this passage are evidently derived from 2 Ki. xix. 34 (= Isa. xxxvii. 35). (*d*) The last passage on our list is the "Miktam of Hezekiah" (xxxviii. 9-20). It was inserted later than (*b*), because only thus can we account for the position of *vv.* 21, 22 at the end of the chapter (p. 213), and later than (*c*), because it is omitted in 2 Ki. xx., where the editor would certainly not have omitted a poem with such a heading, had it been known to him.

II. We may now proceed to inquire, 1. Are there any passages either in the two original narratives or among the insertions which belong to the age of Isaiah?—2. How long after the events described were the two narratives put together?—3. When were these narratives combined?—and 4. When did they receive the latest insertions? 1. There are two passages which have been referred by most (*e.g.* by Dillmann in 1890) to the age of Isaiah, viz. (*a*) xxxvii. 22-32 and (*b*) xxxviii. 9-20. We will examine these. (*a*) Let us first of all consider the oracle in *vv.* 22-29. There are five arguments which, I greatly fear, overthrow the traditional view of Isaiah's authorship. (1) The passage is in direct contradiction to a memorable prophecy (xxii. 1-14) which was most certainly delivered at the supposed period of this poetic oracle. During the blockade of Jerusalem Isaiah did not, so far as we can gather, consider his people worthy of encouragement, nor did he regard the retirement of the Assyrians as either ignominious or final. "National death" was only postponed for a time (xxii. 14). (2) There is no parallel in the age of classical prophecy for such an artificially constructed oracle at the height of a great national crisis. There are indeed two closely parallel taunt-songs in the Book of Isaiah (xiv. 4*b*-21, and xlvii.), but neither of them belongs to the classical period. (3) The writer of *v.* 25 imputes to the Assyrian king, and virtually expresses on his own account, a contempt for the power of Egypt which cannot, at the real or supposed date of the oracle, have been felt. Tirhakah was no despicable antagonist, nor did the clear-sighted Isaiah think meanly of him (see on chap. xviii.). But after Esarhaddon's and

Assurbanipal's conquest of Egypt, a late writer might not unnaturally ascribe to an ideal Assyrian king the proud boast, "With the sole of my feet I dry up all the Nile streams of Egypt." (4) According to *v.* 26, Sennacherib ought to have known that Yahwè had long ago predicted the successes of Assyria, whose king was but an instrument in the carrying out of Yahwè's purposes. This goes much beyond that great prophecy of Isaiah (x. 5-7, 13-14) which seems to have been in the mind of the writer, and it implies the characteristic late idea that Yahwè has given laws and instruction to the nations, which they have nearly or quite forgotten, but which can be recalled to their memory (see xxiv. 5, xl. 18-26, xlii. 4 end ; Ps. ix. 18, xxii. 28, xciv. 10). "Hast thou not heard?" is not the language of a prophet, but of a teacher ; cf. xl. 21, 28 ; Job xx. 4. (5) The style is choicer than we should expect in Isaiah, but the argument from phraseology is comparatively so strong that we need not dwell upon this disputable point. There are no doubt a few points of contact with the true Isaiah (see *vv.* 22, 26, 27), but the diction is on the whole neither Isaianic nor early. Notice לָעַג (*v.* 22) ; first prophetic occurrence in Jer. xx. 7 (לָעַג in Hos. vii. 16 seems corrupt). גִּדֵּף (*v.* 23), as in *v.* 6. Again only in Ezek. xx. 27, Num. xv. 30 (P). Both the verb and its derivatives (see p. 261) are late in use. מָרוֹם "heaven," as xxiv. 21, xxxii. 15, xxxiii. 5, xl. 26 Mic. vi. 6 (post-Isaianic). בְּ=בְּיַד (*v.* 24), prosaic, and in late prophecy and poetry. כַּרְמֶל, though good Heb., is not used by Isaiah (x. 18, xvi. 10, xxix. 17, xxxii. 15, 16 xxxiii. 9, xxxv. 2 being late). קוּר (*v.* 25), only here (Pilpe in xxii. 5). פַּעַם "foot," as xxvi. 6 (see p. 149). יְאוֹרֵי מָצוֹר as xix. 6 (late ; see p. 111). יָצַר, עָשָׂה, and הֵבִיא combined (*v* 26), as xlvi. 11. שָׁאָה Hifil, nowhere else (Qal and Nif. ir vi. 11). נצה Nif. part. in sense of "wasting," as Jer. iv. 7 Qa pass. (nowhere else). קְצִרֵי יָד (*v.* 27), cf. l. 2, lix. 1 ; Num. xi 23 (JE). יְרַק דֶּשֶׁא, cf. xv. 6, 11 (not Isaiah); Ps. xxxvii. 2 רָגַז, Hithp. (*v.* 28), here only. שַׁאֲנָן (*v.* 29), see on xxxii. ς חָח " nose-ring," cf. Ezek. xix. 4, xxix. 4, xxxviii. 4.

What then is this fine poem?[1] Formally regarded, i

[1] On the text, see Bickell and Duhm, and cf. Budde, *ZATW* 1892, pp. 33-37.

must be classed with the two taunt-songs mentioned above, from which however it differs in its want of strophic divisions. It is the first of them to which its resemblance is closest (see p. 74 f.); the king of Assyria described in it is a weaker edition of the grandly impious king of Babylon. But the predictive element which may exist in both the parallel poems is wanting, strictly speaking, in xxxvii. 22-29. This poem is primarily a dramatic lyric (cf. Ps. xlvi., xlviii.), suggested by a profound interest in the great Assyrian crisis, which was regarded after the Exile as a type of the great final struggle with the world-power. In a secondary sense, therefore, it may be called predictive; but the implied prediction is addressed, not to Hezekiah, but to the later church-nation. The poem has no historical value; the writer is entirely dependent for his information on the fragmentary and inaccurate post-Exilic traditions. But what a noble use he makes of his material! The Assyrian king of the poem is unforgetable. He is not the poor Sennacherib of the narratives who hurries home in a panic at the approach of Tirhakah. No, he despises Egypt, and it is Yahwè himself who drags him back like a captive bull to "fall by the sword in his own land." History had forgotten that Sennacherib lived twenty years after his return, and who could guess that his son Esarhaddon, in striking contrast to v. 29, had represented himself on a grand stele holding the conquered kings of Egypt and Tyre by ropes attached to rings in their lips?[1]

We now turn to the prophecy in vv. 30-32. Is it possible to rescue this portion at any rate for Isaiah? Certainly there is an abrupt change in the person addressed. May we, then, view the words, "And let this be the sign unto thee" (v. 30), as the sequel of some prophecy of Isaiah to Hezekiah? No, the first of the five reasons mentioned above applies equally to this passage. Moreover, the ideas and phraseology are not Isaianic. Thus, "house of Judah" (v. 31) takes the place of Isaiah's "house of Jacob," and

[1] See F. v. Luschan, *Mittheilungen aus der or. Sammlung*, Heft i. (Berlin, 1893). The Egyptian king is represented with pronounced negro features. He must therefore belong to the Ethiopian dynasty. The sculptor probably could not distinguish between the different types of dark-coloured men in Ethiopia. On the Egyptian representations of Taharqa, see Birch, *TSBA*, vii. 199.

house of Israel," and שְׁאֵרִית (v. 32) that of Isaiah's שְׁאָר
The high honour given to the "remnant" and to Jerusalem
is in accordance with the later eschatology; see iv. 2, xxviii.
5, 6; Mic. ii. 12, iv. 7, v. 6, 7, vii. 18. As a synonym to 'ש
we have פְּלֵיטָה, which occurs again in Isaiah only in the late
passages, iv. 2, x. 20, xv. 9*b*. Note also that *v*. 32*b* is a
verbal quotation from ix. 6 (post-Isaianic and probably post-
Exilic), while in *v*. 31 we have a striking parallelism to xxvii.
6 (late), and in *v*. 32*a* to ii. 3*b* (merely formal, however). On
the agricultural terms שָׁחִים, or, as 2 Ki. gives it, סָחִישׁ (in
either case an ἄπ. λεγ.), and סָפִיחַ (again Lev. xxv. 5, 11)
no stress need be laid.

(*b*) It was with much hesitation that in 1880 I expressed my doubts of the antiquity of a poem (xxxviii. 9-
20) which so accomplished a critic as Kuenen left unquestioned in the first edition of his *Onderzoek* (ii. 93). In the
present stage of criticism, however, it were false modesty to
speak as if the matter were still doubtful. The plaintive
song referred to cannot be the work of Hezekiah; otherwise
we cannot account for its not having formed part of the
original narrative. It is in fact a *very late* insertion, (1)
because of the character of the style, and (2) because the
heading [1] (*v*. 9) and the appendix [2] (*v*. 20) combine to prove
that this poem was taken (like the "prayer of Habakkuk"
in Hab. iii.) from a late collection of liturgical songs
That *all* the headings of the psalms are of post-Exilic origin
is no longer a doubtful proposition; why then should we
attach the least importance to the title "Miktam of Hezekiah"? How full the poem is of literary reminiscences has
long ago been pointed out. "In the melancholy tone
of its contemplation of death it reminds us partly of
the Psalms (see Ps. vi. 5, xxx. 9, lxxxviii. 10-12, xciv. 17
cxv. 17), partly of the Book of Job (*e.g.* chap. xiv.)—the
latter book, indeed, seems to have influenced not only the
tone, but even the selection of images and phraseology in
the song. The proof of this has been given by Delitzsch

[1] See Drechsler, *Der Proph. Jes.*, ii. 2, pp. 220, 221 (*Anhang* b
Delitzsch).

[2] An early date seems inconsistent with the apparent allusion in *v*. 2
to a fact only supported by the Chronicler [2 Chr. xxix. 30, Hezekiah
superintendence of the temple psalmody].

who infers from this relation of the two works that to ascribe a later date to the Book of Job than the age of Solomon is henceforth an impossibility. As specimens of the close stylistic affinity between our song and the Book of Job, take 'the gates of Sheól,' *v.* 10, comparing 'the gates of Death,' Job xxxviii. 17 ; the image of the body as the house of the soul, *v.* 12, comp. Job vi. 19, 21 (in the latter passage the soul is compared to a tent-rope) ; that of death as the cutting off of the thread of life, *v.* 12, comp. Job vi. 9, xxvii. 8 (*QPB*) ; and of God, when He afflicts man, as a lion, *v.* 13, comp. Job x. 16. Compare, too, the image of the weaver's shuttle in Job vii. 6. For the scattered phraseological parallels, see notes on *vv.* 12, 14, 15, 16."[1] The conviction too gently expressed in 1880 I have found no cause to abandon. To collect the phraseological data in full is however unnecessary ; few who accept the Exilic or post-Exilic date of the Book of Job will question the post-Exilic date of the psalm of Hezekiah. Five decidedly late words may be mentioned. *V.* 11, חֶלֶד, late in use, see *BL*, p. 467. *V.* 12, דּוֹר " dwelling " ; cf. דּוּר Ps. lxxxiv. 11 (Aram.). *V.* 14 (a safe correction ; *RT*), עָשַׁק, cf. Aram. and Talm. עֲסַק " to busy oneself with " (see Klostermann, *St. u. Kr.*, 1884, p. 157, etc.). *V.* 15, אַדַּדֶּה, late, see on Ps. xlii. 5 (*BL*, p. 470). *V.* 18, שֶׁבֶר, only in Ruth, Esther, Psalms ; Qal in Nehemiah. Cf. Aram. סְבַר. Duhm quotes the unemphatic use of אֲנִי (*v.* 10) as reminding us of Qoheleth.[2] But we should compare rather the apparently superfluous אֲנִי in Ps. xxx. 7, xxxi. 23, lxxxviii. 14, cxvi. 11, where there is an implied antithesis. So here there is an antithesis between the speaker who thought himself Godforsaken and Yahwè who was ready to save him from " the pit of destruction " (*v.* 17, note אַתָּה). It is no objection to this view that in *v.* 11 we have אָמַרְתִּי without אֲנִי. The אֲנִי was probably required in *v.* 10 to complete the number of syllables,[3] but would have been superfluous in *v.* 11.

And now to sum up. Formally regarded the poem is a song of which only the beginning and the end (*vv.* 10-13 ;

---

[1] *PI*, i. 228.   [2] Cf. König, *Einl.*, p. 432, l. 18.
[3] So also in the psalm-passages, to which add Ps. xli. 5, cxvi. 10, where there is probably only a metrical reason for the presence of אֲנִי.

vv. 17*b*-19) have been fully preserved. This portion, however, enables us to conjecture the original plan of the work. It consisted probably of six tetrastichs, each containing four stichi. The author was not a great literary artist; he began, as it seems, in syllabic metre, but could not carry it on consistently.[1] *V.* 20 (at the head of which supply רְצֵה, cf. Ps. xl. 14) is a rhythmic liturgical appendix. Next, as to its contents. The speaker is not even in dramatic fiction Hezekiah, but the church-nation, which has lately been brought to the verge of destruction, and even now fears to indulge in the rapture of deliverance. To understand the song, we should read it with Ps. lxxxviii., which is equally full of reminiscences of Job, and of which it may be regarded as the complement, just as Ps. xxx. is the complement of Ps. vi. And the period of both is probably the last century of Persian rule in Palestine.[2]

II. 2. Our second question relates to the date of the two narratives in their (presumably) original form. It may be reasonably supposed that the former (xxxvi. 1-xxxvii. 9*a*, 37, 38) was written considerably before the latter on account of its greater historical simplicity and the absence of a prominent didactic purpose. This point indeed cannot be definitely settled, but we may at any rate be sure that even the first narrative was written long after the time of the events described. That there are points of contact with the true Isaiah may be admitted—cf. xxxvi. 8 with xxxi. 1, etc.; *v.* 10 with x. 5; xxxvii. 32 with ix. 6; *v.* 35 with xxxi. 5; *v.* 36 with xvii. 14. But these simply prove some acquaintance with Isaiah on the part of the writers. And on the other hand, xxxvii. 4 may allude to x. 22, and *v.* 36 to xxxi. 8*a*, both of which are late insertions, and the narratives are full of contradictions to the ideas and descriptions of the prophecies of Isaiah. Nor can it easily be denied that the narratives are strikingly inaccurate, both in chronology and in details.

Instances of this inaccuracy will at once suggest them-

---

[1] In the first and last tetrastich (*a*), (*b*), and (*c*) are taken by Bickell as decasyllabic, *d* as octosyllabic. The middle part, so far as one can judge from the present text, presents a variable rhythm.

[2] See *BL*, pp. 117-118, and cf. Baethgen.

selves. The embassy from Babylon is placed by the second narrator (as there seems no sufficient reason to doubt) soon after the disaster of the Assyrians. But this is a gross error. The embassy must, of course, have preceded the Assyrian invasion. Its real object was, not to congratulate Hezekiah on his recovery [1] (xxxix. 1), but to stimulate the king to join in a revolt against Assyria. The only question is, whether it belongs to the first (722-710) or to the second (702) of Merodach-Baladan's two usurpations of the crown of Babylon. The second, however, was so short (it lasted only nine months) that the Chaldæan prince can hardly have felt strong enough to plan an extended revolt. In 1880 I ventured to place it in 713 or 712.[2] Nearly the same date (711) was given by Hommel[3] in 1885, and by Duhm in 1892, while Tiele placed the event more vaguely in one of the later years of Merodach-Baladan's first period of kingship.[4] Winckler, however, dates it earlier,[5] viz. in 720 or 719, shortly after the great defeat of Sargon by the Chaldæans at Dûr-ilu (see on xiv. 28-32, p. 81), and, if the chronology of Hezekiah's reign will permit, this view is preferable. But at any rate the true period and the object of the embassy were forgotten when the second narrator lived, and this writer must also have been ignorant of Hezekiah's payment of tribute to Sennacherib (2 Ki. xviii. 15). Otherwise why did he not make Isaiah foretell in xxxviii. 6 this nearer and more personal chastisement?[6]

There is no improvement when we pass on to the accounts of the Assyrian invasion. We will not indeed impute to the first narrator the wrong date in xxxvi. 1, nor the belief in the perfidy of Sennacherib which most readers (cf. xxxiii. 8, "he hath broken the covenant") have derived from the collocation of 2 Ki. xviii. 16 and 17. But have we not a right to blame him for his unintelligible account of the mission of the Rab-shakeh, who comes to Hezekiah "with a great host," makes an oration to the citizens of

---

[1] Nor yet "to inquire of the portent that had occurred in the land" (2 Chron. xxxii. 31).
[2] *PI*, i. 205.
[3] *Gesch.*, p. 704.
[4] *Bab.-ass. Gesch.*, p. 319.
[5] *Untersuch.*, pp. 139-142.
[6] On the supposed prediction in xxxix. 6, 7, see *PI*, i. 239-240.

Jerusalem, and then returns to his master, for his ignorance of the plague which (as most critics admit) decimated the Assyrians, and for his misleading notice of the death of Sennacherib?[1] And must we not criticise the second narrator, first, for the anachronism of the theology which he ascribes to Hezekiah; next, for his too edifying version of the king's character, and of the relations between him and Isaiah; and, lastly, for his at once vague and exaggerated account (some will even say, for his invention) of the pestilence in the Assyrian camp?

Yes; any one who approaches these narratives with the prejudice that they have a historical object, may and must criticise them severely. But there is a sufficient excuse for their inaccuracies, viz. (1) that they are probably taken, as we have seen, from biographies (or fragments of biographies) of Isaiah, which aimed first at doing honour to the prophet, and had no direct concern with history; and (2) that these biographies represent a very late phase of tradition, later at any rate than 588 B.C. Can we reach a more precise view of their date? It is possible that the ideas and phraseology of the narratives may enable us to do so. See e.g. xxxvii. 4, where Isaiah is asked to intercede for the "remnant." The term is used technically, without anything in the context to explain it; it is the Isaianic word שְׁאֵרִית (as v. 32; see xiv. 30). The writer may, perhaps, recall x. 22 (Dillm.); at any rate, xxxvii. 4 and x. 22 may be nearly contemporaneous. In xxxvii. 16-20 the conscious monotheism is certainly that of Deuteronomy and the second Isaiah; note especially לְבַדְּךָ, v. 16, and cf. xliv. 24. In xxxix. 6, 7, the belief that prophets like Isaiah predicted distant political events cannot be shown to be pre-Exilic. In xxxvi. 11 the language of Judah is called יְהוּדִית, as in Neh. xiii. 24 (nowhere else). The designation " Jew " occurs in 2 Ki. xvi. 6, xxv. 25, Jer. xxxiv. 9, etc. In xxxvii. 11 (18), cf. xxxvi. 20, occurs אֲרָצוֹת. Apart from these and the parallel passages, this plural form stands in sixty-seven

---

[1] With this writer the assassination of Sennacherib takes the place of the pestilence in the other narrative. For the former is clearly intended as a swift punishment for Sennacherib's blasphemy (cf. xxxvii. 4, 7).

passages, of which all but Gen. xli. 54 (E) occur between the age of Jeremiah and that of the Chronicler. Jeremiah uses it seven times, Ezekiel not less than twenty-seven. In xxxvii. 17, פָּקַח (see p. 266). In xxxix. 2, בֵּית נְכוֹתָו (so read), cf. Ass. *bît nakamâti* (*nakavâti*), "treasure-house," from *nakâmu*, "to heap up."[1] Also מֶמְשָׁלָה, as in xxii. 21 (late), see p. 137. I do not include the form חִזְקִיָּהוּ, though this is proved correct by Sennacherib's inscriptions, because names of this formation occur quite late; nor פֶּחָה, Ass. *paḥat*, "governor," xxxvi. 9, because פַּחַת is clearly a gloss (see Stade, *ZATW*, 1886, p. 182).

In view of this evidence, must we not admit that at any rate the second narrative (including chaps. xxxviii.-xxxix.) is most probably post-Exilic?[2] And if so, our third question is already answered; the combination of the two narratives (2 Ki. xviii. 14-16) and the insertion of the composite narrative in Kings must also be post-Exilic. This is entirely consistent with the relation pointed out on p. 215 between the second narrative (in its fullest extent) and D^2, whom, with Kittel and König, I take to have worked before the close of the Exile. The only question which now remains is, What is the date of the latest insertions in chaps. xxxvi.-xxxix.? This too has been incidentally answered already. The insertions in xxxvi. 1, xxxvii. 8 are clearly editorial. Others, such as xxxvi. 18-20, xxxvii. 4, 6, which are derived from the second narrative, were presumably made before the two narratives were combined.[3] The latest of all appear to be xxxviii. 21, 22, and the "Miktam of Hezekiah," the latter of which may conceivably have been inserted as late as the beginning of the Greek period.

These results may, I fear, seem at first sight to destroy the historical value of the narratives. Such, however, is not the case. Not only do they help to fill out our ideas of the Exilic and post-Exilic age, but they contribute some valuable

---

[1] Paul Haupt, *Zt. f. Assyriologie*, 1887, p. 266.
[2] But of course considerably earlier than Chronicles (see 2 Chron. xxxii.). Wellhausen thinks that xxxix. 5-7 transport us into the time of the Exile (so too Kuenen). But would a post-Exilic writer have expressed himself differently? *I reserve the question as to pre-Exilic elements in these narratives.* [3] Duhm.

material (the amount of which, no doubt, may be differently estimated by different critics[1]) for the history of Sennacherib's invasion. We have *a priori* a right to expect this; even the story of Elijah is admittedly an embroidery of legend on a basis of fact. And whereas the story of Elijah is in the main derived from oral tradition, the lives of Isaiah, of which we have fragments in these chapters, were probably founded on earlier written biographies. It is well, therefore, even from a historical point of view, that we have Jewish traditions of Sennacherib's invasion to put beside the official narratives of the Assyrian scribes. This is what the great king (or one of the temple officers) has to tell us of his famous third campaign (701 B.C.). He spares us this time the record of the difficulties of the route. The fall of Sidon opens his list of his successes. Great was the terror it produced among the petty kings of Palestine, whose plans of an armed coalition had thus been baffled. Sennacherib was not so much too strong as too quick for his opponents. Among the few who still held out were the kings of Ashkelon, Ekron, and Judah. After holding a great durbar, at which all faithful vassals assembled, Sennacherib proceeded to Ashkelon, where the former king had been deposed for his Assyrian propensities, and been succeeded by the nominee of the Egyptian party, Zidkâ. Short was the siege of Ashkelon. Zidkâ, and his gods, and his family went into captivity. The king or chieftain of Ekron was more enterprising. In hot haste he sent for his allies, the kings of Egypt and the king of Melucha (N.W. Arabia); "countless troops they summoned." But the Egyptians were no longer the equals of the Assyrians in warlike skill. A battle took place before the neighbouring city of Altaku (Eltekeh, Josh. xix. 44), in which the Assyrians were victorious. It may be that Sennacherib boasts rather too much of his victory,[2] but at any rate it sealed the fate of Ekron, where the great king took cruel vengeance on the leaders of the

[1] Note among other points that the first narrative gives Shebna the important office of "secretary," in spite of Isaiah's threat of captivity in xxii. 17, 18.

[2] On Sennacherib's excellent strategy, which shows that he knew the geography of S. Palestine, cf. G. A. Smith, *Hist. Geography of the Holy Land*, p. 235 f.

party opposed to Assyria. Now came the turn of Hezekiah. Good reason had he to tremble, considering what a leading part he had taken in the recent political history of Ekron. The matter can be put very briefly. The legitimate king of Ekron, from Sennacherib's point of view, was one Padî who had faithfully kept his oath to Assyria. But the anti-Assyrian party had thrown Padî into chains, and delivered him up to Hezekiah. Would Sennacherib pardon this addition of insult to injury? It was bad enough that Hezekiah revolted himself; it was almost worse that he punished a fellow-king for his loyalty. Sennacherib took sufficient vengeance for both offences. Padî, as he informs us, he "brought out of Jerusalem" (through the Rab-shakeh?) "and made him again ascend the throne of dominion." Then follows in the Prism inscription the account of the invasion of Judah, the opening of which has been quoted already (see p. 4). This is what it tells us of Hezekiah: "Himself I shut up like a cage-bird in Jerusalem, his royal city; fortifications I erected against him, and those who came out of the gate of his city I made to turn back. His cities, which I had plundered, I separated from his land, and gave them to Mititnti, king of Ashdod, to Padî, king of Ekron, and Zilbel (?), king of Gaza; so I diminished his land. To the former tribute . . . I added the tribute which befits my rule, and laid it upon them. Him, Hezekiah, terror at my glorious rule overpowered; the Arabians and his brave (?) warriors, whom he had sent for to defend Jerusalem, his royal city, laid down their arms (?)." Then follows the description of the rich booty which, together with Hezekiah's "daughters" and "palace-women" Sennacherib "caused to be brought after him to Nineveh, the city of his dominion," while Hezekiah "despatched his envoy (?) for the payment of the tribute and for the homage."[1]

There are several points here on which we should be glad to have been informed more fully. Why are only the "kings of Egypt" spoken of? And if the battle of Altaku was really as important as Sennacherib represents, and if, subsequently, Hezekiah was so completely vanquished, why

---

[1] Chiefly after Peiser, *KIB*, ii. 90, 97.

did the Assyrians make no attempt upon Egypt? The new facts which the Biblical narratives report do not by themselves enable us to answer these questions, but they contribute some material to the discussion. (1) We are told in xxxvii. 9 (first narrative) that Tirhakah, king of Cush, had taken the field against Sennacherib immediately before the withdrawal of the latter from Palestine. It seems then that Taharqa had at first entrusted the relief of his Palestinian allies to the petty kings of the Delta, but when these had proved unequal to their charge, he himself "came out to fight with" Sennacherib. (2) We also learn from the first narrative (xxxvi. 2 ; cf. 2 Ki. xviii. 14) that Sennacherib did at any rate advance rather near to the Egyptian frontier, for he captured an important city which commanded the road to Gaza and to Egypt, Lachish. This statement is confirmed by the large bas-relief found by Layard at Kuyunjik,[1] on which Sennacherib is represented, in the words of the inscription, "receiving the spoil of the city of Lachish,"[2] and, as Mr. Flinders Petrie tells us, by the appearance of an ancient wall unearthed at Tell el-Hesy, which was "evidently ruined very shortly after it was built," and which is almost certainly that destroyed by Sennacherib.[3] But why did the king advance no further than Lachish, or, as the second narrative appears to have said, than Libnah? Again, as most critics believe, the Jewish traditions help us. The first narrative says that Sennacherib withdrew in alarm at the approach of Taharqa (xxxvii. 9, 37), the second that "the angel of Yahwè went forth, and smote in the camp of the Assyrians 185,000 ; and when men arose early in the morning, behold they were all dead corpses" (xxxvii. 36), *i.e.* that the whole Assyrian army (or, as Tiele rationalises, all but a "miserable remnant") was destroyed on the very night that Sennacherib's letter reached Hezekiah. These statements are held to be confirmed in part by the Egyptian legend caught up by Herodotus,[4] that when Sennacherib

---

[1] Now in the British Museum.
[2] *KIB*, ii. 115 ; *RP*, n.s., vi. 83. Winckler however has, "and the prisoners . . . marched up before him."
[3] Petrie, *Tell el-Hesy*, p. 28.
[4] ii. 141. Josephus accepts the story (*Ant.*, x. 1, 4).

invaded Egypt and besieged Pelusium in the days of the unwarlike priest-king Sethos,[1] field mice gnawed the quivers and shield handles of the invaders, who precipitately fled. The story of the mice is indeed merely a mythological way of saying that Horus, to whom the field-mouse was sacred, repelled the foes of Egypt in an unaccountable way.[2] But the siege of Pelusium and its sudden and unaccountable raising may belong to a genuine tradition, and they are analogous to the facts reported by the Hebrew narrators. The north-east corner of the swampy Egyptian Delta was the home of the plague,[3] and granting the weakening of the Assyrian forces by pestilence, we can readily understand the uneasiness of Sennacherib at the approach of Taharqa. I wish I could say that this argument was perfectly satisfactory. I am myself not at all sure that the late and strongly didactic second narrative can be trusted. If the mouse story is but a mythic fancy, why may not the story of the pestilence (which is not made use of even in the late psalms, xlvi. and xlviii.)[4] have been spun by a pious scribe from the words of xvii. 14,—

> At eventide, behold terror!
> Before morning, he is no more!
> This is the portion of those that spoil us,¦
> And the lot of those who plunder us!

If Sennacherib's army had been reduced by sickness to a "miserable remnant" (see above), would Hezekiah have troubled himself to send a special envoy with tribute to Nineveh?[5] And may we not sufficiently explain the

[1] Wiedemann identifies Sethos with the Shabataka of the inscriptions (*Aeg. Gesch.*, p. 587). The legend may however mean Taharqa, and confound him with Seti (19th dynasty).

[2] The story of rats or mice gnawing bowstrings belongs to the common stock of mythologies, and is primarily an attempt to justify the worship of these animals (Lang, *Custom and Myth*, pp. 111-114; cf. Sayce, *Herodotos*, p. 204).

[3] G. A. Smith, *Hist. Geography*, p. 157.

[4] Prof. G. A. Smith indeed finds a reference to the supposed calamity of Pelusium in the word "amazed," Ps. xlviii. 6 (*Exposition*, i. 359), but this implies a wrong exegesis of ראו, which in this context can have no other implied object but Jerusalem.

[5] See Prism inscription, as above.

reported failure of Sennacherib to meet Taharqa by his receipt of some bad news from home? In the following year he had trouble enough from the restless Chaldean princes, and an early warning of their machinations may have reached him from Nineveh.

Another point now claims our attention. Is it possible that the Jewish traditions give faint hints of a still more important fact, viz. a second invasion of Palestine by Sennacherib, which, unlike the first, ended in disaster?[1] It may be urged that only one of the Hebrew narratives mentions Taharqa, and that Sennacherib, in describing his third campaign, does not refer to him at all. The incompleteness of the Assyrian record, however, need not be more surprising than that of the Hebrew narratives. It is no doubt, unlike the latter, a contemporary document, but may not our interest in this great episode in the history of Judah lead us to exaggerate its importance to Assyria?[2] Why should Sennacherib record every detail of a campaign which was not probably in his own estimation one of the most important? It is true that if he was overtaken by disaster the Assyrian scribe was not likely to record it; one remembers the patriotic contradiction of the defeat of Dûr-ilu (p. 81). But in the present instance, we have no very satisfactory evidence of Sennacherib's disaster from a non-Assyrian source, and the two best Hebrew traditions (2 Ki. xviii. 14-16, and the first of the two longer narratives) make no reference to it. Is it not possible that Sennacherib omits all reference both to Taharqa and to the pestilence of a late tradition simply because he was not (as xxxvii. 9, 37 suggests) afraid of the one, and knew nothing of the other?

There would be a more plausible argument for a second invasion if it were certain that in 701 Taharqa was simply king of Cush and not in any sense lord of Egypt. For my own part, until better instructed, I follow Meyer, and suppose that Taharqa became virtual suzerain of Egypt in 704, but only ventured to assume the "double crown" of Egypt in 689. In 1880, however, I suggested that "the late compiler of chaps. xxxvi.-xxxix. may have confounded Shabataka with the

---

[1] Winckler, *Untersuch.*, pp. 34-36.
[2] Tiele, *Bab.-ass. Gesch.*, p. 295.

better known Tirhakah."[1] We might also avoid accepting a second invasion by supposing with Wiedemann that Shabataka, himself king of Egypt, summoned his kinsman Taharqa to his aid.[2] But granting that there is some difficulty in harmonising all the facts of the different narratives, are we justified in accepting a theory which, even in Winckler's hands, requires so much explanatory hypothesis? Surely Sennacherib's later campaign against the Arabians is quite intelligible without supposing that it led up to an unrecorded because disastrous invasion of Judah. Indeed, as Hommel remarks,[3] it would at most have taken Sennacherib into the region east of Jordan, not into Judah.

The general effect of our criticism of the parallel records is to confirm the accuracy of the Assyrian account. It is true that Sennacherib exaggerates the significance of the battle of Altaku, which was really, as Wellhausen remarks,[4] merely an interlude in the siege of Ekron, and would only have been important if Sennacherib had been able at once to follow up his success by hastening into Egypt. It is also possible that Sennacherib gives an exaggerated description of the tribute of Hezekiah. The " 800 talents of silver " may perhaps be equal to the 300 Jewish talents mentioned in 2 Ki. xviii. 14, but did Hezekiah really have to send his daughters and palace-women to Nineveh (cf. Isa. iii. 24)? In all other respects Sennacherib's account is both natural in itself, and confirmed by the two earliest of the Hebrew narratives. What is said in 2 Ki. xviii. 14-16 agrees with Sennacherib's own description of his devastation of Judah, except that it fixes the Assyrian headquarters to which Hezekiah sent his message of submission at Lachish (Sennacherib leaves the place uncertain), and that it appears to state that Hezekiah sent his treasure to Lachish, and not (in accordance with precedent) to Nineveh. Again, the language of both the Hebrew narratives confirms the very

---

[1] *PI*, i. 110.   [2] *Gesch. von Alt-Aeg.*, p. 165.
[3] *Gesch. Bab. u. Ass.*, p. 705. Cf. Tiele, *Bab.-ass. Gesch.*, p. 295 ; Meyer, *Gesch. Aeg.*, p. 350; Schrader, *CI*, i. 303-307. See also Winckler, *Untersuch.*, pp. 37-39 ; *Gesch. Bab. u. Ass.*, p. 254-258, and, for Sennacherib's Arabian campaign, Budge, *The Hist. of Esarhaddon*, p. 55.
[4] *Die Composition des Hexateuchs*, etc., p. 292.

precise statement of Sennacherib that he shut up, *i.e.* blockaded, Hezekiah within his city. The first narrative assumes that Jerusalem was not actually besieged; the second makes Isaiah predict that this would be the case. The omissions of Sennacherib are not due to interested motives, but to a certain contemptuous economy of details. It was not the whole Assyrian host which proceeded to Jerusalem; the mass of the army of course remained in the south-west. A small detachment was all that could be spared,[1] and a blockade of the strongest fortress in Judah was all that such a detachment could attempt. Meantime Sennacherib (who knew the country well) went on step by step to the wâdy which was nearest to the longed-for Egyptian frontier. First he took Libnah by storm, then Lachish. And while at Lachish he heard bad news which forced him to return with all speed to Babylon; it was not however the report of Taharqa's approach which disturbed him, but that of expected disturbances in Babylonia. That he crossed the Egyptian border to Pelusium, and that his army, when encamped before the city, was well-nigh destroyed by a plague, so that "he had to return, deserted by almost all, to Nineveh,"[2] is a precarious inference from heterogeneous and equally doubtful legends.

It would be easy to show that, both for the character of Sennacherib and for that of Hezekiah, these results are of the utmost importance. The former is neither perfidious nor (here at least) mendacious, and the latter is a hero, who, unlike Luli of Sidon, clung to his post, and braved the greatest dangers, and only gave way when all friends had failed him, and Jerusalem was "like a booth in a vineyard or a lodge in a cucumber field" (i. 8). The alteration introduced into the portrait of Sennacherib by the Jewish writers is, for the historian, the most unfortunate of their inaccuracies. But who that rightly appreciates the spirit of the later

[1] Wiedemann, *Aeg. Gesch.*, p. 587.
[2] It is an obvious exaggeration when 2 Ki. xviii. 17 makes the Tartan himself accompany the blockading force. The Tartan was of course wanted at Lachish to prepare for the intended march to Egypt. Isa. xxxvi. 2 only mentions the Rab-shakeh, not, however, from superior judgment, but in accordance with the abbreviating tendency of the editor.

Jews can seriously blame them? The cultivation of a frame of mind out of which in due time evangelical religion might spring was of more consequence to them than historical exactness. And, with all this admixture of distorting elements, how much more fact there is than might have been expected! The close of the first narrative in particular has been verified in the main by the Babylonian Chronicle, which states that on the 20th of Tebet (tenth month) 681, Sennacherib was murdered in an insurrection by his son.[1]

[For other treatments of the campaign of 701 see Schrader, *CI*, i. 299-303; art. "Sanherib" in Schenkel's *Bibel-lex.*, v. 176 (connects the reported pestilence in the Assyrian camp with the battle of Altaku); Friedr. Delitzsch, art. "Sanherib," in Herzog-Plitt, *Realencyclop.*, xiii. 384-386 (thinks the pestilence befell the detachment which came to besiege Jerusalem; calls attention to the ambiguity of *usêbilamma*, in Sennacherib's account of Hezekiah's tribute, either "I caused" or "he caused to be brought"); Tiele, *Bab.-ass. Gesch.*, pp. 289-295, 315-319 (very thorough); Wellhausen, *Composition des Hexateuchs*, p. 292 f. ("Sennacherib's inscription speaks only of the first, not of the last and decisive phase of the campaign"), cf. *Hist. of Israel and Judah*, pp. 102-107.]

CHAPTERS XL.-LXVI

INTRODUCTORY

SECTION I.—Arguments, (1) from historic background; (2) from ideas and beliefs, showing that these chapters (if they form a whole) proceed from a late Exilic writer.

THE prophecies in chaps. xl.-lxvi. have commonly been ascribed to Isaiah. They have no heading, however, mentioning the name of the author, and the fact that they come after a narrative section which was evidently intended by an

---

[1] See *RP*, n.s., i. 28; *Zt. f. Ass.*, April 1887, p. 157 f.; Hommel, *Gesch.*, p. 688; F. Brown, *Presb. Rev.*, April 1888, pp. 297-299. The Chronicle only mentions one of the sons of Sennacherib as the murderer, and does not speak of his flight to Armenia (see however Pinches, *RP*, n.s., v. 129).

editor as the close of the then existing Book of Isaiah, justifies a doubt whether the person who placed them there had traditional evidence of Isaiah's authorship. This later editor (who was of course post-Exilic) may have been influenced in his procedure by very uncritical considerations. He may have felt, on the one hand, that the old Book of Isaiah was but a meagre monument of so great a prophet,[1] and, on the other, that without some protecting name, ensuring admission into the canon, the glorious prophecy of restoration would at length pass into unmerited oblivion. Upon this hypothesis, the editor did not himself assert chaps. xl.-lxvi. to be by Isaiah, but was not unwilling that future readers of the Book should do so. There is, however, another possible view. The editor, who doubtless held the later Jewish theory of prophecy, may have inferred from a number of passages, especially xli. 26, xlviii. 3, 6, 14, that the first appearance of Cyrus had been predicted by an ancient prophet,[2] and observing certain Isaianic elements in the phraseology of these chapters, may have identified this prophet with Isaiah. The value of this inference (supposing it to have been drawn) will depend for us on the completeness of the writer's phraseological observations, and on the soundness both of his theory of prophecy and of his exegetical inferences from the passages referred to. But however we explain his procedure, his act determined the belief of succeeding generations. To ascribe these fine prophecies to Isaiah, in accordance with the general heading of the Book, presented no more difficulty to the Jews of the later post-Exilic period than to suppose David to have written the 51st or even (see Sept.) the 137th Psalm. Some faint reminiscence of the composite origin of Isaiah may have lingered among learned men, but, if so, it produced no effect on the commonly taught and commonly received opinion of the authorship of Isa. xl.-lxvi.[3]

[1] So Eichhorn and Ewald; see also Prologue.
[2] See Delitzsch, *Jesaia*,³ pp. 494-495 ; Bredenkamp, *Jes.*¹, pp. 239-240; Klostermann in Herzog-Plitt, p. 599 ; Rutgers, *Echtheid van het tweede Gedeelte van Jesaja* (1866), p. 65 ; and cf. Orelli, *Isaiah*, E.T., p. 215.
[3] According to the original order of the prophetic books (testified in

What then is the critical value of the tradition of the Jewish and the Christian Church relative to the authorship of these chapters ? None whatever. The earliest exponent of this tradition is Ben Sira, who, in extolling the merits of Isaiah states that he 'comforted the mourners in Zion' (Ecclus. xlviii. 24), but such a statement throws no light on the grounds of the combination of the two parts of Isaiah, and is only of value for the history of the prophetic canon. And as soon as the critical spirit began to exercise itself on the Old Testament literature, the great Spanish rabbi Ibn Ezra († 1167) expressed again and again his suspicions of the Exilic origin of Isa. xl.-lxvi.,[1] suspicions which were at length thoroughly justified by the researches of the older German critics, culminating in the great work of Gesenius, *Der Prophet Jesaia* (1820-21). In fact, the argument (1) from the historical background, (2) from the ideas, beliefs, and anticipations, and (3) from the language of chaps. xl.-lxvi. (to mention only the leading proofs) is decisive in favour of the theory that they are not the work of Isaiah, but (if they really form a single book) of a writer who flourished at the close of the Babylonian Exile. Let us consider this threefold argument, before proceeding to examine the question whether we may not have before us the work of more than one author, and of more than one period.

1. *The historical background* is the same as that of xxi. 1-10 and xiii. 1-xiv. 23 (see pp. 68, 128). The people addressed are not the scornful and spiritually insensible contemporaries of Isaiah, but a body of depressed and contrite exiles in Babylonia, who have to be encouraged to trust an all-merciful though " long time silent "[2] God, and to prepare

Baba batra, 14*b*), Isaiah was placed after Jeremiah and Ezekiel, probably from a sense that in its present form Isaiah was a later book than either of the two other prophets (so Lagarde, *Symmicta*, i. 142 ; Stıack, art. " Kanon des A.T." in Herzog-Plitt, *Real-enc.*, vii. 433). The reason given in *Baba batra l.c.* is imaginary.

[1] So Geiger (*Jud. Zt.*, iii. 553-556) ; cf. Friedländer, *Essays on Ibn Ezra*, pp. 67-69 ; Fürst, *Der Kanon des A.T.*, p. 16. Ibn Ezra had, of course, no thought of denying the possibility of predictions.

[2] הֶחֱשֵׁיתִי מֵעוֹלָם, xlii. 16. The *terminus a quo* is probably the fall of Josiah at Megiddo in 608, not the beginning of the Exile (Dillm.). Of the parallel passages cited by Dillm., lvii. 11 ; lviii. 12 ; lxi. 4 ; lxiii. 19,

for a coming deliverance. The very name of the deliverer is given—it is Cyrus, who is referred to as a personage well known to all readers, and of whom the most idealistic picture is given—just such a picture, in short, as Jews, who hoped so much from his liberality, would be likely to give. But why summarise poetical descriptions, so instinct with life and thrilling earnestness, and so familiar to us all? There can be no doubt that the historic background of these chapters is, not that of the age of Isaiah, but rather (if we put aside certain difficult portions, which are at any rate in no respect akin to Isaiah's acknowledged writings) of the close of the Exile. The only question with conservative scholars is, whether Isaiah's exceptional gifts may not have enabled him to write in perfect sympathy with the exiles at Babylon. True, these exiles lived long after his time, but granting Isaiah's fore-knowledge of the Captivity, might he not be able to throw himself into their state of mind, as a tragic poet throws himself into the parts of Ajax and Agamemnon? (The comparison is Chrysostom's.) And may not those difficult portions of chaps. lv.-lxvi., which seem more Palestinian in colouring, be involuntary self-betrayals of a Palestinian prophet.[1] According to this theory, as Dean Bradley has remarked:—

> The Isaiah of the vexed and stormy times of Ahaz and of Hezekiah is supposed in his later days to have been transported by God's Spirit into a time and a region other than his own. . . . The voices in his ears are those of men unborn, and he lives a second life among events and persons, sins and suffering, and fears and hopes, photographed sometimes with the minutest accuracy on the sensitive and sympathetic medium of his own spirit; and he becomes the denouncer of the special sins of a distant generation, and the spokesman of the faith and hope and passionate yearning of an exiled nation, the descendants of men living when he wrote in the profound peace of a renewed prosperity.[2]

This view is akin to that by which both Ibn Ezra and

only the second and third are in point, but all these passages may, and probably do, belong to a later writer or writers, and therefore none of them can here be admitted as decisive. In lxiii. 19 מעולם means, not *seit lange* (Dillm.), but *von urher* (Del., Duhm), in lvii. 11 read מעלם (Sept.).
[1] Cf. *PI*, ii. 227.   [2] *Ibid.*

CHAPTERS XL.-LXVI. (INTRODUCTORY)

Theodore of Mopsuestia interpreted "Davidic" psalms as referring to Exilic times. For many years it was held by the justly honoured Franz Delitzsch, which proves that it is not incompatible with an honest and accurate exegesis. But modern human nature finds this theory more and more difficult to believe. For it implies that the prophet assumed not only the historical point of view, but even the linguistic peculiarities of a later age, or, at the very least, that his "new and grand ideas" forced him to become a great transformer of language, discovering new words and giving new meanings to old ones.[1] Surely it is no "aberration" to say that any such view is "unpsychological."[2] We really ought not to be so unmodern as to exclude all psychological considerations from our criticism. If the newer criticism in England forbids this protest, the newer criticism is still too old, too incomplete. At any rate, no one can venture to assert that such a theory of the range of prophetic vision receives the least support from the undisputed prophecies of Isaiah and his contemporaries. And lastly it is a weighty consideration that Delitzsch himself in 1889, at an age when most men cling tenaciously to old views, bravely abandoned the theory which as late as 1880 he most earnestly defended.

2. *Ideas, beliefs, and anticipations.*—We must here consider chaps. xl.-lxvi. by themselves. With the exception of chaps. xxiv.-xxvii. the other disputed portions of Isaiah contain no religious ideas of any depth, and the ideas of chaps. xxiv.-xxvii. are, as we have seen, so thoroughly peculiar that they cannot be profitably compared with those of chaps. xl.-lxvi. Let us then take the view of the divine nature expressed in the finest parts of II. Isaiah, and compare it with that which we find in the undoubtedly true Isaiah. The two views may not be essentially different, but that in II. Isaiah is manifestly much more developed. According to a not too partial student,[3] its one great blemish is the retention of the popular divine name Yahwè, which some post-Exilic writers show a tendency to abandon, but which

---

[1] Delitzsch, *Schlussbemerk.* to Drechsler's *Jesaja*, iii. 403.
[2] In reply to Davidson, *Expositor*, 1883, p. 91.
[3] Renan, *Histoire*, iii. 504; cf. i. 86. On this whole subject see *BL*, pp. 286-291, 297-304 (where references to other books are given).

the writer (or writers) of Isa. xl.-lxvi. use frequently and, in the first part, with enthusiastic admiration. This criticism, however, goes too far. Although the dear traditional name is retained, it is filled with a meaning of far more than national reference. More especially in chaps. xl.-lv. the writer exhausts language in admiring affirmations of the sole divinity[1] and incomparable wisdom and power of Yahwè, as revealed in creation, in history, in prophecy,[2] and as contrasted with the impotence of the idols of the heathen. The absolute divinity thus claimed for the God of the prophets of Israel necessarily involves eternity. It would therefore be at once a confession of faith in Yahwè, and a definition of the meaning of the name to say, adapting the words of the prophetic writer,

Thou, Yahwè, art the first, and with the last thou art the same.[3]

Biting sarcasms are addressed (cf. p. 299 f.) in these chapters to the makers and worshippers of idols,[4] whose folly consists not in worshipping spiritual powers hostile to the true God (cf. xxiv. 21), but in imagining that "the divinity" (of which they have some faint tradition [5]) can be "like unto gold, or silver, or stone" (Acts xvii. 29), and then trusting in these unworthy images (after they have been made divine by charms, cf. xliv. 11) to deliver them.

God and man are indeed separated by a wide gulf even in the undoubted Isaiah (see esp. vi. 5 ; xxxi. 3*a*). But the acute and constant sense of this separation is peculiar to the Exilic and post-Exilic writers, one of whose chief aims appears to be to find a conception that will bridge over the gulf. It is the conception of the divine breath or spirit, as the organ of the external activity of Yahwè, which serves this purpose both

---

[1] See xlv. 6, 22, 23 ; xlvi. 9 ; liv. 5 (end).
[2] See xl. 12-17, 22-26, 28 ; xli. 21-23 ; xlii. 5 ; xliv. 24 ; xlv. 7, 12, 18-21 ; xlviii. 13, 14 ; li. 13, 15.
[3] xli. 4 ; cf. xliii. 10, 13 ; xliv. 6 ; xlvi. 4 ; xlviii. 12.
[4] Cf. xl. 18, 19 ; xli. 6, 7, 21-24, 29 ; xlii. 17 ; xliii. 9 ; xliv. 9-20 ; xlv. 20 ; xlvi. 1, 2, 5-7. (But are these passages all by II. Isaiah ?)
[5] See Ps. ix. 18, and cf. *BL*, pp. 293, 306. The constant appeals to the אדם in II. Isaiah imply that Jews and Gentiles have a common basis of argument (cf. also xxiv. 5).

CHAPTERS XL.-LXVI. (INTRODUCTORY) 243

to Ezekiel and to the writer (or writers) of Isa. xl.-lxvi.[1] The " spirit " may symbolise the conscious intelligence of the divine activity; for its irresistible might there is a special phrase—Yahwè's " arm."[2] The frequent occurrence of both phrases is significant. It seemed, when the prophet wrote, as if the people of Israel were both outwardly and inwardly dead (Ezek. xxxvii. 11), and incapable therefore of repentance (xlii. 19, 20). It seemed, too, as if Yahwè's recent action had been aimless, as if he had begun by spending great pains on the education of Israel, and then forgotten Israel's right to protection (xl. 27; xlix. 14; lxiii. 11-14), and as if the source either of Yahwè's compassion or of his heroic deeds had been dried up, so that he tamely "gave his glory to another god" (xlii. 8; xlviii. 11; lxiii. 15). Of these appearances it was only the first which was not altogether deceitful. Israel as a nation was in truth dead; the few individuals who sighed for a new national life were incapable of realising their own aspirations. But it was not the fact that Yahwè had been acting blindly, as the whole world would soon have to acknowledge. Israel should not languish much longer in the moral and physical paralysis of exile; the breath or spirit of Yahwè should revive it, and multiply and bless its seed (xli. 17; xliv. 3, 4). The same divine spirit should, moreover, justify the ways of God by intervening in the affairs of Israel and Babylon (xl. 7, 8, by implication); for he who arranged the framework of the world, also directed its history, destroying and building up according to a wise plan, revealed at least in part to Israel by prophecies (xl. 22, 23; xli. 4; xlii. 5, 6; xliii. 12, 13; xlv. 18, 19). At the fit moment the "arm" of Yahwè should "awake" and the great deeds of antiquity should be more than paralleled.

Take (b) the doctrine of the future extension of the knowledge of the true God. The coming ideal age was not a subject to which Isaiah, absorbed by present needs, could often refer. He does indeed speak now and then of a time when there shall be "judges as at the first" (i. 26), and

---

[1] So xl. 7 (by implication), xl. 13, xlii. 1, xliv. 3, xlviii. 16, lix. 21, lxi. 1, and especially lxiii. 10, 11, 14. Cf. Hag. ii. 5.
[2] See xl. 10; li. 5, 9; lii. 10; liii. 1; lix. 16; lxiii. 5, 12.

when, if xi. 1-8, 9, be really his work, a son of David, supernaturally gifted beyond his great ancestor, shall rule peacefully but vigorously in the land which Yahwè has delivered (ix. 7, 8; xi. 1-5), and in which the "knowledge of Yahwè" (cf. Hos. vi. 6) has become universally prevalent (xi. 9). But of the future of the nations outside he has nothing definite to announce. Once he declares that Yahwè's purpose of "breaking Assyria in his (Yahwè's) hand" concerns "all peoples" and "the whole earth" (xiv. 25, 26), and a similar idea seems to be expressed in xviii. 3. But we hear nothing either of a material or of a purely spiritual kingdom of Yahwè with its centre at Jerusalem (xi. 10, and xviii. 7 are certainly late); such ideas do not seem to have attracted the patriotic Isaiah, unless indeed he can be the author of chaps. xlii. 1-4 and lx. For in these and the parallel passages the omission referred to is abundantly supplied. The latter passage gives us the idea of Israel as an imperial power (an idea which prevails in chaps. lvi.-lxvi.), the former attributes a spiritual primacy to the "chosen" people as a nation of world-traversing missionaries (so again and again in chaps. xl.-lv.). And if it be said that the "imperial" idea was not beyond the horizon of Isaiah, who was essentially a monotheist, and who, according to most critics, announces an "increase of the dominion" of Israel under the ideal king (ix. 6), yet the conception of a missionary people is so original and so unparalleled in Hebrew literature except in the hymn book of the Second Temple,[1] that to ascribe its origin to Isaiah is *primâ facie* an improbable view. By what strange circumstances, acting upon a susceptible mind, can the original nationalism of the prophetic writer have been so transfigured? Most of the Jewish exiles, even in their humiliation, retained that hereditary sentiment in its crudest form; nay, the author of chaps. xl.-lv. himself has moods[2] in which he resembles the writer of xiii. 2.-xiv. 23. But the passages in which the personified ideal of Israel is described as the "Servant of Yahwè"[3] are as free from nationalistic

[1] See *BL*, pp. 292-296.
[2] See xli. 15, 16; xlii. 13-15; xlv. 14, 24; xlix. 7, 23. Retribution is still his chief ethical principle, though it is partly neutralised (see xlii. 6; li. 4, 5) by the idea of the "Servant."
[3] See *BL*, pp. 262-264, 274-275.

limitations as was possible at the real or assumed time of their composition. Not to win fame or empire do they in whom this ideal has taken flesh journey to the distant " coastlands " (איים), but to press the acceptance of spiritual blessings upon others. And whether among their own people or among strangers, they seek out by preference those who make the least return,—the sick in body or in mind, the weary and heavy-laden (xlii. 5 ; l. 4). The medicine which they bring is the knowledge of revealed truth (xlii. 4), not, however, as laid up in a book, but as (whether written or not) continually revealed afresh to its preachers (l. 4), so that in some sense the success of the true religion is dependent on these humble Jewish missionaries. Hence a new and striking development in the idea of the divine "righteousness." To Israel as a whole Yahwè shows his "righteousness" by delivering it from its oppressors (xli. 10, etc.), but to those of its members whose ideal is that of the "Servant," by granting them complete success in their work (xlix. 4). *That* is all the reward that these noble Israelites crave, and the prospect of it nerves them (for even those of them who journey as missionaries retain the keenest sympathy with their people) to the willing endurance for Israel's sake of the punishment laid upon Israel (viz. exile and persecution). When by their example or teaching the "blind" and " deaf" portion of Israel has been spiritually changed (liii. 4-6), and recognises that the " Servant of Yahwè " has been as it were Israel's atoning sacrifice, then shall a people worthy of the same great title " rise, be exalted, and be very high " (lii. 13), and to share its blessedness will be the just reward of those faithful preachers. " Therefore will I give him a portion among the great, and he shall divide spoil with the strong " (liii. 12).

Such was the work appointed originally (as we are told) for David,[1] but only to be accomplished by the combined efforts, first, of a company of faithful men within the people of Israel, and then, of the regenerate Messianic people itself. Surely there is much in the description of it which clearly

[1] lv. 3-5. The passage alludes (*a*) to Ps. xviii. 32-45, (*b*) to 2 Sam. vii. Now (*a*) is at earliest of the time of Josiah, (*b*) of that of Hezekiah. See *BL*, pp. 128, 291-292.

points to a late date. Chap. liii. alone goes far to prove that the portraiture of the "Servant" is post-Jeremianic, for here (as also in l. 4-9) it is difficult not to believe that the figure of the martyr-prophet Jeremiah hovered before the mind of the writer; *v.* 7 is at any rate based on Jer. xi. 19.[1] In short, both the doctrines which we have as yet considered imply a preceding period of deep reflection, and the idea of the Servant of Yahwè can (unless we deny historical development altogether) only have arisen in a period of national disintegration.

(*c*) The above are the most remarkable of the ideas in chaps. xl.-lxvi. which require a late date. In conclusion, here are some of the ideas specially characteristic of the latter portion of the Book of Isaiah. In lvi. 4, 6, lviii. 13, we have that reverence for the Sabbath which contrasts so strongly with Isaiah's external way of regarding it (i. 13), and in lviii. 6, 7, that spiritual view of fasting which became a necessity when the prophetic and the legal teaching were alike recognised as authoritative (cf. Zech. vii. 5, etc.). In chaps. lxiii.-lxvi. late ideas become especially prominent. In lxiii. 1-6, and lxv. 15, 16, we have the idea of the great judgment upon the nations embodied in a description which has all the bitterness of the later writers (cf. Ezek. xxxviii. 21, 22; Zech. xiv. 12, 13; Isa. xxxiv.); in lxiii. 10, 11, that of the personal "holy spirit" dwelling within the people of Israel; in *v.* 15-lxiv. 12 the prophetic writer's willing identification of himself with the guilty nation, which contrasts so forcibly with the rebukes of "this people" in vi. 9, viii. 6, xxix. 13; in *v.* 16 a strange allusion to a belief in Abraham and Jacob as semi-divine beings; in *v.* 17 (cf. lxiv. 5) the idea that Yahwè caused the people to "err from his ways"; in lxiv. 8 the combination of the old idea that Yahwè is the "father" of his people, with the new one (xxix. 16 being late) that he is the irresponsible maker and lord of his human creatures; in lxv. 17 the promise of "new heavens and a new earth" (cf. Enoch xlv. 4, 5); in lxv. 20-22 the restoration of patriarchal longevity (as in the document P), somewhat as Zech. viii. 4; in lxvi. 18-22

[1] For parallels in Jeremiah to phrases in xlix. 1-6, l. 4-9, see the commentaries.

CHAPTERS XL.-LXVI. (INTRODUCTORY)

observe eschatological anticipations, implying a strong interest in the temple ceremonies, and an acquaintance with Numbers and Deuteronomy; in lxvi. 23, 24, a description of a concourse of pilgrims of all nations who have come to worship at Jerusalem and behold the endless torments of the still partly conscious bodies of the enemies of Yahwè.

SECTION II.—Arguments from style and diction proving the late date of these chapters.

3. *Style and diction.* This part of the argument was difficult to treat with precision as long as the critical analysis of the Book was still in its first period. It has been said by Ewald that "every kind of style and every variation of exposition is at Isaiah's command to meet the requirements of his subject" (*Prophets*, ii. 10), and Delitzsch assures us that Isaiah's style, in the prophecies which are most certainly his, displays a prismatic radiance, though upon the whole it is more condensed, "lapidary," and plastic than that of chaps. xl.-lxvi., which only in two places (chap. liii. and lvi. 9-lvii. 11a) ceases to be clear and flowing. Such descriptions overlook the broad lines of difference which, as a more thorough criticism can show, separate the first or historical from the second or imagined Isaiah, and, though somewhat less strikingly, the second Isaiah from the writers of the appended chapters. Its improbability is obvious. No second genius equally Protean is known in the ancient literature of the East, and it is surprising that Ewald, who dropped such fruitful hints for the analysis of chaps. xl.-lxvi., should not have stumbled at the similarity of portions of chaps. x., xxix., and xxx. to the great Exilic Prophecy of Comfort. Nor can a trained critic easily believe either that chaps. xl.-lxvi. were written as a whole at the close of the Exile, or that those parts which resist being assigned to such a date were composed on the eve of, or directly after, the Return by the hand which wrote "Comfort ye, comfort ye my people." At first sight, then, it is with a sense of relief (so far as the last eighteen chapters are concerned) that we listen to Klostermann and Bredenkamp, when they assure

us that ancient Isaianic material has been worked up together with his own prophecies by a late Exilic writer.[1] Criticism, however, as it seems to me, is equally opposed to Ewald's theory of the works of Isaiah, and to Klostermann's view of the origin of chaps. xl.-lxvi. With the remains of the true Isaiah before us, we cannot say that any part of them is in the manner of II. Isaiah, and even a very imperfect criticism of chaps. xl.-lxvi. proves that, whatever heterogeneous elements these chapters may contain, none of them can have come from Isaiah. The contrast between the two great documents (not to assume the results of the analysis of II. Isaiah) is indeed most striking. In the former we see the hand of a severely self-restrained religious statesman, of one who stands between God and man, the equal if not the superior of his king, the champion but not the tribune of the common people, a speaker but not an orator, a prophet in the grand, old style, whose aim is not so much to persuade as to impress a divinely revealed message. Hence that terse, compact style—that authoritative manner. On the other hand, the writer of chaps. xl.-lv. (from which section our ideas of II. Isaiah are generally derived) is not, so far as the evidence goes, a prophet in the old style at all. His word is not "like a hammer that breaketh the rock in pieces" (Jer. xxiii. 29) with a declaration of impending judgment and a stern call to repentance, but like "wine and milk without money and without price" (lv. 1). Sometimes, it is true, he hears angelic voices (see *PI*, on xl. 3), sometimes he speaks as in prophetic ecstasy, and always he is conscious that he transmits a sure prophetic promise, which is not merely a repetition of older prophecies, but has new and extraordinary features of its own. But by preference he pleads and argues, and even rebukes from his mouth have nothing that hurts or repels. In short, he speaks like an elder brother rather than like an angel or like a prophet. He has no prophetic model in the proper sense of the word ; the self-suppression of Isaiah would be uncongenial to him. He looks in his heart and writes, and

[1] See Kl.'s article "Jesaja" in Herzog-Plitt, *RE;* and cf. (against Br.) Cheyne, *PI*, ii. 230 ; *JQR*, July 1891, p. 589 ; G. A. Smith, *Exposition*, ii. 205.

CHAPTERS XL.-LXVI. (INTRODUCTORY)

without any direct self-exhibition [1] reveals to seeing eyes a finely developed personality. He is not only Yahwè's spokesman, but feels with and for his people, and is by turns their teacher and their poet.[2]

His work, however, both as teacher and as poet is marked in general by incompleteness. His feelings are too strong and his imagination too lively to permit him to dwell long on any one aspect of his subject. He constantly varies his argument, and once only (chap. xlvii.) does he come near to achieving a perfect lyric song. Perhaps, therefore, one should say that he is a great preacher with a rich lyric and dramatic vein and a wonderful command of expressive and pathetic imagery,[3] rather than a great teacher. Only this must not be taken to imply that he stands in the flesh before a large audience; like the author of the original Deuteronomy he preaches from his scribe's chamber, though he has doubtless been in and out among his people, and knows their thoughts. When, therefore, some critics infer from appeals like those in xl. 21, 26, 28, xliii. 10, xlviii. 8, l. 10, 11 (?), li. 6, 12, 13, that the writer has previously delivered the substance of his discourses in public, this must be pronounced an unnecessary and hardly probable supposition.[4] That such passages appear at first sight to imply this is undeniable; but since there was no public life, no central community, during the Exile, the appearance must be delusive. There is of course no great difficulty in holding that the writer may have first of all practised himself in

[1] xl. 6 only relates, as briefly as possible, the writer's prophetic call. In xliv. 26 read עֶבֶד, and in xlv. 24 perhaps לְיַעֲקֹב (see *RT*). xlviii. 16*b*, even if genuine, only refers back to the prophetic call.

[2] The lyric tone appears in xlii. 10-13, xliv. 23, xlv. 8, xlvii., xlix. 13, li. 9, 17, lii. 1, 2.

[3] See Driver, *Isaiah*, pp. 182-183.

[4] So Dillmann, p. 362, who lays stress in this connection on the anonymity of the prophecy. A great public worker would have been remembered by name, like Ezekiel. So also Ewald, *Prophets*, iv. 229-232; Duhm, *Theol. der Propheten*, p. 278. The opposite view was maintained by Orelli in 1887 (*Isaiah*, E.T., p. 213), Driver in 1888-93 (*Isaiah*, p. 181), and apparently Stade in 1888 (*Gesch.*, ii. 71). Kuenen thinks that addresses to Sabbath assemblies of exiles may lie at the root of the Exilic portion of the book, but that these addresses may have been reproduced with great freedom (*Ond.*², ii. 137),—an unnecessarily vague theory.

religious addresses to his friends and neighbours, but considering that even Ezekiel, though a recognised prophet, seems to have generally confined himself to his own house (Ezek. viii. 1, xiv. 1, xx. 1), it is unsafe to conjecture that one who had only just received his call (xl. 6) had either the wish or the power to attempt more. On the other hand, to suppose that this great writer has had literary practice (in which Isaiah, Jeremiah, and Deuteronomy may have been his models) is only reasonable. His smooth, flowing rhetoric can hardly have been a gift of nature. And if we accept this hypothesis, and further credit the writer with an earnest and affectionate disposition, we can, I think, fully account for his effective appeals. One admission may however be made. If it can be shown that chaps. lv.-lxvi. (either entirely or in the main) were composed in Judah after 536, it will become somewhat more reasonable to suppose that these discourses of a later writer were first of all delivered orally in public assemblies.[1] Probable, however, this view can hardly be called, (1) because circumstances, even after 536, were not favourable to oral prophecy, and (2) because of the highly artificial character of the later prophecy as a whole, which indisposes one to admit exceptions without the strongest grounds, one of which would naturally be a historical tradition of the name and public activity of the author.[2]

I. Proceeding now to particulars, the really important stylistic and linguistic points of contact between I. and II. Isaiah are surprisingly few. A collection of such phenomena was made by Del. (ed. 3, p. 408) to confirm the conservative theory;[3] but it shrivels up vastly on examination. Thus, the phrases יאמר י׳ and דבר י׳ כי פי י׳ are so rare in Isaiah that, instead of proving the use of this prophet by his successor, they might even make us doubt the soundness of the passages of the Second Isaiah in which they occur.

---

[1] lviii. 1 and lix. 1-3 are somewhat in the style of the old prophets. Cf. i. 15-17; Jer. v. 25-28; Mic. v. 8. But the writer does not seem able to keep up this style.

[2] Such a historical tradition we have in the case of Haggai and Zechariah (see Ezra v. 1, vi. 14), but not in that of Malachi and Joel.

[3] These are, strangely enough, repeated in the fourth edition, in spite of the author's changed point of view.

CHAPTERS XL.-LXVI. (INTRODUCTORY)

The truth is that Isaiah but rarely asserts the divine origin of his oracles; even כה אמר י' and נאם י' occur much less frequently in Isaiah than in Jeremiah and Ezekiel and in chaps. xl.-lxvi (lii. 3-5 is an unique passage[1]). As for the interchange of "Jacob" and "Israel" (xl. 27, xli. 8; cf. ix. 8), it is not distinctive of Isaiah. So too the description of Yahwè as "king" (three or four times in II. Isaiah), though it occurs in vi. 5, is specially characteristic only of the post-Exilic age (see p. 254). The phrase "the Arm of Yahwè" (see pp. 243, 255) is only Isaianic if xxx. 30 is so. The figures *Epanaphora* and *Anadiplosis* are rare in Isaiah and in the prophets generally, though frequent in chaps. xl.-lxvi. (see Driver, *Isaiah*, pp. 182, 200). In fact, the only important parallelism indicated by Del. is קְדוֹשׁ יִשְׂרָאֵל (see p. 254).

It may, however, perhaps be urged that Delitzsch's linguistic parallelisms are too few and that a "cumulative argument" for the unity of Isaiah might easily be obtained from a fuller collection of instances. I have therefore collected nearly forty of the most interesting of the parallels which a conservative criticism so much values, mentioning, however, where necessary, the unfavourable verdict of criticism. The critical student will thus be able to judge what proportion of these parallels will stand. At the end I have grouped the divine titles common to both parts of the Book of Isaiah.

אֻמְמוֹן, ix. 13, lviii. 5; also xix. 15, Job xl. 26, xli. 12 (all late passages).

אוּר, xxxi. 9, xliv. 16, xlvii. 14. But see on xxxi. 9 (p. 204).

אִיִּים, "coast-lands," xi. 11, xxiv. 15; also twelve times in chaps. xl.-lxvi. But xi. 11 is late, and אִיִּים (as distinguished from אִי) is post-Isaianic; it occurs nine times in Ezekiel. Fuller details on xi. 11, p. 61.

אֵילִים, "terebinths," i. 29, lxi. 3, (אֵלִים) lvii. 5. Again only in Ezek. xxx. 14. But the tree so called is not uncommon in Palestine.

אָמִיץ, xxviii. 2, xl. 26 (a rare word).

אֶפֶס, "not," or "no more," xl. 17, and ten other passages (including xli. 24) in chaps. xl.-lxvi.; also in xxxiv. 12, and once in the true Isaiah (v. 8). Not one of Isaiah's favourite words.

---

[1] Cf. נאם י׳, thrice in xiv. 22, 23. But does lii. 3-5 come from II. Isaiah?

252 ISAIAH

אֶפְעֶה, "a viper," xxx. 6, lix. 5.

בָּרָא, iv. 5; also twenty times in chaps. xl.-lxvi. But see on iv. 5, p. 21, n. 1.

גֵּוְ, xi. 1, xl. 24. But see p. 64.

דָּרַשׁ, ix. 12, xxxi. 1, lv. 6, lviii. 2.

הָרַי "my mountains" (the mountains of Canaan), xiv. 25, lxv. 9. No inference possible (see p. 79, note 2).

חוּר "hole," xi. 8, xlii. 22 (if correct). But even xi. 8 may be late (pp. 63-66).

חָסָה בְּ, xiv. 32, xxx. 2, lvii. 13. But in lvii. 13 trust in God is referred to—a specially late use ; see Psalms *passim*.

יִבְלֵי מָיִם, xxx. 25, xliv. 4 (if both passages are not late).

יַעֲקֹב, as a synonym for the ethnic name Israel, once (ix. 8) in the true Isaiah in parallelism to "Israel," twice (ii. 6, xvii. 4) out of parallelism ; cf. also viii. 17, 18. It is more frequent relatively in Mic. i.-iii. (see p. 10), and occurs six times in Amos, twice in Hosea ; also in Gen. xlix. 24. After the fall of Samaria, both names are appropriated by Judah, and after 536 B.C. by the Judæan community. In Isa. xl.-lv. (strictly, xl.-xlix.) it is found seventeen times (*e.g.* xl. 27) in, and three times (*e.g.* xli. 21) out of parallelism ; in chaps. lv.-lxvi. twice out of parallelism and once in parallelism to "Judah" (see below). In the later sections of Part I. of Isaiah, four times (x. 20, xiv. 1*a*, xxvii. 6, xxix. 23) in, and seven times (ii. 3, 5, x. 21, xiv. 1*b*, xxvii. 9, xxix. 22 *bis*) out of parallelism. Also thirty-three times in Psalms, eight times in Sirach, and eight in Num. xxiii.-xxiv. (disputed date). In Mal. iii. 6, "sons of Jacob" = "Judah and Jerusalem" (iii. 4) ; cf. Isa. xlviii. 1, lxv. 1 (important critically).

בֵּית יַעֲקֹב, xlvi. 3, xlviii. 1, lviii. 1 ; also in the late passages, ii. 5, x. 20, xiv. 1 (cf. *v.* 2), xxix. 22, but only twice in the true Isaiah (ii. 6, viii. 17). Altogether nineteen times in the prophets (once in the true Amos ; twice in Mic.) ; also in Ex. xix. 3, Ps. cxiv. 1.

לְמַעַן, fifteen times (including xli. 20, lxvi. 11) in chaps. xl.-lxvi ; once (but *only* once) in the true Isaiah (v. 19).

מִי יְשִׁיבֶנָּה, xiv. 27, xliii. 13. But cf. Jer. ii. 24, and מִי יְשִׁיבֶנּוּ, Job ix. 12, xi. 10, xxiii. 13.

מִכְשׁוֹל, viii. 14, lvii. 14. But also eight times in Ezekiel.

מִפְּנֵי for מִן, xlvi. 3 (*bis*), as xxx. 11 *bis* (מִפְּנֵי), Judg. v. 14 (*bis*), but also Mic. vii. 12 (*bis*), seven times in Psalms, eighteen times in Job. [Mostly late. Cf. Stade, *Gram.*, pp. 203, 223.]

נְרֹחֵי יִשְׂרָאֵל, xi. 12, lvi. 8. But see p. 61.

נַעֲצוּץ, vii. 19, lv. 13 ; nowhere else. But II. Isaiah is a lover of trees and shrubs.

נֵצֶר, xi. 1, lx. 21. But see p. 64.

CHAPTERS XL.-LXVI. (INTRODUCTORY) 253

מְעִיפֵי הַפְּלָעִים, ii. 21, lvii. 5.

עַד, 1. "perpetuity," ix. 5 (?), xlv. 17, lxv. 18 ; 2. (adverbially) " for ever," lvii. 15.

עָשֵׁק, xxx. 12, liv. 14, lix. 13 (? see *RT*).

צֶאֱצָאִים, xxii. 24, and five times in chaps. xl.-lxvi. ; also xxxiv. 1, and four times in Job (nowhere else). But *all* the passages are late.

צִפְעוֹנִי, xi. 8, lix. 5 ; also in Proverbs and Jeremiah. See p. 64.

רַהַב, xxx. 7, li. 9. But the latter passage is not influenced by the former. If רהב הם שבת in xxx. 7 is the true reading, and rightly rendered by the commentators, "Rahab" has a different meaning in the two passages. But more probably לכן וגו׳ in xxx. 7 is a late gloss, and certainly the two last words of the clause are corrupt. רהב, " sea-monster," belongs to the mythological apparatus of Job (see Job ix. 13, xxvi. 12); the term is only applied to Egypt in Ps. lxxxvii. 4, lxxxix. 11, and in the gloss just referred to.

רָם וְנִשָּׂא, ii. 13, vi. 1, lvii. 15 (cf. lii. 13, lvii. 7). But in lvii. 15 the phrase is used, not of things, but of the Creator.

שָׁשׂוֹן, xxii. 13 ; also xii. 3, xxxv. 10, li. 3, 11, lxi. 3.

שֹׁרֶשׁ, " a shoot from the root," xi. 10, liii. 2 (both late passages).

תֹּהוּ, xxiv. 10, xxix. 21, xxxiv. 11, xl. 17, 23, lix. 4 (and five other passages) ; also Ps. cvii. 40, Job vi. 18, xii. 24, xxvi. 7, Gen. i. 2 (P), 1 Sam. xii. 21 *bis* (Exilic), Deut. xxxii. 10 (Exilic, or later), Jer. iv. 23. The last passage is the only one which can reasonably be regarded as pre-Exilic, and even this passage is doubtful. On תֹּהוּ cf. Wellh., *Prol.*[8], p. 305.

תּוֹרָה, i. 10, ii. 3, v. 24, viii. 16, 20, xxx. 9, xlii. 4, 21, 24, li. 7 (plural, xxiv. 5). The usage of 'ת is not quite the same in all these passages. In viii. 20, xlii. 21, 24, the reference may be to a larger or smaller law-book (this depends on analytic criticism) ; in viii. 16 a particular written prophecy may be meant, and in li. 7 the spiritual substance of the Deuteronomic law is very probably intended. In the remaining passages 'ת seems to mean the religious directions of the prophets, or the general essence of their teaching. In xxiv. 5 there is an allusion to Gen. ix. 1-17 (P).

תַּעֲלוּלִים, iii. 4, lxvi. 4.

I now give the divine titles in tabular form (cf. a supplementary list on p. 270), and, exceptionally, leave the student to discriminate in A between the true Isaiah and the inserted later passages. The process will be instructive.

A (Chaps. i.-xxxix.).	B (Chaps. xl.-lxvi.).
אֵל,[1] seven times (v. 16, vii. 14, viii. 8, ix. 4, x. 21, xxix. 22 corr. text, xxxi. 3), including Immanuel and El-gibbor	Fourteen times.
אֲדֹנָי, twenty-two times	Once (xlix. 14; cf. li. 22).
אֲדֹנָי יהוה,[2] eleven times	Thirteen times.
יהוה צְבָאוֹת, forty-one times (five times preceded by הָאָדוֹן, including x. 16, and seven times by אֲדֹנָי)	Six times.
מֶלֶךְ, once (vi. 5)[3]	Three or four times (xli. 21, xliii. 15, xliv. 6, cf. lii. 7). Specially late.
אוּר, three times (xvii. 10, xxvi. 4, xxx. 29)	Once (xliv. 8). Also in Deut. xxxii. (six passages), Hab. i. 12.
קְדוֹשׁ יִשְׂרָאֵל, thirteen times (including x. 17)	Fourteen times (incl. xlix. 7). Elsewhere only in Jer. l. 29, li. 5 (late passages), and thrice in the Psalms.

It is needless to dwell further on these parallel words and phrases. Some of them (*e.g.* אוּר, אִיִּים, and בָּרָא to begin with) might be at once transferred to the list of words and phrases which point to a late date, while others (*e.g.* אָפֵס and לְמַעַן) each occurring once in the true Isaiah, but often in chaps. xl.-lxvi., are scarcely less unfavourable to tradition. Let us now turn to the stylistic and linguistic points of difference between the two great sections of Isaiah. These are even embarrassingly numerous, and are irreconcileable

---

[1] For a full summary of passages, see Baethgen, *Beiträge zur sem. Rel.-gesch.*, p. 298 f. Note that Ezekiel only uses אֵל thrice, in allusions to other writers.

[2] It is doubtful whether אדני in this combination is not really a Q'rê to יהוה (see Cornill, *Ezech.*, pp. 172-175; Schwally, *Theol. LZ*, Nov. 1, 1890).

[3] The pre-Exilic prophets in general leave the use of this divine title to non-Israelites (cf. Am. v. 26, Zeph. i. 5 ?). Post-Exilic references: xxxiii. 22, Zech. xiv. 9, Deut. xxxiii. 5, Ps. v. 3, x. 16, xxiv. 7-10, xxix. 10, xliv. 5, xlvii. 3, 7, xlviii. 3, lxviii. 25, and eight passages in Bks. iii.-v. of the Psalms; and cf. Dan. iv. 34.

CHAPTERS XL.-LXVI. (INTRODUCTORY) 255

with the theory of single authorship. I shall not attempt a catalogue of striking Isaianic words and phrases not found in II. Isaiah, because it is the exception to find any such words and phrases in this document. Two important words only shall be mentioned, viz. אֱלִילִים, "idol-gods," found in ii. 8, 18, 20 (*bis*), and in the very doubtful passages, x. 10, 11, xix. 1, xxxi. 7, and שְׁאָר, "the remnant (of Israel)," attested by the name Shear-Yashub (see further on x. 19, p. 52); neither of which occurs in II. Isaiah. We will pause longer (I.) on the rhetorical peculiarities of chaps. xl.-lxvi. There is a striking one at the outset in the repeated summons, "Comfort ye" (xl. 1; cf. fifteen parallel passages, Driver, *Isa.*, p. 182). Soon afterwards (xl. 9, 10) come two personifications, to which there are many subsequent parallels (xlii. 1, xliii. 6, xliv. 23, xlix. 13, 18-23, li. 17-23, lii. 1, 2, 9, liv. 1-6, lv. 12, and the other references to the "Arm" and the "Servant" of Yahwè). There is nothing in Isaiah to prepare us for such bold rhetoric. Note too in chap. xl. the habit of repeating the same word or words in neighbouring clauses or verses (xl. 7-8, 12-13, 13-14, 31-xli. 1, and cf. liii. 3 *bis*, 3-4, and other passages). Also the frequent repetition of favourite short formulæ, such as "Fear not, for," xli. 10, 13, 14, xliii. 1, 5, xliv. 2, liv. 4; "I am the first and I am the last," xliv. 6, xlviii. 12, cf. xli. 4; "I am Yahwè, and there is none else," xlv. 5, 6, 18, 22, xlvi. 9. Also the habit of attaching participial epithets (often in a long series) to the name of Yahwè, *e.g.* creator, stretcher out of the heavens, spreader out of the earth, xl. 28, xlii. 5, xliv. 24, xlv. 7, 18, li. 13; Israel's creator, fashioner, xliii. 1, 15, xliv. 2, 24, xlv. 11, xlix. 5; his deliverer, xliii. 3, xlix. 26, lx. 16; his redeemer, xliii. 14, xliv. 24, xlviii. 17, xlix. 7, liv. 8. And in general, observe the love of honorific descriptions, *e.g.* of Israel, xli. 8, 9, xlvi. 3, 4; of Cyrus, xlv. 1.

II. Features in the syntax of chaps. xl.-lxvi. unfavourable to tradition. Observe first the un-Isaianic articulation of the sentences, and the free irregularity of the constructions,[1] not only in chs. xl.-lv. but also, more or less, in the following

[1] Cf. Hitzig, *Jes.*, p. 472; Budde, *Beiträge* (on Job), p. 105; Driver, *Tenses*,³ pp. 164, 206, 280; *Isaiah*, p. 200; Ges.-K., *Gramm.*, pp. 372, 442 note 2.

chapters. It is in the latter that we find one of the longest and most complex periods of the Old Testament—lxiii. 19*b*-lxiv. 3, and it is not only the prophet of consolation but (as I think) his supplementer who, once at least, prefixes the object, or virtual object, of the verb to the verb itself, which is in the inf., as in Aramaic; see xlii. 24 (late insertion; see p. 299), xlix. 6 (but not xliv. 12). The idiom of *Beth essentiæ*, so frequent (cf. Ges.-Kautzsch, p. 366) in the Psalms, also probably occurs once in both parts of II. Isaiah (xl. 10, lvii. 15 corrected text). More striking characteristics of II. Isaiah and (perhaps) his followers are the omission (nearly sixty times) of אֲשֶׁר in relative clauses (noticeable also in Job), the frequent substitution of the imperf. with simple *waw* for the perf. with *waw* consecutive (*e.g.* xli. 11, 15, 22, xlii. 6, 14, etc.), and the omission of the preposition when more correct writers repeat it (*e.g.* xlii. 22, xlviii. 9, 14, lviii 13, lxi. 7, if the text is sound). But it is only in chaps. xl.-lv. that we find that subordination of the infin. to a previous verb which reminds us so forcibly of Arabic and Syriac idiom (see xlii. 21, and cf. Job xix. 3, xxxii. 22, Lam. iv. 14; see too xlvii. 1*b*, 5*b*), and such a complex expression as כְּמַסְתֵּר פָּנִים מִמֶּנּוּ in liii. 3 (cf. xi. 14, late). And with the exception of lxv. 17 (based perhaps on xliii. 18, 19), all the passages in which adjectives and participles in fem. plur. are used as if neuter substantives, occur in chaps. xl.-lv. (Among these are אֹתִיּוֹת, xli. 23, xliv. 7, xlv. 11; חֲדָשׁוֹת, xlii. 9, xlviii. 6; נְצֻרוֹת, xlviii. 6. See also xli. 21, 22, xlii. 9, 20, xliii. 18, xlvi. 9, xlviii. 3, lxv. 17.) It is in the same section too that we find those descriptive participial clauses (xl. 22, 23, 26, xlii. 5, xliv. 25, etc.) which reminds us of the late book of Job (xii. 17, etc.), Zech. xii. 1, and Dan. ii. 21 f. Among other phenomena it may suffice here to notice in lix. 2 the idiom הָיוּ מַבְדִּלִים, which is contrary to the usage of the early prophets (see on xxx. 20, p. 198 f.), and in lix. 10 the use of the "subjective" cohortative form (נְגַשְׁשָׁה, "we must grope") not found in the prophets before Jer. iii. 25 (cf. Driver, *Tenses*, § 52). Other syntactical peculiarities may be left for notice to the commentators.

III. Uses of pronouns and particles. (*a*) אָנֹכִי, the more primitive form (cf. *anuki* in the Tell el-Amarna tablets) occurs about twenty times, אֲנִי seventy times.¹ [In the other late parts of Isaiah אָנֹכִי occurs once (*i.e.* twice in the same passage, xxi. 8), אֲנִי six times (xiii. 3, xix. 11, xxvii. 3, xxxvii. 24, 25, xxxviii. 10); in the true Isaiah, אָנֹכִי twice (vi. 5 *bis*, viii. 18), אֲנִי twice (v. 5, x. 14).] (*b*) זוּ as a rel. pronoun, xlii. 24, xliii. 21 (inserted passages, Duhm), as in Hab. i. 11 (see Wellh.), and twelve times in post-Exilic poems (Ex. xv. 13, 16, Ps. ix. 16, x. 2, xii. 8, xvii. 9, xxxi. 5, xxxii. 8, lxii. 12, lxviii. 29, cxlii. 4, cxliii. 8). (*c*) מִי as an indef. rel. pronoun, xliv. 10, l. 10, liv. 15 (inserted passages, Duhm). (*d*) אַף, not an old prophetic word, fourteen times in these chapters.² See especially xl. 24, where אַף בַּל (thrice) acquires the sense of " scarcely," and is followed by וְגַם (" when "); also xlvi. 11, where אַף—אַף—אַף = " not only—but also—but also," and xli. 26 the triple אַף אֵין = " neither—nor—nor " (cf. *HL, s.v.*). אַף occurs also in xxvi. 8, 9, 11, xxxiii. 2, xxxv. 2, and eighteen times in Psalms. It exists in Mishnic Heb., also in Phœn. and Aram. (*e*) בַּל, not in early prophets, except once or twice in Hosea (vii. 2, ix. 16 Q'rê). Also once in ch. xiv.; five times in xxvi. 10-18; five times in ch. xxxiii.; once in ch. xxxv.; eight times in II. Isa. (xl. 24, xliii. 17, xliv. 8, 9); thirty times in Psalms; ten times in Prov.; once in Job; once in Chron. (*f*) בְּמוֹ, xliii. 2, xliv. 16, 19; also xxv. 10 Q'rê; five times in Job (including ix. 30 Kt., where Siegfried כְּמוֹ); and Ps. xi. 2. (*g*) לָמוֹ for לוֹ, xliv. 7 (not liii. 8); for לָהֶם, xliii. 8, as xxiii. 1 (where לָמוֹ may be from the editor), xxvi. 14, 16 (not xxx. 7). On final מוֹ cf. Ges.-K., p. 286, n. 2; Cheyne, *BL*, pp. 463, 465 (on Psalms ii., xi.). (*h*) עֲדֵי־עַד, lxv. 18, late; so xvii. 2 (corr. text), xxvi. 4, Ps. lxxxiii. 18, etc. (*i*) אוֹת for אֵת (with suff.), liv. 15, and perhaps lix. 21 (as in Kings, Jer., Ezek., Gen. xxxiv. 2, Josh. x. 25, xiv. 12, 2 Sam. xxiv. 24; due everywhere to late writers). Neither passage however belongs to II. Isaiah (see pp. 304, 336). (*k*) לְעָבְרוֹ " straightforward," xlvii. 15, here only (but cf.

¹ See Giesebr., *ZATW.*, 1881, pp. 251-258; Driver, *J. of Phil.*, xi. 222-227, 232; Holzinger, *Einl. in den Hex.*, p. 95; König, *St. u. Kr.*, 1893, pp. 464-468; *Einl.*, pp. 321, 168, 170, 189. An important admission has been made by König (*Einl.*, p. 417). In poetry אֲנִי may sometimes have been preferred for reasons of sound, and "perhaps to complete the number of syllables." [See further on lvi. 1-8, p. 314, Note 2.]
² Or, more strictly, twenty-one times in fourteen passages.

Ezek. i. 9, 12). (*l*) קוֹל interjectionally, four times (see on ch. xiii., p. 72). (*m*) הֵן "behold," fifteen times at least (Nägelsbach, twenty-one times) in chs. xl.-lxvi., *e.g.* xl. 15 *bis*, xli. 11, 24, 29, xlii. 1, etc.; הִנֵּה only ten times (xl. 9, etc.). The following facts are also of interest in this connection. הֵן "behold" occurs in xxiii. 13 (which is at any rate not in the old prophetic style); also in xxxii. 1, xxxiii. 7, both late passages. הִנֵּה in four other late passages, viz. xii. 2, xxi. 9, xxv. 9, xxxv. 4, but also seven times in generally admitted works of Isaiah, viz. vi. 8, vii. 14, viii. 18, 22, xvii. 14, xx. 6, [xxix. 8 *bis*]. הֵן occurs thirty-two times in Job, הִנֵּה eighteen times (Budde, *Beiträge*, p. 115). (*n*) הֵן "if," liv. 15, as Ex. viii. 22 (J); in later Hebrew almost = אִם (Jer. iii. 1, Hag. ii. 12, Lev. xxv. 20, Job xii. 14, 15, 2 Chr. vii. 13, etc.; see Ges.-K., p. 482). Prov. liv. 15 is a later insertion; observe that הֵן "behold" occurs in *v.* 16. (*o*) בְּעַל, a strengthened בְּ, lix. 18, lxiii. 7 (nowhere else). See *RT*. (*p*) אָכֵן, xl. 7, xlv. 15, xlix. 4, liii. 4. Also four times in Jer., once in Zeph.; nowhere else in prophets. (*q*) זוּלַת with suff., xlv. 5, 21, lxiv. 3; also xxvi. 13, Hos. xiii. 4. (*r*) בִּלְעֲדֵי, xliii. 11, xliv. 6, 8, xlv. 6, 21. Also xxxvi. 10 (late). (*s*) כְּאֶחָד, lxv. 25, for יַחְדָּו (Isa. xi. 6, 7), imitating Aram. כַּחֲדָה (Dan. ii. 35), as Ezra ii. 64, Eccles. xi. 6. (*t*) תָּמִיד, xlix. 16, li. 13, lii. 5, lviii. 11, lx. 11, lxii. 6, lxv. 3; also xxi. 8. (Only thrice in pre-Exilic prophets—Hos., Nah., Jer.) (*u*) לוּא (לֻה), to express a wish, xlviii. 18, lxiii. 19. (*v*) and (*w*) לְמַעַן and אֶפֶס, see p. 251 f.

IV. Uncommon or peculiar forms (nouns and verbs). (*a*) אִישִׁים for אֲנָשִׁים, liii. 3, as Ps. cxli. 4, Prov. viii. 4. (*b*) עוֹלָמִים, xlv. 17, li. 9. So xxvi. 4 (see p. 149). (*c*) חֲשֵׁכִים, l. 10 (חֲשֵׁכָה, viii. 22). (*d*) and (*e*) אֲפֵלוֹת, נְגֹהוֹת, intensive plur., lix. 9 (אֲפֵלָה, lviii. 10, viii. 22; נְגֹהָה not found). (*f*) אוֹנִים "(full) strength," xl. 26, 29. אוֹן in different allied senses is good Hebrew (Gen., Deut., Hos., Job, Ps.); אוֹנִים occurs here only. [In Ps. lxxviii. 51, יָם belongs to the compound phrase, רֵאשִׁית אוֹן; and in Prov. xi. 7 restore sense by reading with Bickell אֱוִילִים, Sept. τῶν ἀσεβῶν.] (*g*) צַחְצָחוֹת "dry places," cf. צִחְצָח, Targ. Isa. xxxii. 4, "brightnesses" (*i.e.* clear language). So צְחִיחָה, Ps. lxviii. 7. Isaiah has צַח חֹם "clear heat," xviii. 4. (*h*) תְּבוּנוֹת, xl. 14, as Prov. xi. 12, xxviii. 16, Job xxxii. 11, Ps. xlix. 4, lxxviii. 72. Borrowed from the

CHAPTERS XL.-LXVI. (INTRODUCTORY) 259

Wisdom-literature, and probably late. (*i*) פִּקְחְקֹחַ, lxi. 1 (corr. text). (*k*) פֵּיפִיּוֹת, xli. 15, as Ps. cxlix. 6. (*l*) חַרְצֻבּוֹת, lviii. 6, as Ps. lxxiii. 4 (Aramaic type; see *BL*, p. 478, on Ps. lxxx. 13). (*m*) הֲרִיסֹת, xlix. 19. On lateness of term. וּת see *BL*, p. 472. (*n*) עוֹנִים [עֹוְנֵכוּ], lxiv. 5, 6 (Baer), as Jer. xiv. 7, Ezek. xxviii. 18, Ps. ciii. 3, Dan. ix. 13 (nowhere else). (*o*) חִיתוֹ and שָׂדַי, lvi. 9 (see introduction to lvi. 9-lvii. 21). (*p*) מִסְתֵּר, liii. 3. (*q*) עֲשֹׁתָיו, liv. 5, plur. on analogy of אֱלֹהִים, cf. Job xxxv. 10, Ps. xlix. 2, Eccles. xii. 1. [Also בָּנַיִךְ, lxii. 5, a probable correction of Lowth.] (*r*) סוּרָה, xlix. 21 (belongs to a small gloss; see Sept.), part. pass. Qal with medial sense. König's other examples (*Lehrgeb.* i. 445) are not all sound readings. (*s*) שְׁכוּל "bereaved of children," xlix. 21 (fem.), for שָׁכוּל. (*t*) שָׁכוּר "drunken," li. 21 (fem.), for שִׁכּוֹר. (*u*) גּוּר, liv. 15, if a collateral form of גרה, in Piel "to stir up (strife)"; cf. Ps. lvi. 7, lix. 4, cxl. 3.[1] (*v*) קֹרָא, Pual, xlviii. 8, lviii. 12, lxi. 3, lxii. 2 (in lxv. 1 point קָרָא). Note that xlviii. 8 probably contains a post-Exilic element. Found nowhere else. (*w*) פָּתַח intrans., *patescere*, xlviii. 8 (if text is correct), lx. 11, cf. Song vii. 13. (*x*) שׁוֹחֵח, Polel, liii. 8, as Ps. cxliii. 5. (*y*) הִתְנַגֵּשׁ, xlv. 20 (but cf. Sept.). (*z*) הוֹלִיד, xlv. 10, lv. 10, lix. 4 (for יָלַד), lxvi. 9, as often in P and Chron. Probably not pre-Exilic in use, Deut. iv. 25 and xxviii. 41 being Exilic, and Judg. xi. 1 having been retouched.[2] (*aa*) יֶאֱתָיוּן, xli. 5, lx. 7, 10; and (*bb*) תִּשְׁבָּבוּן, l. 11. Note archaizing ending (as xvii. 12, xxi. 12, xxxi. 3, xxxiii. 7).

V. Other peculiar forms, due probably to corruption of the text or faulty punctuation (cf. *RT*). (*a*) מִסְכָּן, xl. 20. (*b*) יָרוּץ, intrans., xlii. 4. (*c*) צוּלָה = מְצוּלָה, xliv. 27. (*d*) עֲצָתָיךְ, xlvii. 13. (*e*) בְּזֹה, and (*f*) מְתָעֵב, xlix. 7. (*g*) יְהֵילִילוּ and (*h*) מַבִּיאֵץ, lii. 5. (*i*) מוֹתִים (בְּמֹתָיו), liii. 9. (*k*) הֶחָלִי, liii. 10. (*l*) נִגְאָלוּ, lix. 3. (*m*) מִשְׁתּוֹלֵל, lix. 15. (*n*) תִּלְבֹּשֶׁת, lix. 17. (*o*) אֹתָם lix. 21. (*p*) פְּקַח־קוֹחַ, lxi. 1, cf. iv. (*i*). (*q*) הִתְחַיָּפְרוּ, lxi. 6. (*r*) אֶנְאָלְתִּי, lxiii. 3. (*s*) תְּמוּגֵנוּ, lxiv. 6. (*t*) נָבֵל(וּ), lxiv. 5. (*u*) שֵׂד, lx. 16, lxvi. 11. If it should be admitted that all these forms are corrupt, and may be corrected, so much the better for the style of this great literary monument.

---
[1] In all these places however the reading is disputable; see Cheyne, *Book of Psalms*, critical notes, and cf. Kautzsch's *Bible.*
[2] Cf. Giesebr., *ZATW*, I. 236.

But this does not increase the probability of the authorship of Isaiah!

VI. A selection of words and phrases found in chaps. xl.-lxvi. (but not in the true Isaiah), which are either late (at any rate in prophecy), or, if not, are at least specially frequent in these chapters, and sometimes used in distinctly late senses. [To these may be added several items in the list of verbal parallelisms, p. 251 ff., including the important words אִיִּים, תֹּהוּ, רָהָב, בָּרָא.] A word found but once in chaps. xl.-lxvi. is only inserted when the text-reading appears certain.

אַפְסֵי אֶרֶץ, xlv. 22, lii. 10. Also in 1 Sam. ii. 10 (post-Exilic, *BL*, p. 57), Jer. xvi. 19 (secondary?—Stade, *Gesch.* i. 647), Mic. v. 3 (late; Stade, Wellh.), Zech. ix. 10 (late), Prov. xxx. 4 (late), Psalms (six times, incl. ii. 8), Deut. xxxiii. 17.

קְצוֹת הָאָרֶץ, xl. 28, xli. 5, 9, as Job xxviii. 24 (late).

כָּל־בָּשָׂר "all mankind," xl. 5, 6, xlix. 26, lxvi. 16, 23, 24. The earliest certain prophetic passage for this sense of the phrase is Jer. xxv. 31.

שִׂים עַל־לֵב "to heed," xlii. 25, xlvii. 7, lvii. 1, 11 (as Jer. xii. 11; Deut. xi. 18).

פֶּצַח רִנָּה, xliv. 23, xlix. 13, liv. 1, lv. 12, as in xiv. 7. Cf. lii. 9; Ps. xcviii. 4, and see on רָנַן, p. 268.

עִיר הַקֹּדֶשׁ, xlviii. 2, lii. 1, as Neh. xi. 1, 18; Dan. ix. 24. Cf. Ps. xlvi. 5.

שֹׁד וָשֶׁבֶר, li. 19 (virtually), lix. 7, lx. 18 (as Jer. xlviii. 3).

דּוֹר וָדוֹר, lviii. 12, lx. 15, lxi. 4 (only in late writers; see p. 73).

הַגּוֹיִם וְהַלְשֹׁנוֹת, lxvi. 18; cf. Dan. iii. 4, 7, 29, iv. 1, v. 19, vi. 25, vii. 14 (Zech. viii. 23).

עִנָּה נֶפֶשׁ, lviii. 3, 5, as Lev. xvi. 29, 31, xxiii. 27, 29, 32; Num. xxix. 7, xxx. 14; Ps. xxxv. 13. Phrase taken from P.

דִּבְּרֵי־שָׂרָה, lix. 13 (see p. 333).

אָדַר, Hif., xlii. 21. Nifal part. in Ex. xv. 6, 11 (late). Nowhere else.

אֲנָחָה plur., lviii. 6. Once in Exodus, once in 2 Samuel; also in Am. ix. 6 (in a late insertion).

אָחוֹר "future time," xli. 23, xlii. 23.

אָמֵץ "to grow (a tree)," xliv. 14; cf. Ps. lxxx. 16, 18.

אֱנוֹשׁ, "frail (or, weak) man," li. 7, 12, as in Job, Psalms, 2 Chr. xix. 10 (see *BL*, p. 464).

אָפַק Hithp., xlii. 14, lxiii. 15, lxiv. 1, as Genesis twice (p. 272); 1 Sam. xiii. 12; Esth. v. 10.

CHAPTERS XL.-LXVI. (INTRODUCTORY) 261

אֲרֻכָה, lviii. 8; also Jer. (thrice), 2 Chr. xxiv. 13, Neh. iv. 1.
אָמָה, xli. 5, 25, lvi. 9, 12, and thrice (xli. 23, xliv. 7, xlv. 11) in plur. fem. part. Qal. Babylonian period (see on xxi. 12, 14, p. 129). בַּדִּים, xliv. 25 (see on xvi. 6, p. 85).

בָּרַל Hif., lvi. 3, lix. 2. In pre-Exilic writings four times; in later literature more than twenty times (Giesebr., *ZATW*, i. 248). Cf. Wellh., *Prol.*, p. 406; Driver, *J. of Phil.*, xi. 219.

בֶּהָלָה, lxv. 23, as Jer. xv. 8; Lev. xxvi. 16; Ps. lxxviii. 33.
בוּם Pilel, lxiii. 18, as Jer. xii. 19 (Hithpalel, Ezek. xvi. 6, 22).
בָּחַר "to test," for בָּחַן, as in Aram.; xlviii. 10.
בֶּצַע "unjust gain," lvi. 11, lvii. 17 (if correct), xxxiii. 15, Jeremiah, Ezekiel, Proverbs (thrice in each), Ps. cxix. 36. In Hab. ii. 9 רַע is added.

בָּקַע Nif., "to come forth" (from an egg), lix. 5; cf. Qal, xxxiv. 15.

בְּרִית "(religious) covenant," xlii. 6, xlix. 8, liv. 10, lv. 3, lvi. 4, 6, lix. 21, lxi. 8 (so xxiv. 5). The true Isaiah uses בְּ only in its simple sense, xxviii. 15, 18 (so xxxiii. 8).

בְּשֵׂר, five times in chaps. xl.-lxvi. Nowhere again in prophets, except Nah. ii. 1; Jer. xx. 15 (both probably interpolated passages).[1]

גָּאַל Qal perf., "to redeem," xliii. 1, xliv. 22, 23, xlviii. 20, lii. 9, lxiii. 9. Qal part. act., xli. 14 (+ 12 other passages); pass., li. 10 (quotation), lxii. 12 (?). Nif. imperf., lii. 3.

גָּאַל Nif., "to be defiled," lix. 3 (see *RT*), as Zeph. iii. 1 (date uncertain),[2] Lam. iv. 14 (pointed as in Isa. lix. 3); Piel, "to defile," lxiii. 3 (see *RT*), as Mal. i. 7. Cf. Pual in Mal. i. 7, 12; Ezra ii. 62; Neh. vii. 64; Hithp. in Dan. i. 8. Cf. Aram. עֲגַל.

גִּדּוּפִים, xliii. 28, as Zeph. ii. 8 (cf. גִּדּוּפָה, li. 7, and גְּדוּפָה, Ezek. v. 15). See on xxxvii. 23, p. 222.

גָּדַשׁ "to heap up," Qal and Nif., lvii. 20 (a *certain* conjecture). Talmudic.

גִּלְמוּד, xlix. 21, as Job iii. 7, xv. 34, xxx. 3.

גָּמוּל, lix. 18 (*bis*), lxvi. 6, as iii. 11 (gloss), xxxv. 4; Psalms (four times); Lamentations, Obadiah, and 2 Chronicles (once in each); Proverbs (twice); Joel (thrice); Jer. li. 6; Judg. ix. 16. גְּמוּלָה, lix. 18, as Jer. li. 56; 2 Sam. xix. 37.

---

[1] On Jer. xx. 14-18, cf. Stade, *ZATW*, 1886, p. 153; Dillm., *Hiob*,[4] Einl., p. xxxiii.

[2] The date of Zeph. iii. must be considered with that of Mic. vii. Both chapters are, in my judgment, post-Exilic. Cf. Schwally, *ZATW*, 1890, p. 234 f.; Wellh., *Die kl. Proph.*, p. 153 f. But on the other side, see Budde, *St. u. Kr.*, 1893, p. 396, and cf. Wildeboer, *De Letterkunde*, p. 225.

שָׁשָׁע Piel, lix. 10, ἅπ. λεγ.; Aramaism, = pure Heb. שׁעשׁע.
גאָז with acc., lvii. 11, as Jer. xxxviii. 19 (narrative); same verb absolutely, Jer. xvii. 8; combined with לְ, twice in 1 Samuel; with מִן, Jer. xlii. 16; Ps. xxxviii. 19 (different senses).
היו, eight times (including liii. 8); also in xiii. 20, xxxiv. 10, 17 [xxxviii. 12, "dwelling," Aram.]. In li. 8 הוֹיִם, as Ps. lxxii. 5, cii. 25. See further, p. 73.
עָפָא, lvii. 15, Ps. xxxiv. 19 (xc. 3 = crumbling dust).
וְמוּת, xl. 18, as xiii. 14 (see p. 72). Also once in Daniel, once in Chronicles, fifteen times in Ezekiel, twice in Hex. (P), once in Psalms. In 2 Ki. xvi. 10, however, where Mas. text gives it, we should read with Sept. (Luc.) מְוֹיוֹת (see Klost.). All the trustworthy passages therefore are late. Cf. *BL*, p. 474; Wellh., *Prol.*, p. 407; Lagarde, *Uebersicht*, p. 148; Driver, *J. of Phil.*, xi. 216.
הֵמִי, lxii. 6, 7, as Ps. lxxxiii. 2; cf. הֱמִי, xxxviii. 10.
דְּרָאוֹן, lxvi. 24, as Dan. xii. 2.
הָרוֹה, lxi. 1, as Jer. xxxiv. (four times); Ezek. xlvi. 17; Lev. xxv. 10 (not in the older legislation).
הָגָה "to utter," lix. 3, 13 (corr. text), as in Psalms and late Hebrew.
הִגִּיד, "to announce (prophetically)," xli. 22, 23, 26, xlii. 9, xliii. 12, xliv. 8, xlv. 19, xlvi. 10, xlviii. 3.
הֲדַס, xli. 19, lv. 13, as Zech. i. 8, 10, 11; Neh. viii. 15; but not in the parallel passage Lev. xxiii. 40. [Probably the myrtle was imported after the Return; see *PI*³, i. 258, ii. 226.]
הלל Piel, "to praise (God)," lxii. 9, lxiv. 10, as xxxviii. 8 (so first Jer. xx. 13, xxxi. 7). Cf. on תְּהִלָּה, and see *BL*, p. 467.——Poel, "to befool," xliv. 25, as Job xii. 17; Eccles. xii. 7 (Poal, Ps. cii. 9; Eccles. ii. 2).
חֲרָפָה, xlix. 19 (see above, p. 259). Or read חָרְבָה, see Am. ix. 11 (late; see p. 326, on ch. lviii.).
יָבוּל, lxiii. 15, as 1 Ki. viii. 13 (2 Chr. vi. 2); Hab. iii. 11; Ps. xlix. 15, last line (if correct). Perhaps a revived archaism (see *BL*, p. 212).
זוב, xlviii. 21. In prophets, not before Jer. (xi. 5, xxxii. 22? xlix. 4).
יִקְּיֹח, l. 11, = זִקִּים, Prov. xxvi. 18; Talm. זִיקִין shooting stars.
זִכָּרוֹן, a memorial connected with worship or with some religious practice, lvii. 8; so Zech. vi. 14 (nowhere else in prophecy); Ex. xiii. 9, xxviii. 12, xxxix. 7; and other passages of late history or legislation. The use may of course be old.[1]
זֶרַע, lxi. 11, as Lev. xi. 37. Cf. זֵרַע, Dan. i. 12.

---

[1] See Stade, *ZATW*, 1894, p. 310.

CHAPTERS XL.-LXVI. (INTRODUCTORY) 263

חָדֵל, liii. 3, as Ezek. iii. 27; Ps. xxxix. 5.

חוּל and חִילָל, eight times, also in xiii. 8, xxvi. 17 (late), and in xxiii. 4, 5 (doubtful).

חַלָּמִישׁ, l. 7, as Deut. viii. 15 (Exilic), xxxii. 13 (late Exilic); Job xxviii. 9; Ps. cxiv. 8.

חֵמָה, ten times, and in xxvii. 4, xxxiv. 2.

חֶסֶד "piety," lvii. 1 (a rare meaning; cf. חָסִיד in the Psalms); "goodliness," xl. 6 (unique).

חִפָּזוֹן, lii. 12, as in Ex. xii. 11 (P); Deut. xvi. 3.

חֵפֶץ, (a) "wish," "desire," xliv. 28, xlviii. 14, liii. 10; (b) "business," lviii. 3 (plural), 13, as in Eccles.; analogous to Aram. צְבוּ *negotium*, from צְבָא *voluit*.

חֵקֶר, xl. 28, as in Ps. cxlv. 3; Prov. xxv. 3, 27; Job (seven passages); and Judg. v. 16 (not a prophetic word).

חֹרֶב "wasteness," lxi. 4, as Deut. xxviii. 22, Vulg.; Ezek. xxix. 10 (inserted gloss), Jer. xlix. 13 (gloss); in Zeph. ii. 4 read עֶרֶב with Wellh.

חֲרָצֻבָּה (plural), lviii. 6, as Ps. lxxiii. 4. (The insertion of ר in lieu of dagesh is specially common in Aramaic.)

טָהוֹר, lxvi. 20, as Ezekiel (three times), Zech. iii. 5 (*bis*), Mal. i. 11.

טָהֵר (Hithp.), lxvi. 17; nowhere else in prophets (twelve times in Lev. xiv.).

טוּחַ (unless טָחַח, ἅπ. λεγ.), xliv. 18, as in Ezekiel (six passages); Lev. xiv. 42, 43, 48; 1 Chron. xxix. 4.

יָגָה Hif., li. 23, as xxvii. 8 (corr. text); Lam. (thrice); Job xix. 2; Nif. in Zeph. iii. 18 (late), Lam. i. 4; Piel, Lam. iii. 33.

יָמִין "right hand," xli. 10, 13, xliv. 20, xlv. 1, xlviii. 13, lxii. 8. In ix. 19 "=" (on) the right."

יָעַץ Hifil, lviii. 5, as Ps. cxxxix. 8 (Hofal, xiv. 11; Esth. iv. 3).

יְשׁוּעָה, twenty times (and seven times in other late parts).

יְשֻׁרוּן, xliv. 2, as Deut. xxxii. 15, xxxiii. 5, 26. Honorific synonym for Jacob or Israel. (See Bacher, *ZATW*, 1885, p. 161.)

יַחַד used adverbially, lvi. 12, as Dan. viii. 9; cf. Aram. יַחִיר.

בַּרְכֹּד, liv. 12, as Ezek. xxvii. 16.

כָּנָה Nif., xliii. 2, as Prov. vi. 28 (only).

מוּל (Qal), "to measure," xl. 12 (as in Aram. and Ar.).

מֹעֲנ, xlv. 18, li. 13, lxii. 7; so Hab. ii. 12 (late; see Wellh.). Nowhere else in prophecy. Seventeen times in Psalms, twice in Job, once in Deut. xxxii., Proverbs, and Chronicles; also in 2 Sam. vii. 13, 24 (Deut. period).

פָּלַם in Nifal, xli. 11, xlv. 16, 17, l. 7, liv. 4.

פָּנָה (Piel), xliv. 5, xlv. 4, as Job xxxii. 21, 22. (Aramaic affinities.)

פִּפָּ, lviii. 5, as Ps. lvii. 7, cxlv. 14, cxlvi. 8; Nifal, Mic. vi. 6. (Common in Aramaic.)

בְּרִיתוֹת, 1. 1, as Jer. iii. 8, Deut. xxiv. 1, 3.

מַבּוּעַ, plural c., xlix. 10, as xxxv. 7 and (sing.) Eccles. xii. 6.

מוֹפֵת, lviii. 6 (*bis*), 9, as Jer. xxvii. 2, xxviii. 10, 12, 13 (*bis*); Ezek. xxx. 18, xxxiv. 27; Lev. xxvi. 13; 1 Chron. xv. 15. (Possibly also in Isa. ix. 3, *RT*.)

מוּסָר, pl. c. masc., lviii. 12, as Mic. vi. 2; Jer. xxxi. 37 (both passages post-Exilic [1]); Isa. xxiv. 18; Deut. xxxii. 22; Ps. xviii. 8, lxxxii. 5; Prov. viii. 29; pl. fem., Jer. li. 26, and in *stat. c.*, Isa. xl. 21; 2 Sam. xxii. 8, 16 (= Ps. xviii. 16). Seems largely post-Exilic in use.

מָחָא, lv. 12, as Ps. xcviii. 8; (Piel) Ezek. xxv. 6. Aramaizing.

מְחִתָּה, liv. 14, as Jer. xvii. 17, xlviii. 39; Ps. lxxxix. 41; Proverbs (seven times).

מָלַט Hifil, "to bear a child easily," lxvi. 7; cf. מֶלֶט, xxxiv. 15. Contrast Isaiah's use, xxxi. 5.

מֵלִיץ "mediator" (between God and men), xliii. 27; cf. Job xxxiii. 23 (Elihu); 2 Chron. xxxii. 31.

מַסְגֵּר "prison," xlii. 7, as xxiv. 22 (p. 149).

מַעֲמַקִּים, li. 10, as Ezek. xxvii. 34; Ps. lxix. 3, 15, cxxx. 1.

מַעֲצָד, xliv. 12, as Jer. x. 3 (late). Talmudic.

מִצְעָר "a short time," lxiii. 18; cf. מִזְעָר, x. 25, xxix. 17 (late).

מַצָּה, lviii. 4, as Prov. xiii. 10, xvii. 19. [מַצָּא, xli. 12, ἅπ. λεγ.]

מְרוּדִים, lviii. 7, as Lam. i. 7, iii. 19.

מָרוֹם "the heavenly height," xl. 26, lvii. 15, as xxiv. 18, 21, xxxiii. 5; Mic. vi. 6 (late); Job xvi. 19 (plural); Ps. xviii. 17, xciii. 4.

מָרַט, l. 6, as Ezek. xxi. 14, 16, 33, xxix. 18; Ezra ix. 3; Neh. xiii. 25. (Pual part. in xviii. 2, 7.)

מָשׁוֹשׂ, xxiv. 8 (*bis*), 11, xxxii. 13, 14, lx.-lxvi. (four times). Not in viii. 6 (p. 37).

מִשְׁפָּט "ordinance," "law," used for the true religion in its practical aspect; xlii. 1, 3, 4, li. 4, cf. lviii. 2.

מָתַח "to stretch out," xl. 22 (as in Aram.), ἅπ. λεγ. But אַמְתַּחַת, "sack," occurs already in J (Gen. xliv. 27, etc.).

נָדָה "to loathe" (see Sept.), lxvi. 5, as *nad* in Syriac. The same verb in Amos vi. 3 means "to put far" (in thought). The Talmudic sense "to excommunicate" does not suit in Isaiah *l.c.*

נִבָּץ, lvi. 8, as xi. 12. Characteristically late, p. 61.

---

[1] See Kosters, *Theol. Tijdschr.*, 1893, pp. 269-273 (on Mic. vi.-vii.); Kuenen, *Ond.*[2], ii. 204, and Smend, *AT Rel.-Gesch.*, pp. 239-241 (on Jer. xxx.-xxxi.).

CHAPTERS XL.-LXVI. (INTRODUCTORY) 265

נוֹאָשׁ, lvii. 10, as Jer. ii. 25, xviii. 12.

נְוֵה, subst. lxv. 10 (see on xxvii. 10, p. 146).

נִחֻמִים "comfort," lvii. 18, as Zech. i. 13.

נִיב (or נוּב, Q'rê), lvii. 19, as Mal. i. 12.

נָצוּר "secret," xlviii. 6, lxv. 4 (but read 'נ).

נָקַם, (with reference to Yahwè), xlvii. 3, lix. 17, lxi. 2, lxiii. 4, as in xxxiv. 8, xxxv. 4. [Only once therefore in the Prophecy of Comfort, chaps. xl.-lv. Nowhere in any pre-Exilic prophecy, Mic. v. 14 (A.V., 15) being certainly late (see Stade, *ZATW*, 1881, p. 170). The verb נקם occurs (in Nifal) with reference to Yahwè in Isa. i. 24, but nowhere else in pre-Exilic prophecy before Jeremiah, who uses both נקם (in Nif. and Hithp.) and נְקָמָה (Jer. xi. 20 = xx. 12) of Yahwè. Observe that in later parts of Jeremiah נְקָמָה occurs seven times with reference to Yahwè (chaps. xlvi., l., li.).]

נָשַׁב, xl. 7, as (Hifil) Gen. xv. 11; Ps. cxlvii. 18. In Genesis *l.c.*, however, the pointing is doubtful; the word is more used in Aramaic, and is also found in Talmudic.

נְשָׁמָה "living being," lvii. 16 (plural here only), as Deut., Josh., 1 Kings (once in each), and Ps. cl. 6.

נֶשֶׁף, xl. 24, as Ex. xv. 10 (late). But נֶשֶׁף is classical Hebrew.

נָתַר Hif., "to throw off," lviii. 6, as Job vi. 9; Ps. cv. 20, cxlvi. 7. (So Aram. Afel.)

נָשָׂא, xli. 17, as xix. 5 (see p. 111).

סֵבֶל, xlvi. 4 (*bis*), 7, liii. 4, 11. Cf. סֹבֶל, ix. 3, x. 27, xiv. 25; also סָבַל, Gen. xlix. 15; סִבְלָה, Ex. i. 11, ii. 11, v. 4, 5, vi. 6, 7.

סָגַד, "to worship," xliv. 15, 17, 19, xlvi. 6. From Aramaic.

סְגָנִים = Aram. סִגְנִין (Dan.), a term for Babylonian governors, xli. 25, as Ezek. xxiii. 6, 12, 23; Jer. li. 23, 28. From Ass.-Babylonian.

סַפִּיר, liv. 11, as Ex. (four times in chaps. xxiv.-xl.); Ezek. i. 26, x. 1, xxviii. 13; Lam. iv. 7; Job xxviii. 16; Song v. 14.

עָדַר Nifal, "to be missing," xl. 26, lix. 15, as xxxiv. 16, Zeph. iii. 5.

עוּר imper. Qal, li. 9, liii. 1 (nowhere else in prophets except Hab. ii. 19,[1] Zech. xiii. 7, both post-Exilic). Hifil, xli. 2, 25, xlii. 13, xlv. 13, l. 4 *bis;* also in xiii. 17. Earliest prophetic passage, Ezek. xxiii. 22, Hos. vii. 4 being a gloss (Wellh.); Hithp., li. 17, lxiv. 6 (again only twice in Job).

עֲוֹנוֹת, xlii. 25, as Ps. lxxviii. 4, cxlv. 6.

עֲוֹנוֹת, xliii. 17, as Ps. xxiv. 8 (only).

עֶצֶם, lvii. 16, as (different stems) in Psalms (six times), Lam. (thrice), Jon. ii. 8, Gen. xxx. 42 (used technically).

עַם and קָעָם "mankind," xl. 7 (?), xlii. 5, xliv. 7 (?).

---

[1] See Budde, *St. u. Kr.*, 1893, p. 390.

עֻנּוֹ (Hithp.) and its derivatives, ten times. (But cf. תַּעֲנוּגִים, Mic. i. 16, ii. 9.)

עָנָה Nif., liii. 7, reflexive, as Ex. x. 3 (?); lviii. 10, passive, as Ps. cxix. 107.——Pual, liii. 4, as Lev. xxiii. 29, Ps. cxix. 71, cxxxii. 1.

עָנָו "submissive to the divine will," lxi. 1, as xxix. 19, xxxii. 7 (Ktib). Not pre-Exilic in this sense (see on xi. 4, p. 64 f.).

עָסִיס, xlix. 26, as Amos ix. 13 (late, Wellh.); Joel i. 5, iv. 18; Song viii. 2.

עָצַב Qal, liv. 6 (part. pass.); Piel, lxiii. 10 (again only in Ps. lvi. 6). Both are good Hebrew forms (see derivatives), though nowhere else found in prophecy.

עָצְמָה, xl. 29, xlvii. 9 [lviii. 11, conj.], as Nah. iii. 9 (?).

עֲצָמוֹת "arguments," xli. 21; cf. Mishna phrase, נִתְעַצֵּם בְּדִין.

עֲרָבִים, xliv. 4, as xv. 7 (not Isaiah), Ps. cxxxvii. 2; Job xl. 22; Lev. xxiii. 40. [In xv. 7, however, 'ע may perhaps = "steppes."]

פְּגוּל (plural), lxv. 4, as Lev. vii. 18, xix. 7, Ezek. iv. 14.

פָּגַע Hif., liii. 6, 12, lix. 16, as Jer. xxxvi. 25 (not xv. 11); Job xxxvi. 32.

פָּרָה, (Qal part. pass.) li. 11, from xxxv. 10; xxix. 22; (Nifal) i. 27.

פְּדוּת "redemption," 1. 2, as Ps. cxi. 9, cxxx. 7 (in Ex. viii. 19 it may be corrupt; see Dillm.). Late in prophetic use.

נֹפֶךְ = פּוּךְ, "emerald" (?), liv. 11, as 1 Chron. xxix. 2.

פּוּק exire, Hif., lviii. 10, as Ps. cxl. 9, cxliv. 13, Proverbs (four times).

פּוּרָה, lxiii. 3, as Hag. ii. 16 (only).

פָּחַם, xliv. 12, liv. 16, as Prov. vi. 21, Ps. xi. 6 (conj.).

פֶּלֶס, xl. 12, as Prov. xvi. 11 (the verb only occurs in Psalms and Proverbs, and in Isa. xxvi. 7).

פֶּסֶל, xl. 19, 20; xlii. 17, xliv. 9, 10, 15, 17 [19, conj.], xlv. 20, xlviii. 5. Nowhere in any pre-Exilic prophecy; Jer. x. 14, li. 17, Nah. i. 14 (v. Gunkel, *ZATW*, 1893, p. 223), Hab. ii. 18 (v. Budde, *St. u. Kr.*, 1893, p. 390) are post-Exilic. פְּסִילִים seems preferred by the early prophets.

פְּקֻדָּה "magistracy," lx. 17. In Isaiah "punishment," x. 3.

פָּקַח, used of opening the ears, xlii. 20; and the derivative פְּקַח־קוֹחַ, or rather פְּקַחְקֹחַ (Olsh., *Lehrb.*, § 188b), lxi. 1, of opening prison doors. Elsewhere only of opening the eyes (xxxv. 5, xxxvii. 7, xlii. 7).

פָּרַס "to break" (from a flat loaf of bread), lviii. 7, as Jer. xvi. 7. Cf. Talm. פְּרוּסָא.

פְּצָלָה, xl. 10, xlix. 4, lxi. 8, lxii. 11, lxv. 7.

פֶּשַׁע, ten times, and in xxiv. 20. [פָּשַׁע perf., inf., and part. Qal six times; perf. also in i. 2, and part. once in an interpolation (i. 28).]

CHAPTERS XL.-LXVI. (INTRODUCTORY) 267

צָבָא in metaphorical sense for "hard time," xl. 2, as Job vii. 1, xiv. 14. (Here fem., as in Dan. viii. 12, where however 'צ = "campaign.")

צַבִּים "litters," lxvi. 20, cf. צַב Num. vii. 3 (P). Targ. צִיבָא (Isa. xlix. 22), צַבָּא (Nah. ii. 8). Assyrian ṣumbu (CI, ii. 33).

צַר, lx. 4, lxvi. 12, (six times in Ezekiel; nowhere else in prophets). צֶדֶק (xlv. 19), צְדָקָה (xlv. 23, xlviii. 1), "truth," "sincerity," צַדִּיק, "correct," "truthful," xli. 26.—צֶדֶק, צְדָקָה, (a) God's fidelity to his announced purpose, xlii. 6, 21, xlv. 13; (b) "redress," "success" (Israel's public justification by its God); xlv. 8, xlvi. 13, li. 5, 6, 8, liv. 17, lvi. 1, lix. 14, 17, lxi. 10, 11, lxii. 1. Both senses also frequently in Psalms.—צְדָקוֹת "righteous acts" (of men), lxiv. 5 (see p. 168).

צַהַל, liv. 1, see on xii. 6, p. 58.

צִוָה, xlii. 11, ἅπ. λεγ. (see on צְוָחָה, xxiv. 11).

צוּלָה, xliv. 27 = מְצוּלָה, Zech. i. 8; Job xli. 23; Ps. lxviii. 23, lxix. 3, 16; Jon. ii. 4; also (plur.) Mic. vii. 19; Zech. x. 11; Ps. lxviii. 23; cf. מְצוּלוֹת, Ex. xv. 5; Neh. ix. 11; Ps. lxxxviii. 7. Late in usage.

צִיר (plur.), "image," xlv. 16 = Aram. צוּרָא (the verb צוּר "to form" is Aram., not Heb.; in Pael = "to model, to paint").

צֶמַח, seven times; including xlii. 9, xliii. 19, lviii. 8, where it is used of divinely appointed events which appear as suddenly as the flowers in spring.

צָמַח, lxi. 11, as iv. 2 (late).

צָעָה, li. 14 (not lxiii. 1), as Jer. ii. 20, xlviii. 12.

קָבַץ Nifal, xliii. 9, xlv. 20, xlviii. 14, xlix. 18, lvi. 8, lx. 4, 7 (also xxxiv. 15). Piel, xliii. 5, xlix. 11, liv. 7, lvi. 8, lxii. 9, lxvi. 18 (also xi. 12, xxii. 9). Hithp., xliv. 11.

קָרַח, l. 11, lxiv. 1, as Jer. xv. 14, xvii. 4; Deut. xxxii. 22.

קַדְמוֹנִי, xliii. 18, as Ezek. (four times), Joel ii. 20; Zech. xiv. 8; Mal. iii. 4; Job xviii. 20 (also 1 Sam. xxiv. 14, gloss; see Wellh.).

קַדְרוּת "blackness" = "mourning garment," l. 3, ἅπ. λεγ. (favourite late ending).

קָדֵשׁ (Hithp.), lxvi. 17, as xxx. 29 (probably late), and Ezek. xxxviii. 23. On the use of קדשׁ and its derivatives in chaps. xl.-lxvi., see note, p. 314.

קוּמֶם, xliv. 26, lviii. 12, lxi. 4 (nowhere else, Mic. ii. 8 being corrupt).

קָצַף, six times (Hithp. in viii. 21).

קֶצֶף, liv. 8, lx. 10, as xxxiv. 2 (not in prophets before Jeremiah).

קָרָא "to call" = "to prophesy"; xl. 2, 6, xliv. 7, lxi. 1, 2 (lviii. 1 is a little different); cf. Jon. i. 2; Zech. vii. 7. Also "to sue" (*in jus vocare*), lix. 4, as Job ix. 16, xiii. 22.

268   ISAIAH

קֶשֶׁת, lxiii. 17, as Job xxxix. 16.
רֹאשׁ "beginning," xl. 21, xli. 4, 26, xlviii. 16, as Ezek. xl. 1; Ex. xii. 2; Num. x. 10, xxviii. 11 (all P), Prov. viii. 23.
רֵאשִׁית "beginning," xlvi. 10 (rare sense in early lit.; see Siegfr.-Stade).
רָגַע (Qal), "to stir up," li. 15 (from Jer. xxxi. 35*b*); (Hifil) "to found" (?), li. 4 (or connect with next verse, and render "quickly . . ."; see Sept. and cf. *RT*).
רָנַן Qal and Piel, xlii. 11, and seven times besides, as in xii. 6, xxiv. 14, xxvi. 19, xxxv. 2, 6, all post-Exilic passages. רִנָּה, xliii. 14 (if וְנָהַם may be trusted), xliv. 23, and five times besides, as in xiv. 7, xxxv. 10. There is no sure pre-Exilic instance of רָנַן, Proverbs (see i. 20, viii. 3, xxix. 6) in its present form, as well as Job and Psalms, and Zeph. iii. (see *v.* 14) being post-Exilic. For the same reason, there are no sure pre-Exilic instances of רִנָּה except Jer. vii. 16, xi. 14, xiv. 12 (where the word means "cry of supplication").
רֶפֶשׁ, lvii. 20, ἅπ. λεγ. Talmudic.
רָצָה "to have pleasure (in)," xlii. 1, and רָצוֹן "favour," xlix. 8 (+5 other passages). Class. Heb., but very rare in pre-Exilic writings. Nif., "to be paid off" (of a debt), xl. 2, as in Qal and Hifil "to pay off," Lev. xxvi. 34, 41; 2 Chr. xxxvi. 21.
רִיק, l. 6, as Job vii. 19, xxx. 10.
רָקַע Qal part., xlii. 5, xliv. 24; Piel denom. xl. 19. Elsewhere only (Qal) in Ezek. vi. 11, xxv. 6, 2 Sam. xxiii. 43 (where the word is a late explanatory gloss), and Ps. cxxxvi. 6 (part., as II. Isaiah); also (Piel) in Ex. xxxix. 3, and Num. xvii. 4 (both P), and in Jer. x. 9, and Job xxxvii. 18 (both post-Exilic). That the word is of late Aram. origin, has not been proved (Driver, *Journ. of Phil.*, xi. 212); but in both its senses (1, to stamp, 2, to establish), it is late in use. Cf. Wellh., *Prol.*³, p. 406. (רָקִיעַ is also late in use, but though II. Isaiah, if we may assume his existence, flourished after Ezekiel, he does not use this word.)
שָׂשׂ, lxi. 10, lxii. 5, lxiv. 4 (?), lxv. 18, 19, lxvi. 10, 14, also xxxv. 1; so Deut. xxviii. 63, xxx. 9; Jer. xxxii. 41.
שָׁכַב, lvii. 17, as Jer. iii. 22. (Jer. iii. 14, xxxi. 22, xlix. 4 are late; see Giesebr.)
שָׁוָה Hif., "to compare," xlvi. 5, as Lam. ii. 13.
שַׁחַק "dust," xl. 15. In plur. elsewhere for the clouds, or the sky; and so in sing., Ps. lxxxix. 7, 38.
שָׁלַל Hithpol., lix. 15; Ps. lxxvi. 6. But see p. 333.
שָׁלִישׁ "a tierce" (measure), xl. 12, as Ps. lxxx. 6 (late).
שָׁמֵם Hithpol., lix. 16, lxiii. 5, as Ps. cxliii. 4; Dan. viii. 27; Eccles. vii. 16.

CHAPTERS XL.-LXVI. (INTRODUCTORY) 269

שָׁעָה in Hithp., "to look about" for help, xli. 10, or in astonishment, v. 23. In Qal "to look," xvii. 7, 8, xxii. 4, xxxi. 1. שְׁעִי, xl. 12, as Ezek. xiii. 19; 1 Ki. xx. 10.

שָׁפַט Nif., "to go to law" or "plead together," xliii. 26, lix. 4, lxvi. 16. So Jer. ii. 35, xxv. 31; Ezekiel (four times); Prov. xxix. 9; 2 Chr. xxii. 8; Joel iv. 2. Comp. מִשְׁפָּטֶה, xliii. 26, with נִוָּכְחָה, i. 18. שִׁפְקוּצִים, lxvi. 3 [lvii. 13, conj.], five times in Jeremiah, eight in Ezekiel. Also in Hos. ix. 10 (if genuine there); Nah. iii. 6.

שָׁרַב, xlix. 10, as xxxv. 7. The root is Aramaic = "to be burnt or dried up" (see Ex. iii. 2, 3, Targ. Jon.; Judges xvi. 7, Pesh.; and cf. שְׁרָב "heat, or drought," Isa. iv. 6, xxv. 4, 5, and Ps. xxxii. 4, Targ.). "Nemo negabit," says L. de Dieu, "quin שְׁרָב 'aestus,' hîc metonymicè significet 'terram siccam'" (*Animadversiones*, 1648, p. 527). This sense has been abandoned by most scholars in favour of the rendering "mirage"[1] (cf. Ar. سَرَاب). The old meaning, however, is by far the more defensible one. "Mirage" cannot except by a violent zeugma be reconciled to the verb "to smite" in xlix. 10, and though this sense is not altogether unsuitable in xxxv. 7a, yet "thirsty land" (lit. thirst) in v. 7b rather favours the rendering "parched land" in v. 7a. Moreover (and this is the chief point), since שְׁרָב in xxxv. 7 is borrowed (see p. 208) from xlix. 10, we have no right to impose a meaning upon it there which it will not bear in the original passage. The most natural rendering of שְׁרָב in xlix. 10 is surely "scorching wind"; cf. Jon. iv. 6, when God first summons an east wind, and then the sun "smites" Jonah's head. The word for this east wind in Sept. is πνεῦμα καύσων, and ὁ καύσων is Sept.'s rendering of שְׁרָב in xlix. 7, while in xxxv. 7 the same version gives, with equal insight, ἡ ἄνυδρος (Targ. keeps close to the original word, rendering שְׁרָבָא, שְׁרוּבָא). If in spite of these arguments the sense "mirage" be adopted in Isaiah, we must at any rate give up connecting שְׁרָב with the Aram. root שְׁרַב. Ges. even thinks it probable that سَرَاب and שְׁרָב are of Persian origin (*Jes.*, p. 930).

שָׁרַשׁ (Poel), xl. 24, cf. Jer. xii. 2 (Poal). Piel and Hif. are also late in use.

שָׁרֵת (in religious sense),[2] lvi. 6, lx. 7, 10, lxi. 6. Occurs seventeen times in Ezekiel, four in Joel; also Jer. xxxiii. 21, 22; Ps. ci. 6, ciii. 21, civ. 4, all late passages.

תְּאַשּׁוּר, xli. 19, lx. 13, as Ezek. xxvii. 6 and xxxi. 3 (corr. text).

---

[1] Duhm and Klostermann are exceptions. The latter gives the new rend., "Wüstenbrand."
[2] See Holzinger, *ZATW*, ix. 101-104.

ISAIAH

תְּבוּנָה sing., xl. 28, xliv. 19, as Obad. 1, 8; Jer. x. 12, li. 15 (all late passages).[1] Cf. iv. (*h*), תְּבוּנוֹת.

תַּבְנִית, xliv. 13, as Ezekiel (three times), Ex. xxv. 9 *bis*, 40, Deut. iv. 16-18 (five times), Josh. xxii. 28, 1 Chronicles (four times); Ps. cvi. 20, cxliv. 12; 2 Ki. xvi. 10. All post-Exilic passages except, probably, the last.

תְּהִלָּה, xlii. 8, 10, 12 (+ 8 other passages); also Jer. xiii. 11, xvii. 14, xxxiii. 9, xlviii. 2, li. 41 (Nos. 3 and 5 are at any rate not Jeremiah's), Deut. x. 24, xxvi. 19 (No. 2 not original), Ex. xv. 11 (late), Hab. iii. 3 (late), Nehemiah and Chronicles (twice in each), Psalms (30 times). Cf. on הלל.

תִּכֵּן (Piel), xl. 12, 13 (omitted in Sept.), as Ps. lxxv. 4; Job xxviii. 25.

תַּנְחוּמִים, lxvi. 11, as Jer. xvi. 7; Ps. xciv. 19.

תַּנִּים, xliii. 20, as xiii. 22, xxxiv. 13, xxxv. 7 (but also Mic. i. 8).

תַּצִּין, li. 9, as xxvii. 1.

תַּרְעֵלָה, li. 17, 22, as Ps. lx. 5 (only).

תְּשׁוּעָה, xlv. 17, xlvi. 13 *bis* (only other prophetic passage, Jer. iii. 23).

To these may be added three divine titles found in II. but not in I. Isaiah, viz. (*a*) אֲבִיר יַעֲקֹב, xlix. 26, lx. 16; (*b*) אֱלוֹהַּ (xliv. 8); and (*c*) קָדוֹשׁ (xl. 25, lvii. 15). (*a*) can hardly be imitated from i. 24, for א׳ ישראל there seems deliberately substituted for א׳ יעקב in Gen. xlix. 24. The Second Isaiah (*l.c.*) and a psalmist (Ps. cxxxii. 2, 5) copy the old song in Genesis more closely than Isaiah. Budde regards the phrase in i. 24 as an interpolation,[2] but rhythm is equally satisfied by the omission of י׳ צְבָאוֹת. (*b*) is distinctively late.[3] For (*c*) as a *quasi* proper name, cf. Job vi. 10; Hab. iii. 3; and the use of אַדִּיר in x. 34 (late; see p. 56).

It is hardly too much to say that the late date of chaps. xl.-lxvi. is amply shown by the preceding list. It may indeed be reasonable to urge that on linguistic grounds some

---

[1] See Kuenen's *Ond.*², or Cornill's *Einleitung*.

[2] *ZATW*, 1891, p. 246; on the other side see Duhm.

[3] For statistics of its occurrence, see *BL*, p. 457. I doubt, however, whether Baethgen's theory that the author of Deut. xxxii. invented the singular form אֱלוֹהַּ will hold, for the "Song of Moses" is not improbably later than II. Isaiah. Its frequent occurrence (forty-one times) in Job is remarkable, and may be presumed to have metrical reasons. Cf. König's suggestion to account for the fourteen אָנֹכִי in Job (*Einl.*, p. 417).

CHAPTERS XL.-LXVI. (INTRODUCTORY) 271

portions of the section are more distinctly late than others (the Aramaizing סגד, for instance, only occurs in passages which are, on various grounds, most probably very late insertions), but even those which stand linguistically highest belong obviously enough to an advanced stage of development. If there is such a thing as the history of the Hebrew language, the last twenty-seven chapters of the Book are not the work of the historical Isaiah, but of a much later writer or school of writers.

SECTION III.—Consideration of minor arguments for and against the Isaianic authorship.

How far is this result either confirmed or rendered doubtful by minor considerations, the due treatment of which would have overweighted the preceding argument? For instance, 1. conservative critics have been accustomed to derive a subsidiary argument from the supposed literary indebtedness of certain pre-Exilic prophets to II. Isaiah. They argued thus: Isa. xli. 13, xliii. 5, xliv. 2 are undeniably parallel to Jer. xxx. 10, xlvi. 27, 28. Now, upon an inspection of both groups of passages, it would appear that the latter group is dependent upon the former, and consequently Isa. xl.-lxvi. must be pre-Jeremian. But how uncertain will this inference become, if it can be rendered probable that the passages in Jeremiah are post-Exilic insertions.[1] So, too, the parallelism between lii. 7 and Nah. ii. 1 (A.V., i. 15) becomes useless, if it is probable that the early part of Nahum contains a large post-Exilic insertion, even apart from the fact that Nahum's date cannot be earlier than 663. A similar consideration vitiates the argument drawn by Del. from the parallelism between lxvi. 20 and Zeph. iii. 10, while to argue with this great scholar (even in his fourth edition) that Zeph. ii. 15 is based upon xlvii. 8, 10, because עליז is exclusively Isaianic, ignores the demonstrably Exilic origin of chap. xiii. In fact, the critical value of parallelisms of this sort is now very different from what it used to be. It is greatest to those who hold II. Isaiah to

[1] That this view will be more and more accepted can hardly be doubtful

be a composite work.¹ Such critics are assisted by parallelisms in tracing out the literary and religious circles to which the writers of the several portions of that work belonged. Points of contact with the Hexateuch documents are, however, still as useful as ever. The most obviously important are, of course, those to any portion of Deuteronomy and to the document known as P (and within P to H, *i.e.* to the Holiness-Law, Lev. xvii.-xxvi.). Examples are, xliv. 2 (Jeshurun), cf. Deut. xxxii. 15, xxxiii. 5, 6; xlviii. 4 ("hard"), cf. Deut. ix. 6, 27; lii. 12 (בְּחִפָּזוֹן), cf. Deut. xvi. 3 (Ex. xii. 11, P); lviii. 14 ("riding over the heights of the land"), cf. Deut. xxxii. 13; lix. 10 ("groping like the blind"), cf. Deut. xxviii. 29; lxiii. 9, 14, cf. Deut. i. 31, vii. 7, 8, xxxii. 11, 12; lxv. 22 (form), cf. Deut. xxviii. 30. Such too are lviii. 3 (עִנָּה נֶפֶשׁ), cf. Lev. xvi. 29; lix. 2 (הָיָה מַבְדִּיל), cf. Gen. i. 6; lix. 21 (style), cf. Gen. xvii. 4, ix. 9; lxv. 20*b* (age of primeval patriarchs), cf. Gen. v.; all the passages compared here belong to P. Also xl. 2 (נִרְצָה), cf. Lev. xxvi. 34, 41; this passage belongs to H (Exilic). These phenomena are altogether inconsistent with a pre-Exilic date for chaps. xl.-lxvi., though their importance is by no means exhausted by this remark. The references to J are at first sight less important, for J is undoubtedly earlier than the age of Isaiah. But the number of these references is adverse to a date so early as the eighth century. Here are the parallelisms to passages of J or JE.

Isa. xli. 8, 9 } cf. Gen. xii. 1 (J; cf. xi. 31, P); call of Abraham.
„ li. 2 } Note also the unique mention of Sarah in li. 2, and the reference to Abraham in lxiii. 16.
„ xlii. 14 }
„ lxiii. 15 } cf. Gen. xlv. 1 (J); special use of הִתְאַפֵּק.
„ lxiv. 11 }

---

¹ For instance, almost all the points of contact with Ezekiel occur in passages which some deny to II. Isaiah, viz. in xlviii. 4 (which may be an editorial insertion), and in certain portions of chaps. lvi.-lxvi. The exception is שִׂיחַ מָצִיץ in li. 17, cf. Ezek. xxiii. 34 (but also Ps. lxxv. 9). Ezekiel and the author (?) of Isa. xl.-lxvi. evidently belong to different circles. The former does not ever use בָּרָא, "to create, or produce" (said of God); the latter uses it sixteen times (in thirteen passages).

Isa. xliii. 16, 17	} cf. Ex. xiv. 21-31, JE (P); passage of the Red Sea.	
,, li. 9. 10		
,, lxiii. 11-13		
,, xliii. 27	cf. Gen. xxv. 29-34 (J); xxvii. (JE); Jacob's sins.	
,, xlviii. 19	,, Gen. xxxii. 13 (J); cf. xxii. 17 (R); Israel as the sand.	
,, xlviii. 21	,, Ex. xvii. 5-7, and Num. xx. 7-13 (JE); water from the rock.	
,, li. 3	,, Gen. ii. 8, xiii. 10 (J); "Eden" and "garden of Yahwè."	
,, lii. 4	,, Gen. xlvii. 4, cf. xii. 10 (J); Israel's guest-right in Egypt.	
,, lii. 12*b*	,, Ex. xiii. 21, 22 (J), cf. xiv. 19 (E); Yahwè in the van and in the rear.	
,, liv. 9	,, Gen. vi.-ix., esp. viii. 20-22 (J); the deluge; Yahwè's promise.	
,, lxiii. 9	,, Ex. xxxiii. 14, 15 (J); the delivering presence of Yahwè.	
,, lxv. 25	,, Gen. iii. 14 (J); dust, the serpent's food.	

Now to what period *can* this large number of references belong? Only to the period when Israel became a people which had no present history—to the period which began in 586, and in which the solace of good men was the study and the supplementing of the records of the past. And to this, that as probably[1] no pre-Exilic prophecy refers to Abraham (the earliest seems to be in Ezek. xxxiii. 24), and there is certainly none which refers to Noah (the earliest prophetic mention is in Ezek. xiv. 4) or to Sarah (see p. 272), we may, even on these grounds alone, assume that Isa. xl.-lxvi. is not of pre-Exilic origin.

2. Another argument for the unity of Isaiah has been based on the local colouring of chaps. xl.-lxvi., which has been said to be too Palestinian to be consistent with a Babylonian origin. Before we can admit this argument, however, it must be shown that the whole of chaps. xl.-lxvi. is the work of one man. Provisionally we can consider it with regard to chaps. xl.-lv. Beyond question, the trees and plants there mentioned are not all such as, now at any rate, grow in Babylonia, while such a common Babylonian

---

[1] "Probably" seems to understate the case; see on xxix. 22.

tree as the date-palm is omitted. True, but omissions of trees are unimportant; the palm-tree is only once mentioned in prophecy, and that in Palestinian writings (Jer. x. 5, Joel i. 12). And at any rate, we have the *Populus euphratica* (xliv. 2, see Wetzstein in Del.), which is specially though not exclusively Babylonian, and the myrtle (xli. 19, lv. 13), which was probably imported late into Palestine from Babylonia.[1] As to the trees which are unknown in Judah, they are sometimes equally unknown in Babylonia. That the writer of chaps. xl.-lv has a good knowledge of Palestine may be granted, though Mr. Cobb surely attaches too much importance to the mention of snow in lv. 10.[2] But of what critical value are even the most undoubted references to Palestine as long as the historical situation of the writer is so clearly that of the latter part of the Exile? Even apart from the bare possibility that he was one of the Israelites left behind in Judah, must he not have been familiar with the landscape and climate of Palestine either from personal knowledge or from the national literature? If the Arab lyric poets in Spain delighted in references to Arabian life and scenery, must not those Hebrew writers in Babylonia, whose vein was lyrical or rhetorical, have been animated by a similar religious patriotism?[3] Nor must we omit to notice that one of the chief tree-catalogues (xliv. 19) belongs to a section which may, or even must, be post-Exilic. On the other hand, we may freely grant that a peculiar atmospheric phenomenon known as the mirage, and familiar in Babylonia,[4] is not really referred to in xlix. 10 (p. 269).

3. At any rate, no ingenuity can derive a conservative argument from the geographical ideas of our prophet.

---

[1] On the use of ערבים and הדס, see pp. 262, 266. The right inference in the case of the latter word is obvious.

[2] *Bibliotheca Sacra*, July 1882, p. 528. Delitzsch remarks (*Isaiah*, E.T., ii. 125), "I do not think Cobb has proved Ezekiel betrays Babylonian, and II. Isaiah Palestinian natural surroundings."

[3] Ezekiel was neither a lyric poet nor a rhetorician, and has little interest in nature. Yet even he, when occasion favours, goes beyond the trees of Babylonia (xxvii. 5, 6, xxxi. 3, 8).

[4] Rawlinson, *Anc. Mon.*, i. 30; H. S. Cowper, *Through Turkish Arabia* (1894), p. 178 f.

Putting aside chap. lxvi., it is clear even from chaps. xl.-lv. that the Jews were scattered in many countries, and that our prophet had a wide geographical horizon. He cannot therefore (cf. p. 60) have lived before the Exile. Many have thought that he had even heard of China. The theory that the "Sinim" in xlix. 12 are the Chinese, has, it is true, been disproved by Richthofen and others,[1] but the "Sinim" must at any rate have lived in some comparatively distant region, which had only lately become known to the Jews. The Sept. guessed the Persians; it is better to correct סְוֵנִים, "the inhabitants of Syene" (cf. Ezek. xxix. 10; xxx. 6). We thus obtain, after a very probable *completion* of the text, a mention of the three chief centres of the Jewish dispersion, viz. Babylonia (cf. xli. 9), the sea with its "coast-lands" (cf. xi. 11), and Egypt (Jer. xliv. 1), the southern limit of which was Syene (Aswân), at the first cataract.[2]

4. The allusions to the manner of life of the Babylonians are not as numerous as might have been wished. But the references to the manufacture of idols (xl. 19, xli. 6, 7, xl. 20), to the processions of idols (xlv. 20, xlvi. 1, 2), to the patron deities of Babylon and Borsippa (xlvi. 1), to the traditional wisdom and magic of the priests and astrologers

[1] See especially Terrien de la Couperie, "The Sinim of Isaiah," *Bab. and Or. Record*, 1887, p. 183, etc., and cf. Yule's review of Richthofen's *China* in *Academy*, xiii. 339.

[2] The "Sinim" of Gen. x. 17 (cf. *Sain-arkay*, "the hinder Sin," in the el-Amarna tablets, W. M. Müller, *As. u. Eur.*, p. 289) were too near Palestine, and probably too obscure to be referred to. Even the name of this Sin disappeared in classical times. Sin = Pelusium, which occurs in Ezek. xxx. 15 f., has also been thought of (Saadya, Bochart, and Ewald); but why should the *eastern* frontier town of Egypt have been specified as a chief seat of the Jewish dispersion? Moreover, the phrase "the land of . . ." suits Syene better than Pelusium. For "*properly speaking*, *Syene was the island of Elephantine*" (Budge, *The Nile*, p. 284), which could most fitly be distinguished as an אֶרֶץ. To "from the land of the Syenites" in the extreme south, what should correspond in the parallel line? It must be something nearly equivalent to, but somewhat more definite than, "from afar." Very probably "from the ends of the earth," *i.e.* Babylonia (xli. 9). We may venture, therefore, to read:

Behold, these—from afar do they come [and these from the ends of the earth], And behold, these from the sea, and these from the land of the Syenites.

In *b*, "from the north and" may have been inserted through a reminiscence of Ps. cvii. 3.

(xlvii. 9, 10, 12, 13), to the commercial importance of Babylon (xliii. 14 ?-xlvii. 15), to its river and gates, xlv. 1, 2 (cf. Herod., i. 180), and to its treasures (cf. Æsch., *Persæ*, 53), are perhaps as many as a religious teacher absorbed in the thought of restoration might be required to make.

5. The mythological allusions, too, are as many as we could reasonably expect from a prophet (see *PI*). The pre-Exilic prophets, except in visions (Am. ix. 3, Isa. vi. 2), make none; an Exilic writer, however, could not altogether resist that tendency to a revival of mythology[1] to which we owe the poem of Job, and in no slight degree the story of Jonah, and which has also influenced the language of xxiv. 21, xxvii. 1. The most distinct allusion of this sort in chaps. xl.-lv. is in li. 9. The writer " has probably a kind of half-belief in the myths which speak of a conflict between the god of light and the rebellious monsters of darkness—such myths as are alluded to in Job ix. 13, xxv. 2, xxvi. 12, 13, and are so fully described in the sacred texts of Egypt and Babylon. If Yahwè once for all subjugated these rebels, it must have been in that remote antiquity in which his almightiness was most conspicuously displayed. To this great deed the prophet refers when appealing to Yahwè to put down Babylon, lest this hostile power should quench the light of true religion which shines in Israel in endless darkness " (*BW*). In xlv. 7, too, Babylonian dualism (see *PI*) is contradicted.

6. Driver (*Isaiah*, p. 191) has already called attention to the precious stones in liv. 11, 12, as suggesting the Babylonian origin of the prophecy. If פּוּךְ in liv. 11 = נֹפֶךְ, we have four precious stones mentioned by name. One of these אַקְדָּח is an ἅπ. λεγ.; the use of the three others is recorded in the preceding list. Ezekiel is still more abundant in such references; Isaiah and the older prophets however make no mention of precious stones. (Another argument of Driver—that from the animals mentioned—seems to me more hazardous.)

7. Lastly, we may refer to the obscure superstitions mentioned in chaps. lxv.-lxvi., which manifestly imply a decay of faith in the traditional Israelitish religion, such as can only be understood in an age of political collapse.

[1] See Cheyne, *BL*, pp. 202, 270; *Job and Solomon*, p. 78.

But though, to believers in the unity of chaps. xl.-lxvi., this may be only a subsidiary argument, to those who question the traditional view it becomes an argument of prime importance. We will therefore consider it fully at a later point. It may perhaps be found that these superstitions can best be understood as survivals of northern Israelitish *Aberglaube* in post-Exilic times.

SECTION IV.—Date and place of composition of chapters xl.-lv.

That chaps. xl.-lxvi. were not written before the close of the Exile, is now clear. That they were all written at one time, and even that they were all written by one man, is not so clear; facts enough have been collected which make both suppositions not a little difficult. But at any rate the section, chaps. xl.-lv., or the main part of it, possesses a unity of its own, and we can venture to ask, When and where does it appear to have been written? 1. The *date* of chaps. xl.-lv. is as clearly revealed as the nature of the section (or book) permits. The mention of Cyrus, the vivid poetical descriptions of his conquests, both past and future, and the confident expectation (so far from being literally fulfilled) of his capture of Babylon and vengeance on its inhabitants, forbid us to date the section earlier than 546 or later than 539. It was in 547 ("the ninth year"), as the annals of Nabû-nâ'id (the last king of Babylon) tell us,[1] Cyrus "king of Parsu" crossed the Tigris below Arbela. In the same year it would seem (though the Babylonian annals do not refer to this) that Crœsus king of Lydia formed an alliance against Cyrus with Amasis king of Egypt and (if Herod. i. 77 may be trusted) Labynetus, *i.e.* Nabû-nâ'id, king of Babylon; Sparta also is said to have promised auxiliary troops. But without waiting for his allies, Crœsus crossed the Halys in the spring of 546, entered Cappadocia, and conquered the renowned fortress of Pteria. Cyrus however drove him back into Lydia, and in the autumn of the same year Sardis, the capital of Lydia, was taken, and Crœsus fell into the hands of his enemies. The

[1] *KIB*, iii. 2, p. 134 f.; cf. Halévy, *Rev. sém.*, avril 1894, pp. 88-191.

history of the following years is uncertain, owing to the incompleteness of the Babylonian annals. But we know that in 539-538, after winning a battle in S. Babylonia, the army of Cyrus under Gobryas entered Sippar, and two days later the capital itself, amidst the acclamations of the inhabitants, and without even a street battle. It was probably at intervals during this period (but before the march upon Babylon) that II. Isaiah wrote his book, which says so much of the "coastlands" (of the Mediterranean) and of the "nations" (both far and near), and so clearly gives us to understand that they were deeply interested in the movements of Cyrus. The "large designs" attributed to Cyrus by Herodotus naturally produced a wide-spread excitement in the East. The Jews participated in this. They had everything to hope, and nothing to fear from the successes of Cyrus, and to this, combined with their intense belief in prophecy (Jer. xxix. 10), we owe the splendid composition of the Second Isaiah.

To attempt more than this broad definition of date would be tasteless; we have no right to confound the prophetic writer with a modern newspaper reporter. The passages which to Knobel appear to describe the changing scenes of Cyrus's campaigns, are vagueness itself. The Second Isaiah does not even say plainly to what nation Cyrus belonged, nor is he aware of the dislike to Nabû-nâ'id, as a usurper and perhaps as a religious innovator, which prevailed in Babylon, and accounts for the easy victory of Gobryas; is it likely that we should be able to recover from his prophecy the successive rumours which arrived from the seat of war? But are we sure that even our modest definition is not too precise? Such a cautious critic as Kuenen[1] has doubts whether chaps. l., li., liv., and lv. were not really written after the return of the exiles to Jerusalem, while (not to refer to still more radical critics) Seinecke[2] thinks that the whole of chaps. xl.-lxvi. was written in 536 B.C. between the "edict of Cyrus" and the so-called Return. Not to refer as yet to the probably

[1] *Ond.*[2], ii. 137-139, quoted further on (p. 296 f.).
[2] *Der Evangelist des AT*, pp. 6-16. The hypotheses of M. Verne· and Isidore Loeb need not, I think, be discussed here.

CHAPTERS XL.-LXVI. (INTRODUCTORY)

unhistorical character of the traditional date of the Return (on which see Prologue, Part iv.), it may at once be stated that both scholars rely on unsafe inferences from exegesis. We cannot assert with Kuenen that chaps. l. and li. are addressed to the Jerusalem of the restored exiles, among whom, exposed like them to shame and contumely, the prophet moves about comforting them. First, because in l. 4-9 [1] it is not the prophet who speaks, but the ideal personage called the Servant of Yahwè, and the passage referred to belongs to a cycle of compositions which was probably completed *before* the prophet began to write the work into which these compositions are introduced. Next, because chaps. l. and li. lack that concreteness which we find in Haggai and Zech. i.-viii. (works, according to Kuenen, of the Restoration period), and in possibly or probably post-Exilic portions of Isa. xl.-lxvi. That a change has passed over the spirit of the writer may be granted; but the change begins (as we shall find) to be visible at chap. xlix., which Kuenen himself does not deny to be of Babylonian origin. Besides, l. 1-3 is clearly parallel to other short consolatory utterances, some at least of which begin (like l. 1-3) with "Thus saith Yahwè." As to chaps. liv. and lv. these passages at any rate cannot have been written at Jerusalem. They are altogether idealistic, and are without even that touch of actuality which may reasonably be found in l. 6. The ὕστερον πρότερον, which Kuenen thinks (p. 297) that critics in general wrongly impute to II. Isaiah, does in truth exist. The writer endeavours to awaken his people to a sense of the high mission which awaits it after the Return, and concludes with the promise of a glorious redemption from Babylon. But this is perfectly natural. For *vv.* 10-13 are the close, not of an instruction on the future mission of Israel, but of the whole section (or book), and this close begins already at *v.* 6. The Jews are exhorted, not to "seek Yahwè," by giving up their evil deeds, in order to qualify themselves for becoming apostles of the true religion,[2]

---

[1] *Vv.* 10-11 are probably a very late insertion (p. 302 f.).

[2] The "thoughts" and "ways" of Yahwè are infinite as the heavens (Job xi. 8) and his word or promise as sure as the phenomena of nature

but to claim their share in Yahwè's promise and lose no time in joining all true Israelites, and preparing to return under the divine escort to Judah. In fact, the writer repeats in another form the call and the promise of xl. 3, 4. The Jews are to return through the transformed wilderness, and nature is to share in the glory of the divine manifestation.[1]

Seinecke's hypothesis is much less tenable than Kuenen's. It seems to have been suggested by an imperfect realisation of the intensity of the ancient belief in prophecy, and of the sympathy with the divine purposes which the written records of the ministry of Isaiah and Jeremiah had produced. Jeremiah had said that Nebuchadrezzar was but a servant of Yahwè (Jer. xxvii. 6), and that after seventy years (a round number) the people of "Judah and Jerusalem" should be brought back, penitent and believing, to its own land (Jer. xxix. 10). This prophecy took such hold upon Ezekiel, that fourteen years after the fall of Jerusalem[2] he could prepare a plan of the future temple, which by its minute definiteness was the most positive and dogmatic of all possible prophecies. Nor is this all. Isaiah and Jeremiah had both declared that Yahwè, the divine governor of the world, had chosen the people of Israel to show in its national life what true religion meant, and had pointed to a regeneration of Israel by means of judgment (Isa. i. 24-26; viii. 17, 18; Jer. xxix. 11-13). It was sympathy with the divine purpose of preserving the deposit of true religion which combined with veneration for the last and in a sense greatest of the old prophets to assure the Second Isaiah of the impending fall of Babylon and of the return of faithful Israel. A minute exegesis confirms the ordinary reader's impression that Babylon had not yet fallen when chaps. xl.-lv. were written. Only two passages may seem at

(vv. 10, 11; cf. *BL*, p. 321). Verse 7 is inconsistent with this train of thought, as Duhm has shown. The "thoughts" and "ways" of the "ungodly" (v. 7) are absolutely bad; the "thoughts" and "ways" which are not those of Yahwè (v. 8) are simply imperfect, because earthly. V. 7 was inserted by a post-Exilic editor (see p. 304).

[1] It is strange at first sight that the promise of transformation is limited to the desert which separates Babylon from Palestine (cf. xli. 18, 19). But if the desert becomes like a "paradise" or park of stately trees, how glorious will Canaan itself become! Cf. xxxii. 15.

[2] Smend, *ATRel.-gesch.*, p. 350.

first sight to favour Seinecke's view, viz. xliv. 26-28 and lii. 11. The former passage closes, according to the Massoretic text, with the words,

That saith of Cyrus, My shepherd (is he) | and all my purpose will he accomplish,
And that he should say of Jerusalem, Let it be built, | and (of) the temple, Be thy foundations laid.

To Seinecke this verse looks like a distinct reference to the edict of Cyrus, handed down to us in Ezra i. 2-4 (cf. vi. 3-5). He regards it, that is, as containing a *vaticinium post eventum*. But the historical character of much of Ezra i.-vi. is open to grave suspicion,[1] nor can a cautious critic venture to accept the contents of the so-called edict as authentic or as contemporaneous with the work of II. Isaiah. And even apart from this point, can we believe that any moderately good writer would begin the two halves of the same verses with הָאֹמֵר and לֵאמֹר respectively? Surely Duhm and Klostermann must be right in supposing that *v.* 28*b* is a variant to *v.* 26*b*, which is substantially the same, and runs thus :—

That saith of Jerusalem, Let it be inhabited, and of the cities of
    Judah, Let them be built.

But is there no connection at all between *v.* 28 (as it now stands) and Ezra i. 2-4? Certainly there is. When the addition had accidentally been made to *v.* 28, it was natural for later writers of history (cf. Jos., *Ant.*, xi. 1, 2) to use it in support of the legend of the participation of Cyrus in the building of the temple.

The second passage referred to contains an address to the exiles as "ye that bear the vessels of Yahwè." This, as Seinecke thinks, presupposes the restoration of the sacred vessels described in Ezra i. 7-11. But this restoration is, historically speaking, as doubtful as the edict of Cyrus, and, even apart from this, can we believe that in composing *vaticinia post eventum*, II. Isaiah would have made so little use of

[1] See Prologue, part iv., and cf. especially Stade, *Gesch.*, ii. 115, etc.; Kosters, *Het Herstel van Israël in het Perz. Tijdvak* (1894), pp. 4-49.

an act of such singular liberality?[1] But surely it is more reasonable to suppose that lii. 11, 12 is a purely imaginative description of the return of the exiles.[2] The idea of the prophet is that, as soon as they have quitted Babylon, the exiles will begin again to offer sacrifice to the God who is once more present among them. For this they can be satisfied with very simple appliances.[1] The 5400 chargers and bowls and other vessels of gold and silver can easily be dispensed with; indeed, to the author of xl. 16 they would probably have appeared a barbaric attempt to express the glory of the true God. Probably, however, when the legend of the donation of Cyrus was constructed for the glorification of the temple, this vague and inconspicuous reference to "Yahwè's vessels" was magnified into a prediction of the royal liberality (see Prologue).

2. As to the *place* where chaps. xl.-lv. were written, absolute certainty is unattainable. The author is not a prophet in the same sense as Haggai and Malachi; the poetic and rhetorical character of his style makes it barely possible to hold that he lived at a distance from the main body of exiles. Still the arguments of Ewald for Egypt and of Duhm (so far as one can gather them) for N. Phœnicia are weak. A well-informed man like the author may quite naturally have meditated on the prospects of Egypt (xliii. 3, xlv. 14), and have been acquainted with the name of the Egyptian or the Phœnician Sin (xlix. 12),[2] and with the names of the trees of Lebanon (xli. 19). There is no allusion to Egyptian animal-worship, which, even more than idolatry, must have shocked Jewish exiles in Egypt (see Wisd. xii. 23, 24, and cf. Jer. xlvi. 15 Sept.), nor to the specially Phœnician cultus of Tammuz. Evidently the three regions in which the author is most interested are Judah, Babylonia, and the "coast-lands" of the West. The "coast-

[1] So Dillm. (with hesitation) and Duhm. Del., however, finds an indirect prophecy of the liberality of Cyrus, and Dillm. admits the possibility of a reference to this, if lii. 11, 12 are an interpolation. There are, however, good reasons for rejecting the interpolation theory.

[2] According to Duhm, the isolated mention of the name of a country must have a special reason, and this reason is that II. Isaiah lives in the Phœnician Sin—a hypothesis, as he frankly admits, of despair. Against both Ewald's view and Duhm's, see p. 275, note 2.

lands," however, obviously cannot be his place of residence, being always represented as far-off countries ; and Judah is excluded because only the least cultured classes were left there by Nebuzar-Adan. Babylonia alone remains, and to this all the chief indications point as the temporary abode of the author. It was here that he could best learn those religious and secular characteristics of the great city which he so vividly describes (see p. 275 f.) ; here too that he could best study the various moral types and follow the vicissitudes of hope and fear among the Jewish exiles. May I not add that here too. he could best acquaint himself with the character of Cyrus and with the " large designs " of his ambitious mind ? The language used in xli. 9 respecting the home of Abraham supplies no objection to this view. For it is clear that the writer places himself imaginatively in Palestine (cf. xl. 9), where the home of Abraham would seem as far away as Palestine seemed to the Jewish exiles in Babylonia. As to xl. 9, lii. 7, the expressions are used imaginatively ; the prophet is transported in imagination to Palestine and to the time immediately preceding the fulfilment of the promise. And the same remark explains " thence " in lii. 11 ; " here " in lii. 5 is no doubt inconsistent with this expression, but lii. 3-6, as we shall see, is a late inserted passage, the writer of which has some difficulty in assuming the character of the Second Isaiah.

ANALYSIS OF CHAPTERS XL.-LXVI

" Et c'est ainsi qu'au nom de l'histoire on détruit l'histoire elle-même. Ce qui se passe aujourd'hui pour Esaïe est instructif. Tout ce qui ne cadre pas avec la situation et l'époque adjugée au prophète est impitoyablement retranché. A chaque pas, nous sommes avertis qu'une interpolation a détourné le texte primitif de son sens naturel. La personnalité de l'écrivain finit par disparaître à ce jeu. Encore un petit effort, et nous en serons réduits à penser avec Lagarde que le recueil intitulé faussement Esaïe n'est qu'une chréstomathie de poésies détachées, faite après l'exil."[1]

---

[1] Westphal, *Les sources du Pentateuque*, II. (1892), Préf. p. x. The fancy of Lagarde referred to has had no influence on the course of criticism, and may here be passed over.

The above motto from one of the rising Hebraists of France shows how hard the work is which lies before the critics of the second part of Isaiah. From the root upwards, the critical theory of the average Bible student of England and France needs rectification. The second part of Isaiah is not a whole, nor is it the work of one man, and this result has been practically certain for more than twenty years. Why, then, has it been most conscientiously denied? And what are among the best forms of that critical view which aspires to take the place of its predecessor? Before answering either question, let us survey the history of the analysis of the second part of Isaiah.

The first disintegrator of II. Isaiah was a learned Spanish Rabbi, who showed that that critical tendency which shocks so many religious minds can co-exist with, and even spring out of an ardent love for Biblical religion. Long before Koppe and Eichhorn, he wrote down this observation, in his commentary on Isaiah (finished 1498 A.D.), à propos of Isa. liii., "Nor is there anything remarkable in this prophecy coming in the midst of a series of promises of the future redemption; for the promises in this book are not all of them connected or related to one another, but each separate prophecy and each separate promise uttered by the prophet stands by itself, as may be seen by the contents."[1] This subtle suggestion, however, had no critical consequences. The modern school of fragmentists dates back to Koppe, the author of the notes to the German edition of Lowth's *Isaiah* (1779-1781). This critic was followed by Augusti, Bertholdt, and Eichhorn, the last of whom, led astray by Koppe, too boldly separated the text of Isaiah into eighty-five pieces. Gesenius and Hitzig, however, stood firm on the side of unity, and the words in which the former, whose name is still so justly honoured among us, expressed himself, deserve quotation: "The only concession," he says, "which can be made is that the prophet did not write the whole book straight on, but composed the different sections at different times, after which they were united, or rather, worked up together. Thus, at any rate, lvi. 9-lviii. 14, lxiii. 1-6, and

---

[1] *The Fifty-third Chapter of Isaiah, according to the Jewish Interpreters*, II. Translations by Driver and Neubauer (1877), p. 188.

lxiii. 7-lxv. 25 can be thought of as having a separate existence, though they were afterwards, no doubt, worked up together."[1] Precisely the same view is expressed by Hitzig, who fully admits the fragmentary origin of the book, but insists on the unity ultimately produced when the author brought the separate fragments together, and seeks to strengthen his argument for unity by adopting a bright idea of Friedrich Rückert. This idea was that the book, commonly called the Second Isaiah, was divided by the author himself into three books of nine sections or chapters each, and that the two former books were marked by the closing refrain, "No peace, saith Yahwè (or, saith my God) to the wicked" (xlviii. 22; lvii. 21). There was much wise moderation in the attitude of these great scholars, the old and the young. They candidly admitted an element of truth in the theory of the fragmentists, but could not tolerate the denial of the unity of the book, and the ascription of the sections which composed it to different authors. Their position is, I think, untenable, and yet I am sure that by their policy of moderate conservatism they did good service in their day to criticism. For the analysis of ancient writings requires to be practised with circumspection, and this is a quality in which the early critics were deficient. There were two ways in which the school of Koppe might have sought to justify its procedure. It might have produced either a thorough commentary on Isaiah, or a sketch of Jewish literature in the framework of contemporary history, showing, if possible, that such extreme disintegration was not uncalled for on exegetical and historical grounds. Now, it is true that Eichhorn did translate and comment on the Hebrew prophets, but he aimed more than was right at popularity. He had his reward, for he won the ear of Goethe, but he did not win that of Hebrew scholars like Gesenius. The other work which might have been asked for—a history of Hebrew literature—Eichhorn wisely left unwritten. That was reserved for a younger Göttingen scholar, not a member of any of the existing schools, Heinrich Ewald.

This eminent critic, whose life I have sketched at considerable length elsewhere, has produced one of our greatest

[1] Gesenius, *Der Prophet Jesaja*, II. (1821), p. 15.

books, not indeed in size, but in importance, on the prophetic literature.[1] Here, in spite of his manifest weakness in expounding an argument, Ewald carried the criticism of the Second Isaiah to the furthest point which had as yet been reached. The prophecies of the Second Isaiah originated, according to him, at the close of the Exile, in "fly-sheets, which the surging stream of the time drew forth, one after another, from the prophet."[2] Hence the changes in the prophet's mood, and the references which he makes to the varying effects of his prophecies on the people. These "pamphlets or fly-leaves," however, were collected by the writer in two books, one comprising chaps. xl.-xlviii., and the other chaps. xlix.-lx., to which, as Ewald thinks, the writer added lxi. 1-lxiii. 6 as an epilogue, and after wards lxiii. 7-lxvi. 24 as an appendix. It should be added that Ewald peremptorily rejects the plausible threefold division suggested by Rückert, and adopted by Hitzig and Ruetschi, and afterwards by Delitzsch and (1870) by myself.

This, indeed, is not the whole of Ewald's critical theory. He also felt compelled by exegetical phenomena to recognise in the Second Isaiah a considerable element derived from earlier books. He had already pointed out, in the masterly introduction to his book, that words and thoughts of earlier prophets were continually revived by more recent prophetic writers, including the Second Isaiah. In the section on Isa. xl.-lxvi. he showed how this theory worked. Creative as the prophetic writer is, he often does not disdain to imitate models; nor, says Ewald, "on closer consideration is it possible not to see that he also inserts whole passages of some length from older prophets with little or no alteration, which can be plainly distinguished as regards their primary meaning and the time of their origin."[3] These passages are xl. 1, 2, lii. 13-liii. 12, lvi. 9-lvii. 11, in which Ewald finds a great similarity to Mic. vi., vii., and which, like that prophecy, or these prophecies, he ascribes to a prophet of

[1] *Die Propheten*, ed. 1, 1840-41; ed. 2, 1867. Translated by J. F. Smith, in five vols., 1875-81.
[2] *The Prophets* (E. T.), iv. 254; cf. i. 90.
[3] *Ibid.*, i. 82-83.

the reign of Manasseh; and further, lviii. 1-lix. 20, and some smaller passages, which are, he thinks, introduced from a writer closely allied to Ezekiel, and probably contemporary with that prophet.

It will at once be noticed that in this complicated theory Ewald makes more concessions to the fragmentists than either Gesenius or Hitzig. He will only admit an imperfect unity in the book; for lxi. 1-lxiii. 6, and lxiii. 7-lxvi. 24, he views as additions representing after-thoughts of the writer, and several passages in the body of the work he regards as extracts from older prophetic writings. In this increased complication we must, I think, acknowledge a sign of progress. Gesenius and Hitzig had gone too far in their natural rebound from the pernicious extreme of the fragmentists; the right mean was seen as if at a glance by Ewald. No unprejudiced reader of the Second Isaiah, if he has any literary tact, can fail to admit this. It still remained to examine the different sections of II. Isaiah more closely, both from the point of view of ideas and from that of style, taking account of the best of Ewald's suggestions, and modifying them, as might be necessary, in accordance with deeper study, both of Isa. xl.-lxvi. and of other monuments of Babylonian or Persian period.

This re-examination of II. Isaiah I long ago began to attempt to institute. But several scholars before me declared their agreement with Ewald's principles, and sometimes indicated a disposition to advance further. The soberminded Bleek (*Einl.* 1860) fully admitted the fragmentary character of the latter part of the so-called II. Isaiah. Some at least of the later prophecies were written, he thought, between the capture of Babylon and the edict of Cyrus, and the very latest (*i.e.* certainly chaps. lxiii.-lxvi., and perhaps from chap. lviii. onwards) were written as separate works, probably by II. Isaiah, after both prophet and people had returned to Palestine. The acute Jewish scholar, Abraham Geiger, still more strongly felt the necessity of disintegration. In 1868 he described the later Isaiah as "not an individual, but a collective figure, a succession of inspired seers from the call of Cyrus to the Greek period."[1] In 1875 he repeated

[1] *Jüd. Zeitschrift*, vi. 90.

the same theory in more guarded terms :—" The second portion of Isaiah belongs, on the whole, to the time of the Return and to the following period, but is made up of different parts."[1] Nowhere, however, does he give even a fragmentary justification of this seductive thesis. The next scholar to reassert the want of unity of the Second Isaiah's work was Oort, in *The Bible for Young People* (vol. IV., Engl. trans., 1875), who, in his general view, reminds us of Bleek, but in his details anticipates the bolder criticism of Kuenen. The views of Stade are to be found in some of the notes to chap. vii. of Part II. of his history. His concessions to disintegrating criticism are not as great as might have been expected ; he speaks of lvi. 1-8 as in the full sense deutero-Isaianic, and assumes a deutero-Isaianic basis for the later or even the latest chapters.

It was in 1880-81 that I began, on a larger scale and with more definiteness than my predecessors, to set forth the data and some of the results of such a criticism, partly in a work called *The Prophecies of Isaiah*, partly in the article " Isaiah" in the *Encyclopædia Britannica*. In the former (experience having proved the unpreparedness of the general public) I used all the delicate reserve which the situation demanded, and though incidentally I presented the data of criticism as fully as I could in a commentary, and in an appended essay described the state of the critical controversy, I left the reader free to form his own critical theories for himself. To save my conscience, however, and in the hope of benefiting a few, I gave my own provisional results in the article referred to. The main conclusion was that the appearance of unity in chaps. xl.-lxvi. (which had misled me in *ICA* into treating those chapters as a literary whole) was fallacious, and that these chapters contained not less than nine inserted or appended passages belonging to different periods. In 1884 it occurred to me that the time had come to incorporate the results of my article into vol. ii. of my book on Isaiah, but in deference to the opinion of my friends Dr. Sanday and the present Bishop

---

[1] *Jüd. Zeitschrift*, xi. 40. Elsewhere Geiger speaks of "der Dichterkreis im jüngeren Jesaias" (*Nachgelassene Schriften*, iv. 170). Cf. Isidore Loeb (below).

CHAPTERS XL.-LXVI. (ANALYSIS) 289

of Peterborough (who feared that the usefulness of the book might be injured) I gave up the idea. I have often doubted of late whether I was not too yielding. But at any rate it has become clear to me since that the student-world is now more friendly to criticism than of old, and I have therefore taken every opportunity of putting the state of Isaianic criticism before the public (see especially two articles in *JQR* for July and October 1891). Allies have not been wanting, though almost entirely on the Continent.

First among these, as in duty bound, I mention Kuenen, whose death, in December 1891, at the height of his activity and intellectual development, is the greatest blow save one which has befallen Old Testament criticism in recent years. Whenever the history of Biblical criticism in the nineteenth century is written, the singular freedom from bondage to his temporary conclusions which distinguishes this truly judicial critic will not fail to be recognised. In the first edition of vol. ii. of his *Onderzoek* (1865), Kuenen advocated a view of the origin and arrangement of Isa. xl.-lxvi. which would now be called in a high degree conservative, and in his *Godsdienst van Israël* (1869-70), he still declares that " we know for certain that the last twenty-seven chapters of Isaiah are the production of a later prophet who flourished in the second half of the 6th century B.C."[1] But in the second edition of the former work (Part II., 1889), he not only presents the results of a thorough-going analysis of these chapters, but gives in a connected form the chief arguments in favour of his new conclusions. The Prophecy of Restoration consists, according to him, of chaps. xl.-xlix., lii. 1-12, and perhaps lii. 13 to liii. 12. The remaining portions of the second half of Isaiah, which all presuppose a Palestinian Jewish community, were written, he thinks, after the Return, some by the Second Isaiah, but more by writers who belonged to the same circle, or who, if they were of the next generation, held in honour and sought to propagate the traditions of this circle. With regard to lvi. 9-lvii. 11*a*, he says that it may very likely be a pre-Exilic passage, but that if so, lvii. 11*b*-20 must be addressed to persons who, in some respects, resembled the pre-Exilic Jews, *i.e.* who had a national existence in Pales-

[1] *Religion of Israel* (Eng. trans.), i. 15 (= i. 17 *G. v. I.*).

tine, and were not wholly free from the sins which the older prophet had denounced. Another important critical remark is that lxiii. 7-lxiv. is most naturally explained by "the facts related in Neh. i. 3, or still later occurrences of the same kind." The caution which prompts this critic not to lay too much stress on a doubtful even though probable explanation of Neh. i. 3 should be noted. Probably in the sixth century, he thinks, all the prophecies were brought together in a volume and arranged.

I have next the pleasure of referring to the last and not the least able of the commentaries of Ewald's most distinguished disciple, August Dillmann. "It would not be difficult, I admit, to find something to carp at. The author is not quite in touch with the most recent critics, and it would be not unnatural that some who feel that there has been a danger of stagnation in Old Testament criticism should be annoyed at his attitude towards them. But I confess that I am myself not so much displeased that he has adopted so little from the more 'advanced' school as grateful that he has assimilated so much. It is not impossible that conservative scholars may soon begin to quote Dillmann against progress in Isaiah criticism. I venture, in anticipation, to controvert their position, and to claim him as an ally. This great scholar sees clearly enough that Isaiah xl.-lxvi. does not, as it stands, form a true whole. But the unity of form, and that of tone and subject-matter, are, he admits, very imperfectly present. As to the former, there are considerable differences of style. In lii. 13-liii. 12, in lviii. and lix., and, most clearly of all, in lvi. 9-lvii. 13*a*, the language of earlier prophets appears to have been more or less adopted, and there is much reason to doubt whether lxiii. 7-lxvi. 24 has escaped later alterations. Chap. lxvi., in particular, from the abruptness of its transitions, and in *vv.* 18-24 the strangeness of the style and ideas, is liable to this suspicion. And, as to the latter kind of unity, it is clear from Part II. of Isaiah xl.-lxvi. that the author had had to moderate the high hopes with which he started. A general amendment of Israel had proved to be hopeless, and the prophet accordingly devoted himself to a criticism, which became continually sharper, of the moral state of the people. The promised redemption was delayed, and of this Israel's wickedness was the cause. Part II. (l.-lxii. 12) must, therefore, be placed between 549 and 539-8 B.C. The appendices in chaps. lxiii.-lxvi. moreover contrast with Part II. as much as Part II. contrasts with Part I. They reveal an intense sorrow in the prophet at the vanity of his previous exhortations, and are indirectly a record of affairs on the eve of Israel's restoration. In chap. lxvi., indeed, the permission of Cyrus to return seems to be pre-supposed, and the prophecy is apparently addressed to those who are taking steps to avail themselves of it. It is impossible not to see in all this that Dillmann has been moved almost in spite of himself by the most recent current of criticism."[1]

A Scottish scholar, Prof. G. A. Smith, has now to be mentioned. His work on Isaiah in the *Expositor's Bible* has been called incomplete and discursive. The wonder is, however, that with the limitations imposed upon him by his plan he was able in vol. ii., however tentatively, to treat the criticism of II. Isaiah in a progressive spirit. I have the more pleasure in welcoming him as an ally, because of the conservative position taken up in 1888 and again in 1891 by Dr. Driver.[2] Prof. Smith's main result is expressed in these words: "Second Isaiah is not a unity, in so far as it consists of a number of pieces by different men, whom God raised up at different times before, during, and after the Exile, to comfort and exhort amid the shifting circumstances and tempers of His people; but it is a unity in so far as these pieces have been gathered together by an editor very soon after the Return from the Exile, in an order as regular, both in point of time and subject, as the somewhat mixed material would permit."[3] Obviously this is a somewhat more "advanced" view than Dillmann's, who (followed by König) denies that even chaps. lxiii.-lxvi. were written after the first partial return of the exiles to Palestine. It must

[1] I quote this passage unaltered from *JQR*, Oct. 1891, for obvious reasons.

[2] See *Isaiah* (1st and 2nd ed.), chaps. 3-5; *Introduction*, pp. 271-230. In the appendix to the 5th edition (1894), some account is given of the views of recent Isaiah critics, not however of Duhm's.

[3] *Exposition of Isaiah*, ii. 21. I do not understand "*before* the Exile."

be added however that though Prof. G. A. Smith does not insist upon the unity of authorship after chap. xlix., nor upon that of tone and situation, he is not convinced that any considerable part of Isa. xl.-lxvi. was written in Palestine after the Return.[1]

At this point I may briefly sum up the critical results which I had reached in 1891 as given in *JQR* for July and October of that year. The solution of the problem which seemed to me the fairest was this: The work of the Second Isaiah, *i.e.* the prophecy of the restoration of the Jews from Babylon, consists of two parts, viz. (1) a continuous series of discourses, chaps. xl.-xlviii.; and (2) a broken collection, composed of chaps. xlix. 1-lii. 12; lii. 13-liii. 12 (a later insertion by the author), liv., lv., lvi. 9-lvii. 21 (beginning with a long passage from an older prophet, which may either have been prefixed by the author, or more probably worked up with a deutero-Isaianic fragment by the editor), and lx.-lxii. Just as Book I. closed with, "Go ye forth of Babylon, flee ye from Chaldea," etc., so Book II. ends with, "Pass ye, pass ye through the gates; clear ye the way of the people," etc. The second book was probably, like Ecclesiastes, left incomplete by the author. This would make it all the easier for the Soferim, or students and editors of the religious literature, to insert or to append prophetic writings of later origin. Such inserted or appended passages are lvi. 1-8, lviii., lix., lxiii.-lxvi. The editorial process, I conjectured, might have been completed in the second half of the fourth century, when the second half of Isaiah assumed the form which it still bears.

In the same year Karl Budde and C. H. Cornill expressed clear opinions. The former, in the course of one of his pioneering essays on the "elegiac" rhythm, made these observations :—

"Very different opinions are held as to the amount of literary material which belongs to the very peculiar writer called the Second Isaiah. This is not the place to give the grounds for my own view upon which I base my present conclusions as to the rhythm of II.

---

[1] In his *Historical Geography* (p. xxiii.) Prof. Smith gives as the period of the Second Isaiah 538-515 B.C., which suggests a more advanced view than that taken in the *Exposition*.

Isaiah. In essential agreement with Cheyne, I assign to the writer called II. Isaiah, chaps. xl.-lv., lx.-lxii. As to chap. lxi., indeed, I am not quite certain."[1]

The latter, in his brief but valuable *Introduction*, divides the latter part of Isaiah into three sections. Chaps. xl.-xlviii. were written between 546 and 538 in Babylonia; chaps. xlix.-lxii. by the same author after a considerable interval, and most probably in Palestine after the Return; chaps. lxiii.-lxvi., which consist of several obscure and seemingly unconnected passages, cannot, as Cornill declares in the words of Stade, "at least in their present form be ascribed to the author of chaps. xl.-lxii." Cornill also admits the probability that even chaps. xl.-lxii. possibly or probably contain several inserted passages, such as xlii. 1-7, lvi. 9-lvii. 13, lix.[2]

Duhm's great work marks the year 1892, and, in spite of some not inconsiderable drawbacks which have somewhat obscured its far greater merits, is certainly the most important work on our subject since the appearance of Ewald's *Prophets*.[3] As regards chaps. xl.-lxvi., Duhm has not only put forward the critical problem more clearly and completely than any one before him, but also offered solutions which, in many respects, are an improvement upon those of all his predecessors. He admits upon the whole the unity of chaps. xl.-lv., which he thinks were probably written in N. Phœnicia, but believes that important insertions have been made which have lengthened the original work by about one quarter. These insertions include the Songs of the Servant of Yahwè (on which more anon) and some much inferior post-Exilic passages. Chaps. lvi.-lxvi. form, according to Duhm, an independent work, written in Jerusalem during the first half of the Persian period, and presenting the strongest possible contrasts to II. Isaiah, by which, however, as well as by other books (especially Ezekiel), it is influenced. Even chaps. lx.-lxii., thinks Duhm, have only an external

---

[1] *ZATW*, 1891, p. 242.   [2] *Einleitung*, pp. 148-152.
[3] In justification of this view, see the present writer's reviews of Duhm in *JQR*, Jan. 1893, p. 295, etc., and *Academy*, Dec. 25, 1892; cf., however, A. B. Davidson, *Critical Review*, Jan. 1893, p. 12, etc.

resemblance to the genuine II. Isaiah ; the phrases or ideas which are borrowed from that work acquire a somewhat different meaning through the change which is presupposed in the historical situation. Though living before the constitution of Ezra, the author attaches the greatest importance to forms and ceremonies, and to the law, and consequently is in the strongest opposition to the half-Israelites, afterwards called the Samaritans, and the not too orthodox Judahites who had escaped deportation to Babylon, and were found in the land by the restored exiles. He belongs in fact to the school which was founded by Ezekiel and promoted by Haggai and Zechariah, though it only became dominant through Ezra. His work is therefore a pendant to the Book of "Malachi," and a prelude to the priestly codex. He may himself be called the Trito-Isaiah. It was at a still later time that the chief insertions in the genuine Deutero-Isaiah were made, and the same editor who is responsible for these, very probably transposed the two parts of the Trito-Isaiah, chaps. lvi.-lx. having originally stood after chaps. lxi.-lxvi. Two valuable allies have in 1893-94 expressed their adhesion to the most important of Duhm's results, viz. Smend (*AT Theol.*, pp. 260, 369), and Marti in his revision or recast of A. Kayser's *Theologie des AT's* (1894), pp. 116, 191, 202, while Ryssel admits that chaps. lxiii.-lxvi. may possibly have been "composed or redacted" in Jerusalem after the Return by members of the school of II. Isaiah.[1] Lastly, Wildeboer in his excellent survey of the present state of criticism (*De Letterkunde des OV*, 1893, p. 322 f.) expresses views very similar to those of Cornill. If this able writer is correct, the average of critical opinion among competent scholars has risen considerably within the last ten years. Nor can the scantily justified moderation of König[2] (*Einleitung*, 1893, p. 325 f.) seriously affect this judgment, which is confirmed by the recent unexpected

[1] See the new translation of the O.T., edited in accordance with the best results of criticism by Kautzsch (1893-94), p. 489.

[2] Chapters lxiii.-lxvi. written in Babylonia after the publication of the edict of Cyrus. lxv. 20, lxvi. 13 are said to point away from Jerusalem; lxv. 3, 4, 11, lxvi. 1-2, 3, 17 are explained with Feilchenfeld of an inclination of Israelitish renegades to the "Persian cult."

CHAPTERS XL.-LXVI. (ANALYSIS) 295

declaration of Wellhausen [1] that the later origin of chaps. lvi.-lxvi. seems to him to have been proved.

I must not conclude, however, without a brief reference to Isidore Loeb. This lamented scholar, whose eminence in other branches of Jewish lore is incontestable, has not been equally successful in his treatment of Isaiah.[2] His theory of the composition of the second part of the book deserves some attention however, for, crude as it may be, it is the result of observations which are not altogether incorrect. He refers the whole of chaps. xl.-xlvi. to the period of the Second Temple, but not to one and the same writer. It is the latter point which interests us most. Loeb thinks, partly developing the ideas of Geiger, that from lii. 13 to the end of chap. lxvi. we have the work of different authors—" une collection factice, où les chapitres se sont plus ou moins rangés d'eux-mêmes et un peu au hasard." He remarks, strikingly enough, how admirably the preceding "collection" would close, or the new "collection" open, with the unique 53rd chapter, but makes the questionable admission that several of the passages in liii.-lxvi. might easily be attached to the first part of the book (xl.-lii.). On lxiii. 7-19 he says, It is evidently a psalm which has slipped by mistake into the collection. lvi. 9-12 may also, he thinks, be an interpolation; cf. Jer. xii. 9-12; Ezek. xxxiv. 8-10. Finally he observes, " Quand même le livre du second Isaïe serait une cours collective, elle n'en serait pas moins admirable; au contraire." This remark, which reminds us of Goethe's well-known epigram on Homer, may be fairly opposed to the hasty assertions of another French scholar in the passage cited at the opening of this chapter. We have indeed not lost the personality of the Second Isaiah, and we have gained probably more than one eminent writer, whose works may be utilised as records of a too little known age.

[1] *Israelitische und jüdische Geschichte* (Oct. 1894), p. 114. The statement indicates some suspense of judgment as to details. In Dec. 1893 Wellhausen still spoke of "the author of Isaiah xl.-lxvi." ("The Babylonian Exile," *New World*, ii. 601-611).
[2] See *La littérature des pauvres* (1892).

Analysis of Chapters XL.-LV

It has been shown that what might formerly have been described as the eccentricity of a few isolated individuals, has succeeded in obtaining a large amount of support from recent critics. The composite character of the second half of Isaiah is, we may already assume, so reasonable that the rashness is on the side, not of those who proclaim it to be certain, but of those who, like the French scholar quoted on p. 283, deny it altogether. The fact that Duhm (to mention only one member of the advanced school) has not conveyed to other students the sense of certainty which he possesses himself may be simply due to the synthetic form in which his work is cast, and when these students have analysed II. Isaiah for themselves, the doubt which they at present feel may be transformed into an assured conviction. Let me, then, for their benefit, proceed to analyse chaps. xl.-lxvi. I will begin with the first half of this fasciculus, the greater part of which at any rate undoubtedly belongs to the Exilic prophet called II. Isaiah. Two questions have to be asked: (I.) May the work of some later writers of II. Isaiah's school have made its way into chaps. xl.-lv.!? And (II.) may even II. Isaiah himself have inserted passages from kindred, and of course earlier writings? In the analysis required for answering the first of these questions, I am more indebted to Duhm than perhaps anywhere else, not having previously made such an analysis of chaps. xl.-lv. for myself.

I. The passages which Kuenen marks as later insertions are chaps. l., li., liv., lv. The grounds on which this analysis is based[1] are not phraseological, but embody Kuenen's impression respecting the object of these discourses. " The dispute alluded to in l. 1-3 is in no relation to the great question which preoccupied all minds before 538, and is such as might be carried on in a settled Jewish community, *i.e.* after 536. . . . Chap. li. makes the impression of a consolatory discourse addressed to the scanty population of the

[1] *Ond.*², ii. 138 (§ 49, n. 5).

new Jerusalem, which, according to *vv.* 17-20, has suffered much through a series of misfortunes. . . . Chap. liv., too, refers to the expansion of Jerusalem and the increase of its population, and, in *vv.* 14-17, to the plots of the enemies of the new community. The foundation of the community itself is not referred to ; must it not be already a thing of the past? . . . Chap. lv. ends with the announcement of a brilliant procession from the land of captivity to Jerusalem ; the preceding address is meant for an already existing Israelitish community. If the formation of the latter was still future, would not the prophet have fallen into a singular ὕστερον πρότερον ? All is in order, however, if *vv.* 12-13 refer to a second and grander return, viz. that of the Diaspora." These impressions of Kuenen will not, I fear, bear the weight laid upon them. In another context I have had to refer to them already (p. 279), and need only now adduce certain supplementary arguments which appear to me decisive. As to chap. li., only the very strongest argument from ideas would justify us in separating it from lii. 1-2, 7-12, with which, phraseologically and rhythmically, it is connected, and which certainly belongs to II. Isaiah. But does Kuenen supply such an argument ? If a band of exiles did return to Jerusalem in 536, it can only have been a very small one indeed, and, if he foresaw this, the prophet might well address to those who longed to see Zion again, the assurance of their thousandfold multiplication and of Zion's glorification. That he idealises such persons as the " people in whose heart is Yahwè's law " (*v.* 7), confirms the view that the prophecy is not of a later date than 538. For the complaints of Haggai and Zechariah prove that the Jerusalem of their day was not such as II. Isaiah could have addressed in these terms. Chap. liv. is the natural continuation of lii. 7-12 (see p. 306). In the divine purpose Zion is already redeemed ; as a believer in this purpose the prophet naturally addresses the restored and glorified Zion at the beginning and end of his prophecy. (For if any part of chaps. lvi.-lxvi. may be assigned to II. Isaiah, it can only be as an appendix to his great work.) Still he does not altogether forget the place where he writes. " Wherefore do ye spend money for that which is no bread " (lv. 2) would certainly not have been addressed to an early post-Exilic community at Jerusalem. Verses 12-13 (cf. xl. 11, lii. 12, xli. 19) may belong in part to the Diaspora, but the Jewish exiles in Babylon must of course be included in the reference. Indeed, if II. Isaiah writes in Babylon, he naturally thinks of his fellow-exiles in the first instance. That liv. 15 is suspicious, may be admitted.

A much more thorough analysis of these chapters has been made by Duhm. Granting that Jewish editors interfered systematically with the texts before them, partly with the view of filling up illegible passages, partly for edification, there is little that can be objected to the following list of *later insertions.*

1. xl. 5, " And the glory of Yahwè shall be revealed, and all flesh shall see it together, for Yahwè's mouth hath spoken it." This is the first of a number of insertions due to one or another of the editors of II. Isaiah. Verses 12-26 are manifestly a first elaboration of the theme in verses 6-8, which must therefore at one time have stood immediately before *vv.* 12-26. Verses 9-11, on the other hand, are connected as closely with *vv.* 3 and 4, of which they are the natural continuation. Restore the respective passages to their right positions, and *v.* 5 becomes superfluous. It is really a later insertion, made at a time when *vv.* 6-8 had already been placed before *v.* 9, and intended to round off the now isolated oracle in *vv.* 3, 4. It was suggested by lii. 10. The correctness of this theory of Duhm is shown by the rhythmic difference between *v.* 5 and its context. The phrase " the glory of Yahwè " occurs again (in chaps. xl.-lxvi.) only in the disputed passages lviii. 8, lx. 1, 2, lxvi. 18. The rare formula " for Yahwè's mouth," etc., recalls lviii. 14 (disputed); cf. i. 20. How strangely *v.* 5*b* contrasts with *v.* 6*b*, " All flesh is grass," etc. ! [There is also a late insertion at the end of *v.* 7. The words, " Surely the people is grass," weaken the sense, and mar the symmetry of the double tetrastich. In spite of the deutero-Isaianic אָכֵן, they are a gloss. The view of Budde (*Theol. LZ*) that the whole of *v.* 7 is a later insertion, seems to impair the effectiveness of the context.]

2. xli. 5,

The coastlands saw it, and feared; the ends of the earth trembled; They drew near and came [together to the judgment-seat].

I had myself pointed out in *PI* that something must have dropped out of the text between xl. 19 and 20. Duhm has now made it probable that the missing passage is xli. 6, 7, which has no natural connection with its present context; note לֹא יָמוֹט both in xl. 20 and in xli. 7. This seems an improvement on the suggestions of Oort[1] and T. K. Abbott[2] that xli. 6, 7 should come after v. 20 (cf. *RT*). It involves the supposition that v. 5 was inserted to patch up a connection between xli. 4 and 6-7, when these two latter verses had already been transferred to their present position. It was suggested by the חָזַק in v. 6.

3. xlii. 24 (from הֲלֹא to בְּתוֹרָתוֹ) and xliii. 20*b*, 21. Note (1) the change of rhythm, (2) the late uses. זוּ as a relative pronoun (p. 257); הָלוֹךְ after instead of before בְּדָרְכָיו (Aramaizing; Ges., Hitz.).

4. xliv. 9-20 (21*b*, 22*b*), xlvi. 6-8. Two controversial passages directed against idolatry, which at once become natural and interesting, when viewed as specimens of Jewish witnessing for monotheism in an advanced part of the post-Exilic (pre-Maccabean) period, but which contrast very strongly with II. Isaiah's work. Their tone (like that of Jer. x. 1-16; Hab. ii. 18, 19, kindred passages) is sarcastic (contrast the spirit of xlii. 3, l. 4), and they fail to convey a compensating impression of the majesty of the God whose sole existence they preach (contrast xl. 19, xli. 6, 7, xl. 20, and xlvi. 3-5, 9). The former passage is the more elaborate of the two, but withal how cold it is! and how unlike is the rhythm (if rhythm it can be called) to that of II. Isaiah in the context! Clearly it is an insertion. Indeed, how can *v.* 21*a* be understood except as the continuation of *vv.* 6-8? "Remember these things," says II. Isaiah,—viz. that Yahwè alone is a Rock, and alone can prophesy,—"for thou art (indeed) my servant." Then we should expect to read, "Thou hast nought to fear; my salvation is at hand." But the next line had become illegible. After this followed an

---

[1] *Theol. Tijdschr.*, 1886, p. 310; 1891, p. 463.
[2] *Essays*, 1891, p. 222.

assurance (happily preserved correctly) that the sins which hindered redemption had been blotted out; but the second half of this distich was effaced. The supplementer did his best to fill up the lacunæ. Taking "these things" in v. 21 to mean the foolish practices of the idolaters (cf. on xlvi. 6-8), he introduced two lines (vv. 21b, 22b), containing an appeal to Israel not to give up its God, and sink to the level of the persons just described. Let any Israelites who have fallen away (cf. xlvi. 8) return to Israel's Redeemer.—Passing on to the latter, we notice again that II. Isaiah's train of thought is broken. הַזֻּלִים cannot be in loose apposition to "ye" implied in the imperfects of v. 5 (Dillm.); it means, "How foolish are those yonder who," etc., and is not the proper sequel of v. 5. Nor can v. 8 be said to be followed naturally by v. 9; זָכְרוּ in the two verses has an entirely different object (cf. on xliv. 21b). The descriptions in both these passages are intended for the instruction of post-Exilic Jews. The writer seems to have lived in the neighbourhood of cities where idol-factories existed, but he knew that many of his own people were inclined to idolatry, and therefore warned them of the danger of such backsliding. This view of the religious state of the Jews may be confirmed by many late passages,[1] which prove that superstitious and idolatrous practices were surprisingly prevalent in the Persian, and especially in the early Greek period. In xlvi. 8 such persons are fitly called פּוֹשְׁעִים, even if they happen to conform to the temple ritual.—The *phraseology* of these passages deserves a careful study in connection with the list on pp. 256-270. In xliv. 9 we have לֹא = בַּל thrice, and חֲמוּדִים; in v. 14 אֹמֶץ; in v. 20a, an unusual gnomic style; in xlvi. 6 וְלִים and קָנֶה ("balance-beam"); in both passages the late word סָגַד (xliv. 15, 17, 19, xlvi. 6), הֵשִׁיב עַל־לֵב (xliv. 19, xlvi. 8), and, virtually the same phrase, יֵצֶר אֵל (xliv. 10), פָּעַל אֵל (xliv. 15), עָשָׂה אֵל (xlvi. 6), nowhere in II. Isaiah. Conjectures.

---

[1] See the passages quoted on p. 316, and cf. Loeb, *La litt. des Pauvres*, pp. 231-233. The facts presented by Ewald, *Gesch.*, iv. 304, Droysen, *Gesch. des Hellenismus*, ii. 598-601, show how easy it was for Jews to become infected with idolatry in the early Greek period. No barrier could altogether keep out ideas which were in the air, and the "hedge" about the law defeated its own object with those who "delighted in scorning."

In xliv. 11 read חֹבְרָיו (Deut. xviii. 11, Ps. lviii. 6) "his charmers," and חָרָשָׁיו (cf. Aram. חָרָשׁ "enchanter," and חֲרָשִׁים "enchantments," Isa. iii. 3) "his enchanters"; and in xliv. 19 פֶּסֶל, for בּוּל, cf. *vv.* 15, 17. In xlvi. 8 הִתְבֹּשָׁשׁוּ; cf. Gen. ii. 25 (nowhere else). "Pedestris sermonis fuisse videtur" (Ges.).

5. xlviii. 1-11, 17-19, "The genuine part of this chapter is largely made up of repetitions. Before venturing on fresh teachings, the writer would fain once more impress the argument from prophecy and the doctrine of Yahwè's creatorship on his readers. The post-Exilic editor, however, was dissatisfied, and actually interlaced the Second Isaiah's work with severe reproachful remarks addressed to his contemporaries, who had fallen back, as he considered, into obstinate unbelief. The largest mass of inserted matter is in *vv.* 16-19, where the editor (uttering, as he thinks, the mind of the original writer) makes what he regards as a new and confidential announcement. This passage must be taken together with Ps. lxxxi. 6*b*-17, a lyric fragment of the Persian period. The foes of Israel are as powerful as ever, and even the national existence seems threatened. In touching language (for here he is himself, and not a mere interpolator) the writer, who is conscious of inspiration (*v.* 16), and can therefore speak for his God, expresses the sorrow of Yahwè for the disobedience which has rendered this punishment necessary" (*BW*). This view of the passage is due to Duhm, though Bredenkamp before him had divided chap. xlviii. between Isaiah and II. Isaiah, the former receiving *vv.* 1-11 as his share, and the latter *vv.* 12-22. Dr. C. H. H. Wright has also lately taken up a position which reminds us of both scholars. "The phraseology," he says, "is Isaianic, worked over by a later hand, prophetic text and prophetic comment being so intermixed that they cannot be separated." This "later hand" is post-Exilic, and is also "seen in the exhortations, *vv.* 12-22," though "the thoughts and verbiage (?) are still mainly Isaianic."[1] It is plain that neither Bredenkamp's view nor that of Wright is tenable; both involve concessions to modern criticism, which are either much too large or much too small. Duhm, however,

[1] Smith's *DB*,[2] i. 1469.

is not as clear in his exposition of our passage as could be wished. The view of the interpolator appears to be that Israel's whole history, both before and after the Exile, has been one long series of lapses into idolatry, interrupted by short repentances and deliverances. He knows full well that the original author wrote at the close of the Exile, and he expresses what he thinks II. Isaiah must have meant, viz. that the "house of Jacob" was as obstinate and unbelieving as ever. But he also addresses his own contemporaries, whom he with perfect accuracy describes as Jews, who delighted to call themselves Israelites ; the name of "Israel" in fact belonged to Jews as such, to those of the Dispersion as much as to those of Judah. And the men of Judah to whom he speaks (II. Isaiah never mentions the name of Judah [1]) are as unbelieving, he implies, as the exiles addressed by his predecessor. Hence another sure judgment will still be necessary before the promises of II. Isaiah can be adequately fulfilled. See further on the parallel passage, x. 20-23 (pp. 53, 54), which expresses or implies the same ideas. In the phraseology, note the affinity to Ezekiel (ii. 4, iii. 7) in v. 4, the use of לוא in v. 18 (p. 258), and the late words חטם (?), v. 9, בָּחַר = בָּחַן, v. 10 (p. 261), and מְעוֹת (plur.), v. 12.

6. xlviii. 16b. A gloss which (1) is unrhythmical, (2) implies a wrong view of the preceding words (see *BW*), and (3) introduces a reference (unique in chaps. xl.-lv.) to the person of the speaker as endowed with the divine spirit (cf. lxi. 1). Nägelsbach, too, sees at least that v. 16 and vv. 17-19 do not look quite right ; he quiets his scruples with the remark that they are probably misplaced.

7. xlix. 3, "Israel." As Gesenius long ago suggested, this is an interpolation (from xliv. 23) like "Israel" and "Jacob" in Sept. xlii. 1.[2]

8. l. 10, 11. The passage only becomes clear when viewed in the light of post-Exilic statements relative to the persecution of true believers ; there is nothing like it in the undoubted work of II. Isaiah (so Duhm). The character

---

[1] "Judah" occurs again only in lxv. 9 (post-Ex.).
[2] In the notes to his translation, however, Ges. retracted this view (see 2nd ed. 1829).

described is that of the later Jerusalem community; cf. lvii. 15, lxvi. 2. The phraseology is *almost entirely unlike that of II. Isaiah*. At the very outset, the use of מִי recalls xliv. 10, liv. 15 (insertions); יְיָ רָא׳, Mal. iii. 15, 16, Psalms (often); בְּיִ׳ בָּטַח, xxvi. 4 (cf. p. 321); יְיָ שֵׁם (p. 313); הָלַךְ with acc., lvii. 2 (xxxiii. 15); חֲשֵׁכִים *ἅπ. λεγ.* (p. 258); use of שָׁעַן (Nif.), x. 20 (p. 54); הֵאִיר קָדַח "to set on fire," אוּר, זִיקוֹת, מַעֲצֵבָה (see pp. 251, 262). Note especially the sharpness of the rebuke; cf. the persecution psalms (xi. 2, lvii. 5, etc.), and the apostrophe in lvii. 3. Also the allusion to Gehenna at the end; cf. lxvi. 24. In *Kohel. rabba*, 66*d*, 67*a*, the ungodly in Gehenna receive a title drawn from *v*. 11*a*.

9. li. 15, 16. The former verse, apart from the opening words, occurs again in Jer. xxxi. 35*b*. Giesebrecht regards the words there as a quotation from Isa. li. 15, inserted simply to fill up the verse. But it is still harder to account for them in our passage, if they were written by II. Isaiah to follow *vv*. 12-14. Considering that *v*. 14 and the latter part of *v*. 13 are evidently corrupt, is it not more probable that *v*. 15 is an artificial substitute for an illegible passage, and that part of it is a quotation? Of course the source of the quotation may be some third writing, but is it so clear that Jer. xxxi. 35*b* has no connection with the first half of the verse? May not the sea be the upper ocean which was the scene of the mythic contest between Yahwè and the sky-dragon (cf. Job xxvi. 12, where רֹגַע הַיָּם certainly refers to this)? In this case the association of ideas in Jer. *l.c.* is natural. That Jer. xxxi. 35-40 is post-Exilic, may be safely assumed (see Giesebr.).—In *v*. 16 we have no less than three quotations, from lix. 21, xlix. 2, Hos. ii. 25 respectively.

10. lii. 3-6. One of the worst written passages in the Old Testament. Note the accumulation of formulæ asserting a divine revelation (p. 251), and the repetition of "my name," also the strange declaration of Israel's innocence. Assyria, too, is nowhere else mentioned in these chapters. In *v*. 5 "here" is, strictly speaking, inconsistent with "thence" in *v*. 11—a pardonable oversight in an interpolator. Observe the strange idiom בְּאֶפֶס (*v*. 4), and the strange form מְנֹאָץ (*v*. 5), a combination of two vocalisations (see *RT*). נְאֻם itself is suspicious, being found again in these chapters only in lx.

14 (Piel). Note also the interpolator's formula בְּיוֹם הַהוּא (v. 6), nowhere again in chaps. xl.-lxvi.

11. liv. 15. An insertion, weak in style and late in phraseology. Note הֵן "if," אוֹתִי for אִתִּי, גּוּר = גָּרָה. The original line must have become illegible.

12. lv. 7. Verses 7 and 8 are inconsistent (see p. 279, note 2). The insertion of v. 7 obscures the division into double tetrastichs. It is more in the style of the pastor-prophet Ezekiel than of II. Isaiah, and was suggested partly by a regard for edification (the writer addresses the wicked men of Jerusalem), partly perhaps to prepare the way for the demands of a stricter morality in chaps. lvi.-lix. The same editor probably inserted lix. 5-9, where note the use of the expression "thoughts" (of the wicked) in v. 7.

The second question (p. 296) is answered in the affirmative, not indeed by Kuenen, but by Ewald, who regards it as a characteristic of the " new race of prophets which arose towards the end of the captivity " that they " weave many passages of older prophets into their own writings."[1] The older passages which Ewald finds in chaps. xl.-lv. are xl. 1, 2 and lii. 13-liii. 12, which he refers to a prophet of the reign of Manasseh. Of these, it is only the latter which can any longer be viewed as possibly a quotation; in the former, the use of צָבָא and רָצָה (p. 267 f.), and the allusion in v. 2c to Jer. xvi. 18 point to a later writer than Ewald supposes, and both form and contents of the passage suggest II. Isaiah as the author. It is in fact a prelude such as a rhetorical writer would naturally prefix to his work. For the theory that lii. 13-liii. 12 was taken from an earlier writing, very much more may be urged (see below). Hence both in 1881 and 1891 I accepted this part of Ewald's view, supposing chap. liii. to have been in its original form either a half-encomium, half-threnody on some martyr of the higher religion of Israel (possibly Jeremiah), or " the first sketch as it were (Job in the poem which bears his name being another) of the Servant of Yahwè."[2] The theory should not be too hastily rejected. The passage may indeed in its present form be too theological for either of the purposes referred to,

[1] *The Prophets*, E.T., i. 83.
[2] *EB*, xiii. (1881), p. 380; *JQR*, July 1891, p. 598.

but we may admit that II. Isaiah when he adopted it, and also probably a later editor,[1] altered it in some important respects. And no critic can deny the plausibility of that form of the theory which assumes the influence of the life of the martyr-prophet Jeremiah. Every commentary on Isaiah points out the striking features common to Jeremiah's self-revelations and to chap. liii., and every work on the Psalms refers to the influence of that prophet's works on a group of psalms. Certainly it is as clear as the day (1) that the Servant of Yahwè is more like an individual in chap. liii. than elsewhere, and (2) that the unique personality of Jeremiah was well worthy of being taken, and in certain psalms was taken, as a type of the noblest section of the Jews. There is also an excellent analogy for the course attributed to II. Isaiah in the development of the story of Job, who in the original legend was an individual, but who comes before us in the poem as a symbol of humanity and of Israel.[2] Still, considering that the rhythm of lii. 13-liii. 12 (except where the text is corrupt or imperfect) agrees with that of most of the other passages on the Servant, and disagrees with that which seems properly to belong to threnodies, and that this passage is by no means devoid of points of contact, other than rhythmical, with the other descriptions referred to, it seems to me now unsafe to separate this portrait of the Servant from those which precede and follow it. And a fuller study of the Servant-passages reveals the striking fact that they form a connected cycle of poetical meditations (influenced no doubt, especially in the two last, by an idealistic view of Jeremiah), so that the further question arises, May not this cycle of poems once have had a separate existence?

Now it can, I think, be made in the highest degree probable that lii. 13-liii. 12 was inserted by II. Isaiah from some other work after the preceding and following sections had been written.[3] We need not lay stress on the stylistic

---

[1] The former admission is made by Dillmann. But it is not enough. The unrhythmical character of some parts of chap. liii. suggests that an editor, in dealing with a scarcely legible part of his manuscript, involuntarily obscured the meaning (hence perhaps עיר in v. 10).

[2] Cf. *BL*, p. 275; Giesebrecht, *Beiträge*, p. 184.

[3] It is no objection to my theory (see p. 309) that xlix. 7 seems to presuppose the writer's acquaintance with liii. 13, 14.

argument. The harshness and obscurity which characterise some parts of the passage, and which are unfavourable to the authorship of II. Isaiah, are sufficiently explained on the hypothesis of corruption of the text. But few will deny that in tone, subject, and rhythm the passage contrasts very strongly with the discourses between which it is placed, and though Wellhausen thinks that liv. 1-lvi. 8 is "clearly, to a certain extent, a sermon on the text lii. 13-liii. 12,"[1] it is a much more defensible view that "Be jubilant, O barren, thou that hast not borne" (liv. 1) was written to follow the section which begins "Awake, awake, put on thy strength, O Zion" (lii. 1).[2] Now if lii. 13-liii. 12 has the origin which we have supposed, it follows that the other poems of the cycle must also have been inserted from elsewhere, though not necessarily after the composition of their contexts. These poems are xlii. 1-4, xlix. 1-6, l. 4-9, the two former of which are, like lii. 13-liii. 12, in a rhythm which differs from that of the neighbouring discourses, while all of them maintain an elevation of tone in no respect inferior to that of the last of the series, but decidedly above the average tone of the rest of II. Isaiah's book. In his very thoughtful early work, *Die Theologie der Propheten* (p. 289), Duhm suggested that the passages in question might perhaps come from a separate work on the life and ministry of Jeremiah, with which II. Isaiah became acquainted after he had already written the first part of his work, so that the passage xlii. 1-7 was inserted by an afterthought. Now, however, this acute critic supposes that the Servant-passages were both written and introduced into II. Isaiah in post-Exilic times. I will not distract the reader's attention by criticising this assignment of date. The point on which I would here lay stress is this—that a theory which has stood the test of seventeen years' examination[3] cannot be lightly set aside,

[1] *Prolegomena*,[2] p. 426. Perhaps Wellh. thinks of what Ewald has said (*Prophets*, iv. 315); but the question is not whether the ideas of the two passages can here and there be brought into connection, but whether the natural sequence is, or is not, broken by lii. 13-liii. 12.
[2] See *PI*, ii. 53 ; Duhm, *Jes.*, p. 378. König clearly goes too far when he asserts that lii. 13-liii. 12 is, by its contents, organically of the same growth as the preceding discourses (*Einl.*, p. 325).
[3] The *Theol. der Proph.* is dated 1875 ; the *Jesaia* 1892.

and, for my own part, having long been convinced that lii. 13-liii. 12 is most naturally viewed as a passage taken by II. Isaiah from an earlier work, and recognising now that this grand composition cannot be separated from the other Servant-passages, I have felt bound to give the theory in its least complicated form the fairest and most thorough examination. My result is that "there is" much "which makes it impossible for" any of the Servant-passages "to have originally sprung, each at the place at which it now stands, from the progress of the prophet's thoughts,"—just the opposite view to that which Prof. G. A. Smith has formulated.[1] I should regret this divergence of view from a friendly scholar, if I did not feel confident that the observations upon which he bases his opinion should lead up rather to a more complicated but a sounder theory. A strict exegesis permits, as it seems to me, no other conclusion than this, viz. (1) that all the Servant-passages are, properly speaking, independent of their present contexts, and must once have been separate from them, and (2) that they have in general exercised such an influence on the following sections that they cannot well have been inserted by any one but II. Isaiah himself. It is the practice of that writer, when he needs a stimulus for a fresh oratorical start, to take up one of the Servant-passages as a suggestive theme, though it must be confessed that the development of the theme which follows (see xlii. 5-9, xlix. 7-12, li. 7, 8 ?) is thin and superficial. The exception to the rule is, as we have seen, in chap. liv., which, though it succeeds the most striking of all the Servant-passages, presents nothing that can fairly be called a development of any part of lii. 13-liii. 12 (unless indeed the isolated mention of the righteousness of all Zion's children in liv. 13*a* may be reckoned as such), and suggests that this particular poem on the Servant was inserted, not during, but after the composition of the section which includes li. 9-lii. 12 and chap. liv. That the phrases (*a*) "my servant," and (*b*) "his servant," occur not only in the Servant-passages but (*a*) in xli. 8, xlii. 19, xliii. 10 ?—xliv. 1, 2, 21, xlv. 4, (*b*) in xliv. 26 ?—xlviii. 20 [l. 10], is no objection to the separatist theory, for in these passages it is

[1] *Exposition*, ii. p. 315.

the Israel of experience, without any admixture of transcendentalism, which is referred to. The inference that all the passages in which a servant of Yahwè is spoken of belonged from the first to the same book, will therefore not hold. We need not now be surprised at another and a much more glaring inconsistency between the Servant-passages and the surrounding discourses, viz. that the writer of the latter too often treats the nations outside Israel as an odious and an inferior race. Even in chap. xlii., which opens with the noble description of one who will not " break the cracked reed," and who will persuasively teach the nations, we are shocked by the awful picture of the warrior who stirs up his slumbering jealousy that he may lay waste mountains and hills, and put to shame those who trust in graven images (*vv.* 13-17), and the surprising assurance that no one is so blind and deaf as the Servant of Yahwè. (See further on p. 244 f.)

As to the *date*. Duhm makes the Servant-passages post-Exilic, and denies them to II. Isaiah—(1) because the quiet concentrated character and the missionary and pastoral activity described in them seem to him to suit the age of the Scribes rather than the period of the close of the Exile ; (2) because in chap. liii. the problem of the suffering of the innocent is treated so much more profoundly than in Job (itself post-Exilic) ; (3) because liii. 10 alludes to the recovery of Job described in Job xlii. ; and (4) because liii. 12 presupposes the possibility of a dead man's return to life. To (1) my reply would be that we may admit different schools even among the Jewish exiles ; to (2) that others (*e.g.* Kuenen) think that the author of Job was influenced and stimulated to further reflection by the portrait of the Servant in II. Isaiah ; to (3) that there *need* be no indebtedness on either side ; and to (4) that the possibility of a return from the world of the dead may well have been surmised under Babylonian influence during (or even before) the Exile. If, however, the influence of the story of Job be still insisted upon, I would urge that even such an extremely cautious critic as König admits [1] that the Book of Job has passed through several phases. It seems to me quite possible

[1] *Einl.*, pp. 413-415 ; cf. Hoffmann, *Hiob*, p. 22 ; Cheyne, *Job and Solomon*, p. 66 ; *Critical Review*, May 1891, p. 252 f.

that the singular description of the ideal righteous sufferer as a leper in liii. 4, 5 comes from an earlier Book of Job, and if it should be wished to connect other features in the portrait of the Servant with the story of Job, it will be plausible to assume that these parts of the Job-story already existed in the earliest narrative. But here we are on slippery ground. At any rate, I think it safest to hold that all the Servant-passages in II. Isaiah are Exilic (the soliloquies in lxi.-lxii. are however post-Exilic; see p. 344). That they come from the school of II. Isaiah is clear, nor is it, I think, at all impossible that they may be the work of II. Isaiah himself. I admit that this makes that great writer extremely inconsistent, but I do not see that this objection is decisive. As Duhm frankly states, the passages "have very close points of contact, both in word and in thought, with II. Isaiah." May they not have been written in a quieter time than the prophecy of restoration in which they are now enshrined? The nearer the goal of II. Isaiah's wishes seemed to come, the harder it must have been to maintain his serenity of mind. But at least he has had the candour to preserve those records of noble aspirations, which have left an ineffaceable mark, not only on the restoration prophecy, but on some of the finest of the post-Exilic psalms.[1]

[Prof. Briggs' theory of the composition of chaps. xl.-lxvi. out of two different writings is mentioned here, because it appears partly to spring from observations like those of Duhm. It seems to this excellent scholar and teacher "that there was an earlier prophecy with the trimeter movement, whose great theme was the divine deliverance of the servant of Jahveh; and that this was taken up into a larger prophecy (in pentameters and hexameters) in a second edition and associated with a parallel theme, the divine deliverance of Zion, the wife of Jahveh."[2] To judge of this theory without a special rhythmically arranged edition of the text, is difficult. It seems at first sight impossible that chaps. lviii.-lix. should be in the same rhythm as xl.-xli. 10, not to mention that

[1] Cf. especially Smend, *AT. Rel.-gesch.*, p. 260 f., who also holds the Servant-passages to be older than II. Isaiah.
[2] *Messianic Prophecy* (1886), p. 340.

the latter section as it stands does not seem to present a uniform rhythm. Exegetical objections are still more obvious. That a connection can be devised between lii. 13-liii. 12 is undeniable; but who can forge a link of union between this and the next "trimeter poem," chap. lv.? That lii. 7-12 and chap. liv. are brought close together is however helpful.]

ANALYSIS OF CHAPTERS LVI.-LXVI.

We now enter upon a fresh part of our analysis. That chaps. lvi.-lxvi. are not a direct continuation of chaps. xl.-lv. is obvious; with the exception of chaps. lx.-lxii. there is no portion of this group of chapters which can even plausibly be regarded as forming part of the great Prophecy of Restoration. But may they not in spite of this have been written by the author of that prophecy, under somewhat altered circumstances, as appendices? That is one question that we have to answer. It is, however, as we shall presently see, not the only one; there is another equally reasonable theory. Considering the activity of the post-Exilic editors, it is far from inconceivable that just as a continuous work of Exilic origin (chaps. xl.-lv.) was appended to chaps. i.-xxxix., so a continuous or almost continuous composition of post-Exilic origin, or a group of nearly contemporary though separate post-Exilic writings, may have been appended to chaps. xl.-lv. The collection of the prophetic writings appears to have been made sometime in the third century B.C. Before this event there was ample time for such a work, or such a group of works, to win popularity and to obtain insertion in II. Isaiah, or in the combined prophetic volume of I. and II. Isaiah. Nor can we exclude the possibility that small additions were made even after 200 B.C. (cf. the long-continued supplementing of the text of the Hexateuch, on which see Kuenen, *Hexateuch*, pp. 313-317).

CHAPTER LVI. 1-8

The situation of the prophecy is briefly this. The

religion of Israel has begun to attract foreign proselytes, who zealously practice the worship ("love the name") of Yahwè and "keep his Sabbaths." But at Jerusalem a new spirit of exclusiveness has begun to show itself; legal objections are raised to the admission of non-Israelites. There are also a number of faithful Israelites who have been forced to become eunuchs at the court of the "great king" (cf. xxxix. 7), and who, though admitted into the community, have to deplore their loss of the "heritage and gift that cometh of the Lord." For both classes the writer has comfort, but it is in part very obscurely expressed, and it is by no means what we should expect from the spiritually-minded II. Isaiah. It is very strange too that the writer should seek to fortify his position ($v.$ 8) by a revelation which he represents as a specially striking one, but which is really by no means new (see xliv. 5, lv. 5). Surely this implies that the teaching of the Second Isaiah has fallen into some neglect.

The date of this prophecy seems reasonably certain.[1] The *circumstances* are evidently not those of II. Isaiah. The first return of the exiles is past ($v.$ 8a refers to the future; cf. xi. 12), the temple has been rebuilt[2] ($vv.$ 5, 7), and an exclusive and strictly legalist tendency prevails at Jerusalem. The writer himself, however, is far less exclusive than his neighbours; he reminds us rather of 1 Kings viii. 41-43 than of Ezra ix. 1-4, Neh. xiii. 1-3. He even claims a divine sanction for cancelling the order for the exclusion of foreigners. But he is at one with the legalists (and also no doubt with Ezekiel, their forerunner) in emphasising the religious duty of Sabbath-keeping ($vv.$ 4, 6; cf. lviii. 13, 14, Neh. x. 31, xiii. 15-22). Surely this places us in the age of Nehemiah. That patriotic man may indeed very possibly himself have been one of the eunuchs referred to, for he served wine in the presence of the queen;[3] we might almost take the promise in $v.$ 5 as an answer to the ejaculations in

---

[1] So *EB*, xiii. 380; *JQR*, July 1891.
[2] König (*Einl.*, p. 325) objects that Yahwè says, "I will bring them," and "my house shall be called." But יִקָּרֵא means "is called," liv. 5, and the "holy mountain" is the temple-hill, not Jerusalem, nor yet the whole mountain-country of Palestine.
[3] So Grätz, Renan, and Paul Haupt, who also think that Ps. cxxvii. is directed against Nehemiah.

Neh. v. 19, xiii. 14, 22, 31. At any rate, it may be readily believed that Jewish eunuchs followed Nehemiah from the Persian court. The fact that deliverance from an oppressor is still needed (*v.* 1) is not opposed to this date, for it was precisely the "great affliction and reproach" of Jerusalem which induced Nehemiah to leave his important post at the court. The earliest admissible date, on this hypothesis, is 444 B.C. But considering that strict Sabbath observance was not carried out till Nehemiah's second visit in 432 (see Neh. xiii.), it is not impossible to bring down the date to that year.[1]

That the *ideas*, *style*, and *language* are in the main too late for II. Isaiah, is also clear. Of the ideas something has been said already. In so far as the circumstances differ from those of chaps. xl.-lv., the ideas are also different. The age of idealism seems to have passed; a certain practical moderation is now more in request even with the noblest Jews. II. Isaiah, it seems, had nothing to say about the Sabbath, agreeing herein with Jeremiah (for Jer. xvii. 19-27 is a post-Exilic insertion[2]). Our prophet, however, actually uses P's phrase, "my (*i.e.* Yahwè's) Sabbaths" (*v.* 4); see Ex. xxxi. 13, cf. 16; Lev. xix. 3, 30; xxvi. 2. Other phrases are equally significant of a change of ideas. שָׁמַר, used five times (in a religious sense), is a favourite word of Deuteronomy and Ezekiel. In *v.* 1*a* מִשְׁפָּט and צְדָקָה mean "lawful and right courses of action." Not exactly so in chaps. xl.-lv. We do find, however, II. Isaiah's use of צְדָקָה for righteousness as a principle determining the divine action (cf. p. 267) in *v.* 1*b;* also גָּלָה in Nifal, as used four times in chaps. xl.-lv. Indeed the whole verse-half resembles li. 5. *V.* 2, notice the poverty of the style. חִלֵּל is a legal term (Lev.; Ezek.). *V.* 3, בֶּן־הַנֵּכָר, here only (and in plural in *v.* 6) with art. 'בְּנֵי־נ, lx. 10, lxi. 5, lxii. 8. The writer knows the ancient usage, according to which גֵּר might be used of an Israelitish sojourner from another "tribe,"[3] and

[1] Cf. Kosters, *Het Herstel van Israël*, p. 82 f. (on the order of events).
[2] Kuenen, *Ond.*[2], ii. 176 f.; Cheyne, *Jeremiah* (commentary), i. (1883), p. 418 ("introduced to assist the reforming movement of Ezra and Nehemiah").
[3] See Judg. xvii. 7, 8, and cf. Stade, *Gesch.*, i. 400.

CHAPTER LVI. 1-8

therefore avoids this word, which, however, is used in xiv. 1, a passage of presumably later date, in which, as in P, גֵּר is on the way to assuming the new sense of "proselyte." הַגִּלְוָה (so to be pointed; see v. 6) is added; a point of contact with xiv. 1 (see p. 75). בָּדַל, see p. 261, and cf. Neh. ix. 2, וַיִּבָּדְלוּ. הֵן, the favourite form throughout chaps. xl.-lxvi. V. 4, כִּי כֹה וגו׳, a favourite phrase of II. Isaiah. "My Sabbaths"; see above. בָּחַר בְּ, in a religious sense, as in xli. 24, xliv. 1, lxv. 12, lxvi. 3, 4 (*bis*). Also in i. 29 (Isaiah). בְּרִית, not in the same shade of meaning as in lv. 3 (lxi. 8). There it refers to the promises of Yahwè; here, to practical injunctions as to daily life. V. 5, יָד = *stele*, as 1 Sam. xv. 12, if correct text, 2 Sam. xviii. 18 (also important for connection of בָּנִים, יָד, and שֵׁם); elsewhere "name" and "seed" are connected, xlviii. 19, lxvi. 22. "Name ... cut off," as lv. 13 (end). V. 6, שֵׁרֵת, see list, p. 269. שֵׁם יהוה, in the Book of Isaiah, only occurs in passages which are probably post-Exilic, viz. xviii. 7, xxiv. 15, xxx. 27, xlviii. 1 (added portion?), l. 10, lvi. 6, lix. 19, lx. 9. Of the passages in which שְׁמִי, שִׁמְךָ occur (with reference to Yahwè), three, viz. xli. 25, xlii. 8, xlviii. 11*a*, belong undoubtedly to II. Isaiah; the remainder, xxvi. 8, 13, xxix. 23, xlviii. 9, lii. 5, 6, lxiii. 16, lxiv. 1, 6, lxvi. 5 are probably post-Exilic. Five closely related senses of the phrase "name of Yahwè" emerge from these passages, (1) the name Yahwè, considered as expressing sufficiently for its purpose the divine nature; (2) the bright and awful physical and moral manifestation of the divine Being which is also called כָּבוֹד (xxx. 27, lix. 19); (3) the praise and honour which this manifestation brings to Yahwè from men (xlviii. 9; also one of the senses of כְּבוֹד י׳); (4) the place where Yahwè gives such a manifestation of himself (lx. 9); and (5) the worship offered to Yahwè at such a place (xviii. 7; so Zech. xiv. 9). It is the fifth of these senses which alone suits in lvi. 6 (cf. 1 Ki. viii. 29); the three passages of II. Isaiah (and the disputed passage xlviii. 1) require the first. V. 7, this verse is somewhat different from Mal. i. 11, where it is said that everywhere among the nations offerings are (even now) made to Yahwè; it seems to represent a middle view between Malachi's theoretic breadth and the old narrow view of tradition. But it also differs from the vague statements of II. Isaiah. Cyrus "calls upon Yahwè's name" (xli. 25), but it is nowhere said (see on chap. lx.) that he will worship in the temple of Yahwè. קְדֹשׁ, a characteristic word of chaps. lvi.-lxvi. (see below). "My holy mountain"; a distinctively late expression (see on xi. 9, p. 67). "Make them rejoice"; cf. Deut. xii. 7, 12, 18. "House of prayer," etc.; cf. 1 Ki. viii. 29, 43 (post-Exilic; Cornill, *Einl.*, p. 128), Ps. lxv. 3; prayer taking precedence of the ritual sacrifices, as in Psalms l. and li. לִרְצוֹן, as lx. 7, Jer. vi. 20, Ex. xxviii. 38, Lev. xxii. 20, 21, Ps. xix. 15 (late).—*V*. 8, נְאֻם י׳, thirteen times in chaps. xl.-lxvi., but nowhere else as an introductory formula (cf. i. 24, Zech. xii. 1, Ps. cx. 1). Here, however, we have אֲדֹנָי י׳; see list, p. 254. "That gathereth (or, will gather) Israel's outcasts"; cf. xi. 12, and, for "outcasts," Ps. cxlvii. 2. No passage is more clearly post-Exilic than *v*. 8. But can we separate *v*. 8 from its context?

Note 1. *On* קדשׁ *and its derivatives.*—An examination of the use of these words gives some remarkable facts. קדשׁ, Qal, or rather (*RT*) Piel, occurs in lxv. 5; Hithp. in lxvi. 17; no form of this verb in chaps. xl.-lv.—קָדוֹשׁ is used of Yahwè fourteen times in xl.-lv.; only thrice in lvi.-lxvi. (viz. lvii. 15 *bis*, lx. 9). Of the Sabbath, lviii. 13; of Zion, lx. 14. קֹדֶשׁ only twice, certainly, in xl.-lv. (viz. lii. 1, "holy city," and lii. 10, "his holy arm"); for xliii. 28 is corrupt, and xlviii. 2 interpolated. But thirteen times in lvi.-lxvi. (eleven times of objects consecrated to Yahwè, and twice of Yahwè's spirit). מִקְדָּשׁ, twice in lx. 13, lxiii. 18, nowhere else in the second half of Isaiah. Is it probable that this second half is all by one author?

Note 2. *On the use of* אָנֹכִי *and* אֲנִי.—The statistics given on p. 257 (top) need to be supplemented, now that we are entering on the study of chapters of specially disputed date. According to König's list (*Einl.*, p. 321) *all but two* of the instances of אָנֹכִי occur in chaps. xl.-lv., and of these two (lxvi. 13, 18) the former is probably produced (see Duhm; *RT*) by the intrusion of a gloss based upon II. Isaiah's words in li. 12, while the latter occurs in a passage of more than ordinary solemnity, where אֲנִי unsupported would be too weak. אֲנִי occurs altogether sixteen times in chaps. lvi.-lxvi.; it is absent from only two of the sections.

CHAPTERS LVI. 9-LVII. 21

This obscure passage, which opens with a denunciation of the rulers of the Jewish community for their incapacity, slothfulness, and greed, closes with a message of delicately expressed consolation and encouragement to the whole Jewish people, "to the far-off and to the near." Midway comes an invective, in still more vehement terms than the introduction, against a community distinct (as it would seem) from that of Jerusalem, and addicted to the most various forms of heathenism.—The first question to ask is, whether this passage is a whole, or whether two writers have been concerned in producing it. The detailed evidence will be given presently, but even a hasty inspection ought to convince the student that lvi. 9-lvii. 13a, which reminds us so forcibly of Ezekiel, was not written to be followed by lvii. 13b-21, which not less strikingly recalls the author of chaps. xl.-lv. (who has hardly any clear points of contact with Ezekiel). The next question is, whether the period of the first and longer part, viz. lvi. 9-lvii. 13a (or, as Ewald less probably fixes the close of the fragment, lvii. 11a), is before, during, or after the Exile. Most critics [1] have followed Ewald in replying that it is pre-Exilic. The Palestinian colouring of lvii. 5, 6, the probable reference to persecution in lvii. 1, and the correspondence of the sins imputed to the community with those of Israel before the Exile, have been felt to be unfavourable to a late Exilic date,[2] and so even Kuenen has supposed the question to have been settled. A doubt has indeed been expressed by Dillmann whether the passage can have been earlier than the time of Jeremiah (Ewald had referred it to the reign of Manasseh [3]), and

[1] *E.g.* Bleek, Grätz, Kuenen, Dillmann, Cornill, Ryssel, Wildeboer. In *PI*, *EB*, and *JQR* I have myself adopted this view, and accepted Ewald's date.
[2] An Exilic date was defended by the writer in *ICA*, and by Riehm in his posthumous Introduction (ii. 141); it is still held by König (*Einl.*, p. 325). Against the former, see *JQR*, July 1891, p. 596. König conjectures that lvii. 5 may have been true of some of the exiles, and appeals to Ezekiel, as showing that similar descriptions were written during the Exile. A very slender argument!
[3] Luzzatto (who ascribes all the rest of the book to Isaiah) agrees;

whether (like the original of chap. liii.) it has not been retouched by the Second Isaiah,[1] who may even have worked up more than one pre-Exilic passage, but the possibility of a post-Exilic date has not till very lately been considered.

Why indeed should a post-Exilic date be discussed, unless it can be shown to have some plausibility? If the editor and supplementer of the inserted passage be the Second Isaiah, it is clear that that passage must at latest be Exilic. And if there was no such heathenish community in Palestine after the Exile as that addressed in lvii. 3-13a, it is clear that it must even be pre-Exilic. For though the sins of the fathers might, according to lxv. 7, be visited upon the children, this was only on the supposition that the children had not broken away from the transgressions of their fathers. To me the latter argument appeared more important than the former. It seemed possible to hold that lvi. 9-lvii. 13a was incorporated into II. Isaiah by a late editor, who worked it up with a fragment of II. Isaiah's work. Had this passage been inserted by that great writer himself, one would have expected him to alter the phraseology more, and so make the passage his own.[2] But how, if even the latter argument is based upon a misapprehension? From a number of passages which recent criticism reasonably claims as post-Exilic, it follows that the Jews of the Persian, and still more those of the Greek period were by no means free from heathenish superstitions; see especially Ps. xvi. 4, lxxxi. 6b-17;[3] Mic. v. 9-14; Zech. x. 2, xiii. 2; Isa. xxvii. 9, and most of the didactic passages inserted in the prophecies of Isaiah and II. Isaiah, e.g. ii. 20, xvii. 7, 8, xxx. 22, xxxi. 6, 7, xlvi. 6, 7, xlviii. 5b, etc.; cf. also parallel references for xiii. 21 (p. 70), and the prohibitions of heathenish customs in Lev. xvii.-xxvi. retained in the Levitical legislation. And very near the Jews themselves were the Samaritans, i.e. the

---

vv. 1, 2 he regards as a dirge upon Isaiah, who, according to the legend, was sawn asunder by order of Manasseh.

[1] Some expressions in lvii. 11, 12 and (הֵם הֵם) in *v*. 6, and the pictures in lvii. 1, 2, and 4 seem to Dillm. deutero-Isaianic.

[2] *JQR*, July 1891, p. 597 f.; cf. my former view of lii. 13-liii. 12.

[3] It is very strange that, against the linguistic evidence, Baethgen should refer Ps. lxxxi. to the last years of the kingdom of Judah because of its warning against idolatry. Cf. *BL*, p. 478.

descendants of the N. Israelitish remnant and of the Assyrian, Babylonian, and Arabian colonists, who worshipped Yahwè as the "god of the land" (2 Ki. xvii. 24-28, 41; Ezra iv. 9, 10; cf. 2 Ki. xxiii. 15; Jer. xli. 4), but who, until the erection of the Gerizim temple and the adoption of the Jewish law-book, cannot have altogether given up the heathen practices of their ancestors.[1] We might therefore suppose the invective in lvii. 3-13 to be addressed either to the lukewarm Jewish community of the times before 432, or to the Samaritans. The opening words, however, are certainly more favourable to the latter alternative; the community addressed (note the fem., from *v.* 6 onwards) seems to be distinct from that whose leaders are spoken of in lvi. 10-12, and the words "an adulteress and a harlot" (see *RT*) gain in force when explained of the mixed origin as well as of the impure religion of the Samaritans. Moreover, with Haggai and Zech. i.-viii. before us, it is scarcely credible that, even in imitation of Ezek. xvi. 3, 45 (written before Zedekiah's captivity), such strong expressions could have been used of the post-Exilic *Jewish* community. (Cf. on chaps. lxv., lxvi.)

Hitherto we have considered only lvii. 3-13*a*. But what of lvi. 9-lvii. 2? Does the description necessarily involve a pre-Exilic date? The apparent reference to persecution in lvii. 1 seemed to me formerly to recommend, and to Ewald seemed almost to enforce the reign of Manasseh as the period of this passage as well as of the parallel description in Mic. vii. 2. A more thorough study of the Psalms, however, has convinced me that (even allowing for some exaggeration in the psalmists' expressions) there were times when poor and pious Jews were exposed to something like persecution, even after the Return, and that their oppressors were not merely

---

[1] The writer of 2 Ki. xvii. 41 expressly asserts this to have been the case "unto this day" (*i.e.* to a date shortly before the Exile), and there was nothing until the great event mentioned above to hinder this impure, inconsistent religion. On the composition of the Samaritan population, see Kautzsch in *Realencyclop.*[2], xiii. 340, etc.; Stade, *Gesch.*, ii. 189-191; Winckler, *Untersuch.*, pp. 97-107; Kosters, *Het Herstel van Israël*, p. 66; and on the composite narrative in 2 Ki. xvii. 24-41, Kittel, *Gesch.*, ii. 188 f., and cf. 2 Ki. *l.c.* in Kautzsch's edition of the O.T.

foreigners, but also rich and lawless Jews;[1] it has also become very doubtful whether the whole of Mic. vii. is not post-Exilic, and though the sins rebuked in lvi. 11, 12 are old ones among the priests and prophets (see *e.g.* xxviii. 7, Mic. iii. 5, 11, and cf. Ezek. xiii. 19), yet the rebuke of the priests in "Malachi" (ii. 1-8) and the story of Shemaiah in Nehemiah (vi. 11, 12) show us that the later priests and prophets were not exempt from the traditional errors of their class. Zeph. iii. 1-4 may also supply evidence of this fact, for the section to which it belongs is most probably post-Exilic. Note also the sad description of the rulers (who may be included under "watchmen" in lvi. 10) in Neh. v. 1-5. Altogether it is clear that for this introductory portion also a post-Exilic date is thoroughly tenable. If, therefore, it can be shown by fresh evidence that a pre-Exilic date is impossible, we need no longer hesitate to regard the passage as a post-Exilic invective against the half-Jews or Samaritans and their Jewish allies.

It now becomes important to make a strict examination of the literary evidence. The following are among the more important parallelisms. lvi. 9 closely resembles Jer. xii. 9*b* (cf. Ezek. xxxiv. 5, 8, xxxix. 17), while lvi. 11-lvii. 1 reminds us of Zeph. iii. 1-7, Mic. vii. 1-6 (both late passages?), and Ps. x. 1-11 ("doubtless from the same period," Ewald), xii. 2, xiv. 1, etc. The description in lvii. 5, etc. recalls similar passages in Jer. ii., and Ezek. xvi., xxiii.; the contrast in lvii. 6 between the "portions" of the two classes of persons, and the reference to "libations," suggests Ps. xvi. 4, 5. There are also four points of contact with II. Isaiah, viz. (*a*) in lvi. 11, cf. liii. 6; (*b*) in lvii. 1, cf. liii. 8; (*c*) in lvii. 12, cf. xli. 29; and (*d*) in lvii. 13 ("the wind shall carry them all away") with xli. 16, 29. [I do not add lvii. 11, for there we should read, not וּמֵעוֹלָם (cf. xlii. 14), but וּמֵעֹלָם (see below); nor lvii. 6, for the repetition of הֵם is merely rhetorical (cf. *vv.* 14, 19); nor lvii. 12, for "thy righteousness" means, not "thy salvation"[2] (cf. xlvi. 13), but "thy

---

[1] See *BL*, pp. 121, 226, etc. Those who, like the author formerly, refer some of the persecution-psalms to the age of Jeremiah, may be inclined to follow Dillmann, who ascribes our prophecy to the same period. Cf. Jer. ix. 8, xi. 21, xxvi. 23, xxxvi. 26.

pretended religious correctness" (cf. Ezra iv. 2).]—Let us now look at the more minute facts. In lvi. 9 (twice) note חַיְתוֹ; Jer. xii. 9 has חַיַּת. The fuller form occurs in Gen. i. 24; Zeph. ii. 14; Ps. l. 10, lxxix. 2, civ. 11, 20. According to Dillmann, all the other passages imitate Gen. i. 24 (contrast *v*. 30). Cf. the same ending in Num. xxiv. 3, 15; Ps. cxiv. 8. It does not look as if the author of this passage were either Isaiah or II. Isaiah.—Joined to 'ח note שָׂדָי. Jer. *l.c.* has הַשָּׂדֶה (but see Jer. iv. 17, xviii. 14). The form occurs twice in Hos.; once in Joel and in Lam.; 5 times in Psalms; also in Deut. xxxii. 13. Combined with חַיְתוֹ it has an air of lateness; the combination occurs again only in Ps. civ. 11.— אָתִיוּ (again in *v*. 12); Jer. *l.c.* has הֵתָיוּ. Both forms occur again in xxi. 12, 14 (see p. 129). אָתָה Aramaizing, for בּוֹא. *V*. 10, צֹפִים "watchmen," *i.e.* the members of the three leading classes, "princes," priests, and prophets (cf. Zeph. iii. 3, 4). This sense alone suits the figure of the flock (as the gloss וְהֵמָּה רֹעִים rightly suggests; cf. Ezek. xxxiv. 2-5). The same term in Jer. vi. 17, Ezek. iii. 17, xxxiii. 7, Isa. lii. 8, has the narrower sense of prophets. The more extended meaning is presumably late. נָבֹחַ ἅπ. λεγ.; so also הֹזִים, cf. Talmudic.—*V*. 11, פָּנוּ לְדַרְכָּם; cf. liii. 6. From Hab. onwards, unjust gain is specially rebuked by the prophets. —*V*. 12. יֶתֶר adverbially, as Dan. viii. 9 (יִתְרָ). בֶּצַע, as lvii. 17 (?); cf. xxxiii. 15; Jer. vi. 13, viii. 10; Ezek. xxii. 27, xxxiii. 31; Ps. cxix. 36.

lvii. 1, אָבַד; so Mic. vii. 2 (similar context). שָׂם עַל־לֵב; Jer. xii. 11, Isa. xlvii. 7. חֲסִידִים = אַנְשֵׁי חֶסֶד, which became the party name of the legalists. חֶסֶד "piety," rare. Cf. Hos. vi. 4, 6; Neh. xiii. 14 (plur. = good deeds). בְּאֵין מֵבִין, idiom as in Prov. xxvi. 20.—*V*. 2, מִשְׁכָּב = the grave, as Ezek. xxxii. 25. הֹלֵךְ נְכֹחוֹת (so read), idiom as in xxxiii. 15.—*V*. 4, הִתְעַנַּג, as lv. 2, lviii. 14 (but in different sense).—*V*. 5, אֵלִים = אֵילִים, i. 29 (see also on lxi. 3). "Under every green tree," as Deut. xii. 2, Kings (thrice in Deuteronomic passages), Jer. (thrice), Ezek. (once). רעננ, 6 times in Jer. שָׁחַט of sacrifices of children, as Ezek. xvi. 21. "Clefts of the rocks"; Isaianic (ii. 21); cf. *v*. 7.—*V*. 6, חֵלֶק (so point), as 1 Sam. xvii. 40. חֵלֶק and גּוֹרָל in a religious sense, as Ps. xvi. 5; cf. Deut. iv. 19. In form the concluding question resembles Jer. v. 9, 29, ix. 8.—*V.* 7, גְּבֹהַּ וְנִשָּׂא; cf. ii. 12-15.—*V.* 8, מְזוּזָה; cf. Deut. vi. 9. זִכָּרוֹן, late; see p. 262. In *d* supply from Ezek. xvi. 25f; cf. Sept. Isa. lvii. 9 (Duhm ; *RT*).—*V.* 9, Is there any trustworthy passage for שׁוּר "to journey"? Jer. v. 10 and Ezek. xxvii. 25 are both corrupt. If we read here וַתְּסוּרִי (*RT*), we can more easily account for בְּ. See Ezek. xvi. 9, and cf. xxiii. 40*b*. רְקָחִים, *ἅπ. λεγ.* רקח and its derivatives occur almost exclusively in Exilic and post-Exilic writings (see esp. Ex. xxx. 25, 35, P).—*V.* 10, נוֹאָשׁ, as Jer. ii. 25, xviii. 12.—*V.* 11, דָּאַג with accus., Jeremianic (see p. 262). מַחְשֶׁה, of Yahwè's longsuffering ; cf. the same use of a synonymous term, Ps. l. 21. מֵעֹלָם (so point with Sept.); a synonymous term is used in the same way, Ps. x. 11. The very idiom occurs in Ps. x. 1, but in a different sense.—*V.* 12, מַעֲשַׂיִךְ, of false religious practices, as xli. 29 (probably). הוֹעִיל with negative, of heathenism, as xliv. 10 (late).—*V.* 13, Read שִׁקּוּצַיִךְ with Weir (as in *PI*) ; see p. 269.

All these phenomena taken together justify a definite conclusion. Note especially the points of contact with Jeremiah and Ezekiel, which (putting aside those produced by corrections of the text) are so numerous as to imply a peculiar affection on the part of the writer for these prophets. A pre-Exilic date is therefore excluded, and we are shut up to the view of the date and meaning of the passage indicated above. The affinities to II. Isaiah and necessarily late psalms supply subsidiary evidence in favour of this result.

The supplementary portion, lvii. 13 *b*-21, has still to be considered. That it was worked up with the (incomplete) earlier passage is, as I have already suggested, not unplausible. I can now go further and maintain that this is an absolutely necessary view, and that the editor is not II. Isaiah, but a later writer of his school, who may indeed also have left his mark on the close of the preceding denunciation. It is a prophecy of consolation that he gives us, but it does not flow as gently as the honeyed rhetoric of his predecessor. At first he may seem to write like II. Isaiah, but he soon falls into other grooves, and neither his phraseology nor his ideas are altogether deutero-Isaianic. Even at the outset, הַחוֹסֶה בִי (*v.* 13) strikes one as strange. There are only two

CHAPTERS LVI. 9-LVII. 21

passages in chaps. xl.-lv. where trust in Yahwè is either enjoined or distinctly presupposed, and both these passages occur in late contexts (xlviii. 2*b*, l. 10*b*); nor is the phrase there used בְּ חָסָה. The quality of trustfulness is one which grew up among the "fearers of Yahwè" under the combined discipline of the law and of an oppressive foreign yoke (cf. xxvi. 3, 4, and Psalms *passim*), and the phrase בְּ חָסָה is rare in the earlier literature (Judg. ix. 15; Isa. twice; see p. 252). נָחַל אֶרֶץ reminds us of יָרַשׁ אֶרֶץ (see on lx. 21); cf. נָחַל in xlix. 8. הַר קָדְשִׁי; as lvi. 7. In *v*. 14 the command to prepare a highway is an echo of xl. 3, 4, and the opening word וְאָמַר, whether due to the writer or to a glossator, seems to be a reminiscence of xl. 6. The form of the command, however, is more closely parallel to lxii. 10, which also occurs in a passage with affinities to II. Isaiah, but (as we shall soon see) not the work of that writer. מִכְשׁוֹל (*v*. 14) and רָם וְנִשָּׂא (*v*. 15) are Isaianic; but see p. 252 f. עַד and קָדוֹשׁ (as a proper name) are deutero-Isaianic (pp. 253, 270). The repetition of קָדוֹשׁ however (read בְּקָדוֹשׁ, " as a holy one," with Klost.) in the next line is unlike II. Isaiah, and altogether the series of divine titles is not in the manner of that writer. דַּכָּא, in an ethical sense, recalls Ps. xxxiv. 19. נִדְכָּא, cf. נִדְכֶּה, Ps. li. 14. The whole description in *v*. 15 is unlike anything in chaps. xl.-lv., and this applies alike to the series of divine titles, to the striking combination of the ideas of the divine transcendence and immanence (cf. Ps. cxxxviii. 6), and to the picture of the Jewish community as "crushed and lowly" (cf. lxi. 1, lxvi. 2; Ps. xxxiv. 19, li. 18, cxlvii. 3). מָרוֹם אֶשְׁכּוֹן; same phrase in xxxiii. 5 (late). *V*. 16 opens, no doubt, in the manner of liv. 8, but the great idea of chap. liv. finds no expression. The idea of *v*. 16*b* is also that of Num. xvi. 22, xxvii. 16 ("God of the spirits of all flesh"), which belong to P, and of Zech. xii. 1 (post-Exilic). עָטַף "to faint," as Ps. lxi. 3, cii. 1 (cf. p. 265). נְשָׁמָה (unique case of plur.), as in xlii. 5, but in different sense (see p. 265). *V*. 17. The text needs several corrections (see *RT*), the chief of which is בַּעֲוֹנוֹ רֶגַע (Klost.). The writer (who is surely not II. Isaiah) distinctly alludes to liv. 8. The last clause of *v*. 17 and the first of *v*. 18 may allude to Jer. iii. 21, 22. In *v*. 18 note נִחֻמִים and אֲבֵלִים, neither of which occurs in chaps.

xl.-lv. The alternative expressions at the end remind us of lvi. 8. V. 19 as it stands is very ill-connected. The opening words may be taken as an admiring exclamation in the style of II. Isaiah (see xl. 22, 23); but the phrase seems too obscure and artificial for that great writer (cf. Hos. xiv. 3). שָׁלוֹם repeated reminds us of the repetitions in vv. 6, 14. וּרְפָאתִיו seems a variant to וְאֶרְפָּאֵהוּ (v. 18). The phrase "the far off and the near" (viz. with regard to the temple) is not only conclusive against II. Isaiah's authorship, but, occurring again as it does in Dan. ix. 7, suggests a somewhat late date. In v. 20 we even find two late Hebrew words of Talmudic affinities, viz. רֶפֶשׁ, and, one cannot hesitate to add, גָּדַשׁ "to heap up" (part. Nif., and imperf. Qal or Piel).[1]

The easiest critical hypothesis seems to be, that we have in lvi. 9-lvii. 13a the work of a friend of reform at Jerusalem, who wrote before the arrival of Ezra and the introduction of the law-book. Possibly he had come to Jerusalem in the train of Nehemiah, and been violently shocked at the religious abuses which were still practised in Jerusalem or its neighbourhood. No doubt it is to the Samaritans that the greater part of this prophecy (cf. chaps. lxv., lxvi.) is specially addressed, but inhabitants of Jerusalem, who in any degree identified themselves with the detested half-Jews, would share the same punishment.

So far our view agrees with that of Duhm. But at v. 13 we have to part company with this acute critic, for here we begin to trace a new writer, who is strongly affected by II. Isaiah, but from a literary point of view is greatly inferior to that writer. He has nothing to say about the return from Babylon, because it is a thing of the past, but looks forward, like the other post-Exilic writers, to a still future return from the other countries of the dispersion, so that the promised land, within its widest limits, may be occupied by none but Israelites. This, however, at present is but a dream, and as such quickly dismissed; what chiefly engages

---

[1] Read וְנִגְדַּשׁ and וַיִּגְרְשׁוּ. A similar emendation is required in Am. viii. 8, where, however, וְנִגְרְשָׁה should be excised as a gloss; see Am. ix. 5, and cf. Talm. *Sota*, 34a, which makes doubt impossible. See G. Hoffmann *ZATW*, iii. 122, who only omits to refer to *Sota, l.c.*

the writer's thoughts is the depressed condition of the faithful at Jerusalem (cf. lxi. 1, lxvi. 2). The ideas of II. Isaiah have therefore been modified by him to suit the times. That great teacher assures us (xlii. 3) that the prophets of the true religion will comfort the sorrowful and be gentle to "bruised reeds" (xli. 1, xlii. 3). But this new writer recognises no genuine Israelites who are not crushed in body and mind by trouble. He cannot fix his hopes on any "Servant of Yahwè"; only Yahwè himself can revive the failing spirit of Israel. And the reason which he gives (lvii. 16) for his expectation of the divine mercy is not that which we find in II. Isaiah, viz. that Yahwè has called or chosen Israel, and cannot be untrue to his word, but that, being the Creator, he cannot and will not punish weak man too severely (cf. Ps. lxxviii. 39, xc. 5-12, ciii. 9, 13-16). We may indeed find the germ of lvii. 16 in xlii. 5,—

> Who giveth breath to the folk upon it, and spirit to those who walk thereon,

but the Second Isaiah follows up these fine expressions with the assurance that Israel has received special privileges from Yahwè. The new writer, for the present at least, appeals not to God's lovingkindness (חסד) but to his compassion (רחמים). The emphasis in *v.* 17 on the sin of covetousness is remarkable. Duhm sees an allusion to facts like those described in Neh. v. ; but בִּצְעוֹ is probably corrupt (*RT*). It should be added that lvii. 13*b*-21 contains nothing like a definite reference to the Samaritans ; רְשָׁעִים in *vv.* 20-21 is the ordinary expression (see Psalms) for the lawless party among the Jews. The close point of contact with Daniel in *v.* 19, and the two seemingly very late words in *v.* 20 suggest perhaps an even later date than the age of Nehemiah and Ezra.

CHAPTER LVIII.

This and the next chapter are treated by Ewald as a single prophecy of five strophes. It would be more natural to regard them as a pair of related prophecies, written at nearly the same time; only we must first of all be sure that they are not of composite origin. That lviii. 13, 14 is a later addition was long ago pointed out by Koppe. The duty of the Sabbath-rest has no proper connection with the duty of performing works of mercy. The passage reminds us of lvi. 2, 4, 6 (the only other passage in chaps. xl.-lxvi. in which the Sabbath is referred to), and gives a full description of what may be meant in lvi. 2 by "profaning" that holy day. The extreme to which respect for the Sabbath (which is even personified as קְדוֹשׁ יהוה [1]) is carried, equally favours a late date, and the forced character of the expressions and the reminiscences in v. 14, of Job xxii. 26, and Deut. xxxii. 13 [2] (both post-Exilic), makes it difficult to defend an earlier date than the age of Nehemiah. Need the preceding composition be as late?—or rather, do the social circumstances presupposed, the ideas, and the phraseology justify us in placing it much earlier? Let us first examine the evidence.

1. *Circumstances and ideas.*—The prophecy in lviii. 1-12 is addressed to a people which is not detained by force in a foreign country, but dwells in the land of its fathers. In other words, a number of the exiles have returned from Babylon, but they are not numerous enough to rebuild the "ancient ruins," nor is their condition such as corresponds to the character of Yahwè's faithful servants. Their uppermost thought, therefore, is how to obtain such legal righteousness as will ensure the fulfilment of the promises. The prophetic discourse starts (like several of the sections of "Malachi") from a question of the Jews who, unlike the persons referred to in lxv. 1, display great inquisitiveness respecting the divine will. "Me indeed they consult daily, and to know my ways is their delight, as a nation that hath done righteousness, and hath not forsaken the law of its God! They ask me concerning ordinances of righteousness" (*i.e.* the ordinances which will produce righteousness), v. 2. Nor does the prophet deny that the Jews are equally assiduous in observing the prescribed forms of worship. How often has he noticed

---

[1] This goes beyond Neh. ix. 14, Ex. xvi. 23 (P).

[2] The idea conveyed in "riding over the heights of the land" is more briefly expressed in יוֹרֵשׁ הָרֵי, lxv. 9.

CHAPTER LVIII.

them on a fast-day "drooping the head like a bulrush" (in the manner of Eastern devotees), and murmuring their prayer-formulæ.[1] Hence he adds (in *v*. 2), "to draw nigh to God is their delight." But he has also noticed how, in the intervals of the public litanies, these well-instructed formalists greedily seize on worldly "business," in which they are far from "despising the gain of oppressions" (xxxiii. 15, post-Exilic). Quarrels, too, are, naturally enough, of frequent occurrence, and the worst cause is supported by the heaviest blows. Meantime, many a brother-Jew is languishing in a debtor's prison or in slavery, or begs his bread as a homeless wanderer (*vv*. 3-7), for the quickest way for a rich man to become richer is to lend money at a ruinous rate of interest (cf. on Ps. xv. 5). No wonder that the Messianic promises remain unfulfilled; "righteousness" must be understood in a far deeper sense before the "light" of the new Jerusalem can dawn (*v*. 8, cf. lix. 9, lx. 1-3).

2. *Style and phraseology.*—How unlike is the style to that of II. Isaiah! *V*. 1 opens in the old prophetic manner; cf. Hos. viii. 1; Mic. iii. 8 (especially). "House of Jacob," as xlvi. 3, xlviii. 1. But at *v*. 2 the writer passes at once into the quiet, expostulating style of Malachi.— *V*. 2, י׳ דרש, as lv. 6. עשׂה צדקה, as lvi. 1. משׁפטים here only in chaps. xl.-lxvi.; often in Ezek., and fifteen times in Ps. cxix. The Second Isaiah had certainly a simpler conception of the *mishpat* of Yahwè (xlii. 1). קרבת אלֹ֗ and (*v*. 3) ענה נפשׁ, see above. חפץ "business"; so in plur., *v*. 13 (a late sense; see p. 263). עצב (plur.), ἅπ. λεγ.—*Vv*. 4-10, יצע, כפף, מצה, נגה, הפיק, ארכה, מרודים, פרס, מוטה, אגדה, התיר, חרצבות,

---

[1] קרבת אלהים (so Ps. lxxiii. 28). The usual modern rendering "the approach of God" (*i.e.* His advent as Judge, cf. Mal. ii. 17, iii. 1), adopted in *PI*, must, I think, be abandoned in favour of that of Sept., Pesh., Targ., Vulg.; cf. G. A. Smith, *Exposition*, p. 147. Ἐγγίζειν θεῷ suits the verb חפץ best, and is more in accordance with usage. קרב is the word used of sacred ministrations (Lev. xvi. 1, 1 Sam. xiv. 36), and also specially of prayer (1 Ki. xviii. 36; Ps. *l.c.*, and perhaps Zeph. iii. 2). In the post-Exilic period, [prayer in the sanctuary was the chief means of "drawing near" to God (see lvi. 7, and cf. Ps. cxix. 169, "Let my cry come near before thee"). There is a parallel development in Assyrian; *ikribu* = prayer. Cf. קרובות, the name for certain extraordinary prayers in the Jewish service. See Feuchtzwang, *Zt. f. Ass.* 1887, p. 340.

see list of late or rare words, pp. 260-270; all these words point away from II. Isaiah. In v. 8b there are allusions to lii. 12, lx. 1, and in v. 10b (less distinctly) to Job xi. 17. But note that "righteousness" in v. 8b means probably inward, personal righteousness; had "thy righteousness" taken the place of "Yahwè" in lii. 12, it would certainly have meant "thy outward justification," i.e. "thy prosperity." V. 10, חֹשֶׁךְ and אֲפֵלָה as Joel ii. 2; cf. also lix. 9. V. 11, Yahwè's leadership, as lvii. 18. צִחְצָחוֹת only here; cf. צְחִיחִים, Neh. iv. 7, עֲצָמְתְךָ יַחֲלִיף. Secker and Lowth had no thought of helping the higher criticism. But either as a whole or (see PI) in part this correction *must* be accepted; the writer was thinking of xl. 29, 31 (or at least of xl. 31). "As a well-watered garden"; so Jer. xxxi. 12 (post-Exilic? see Giesebrecht).—V. 12, May we follow Weir (see PI), and read וּבָנוּ בָנֶיךָ? If so, the writer may remember liv. 13, where בָּנַיִךְ and בָּנָיִךְ stand, according to Duhm's excellent correction, in close proximity. חרבות reminds us of xliv. 26, עולם (if the prophecy be taken as Exilic) of xlii. 14; but מוֹסְדֵי דוֹר וָדוֹר, if statistics may be trusted, has a very post-Exilic appearance (pp. 73, 260, 264). קוֹמֵם comes from xliv. 26 (p. 267). The whole passage, which, if put late, gains in force, has a close parallel in lxi. 4a. קֹרָא (Pual) only occurs in chaps. xl.-lxvi. (6 times) and in Ezekiel (once). גֹּדֵר פֶּרֶץ, Israel's new name, reminds us of the post-Exilic passage on Israel's regeneration appended to Amos[1] (Am.ix. 8-15), where not only does the same phrase occur (v. 11), but as a parallel to פְּרָצֶיהָ we find הֲרִסֹתָיו, which suggests a necessary correction of the troublesome נְתִיבוֹת in lviii. 12 (נְתִיצוֹת; see RT).

The right inferences cannot be doubtful. (1) Not only a pre-Exilic, but an early Exilic date, such as Ewald proposes, for chaps. lviii.-lix. is excluded. We grant the parallelism between lviii. 6-7 and Ezek. xviii. 7-8, but this only proves the influence of Ezekiel, which is plainly traceable in other probably or certainly post-Exilic passages (*e.g.* ch. lvii.), and the observance of the Sabbath is urged in lviii. 13-14 in terms which presuppose an advance in strictness beyond the

---

[1] Am. ix. 8-15 was probably substituted by the editor of Amos for a genuine but too painful passage. See Wellhausen, *Die kl. Proph.*, p. 94; Smend, *AT Rel.-gesch.*, p. 183 f.; Schwally, *ZATW*, x. 227.

requirements of the great prophet of the Exile. (2) A very late Exilic date (Dillm.; G. A. Smith) for these chapters is even more inadmissible.[1] How unlike is this writer with his loud, imperious manner (contrast v. 1 with xlii. 2) to the author of chaps. xl.-lv.! And what reason have we to suppose that the exiles in Babylon formed such a highly organised community as we meet with here, or that their state of mind was such as is here described? Clearly, some of the exiles have already returned (see above), and formed, or joined with the remnant of the old nation in forming, a civic community. The most illustrative passage (Zech. vii. 1-14) is early post-Exilic. We there find Zechariah consulted on the question of the retention or abolition of the special fast-days, and replying that, if the Jews will but obey the constant command of God by the "former prophets," the hoped for turn in their fortunes will arrive, and the fasts become days of "joy and gladness." The "former prophets" are, of course, the prophets of the earlier period, from Amos to Jeremiah. For to suppose with Renan[2] that Zechariah specially refers to this very chapter (lviii.), which must, therefore, be pre-Exilic, would be arbitrary in the extreme. And does not the description of the impoverished Jews in vv. 6, 7 remind us of Neh. v. 1-13 (comp. e.g. "thine own flesh," v. 7, with the opening words of Neh. v. 5), and the exhortation to "break bread to the hungry" of the noble example set by Nehemiah (Neh. v. 17)? The view of fasting, too, recalls the importance attached to a public fast in Joel, and the explanation of a fast as "a day when a man humbleth his soul" (v. 5 ; cf. v. 3) reminds us of passages in the Levitical legislation (e.g. Lev. xvi. 29, 31), though we have not yet reached the latest and shortest technical term for fasting, תַּעֲנִית "humiliation," which is found in Ezra ix. 5. So too the statement that the formalists addressed "seize on business" and "drive all their workmen" (Jewish as well as Gentile), even on the fast-day, suggests that the writer, like Zechariah, is not yet

---

[1] Dillm. is of opinion that in lviii. 3-8 the writer was influenced by earlier moral descriptions (e.g. Ezekiel's), but that, on the whole, he gives us a criticism of the moral condition of the exiles. Against the latter part of his theory, I venture to refer to my review of Prof. G. A. Smith's *Exposition* (Part II.) in the *Expositor*, 1891 (1), p. 156.

[2] *Histoire*, iii. 475, note 2.

acquainted with the law of the Day of Atonement in P.[1] Note in conclusion that the expression "ancient ruins" (v. 12) is more forcible in the age of Nehemiah than in that of II. Isaiah. Indeed, the new name given to the community in v. 12 seems specially applicable to those who were "stopping up the breaches" in the wall at Nehemiah's instance, and the "darkness" and "obscurity" spoken of in v. 10 may well be the despondency caused by the design of the Samaritans and their allies "to come and attack Jerusalem, and to cause confusion there" (Neh. iv. 1, 2 = A.V. 7, 8). For every single detail we can find an illustration in the post-Exilic writings, especially in Nehemiah, where we even find the rare word אֲרוּכָה, which in lviii. 8 has the general sense of recovered prosperity, applied with special reference to the restoration of the walls (Neh. iv. 1). And this sort of "recovery" was certainly in the foreground of the writer's thoughts, for he closes his work with a reference to it (v. 12). Still, not to be too precise, let us date the prophecy between 450 and 444 (the latter year, that of the rebuilding of the walls), and put the appendix soon after the return of Nehemiah in 432 (Neh. xiii. 15, etc.). We cannot say whether the same writer produced lvi. 1-8 and lviii.-lix. 1-15a, but it is not impossible. There is some affinity between them.

CHAPTER LIX

"This chapter continues the subject of chap. lviii. With all their observance of the outward forms of religion, the prophet's contemporaries are guilty of open violations of the moral law (vv. 1-8). But soon the prophet assumes that his admonitions have borne fruit. The Jews penitently confess their sins, and their breach of the covenant with [Yahwè]; they lament their unhappy state, and own that they have no claim upon their God for assistance (vv. 9-15a). Then follows a splendid theophany. As there is no other cham-

---

[1] See Lev. xvi. 29. Some Jewish scholars have supposed the discourse to have been delivered on the Day of Atonement (Sachs, *Kerem Chemed*, vii. 124 ff.; Hoffmann, in Berliner's *Magazin*, 1876, p. 5 f.), and have even urged this in defence of Isaiah's authorship.

pion [Yahwè] interposes. The last verse communicates a special word of promise to the true Israel."[1] If this summary of contents is correct, two things are at once clear, (1) that this chapter, or part of it, is probably contemporaneous (or nearly so) with the preceding one, and (2) that it is very badly put together.

Let us first of all consider the question of the unity of the passage. So much is clear at the outset, that *vv.* 5-8 both interrupt and obscure the context. The two preceding verses bring a definite charge against the Jews, viz. the commission of gross acts of injustice both in private and in public life, and *v.* 9 says that in consequence of the sins which have been mentioned God still permits the Jews to be under a foreign yoke. Later on, in *vv.* 13-14, the principal sins of the people are once more summed up, and they turn out to be the same of which we have already heard in *vv.* 3-4, with the addition of the sin of "apostasy and denial of Yahwè," which however is in reality only a general and more directly religious expression for the moral aberrations of the people. Now, considering the fondness of the post-Exilic Jews for proverbial composition, and the Septuagint insertions in Proverbs, is it not very probable that *vv.* 5-8 were inserted by an early editor? May they not be a quotation from some favourite book of moral teaching, or, as Duhm suggests (cf. Ps. xiv. in Sept.), from some very late psalm? It is noteworthy that *v. 7a* has been inserted in the Massoretic text of Prov. i. (though not found in Sept.), where it stands as *v.* 16, to the great detriment of the connection and the interruption of the metre. We have no reason in either case to ascribe the insertion to the author of the work which has received the quotation.[2] At any rate, the writer of chap. lviii. would have felt the exaggeration of the language of *vv.* 5-8 when applied to the leading members of the Jewish community. There is, in short, an internal discord between the latter passage and its context.

[1] *PI*, ii. 81.
[2] The insertion in Proverbs *l.c.* was clearly suggested by the words רַע and נְתִיבוֹת, and that in Isa. lix. by the gloomy tone and proverbial style of the last stichos of *v.* 4. In Ps. xiv. Sept., where bits of Isa. lix. 7, 8 enter into the great interpolation, the insertion was in a high degree natural.

This remark, if correct, is of considerable importance. It can hardly be denied that, though *v.* 9 connects much better with *v.* 4 than with *v.* 8, the transition from *v.* 4 to *v.* 9 is somewhat abrupt. In *vv.* 1-4 the prophet stands apart as a moral censor, but from *v.* 9 onwards he unites himself (in the manner of Ezra in Ezra ix.) to the guilty members of the community. But we may not simply on that account assert that *vv.* 1-4 and *vv.* 9-15*a* come from different writers. We must be on our guard against plainly unnecessary disintegration, and remember that the later writers (if such there were) in chaps. xl.-lxvi. were presumably not the equals of the Second Isaiah in literary skill. The case is different when we come to *vv.* 15*b*-21 (or 20). Surely the description of the theophany and its glorious consequences takes off the edge of the preceding denunciation as much as the somewhat parallel picture in xxx. 27-33 weakens the effect of xxx. 1-17. A sense of this seems to underlie Duhm's too bold emendation of *v.* 20. The text, as it stands, conveys this meaning :—

And for Zion there cometh a redeemer, and for them that turn from rebellion in Jacob.

But Duhm[1] transforms it thus :—

And from Zion shall come the redeemer, and put away rebellion from Jacob.

Of course, he also renders מִשְׁפָּט in *v.* 15 "(public) justice," but this is neither suitable to the context nor to the parallel passage in lxiii. 5. A natural exegesis seems to me only possible if we recognise that *vv.* 15*b*-21 (or 20) in part, and lxiii. 1-6 altogether, are visions of the deliverance from foes without and false brethren within, which was to usher in the Messianic felicity (cf. chaps. xxxiii., lxvi.). But we must, I think, agree with Duhm that the closing words of *v.* 18 are an incorrect gloss, and should be excised. There is no reason why the far-off coast-lands should be specified as the foes of Yahwè. The enemies whose overthrow the writer foresees are (if his work is post-Exilic) the Persians, and also

[1] Relying on the Greek renderings of Sept. and Rom. xi. 26. See however i. 27 (post-Exilic).

the Samaritans, and the aristocratic party among the Jews which favoured their pretensions. We must suppose, then, that lix. 1-15*a* and *vv.* 15*b*-21 (or 20) are two incomplete works, one of which lacked its close, and the other its commencement, and which were fitted together by an editor. This editor may perhaps have interpreted *vv.* 15*b* and 16*a* in the sense suggested by Ezek. xxii. 30 ; Jer. v. 1.

The only other passage which may possibly or even probably be a later insertion is *v.* 21. But before considering this, we must examine the circumstances, ideas, and phraseology of both the earlier sections.

I. *Vv.* 1-15*a*. 1. *Circumstances and ideas.*—The social circumstances agree with those described in chap. lviii., though the vehemence of the prophetic orator (for such he professes to be) has become greater. It is as if the calamities of the time had increased, and the prophet accounted to himself for this by assuming an increase of guilt (cf. lxiii. 17, lxiv. 4, 5 [1]). His description of the prevalent immorality may therefore be somewhat exaggerated, but the basis of fact which we cannot help recognising is in harmony with the theory of a post-Exilic date. Thus, according to the prophet, murder was of common occurrence, and certainly we have no reason to suppose that this besetting sin of passionate natures was eradicated by the discipline of the Exile (cf. Ecclus. xi. 32, xii. 13). Not to dwell now on lvii. 1, there is a post-Exilic passage in the first part of Isaiah which says that only a special divine energy could wash out the blood-stains of Jerusalem (iv. 4 ; see p. 22), and in a post-Exilic psalm Israel personified prays to be delivered from bloodguiltiness (Ps. li. 16 ; cf. Ps. lix. 3, cxxxix. 19). The commission of murder by a rich man was too easily condoned by the judges, says the post-Exilic writer of Mic. vii. 2, 3, and so our prophet tells us that judicial proceedings have become utter distortions of justice. The phraseology of lix. 4 reminds us, too, of that of xxix. 21 (post-Exilic), and the description in *v.* 14 of a striking passage in an obviously late psalm, which closes thus—

Oppression and fraud withdraw not from its public place (Ps. lv. 12).

---

[1] Here, however, the idea is not quite the same (*BL*, p. 357).

Indeed, as I have remarked elsewhere,[1] the moral scenery of Isa. lix. recalls that of Psalms lii.-lix., which cannot be adequately explained by any pre-Exilic or Exilic circumstances.

I have ventured to suspect that there may be some exaggeration. This is surely a not unnatural inference from the confessions in *vv.* 9-15*a*; there is perhaps an even greater exaggeration in a later liturgical confession (lxiv. 6, 7). Those who could say with sincerity, "We are conscious of our transgressions, and as for our iniquities we know them" (*v.* 12), were very unlike the heartless formalists described in lix. 2-4, lviii. 2-4. There is however a strange omission in their confession which helps to confirm a post-Exilic date. Ewald has already compared *v.* 12 with Ps. li. 5 (A.V. 3), but the confession in chap. lviii. differs from Ps. li. in some important respects. It contains, that is, no appeal to Yahwè's covenant love, no petition for a cleansing better than that of hyssop, no vow of self-devotion to God's service. Such an omission would hardly have been made by the Second Isaiah. All that we can urge in arrest of judgment is (1) that the composition is probably fragmentary, and that it may originally have contained at least such an appeal to the Father and Redeemer of Israel as occurs in lxiii. 16, lxiv. 9 (8), and (2) that the national distress when chap. lix. was written seems to have been greater than that of the Second Isaiah and his companions. The trouble was indeed so great that God seemed to have hidden His face from His people (see below), and many said in their hearts, "It is vain to serve God, he destroyeth the perfect and the wicked" (Mal. iii. 14; Job ix. 22), which came perilously near to atheism (כחש ביהוה), and led some to open contempt for law. Certainly a post-Exilic phenomenon.[1]

2. *Phraseology.*—Notice first the lax construction in *v.* 2, "your sins have caused the face to be hidden from you." On the analogy of liii. 3, this might mean, "your sins have caused men to hide the face from you." But the writer probably has in his mind a current saying of the Jews, "Yahwè hath hid the face from us" (see Job xxxiv. 29 and cf. Ps.

[1] *BL*, p. 123.

xliv. 25, lxxxviii. 15), and puts פָּנִים instead of פָּנָיו.[1] The Second Isaiah would surely have been more careful. Nor is it likely that this writer would have used the somewhat heavy phrase הָיוּ מַבְדִּילִים, which reminds us of Gen. i. 6 (see p. 198 f.), and though not necessarily an allusion to that passage must at any rate belong to the same linguistic period with it. בָּדַל itself is a suspicious word (p. 261); it seems to belong to a later linguistic stage, or at any rate to a different circle from that of the undoubted II. Isaiah. The same remark applies to נגאל "to be defiled," גשש "to grope," הגה "to utter" (see p. 262), to the Hifil form הוֹלִיד (especially when used carelessly, as here, for יָלַד; see p. 259); and to the strange expression מִשְׁתּוֹלֵל, v. 15, which (if the reading be correct) must be an allusion to Ps. lxxvi. 6a, for how otherwise should such an expression have been thought of?[2] דִּבֶּר־סָרָה, v. 13, is also scarcely II. Isaiah's. סוּר in a moral or religious sense never occurs in chaps. xl.-lv.; the phrase is borrowed from Jer. xxviii. 16, xxix. 32, Deut. xii. 16, where however it refers to the teaching of the false prophets. (From Jeremiah, too, comes כַּחֵשׁ בַּיהוה, v. 13, cf. Jer. v. 12, though the practical atheism spoken of takes a different form in each writer). On the other hand, we have II. Isaiah's favourite form הֵן (see p. 258), and can here and there recognise parallelisms to chaps. xl.-lv. Compare e.g. lix. 1 (the "shortened hand") with l. 2; v. 7 (שֹׁד וָשֶׁבֶר) with li. 19; v. 9 (מִשְׁפָּט and צְדָקָה) with xl. 27, xlvi. 13; also (words for light and darkness) with l. 10 (on the intensive plurals, see p. 258); v. 15 (נֶעְדָּרֶת) with xl. 26. תֹּהוּ, v. 4, is such a favourite post-Exilic word (p. 253), that we can hardly quote it in favour of II. Isaiah's authorship.

[1] My former view (PI, ii. 82), viz. that פָּנִים is used technically for the Face of God (cf. הַשֵּׁם, שֵׁם, Lev. xxiv. 11, 16), though adopted by Duhm, seems too hazardous. There is no evidence elsewhere for such a use; in lxiii. 9 we find "his face."

[2] Even apart from the Ethpoel in v. 6, Ps. lxxvi. is clearly post-Exilic. See BL, pp. 165, 478; Nowack-Hupfeld, Psalmen, ii. 243; Beer, Indiv. und Gemeindepsalmen, p. xlvi. But in Isa. lix. 15 we should rather read with Klost. מִשְׁתַּפֵּל, and render thus, "So that truth hath become missing (from the civic register), and one that avoideth evil giveth himself out (or putteth himself down, viz. in the register) as childless," a fantastic way of saying that the race of good men and true has died out (BW).

Among the parallelisms to other writings, compare *v.* 10 with Zeph. i. 17, and esp. Deut. xxviii. 29 (Exilic); *v.* 12 with Ps. xc. 8, li. 5; and *vv.* 14 (Truth and Righteousness) with xxxii. 16, Ps. lxxxv. 11, 12, 14. Lastly, with regard to the insertion (*vv.* 5-8), note in *v.* 5 the rare use of נבקע "to come out of an egg" (p. 261); in *vv.* 7-8 the four words for "way," all found in Proverbs; and in *v.* 8 the use of עקשׁ, cf. Prov. x. 9, xxviii. 18, ii. 15.

II. *Vv.* 15*b*-20. 1. *Circumstances and ideas.*—According to our theory, this fine fragment is half-vision, half-prophecy. The perfects in *vv.* 15*b*-17 belong to the vision; the imperfects in *vv.* 18-20 to the prophecy. The common subject of both is the great final destruction of the foes of Yahwè and of Israel. As to the circumstances of the Jews when the passage was written, no direct information is given us. So much at least, however, is clear—that the Jews (or some of them) have returned to "Zion" (*v.* 20), but that they still complain of oppression, and that there is no human helper, no Cyrus, on the horizon. It may also be inferred from *v.* 20 that religious reforms are fervently hoped for, or even that they are already in course of being effected. The ideas of the passage are most certainly those of the post-Exilic period; the brief description of the judgment and its consequences may be filled up or illustrated from other passages. From the companion passage we learn that the foes of Yahwè are the "peoples" of the world, none of whom have placed themselves on the side of Israel's God (lxiii. 3); and from lx. 3, Ps. cii. 15, 16, that it is not the awful glory of the destruction of the foes, but the bright radiance of the new Jerusalem which attracts the gaze of the nations (*i.e.* of those outside the circle of the hostile peoples, cf. lxvi. 19). And the brief reference in *v.* 20 to the connection between moral amendment and external redemption is illustrated by lviii. 6-12; Zech. viii. 16-19. Our passage differs, it is true, from some parallel passages (see especially lvi. 9-lvii. 13*a*, and cf. the gloss in i. 27, 28) in the absence of any direct mention of the punishment of unfaithful Jews, but there is at any rate an indirect allusion to this in the words "unto them that have turned from rebellion in Jacob" (*v.* 20).

CHAPTER LIX

2. *Phraseology.*—The following words are adverse to the authorship of II. Isaiah: יִשְׁתּוֹמֵם (*v.* 16), עָטָה Hif. (*v.* 17), בְּעַל and גְּמוּלוֹת (*v.* 18), נְסָכָה (*v.* 19). On the former, see pp. 268, 258, 261. The last is ἅπ. λεγ.; cf. נוּם in Ps. cxiv. 3 = "to be driven in a new direction." Note also the defining use of ן in *v.* 20, as with a similar reference in lvii. 18. No stress need be laid either on the ἅπ. λεγ. תִּלְבֹּשֶׁת, *v.* 17, though post-Biblical in form (see Del.), or on מָצֹר, which should perhaps be read instead of צָר in *v.* 19, for the former may be corrupt, and the latter is only a highly probable conjecture.[1] Points of contact with the undoubted II. Isaiah are, of course, not wanting. In *v.* 16 מַפְגִּיעַ reminds us of liii. 6, 12 (Hif. perf. and imperf., but in different senses). See also xlii. 13 (Yahwè, a warrior), li. 9 and lii. 10 (Yahwè's arm), xliii. 5 and xlv. 6 (east and west), xl. 7 (breath of Yahwè), xli. 14 ("Redeemer"), xli. 14, etc. (נְאֻם י״י). But cf. also *v.* 16 with lxiii. 5; *v.* 20 ("Redeemer") with lxiii. 4; *v.* 16 (Yahwè's arm) with lxiii. 12; *v.* 18 with lxvi. 6; *v.* 19 with Ps. cii. 15, and especially with Isa. xxx. 27, 28 (see p. 199), also ("name of Yahwè") with lxiv. 1, and ("see . . . his glory") lxvi. 18.

Surely the right inference from these facts is clear. To assert with Bredenkamp and C. H. H. Wright[2] that the imagery, literary allusions, and social circumstances conclusively prove a pre-Exilic date, and favour the authorship of Isaiah, or of a disciple of Isaiah, implies a superficial study of the evidence, and in particular assumes a correctness of morals among the post-Exilic Jews which is both improbable in itself and at variance with other critical results. The only possible date is a post-Exilic one. The affinity between chaps. lviii. and lix. 1-15*a* forbids us to separate

---

[1] See *RT*. If, with Klost., we read כִּנְהַר מָצֹר, *v.* 19*b* will run thus:—
"For he cometh like the river of Egypt, when Yahwè's breath driveth it on." The "overflowing torrent" of xxx. 28 (in the passage which is imitated) becomes the Nile, to suggest thoughts of joy and confidence (cf. lxvi. 12). The overflow of the Nile is also referred to in Am. viii. 8, ix. 5, Jer. xlvi. 7 (the two latter passages are late). On the late form מָצֹר, see p. 111, and cf. *RT* on lix. 19.

[2] Bred. *Jesaia*, pp. 227, 333; Wright, art. "Isaiah," Smith's *DB*,[2] vol. i. part 2, p. 472. Both scholars agree in holding that Isaiah's authorship is clearer in the case of chap. lix. than in that of chap. lviii.

them by too long an interval. Possibly the Samaritans had gone to a greater length in their outrages when the latter passage was written. The vision and prophecy of deliverance, and also presumably the companion-passage lxiii. 1-6, may most naturally be dated in 432, if this is the year in which those who had "turned from transgression in Jacob" formed themselves into a *ḳāhāl* or religious community (Neh. ix., x.).[1]

The abruptness of the transition in *v.* 21 justifies us in regarding this verse as a later insertion. At any rate it was written most probably after the publication of P by Ezra, for its opening words, אתם [2] ואני זאת בריתי, can hardly help being an allusion to Gen. xvii. 4 (cf. ix. 9). It contains virtually a declaration that the קָהָל, the true Zion, which has now come into existence (Neh. ix., x.), is the Servant of Yahwè spoken of in xlii. 1, xlix. 1-3.[3] The "spirit" is the "good spirit" which God has given to "instruct" His people (Neh. ix. 20), and to bring "wondrous things out of His law" (Ps. cxix. 18). And the "words" are those of the law (cf. lxvi. 2, 5), in which the good man is to "meditate day and night" (Ps. i. 2), and the study of which is the pledge of the permanence of the church-nation (Ps. cxix. 92). How Klostermann can suppose that the author of *v.* 21 is a disciple of Isaiah who has assumed his master's mantle,[4] it is difficult to see. No old writer could have had these ideas or expressed them so badly. Much more reasonable (though incorrect) is the view of Ewald that this verse was written by II. Isaiah to connect the inserted passage (lviii.-lix.) with the prophecy of the Servant of Yahwè.

CHAPTER LX

Ewald's view of chaps. lx.-lxiii. has been already men-

---

[1] See Kosters, *Het Herstel*, etc., pp. 98-102.
[2] The right Mas. reading is אֹתָם (see Baer's ed.), which may be a mistake for אִתָּם (Klost.). At any rate, no safe argument for a late date can be based upon it.
[3] Chap. li. 16, however, in spite of one parallelism, is later than our passage (see p. 303).
[4] *Zt. f. luther. Theol.*, 1876, p. 46.

CHAPTER LX

tioned (p. 286). Chap. lx. he regards as the close of Book II. of the Second Isaiah's main prophecy, and lxi. 1-lxiii. 6 as a first appendix, in which chaps. lxi.-lxii. are the work of that great writer himself, and lxiii. 1-6 is an inserted passage, by the author of lviii. 1-lix. 20. How much of this theory is correct? So much at least is clear, that chaps. lx. and lxi. are not continuous, and that on the analogy of chap. xlvii. we may fairly assume chap. lx. to be at least a provisional close of something that has gone before. But we are not bound to suppose that the song upon glorified Zion was originally intended to follow chaps. lviii.-lix., which, having regard to the contents of those chapters, is extremely improbable. It is also clear that if chaps. lxi.-lxii. are II. Isaiah's work, they must be an appendix to his main work, for, as Ewald remarks, "we see nothing essentially new in this passage," though when he continues, "nor is any progress observable in the development of events," we must take the liberty of questioning this. What we have to inquire therefore is, (1) Are chaps. lx.-lxii. by II. Isaiah?—and (2) Even if not by that writer, is it probable that they stand in some special relation to the Prophecy of Restoration (chaps. xl.-lv.)? To lxiii. 1-6 I need not at present refer, beyond reminding the reader that we have found strong reason to suspect the date to be post-Exilic.

Let us first of all study chap. lx. It is a song upon glorified Zion in ten stanzas of four double lines each. A few interpolations indeed mar the symmetry of the lines (see *vv.* 6, 12, 14, 17 in *BW*), but only one of these is of much importance, viz. the second. *V.* 12 is altogether intrusive, and may be based on Zech. xiv. 16-19; its unrhythmical, prosaic character is obvious (see further, p. 344). Twice, according to Budde, the author adopts the Kîna or elegiac rhythm [1] (viz. in *vv.* 14-15 and 17*b*-20), but it is doubtful whether he had any such intention. 1. As to the *circumstances* implied, several striking points justify the suspicion of a late date. The poet speaks as if he were a resident in Jerusalem. Of late the holy city has been cut off from the rest of the world (*v.* 15), poverty-stricken (cf. xxiii. 18), ill-governed (cf.

[1] *ZATW*, 1891, p. 241 (the theory involves excising an important word in *v.* 14 : see below).

lviii. 4), and ill-defended (*vv.* 16-18). Its population has been small (*v.* 4), and its walls and gates have yet to be rebuilt (*vv.* 10-11). The temple indeed has already risen from its ashes, for the "proleptic" theory of Dillmann is most unreasonable, but it is altogether unworthy of its object, and sorely needs expansion and beautification, while the dignity of the sacrificial rites requires a far larger supply of victims (*vv.* 7, 13). But the present misery will shortly disappear. The exuberance of the writer's anticipations shows on the one hand that the existing distress is deep, and on the other that a gleam of hope has visited the minds of pious patriots.

2. *Ideas.*—The leading idea is that, though the temple has been rebuilt, Yahwè has not yet, in any satisfying sense of the word, "come to his temple," his presence is still unfelt, his glory unseen (Zech. ii. 10, Mal. iii. 1). But, when the time has fully come, there will be a great change. The nations have been hitherto in the light, the Jews in the darkness (cf. lviii. 10, lix. 9); now the Jews are to enjoy a light such as man has never yet seen, while the nations are in thick darkness, from which they can only escape by voluntarily enslaving themselves to the Jews. Nothing is said of a Messianic king; as another writer says, "Yahwè is our judge, our marshal, our king; he will deliver us" (xxxiii. 22). Not the royal palace, therefore, but the temple is the goal of the tribute-bearing companies, and presumably the store-chambers of the temple (like those of the temple of Amen at the Egyptian Thebes) are to receive the newly acquired treasures (cf. xxiii. 18, p. 139). Nothing too is said of a yearning of the nations for moral instruction (xlii. 4, end; the supposed allusion to this in lx. 9 is based on a corruption of the text), nor of attempts of the Jews to raise their new subjects to a higher spiritual level (xlii. 1). The only gentle thought which the writer expresses is that the nations will of their own accord bring the scattered Israelites home to Canaan—to a glorified Canaan (*v.* 19), and vie with each other in offering their richest gifts—" their kings leading the train "[1] (*v.* 11). The great idea of the moral regeneration of Israel is barely touched upon (*vv.* 18*a*, 21*a*); it would

[1] Read with Duhm נְהוּגִים.

CHAPTER LX

appear as if Israel had many privileges, but few important duties except that of keeping up the temple services (*vv.* 7, 9). The most ardent love is lavished upon Zion; to be friendly to Israel is to love Jerusalem (cf. lxvi. 10), and the writer even coins this strange phrase as an honorific appellation of the capital—"the Zion of the Holy One of Israel." In *v.* 19 there seems to be an allusion to the hope of "new heavens," fully expressed in lxv. 17.

3. *Style and phraseology.*—The style is poor, and contrasts painfully with that of chap. xlvii. The arrangement is laboured; and there is a great want of variety in the expressions (see *vv.* 7, 10, 13, 16, 19, 21); even the sense is not always clear. The images are wanting in originality. Once however (lx. 8, 9) there is a happy development or adaptation of a figure in Hos. xi. 11, and the genuineness of the feeling makes up for the poverty of the style, except where the moral sense of the reader protests.—Points of contact both with chaps. xl.-lv. and with other late parts of Isaiah abound. The image of the prostrate woman (*v.* 1) reminds us of li. 17, lii. 2; and the phrase "the glory of Yahwè" of xl. 5 (p. 298). Cf. also *v.* 3 (the surprise of the kings), xlix. 7, 23; lii. 15;—*v.* 4, xlix. 18, 22, xxi. 12, lxvi. 20;—*v.* 6 (end), xlii. 10-12;—*v.* 7 (Kedar), xlii. 11;—*vv.* 9, 10, xiv. 2;—*v.* 9*b*,[1] lv. 5*b*;—*v.* 10*b*, liv. 7, 8;—*v.* 11 (פְּתִחוּ), xlviii. 8 (?);—*v.* 13, xli. 19*b*, lv. 13, where, however, the trees of Lebanon serve a very different purpose from that indicated in the Song;[2]—*v.* 16*a*, xlix. 23;—*v.* 16*b*, xlix. 26*b*;—*v.* 18, שֹׁד וָשֶׁבֶר, as lix. 7, from li. 19;—*v.* 21, liv. 13, cf. xxvi. 2; also lvii. 13; and note לְהִתְפָּאֵר, as lxi. 3, from xliv. 23, xlix. 33. Also *v.* 13 ("glory of Lebanon"), xxxv.

---

[1] *V.* 9*a* suggests a comparison with xlii. 4, li. 5. But we should rather read יְקַוּ צִיִּים, with Duhm, supplementing a conjecture of Luzzatto (*PI*, ii. 90). יְקַוּ is not indeed happily chosen for the context, but the writer is a copyist.

[2] In lx. 13 the meaning probably is that the timber derived from Lebanon shall be used in the buildings of Jerusalem, especially the temple. "The place of my sanctuary" = "the whole place of Mount Zion" (*i.e.* Jerusalem) in iv. 5. The rival view (Dillm.) that the city, especially the approaches of the temple, are to be planted with beautiful trees, is less in harmony with the spirit of the poem. The strange statement in *v.* 17, line 2, is probably an interpolation; it contradicts lvi. 11, 12.

2 ;—v. 18b, xxvi. 1 ;—v. 19, xxiv. 23, iv. 5, xxx. 26 ;—v. 21 ("the work of my hands"), lxiv. 7, xix. 25 ;[1]—v. 22, עֵת (with suffix), the time of the fulfilment of some prophecy, lx. 22 as xiii. 22.—Outside the Book of Isaiah, comp. especially v. 1 with Mal. iii. 20 ;—v. 9 (לְשֵׁם "to the place of the name," and יְקָרוּ),[2] Jer. iii. 17 ;—v. 13 (the temple, or Jerusalem, God's footstool), Ezek. xliii. 7, Lam. ii. 1 ;—v. 14 ("city of Yahwè"), Ps. xlvi. 5, xlviii. 2, 9 ;—v. 15, "hated," Ps. xxxv. 19, lxix. 5, "that hate me without a cause." Looking at the vocabulary, we find many words not used in chaps. xl.-lv. Some of them are more or less characteristic of these closing chapters of Isaiah. V. 3, נֹגַהּ ; so v. 19, lxii. 1, also l. 10 (post-Exilic insertion). זָרַח, ἅπ. λεγ.—V. 5, נָהַר "to be radiant (with joy)," as Ps. xxxiv. 6. פָּחַד, "to tremble (for joy)," as Jer. xxxiii. 9, Hos. iii. 5 (post-Exilic insertion). הָמוֹן, "riches," as Ps. xxxvii. 16, Eccles. v. 9.— V. 6, שִׁפְעָה with כִּסָּה, as Ezek. xxvi. 10, Job. xxii. 11. בֶּכֶר, ἅπ. λεγ.; fem. form in Jer. ii. 23 (only). תְּהִלָּה, five times in chaps. lx.-lxii. ; on the usage, see pp. 262, 270. The plur. ("praiseworthy deeds") again in lxiii. 7, Ex. xv. 11, Ps. xxii. 4, lxxviii. 4 ; a late use. בִּשֵּׂר, as lxi. 1, and thrice in chaps. xl.-lv. (see p. 261).—V. 7, שֵׁרֵת, as v. 10, lvi. 6, lxi. 6 (see p. 269) ; note archaizing plural form (p. 259). עַל־רָצוֹן, see on lvi. 7. V. 8, אֲרֻבּוֹת, as xxiv. 18.—V. 10, בְּנֵי־נֵכָר, a characteristic phrase of this and the neighbouring chapters (see p. 312).—V. 13, מִקְדָּשׁ, as lxiii. 18 (nowhere else in chaps. xl.-lxvi.).—V. 14, "the Zion of Israel's Holy One." Del. compares "Bethlehem of Judah," "Gibeah of Saul." But in each of these cases there was a geographical reason for the distinctive addition. Here, however, unless we suppose an allusion to a barely possible etymological meaning, "citadel,"[3] there is no obvious reason but the desire to produce a perfectly new name for Jerusalem. Considering the writer's arbitrary use of שֵׁרֵת in v. 7, and of שֹׁד (or שַׁד) in v. 16, this seems probable enough. Budde, for rhythmical reasons,

---

[1] In lx. 21, lxiv. 7 the work of Yahwè's hands is Israel ; but in xix. 25 Assyria. Note the more advanced development implied in the last passage. פֹּעַל יָדָיו, xlv. 11, has an entirely different meaning (see BW).

[2] See p. 339, note 1.

[3] See Ges.-Rödiger, *Thesaurus*, s.v.

excises צִיּוֹן,[1] but the existence of Kîna-rhythm in *vv.* 14-15 is questionable (see p. 337).— *V.* 15, מָשׁוֹשׂ, as lxii. 5, lxv. 18, lxvi. 10, xxiv. (twice), xxxii. (thrice). דּוֹר וָדוֹר, as lxi. 4, lviii. 12.— *V.* 16, שַׁד, see p. 259.— *V.* 17, פְּקֻדָּה, as a collective, here only.— אֲבָל (*v.* 20) and מֶטַע (*v.* 21), as lxi. 3 (here only in Isaiah). נֵצֶר (*v.* 21), see p. 64.

It is now time to sum up. Under each of the above three heads sufficient evidence has been given to justify a post-Exilic date. The late summer which produced the masterpiece of the Second Isaiah is over; imitators and copyists have taken the place of that soaring religious genius. In other fields conquests may yet be won, or contrary to expectation some isolated writer may yet rise above the crowd, but to all appearance a school of writers, who look up to the Second Isaiah as one of their models, alone maintains some at least of the prophetic traditions. We shall presently be able to go further than this. But it is something to have already reached the assured result that chap. lx. is post-Exilic, and not (as the writer supposed in *JQR*) a misplaced chapter of II. Isaiah.

CHAPTERS LXI.–LXII

A mixture of soliloquy and prophecy, followed in lxii. 10-12 by an ill-connected little poem on the return of the Jews. As Budde and Duhm have seen, lxii. 4-12 is in what the former calls elegiac rhythm. The writer seeks to compensate for poverty of thought by variety of form. For it is difficult to admit that *vv.* 4-12, or even *vv.* 4-9, form a separate poem from that which precedes. lxi. 10, however, which interrupts the context, is no doubt an insertion from some other source. It looks like the beginning of a liturgical composition in which Zion (to whom the Targum assigns the verse) is the speaker; cf. lxiii. 7. The imagery of line 2 reminds us of lix. 17.

1. *Circumstances.*—The land of Judah is in part repeopled, and the temple rebuilt (lxii. 9 " in my holy courts ") but the Jews are still despised of all men (lxi. 11, lxii. 7;

[1] Budde, *ZATW*, 1891, p. 241.

cf. lx. 15 "hated"). "Ancient ruins" still need to be restored (lxi. 4; cf. Zech. i. 12), and among these we are justified in including the broken-down walls of Jerusalem (lxii. 6; cf. lx. 10, 11). There are but few men capable of bearing arms, for cornfields and vineyards are ravaged by enemies with impunity (lxii. 8). Meantime the mass of the Jewish people still languishes, afar from Palestine, in literal or metaphorical slavery (lxi. 1; cf. xlii. 7, 22, xlix. 9; Joel iv. 8; Deut. xxviii. 68). Liberty has once more to be proclaimed, and the "way of the people" again and more effectually to be prepared (lxi. 1, lxii. 10). The return of the exiles, in a full and worthy sense, has still to take place.

2. *Ideas.*—The circle of ideas is the same as in chap. lx. Neither Israel nor Israel's God has in any full sense returned to the promised land (lxii. 10, 11, interpreted by xl. 3, 9, 10). But the "prophecy of restoration" cannot have failed. Nay, it is re-announced, with fitting modifications, and with the addition of a specially guaranteed promise with regard to the harvests and vintages of Palestine (lxii. 8, 9). It delights the writer to think of the strictness with which the law of retribution will be carried out. The former taskmasters of the Jews will become their ploughmen and vinedressers (lxi. 5), so that the Jews will have all their time for "ministering" to their God.[1] In liv. 13 the children of glorified Zion were described as all disciples of Yahwè, *i.e.* as all prophets (cf. Num. xi. 29), but according to lxi. 6 they will be a lordly and wealthy priesthood. Whether their functions will extend to the moral instruction of the conquered millions (cf. ii. 3), we are not told. And should Yahwè still delay his coming, there are those who by ceaseless prayer will rouse him from his inactivity, lxii. 6, where the "watchmen" may be either interceding angels (a late idea, cf. Zech. i. 12; Job xxxiii. 23; so *PI*, ii. 99 and Duhm), or (better) interceding prophets (see li. 9, and cf. the institution of the Levites called *meorerim*, or "awakeners," who cried to

---

[1] We can now understand שרת in lx. 10 better. The Jews in the day of their triumph have become sacred persons (cf. lxii. 12) to their former oppressors, so that the building work done for them by the kings is sacred "ministration."

Yahwè to awake).¹ If these anticipations seem to betray a colossal spiritual arrogance towards men, yet side by side with this we notice a humility towards God,² and a patient endurance of injuries as willed by Him, which are foregleams of Christ's religion, and specially characteristic of the age of the Psalter, *i.e.* post-Exilic (cf. on lvii. 13*b*-21, p. 321).

3. *Style and phraseology.*—As in chap. lx., there is a striking want of continuity in the style and a laboured use of phrases which betokens the imitator. Observe too how, from his poverty of invention, the writer three times refers to the new name of glorified Zion (xli. 3, 4, 12). The opening and the closing words of lxi. 1 allude to xlii. 1 and 7 respectively; and the solemn phrase "Lord Yahwè" recalls the soliloquy of the Servant in l. 4-9. *V.* 2 repeats the antithesis of lxiii. 4 (whereas xxxiv. 8 is only in part parallel); cf. also xlix. 8. "A failing spirit" (רוּחַ כֵּהָה) recalls xlii. 3, and the close of *v.* 3 agrees almost verbally with lx. 21*b*; in the latter case, presumably, the author repeats himself. "Ancient ruins" (*v.* 4) alludes to, or is alluded to in lviii. 12. *V.* 7*a* alludes to xl. 2; Jer. xvii. 18. In *v.* 8 "an everlasting covenant" alludes to lv. 3. *V.* 9*b*, cf. lxv. 23*b*. *V.* 11, יַצְמִיחַ צְדָקָה, cf. xlv. 8*b*.—In chap. lxii., *v.* 1 repeats the image of lx. 1-3, while *vv.* 1, 2 contain צֶדֶק in II. Isaiah's favourite sense of "victory." *V.* 4 (figure), cf. liv. 5. In *v.* 8 the oath of Yahwè suggests xlv. 23, liv. 9, while the promise in *v.* 9 is at any rate parallel to that in lxv. 21, 22. *Vv.* 10-12 consist of echoes of xl. 3, 10, xlix. 22, xlviii. 20; cf. also lvii. 14. The name "the holy people" reminds us of Ex. xix. 6 (late); lxiv. 18 cannot safely be quoted (*RT*). The companion name recalls lxiii. 4, xxxv. 10.—Nor must somewhat more minute phenomena be omitted; often they are critically important. Note first three highly probable though conjectural points of contact with chaps. xl.-lv. In xli. 7*b* should we not, with Klost., read וָרֹק for יָרְבּוּ, cf. l. 6; in lxii. 4 שְׁמָמָה, with Oort, Klost., and Duhm, for שְׁמָמָה, cf. liv. 1 (Lam. i. 13); and in lxii. 5 בֹּנַיִךְ (p. 259), with Lowth, Briggs, Oort, and Duhm, for בָּנָיִךְ, cf. liv. 11, Ps. cxlvii. 2?

¹ See Delitzsch, Introd. to Ps. xlv.
² Duhm (p. 404) depreciates this "humility" on the ground of its connection with physical states. But this seems unfair. See *BL*, p. 343 f.; Montefiore, *Hibbert Lectures*, p. 444.

Then, apart from conjecture, note בַּשֵּׂר (v. 1). This is certainly one of II. Isaiah's words (see on lx. 6, p. 340), but עֲנָוִים is not (p. 64 f.), nor probably is יַעַן (found in lxv. 12, lxvi. 4). נִשְׁבְּרֵי־לֵב recalls Ps. xxxiv. 19, li. 19 (post-Exilic), also cxlvii. 3, which seems to allude to our passage;[1] cf. also lxvi. 2, lvii. 15 (all these passages must be nearly contemporaneous). קְרָא דְרוֹר " to proclaim liberation "; on this see p. 262. פְּקַח־קוֹחַ, see pp. 259, 266. אֲבֵלִים, vv. 2, 3, as lvii. 18 (p. 321). שָׂשׂוֹן, as li. 3, 11 (Ps. li. 10). מַעֲטֵה, ἅπ. λεγ., but cf. עָטָה, lix. 17, lxi. 10 (nowhere else in Isaiah). קְרָא, as lxi. 3, lviii. 12—V. 4, קוֹמֵם (p. 267). חָדָשׁ, ἅπ. λεγ. חֹרֶב "wasteness" (rare and late; p. 263).—V. 6, מְשָׁרְתֵי אֱלֹ, as Joel i. 9, ii. 17; Jer. iii. 21. הִתְיַמֵּר, ἅπ. λεγ.; Kl. corrects תִּתְהַדָּרוּ (cf. Prov. xxv. 6). V. 7, עוֹלָה (so point, of course), as lix. 3. "Seed" and " offspring," as xliv. 3, xlviii. 19, liv. 3.—V. 10, שׂוֹשׂ אָשִׂישׂ (cf. lxii. 5) points away from II. Isaiah (p. 268). —In lxii. 3, note מְלוּכָה, as xxxiv. 12. The undoubted II. Isaiah, like Isaiah (xvii. 3), only has מַמְלָכָה. In lx. 12 we find the latter form, but that verse is *interpolated* (see p. 337). —V. 6, שֹׁמְרִים. If a term for the interceding angels (see above), we may compare the "watchers" of Dan. iv. 13, Enoch i. 5. If = prophets, cf. xxi. 8, 11. The latter view seems to me on a re-examination the more probable view; compare xxi. 8, 11 (מִשְׁמַרְתִּי . . . שֹׁמֵר), and note the parallelism between כָּל־הַיּוֹם . . . תָּמִיד and expressions in xxi. 8 (p. 126). דָּמִי, as v. 7 (late; p. 262).—V. 7, כּוֹנֵן, II. Isaiah (p. 263).—V. 8, יָגַע בְּ, as xlvii. 12, 15.—V. 9, הִלֵּל "to praise (God)," as lxiv. 10 (p. 262).—V. 12, קֹדֶשׁ, very rare in chaps. xl.-lv. (p. 314). לֹא נֶעֱזָבָה "unforsaken," cf. liv. 11a.

" A threefold cord is not easily broken." Not only chap. lx., but chaps. lxi.-lxii., must be post-Exilic. It is now time to verify the assurance given above that we can go still further, and determine with probability the date and the meaning of these two closely connected sections. Let us turn back to lix. 15b-20. We have seen that this incomplete passage either presupposes or anticipates the near approach of that separation of the stricter religious elements in the society of Jerusalem from those which favoured a heathenish reaction. It may in fact be most fitly dated in the year of

[1] Rahlfs.

CHAPTERS LXI.-LXII

the formation of the *kāhāl* or religious community, *i.e.*, let us provisionally say, in 432. Surely the Song in chap. lx. is highly appropriate for those who had now, as they believed, removed the obstacle to the fulfilment of II. Isaiah's promises. And if we may further follow Kosters in the view that this formation of the *kāhāl* took place soon after the arrival of Ezra and his fellow-exiles with rich gifts for the temple from Babylonia,[1] we can well understand the high hopes which the Song expresses of a general return of exiled Jews in connection with a great world-revolution. Surely, too, the thought expressed in chaps. lxi.-lxii. are just those which would be natural on the arrival of Ezra and his caravan, which (as Kosters appears to have shown) is to be placed after and not before the (second) arrival of Nehemiah. Already in 444 the latter, according to Neh. i. 5-11, had been deeply impressed with the non-fulfilment of the prophetic promise of restoration.[2] Already, too, if our previous results are correct, religious writers had begun, feebly enough, to copy the phraseology of chaps. xl.-lv., and to point to an approaching manifestation of the divine glory. Is it surprising if the most enthusiastic of these disciples of II. Isaiah in or about 432 conceived the idea of providing the Prophecy of Restoration with an appendix? This is the date, and this the theory, which appears to answer best to all the requirements of chaps. lx.-lxii. Chap. lx., with its self-evident allusions to chaps. liv.-lv., was not unnaturally placed first; it forms, in fact, as Delitzsch has pointed out, the climax of a series of passages addressed to prostrate Zion, viz. li. 17-23, lii. 1-2 (incomplete; see Duhm), lx. The "Zion" to which it is addressed is the company of those who "feared Yahwè," and "spake often one to another" (Mal. iii. 16), or, in the language of Neh. x. 28, "all those who had separated themselves from the עַמֵּי הָאָרֶץ[3] unto the law of God." It is only to such persons that the radiant dawn of the "Sun of righteousness" is promised in Mal. iii. 20; Isa. lx. 1. They are the "trembling listeners to Yahwè's word"

---

[1] Kosters, *Het Herstel*, etc., pp. 130, 144 f.
[2] It is true, the reference in Neh. i. 8, 9 is not to II. Isaiah, but to Lev. xxvi. 33; Deut. xxx. 4.
[3] *I.e.*, the children of the Judahites and Israelites who had remained in the land during the Exile.

spoken of in lxvi. 2 (Ezra ix. 4, x. 3), and also the עֲנָוִים of lxi. 1, and the "good news" for which they crave relates to the "year of favour" and the "day of vengeance" which shall remove the distressing anomalies of the present order of things.

Now perhaps we can understand the form of the section lxi.-lxii. It was the Servant of Yahwè[1] who was appointed "to revive the weary" (l. 4), and "to say to the bondmen, Go forth; to those who are in darkness, Show yourselves" (xlix. 9). Hence the writer of chaps. lxi.-lxii., in the manner of his great model, introduces three soliloquies of this ideal personage, the first describing the evangel with which he has been intrusted, the other two the ardour with which he importunes Yahwè to fulfil his promise. The speaker is not indeed expressly designated Yahwè's Servant, but the same omission is made in l. 4-9, the poem which is not improbably the source of the divine title Adonai Yahwè[2] in lxi. 1. It is true, the writer uses some expressions which belong more properly to a prophet than to the Servant of Yahwè, but this is only an additional proof that he is a later disciple of the Second Isaiah, and not that great writer himself. He regards the Servant of Yahwè as personifying the company of prophets (מְבַשֶּׂרֶת צִיּוֹן, xl. 9), and so in the third soliloquy he makes the Servant declare that he has set watchmen or guards over the (still ruined) walls of Jerusalem (lxii. 6), i.e. that individual prophets, or prophetically minded teachers, derive their commission from the ideal which gives unity to the prophetic band. The other exegetical interpretations, viz. that in the first soliloquy the speaker is the prophetic writer, in the second and third either Yahwè or the prophet, are more difficult. The difference of rhythm between the first and the two last soliloquies is no reason for supposing a difference in the speaker, for the same difference of rhythm exists in the Ebed-Yahwè songs. More particularly, if the שֹׁמְרִים in lxii. 6 are prophets (which it now seems to me hazardous to deny), the speaker in v. 6a´ can

---

[1] True, xlix. 9 forms no part of the second Ebed-Yahwè song. But the passage to which it belongs gives us at any rate II. Isaiah's interpretation of the theme in vv. 1-6.

[2] Sept. however has simply Πνεῦμα Κυρίου.

hardly be either Yahwè or any individual prophet. The phraseological influence of II. Isaiah, manifest throughout the composition, becomes still stronger at the close of the work, which, except *v.* 12, is little more than a mosaic of shreds of the Prophecy of Restoration (see above). How mechanical is the new writer's procedure is clear from the absence of any object to הִשְׁמִיעַ (supply "redemption" from xlviii. 20), and of any words explaining the subject of "his wage" and "his recompense" (*v.* 11).

Note.—In lxi. 10 the speaker is the Jewish community, and the passage may be a misplaced fragment of a prophecy, in which the writer adopted the style of liturgical poetry (see *BW*). Line 2 seems to allude to lix. 17.

CHAPTER LXIII. 1-6

These six verses contain a dramatic dialogue (which reminds us of Ps. xxiv. 7-10) between an imaginary bystander and a victorious warrior (*i.e.* Yahwè) returning from the field of battle. To regard this passage, with Ewald, as having even an artificial connection [1] with the preceding sections, is hazardous. But in one point this keen critic sees more clearly than Dillmann, for he distinctly denies the authorship of II. Isaiah. The latter may not indeed always have been consistent with himself (see xli. 15, xlii. 13-15, xlix. 26), but could not, as Smend truly remarks, have displayed such elaborate ferocity as we find here. The phraseological points of contact with II. Isaiah which Dillm. points out are not all real. Take מִי־זֶה in *v.* 1. This reminds us of מִי־אֵלֶּה in lx. 8, but chap. lx. cannot be II. Isaiah's, and the מִי־זֶה of Ps. xxiv. 8 is a still closer parallel. הָדוּר is not paralleled by הֲדוּרִים, xlv. 2, for the latter word is corrupt (see *RT*). Nor is צָעָה to be matched by the same word in li. 14, for 'צ there is used differently; or rather because in our passage we should read צָעַד (Vulg., etc.). בּוּס (*v.* 6) occurs again in xli. 25 (corr. text), but also with a similar reference

---

[1] How, if the homeward march of the redeemed were opposed by jealous neighbours like the Edomites?—is Ewald's imaginary link. Similarly Dillmann.

in late psalms. אִתִּי (v. 3) is found in xliv. 24, and צְדָקָה "truth" (v. 1) in xlv. 23. The few resemblances are certainly far outweighed by the singularities of expression. And as to the imagery, Yahwè no doubt appears as a warrior in xlii. 13, but how common is this figure! The love of theophanies is characteristic of the whole later period. We find the image of the winepress (with the same reference) in Joel iii. 13 (post-Exilic), and the description of the carnage wrought by Yahwè is in accordance with xxx. 25, Ps. lxviii. 22, 24, cx. 5, 6, all late passages.

The composition must be grouped with lix. 15*b*-20, which in subject, imagery, and phraseology it so strikingly resembles (p. 334 f.). It has also a phrase in common with chap. lxi. and the grim prophecy in chap. xxxiv. ("day of vengeance," v. 4, cf. lxi. 2, xxxiv. 8), which at least suggests that all these are products of the same school. Some writers stumble at the singling out of Edom as the representative of the foes of Yahwè, and following Lagarde (*Proph. Chald.*, p. l.) emend מֵאֱדוֹם into מֵאָדָם (Nah. ii. 4), and מִבָּצְרָה into מִבָּצֵר. To this course, however, there are strong objections. (1) The text as it stands is in a high degree Hebraic. Edom suggests the idea of red (*'ādōm*), Bozra that of a vintage (*bāçīr*). "There are indeed no more wine-vats of Bosra, but her fields are fruitful vineyards" (Doughty, *Arabia*, i. 38). (2) The proposed text is unsatisfactory. מֵאָדָם should rather be followed by מִדַּרְךְ (see Judg. ix. 27), and the supposed anticipative mention of the grape-treading spoils the effect.[1] And as to the mention of Edom and of Bozra, is there not an analogy for this in chap. xxxiv., where the judgment is upon Edom, and especially Bozra (*vv.* 5, 6), also upon "all nations"? It is true, Duhm would like to eliminate Edom from chap. xxxiv., but he wisely gives no effect to the wish. Even if Joel (iv. 12) places the destruction of the hostile nations in the valley of "Jehoshaphat," which was presumably near Jerusalem, there was no reason why other writers should not vary the scene. Indeed, in our

[1] So Dillmann. Duhm refers to Sept.'s ἐκ Βοσόρ as proving the reading מִבָּצֵר. But Sept. has ἐν Βοσόρ in xxxiv. 6, where a difference of reading is impossible. Kuenen (*Ond.*[2], ii. 140) holds his judgment in suspense, but his treatment of the whole question is extremely slight.

study of chap. xxxiv., we have seen (pp. 209-210) that there was probably a very special reason why Edom should have been singled out in the way referred to. It may reasonably be held that fresh bands of Edomites occupied parts of S. Judah between 450 and 400 B.C., and that this renewed the old irritation at the self-seeking conduct of this kindred people.

We have now therefore also gained a probable date for this little work, and it accords with that suggested by the parallelism between it and lix. 15b-20 and chap. lxi. (see pp. 336). We have also virtually determined the right interpretation of the passage. Chap. lxiii. 1-6 is not an ideal picture of the defeat of the expected attempt of the Edomites to hinder the return of the Jewish Exiles (Dillmann), nor a prediction of the successes of Judas Maccabæus or John Hyrcanus (Grotius, against whom see Lowth), but a description of Yahwè's final judgment upon Edom and all other foes. Both "Edom" and "Bozra" are used conventionally as in chap. xxxiv. (p. 211).

This view of lxiii. 1-6 throws a fresh light on the parallel passage, Ps. xxiv. 7-10, which is also post-Exilic (note עזוז), and should presumably be interpreted eschatologically. Indeed, the two passages might almost be combined, Ps. xxiv. 7-10 being taken as a poetic description of a later point in Yahwè's return to Zion on "the day of the great slaughter"[1] (xxx. 25).

CHAPTERS LXIII. 7–LXIV

A liturgical thanksgiving, confession of sin, and supplication, full of interesting peculiarities. The text has been rather ill preserved, but much has been done for its correction. I quote the opening lines, in which Budde recognises what he, with doubtful appropriateness, calls Kîna-rhythm. The student will notice with interest in $v.$ 9 the correction to which both Budde and Duhm have been led by rhythmical considerations, and which has the support of the Septuagint, and in $v.$ 11 the substitution of a phrase from a favourite

[1] *BL*, p. 203.

poem of the author (Deut. xxxii. 7) for the two intrusive glosses מֹשֶׁה עַמּוֹ.

7. Yahwè's loving acts will I praise, Yahwè's deeds of renown,
   In proportion to all that Yahwè so rich in goodness hath wrought for us,
   That he hath wrought for us according to his compassion and his manifold loving-kindness.
8. He said, Surely they are my people, sons that will not prove false;
   So he became to them a deliverer from all their distress.
9. Not an angel-messenger, (but) his presence it was that delivered them,
   And that took them up and carried them all the days of old.
10. But they resisted, and pained his holy spirit,
    So he changed for them into an enemy, he himself fought against them.
11. Then (Israel) remembered the days of old, [the years of past ages,] (saying,)
    Where is he that brought up from the sea the shepherd of his flock?
    Where is he that placed within it (viz. his flock) his holy spirit?
12. He that made his glorious arm to proceed at the right hand of Moses?[1] . . .

This retrospect of the times of Moses and Joshua continues till *v.* 15. Then, as in Ps. lxxxix. 39, delight in the traditional glories of Israel gives place to deep despondency at the calamities of the present. The Church supplicates Yahwè, as being still the "father" of his people, to take notice of its distress. He has, as it appears, deserted his people, and given up his sanctuary to the foe. But if he would but "look hither," he would no longer restrain his fatherly compassion. He would surely "rend the heaven and come down," and exceed even the wonders of old time. Not that Israel claims righteousness; on the contrary, it confesses its ingrained sinfulness. But, says the writer, is it not Yahwè who "causeth us to err from his ways" by his excessive anger, which seems to make the more or less of sin a matter of indifference? Then, in case the voice of fatherly com-

[1] Budde traces "elegiac rhythm" as far as *v.* 12 (*ZATW*, 1891, p. 241). His arrangement leads him to a correction in *v.* 9, which produces this fine passage.

passion should continue mute, the almost despairing Church makes a fresh appeal to Yahwè on the ground of his reasonableness. Does the potter lightly break a vessel on which he has lavished his utmost skill? And can Yahwè bear to see his own "holy cities" and the house of prayer and praise lying waste?

1. The *circumstances* indicated in this unique composition, and the tone in which they are referred to, are absolutely and entirely inconsistent with those of the author of chaps. xl.-lv. "Thy holy people,"[1] we read in lxiii. 18, "possessed it but a little while; our adversaries have trodden down thy sanctuary." And in lxiv. 10-11 we are told that Jerusalem and the other "holy cities" have become a wilderness, and that the temple itself has been "burned with fire." Such are the most prominent facts in the writer's mind. They fill him with consternation, and in strong excitement of feeling he even permits himself (not indeed as an individual, but as the spokesman of the Church) to accuse Yahwè of being unmerciful and unreasonable. Can the Second Isaiah have felt and written thus? This writer knows indeed that Jerusalem and the temple are in ruins, but his mind is at ease, he is more than comforted, for Zion and the sanctuary will arise from their ashes in more than their pristine splendour, and so far is he from accusing Yahwè, that he emphasises the depth of his compassion and the wisdom of his arrangements. He alludes indeed to those who ventured to pass censure upon Yahwè. But, almost as if he anticipates the complaints of lxiii. 15-lxiv., he bursts out with this indignant reproof:—

Ha! one that striveth with his fashioner—a potsherd like (other) potsherds of earth!
Doth the clay say to its fashioner, What canst thou make? and his work, Thou hast no hands![2]

2. The *ideas*, too, and the *forms of belief* are hardly less inconsistent with II. Isaiah's authorship. (*a*) The idea of the spirit (or the holy spirit) of Yahwè, dwelling within the

---

[1] For a different reading see *RT* (or *PI*).
[2] xlv. 9, reading יֹּעֲשֵׂנִי and לֹו with Koppe, Dillm., and Duhm.

community,[1] is indeed not opposed to xlii. 1 (where the spirit of Yahwè is said to have been put upon his commissioned Servant), but, if it is at all related to this passage, and is not rather suggested by Num. xi. 29 (E^2), it implies the exegesis of a later generation, to which (cf. lix. 21) the Servant of Yahwè meant the church or "congregation" which had pledged itself to obey the law-book of Ezra. At any rate, the hypostatising of the divine or "holy" spirit as the equivalent of Yahwè points to a later stage in the personifying process, and contrasts with xliv. 3, where the spirit of Yahwè is described as a poured-out stream of blessing (Neh. ix. 20 will then represent at once a more sober and a more conservative position). (*b*) The half-acceptance of a popular belief in the semi-divine character of Abraham and Israel[2] (or Jacob), which is implied in the words (lxiii. 16)—

. . . for (only) thou art our father,
For Abraham knoweth us not, and Israel doth not regard us;
Thou, Yahwè, art our father; our redeemer from of old is thy name,

would be equally strange in the Second Isaiah. What this writer thought of Jacob is not a matter of doubt. "Thy first father," he says, "sinned" (xliii. 27), and this, we learn, was one of the causes of the calamities of his descendants. How, then, could the Second Isaiah associate himself in thought with those who invoked Jacob-Israel as a divinity?[3] But the truth is that he nowhere suggests that the Jewish exiles practised any Palestinian worships in Babylon but that of Yahwè. Nor can we easily imagine their doing so. That Yahwè had ceased, even for less advanced Israelites, to be merely the god of Canaan is certain (cf. Jer. xliv.), but we can hardly suppose the invocation of Abraham and

[1] lxiii. 11, 14, 10. Cf. *v.* 11 with Hag. ii. 5, "and my spirit abideth in your midst."
[2] How else can Abraham and Israel be introduced in this connection? It would be a "platitude to say that the remote ancestors of the Jews could not help them unless there was some chance that they might both sympathise and powerfully co-operate with their descendants —unless in short they were regarded somewhat as demi-gods" (*PI*, ii. 108; cf. 308).
[3] In xliv. 5 read יִקָּרֵא with Duhm. Symm., $κληθήσεται$.

Israel to be dissociated from their sacred burying-place at Machpelah. Abraham, too, is mentioned by II. Isaiah (li. 2) as the "father" of the Israelites, and the terms in which he is referred to seem to show that there was then at least no probability of his being appealed to for help. Yahwè might indeed seem to have "forgotten" Israel (xlix. 14), but no minor divinity had replaced the Most High in Israel's regard. But in post-Exilic times it became possible for at any rate a pale reflection of the cultus of Abraham and Israel to exist side by side with the worship of Yahwè. Nor is it impossible that when Eliphaz says to Job:

Call now, if there be any that will answer thee,
And to which of the holy ones (= *elohim*) wilt thou turn?

the writer, who is more Hebraic in thought than some have supposed, is thinking not only of angel- but of patriarch-worship. If it be asked how the later Jewish community can have been so inconsistent as to revert to the cultus of patriarchs, the answer is that other not less superstitious usages are known to have existed after the Return;[1] it was impossible to do as the reformers wished, and altogether avoid the influence of the עַמֵּי הָאָרֶץ. The latest trace of the superhuman character of the "fathers" is the doctrine of the Targum and the Talmud that the Messianic redemption would be the recompense of their merits (Jacob and Joseph are specially mentioned), or of the prayers of Rachel.[2]

(*c*) The intense consciousness of guilt, the strange excuse for it (see above), and the reference to Levitical uncleanness (lxiii. 17, lxiv. 4, 5), have their parallels, not in chaps. xl.-lv., but in Ps. li. (*vv*. 4, 7, 9), which, being Deutero-Isaianic, is (even if for no other reason) post-Exilic. (*d*) The idea that foreign oppression is due to a suspension of Yahwè's lordship over Israel is expressed in lxiii. 19 with a terrible force, which can be illustrated, certainly not by xlvii. 6, but only by xxvi. 13*a* (post-Exilic).

3. *Style and phraseology.*—As Delitzsch has already

---
[1] See p. 316, and add to the passages there quoted viii. 19 (a late insertion) and 2 Macc. xii. 40. The prohibition of cuttings for the dead, Lev. xix. 28, etc., also points to the continued danger of ancestor-worship.
[2] Cf. Ibn Ezra and Kimchi on lxiii. 17.

remarked, the tone of the poem is that of the synagogal *widdui*, or confession of sin. There is no parallel to it in chaps. xl.-lv.; the morsel of collective confession in xlii. 24 would be too slight to adduce, even if it were not most probably a late insertion (see p. 299). It is, however, like the short but very distinct church-confession in lix. 9-13, and in contents it resembles the long prayers of the Church in Neh. ix., Dan. ix. 4-13, only it rises into a higher style. It has also a striking affinity (*a*) to those psalms in which the Church, for purposes of edification, takes a retrospect of Israel's fortunes in antiquity, such as Ps. xliv., lxxviii., lxxx., lxxxi., lxxxix., cv., cvi., cxxxvi.; (*b*) to those which consist of, or contain, church-confessions of sin, whether the Church is represented as a group of individuals (so in Ps. cvi. 6, 7), or as having itself a kind of personal existence (so undoubtedly in Ps. li.); (*c*) to psalms of complaint under an oppression which almost kills the national life, such as xliv., lxxiv., lxxix., lxxx., lxxxix.[1] And among these note especially Ps. lxxxix., which, like our poem, opens with an eulogy of Yahwè's loving-kindness, and passes midway into a melancholy contemplation of the miseries of the present, Ps. lxxiv., which, like our poem, refers with all the pathos of an eye-witness to the destruction of the temple by fire, and Ps. li., which, in addition to the parallelisms mentioned already (p. 353), contains the phrase "holy spirit" (Ps. li. 13, cf. Isa. lxiii. 10, 11). Nor are less conspicuous points of resemblance to the psalms wanting. In lxiii. 8 note שָׁקֵר *perfide egit*, as Ps. xliv. 8, lxxxix. 34; in *v.* 10 מרה and עצב combined, as in Ps. lxxviii. 40; in *v.* 11 the "remembering" which is a characteristic feature of the later books of the Psalter (see Ps. lxxvii. 12, lxxviii. 35, cv. 5, cxliii. 5), also the representation of Moses as Israel's shepherd, as in Ps. lxxvii. 21; in *v.* 13 תְּהֹמוֹת, as eight times in the Psalms; in *v.* 14 (corr. text) the spirit of Yahwè leading the people, as in Ps. cxliii. 10; in *v.* 15 the phrase "look from heaven," as in Ps. lxxx. 15 (and nowhere else); in lxiii. 19*b*, prayer for a theophany as in Ps. cxliv. 5; in lxiv. 2 נוֹרָאוֹת, as in Ps. cvi. 22, etc.; in *v.* 3 "waiting" for Yahwè, as in Ps. xxxiii. 20 (cf. Isa. xxx. 18); in *v.* 5 the complaints of a mortality

---

[1] *JQR*, Oct. 1891, p. 104.

among the people which is the punishment of its sins, as in Ps. xc. 5-7; in *v.* 11 the temple psalmody emphasised, as in Ps. xxii. 4, lxv. 2. Among other writings which present affinities to our poem are Lamentations, Job, and Deut. xxxii. Compare *e.g.* lxiii. 15 with Lam. iii. 50; lxiv. 4*b*-6 (5*b*-7) with Lam. iii. 42-44; lxiv. 10 (11) מַחֲמַדֵּינוּ with Lam. i. 10; also lxiv. 5 (figure) with Job xxvii. 21, xxx. 22;[1] lxiv. 7 with Job x. 9; also lxiii. 8 with Deut. xxxii. 5; lxiii. 9, 14 with Deut. xxxii. 11, 12; lxiii. 11 with Deut. xxxii. 7; lxiii. 16 with Deut. xxxii. 6. Cf. also the form of the pathetic exclamation in lxiii. 19 (lxiv. 1) with that in Deut. xxxii. 29, Ps. lxxxi. 14, and Isa. xlviii. 18 (in an inserted passage). That there are points of contact with II. Isaiah is undeniable. Note *e.g.* the use of נָטַל and נָשָׂא, lxiii. 9, as xl. 15, xlvi. 3, 4; מָרָה, lxiii. 10, as l. 5; שֵׁם עוֹלָם, lxiii. 12, cf. lv. 13; הִתְאַפֵּק, lxiii. 15, lxiv. 11, as xlii. 14 (p. 260); גֹּאֲלֵנוּ, lxiii. 16, as xlvii. 4; הִתְעוֹרֵר, lxiv. 6, as li. 17. But there are so many linguistic affinities to other religious writings, both old and new, that this counts for little; compare, besides points mentioned above, פָּנָיו, lxiii. 9 (corr. text, see p. 350), with Ex. xxxiii. 14, 15; תְּנִיחֵמוּ, lxiii. 14, with Deut. xxv. 19; זְבֻל,[2] lxiii. 15, with 1 Ki. viii. 13 (*BL*, p. 212), Ps. xlix. 15, Hab. iii. 11; בּוֹסֵם, lxiii. 18, with Jer. xii. 10; כָּעַל, lxiii. 7, as lix. 18 (nowhere else); קִנְאָה, lxiii. 15, as lix. 17; הַר־קָדְשֶׁךָ, lxiii. 18 (corr. text), cf. lvi. 7, lvii. 15, lxv. 11, lxvi. 20; צָרֶיךָ צָרֵינוּ, lxiii. 18, lxiv. 1, as lix. 18, xxvi. 11 (צָרִים, of Yahwè's or Israel's foes never occurs in chaps. xl.-lv.). צְדָקוֹת, of righteous acts of men, lxiv. 5, as xxxiii. 15 (p. 168); עֲוֹנִים, lxiv. 5, 6, see p. 259; מִגֵּן, lxiv. 6 probably, as Hos. xi. 8; קָצַף, lxiv. 8, common since Deuteronomy (p. 267). Note also עָרֵי קָדְשֶׁךָ, lxiv. 9 (10). The phrase is unique, elsewhere Jerusalem is "the holy city" (xlviii. 2, lii. 1); Sept. and Vulg. correct "thy holy city."[3] The first writer who represents the entire land of Judah as

---

[1] This passage suggests a probable correction of תְּמוּנֵנוּ in lxiv. 6.

[2] On the Assyrian affinities of this word see *PI*, ii. 173. Dillmann rather dogmatically contradicts. But the sense of "palace" suits excellently well.

[3] The correction is suggested by the next line, "Zion is becom a desert," which is really, however, a variant to the first line (Duhm; *RT*).

holy is Zechariah (ii. 16, A.V. 12). On the use of הֵלֵל, see p. 262; on מַחֲמַדִּים, see *PI*, ii. 113. לְחָרְבָּה occurs elsewhere only in Jer., Ezek., and Lev. xxvi. 31, 33. עֵדִים, lxiv. 5, is an ἅπ. λεγ.; for the figure in this passage, cf. xxx. 22 (late). הָמְסִים, lxiv. 1, is due to corruption.[1]

So the liturgical poem before us is post-Exilic, as indeed is granted (with the qualification "probably") by the most learned and candid of English conservative scholars, Dr. C. H. H. Wright.[2] One objection may, however, be raised: why does the retrospect of Yahwè's past loving-kindnesses keep silence respecting the fall of Babylon? The Exodus from Egypt and the accompanying wonders are described in pathetic language (lxiii. 11-14); why not also the Exodus from Chaldæa? "The man who wrote *vv.* 11-15 of chap. lxiii.," says Prof. G. A. Smith, "had surely the Return still before him; he would not have written in the way he has done of the Exodus from Egypt unless he had been feeling the need of another exhibition of divine power of the same kind. The prayer, therefore, must come from pretty much the same date as the rest of our prophecy,—after the Exile, but while the Return had not taken place."[3] A similar objection has been raised in England to the post-Exilic date of the historical psalms. The answer is twofold:—(1) The "wonders of old time" are the highest examples of what Yahwè can do for his people. They are referred to, not because the writer feels the need of exactly similar divine manifestations, but to revive Israel's faith (cf. xliii. 16, 17). The need of Yahwé's people is that he would make his power felt by the enemies who have laid waste his holy mountain. And (2) If the Return is not expressly referred to, it is because it was accompanied with so many disappointments, and so unlike what II. Isaiah had described, as to be a hindrance and not a help to faith.

It only remains to seek a suitable home for this remarkable work in the post-Exilic period. May we then place it, as so many critics have placed Ps. lxxiv., among the monuments of the Maccabæan movement, or at least of the dark years

---

[1] Read, with Klost., כְּקֹרֵחַ אֵשׁ חֲשָׁשׁ מָשְׁמַיִם תִּבְעַר־אֵשׁ.
[2] Art. "Isaiah," Smith's *DB*,[2] i. 1473.
[3] *Exposition*, ii. 447.

which preceded it? This is virtually the hypothesis of Grotius; but I hesitate to accept it. First, because the passage can be shown to stand among compositions of the Persian age, one of which contains a confession of sin (lix. 9-15a) rather closely parallel to that in lxiii. 17-lxiv. 6; and next, because it speaks of the temple as having been burned, whereas there is no evidence that the work of Judas Maccabæus in 165 went beyond purifying and repairing the still existing sanctuary.[1] But is there any part of the Persian period to which we can venture to assign our poem? Since the temple has been destroyed, one might think first of all of an early year after the reported edict of Cyrus (so Bleek), *e.g.* of 521 B.C., the year before Haggai stirred the people up to rebuild the temple. This however will not suit the statement that "Jerusalem is a desolation" (lxiv. 9), nor were the Jews in Judea at that time conscience-stricken penitents. The striking words of Zechariah (i. 12) must not be pressed too far. There is already a settled population, some of whom have costly houses, oliveyards and vineyards, while the rest serve as day-labourers (Hag. i. 3-6, ii. 19; Zech. viii. 10-12). Next, we might, with Kuenen in 1889, suppose the occasion to have been a catastrophe which was still recent in 444 (see Neh. i. 3). "What led to the destruction of the walls of Jerusalem, and the burning of her gates, we do not know for certain. But the discontent which had already begun to prevail in the more remote provinces of the Persian empire, and in which the Jews may have been involved, even against their will, is quite enough to account for such an occurrence." It is in fact a natural conjecture that the Samaritans and their allies broke down the walls (assuming that these had been erected), just as upon Nehemiah's arrival they united to oppose their being rebuilt, and that this took place during the disturbances produced by the revolt of Megabyzus in Syria.[2] This tempting hypothesis was however with good reason abandoned by Kuenen himself in 1890,[3] and that cautious critic, were he

---
[1] This involves a modification of the argument in *JQR*, *l.c.* The reason of the change will be seen presently.

[2] Kuenen, *Ond.*², i. 507, ii. 140; *Religion of Israel*, ii. 224; cf. *BL*, p. 231 f.

[3] Kuenen, *Chronologie van het Perz. Tijdvak*, p. 26 f. (*Abhand-*

still among us, could perhaps explain both Neh. i. 3 and Isa. lxiv. 9 of the desolation of Judah caused by the Babylonians, and in 444 still to a great extent unremedied. Thus the date given by Kuenen would be retained, and the poem would seem to stand in its proper place among other works of the age of Nehemiah. There is, however, one fatal objection to this date—that it compels us to give an unnatural interpretation to lxiii. 18 and lxiv. 10. Duhm, for instance, assures us that "our holy and beautiful house, where our fathers praised thee" (lxiv. 10) means, not the miserable second temple, but the stately one destroyed by Nebuchadrezzar, and refers to the pathetic scene in Ezra iii. 12, 13, when shouts of joy and cries of lamentation mingled together as proving the poverty of the new temple. But (1) it seems exegetically unfair to explain *v.* 9 of an event which lasts on in its effects to the present, and *v.* 10 of one which has found at any rate an initial remedy. (2) No Hebrew writer of generally accepted orthodoxy would deny the sanctity, or even, to the eye of faith, the "beauty" of the existing temple. To which we may add (3) that the section, Ezra iii. 8-13, is of very doubtful historical value.[1] Nor does the language of chap. lix., parallel though in some respects it is, show as much passionate excitement, and such a depth of almost hopeless misery as that of lxiii. 15-lxiv. 11. Consequently we are obliged to look further, and see if there is any part of the Persian period when the Jews were in greater straits than in the time of Nehemiah, and when the temple really was in all probability destroyed by fire.

Such a crisis it has long appeared to me that we can find, and even while I accepted Kuenen's hypothesis in explanation of Neh. i. 3, I could not help urging that a still greater calamity than that inferred from Neh. i. 3 was needed to account adequately for lxiii. 7-lxiv. 11.[2] The theory which I urged in 1891 I once more offer for consideration, and though Prof. Davidson assures us that "a hypothetical burning under Ochus, on which history is silent, is not here"[3]

lungen, ed. Budde, p. 232). Cf. Kosters, *Het Herstel van Israël*, p. 71 f.

[1] Kuenen, *Ond.*[2], i. 501; Kosters, *Het Herstel*, etc., p. 16.
[2] *BL*, p. 160; *JQR*, Oct. 1891, p. 107.
[3] *Critical Review*, Jan. 1893, p. 19.

(*i.e.* in lxiv. 10), most scholars will agree that in dealing with the history of the Jews in the Persian period a certain amount of inferential reconstruction is legitimate and necessary. What Artaxerxes Ochus was we know only too well. He was "one of those great despots who can raise up again for a time a decayed Oriental empire, who shed blood without scruple, and are not nice in the choice of means."[1] At the very outset he proved this by the massacre of his nearest relations, and his reputation for bloodthirstiness was such that to avoid falling into his hands the citizens of Sidon set fire to their houses, and perished with their wives and children in the flames. To the Egyptians, too, as Nöldeke also remarks, " he made the *væ victis* thoroughly clear, and treated even their religion with little more respect than Cambyses before him."[2] How can we suppose that such a tyrant (or his worthy instrument) would abstain from destroying the temple, if he had occasion to be displeased with the Jews? A Scottish scholar has, I am aware, taken much pains to make out that such an occasion cannot be proved to have existed.[3] It is certain however that no historical specialist (not even the sceptical Nöldeke) doubts that our very inadequate reports of the oppression of the Jews have only too much justification. Between 363 and 345 there were two Palestinian rebellions against Persia, and the Jews could no more have helped taking some part in these than on other similar occasions.[4] Tradition says much of the sufferings of conquered Phœnicia and Egypt, but very little of those of Judæa. What it does tell is significant, even if it be not as minutely exact as we could wish. It speaks of a conflict of the Persians with the Jews which ended in the capture of Jericho (?) and the transportation of

[1] Nöldeke, *EB*, xviii. 580. [2] *Ibid.*
[3] Prof. A. R. S. Kennedy, *Expository Times*, March 1892, p. 247 ; cf. the writer's reply, *Exp. Times*, April 1892, p. 320.
[4] Judeich (*Studien*) mentions five wars of Persia against the Egyptian revolters; in three of them Ochus played a leading part. The captivity of the Jews is connected by this historian with the second Egyptian campaign of Ochus ; the violent acts of Bagôas (= Bagôses) with the third (p. 176). I have ventured to bring the whole chastisement of the Jews into the latter period (*i.e.* between 348 and 340). Cf. Nöldeke, *Aufsätze zur pers. Gesch.*, p. 78.

a part of the Judæan population to Hyrcania and Babylonia.[1] Two scholars have also independently suggested that the strange narrative (Jos. *Ant.* xi. 7, 1) of the pollution of the temple by Bagôses in the reign of "the other Artaxerxes" is really a much altered version of the outrages committed by the eunuch Bagôses, who ever fanned the flame of revenge in the breast of Ochus, and would naturally be entrusted by him with the duty of punishing the Jews. "The whole Bagôses story," remarks Robertson Smith,[2] "looks like a pragmatical invention designed partly to soften the catastrophe of the Jews, and partly to explain it by the sin of the high priest." That this is dealing very freely with tradition, must be admitted. But, unwilling as they may be to provoke the scoffs of opponents, some critics will be ready to stake their reputations on the soundness of this reconstruction of history.

These terrible events, indeed, though but faintly echoed in history, have not failed to find some reflection in contemporary religious literature.[3] I have already expressed the opinion that the gloomiest of the psalms of persecution belong to this period, and even the most cautious scholars must admit the great probability that at any rate Book III. of the Psalms contains some implied references to the oppression of Ochus. Among these it is natural in the first instance to think of Ps. lxxxix., on the affinities of which to the composition before us I have remarked already (p. 354; cf. *BL*, p. 130). Robertson Smith however in 1886 (*EB*, xx. 31) preferred to assign Psalms lxxiv. and lxxix. (as well as Ps. xliv. in Book II.) to this sad period. The plausibility of this theory was obvious. It seemed satisfactorily to explain many parts of these psalms, and it had the advantage of providing for them a relatively early date. Still it seemed strange that some report of the destruction of the temple did not reach Josephus, who had heard of a much less severe blow to the sanctuary (the "defilement" by Bagôses), if the event were really historical, and so Robertson Smith's sug-

---

[1] Syncellus (Dindorf), i. 486; cf. Solinus, xxxv. 6.
[2] *OTJC*[2] (1892), p. 438. So too, I presume, Judeich (1891). Wellhausen, too, goes half-way with Robertson Smith (*Isr. u. jüd. Gesch.*, 1894, p. 148).
[3] *BL*, p. 72, 118, 130, 229.

gestion, like Ewald's before it, found no immediate acceptance among students.[1] It was this lamented scholar's renewal of his suggestion in 1892, with a brief but forcible justification, which induced the writer almost at once to profess his adhesion to this virtually new view.[2] The objection which formerly led him to reject it was removed by the remark of Robertson Smith quoted above; the collectors of Jewish traditions threw a veil over the inexplicable mystery of a second pollution and destruction of the temple by a heathen enemy. He admitted it therefore to be probable "that after glutting his revenge on Sidon, Ochus sent his general Bagôas (a name easily confounded with Bagôses) to chastise the Jews (cf. Judeich, *Kleinasiatische Studien*, p. 176), and that the temple was not only desecrated but destroyed." But he held his judgment in suspense with regard to Ps. xliv., which seemed more easily explained by some recent defeat of the Maccabees than by the events connected with the oppression of Ochus.

Let us now consider the parallelisms between lxiii. 7-lxiv. 11, and Psalms lxxiv. and lxxix., for these are certainly the psalms which (with lxxxix.) have the largest amount of affinity to the work now before us. There would probably be more points of contact, but for the alterations which the two psalms have evidently received from the temple editors.[3]

Ps. lxxiv. 1 } (Israel, a flock); cf. Isa. lxiii. 11.
„ lxxix. 13 }
„ lxxiv. 2 ("the tribe of thine „ „ 17 ("the tribes ...").
  inheritance");
„ „ „ (reference to Mount „ „ 18 (Sept.).
  Zion).

---

[1] Cf. *BL*, pp. 91, 102.
[2] *New World*, Sept. 1892 (review of *OTJC*²); *Founders*, pp. 220-223. Beer (*Gemeinde-Psalmen*, 1894, pp. liv.-lvi.) also adopts the new theory, and refers several other psalms (as well as Robertson Smith's three) to the same period. Should the writer find another occasion to refer to this subject, he would study Ps. xliv. in connection with the neighbouring Korahite psalms with a view to clearing up the date. Is Ps. xlv. of the Persian or of the Greek age?
[3] Ps. lxxiv. 12-17 and lxxix. 6, 7 are undoubtedly later insertions.

Ps. lxxiv. 3-7	(outrages on the temple, culminating in its burning).	cf. Isa. lxiii. 18, lxiv. 10.	
„ lxxix. 1			
„ lxxiv. 8	(all "God's meeting-places" burned up).	„ lxiv. 9,	Yahwè's "holy cities are a desert."[1]
„ lxxiv. 20 (הַבְּ)		„ lxiii. 15, lxiv. 8.	
„ lxxix. 8	(let not Yahwè remember inherited guilt).	„ lxiv. 8	(same idea implied).

It may be objected that there is no evidence in lxiii. 7-lxiv. 11 that the Jews are suffering (in part at least) for their religion, whereas this is clearly implied in Psalms lxxiv. and lxxix. In the former passage we even find the most complete abasement for sin. But the two states of mind, that of abasement for sin and that of consciousness of suffering for the name of Yahwè, may have co-existed among the Jews, and have found expression in different liturgical poems. For the exaggeration of the confession in lxiv. 5-7 proves that the guilt spoken of was not altogether the product of sins consciously committed and remembered by the speakers, but partly inferred from the extremity of the national distress (lxiii. 17). With their long-proved zeal for the law, the Jews could not but consider themselves *hasîdîm* ("pious ones"), and yet, when so savagely treated by Ochus, they would feel as if Yahwè were smiting them through him, not altogether for the known, but also for the unknown sins of that generation, and in part, too (lxiv. 8), for the sins of their forefathers (cf. p. 364), which had not yet been sufficiently punished. A distinct reference to the latter occurs even in Ps. lxxix. 8. Ochus, however, had no conception that he was the rod of Yahwè. Unlike Cyrus and Darius, he scorned and hated the religions of Egypt and Palestine. Hence, while on the one hand he intensified by his ὕβρις the Jewish sense of close connection with Yahwè, which is by no means absent from lxiii. 7-lxiv. 11, he revived the sense of being under God's wrath which is expressed even in Ps. lxxiv. (*v.* 1) and Ps. lxxix. (*v.* 5), though in the former Israel is described

---

[1] The "meeting-places of God," which supplanted the old *bāmōth*, consecrated the cities.

as an innocent turtledove, and in the other as a people of *hasîdîm*.

If this view of the occasion of lxiii. 7-lxiv. 11 and Psalms lxxiv. and lxxix. be accepted, we once more gain from the prophetic literature some valuable additions to and corrections of our historical information. Solinus (xxxv. 6, Mommsen) tells us that Jericho, which succeeded Jerusalem as the capital of Judæa, was subdued by Artaxerxes (Ochus).[1] But Isa. lxiv. 9 and Ps. lxxiv. 8 are more precise. Wherever Yahwè had been worshipped, smoking ruins marked the passage of a blasphemous foe. The "city of palm-trees" naturally could not escape, but the "holy city" was pre-eminent in suffering. This fact may be confirmed from a prophetic fragment which we have already referred to this period, xxvii. 7-11. Let the reader turn to this passage; it will serve as a commentary on lxiv. 9 (see p. 156). Indeed, a great part of chaps. xxiv.-xxvii. is best explained by the troubles under Ochus, and therefore illustrates our present subject. For some further suggestions in defence of our critical theory, see Prologue.

CHAPTER LXV.

Chaps. lxv. and lxvi. are no doubt connected, but must be treated provisionally as separate pieces. The former consists of alternate threatening and promise, the one addressed to persons such as we have already met with in chap. lvii., the other to faithful Jews. It has been usual to regard this composition (which falls into two parts, dividing at *v.* 13) as the answer of Yahwè to the preceding liturgical prayer. I have more than once given my reasons for believing that the opinion of the majority of expositors is mistaken, nor has Dillmann, so far as I can see, impaired the force of my arguments. Indeed, this scholar's own exegesis is (owing to his prejudice in favour of unity of authorship) in some respects so arbitrary that one may be content with putting over against it a summary

[1] Judeich accepts the destruction of Jericho as a fact; so too Hitzig. For myself, while not denying the possibility of the statement, I would rather not trust too much to the accuracy of the name "Jericho."

of the circumstances and ideas of the writer of chap. lxv., which require us to separate it absolutely from lxiii. 7-lxiv., and also (when supported by the phraseological argument) to assign it, like all the preceding sections from chap. lvi. onwards, to the post-Exilic period. We may well be thankful thus to "disburden the great prophecy of the Restoration from the imputation of cherishing the (often) morbid and conflicting thoughts which meet us in the last of the appendices to the Book of Isaiah."[1]

1. *Circumstances.*—Great bitterness of feeling prevailed among the Jews when chap. lxv. was written. A body of men of Israelitish extraction (for they are spoken of as "your brethren," lxvi. 5) had obstinately refused to give up their inherited customs and unite themselves to the faithful servants of Yahwè (lxv. 1, 2). To all appearance, the bad religious customs referred to had gone on for a long period without drawing down any divine wrath upon the perpetrators, for a prophetic oracle declares that "their iniquity and the iniquity of their fathers who burned incense upon the mountains and dishonoured Yahwè upon the hills" still waits to be punished (*vv.* 6, 7). Thus we already find reason to suppose that a part of the Jewish exiles has returned to Palestine, and that the hostile neighbours mentioned are the Samaritans, who continued the northern Israelitish religious tradition without receiving the violent check of captivity. The bitterness with which the writer announces the long-delayed punishment confirms this view. Clearly it cannot be altogether explained by indignation at the "dishonour" to Yahwè. Such words as these:—

And ye shall leave your name for a (form of) cursing to my chosen ones (namely), 'And let the Lord Yahwè slay thee [as he slew this and that sinner];'
Your brethren that hate you, that loathe you for his name's sake;
And as for me their works and their thoughts (or, plots),

betray both vindictiveness and fear. The persons spoken of must have plotted against the faithful servants of Yahwè, and from lxv. 8, where the latter are compared to the few good

[1] *Expositor*, 1891 (1), p. 160.

grapes in a cluster, we may infer that their opponents were very superior in numbers. It is true that, according to lxv. 1 and 11, these "disobedient" people did not "call on the name" of Yahwè, and even "forsook" him, but (not to refer yet to lxvi. 3) this must be understood in the light of Jer. xliv., where the Jewish refugees in Egypt pay practical homage to the "queen of heaven," but continue to use the name of Yahwè in their oaths.[1] The watchword of the writer and his friends was Deut. vi. 4, "Yahwè, our God, Yahwè is one," and to "prepare a table for Gad and pour out mixed drink for Menî" (lxv. 11) was to "forsake" or deny the Yahwè who alone deserved the name.[2] We are also told that the opponents "forgot Yahwè's holy mountain" (lxv. 11), a phrase which would be meaningless unless they might have been expected to remember the temple, and which is by no means a reminiscence (as Dillmann supposes[3]) of Ps. cxxxvii. 4. The writer sees no remedy for this miserable division of the Holy Land between the true and the false worshippers of Yahwè (as he would call them) than a complete extirpation of the latter. Then the true "seed" will come out of Jacob or Judah (for the complete purification of the Jewish community has not yet been effected), and will occupy the whole of Yahwè's mountains" (lxv. 9).

But the religious customs in this and in the next chapter (for chap. lxvi. cannot be treated altogether separately) require a closer investigation. (*a*) From lxv. 11 we learn that tables laden with food were spread before the heathen gods Gad ("Fortune") and Menî ("Destiny"). Nowhere perhaps is the weakness of Dillmann's argument for the

[1] Jer. xliv. 26; cf. Cheyne, *Jeremiah, his Life and Times*, pp. 195-199.

[2] If it is the Samaritans who are meant here, may not they, as well as unfaithful Jews, be referred to in i. 28, "and they that forsake Yahwè shall perish"? That i. 27, 28 is a late insertion we have seen already (p. 6 f.).

[3] So G. A. Smith, *Exposition*, ii. 458. But the mention of "my holy mountain" (which in this connection must refer to the temple) implies that it is the neglect of the temple ritual which is the sin imputed to the opponents, not merely an indifference to the low estate of Zion during the Captivity. Besides, no sufficient proof has been offered of the Exilic date of Ps. cxxxvii., Budde's argument from the Kîna rhythm (*New World*, March 1893) being extremely improbable.

ascription of these chapters to Isaiah more manifest than here. Both Gad and Menî were, as is well known, Syrian deities,[1] connected with the planets Jupiter and Venus as the dispenser of fortune and the arbitress of destiny respectively. The prevalence of the worship of the former is attested by the names Baal-gad and Migdal-gad. In later times "Gad" became so popular that his name acquired the wider sense of "genius," "godhead," cf. גד דביתא, "the good genius of the house"; לגד דהר, "to the godhead of the mountains"; ערסא דגדא, "couch of the protective genius."[2] The name Menî has been found in compound proper names on coins of the Achæmenidæ (e.g. עבדמני). It is a masculine form, but there may have been, as in Babylonia, a masculine as well as a feminine Venus; Manât (*Koran*, Sur. liii. 19-23) and Menâat (Doughty's *Inscriptions*) may be analogous feminine forms. To urge with Dillmann that "possibly Gad and Menî are merely Hebrew appellations of divinities which had other names in Babylonia" is scarcely judicious (see Delitzsch's conclusive summary of evidence, *Jes.*, p. 620).

(*b*) lxiii. 3-5, "That sacrifice in the gardens, and burn incense upon the bricks; that tarry in the graves, and lodge in the secret places; that eat swine's flesh, and in whose vessels is broth of unclean meats; that say, Keep by thyself, come not too near me, else I shall sanctify thee." Worship among the trees of "gardens" is of course a native Palestinian custom (cf. lvii. 5, p. 315). What "burning incense upon the bricks" means, we do not yet know. "Tarrying in the graves" points in the first instance to Palestine, where the rock-graves have in all ages been used upon occasion as dwellings (cf. Mark iii. 5). The special object of the persons referred to was to get inspired dreams (by *incubatio*) or, possibly, necromantic oracles.[3] Swine's flesh was eaten in sacrificial meals, though probably tabooed on other occasions. There is no necessity whatever to suppose that the custom had been lately borrowed either from Babylonia or from

[1] See *PI*, ii. 118; Mordtmann, *ZDMG*, xl. 44-46; Siegfried, *JPT*, 1875, pp. 356-367.
[2] See the Talmudic lexicons of Levy and Jastrow.
[3] Cf. Talm., *Chagiga* 3*b*, "As for him who passes the night in a cemetery, it may be said, He does it that there may rest upon him a spirit of uncleanness" (cf. Zech. xiii. 2); Streane's transl.

Egypt. Indeed, it is not so easy to say where the pig did not occupy an honourable place among sacrificial animals, except indeed among strict Jews.[1] The other points must be taken in connection with (*c*).

(*c*) lxvi. 3, 17. "He that slaughtereth an ox, (but also) slayeth a man;[2] he that sacrificeth a sheep, (but also) strangleth a dog; he that bringeth an oblation, (but also) swine's blood; he that burneth incense, (but also) blesseth an idol. . . . They that consecrate and purify themselves for the gardens . . . that eat swine's flesh, and the swarming creatures, and mice, together shall they come to an end, saith Yahwè." It is not expressly said that the oxen and the sheep, the oblation and the incense were offered to Yahwè. But we may presume that this is what the writer means. The persons spoken of seem to have combined certain offerings and rites of the heathen with those that were sanctioned by the general Yahwistic tradition. "The reference is to certain exceptional sacrifices offered on special occasions, and accompanied with meals in which the worshippers partook of the flesh of the victims with the blood (cf. lxv. 4; Zech. ix. 7). The victims selected were such as were strictly tabooed (*i.e.* virtually unclean) in ordinary life. Human sacrifices (lvii. 5) may have been the rarest; at any rate, chaps. lxv. and lxvi. contain no references to cannibalism" (*BW*). It is a reasonable conjecture that these rites were practised by the Samaritans in the fifth century B.C., at least until greater regularity was introduced into the Samaritan cultus, which we may plausibly attribute to the arrival among the Samaritans of Sanballat's Jewish son-in-law, and the erection of the temple on Mount Gerizim. For the statement of tradition that the non-Jewish immigrants into Samaria brought heathen rites with them is very precise, and though the Persian governor would doubtless have forbidden sacrifices of men and of dogs had he been aware of them, yet we know from experience how easily under such

[1] Cf. W. R. Smith, *Religion of the Semites*, p. 372; *Kinship*, p. 308 f.; Hewitt, *Journal of R. A. S.*, April 1890, p. 439. For Egypt, see the paintings in the tomb of Renni at El-Kab. Renni was a prophet of Hebent, and had to provide swine to be sacrificed to his goddess.

[2] So (of human sacrifices) Lowth and W. R. Smith (*Kinship*, etc., p. 308).

circumstances the strangest rites may escape the notice of the rulers. On the other hand, that the existence of such rites should be no secret to the Jews at Jerusalem would not be strange, considering the intermarriages between Jewish and Samaritan families (cf. on lvi. 9-lvii. 13*b*). And clearly the offences complained of would be far more provocative of prophetic indignation in the land of Judah, after a regular sacrificial system had been established, than in Babylonia (according to Dillmann's theory) during the Exile, when (apart from any obscure heretical rites) sacrifices were necessarily in abeyance.

There is still, however, one very important feature in the description which calls for notice. It is evident that there was not complete uniformity in the religion of the "disobedient people." In lxv. 5 the partakers of the sacred meal warn certain other persons not to come too near them, lest they should themselves become "holy,"[1] and be incapacitated for secular business. Great light has been thrown upon this statement, in connection with the strange religious rites and meals spoken of by my friend the late Prof. Robertson Smith in several suggestive passages of his archæological works.[2] The persons who "purified themselves for the gardens," and who, after the sacrifices had been offered, partook of the sacred meals, were the initiated members of special religious brotherhoods, whose rites were derived from a primitive tribal heathenism, not without strong affinities to totemism, and the existence of which in Judah at the close of the period of independence is attested by Ezek. viii. 10, 11. The members of these brotherhoods met on stated occasions to perform their mysteries, which centred in the exceptional sacrifices referred to above. These were of course accompanied by meals, the object of which was to give the worshippers a mystic communion of the body and blood of a divine animal. According to Robertson Smith, Isa. lxv. 3-5 and the parallel passages are monuments of a syncretism which sprang up about the time of the Assyrian captivity (2 Ki. xvii. 24, 25). It was the time

---

[1] Read קְדַשְׁתִּיךָ (see *RT*).

[2] *Kinship and Marriage in Early Arabia*, pp. 307-310; *The Religion of the Semites*,[2] pp. 343, 357-368.

CHAPTER LXV

when the national religions were breaking up ; the gods of the peoples overcome by Assyria and Babylonia had proved unable to avert destruction, and men looked with sinking hearts for other helpers, and sometimes revived old, sometimes adopted new and foreign superstitions, which promised to be efficacious. The phenomenon is not an uncommon one ; in seasons of public anxiety a recrudescence of superstitious feeling and practice has often been noted. Prof. Burnet has lately pointed out [1] that Hellas passed through such a stage in the fifth century, when it was threatened at once by Persians on the east and Carthaginians on the west. "An age of despondency and even of despair," he remarks, "was setting in, and this has left its mark on all the thought of the time."

This description is fully applicable to Palestine and other Asiatic countries. The only weakness in Robertson Smith's suggestive exposition of the facts is his tacit assumption that chaps. lxv.-lxvi. are of Exilic origin. This acute scholar wished perhaps to bring them as near as he could to the earlier links in the chain of evidence for his theory of totemistic survivals. But is it not much more natural to suppose that lxv. 3-5 and the parallel passages refer (equally with lvii. 3-11) to the descendants of Sargon's and Assurbanipal's colonists in N. Palestine in the fifth century than that it relates to the Jewish exiles in Babylon in the sixth? The latter were not so doubly dyed with superstition as the former, and were outwardly not altogether unprosperous. On the other hand, the condition of the Samaritans was probably, as Winckler has pointed out,[2] the reverse of fortunate, and whatever troubles befell the Syrian satrapy must have been as much felt by the Samaritans as by the Jews, and have strengthened the idea (so favourable to superstition) of the weakness of Yahwè. Hence a slight modification of Robertson Smith's theory seems necessary. And the view here advocated is confirmed by the fact that the list of foods forbidden to faithful Jews (which, as this scholar has made highly probable, is directed against the sacrificial meals of the Semitic mysteries) is found not only

---

[1] *Early Greek Philosophy*, p. 84.
[2] *Untersuch.*, p. 106 f.

in Deut. xiv., but in a slightly revised form in Lev. xi., *i.e.* in the post-Exilic document known as P.

The phrase in lxvi. 17 (restored by Klostermann), אֶחָד אַחַד בַּתָּוֶךְ, *i.e.* "one (consecrating) the other, on the tip of the ear," must be explained by Ex. xxix. 20, 21 ; Lev. viii. 23, 24, xiv. 14-17. The sacred blood was applied to the extremities of the body, which were most in danger of desecration, to represent the renewed bond between the god and his worshipper (comp. W. R. Smith, *Rel. of Sem.*², p. 344).

2. *Ideas.*—Note (*a*) the idea of the renovation of the universe (lxv. 17), to which there has been already an allusion in lx. 19 (li. 16); cf. also iv. 5, xxiv. 23, xxx. 26. This is a step beyond the author of xi. 6-9, who only drew the animal world of Palestine within the range of his eschatological hopes. According to him the moral purity of the human population of Yahwè's mountain-land (itself brought about by human agency)[1] will produce a reflection of itself in the lower animals (cf. Muir's quotation from the Mahabharata, *Sanskrit Texts*, iv. 158). But this new writer conceives the idea of a purely physical miracle, "created" as something which has no human connection, and as a new and unexpected favour. Just as, according to xxxii. 15, the moral regeneration will be produced by a special divine influence, so by creative energy a corresponding physical scenery for this will be provided, viz. "new heavens and a new earth," which, unlike the old (li. 16), will "stand perpetually before" Yahwè (lxvi. 22). A foregleam of this great idea may be found in li. 16, where, however, the language is metaphorical, and not, as here, semi-dogmatic. Dr. A. Kohut's supposition that the idea is of Zoroastrian origin is altogether gratuitous. Still it *is* easier to understand its appearance in Judah under the Persian rule (for Jewish ideas must have been at least indirectly affected by Zoroastrianism[2]) than in Babylonia at the close of the Exile.

[1] It is true that the ideal king of xi. 1-5 is to be endowed with supernatural gifts. Still it is a man who is thus endowed, and the result of his activity is therefore not a new divine creation. The picture is half-way between that which visited Isaiah's mind in i. 16, 17 and that of the passages considered above.

[2] See p. 152, and cf. note 2 (on Jewish doctrinal developments).

CHAPTER LXV

The description which follows is no doubt a poor one, and shows that the devout imagination had yet much to do to fill up its canvas worthily. The writer is satisfied with a mere renewal of the idyll of Paradise, and by a strange slip even speaks (*v.* 20) of sinners in the new Jerusalem. Death, it appears, will not be excluded from the joyous city, though it will be deprived of its evil character (*vv.* 20, 22, 23). Hence the author does not belong to the same school, and probably not to the same period, as the writer of xxv. 8, line 1, which is indeed probably a later insertion (p. 152), nor is there any foregleam in his words of a doctrine of resurrection. He reminds us of a writer in the Book of Enoch (cf. *vv.* 20, 22 with Enoch v. 9, and *vv.* 19, 20 with Enoch xxv. 6), whom Mr. Charles[1] has conjecturally assigned to a period preceding that of Antiochus Epiphanes. He must, however, be earlier than that writer, who, like the Targumist, interprets הָעֵץ in lxv. 22 of the tree of life. (*b*) The idea that the iniquities of the fathers are visited upon the children (lxv. 7) was one of those most prevalent in the Exilic or post-Exilic age (see Lev. xxvi. 39, 40; Lam. v. 7; Ps. cix. 14; Neh. ix. 2; Dan. ix. 4-8). The prophet of restoration, however, has no occasion to refer to it. (*c*) The idea of the heavenly book or register (*v.* 6) was a special favourite of later writers (see *e.g.* iv. 3, Mal. iii. 16, Ps. lvi. 9, Dan. vii. 10).

3. *Style and phraseology.*—The excitement of the writer affects his style and his rhythm, which are equally defective. The oversight in *v.* 20 has been already referred to. The strange phrase "the God of the Amen" (*v.* 16), however, which would at once prove a very late date, is probably due to faulty pointing. Point אֱלֹהֵי אֹמֶן (*PI*, ii. 119), and comp. xxv. 1. כְּאֶחָד for יַחְדָּו (*v.* 25) certainly belongs to a very late linguistic period (see p. 258), and to the lax construction with אֲשֶׁר in *v.* 18 (cf. xxxi. 6, late) there is no parallel in II. Isaiah. Among the parallelisms, note especially these:—
v. 7, שַׁלֵּם אֶל־חֵיק, Jer. xxxii. 18 (late), cf. Ps. lxxix. 12;
רִאשֹׁנָה, Jer. xvi. 18 (late);[2]—*v.* 14, שֶׁבֶר רוּחַ, cf. lxi. 1;—*v.* 15 (formula), Jer. xxix. 22, ("another name"), lxii. 2;—*v.* 16, הִתְבָּרֵךְ בְּ, Gen. xxii. 18, xxvi. 4, Jer. iv. 2, Ps. lxxii. 17

---

[1] *The Book of Enoch* (1893), p. 56.
[2] Sept. omits 'ר in both passages.

—*v.* 21, Deut. xxviii. 30, cf. lxii. 8 f.;—*v.* 22 (trees), cf. lxi. 3 ;—*v.* 24, lviii. 9, xxx. 19 ;—*v.* 25*a*, condensed quotation from xi. 6, 7 ; and *v.* 25*b*, quotation from xi. 9*a* (p. 66). The statement as to the serpent (cf. Gen. iii. 14) is most probably a later insertion. It spoils the context, and is also against the rhythm.[1]

Less striking but still noteworthy parallelisms. *V.* 1, קָרָא בְּשֵׁם יי׳ (קָרָא of Mas. text must be wrong), as lxiv. 6 (the parallelism, however, seems illusory) ;—*v.* 2, דֶּרֶךְ לֹא־טוֹב, as Prov. xvi. 29, Ps. xxxvi. 5 ;—*v.* 3, הַכְעִים, a specially Deuteronomistic word ;[2]—*v.* 4, נְצוּרִים " secret places," cf. xlviii. 6 ;[3] מָרָק (so read with Q're), again only Judg. vi. 19, 20 ; פִּגֻּלִים, as Ezek. iv. 14, Lev. (twice) ;—*v.* 6, לֹא אֶחֱשֶׂה, as lxii. 1 (but how much more appropriately there !), cf. lvii. 11 ;—כִּי־אִם, used as lv. 10 ;—*v.* 9, הָרַי, as xiv. 25 (p. 252) ;—*v.* 10, גְוָה, late in use (p. 146) ;—רְבָץ, as xxxv. 7 ;—*v.* 11, וְאַתֶּם, cf. lvii. 3 ; מְלֵא, and *v.* 20, as xxiii. 2, xxxiii. 5 ;—מִמְסָךְ, as Prov. xxiii. 30 (nowhere else) ;—*v.* 14, טוּב לֵב, as Deut. xxviii. 47 ;—*v.* 17, בָּרָא, as II. Isaiah (p. 252) ;—*v.* 18, שׂוֹשׂ and מָשׂוֹשׂ, see p. 268; עֲדֵי־עַד, as xxvi. 4 (p. 148) ;—*v.* 19, וְעָקָה, as xv. 5, 8 (nowhere else in this book ; but cf. יָעַק, xxx. 19, lvii. 13) ;—*v.* 20, עוּל, as xlix. 15 (nowhere else in O. T.) ; קָלֵל, again only in Job xxiv. 18, Ps. xxxvii. 22 ;—*vv.* 22, 23, allusions to Job xxi. 13 (בָּלָה, " to enjoy the full use of ") and 8 (happiness in seeing one's children grow up) ;—*v.* 23, לָרִיק, as xlix. 4 ; בֶּהָלָה, as Jer. xv. 8 (see p. 126) ; צֶאֱצָאִים, as xliv. 3, lxi. 9 (p. 253). Note also in *v.* 24 וְהָיָה, found again in lxvi. 23, but nowhere else in chaps. xl.-lxvi ; also in *v.* 9 " Judah," found also in xlviii. 1 (in a late insertion), but nowhere else in these chapters, and in *v.* 10 " (the) Sharon," found only twice again in Isaiah, viz. in xxxiii. 9, xxxv. 2.

To sum up. The only date that accords with the evidence is a post-Exilic one, and there is very strong reason to think that the persons denounced in chap. lxv. (and chap. lxvi.) are those half-Jews or Samaritans who, in the time of Nehemiah, were such great adversaries of the faithful Jews.

---

[1] So Duhm (*RT*). Dillmann thinks that the whole verse is a later addition. But his chief reason, viz. that כאחד is a late idiom, has no force if the rest of the chapter is certainly post-Exilic.

[2] See Driver, *Introd.*, p. 191 (No. 26).

[3] In both places, however, ו may be an error for ב (see *RT*).

CHAPTER LXV

If so, a valuable addition is made to our illustrative material for the religious history of this period; let the relative uncertainty of this be noted by all means, but let us not refuse to supplement what we know from other sources by probable inferences from these important documents. When these passages were written, the Jews, as it would appear, had not entirely broken off relations with the Samaritans, and some of them had made great efforts to induce the latter to conform to a more consistent Yahwism. The Samaritans, however, refused, and displayed a religious "loathing" for their stricter "brethren" (lxvi. 5), which these returned in full measure.

This view of the relations between the Jews and their neighbours may no doubt seem inconsistent with that given in Ezra iv. 1-5, where we are told that the Samaritans in 535 asked leave to join the exiles ("the sons of the *gôla*") in rebuilding the temple, on the ground that they worshipped the same God as the Jews, and had offered sacrifice to him ever since Esar-haddon had "brought them up thither." It appears, however, that both on the chronological point, and probably even on the statement as to the king who colonised Samaria, Ezra iv. 1-5 is an unreliable authority,[1] so that we *need not* attach great weight to its assertion of the willingness of the Samaritans to co-operate with the Jews. And even if this be thought exaggerated scepticism (see Jer. xli. 5), it is not hard to reconcile this assertion with the view which we gain from lxv. 1, 2. The Samaritans may have expressed a sincere desire to assist the Jews (not however in 535, but in 520), and the Jews may have consented to this, but this consent must have been coupled with conditions (cf. lvi. 6) which made it seem to the Samaritans no better than a refusal. And so at a later date some of the Jewish prophets may have endeavoured to induce the Samaritans (through the friends of the latter at Jerusalem) to accept the prescribed conditions, but there neither was nor could be any satisfactory result. This view seems in itself a reasonable

---

[1] See Kuenen, *Ond.*², i. 505; Kosters, *Het Herstel*, p. 16; and, on the Assyriological point, Schrader, *CI;* Sayce, *Criticism and the Monuments*, pp. 543-545; and on the opposite side, Winckler, *Untersuch.*, pp. 97-100, and Kosters, *l.c.* note 1.

one. As Palestine had no longer any sanctuary of high reputation,[1] it would be natural for its Yahwè worshippers to wish for a restoration of their old privileges at Jerusalem (see Jer. *l.c.*). There were also obvious reasons why the Jewish leaders should desire an increase in the number of faithful Yahwists. For if any Jewish exiles did return in 536, they must have been very few in number, and wofully inadequate to the great works devolving upon them.

We need not, however, discuss this further. The main point is, that the persons denounced in chap. lxv. (as in lvi. 9-lvii. 13*a*) are the Samaritans, an important addition to the theory which I maintained in 1891, and due entirely to the keen insight of Duhm. It will be observed that the view thus modified increases the probability that Psalms xxii., xxxv., and lxix. belong to an early period in the growth of the feud between the Jews and the Samaritans.[2] Nehemiah's account of this period is no doubt truthful, but it is bald and one-sided. It portrays the man of affairs rather than the promoter of religious truth and unity. But from these psalms and prophecies, which, though by no means free from bitterness, seem to show that kindlier feelings once prevailed among the Jews, we gain a much more satisfactory and psychologically interesting view of a critical period.

CHAPTER LXVI.

The results of the examination of this chapter have to some extent been already indicated. Chaps. lxv. and lxvi. must clearly be referred to the same period, and some of the most important critical data are derived from the latter chapter. But may we assume that chap. lxvi. forms a literary whole, belonging in all its parts to the same period?

---

[1] Renan, *Hist.*, iv. 151.

[2] See *BL*, pp. 231-233. In *BL*, p. 65, I have suggested that Ps. cix. may also be referred to this period, "or even perhaps to the close of the Persian age." The latter date is somewhat recommended by the plural from מֵעִים, *v.* 8 (again only in Eccles. v. 1), but opposed by the parallelisms between Ps. cix. and Psalms xxxv. and lxix. (in which observe the late form בִּרְיָה). Cf. also Neh. iv. 4, 5, xiii. 25. Against a Maccabæan date, see *BL*, p. 47 ; but cf. Baethgen and Beer.

CHAPTER LXVI

We will not lay much stress on the poverty of the rhythm; that may well be accounted for by the incapacity or excitement of the writer. But there are several breaks in the connection which appear to indicate the composite origin of the chapter. Verses 5 and 6, for instance, are not properly consecutive. The former verse closes with a declaration that the scoffing and malignant neighbours of the Jews (the Samaritans) shall find that the high hopes of Yahwè's servants are only too well-founded, while "they themselves shall be put to shame." Then follows in v. 6—

Hark! a roaring from the city; hark! from the temple (it cometh); Hark! Yahwè who rendereth (their) deserts to his enemies.

Who are these enemies? Have we any more right here than in the parallel passage lix. 18 to say with Duhm that they are the unfaithful servants of Yahwè, viz. the half-Jews and the false-Jews? Surely it is much more probable that they are the hostile peoples who, it was expected, would gather in the latter days to the siege of Jerusalem (cf. Joel iii. 2, 12; Zech. xiv. 2).

This alone gives sufficient occasion for the awful description in vv. 15, 16—

For behold, Yahwè will come as a fire (בְּאֵשׁ, Sept.), and as a whirlwind (will be) his chariots, to pay back his wrath in burning heat, and his rebuke in flames of fire. For by fire will Yahwè hold judgment, and by his sword upon all flesh, and many will be the slain ones of Yahwè.

Here "all flesh" certainly means "all the human race," and Sept. is most probably right in reading נִשְׁפָּט אֶת־כָּל־הָאָרֶץ, which completes the parallelism; if any doubt be felt, it will be removed by comparing Jer. xxv. 31.[1] Shall we then suppose, in order to connect vv. 6-18a with v. 5 that the writer mechanically adopts the usual description of the judgment on the nations, but is only thinking of the fate of the false brethren? Surely this would be purchasing unity at too high a price. It is true that the writer is not a very clear

[1] That this passage is late admits of no doubt. Jer. xxv. is largely interpolated (see Giesebr.).

thinker, so far as we can judge from his ill-digested exposition. But we must not admit that he could express himself in such a misleading way as this theory would seem to imply. May we, then, assume that a description of the opposite fates [1] of Jerusalem and the hostile nations has been attached to a short prophecy relative to the Samaritans (*vv.* 1-5)? But even this will not fully meet the circumstances of the case. For *v.* 17 and the opening words of *v.* 18 clearly refer to the Samaritans. Obviously too this passage does not cohere with the context, which gains by its removal. Verse 17 is the natural supplement of *v.* 3; it tells us more about the same strange rites which are there referred to, and with the accompanying imperfectly preserved threat, "And as for me, their works and their plots . . ." [2] forms a suitable close to a short prophecy on the unimportance of material temples, and on the wickedness and the consequent punishment of the Samaritans (*vv.* 1-5, 17-18*a*). *Vv.* 6-16 will then constitute an independent composition, which is very naturally introduced by the interjectional קוֹל (cf. xl. 3).

That several hands have been engaged on chap. lxvi. is at any rate more than probable. In 1891 I suggested [3] that not only *vv.* 1-4 and 17, but *vv.* 18-24 were probably introduced later, and scarcely by the same writer. Dillmann and Duhm, too, are both agreed that *vv.* 18-22 have been tampered with by a later hand, and Duhm also thinks that *vv.* 23-24 are a later addition by the editor of chaps. xl.-lxvi. Let us consider the latter passage first. It is clumsily connected with the context by וְהָיָה, which is a favourite formula of interpolators, and is used thus nowhere else in these chapters. It is also, regarded as a conclusion of the section, altogether superfluous. *V.* 22 is a fully adequate close (cf. lix. 21); why should the writer, who has apparently done with the temple in *v.* 21, return to the subject here? And why should he mar the effect of his former statements

[1] At the beginning of *v.* 7 וְהָיָא seems to have dropped out (Duhm).

[2] בָּאָה which follows is perhaps a fragment of כִּי־הִנֵּה בָאָה הָעֵת, so that immediately after the prediction of Yahwè's judgment upon "all flesh," and his many victims, will come the explanation, "[For behold the time] cometh that I will gather all nations and tongues," etc.

[3] *JQR*, Oct. 1891, p. 122.

by the awful declaration of *v.* 24? There are also two points in which he differs from the writer of the preceding section (if *vv.* 6-16, 18*b*-22) may be taken together. In *vv.* 15-16 the victims of Yahwè's vengeance are certainly non-Jewish, but הַפֹּשְׁעִים in *v.* 24 clearly refers to unfaithful Jews (cf. xliii. 27, xlvi. 8, xlviii. 8, liii. 12, lix. 13). And again, in *v.* 16 "all flesh" means "all mankind" (*i.e.* the hostile nations who are destroyed), but in *v.* 23 it refers to the whole community of servants of Yahwè in Judah (as in Joel iii. 1, A.V. ii. 28). This is clear from the statement that they will offer weekly worship in the temple. Add to this that in *v.* 24 we have a word (דֵּרָאוֹן) which occurs elsewhere only once, viz. in Dan. xii. 2. Now let us turn to *vv.* 18*b*-22. In *v.* 19 from הַגּוֹיִם to יָוָן is certainly an interpolation, like that in xi. 11; the list of the seven nations[1] is quite needless, and spoils one of the best constructed sentences in the chapter. A similar remark applies to the catalogue of animals and vehicles in *v.* 20. In *v.* 21 Dillm. suspects that לְלִוִּים has been interpolated, to conform the language to the then recognised legal standard (see Deut. xvii. 9, xviii. 1). König[2] also thinks this not improbable, but proposes as an alternative view that לְלִוִּים was the gloss of a scribe who understood the reference to be to Gentile proselytes, and therefore moderated the privilege in store for them by adding "(or rather) for Levites." Both Dillm. and König, however, appear to be influenced by a prejudice in favour of II. Isaiah's authorship. The most natural correction is certainly that of Kuenen[3] and Duhm, לְכֹהֲנִים לְוִיִּם "for Levite priests." For II. Isaiah such a statement would seem to be too prosaically precise. Therefore, though לְכֹהֲנִים needs some word or words to support it at the close of Yahwè's oracle, it is accepted as the true reading by these critics. Our choice, however, really lies between the best attested reading לכ' וללוים and the simpler but unattested one proposed by Kuenen and Duhm. The former accords with the later distinction between priests and Levites; the latter with the Deuteronomic law.

---

[1] Reading "Meshech, Rosh," for משכי קשת (the final ח in קשת comes from תובל). Cf. Ezek. xxvii. 13, xxxviii. 2, 4. Cf. Lowth and Duhm.
[2] *Einl.*, p. 233 f.   [3] *Ond.*², i. 200.

But even after these interpolations have been removed, can we be sure that *vv.* 18*b*-22 were written by the same author, and at the same time as *vv.* 6-16? In *v.* 18 we find a phrase, "all nations and languages," which is specially characteristic of the Maccabæan Book of Daniel (Dan. iii. 4, 7, 29; iv. 1; v. 19; vi. 25; vii. 14). May not *vv.* 18*b*-22 (for *v.* 18*b* cannot be separated from the rest) belong to the same period as *vv.* 23-24, and therefore to a different author from the preceding passages? This conclusion would be in harmony with the best attested, though not the most probable reading in *v.* 21, "for priests and for Levites," which would require us to date the passage to which *v.* 21 belongs after the introduction of Ezra's law book. It is however not in itself a very plausible one, for nothing else in the passage suggests quite so late a date. And it so happens that in Zech. viii. 23 we find a phrase, "all languages of the nations," which is sufficiently near to account for the use of the phrase in *v.* 18 long before the date of Daniel. It is safer to suppose that *vv.* 18*b*-22 are a first appendix to *vv.* 6-16, written not long afterwards, and not improbably by the writer of that passage. The earlier prophecy is indeed complete without the appendix, for it describes or alludes to most of the facts described in *vv.* 18*b*-22, viz. the happy change in the fortunes of the Jews, and the devoted attentions paid to them by the Gentiles, who have evidently come to Jerusalem to see the divine glory. Nevertheless the writer of *vv.* 6-16, or a like-minded companion, may have felt that more explanation was desirable. And so he begins with a statement that Yahwè will soon gather "all nations," *i.e.* those which have not been affected by the recent judgment, and becoming immediately conscious that this statement is itself obscure, he explains that those who have escaped in the great catastrophe will go to the more distant nations, and relate what they have experienced of Yahwè's glory, including a wonderful sign (cf. Joel iii. 15, 16, 18; Zech. xiv. 4-10) which can leave no doubt in any one's mind who it is that has interposed in human affairs. Upon this the peoples of the far-off "coastlands" will conduct the Jews of the dispersion with reverential awe to that bright spot of light and glory, Jerusalem. Lastly, to prevent the jealousy of the priests of Jerusalem, it is declared to be Yahwè's will that some of these restored exiles [1] should be admitted into the priesthood. One may presume (for we have no reason to suppose a liberalising tendency in the writer) that only born Levites are referred to.

We have now to consider the dates of these several passages. From what has been said above it will be at once clear that *vv*. 23-24 must have been written a good deal later than the age of Nehemiah. A sense of this led me in 1891 to conjecture that chaps. lxv.-lxvi. were most probably written not earlier than the time of the Syrian and Egyptian campaign of Artaxerxes Ochus.[2] That this view was not free from difficulty I was well aware. The tone of chaps. lxv. and lxvi. was certainly not the same as that of lxiii. 7-lxiv. Still the ideas and situations implied in the two sections did not appear to be irreconcileable, and at other periods too there were superficial differences between prophetic writers. I believe that I was right in asserting (both in 1881 and in 1891)[3] that these two chapters in their entirety, as well as most of chaps. lvi.-lxiv., were of post-Exilic origin, though my analysis and my dating were alike imperfect; and I think, too, that this view is the only tenable alternative to that which, as its natural development, I am now advocating. To refer chaps. lxv.-lxvi. to the Second Isaiah has surely become impossible. Such a theory is equally opposed to the circumstances, the ideas, and the language of the writer or writers of these chapters. I need not therefore trouble myself once more to give a serious discussion of it. How embarrassed its present supporters are, may be seen from a remark of König in his learned and not uncritical *Einleitung* (p. 326). Chaps. lxv. and lxvi. cannot, we are assured, have been written in Jerusalem, because in lxv. 20 מִשָּׁם = from Jerusalem, and in lxvi. 13 the Jews are promised that they shall be comforted "in Jerusalem." And since the writer certainly lives at the chief centre of Jewish life, where can he be but in Babylonia?

---

[1] It is sad to have to abandon the theory (so pleasing but so inconsistent with the context) that מֵהֶם refers to converted Gentiles (*PI*, ii. 131; so Ges., Ew., Del., Kay, Dillm., Baudissin).

[2] *BL*, p. 160; *JQR*, Oct. 1891, pp. 111-122.

[3] *JQR*, as above; cf. *Expositor*, 1891 (1), p. 159 f.

König also observes that "not without reason has Feilchenfeld (1890) explained lxv. 3, 4, 11, lxvi. 1, 2, 3, 17 by pointing out the inclination of the rebellious in Israel to the Persian cultus." The latter argument seems to indicate some peculiar and unsound theory respecting Persian religion, and may be safely disregarded (see above). The former one leaves out of sight the special fondness of later writers for the name Jerusalem. The post-Exilic Jews, to whom Zion was "the perfection of beauty" (Ps. l. 2), could not repeat the name too often (cf. p. 339 f.), and considering that in lxv. 18, 19*a* the writer had twice named Jerusalem, why should he not, in *v*. 19*b*, say "from thence" instead of "from Jerusalem"? As to lxvi. 13, a comparison of lx. 4 suggests that when he wrote "in Jerusalem" the author was specially thinking of the Jews of the dispersion, in comparison with whom the Jews at Jerusalem, even when reinforced by Ezra and his companions, were of altogether trifling importance.

How much later than the time of Nehemiah, lxvi. 23-24 was written, cannot be absolutely determined. The ideas expressed in it, however, imply a considerable development of the simple primitive belief in Sheól which we still find in several of the psalms. "The souls of rebels, he says, will suffer penal tortures as violent as those which the worm and the fire would cause to their bodies, if consciousness remained."[1] A hint of a similar view is given in l. 11, לְמַעֲצֵבָה תִּשְׁכָּבוּן, "in a place of pain shall ye lie down" (Sept. κοιμηθήσεσθε), which probably refers to Gehenna. This passage, as we have seen, comes from a supplementer, and probably to the same person (the editor of Isa. xl.-lxvi.?) the closing verses of chap. lxvi. are also due. Considering that Dan. xii. 2 presupposes an already somewhat definite doctrine of future rewards and punishments, we need not date either passage later than 200 B.C.

The two originally separate but related prophecies (*a*) lxvi. 1-5, 17-18*a*, and (*b*) lxvi. 6-16, together with (*c*) the first appendix, lxvi. 18*b*-22, have now to be considered. Let us take (*b*) and (*c*) first. The circumstances are briefly these. The temple has been rebuilt (*v*. 6), but the nation is

[1] *BL*, p. 405; cf. *PI*, ii. 132-134; Schwally, *Das Leben nach dem Tode*, p. 134 f.

CHAPTER LXVI

still but half-born (*v.* 9; cf. xxvi. 17), and the group of poor depressed Jews which exists at Jerusalem is oppressed by its enemies. The writer comforts himself by certain great beliefs and expectations. Not only one particular foe (such as the Samaritans or the Edomites), but all the dangerous nations round about shall be destroyed. Jerusalem shall be glorified at the expense of the still remaining and now converted nations of the earth, and Levites of the dispersion shall be admitted to the privileges of the Jerusalem priesthood (p. 379). The rhythm is imperfect and intermittent; the phraseology is that of a late period, and sometimes betrays the influence of other decidedly post-Exilic passages. Cf. the last words of *v.* 6 with the gloss in lix. 18*b*. *V.* 7, הִמְלִיט "to bring forth" (a son), only here (see p. 264). *V.* 8, יוּחָל, Hofal only here. *V.* 9, הַשְׁבִּיר, cf. xxxvii. 3. *V.* 10, שִׂישׂוּ (p. 268); מִתְאַבֵּל (20). *V.* 11, שֹׁד; see on lx. 16. תַּנְחֻמִים (p. 270). הִתְעַנֵּג (p. 266). וִיז "udder," nowhere else in this sense (see *BL*, p. 472 f., on Ps. l. 11). מֶצַץ, here only. *V.* 12, נָחַל שׁוֹטֵף, as xxx. 28 (late). צַד (p. 267); שָׁעֲשַׁע Pulpal, here only; cf. xi. 8, v. 7. *V.* 14, את, used as in Ps. lxvii. 2. *V.* 16, נִשְׁפַּט, as Ezek. xxxviii. 22; Joel iv. 2. *V.* 18*b*, late idiom (above). כָּבוֹד יי׳, only in late insertions (p. 298). *V.* 19, פְּלֵיטִים, cf. xlv. 20. שֵׁמַע, as xxiii. 5 (nowhere else in Isaiah). (In the gloss in *v.* 20 note צַב "litter"; in this sense only again in Num. vii. 3. Also כִּרְכָּרוֹת "dromedaries," ἅπ. λεγ.) Other parallelisms. *V.* 6, קוֹל interjectionally, as xiii. 4, xl. 3; מְשַׁלֵּם, cf. lxv. 6; *v.* 10, cf. lxv. 18; *v.* 22, cf. lxv. 17. Also cf. *v.* 7 (sudden regeneration of Zion) with xlix. 17-21, liv. 1; *v.* 9, יֹאמַר with xl. 1;—*v.* 11 with lx. 5, 16, lxi. 6;—*v.* 12 with lx. 4, xlix. 22, 23;—*v.* 14 (figure) with xliv. 3, 4, lviii. 11 (?);—*v.* 16 with Jer. xxv. 33;—*v.* 16 (Yahwè's sword) with xxxiv. 5, 6, xxvii. 1 (p. 151);—*v.* 20 with lx. 3, 4 (a different picture);—*v.* 21 with lxi. 6 (the two views of "priesthood" are reconcilable; but is it likely that they came from the same writer?);—*v.* 22 with Jer. xxxi. 35, 36, xxxiii. 25, 26.

We must therefore group this composition with the others which have been assigned to the age of Nehemiah and Ezra. It would appear from its allusions to have been written after lix. 15*b*-20 and chap. lx. (*i.e.* after the arrival of Ezra in 432 ?), either by the author of those passages, or by a like-minded companion, and to have been occasioned by the general pressure of difficult circumstances. It must however have been composed before the introduction of the priestly lawbook by Ezra, for (if our view of lxvi. 21 is correct) it still maintains the Deuteronomic point of view (as Mal. ii. 1, 4, 8) with regard to the priesthood. These results are perfectly consistent, for neither the prayer in Neh. ix. 7-37, nor the covenant in Neh. x. 33-40, which accompanied the formation of the new *kahal*, betray the influence of P; in other words, the legal basis is Deuteronomic.[1] Before we pass on, let us observe that in lxvi. 20 the phrase "your brethren" refers to the faithful Jews of the dispersion, but in *v.* 5 to the "disobedient" half-Jews. A fresh evidence that the two prophetic works interwoven (as it seems) in chap. lxvi. have not the same occasion.[2]

The remaining prophecy (*a*) seems to have had a more special occasion, and it is not at all easy to understand it. The high spirituality of *vv.* 1, 2 and, as some think, of *v.* 3, suggests a comparison of psalms like xl. 2-12, l., li. 3-19, which, interpreted naturally, express the sentiments of students of Isaiah and Jeremiah, to whom temple and sacrifice were religiously indifferent.[3] On the other hand, these verses stand in a context which positively thrills with an excitement produced by trying circumstances, so that it is hardly probable that *v.* 1 is merely an emphatic declaration that Yahwè "dwelleth not in houses made with hands" (*PI*). If the composition to which *vv.* 1-2 belong was written (as even Dillm. thought that it was) in Babylonia at the close of the Exile, we must surely suppose, with Hitzig and Knobel, that *vv.* 1-3 are directed against certain Jews who wished to build a temple to Yahwè in Chaldæa.[4] But

[1] See the evidence in Kosters, *Het Herstel*, etc., p. 98 f.

[2] *V.* 20 however belongs, as we have seen, to the first appendix.

[3] *EB*, xiii. 380; *BL*, pp. 364-368; Beer, *Gemeinde-psalmen*, p. l. etc. It is the same observation of the affinities of this passage which induces Bredenkamp to ascribe *vv.* 1-6 to Isaiah; *vv.* 7-14 he regards as Exilic, though in *vv.* 7-9 perhaps following an Isaianic model. Very crude criticism, vaguely reproduced by Dr. C. H. H. Wright in Smith's *DB*,[2] i. 1473.

[4] Dillmann's own interpretation of *vv.* 1-2 is, "Ye heathenish uncon-

what if the composition is post-Exilic? In this case it seems at first sight as if the writer were an opponent of Haggai and Zechariah, who urged the rebuilding of the temple, and also of the writer or writers of passages like lvi. 7, lx. 7, lxii. 9.[1] This view however is too difficult (cf. p. 358, on lxiv. 10). We must therefore either follow H. Schultz, who, though a believer in the unity of chaps. xl.-lxvi., acutely suggests that lxvi. 1-3 is directed against the partizans of the old local sanctuaries (*AT Theol.*[4], p. 190), or agree with Duhm that the persons described in *vv.* 1-3 are the Samaritans, and that *vv.* 1-2 were called forth by the first announcement of the plan of a Samaritan temple. Now since the first part of Duhm's theory has as nearly as possible been demonstrated, I do not see how we can help giving a favourable consideration to the latter. It is true, the historical temple on Mt. Gerizim was probably built for that unnamed member of the high-priestly family whom Nehemiah "chased" from Jerusalem because he refused to put away his Samaritan wife.[2] "But the plan of such a temple may have been formed earlier. The prophet seems to be aware of this plan, and takes high spiritual ground in dealing with it. No temple, he says, is worthy of Yahwè, whose footstool is not merely the sanctuary (lx. 13) but the whole earth. He permits indeed the temple at Jerusalem, as he permits the sacrifices, but only out of condescension to the human craving for symbols.[3] And if there is to be a

verted Israelites, who are preparing to return and join in rebuilding the temple, and who contemn your stricter brethren—from you Yahwè will accept no services." How improbable this is, Prof. G. A. Smith (on the whole, a follower of Dillmann) has evidently seen, but his own view (*Expos.*, p. 388), that the question in *v.* 1 "implies a house already built," is very difficult.

[1] So *BL*, p. 152; cf. 375; *EB*, xiii. 381; Beer, *Gem.-psalmen*, p. 48.

[2] Comparing Neh. xiii. 28 (see Ryle's note) with Jos., *Ant.*, xi. 7, 8.

[3] "The writer does not say this, nor would he have so formulated his thought, but something like this lies at the root of the (seemingly) anti-sacrificial psalms (*BW*)." He would not of course have refused compliance to any legal precept, but when he spoke from his heart he showed that he had risen above outward forms. Strict consistency is not to be expected in transitional times. But if so, how came this writer's work to be accepted? Because canonisation did not depend on a single individual or even school. Ruth and Jonah became canonical

384   ISAIAH

temple at all, the only acceptable worshipper is the humble-minded and obedient Jewish believer" (*BW*). It is true, in his excitement the writer has provided no visible link between *vv*. 1-2 and *v*. 3. But the Samaritans being referred to in *v*. 3, it is clear that the reproof in *vv*. 1-2 must be intended for them. The reader will judge for himself whether Hitzig's view of lxvi. 1-2 is half as probable as the view which is here put over against it. And even were its plausibility greater, we must remember that nothing but the strongest evidence from language could justify us in separating lxvi. 1-5, 17-18*a* from chap. lxv. If chap. lxv. is post-Exilic, the other prophetic work must be so too, for the same ideas are presupposed and the same superstitions are referred to in both. The only special peculiarity of the later prophecy is the spirituality of *vv*. 1-2, which are exactly parallel to lvii. 15 and 1 Ki. viii. 27 (probably post-Exilic) and strongly contrast with xl. 13, 14. Let us now consider the phraseology of lxvi. 1, etc. In *v*. 1, מְנוּחָה, see on xi. 10, p. 61. In *v*. 2 note the descriptive terms (the sing. is collective ; cf. xxvi. 6). First, עָנִי, the most common epithet of the post-Exilic Jews (see Psalms). Next, נְכֵה־רוּחַ, cf. דַּכָּא, lvii. 15 (p. 321), also רוּחַ נְכֵאָה, Prov. (thrice). Lastly, חָרֵד עַל־דְּבָרִי (*v*. 5 again, with אֶל for עַל), cf. Ezra ix. 4, x. 3. Clearly this description, not less than those in lvii. 15, lxi. 1, must be post-Exilic. שֹׁחֵט, of human sacrifices, as lvii. 5. מַזְכִּיר, "one that offereth an *azkâra*" (or offering of incense ; see Dillm. on Lev. ii. 2) ; cf. the liturgical expression, לְהַזְכִּיר, Ps. xxxviii. 1, lxx. 1 ; 1 Chr. xvi. 4, = "to be used at the offering of an *azkâra*." This phrase presupposes the organisation of the cultus of Yahwè. שִׁקּוּצִים, Ezek. and Lev.; cf. Zech. ix. 7.   *V*. 4, תַּעֲלֻלִים (rare ; see iii. 4) ; the end of the *v*. nearly as lxv. 12.   *V*. 5, נִדָּה, in Am. vi. 3 "to put afar in thought"; here "to loathe" (Sept. βδελυσσομένοις). Cf. נִדָּה "impurity," Ezek., Lev., Num., Zech.   *V*. 17, הִתְקַדֵּשׁ (p. 267). הִטַּהֵר, eleven times in Lev. xiv. ; שֶׁקֶץ, eight times in Lev. xi.

in spite of their very free spirit, and so too the "Puritan psalms" and the opening verses of Isa. lxvi. Kautzsch (*St. u. Kr.*, 1892, p. 587) and König (*Einl.*, p. 401) seem hardly to have considered these points enough.

CHAPTER LXVI

The two text-corrections, שֶׁרֶץ and תְּנָךְ (p. 370), are also words of Leviticus; for the former see also Deut. xiv. 19.

We return then with renewed confidence to the second of the two theories mentioned above. From chap. lxv. we inferred that some of the prophets of Jerusalem (cf. Neh. vi. 14) had endeavoured to persuade the Samaritans to become strict worshippers of Yahwè like themselves. From lxvi. 1-5, 17-18a, we learn in addition that the Samaritans not only rejected these overtures, but formed the plan of erecting a rival temple to Yahwè in their own territory. The irritation which this news produced at Jerusalem is very intelligible. Had the Samaritans simply confined themselves to their local cults, it is possible that in course of time the schism among Palestinian Jews would have been healed. As a matter of fact the Samaritans did accept the Deuteronomic Law; might they not afterwards have assimilated themselves still further to the more progressive section of the Jewish race? But the erection of a rival temple made the religious and social separation permanent. There is no necessity to suppose that our two prophecies were written *after* the introduction of Ezra's lawbook. The parallelisms with Leviticus are such as can easily be explained from the traditional usages of the Jews. It is highly improbable that overtures would have been made to the Samaritans after the introduction of the priestly code. The parallelisms with Ezra ix. 4, x. 3 suggest that, though Ezra had arrived at Jerusalem, he had not yet gone beyond attempting to separate the pure from the impure members of the Jewish community, as is described in Ezra ix., x. (the latter chapter must be read critically, owing to certain traces of editorial manipulation [1]). The formation of the *kahal* and the introduction of P, as well as the expulsion of Sanballat's son-in-law (Neh. xiii. 28), are still in the future.[2] Whether Judaism can be established on a secure basis is still quite uncertain. So ends the composite book, which was begun amid such high hopes in the land of exile.

[1] See Kosters, *Het Herstel*, etc., pp. 117-124.
[2] On the chronological order of the events described in these chapters, see Kosters, p. 139.

TRANSLATION OF I. AND II. ISAIAH
(APPENDIX)[1]

Note.—It should be understood that the following translation of the supposed genuine parts of I. and II. Isaiah is merely provisional. It is designed to illustrate and exhibit synthetically some of the most important results of the critical discussion in the previous pages. It does not embody the author's final conclusions on the form, metre, and meaning of the text, which must be sought elsewhere (see p. xii). The textual corrections appearing here that are new are derived from the pages of the *Introduction* itself. To this rule, at any rate, there are very few exceptions, and for these the author is responsible. To economise space no parallelistic arrangement has been attempted. The translation, it should be added, is mainly based upon those given in *PI* and *ICA*.

Italic type in the text of the translation, except where otherwise explained, denotes that the passage so printed is either editorial, or of doubtful origin.

* . . . . * Words between two stars denote translation from a corrected Hebrew text.

(. . . .) Round brackets enclose additions in the text of the translation to which there is nothing corresponding in the received text of the original.

[. . . .] Square brackets denote that the enclosed words should probably be deleted from the text as glosses or later additions.

. . . . Dots in the translation denote that some words, which cannot be recovered, have probably fallen out of the original text.

[1] The author's warm thanks are due to Mr. G. H. Box, B.A., of St. John's College, Oxford, who has prepared this Appendix.

PART I

THE GENUINE PROPHECIES OF ISAIAH I

CHAPTER I

Isaiah's preaching of repentance during Sennacherib's invasion (before the siege of Jerusalem)

I

(*a*) *vv.* 2-4. Uncertain date

² HEAR, O heavens, and give ear, O earth, for Yahwè speaketh: Sons have I reared and brought up, and they have rebelled against me. ³ *An ox knoweth his owner, and an ass its master's crib: Israel is without knowledge, my people without understanding.* ⁴ *Ah sinning nation, people burdened with guilt, race of evil-doers, sons that do corruptly: they have forsaken Yahwè, spurned Israel's Holy One, withdrawn backward.*

II

(*b*) *vv.* 5-9. 701 B.C.

⁵ On what part can ye still be smitten, while revolting more and more? The whole head is sick, and the whole heart faint. ⁶ From the sole of the foot even to the head there is no soundness in him—wounds and wales and festering sores—they have not been pressed, nor bound up, nor softened with oil. ⁷ Your land—a desolation, your cities—burnt with fire, your tillage—in your very presence strangers devour it; and it is a desolation like the ruined land of *Sodom.* ⁸ And the daughter of Sion is left, like a booth in a vineyard, like a lodging in a cucumber-field, like a besieged city. ⁹ Except Yahwè Sebáoth had left us a remnant, we should almost have been as Sodom, we should have been like unto Gomorrah!

III

(*c*) *vv.* 10-17. 701 B.C.

¹⁰ Hear the word of Yahwè, ye rulers of Sodom, give ear to the instruction of our God, ye people of Gomorrah! ¹¹ Of what avail to me

is the multitude of your sacrifices? saith Yahwè; I am sated with burnt-offerings of rams, and fat of fed beasts, and in the blood of bullocks and lambs and he-goats I have no delight. [12] When ye come *to behold my face,* who hath required this at your hands—the trampling of my courts? [13] Bring no more oblations, vain is the incense (of sacrifice), it is an abomination unto me; new moon, and Sabbath, calling of assemblies—I cannot away with iniquity hand in hand with the solemn meeting. [14] Your new moons and your set days my soul hateth; they are an encumbrance to me, I am weary of bearing it. [15] And if ye spread forth your hands I hide mine eyes from you : even if ye make many prayers, I do not hear! your hands are full of blood. [16] Wash ye, make you clean, take away the evil of your doings from before mine eyes, cease to do evil, [17] learn to do well; seek out justice, set right the violent man, do justice to the orphan, plead for the widow.

IV

(d) vv. 18-20.   701 B.C.

[18] Come now, and let us argue together, saith Yahwè. Though your sins be as scarlet, they may become as white as snow; though they be red as crimson, they may become as wool. [19] If ye be willing and obedient, the good of the land shall ye eat; [20] but if ye refuse and rebel, by the sword shall ye be eaten, for the mouth of Yahwè hath spoken it.

V

(e) vv. 21-26.   702-701 B.C.

[21] How is she become an harlot—the faithful city, she that was full of justice, where righteousness was wont to lodge [but now murderers]! [22] Thy silver is become dross, thy wine weakened with water. [23] Thy rulers are unruly, and partners of thieves; every one loveth bribes, and pursueth rewards; to the orphan they do not justice, neither doth the cause of the widow come unto them. [24] Therefore this is the oracle of the Lord, Yahwè Sebáoth, the Hero of Israel : Ha! I will appease me of mine adversaries, and avenge me on mine enemies, [25] and I will bring back mine hand upon thee, and will smelt out *in the furnace* thy dross, and will take away all thy alloy; [26] and I will bring back thy judges as at the first, and thy counsellors as at the beginning : afterwards thou shalt be called, Citadel of Righteousness, Faithful city.

VI

(f) vv. 27-28

Editorial addition

APPENDIX

VII

(g) vv. 29-31.   Before 722 B.C.

Fragment against Tree-worship

²⁹ For * ye * shall be ashamed because of the terebinths in which ye have had pleasure, and shall blush for the gardens ye have chosen; ³⁰ yea, ye shall be as a terebinth whose leaves are withered, and as a garden that hath no water; and the strong one shall become tow, and his work a spark, and they shall both burn together, with none to quench them.

CHAPTERS II.-IV

THE FIRST COLLECTION OF ISAIAH'S PROPHECIES

CHAPTER II

[v. 1, Editorial]

I

A. vv. 2-5

Post-Exilic

II

B. vv. 6-22

The impending Day of Yahwè

(a) vv. 6-10 and 18-21.   Soon after 740 B.C.

⁶ Yea, thou (O Yahwè) hast cast off thy people, the house of Jacob, because they are replenished from the East, and are soothsayers like the Philistines, and with the children of aliens do bargain. ⁷ And his (Israel's) land is become full of silver and gold—endless are his treasures; and his land is become full of horses—endless are his chariots; ⁸ and his land is become full of idols, to the work of his hands he doeth homage, to that which his fingers have made; ⁹ and so humanity is bowed down, and man is brought low, and thou—forgive them not! ¹⁰ Go into the rock, and hide thee in the dust, at the terror of Yahwè and the splendour of his majesty (when he ariseth to overawe the earth).

vv. 18-21

¹⁸ And the idols shall utterly vanish; ¹⁹ and men shall go into caverns of rocks, and into holes of the ground, at the terror of Yahwè and the

390   ISAIAH

splendour of his majesty, when he ariseth to overawe the earth. ²⁰ In that day shall man cast his idols of silver and gold which they made to do homage unto, to the * moles * and to the bats, ²¹ to go into the clefts of the rocks and into the rents of the cliffs, at the terror of Yahwè and the splendour of his majesty, when he ariseth to overawe the earth.
[v. 22 a late gloss : omitted in lxx.]

(b) vv. 11-17. Soon after 740 B.C.

¹¹ The haughty eyes of humanity shall be brought low, and the loftiness of men bowed down, and Yahwè alone shall be exalted in that day. ¹² For a day hath Yahwè Sebáoth on all that is proud and lofty, and on all that is lifted up that it be brought low ; ¹³ and upon all the cedars of Lebanon, the lofty and uplifted, and upon all the oaks of Bashan ; ¹⁴ and upon all the mountains, the lofty, and upon all the hills the uplifted ; ¹⁵ and upon every high tower, and upon every fenced wall ; ¹⁶ and upon all the ships of Tarshish, and upon all the choice works of imagery ; ¹⁷ and the haughtiness of humanity shall be bowed down, and the loftiness of men brought low, and Yahwè alone shall be exalted in that day.

CHAPTER III. 1-15

The fall of Judah: its causes indicated

C. vv. 1-15.   *Circa* 735 B.C.

For behold, the Lord, Yahwè Sebáoth, removeth from Jerusalem and from Judah stay and staff—† ² *hero and man of war, judge and prophet, and diviner and elder;* ³ *captain of fifty and man of reputation, counsellor and magician, and expert charmer.* ⁴ And I will make boys their princes, and childish wilfulness shall rule over them. ⁵ And the people shall tyrannise over one another, man over man, and neighbour over neighbour ; they shall be insolent, the boy to the aged, and the mean man to the honourable. ‡ ⁶ *When one man taketh hold of his brother in his father's house (saying), Thou hast (still) an upper garment, thou shalt be our chieftain, and let this ruin-heap be under thy hand;* ⁷ *he shall cry out in that day, saying, I will not be the binder-up; for in my house is neither bread nor upper garment; ye shall not appoint me chieftain of the people.* ⁸ For Jerusalem is ruined, and Judah falleth, because their tongue and their deeds are against Yahwè, to defy the eyes of his glory. ⁹ Their respect of persons witnesseth against them, and their sin they make known like Sodom, undisguisedly.   Alas, for them ! for they have wrought themselves misfortune.   [vv. 10-11 probably an editorial attempt to replace four lines which had become illegible.] ¹² My people —his governor is a wilful child, and women rule over him : my people ! thy guides lead thee astray, and the way of thy paths they have brought into confusion. ¹³ Yahwè stationeth himself to plead : he standeth to

† vv. 2-3 may have an Isaianic basis.
‡ vv. 6-7 may have an Isaianic basis.

defend the cause of * his people.* † ¹⁴ Yahwè entereth into judgment with the elders of his people and the princes thereof (saying), And ye— ye have devoured the vineyard, the spoil of the afflicted is in your houses. ¹⁵ What mean ye that ye crush my people, and grind the face of the afflicted? saith the Lord, Yahwè Sebáoth.

CHAPTER III. 16–IV. 1

The Punishment of the Proud Ladies of Jerusalem

D. *vv*. 16-iv. 1. 735 B.C.

¹⁶ *And Yahwè said:* Because the daughters of Zion are haughty, and go with outstretched neck and leering eyes—go tripping along, and make a tinkling with their anklets ; ¹⁷ the Lord will smite with a scab the crown of the head of the daughters of Zion, and Yahwè will make bare their shame. [*vv*. 18-23 a later insertion.] ²⁴ And it shall come to pass : instead of perfume there shall be rottenness, and instead of a girdle, a rope ; and instead of curled hair, baldness, and instead of a mantle, girding of sackcloth—a brand instead of beauty.

[*vv*. 25-26 a later insertion.]

IV. ¹ And seven women shall take hold of one man in that day, saying : Our own bread will we eat, and our own clothing will we wear : only let us be called by thy name, take away our disgrace.

[E. iv. 2-6 : a Messianic appendix (post-Exilic).]

CHAPTER V

I

The Parable of the Vineyard

A. *vv*. 1-7. *Circa* 735 B.C.

I

¹ Come let me sing of my friend, (sing) my friend's song on his vineyard. A vineyard had my friend, on a fruitful fertile height ; ² and he digged it and cleared it of stones, and planted it with choice vines, and built a tower in its midst, yea, and hewed out a wine-vat therein, and he looked for it to bear grapes, but it bore wild grapes.

2

³ And now, O inhabitants of Jerusalem, and men of Judah, judge, I pray you, betwixt me and my vineyard ! ⁴ What is there still to be done in my vineyard which I have not done in it ? Wherefore, when I looked for it to bear grapes, did it bear wild grapes ?

† *v*. 13, read יסבּ (see p. 18).

3

⁵ And now, let me tell you, I pray, what I will do to my vineyard,—I will take away its hedge, and it shall be devoured, and I will break down its walls, and it shall be down-trodden. ⁶ And I will lay it utterly waste, it shall neither be pruned nor digged, and shall shoot up in thorns and briars, and the clouds will I enjoin that they rain no rain upon it. ⁷ For the vineyard of Yahwè Sebáoth is the house of Israel, and the men of Judah his darling plantation ; and he looked for justice, but behold, bloodshed, for righteousness, but behold, an outcry.

II

A sixfold Denunciation

B. *vv.* 8-24. Same date

1

⁸ Ha ! they that join house to house, that lay field to field, till there is no more room, and ye are made to dwell alone in the midst of the land ! ⁹ (Therefore thus) hath Yahwè Sebáoth (revealed himself) in mine ears : Surely (your) many houses shall become a desolation, great and fair ones without inhabitant ; ¹⁰ for ten acres of vineyard shall yield (but) a bath, and the seed of an homer shall yield (but) an ephah.

2

¹¹ Ha ! those who rise up at dawn to pursue strong drink, that linger in the twilight, inflamed with wine ; ¹² and lute and harp, timbrel and flute, and wine, make their banquet ! But Yahwè's work they regard not, and the operation of his hands they do not see ! ¹³ Therefore my people goeth into exile unawares, and his honoured ones are * sapless from * hunger, and his riotous throng parched with thirst. ¹⁴ Therefore Sheól enlargeth her greed, and openeth her mouth without measure, and down go her splendour and her throng, and her uproar, and he that is jubilant in her ; † ¹⁷ and lambs graze * upon their wilderness, and their ruined places kids shall devour.*

3

For *vv.* 18-19, see p. 184, note 1

¹⁸ Ha ! they that draw guilt (to themselves) with cords of ungodliness, and sin as with traces of a wain ; ¹⁹ that say, Let his work hasten, let it speed that we may see it, and let the purpose of Israel's Holy One draw nigh and come, that we may perceive it !

4

²⁰ Ha ! they who call evil good, and good evil, that put darkness for light, and light for darkness, that put bitter for sweet, and sweet for bitter !

† *vv.* 15-16 quotation of ii. 11, 17, intruded from the margin.

APPENDIX

5

²¹ Ha ! they that are wise in their own eyes, and clever in their own conceit ! . . . .

6

²² Ha ! they that are heroes for wine-drinking, and valiant ones for spicing strong drink !   † ²³ *That declare the wicked righteous for a bribe, and take away the righteousness of the righteous from him !* . . . .
²⁴ Therefore, as the fire's tongue devoureth stubble, and (as) hay sinketh down in a flame, their root shall become as rottenness, and their blossom go up as dust, because they have despised the direction of Yahwè Sebáoth, and spurned the word of Israel's Holy One.

III

v. 25 mainly editorial

²⁵ *Therefore is Yahwè's anger kindled against his people, and he stretcheth out his hand over it, and smiteth it, so that the mountains tremble, and their carcases become as refuse in the midst of the streets.* For all this his anger turneth not away, and still is his hand outstretched. [*Note.—v.* 25 was designed by the editor to link v. 1-24 with ix. 7-x. 4 and v. 26-30.]

IV

C. *vv.* 26-30

[These verses should follow ix. 7-x. 4. See below, p. 399.]

CHAPTERS VI.-IX. 6.   SECOND PROPHETIC COLLECTION

CHAPTER VI

Circa B.C. 734

Isaiah's Account of his inaugural Vision

¹ In the year that King Uzziah died I saw the Lord sitting upon a high and uplifted throne, and his train filled the (heavenly) palace. ² Seraphim stood above him ; each one had six wings ; with two he covered his face, and with two he covered his feet, and with two he did fly. ³ And the one kept crying to the other, and saying : Holy, holy, holy, is Yahwè Sebáoth, The whole earth is full of his glory. ⁴ And the foundations of the thresholds shook at the voice of him that cried, and the house filled with smoke. ⁵ And I said : Woe is me, for I am

† *v.* 23 probably comes from another context.

undone, for a man of unclean lips am I, and in the midst of a people of unclean lips do I dwell, for the King, Yahwè Sebáoth, have mine eyes seen. ⁶ Then flew unto me one of the seraphim, with a (hot) stone in his hand, which he had taken with tongs from off the altar; ⁷ and he touched my mouth with it, and said, Lo, this hath touched thy lips; and so thine iniquity is gone, and thy sin forgiven. ⁸ And I heard the voice of Yahwè, saying: Whom shall I send, and who will go for us? And I said, Here am I, send me. ⁹ And he said: Go and say to this people, Hear on, but understand not, and go on seeing, but perceive not. ¹⁰ Make fat the heart of this people, and their ears make heavy, and their eyes besmear, lest they should see with their eyes, and hear with their ears, and their heart should understand, and they should turn and be healed. ¹¹ And I said, How long, O Lord? And he said: Until the cities be waste without inhabitant, and the houses without men, and the land be *left* a desolation, ¹² and (until) Yahwè have removed the men afar off, and the deserted region be large in the midst of the land. ¹³ᵃ And should there still be a tenth in it, this must again be consumed; like the terebinth and like the oak, of which at the felling a stock remaineth.†

CHAPTERS VII.-IX. 6

A. CHAPTER VII

I

(a) *vv.* 1-16. B.C. 734. Edited late

The Invasion of Rezin and the Reign of Immanuel

‡ ¹ *And in the days of Ahaz, son of Jotham, son of Uzziah, King of Judah, Rezin, King of Syria, together with Pekah, son of Remaliah, King of Israel, went up to Jerusalem to storm it—but he was not able to storm it.* ² And it was told the house of David, saying, Syria hath lighted down upon Ephraim; and his heart shook, and the heart of his people, as the trees of the forest shake before the wind. ³ And Yahwè said unto Isaiah: Go forth now to meet Ahaz, thou, and Shear-Yashub thy son, at the end of the conduit of the upper pool, at the highway of the fuller's field, ⁴ and say unto him, Take care, and keep calm; fear not, neither be faint-hearted, because of these two stumps of smoking firebrands, in spite of the fierce wrath of Rezin and Syria and of the son of Remaliah. ⁵ Because Syria hath purposed evil against thee (with) Ephraim and the son of Remaliah, saying, ⁶ Let us go up against Judah and *distress* it, and win it for ourselves, and appoint to be king in the midst of it the son of Tabel: ⁷ thus saith the Lord Yahwè, It shall not stand, neither shall it come to pass. ⁸ᵃ For the head of Syria is Damascus, and the head of Damascus is Rezin

† 13*b* a post-Exilic addition.
‡ *v.* 1 Exilic, dependent on 2 Kings xvi. 5.

APPENDIX

[⁸ᵇ a gloss], ⁹ and the head of Ephraim is Samaria, and the head of Samaria is Remaliah's son. . . . If ye hold not fast, verily ye shall not stand fast.† . . . ¹⁰ And Yahwè spake further unto Ahaz, ¹¹ Ask thee a sign of Yahwè thy God, deep unto Sheól or high unto heaven. ¹² But Ahaz said, I will not ask, neither will I put Yahwè to the test. ¹³ And he said, Hear now, O house of David ; is it too little for you to weary men, that ye weary my God also ? ¹⁴ Therefore the Lord himself shall appoint you a sign ; behold, whenever (henceforth) a young woman conceiveth and beareth a son, she shall call his name Immanuel. [*v.* 15 a gloss.] ¹⁶ For before the boy knoweth how to refuse the evil and choose the good, the land, of whose two kings thou art in terror, shall be deserted.

II

(*b*) *vv.* 17-20 uncertain date. Partly recast by a late editor

Fragments on the havoc wrought by the Assyrians

[*v.* 17 editorial.]

¹⁸ *And it shall come to pass in that day* that Yahwè shall hiss to the flies and to the bees, ¹⁹ and they shall all of them come and settle on the steeply-walled torrent-valleys, and on the clefts of the rocks, and on all thorn bushes, and on all pastures. ²⁰ *In that day* shall the Lord shave with the razor that is hired on the banks of the River, the head and the hair of the feet, and the beard also shall it sweep away. . . .

III

[*vv.* 21-25 un-Isaianic : " possibly, however, shreds and patches of Isaiah may be imbedded in them."]

CHAPTER VIII

I

B. *vv.* 1-4. 734 B.C.

The Ruin of Syria and Ephraim

¹ And Yahwè said unto me : 'Take thee a large tablet, and write thereon in plain characters, Swift—spoil—speedy-prey ; ² and *take* for me, as credible witnesses, Uriah the priest, and Zechariah the son of Jeberechiah. ³ And I went near to the prophetess, and she conceived, and bare a son. ⁴ And Yahwè said unto me : Call his name

---

† Probably between *vv.* 9 and 10 a passage should intervene which has been lost. See p. 32 f.

Maher-shalal-hash-baz; for before the boy shall know how to cry, My father, and My mother, they shall carry the riches of Damascus and the spoil of Samaria before the King of Assyria.

II

C. *vv.* 5-10.   734-723 B.C.

The Assyrian Invasion; Yahwè's Warning to Isaiah

(1)

⁵ And Yahwè spake still further unto me, saying: ⁶ Forasmuch as this people hath rejected the waters of Shiloah which flow softly, and † *despond because of* Rezin and Remaliah's son, ⁷ᵃ therefore, behold, the Lord bringeth upon them the waters of the River, the mighty and the great, and it shall come up over all its channels, and go over all its banks, ‡ ⁸ and shall sweep on into Judah, shall overflow and pass over, reaching even to the neck.

(2)

(*Appendix added by Isaiah*)

§ ⁸ᵇ. . . . . And his outstretched wings shall fill the breadth of *the land. For* with us is God.   ⁹ *Take knowledge,* ye peoples, and . . . . ; and give ear, all ye of far countries!   Gird yourselves, and break to pieces, gird yourselves and break to pieces!   ¹⁰ Purpose a purpose, and it shall come to nought, form a resolve, and it shall not stand, for with us is God.

III

D. *vv.* 11-18.   *The same subject*

(1)

This prophecy is slightly earlier than the preceding

¹¹ For thus said Yahwè unto me with a strong pressure of his Hand (upon me), and warning me not to walk in the way of this people:— ¹² Call ye not conspiracy all that this people calleth conspiracy, and that which they fear, fear not ye, neither account it dreadful.   ¹³ Yahwè Sabáoth—him shall ye count holy, and let him be your fear, and let him be your dread.   ¹⁴ And he shall be for a stone to strike against and for a rock of stumbling to both houses of Israel, for a gin and for a snare

---

† *v.* 6*a*, see p. 37, note 1.
‡ *v.* 7*b* a gloss.
§ For *vv.* 8*b*, 9, and 10 see p. 39 and note 1.

APPENDIX

to the inhabitants of Jerusalem.   15 And many shall stumble *at it,* and fall, and be broken, and snared, and taken.

(2)

vv. 16-18.   ? 701 B.C.

Epilogue to recent prophetic revelations (from vii. 3 *onwards)*

16 (I will) bind up the admonition (and) seal the testimony among my disciples ; 17 and I will wait for Yahwè, who hideth his face from the house of Jacob, and hope in him.   18 Behold, I and the children whom Yahwè hath given me are for signs and for omens in Israel from Yahwè Sebáoth who dwelleth on Mount Zion.

IV

E. *vv*. 19-ix. 6

(1)

(*a*) 19-22, 23*a*.   734 B.C.   Edited late

A fragment on the despair of the people of Judah

19 And when they say unto you, Consult the ghosts and the familiar spirits that chirp and that moan (give this answer), Should not a people (rather) consult its god ?   On behalf of the living should men consult the dead ?   20a To the direction and the testimony !   Surely they shall speak according to this word,† 20b for whom there is no dawn.   21 And he shall pass through it, hard pressed and famishing ; and it shall be, when he is famishing, he shall be deeply angered and curse his king and his god, and look upwards.   22 And he shall look unto the earth, and behold, distress and gloom, a thick veil of affliction. . . . . 23a . . . . .

(2)

(*b*) *The ideal King* (viii. 23*b*, ix. 1-6) : *First description*

[*v*. 23*b* editorial insertion to connect viii. 21, 22 with ix. 1-6.]

CHAPTER IX. 1-6 (cf. xi. 1-8)

If Isaianic, 734 B.C. ; but the passage is perhaps post-Exilic

1 *The people that walk in gloom see a great light, they that dwell in*

† *v*. 20*b* is Isaianic.   Some lines must have fallen out or become illegible before it.   The editor made good the deficiency by inserting 20*a*.

the land of deep shadow, upon them hath the light gleamed. ² Thou hast multiplied *exultation, thou hast increased joy,* they rejoice before thee as with the joy of harvest, as men exult when they divide the spoil. ³ For his burdensome yoke, and the staff of his back, his task-master's rod —thou hast broken as in the day of Midian. ⁴ Yea, every boot of him that is booted noisily, and the cloak rolled in blood—they are destined for burning, (for) fuel of fire. ⁵ For a child is born unto us, a son is given unto us, and the government is upon his shoulders, and his name is called, Wonder-Counsellor, God-Hero, Father of booty, Prince of Peace : ⁶ *increased* is the government and of peace there is no end, upon the throne of David and over his kingdom, in establishing and supporting it by justice and by righteousness from henceforth even for ever. The zeal of Yahwè Sebáoth will accomplish this.

CHAPTERS IX. 7 (8)-20 ; X. 1-4 ; V. 26-30

735 B.C.

Successive stages of the judgment upon all Israel

CHAPTER IX

1

⁷ A word hath Yahwè sent into Jacob, and it shall light down in Israel, ⁸ so that the whole people shall feel it, (and first of all) Ephraim and the inhabitants of Samaria; (who have stiffened their neck) in pride, and in elation of heart, saying, ⁹ Bricks have fallen down, but with hewn stones will we build up ; sycamores have been cut down, but with cedars will we replace them. ¹⁰ And so Yahwè set on high *his adversary* against him, and his enemies he spurred on ; ¹¹ Syrians on the east and Philistines on the west, and they devoured Israel with open mouth. For all this his anger turneth not away, and still is his hand outstretched.

2

¹² But the people turned not unto him who smote it, and Yahwè Sebáoth they did not consult. †¹³ So Yahwè cut off from Israel head and tail, palm-branch and rush in one day. † ¹⁴ The elder and the man of influence, he is the head; and the prophet who teacheth lies, he is the tail. ¹⁵ And the guides of this people became misleading ones, and they that were guided by them were stricken with confusion. ¹⁶ Therefore Yahwè *spareth not* its young warriors, and upon its orphans and its widows he hath no compassion, because everyone is profane and an evil-doer, and every mouth speaketh folly. For all this his anger turneth not away, and still is his hand outstretched.

† These verses probably editorial substitutes. See p. 46, note 2.

APPENDIX

3

¹⁷ For like a fire doth unrighteousness burn, thorns and briars it devoureth, and it kindleth the thickets of the forest, so that upward they roll in a column of smoke. ¹⁸ᵃ By the fury of Yahwè Sebáoth the land was †*burned up*; and the people became as fuel of fire; ¹⁹ᵃ they sliced on the right hand, and are (still) famished; and devoured on the left, and are (still) unsatisfied; ¹⁸ᵇ they had no pity on each other, ¹⁹ᵇ every one devoured the flesh of his helper—²⁰ Manasseh (devoured) Ephraim, and Ephraim Manasseh—(but) both of them together were against Judah. For all this his anger turneth not away, and still is his hand outstretched.

4

CHAPTER X. 1-4

¹ Ha! they that decree unjust decrees, and the scribes that scribble oppression, ² to turn aside the helpless from judgment, and to rob of their right the afflicted of my people, that widows may be their prey, and that they may spoil the fatherless. ³ What then will ye do in the day of visitation, and of crashing ruin which cometh from far? To whom will ye flee for help, and where will ye leave your wealth? ⁴ (They can do nought) except crouch under the captives, and fall under the slain. For all this his anger turneth not away, and still is his hand outstretched.

5

CHAPTER V. 26-30 (see p. 25 f.)

²⁶ And he shall lift up a banner to a far-off *nation,* and hiss to it from the end of the earth; and, behold, speedily, swiftly it cometh. ²⁷ There is none weary and none that stumbleth therein [they slumber not and sleep not]; and the girdle of their loins is not loosened, nor is the thong of their sandals torn; ²⁸ they, whose arrows are sharpened, and all their bows bent, whose horses' hoofs are accounted as flint, and their wheels as the whirlwind—²⁹ a roar have they like the lion's, they roar like the young lions, and growl, and seize the prey, and carry it off safe, none rescuing (it). [*v.* 30, editorial: modelled on viii. 22.]

CHAPTERS X. 5–XII. 6

A. (x. 5-34)

CHAPTER X

I

(*a*) *vv.* 5-15. 711 B.C.

(*The Plan of Assyria and the Plan of Yahwè contrasted*)

⁵ Ha! Assyria, the rod of mine anger, and the staff in whose hand

† Reading נצתה, see *PI*, critical note.

is mine indignation! ⁶ Against an impious nation am I wont to send him, and against the people of my wrath to give him a charge to take spoil and to seize booty, and to make it a trampling like mire in the streets. ⁷ But he—not so doth he plan, and his heart, not so doth it reckon; for to exterminate is in his heart, and to cut off nations not a few. ⁸ † *For he saith*, Are not my captains all of them kings? ⁹ Is not Calno as Carchemish? or is not Hamath as Arpad? or is not Samaria as Damascus? [*vv.* 10-12 editorial, probably designed to conceal a gap in the Isaianic material.] ¹³ † *For he hath said*, By the strength of my hand have I done it, and by my wisdom for I am discerning; and I removed the bounds of the peoples, and their treasures I plundered, and brought down like an hero them that were enthroned; ¹⁴ And as unto a nest mine hand hath reached the riches of the peoples, and as one gathereth forsaken eggs have I gathered all the earth; and there was none that fluttered the wing, or opened the beak and chirped. [*v.* 15 a later insertion.]

II

(*b*) *vv.* 16-23

The Judgment upon Assyria and its consequences for Judah; first description, followed by a promise

The whole passage, as it stands, is post-Exilic. *vv.* 16-19 *may* embody some Isaianic material; but the passage cannot be analysed.

III

(*c*) *vv.* 24-34

The same subject, preceded by a promise

722 B.C.   Edited late

[*vv.* 24-27 a later insertion.] ²⁷ᵇ His burden shall remove from off thy back, and his yoke from off thy neck * shall cease. ²⁸ A destroyer hath come up from the north,* he hath invaded Aiath, he hath passed through Migron. At Michmash he layeth up his baggage. ²⁹ They go through the pass, in Geba they have taken up their lodging; Ramah trembleth, Gibeah of Saul fleeth. ³⁰ Shriek, O daughter of Gallim; listen, Laishah. Answer her, Anathoth! ³¹ Madmenah is in mad flight; the inhabitants of Gebim gather their goods to flee. ³² This very day he will halt in Nob; he swingeth his hand against the mount of the Daughter of Zion, the hill of Jerusalem.

[*vv.* 33-34, editorial supplement.]

† Editorial.

APPENDIX

CHAPTERS XI.-XII

B. (chaps. xi.-xii.)

CHAPTER XI (cf. ix. 1-6)

I

(*a*) *vv.* 1-9. ? 720-715 B.C. Edited late

The Ideal King; second description

¹ *And a shoot shall come forth from the stock of Jesse, and a scion from his roots shall bear fruit,* ² *and the spirit of Yahwè shall rest upon him, a spirit of wisdom and discernment, a spirit of counsel and might, a spirit of knowledge and of the fear of Yahwè.* ³ *And he shall not judge according to that which his eyes have seen, nor arbitrate according to that which his ears have heard,* ⁴ *but with righteousness shall he judge the helpless, and arbitrate with equity for the humble in the land; and he shall smite *tyrants* with the rod of his mouth, and with the breath of his lips shall he slay the ungodly.* ⁵ *And righteousness shall be the girdle of his loins, and faithfulness the girdle of his reins.* ⁶ *And the wolf shall lodge with the lamb, and the leopard lie down with the kid, and the calf and the young lion and the fatling together, whilst a little child leadeth them.* .⁷ *And the cow and the bear shall feed, together shall their young ones lie down, and the lion shall eat straw like the ox;* ⁸ *and the suckling shall play at the hole of the asp, and the weaned child shall stretch out his hand to the eyeball of the basilisk.*

[*v.* 9 editorial link.]

II

[(*b*) *vv.* 10-16 a late appendix.]

III

[(*c*) xii. 1-6 a late appendix.]

CHAPTER XIV. 24-27

Probably the misplaced conclusion of the Isaianic prophecy on the plan of Assyria in x. 5-15

711 B.C.

²⁴ Sworn hath Yahwè Sebáoth, saying, Surely, according as I have planned, so shall it be, and according as I have purposed shall it stand; ²⁵ to shatter Assyria in my land, and upon my mountains to tread him under †foot. ²⁶ This is the purpose which is purposed concerning the whole earth, and this the hand that is stretched out over all the nations. ²⁷ For Yahwè Sebáoth hath purposed, and who can annul it? And his is the outstretched hand, and who can turn it back?

† 25*b* (*and his yoke shall remove from off them, and his burden remove from off his neck*) = x. 27, *and is a marginal gloss.*

CHAPTER XIV. 28-32

The Fate of the Philistines

720 B.C.

²⁸ *In the death year of King Ahaz came this *word.** ²⁹ Rejoice not, entire Philistia, that the rod which smote thee is broken! For out of the serpent's root shall issue a basilisk, and its fruit is a flying dragon. ³⁰ And *on my meadows* the poor shall feed, and the needy shall lie down securely; but I will kill thy root with famine, and thy remnant will *I* slay. ³¹ Howl, O gate; cry, O city; faint, entire Philistia! For out of the north a smoke cometh, and there is no straggler in his companies. ³² And what shall (the king of my people) answer (when) the messengers of the nation (shall speak unto him)?—That Yahwè hath founded Zion, and therein the afflicted of his people find refuge.

CHAPTER XVI. 13-14

An Isaianic fragment (?) Cf. p. 89

711 B.C. Edited late

¹³ †*This is the word which Yahwè spake concerning Moab heretofore.* ¹⁴ *And now Yahwè hath spoken, saying,* Within three years, as the years of an hireling, shall the glory of Moab be disgraced, with all the great multitude, but the remnant *in a very little while will I bring unto honour.*

CHAPTER XVII. 1-11

The Downfall of Syria and Israel

Before 734 B.C. Edited late

[*vv.* 1-3 have been retouched by the editor.]

1

¹ Behold Damascus is about to be removed from being a city, and becometh *a ruin.* ² Forsaken shall the cities *thereof* be *for ever*; they shall be given up to flocks, which shall lie down there, none making them afraid. ³ And the fortress shall cease from Ephraim, and the kingdom from Damascus; and the remnant of Aram — like the glory of the children of Israel shall they be, saith Yahwè Sebáoth.

2

⁴ In that day shall the glory of Jacob be attenuated, and the fatness of his flesh wax lean. ⁵ And it shall be as when the harvestman gathereth standing corn, and his arm reapeth the ears; yea, it shall be as when one gleaneth ears in the vale of Rephaim. ⁶ And gleanings

† Editorial.

APPENDIX

shall be left thereof, as at the striking of an olive tree, two or three berries at the uppermost point, four or five on the branches *of the* fruit tree, saith Yahwè, the God of Israel.

3

[*vv.* 7-8, editorial, replacing a missing strophe which had become illegible.]

⁷ *In that day shall mortal man look unto his maker, and his eyes have regard to the Holy One of Israel;* ⁸ *and he shall not look unto the work of his hands, and that which his fingers have made he shall not regard.*

4

⁹ In that day shall *thy* fortress cities be like the deserted places of the Hivites and the Amorites, ¹⁰ because thou hast forgotten the God of thy welfare, and the rock which is thy fortress thou hast not remembered. Therefore thou mayest plant plantations of Adonis, and with slips of a strange (God) mayest stock them ; ¹¹ as soon as thou plantest them thou mayest hedge them in, and in the morning bring thy seed to blossom— yet (for all that) shall the harvest flee in a day of sickness and desperate pain.

CHAPTER XVII. 12-14

The Preservation of Judah (Appendix added by Isaiah)

Circa 723 B.C.

¹² Ha ! the booming of innumerable peoples—like the boom of the sea is their booming ! And the din of nations—like the din of mighty waters is their din ! ¹³ Nations—their din, like the din of many waters may it be, but he checketh it, and it fleeth afar, and is driven away like chaff on the mountains before the wind, and like whirling dust before the hurricane. ¹⁴ At eventide, behold terror ! before morning, it is gone ! This is the portion of those who spoil us, and the lot of those who plunder us.

CHAPTER XVIII

The Destruction of the Assyrian Army ; an address to Ethiopia

702 B.C.

1

¹ Ha ! the land of the rustling of wings, ² which sendeth ambassadors on the sea, and in skiffs of reed on the face of the waters ! Go, ye fleet messengers, to a nation tall and glossy, to a people dreaded far and wide, a nation strong and all-subduing, whose land the rivers divide. ³ O all ye inhabitants of the world and dwellers on the earth, when a

banner is raised on the mountains, look; and when a trumpet is sounded, hearken.

2

⁴ For thus hath Yahwè said unto me, I will be still and look on in my place, as still as the clear heat in sunshine, as the dew-cloud in the heat of harvest. ⁵ For before the harvest, when the blossom is over, and the bud becometh a ripening grape, he shall lop off the branches with pruning-knives, and the tendrils shall he hew away. ⁶ They shall be left together to the mountain birds of prey, and to the beasts of the land; and the birds of prey shall summer thereon, and all the beasts of the land shall winter thereon.

[*v.* 7 post-Exilic appendix.]

CHAPTER XX
The Captivity of Egypt and Ethiopia
Circa 711 B.C.

¹ In the year when the Tartan came to Ashdod—Sargon, king of Assyria, having sent him—and stormed Ashdod, and took it, † ³ Yahwè said: According as my servant Isaiah hath gone unclad and barefoot three years for a sign and an omen against Egypt and against Ethiopia, ⁴ so shall the king of Assyria lead away the captives of Egypt and the exiles of Ethiopia, young and old, unclad and barefoot, and with buttocks uncovered—Egypt's shame! ⁵ And they shall be dismayed and ashamed because of Ethiopia, their expectation, and because of Egypt their pride. ⁶ And the inhabitants of this coast-land shall say in that day, Behold (if) thus hath our expectation fared, whereunto we fled for help to get deliverance from the king of Assyria; how can we escape?

CHAPTER XXI. 11-12, 13-17

Fragments on the doom of Edom and Kedar: two oracles (vv. 11-12, 13-15) of unknown authorship, date 589 B.C. (?) To these an Isaianic fragment (vv. 16-17) was attached after the Exile.

711 B.C. Edited late

¹⁶ For thus hath the Lord said unto me, Within a year, as the years of an hireling, all the glory of Kedar shall fail; ¹⁷ and the number that is left of the * mighty archers,* the sons of Kedar, shall become small; for Yahwè, Israel's God, hath spoken (it).

CHAPTER XXII. 1-14
The Inexpiable Sin
701 B.C. (After the raising of the blockade of Jerusalem)

I

¹ What aileth thee, then, that thou art wholly gone up to the house-

† v. 2 a later insertion.

tops, ² thou that art full of uproar, tumultuous city, exultant town ? thy slain are not the slain of the sword, nor the dead in battle. ³ All thy chieftains have fled together, bowless have they been made prisoners ; all of thine that were seized have together been made prisoners, though they fled far away. ⁴ Therefore I say, look away from me, let me weep bitterly ; be not urgent to comfort me for the destruction of the daughter of my people. ⁵ For a day of riot, and of repression, and of rout hath the Lord, Yahwè Sebáoth, in the valley of vision they undermine the wall, and the crying (soundeth) unto the mountains.

2

(*vv.* 6-14 *derived from another nearly contemporaneous prophecy of Isaiah's*)

† . . . . ⁶ And Elam took up the quiver, with troops of men, of horsemen, and Kir uncovered the shield,† . . . . ⁷ And when thy choicest valleys were full of chariots, and the horsemen had set themselves in line towards the gate † . . . . ⁸ and (the enemy) had drawn aside the screen of Judah, thou didst look in that day to the armour of the forest-house, ⁹ᵃ and ye saw that the breaches of David's city were many ; ‡ ¹¹ᵇ but ye looked not unto him who prepared it, and him who fashioned it long since ye did not regard. ¹² And the Lord, Yahwè Sebáoth, called in that day to weeping and to lamentation, to baldness and to girding with sackcloth ; ¹³ but behold, joy and gladness, killing oxen and slaughtering sheep, eating flesh and drinking wine, for "to-morrow we may die." ¹⁴ And Yahwè Sebáoth hath revealed himself (thus) in mine ears : Surely this iniquity shall not be cancelled unto you till ye die, saith the Lord, Yahwè Sebáoth.

CHAPTER XXII. 15-25

A wily Politician denounced

704-701 B.C.

¹⁵ᵇ*Against Shebna who was over the palace.* ¹⁵ᵃ Thus saith the Lord, Yahwè Sebáoth : Go, get thee unto this prefect (and say) ; ¹⁶ What (right) hast thou here, and whom hast thou here, that thou hewest thyself out a sepulchre here ? (thou man) that heweth his sepulchre on high, that carveth himself out in the rock a habitation ! ¹⁷ Behold, Yahwè will hurl, will hurl thee, O mighty man, and clutch thee tightly ; ¹⁸ he will roll, will roll thee up, (and toss thee) as a ball into a broad broad land ; thither shalt thou go to die, and thither shall go thy glorious chariots, thou disgrace of the house of thy lord !

[*vv.* 19-23 a late appendix.]
[*vv.* 24-25 a later appendix.]

† Something has fallen out of the text.
‡ *vv.* 9*b*-11*a* a prosaic interpolation.

ISAIAH

CHAPTER XXIII

The Fall of Tyre

725 B.C. Edited late

1

¹ Wail, ye ships of Tarshish, for * your fortress * is laid waste, so that there is no house, no entering in ! ² Be dumb, ye inhabitants of the coast, ye merchants of Zidon. . . . [*v.* 3 gloss ?]. ⁴ Be ashamed, O Zidon, for the sea, the fortress of the sea, speaketh saying, I have not travailed nor brought forth, neither have I reared youths, nor brought up virgins. [*v.* 5 a prosaic gloss.]

2

⁶ Pass ye over to Tarshish ; wail, ye inhabitants of the coast ! ⁷ Fareth it thus with your joyous one, whose origin is of ancient days, whose feet were wont to carry her afar off to sojourn ? ⁸ Who hath devised this against Tyre, the dispenser of crowns, whose merchants were princes, whose traffickers were the most honoured of the earth ? ⁹ Yahwè Sebáoth hath devised it, to profane the pride of all splendour, to disgrace all the most honoured of the earth.

3

¹⁰ Overflow thy land as the Nile ; O daughter of Tarshish, thy dikes are no more. ¹¹ His hand he stretched out over the sea, he made kingdoms to tremble ; Yahwè Sebáoth gave charge concerning Canaan, to destroy the fortresses thereof. ¹² He said, Exult no more, thou ravished virgin-daughter of Zidon ; arise, pass over to Chittim ; there too thou shalt have no rest ! [*v.* 13 later insertion.] ¹⁴ Wail, ye ships of Tarshish, for your fortress is laid waste !

[*vv.* 15-18 a later prosaic addition.]

CHAPTERS XXVIII.-XXXIII. (see p. 162 f.)

A. *Post-Exilic Appendices*

[(*a*) Chap. xxxii. 1-8 }
 (*b*)   ,,   ,,   9-20 } see p. 172 f.
 (*c*)   ,,   xxxiii. see p. 163 f.]

B (Chaps. xxviii.-xxxi., see p. 180 f.)

CHAPTER XXVIII

1

(*a*) *vv.* 1-6

The Imminent Fall of Samaria

723 B.C. Edited late

¹ Ha ! the proud crown of the drunkards of Ephraim, and the fading

flower of his beauteous splendour, which is on the head of the fat valley of the smitten with wine ! ² Behold, a strong and unflinching one hath *Yahwè* like a storm of hail, a destroying tempest; like a storm of mighty, overflowing waters, he casteth it down to the earth with violence. ³ With the feet shall it be trampled upon—the proud crown of the drunkards of Ephraim; ⁴ and the fading flower of his beauteous splendour, which is on the head of the fat valley—like an early fig before the fruit-harvest shall it be, which when a man seeth, as soon as it is in his hand, he swalloweth it.

[*vv*. 5-6 a post-Exilic insertion.]

II. and III

Warnings to Jerusalem, suggested by the earlier prophecy (*vv*. 1-4)

(*b*) *vv*. 7-13 and (*c*) *vv*. 14-22.   703 B.C.

II

⁷ And these also reel with wine and stagger with strong drink; priest and prophet reel with strong drink, they are confused through wine, they stagger through strong drink, they reel in the vision, they totter in judgment ! ⁸ For all tables are full of filthy vomit; there is no place (clean). ⁹ " Whom would he teach knowledge ? and to whom explain a revelation ? Those who are weaned from the milk—parted from the breast ?   ¹⁰ For (he is ever stammering) 'Correct, correct, correct, correct; direct, direct, direct, direct; here a little, there a little.' " ¹¹ (Yea, verily), for with stammerers in speech and with another tongue will he speak to this people; ¹² he who said unto them : This is the (true) rest, give ye rest to the weary; and this is the (true) refreshment —but they would not listen.   ¹³ So the word of Yahwè shall (indeed) be unto them, " Correct, correct, correct, correct; direct, direct, direct, direct ; here a little, there a little," that as they go they may stumble backward and be shattered, that they may be snared and be taken.

III

(*c*) *vv*. 14-22

¹⁴ Therefore hear the word of Yahwè, ye men of scorn, rulers of this people which is in Jerusalem; ¹⁵ because ye have said, We have entered into a covenant with Death, and with Sheól have we made a compact; the overflowing scourge, when it passeth along, shall not reach us, for we have made a lie our refuge, and in falsehood have we hid ourselves : —¹⁶ Therefore, thus saith the Lord Yahwè : Behold I *found* in Zion a stone, a tried stone, a precious corner-stone; he that believeth shall not *give way.*   ¹⁷ And I will make justice a line, and righteousness a plummet, and hail shall sweep away the refuge of lies, and waters shall overflow the hiding-place *of falsehood*; ¹⁸ and your covenant with death shall be *annulled*, and your compact with Sheól shall not stand : when the overflowing scourge passeth along, ye shall be trodden down

by it. ¹⁹ As often as it passeth along, it shall take you away, for morning by morning shall it pass along, by day and by night; and (then) it shall be unmingled terror to understand the "revelation." † ²¹ For Yahwè shall arise as on Mount Perazim, he shall be wroth as in the vale of Gibeon ; to do his work—alien is his work, and to carry out his task —strange is his task. ²² And now, behave not as scorners lest your bands become tight, for a consummation and a doom have I heard from the Lord, Yahwè Sebáoth [upon the whole earth].

IV

(*d*) *vv*. 23-29 : a post-Exilic addition

CHAPTER XXIX. 1-14 (see p. 187 f.)

I

vv. 1-8 (see p. 189)

The Strange Fate of Arial

703 B.C.   Edited late

¹ Ha ! Arial, Arial, city against which David encamped ! Add year to year ; let the feasts again run their course ; [here probably a passage has been lost]; ² Then will I distress Arial, so that there will be moaning and bemoaning, and it will become unto me a true Arial ; ³ I will encamp like David [so Sept.] against thee, and close thee in with entrenchments, and set up forts against thee ; ⁴ and being humbled thou wilt speak from the ground, and thy speech will come submissively from the dust. [*v*. 4*b* gloss : *v*. 5 a post-Exilic insertion.]   ⁶ And then— suddenly, full suddenly, it shall receive doom from Yahwè Sebáoth with thunder and with earthquake and a great noise, with whirlwind and hurricane and flame of devouring fire.   [*vv*. 7 and 8 later insertions : "*v*. 7 may contain some Isaianic phrases—the remnant of a lost passage respecting the siege of Jerusalem."]

II

The Blindness of the Rulers

vv. 9-12.   Same date

⁹ Feign astonishment, and ye shall be astonished indeed ; feign blindness, and ye shall be blind indeed.   They are drunken, but not with wine, they stagger, but not with strong drink.   ¹⁰ For Yahwè hath poured out upon you a spirit of deep slumber, and hath closed up your *eyes which see, and your heads* hath he covered, ‡ ¹¹ *so that the vision throughout is become unto you as the words of a sealed book which if one*

---

† *v*. 20 an interpolation, see *PI*.
‡ *vv*. 11-12, if Isaianic, have been recast.

APPENDIX

delivers to a scholar, saying, Pray read this, he saith, I cannot, for it is sealed; [12] *and should one deliver the book to one that is not a scholar, saying, Pray read this, he saith, I am not a scholar.*

III

The Punishment of Formalism

vv. 13-14. Same date

[13] *And the Lord said:* Because this people draweth near, with their mouth and with their lips honouring me, but their heart they keep far from me, and their religion is a rote-learned precept of men. [14] Therefore, behold, I will go on dealing with this people wonderfully, yes, wonderfully, so that the wisdom of their wise men shall perish, and the discernment of their sagacious men shall be hid.

CHAPTER XXIX. 15-24 (see p. 190 f.)

I

The Egyptian Alliance: First Fragment

v. 15. Same date

[15] Ha! those who hide deeply their purpose from Yahwè, so that their work is done in the dark, and who say, Who seeth us, and who noticeth us? . . . .

II

[*vv.* 16-24 post-Exilic insertion by the writer who inserted the Appendix xxxii. 1-8.]

CHAPTER XXX

I

(*a*) *vv.* 1-7

(1)

The Egyptian Alliance: Second Fragment

703 B.C.

[1] Ha! the unruly sons! saith Yahwè, carrying out a purpose which is not from me, and making a league without my spirit, that they may add sin to sin; [2] who set forth to go down to Egypt, and have not asked my counsel, to flee unto the protection of Pharaoh, and to take refuge in the shadow of Egypt. [3] And so the protection of Pharaoh shall be unto you for shame, and the refuge in the shadow of Egypt for confusion. [4] For though his princes appear in Zoan, and his messengers

reach Hanes, ⁵ only shame shall all get from a people who cannot profit them, who are not for help nor for profit, but for shame and also for reproach.

(2)

Same subject: Third Fragment

Same date

⁶ *Oracle of the beasts of the south country* . . . . through a land of distress and difficulty, whence (come) lioness and lion, viper and flying dragon, they carry their wealth upon the backs of young asses, and upon the humps of camels their treasures, to a people who cannot profit (them), † ⁷ᵃ whose help is (but) vapour and emptiness. [⁷ᵇ Therefore do I name this, Rahab Sit-still.]

II

The Impending Ruin of the State

(*b*) *vv*. 8-17. Same date

⁸ Now go in, write it down on a tablet before them, and inscribe it on a scroll, that it may serve to an after-day for *a testimony* for ever. ⁹ For it is a rebellious people, lying sons, sons that will not hear the direction of Yahwè, ¹⁰ who say to the seers, See not, and to the prophets, Prophesy not unto us right things; speak unto us smooth things, prophesy illusions, ¹¹ turn aside from the way, decline from the path, ease our society of the Holy One of Israel! ¹² Therefore thus saith the Holy One of Israel, Because ye reject this word, and trust in *wile* and policy, and rely thereon, ¹³ therefore this iniquity shall be unto you as a rent ready to fall, bulging out in a high wall, the breaking of which cometh suddenly in a moment; ¹⁴ and one breaketh it, as an earthen pitcher is broken, shivering it unsparingly, so that not a sherd is found among its shivered pieces for taking fire from the hearth, or for drawing water from a cistern. ¹⁵ For thus hath the Lord Yahwè, the Holy One of Israel, said: By returning and resting ye would be delivered, in quietness and confidence would be your (true) strength; but ye have refused ¹⁶ and said, No, but on horses will we fly,—therefore shall ye flee! And on the swift will we ride,—therefore swift shall your pursuers be! ‡ ¹⁷ᵇ At the menace of five shall ye flee, till ye be left as a pole on the top of a mountain, and as a banner on a hill.

III

[(*c*) *vv*. 18-26 post-Exilic insertion.]

IV

[(*d*) *vv*. 27-33 also post-Exilic.]

† וּמִצְרַיִם a gloss.   ‡ 17*a* a gloss.

CHAPTER XXXI

The Egyptian Alliance: Fourth Fragment

B.C. 702

¹ Ha! those who go down to Egypt for help, and who rely on horses, and put their trust in chariots because they are many, and in horsemen because they are a host, but look not unto Israel's Holy One, neither consult Yahwè! ² Yet he also is wise, and bringeth evil to pass, and his words he hath not recalled, and he will arise against the house of evil-doers, and against the help of those that work wickedness. ³ Yea, the Egyptians are men and not God, and their horses flesh and not spirit; and when Yahwè stretcheth out his hand, the helper shall stumble, and the holpen shall fall, and they all shall be consumed together. ⁴ For thus hath Yahwè said unto me: As the lion with the young lion growleth over his prey, when there is summoned against him a full band of shepherds—at their cry he is not dismayed, and at their noise not daunted—so shall Yahwè Sebáoth come down to fight against Mount Zion and against the hill thereof. ⁵ᵃ Like fluttering birds . . . [The following words had probably become illegible when the prophecy was edited after the Exile. *vv.* 5*b*-9 due to a post-Exilic editor.]

END OF PART I

PART II†

THE GENUINE PROPHECIES OF ISAIAH II

Israel's Redemption and Destiny: their basis in revealed religion (Chaps. XL.-LV.): 545-539 B.C.

I

Good News for the Exiles

CHAPTER XL. (see p. 298 f.)

1

vv. 1-5

¹ Comfort ye, comfort ye my people, saith your God. ² Speak ye tenderly to Jerusalem, and cry unto her, that her warfare is accomplished, that her guilt is paid off, that she hath received from Yahwè's hand double for all her sins. ³ Hark! one calleth: "Clear ye in the wilderness the way of Yahwè, make level in the desert a highway for our God. ⁴ Let every valley be uplifted, and every mountain and hill be brought low, and let the steep become a table-land, and the ridges a plain." (*v.* 5 an insertion.)

vv. 9-11

⁹ Get thee up on a high mountain, O company that bringest good tidings to Zion, lift up mightily thy voice, O company that bringest good tidings to Jerusalem; lift it up, be not afraid; say unto the cities of Judah, Behold your God! ¹⁰ Behold the Lord Yahwè cometh as a strong one, his arm ruling for him; behold his reward is with him, and his recompense before him. ¹¹ As a shepherd will he shepherd his flock, with his arm will he gather (it), the lambs in his bosom will he carry, those which give suck will he lead.

---

† In the text of Part II., italic type, with one or two unimportant exceptions, is confined to the *Servant passages*, on which cf. p. 304 f.

APPENDIX

2

vv. 6-8

⁶ Hark! one saith, Cry; and *I say,* What shall I cry? All flesh is grass, and all the grace thereof like the flowers of the field; ⁷ the grass withereth, the flowers fade, because the breath of Yahwè hath blown thereon [*v*. 7 end a gloss]. ⁸ The grass withereth, the flowers fade, but the word of our God standeth for ever.

vv. 12-26

¹² Who hath measured the waters in the hollow of his hand, and meted the heavens with a span, and comprehended the dust of the earth in a tierce, and weighed the mountains with scales, and the hills with a balance? ¹³ Who hath meted out the spirit of Yahwè, and being his counsellor given him knowledge? ¹⁴ With whom hath he taken counsel that he might endow him with discernment, and teach him as to the path of right, and teach him knowledge, and give him knowledge of the way of perfect discernment? ¹⁵ Behold, the nations are as a drop in a bucket, and as fine dust on a balance are they reckoned; behold he lifteth up the islands as a straw; ¹⁶ and Lebanon is not sufficient for fuel, nor its beasts sufficient for burnt-offerings. ¹⁷ All the nations are as nothing before him; as nothingness and chaos are they reckoned by him. ¹⁸ To whom, then, will ye liken God, and what sort of likeness place beside him? ¹⁹ An image! a craftsman hath cast it, and a goldsmith overlayeth it with gold, [and forgeth (for it) chains of silver]. ˣˡⁱ· ⁶ One helpeth the other, and saith to his fellow, Be of good courage. ˣˡⁱ· ⁷ And the craftsman encourageth the goldsmith, he that smootheth with the hammer him that striketh the anvil, saying of the soldering, It is good, and he fasteneth it with nails, that it may not totter. ˣˡ· ²⁰ †He that is impoverished in offerings† chooseth a wood that decayeth not, seeketh for himself a skilful craftsman, to set up an image that will not totter. ²¹ Can ye not perceive? Can ye not hear? Hath it not been told you from the beginning? Have ye not discerned (it) from the foundation of the earth? ²² (It is he) that sitteth above the vault of the earth (so high) that its inhabitants are as locusts, who hath stretched out the heavens as fine cloth, and spread them out as a tent to dwell in: ²³ (It is he) who bringeth princes to nothing, who maketh the judges of the earth as chaos—²⁴ Scarcely have they been planted, scarcely have they been sown, scarcely hath their ‡scion‡ taken root in the earth, when he bloweth upon them, and they wither, and like stubble a tempest carrieth them away. ²⁵ To whom then will ye liken me, that I should be equal to him? saith the Holy One. ²⁶ Lift up your eyes on high, and see; who hath created yonder? He who bringeth out their host in (their full) number, who calleth them all by name; for fear of *him* who is so powerful and mighty not one is missing.

† Text obscure and probably corrupt.
‡ See p. 63.

3

vv. 27-31

²⁷ Why sayest thou, O Jacob, and speakest, O Israel, My way is hidden from Yahwè, and my right is passed over by my God? ²⁸ Hast thou not perceived, hast thou not heard? An everlasting God is Yahwè, the creator of the ends of the earth! He fainteth not, neither doth he grow weary; unsearchable is his discernment; ²⁹ he giveth strength to the weary, and maketh the feeble powerful; ³⁰ youths may faint and grow weary, and young warriors may stumble, ³¹ but they that wait for Yahwè shall renew their strength, they shall put forth as it were eagles' wings; they shall run and not grow weary, they shall go on and not faint.

II

Yahwè the only true God, proved as such by the prediction of Cyrus

CHAPTER XLI

¹ Listen silently unto me, ye coastlands, †and let the peoples renew their strength†; let them draw near, then let them speak; together let us approach the tribunal. ² Who stirred up from the East him whom victory meeteth at every step, (who) giveth up nations before him, and maketh him trample upon kings? His sword *maketh them* as dust, his bow as driven stubble. ³ He pursueth them, passeth on in safety; the path with his feet he doth not tread. ⁴ Who hath wrought and performed this? He who called forth the generations from the beginning; I, Yahwè (who) am the first, and with the last I am the same. [*v.* 5 a later insertion.]

⁸ But thou, Israel my servant, Jacob whom I have chosen, seed of Abraham my friend, ⁹ thou whom I fetched from the ends of the earth, and called from its uttermost parts, and to whom I said, My servant art thou, I have chosen and not rejected thee; ¹⁰ fear not, for I am with thee; look not dismayed, for I am thy God; I strengthen thee, yea, I help thee; yea, I uphold thee with my right hand of righteousness. ¹¹ Behold, ashamed and confounded shall they all be, that were enraged against thee; they shall become as nought and perish—the men that strove with thee. ¹² Thou shalt seek them but find them not—the men that contended with thee; they shall become as nought and as nothingness—the men that warred with thee. ¹³ For I, Yahwè thy God, hold fast thy right hand; I who say unto thee, Fear not, *I* do help thee. ¹⁴ Fear not, thou worm Jacob, ye petty folk of Israel; *I* do help thee, saith Yahwè, and thy redeemer is the Holy One of Israel. ¹⁵ Behold, I make thee a threshing-sledge, sharp, new, furnished with teeth; thou shalt thresh mountains and crush them, and shalt make hills as chaff. ¹⁶ Thou shalt winnow them, and the wind shall carry them away, and the tempest shall scatter them; but thou shalt exult in Yahwè, and

† Text probably corrupt.

APPENDIX

in Israel's Holy One shalt thou make thy boast. [17] The afflicted and the poor who seek for water, and there is none, whose tongue is parched with thirst—I Yahwè will answer them, I the God of Israel will not forsake them. [18] On bare hills I will open rivers, and fountains in the midst of plains; I will make the wilderness a brimming lake, and dry land springs of water. [19] I will place in the wilderness the cedar, the acacia, and the myrtle, and the oleaster; I will set in the desert the pine, the plane, and the sherbin-tree together, [20] that men may see and acknowledge, and consider and understand at once that Yahwè's hand hath performed this, and Israel's Holy One created it.

III

Dispute between Yahwè and the Idol-gods

[21] Bring forward your cause, saith Yahwè; produce your strong reasons, saith Jacob's King. [22] Let them produce (them) and announce unto us what shall happen : the former things, what they be, do ye announce, that we may reflect upon them and mark their issue; or else the future things do ye declare unto us. [23] Announce the things that are to come hereafter, that we may know that ye are gods; yea, do something good or bad, that we may at once look amazed and have somewhat to see. [24] Behold ye are of nought and your work is of *nothingness* : an abomination is he that chooseth you.

[25] I have stirred up one from the north, and he is come; from the sun-rising one who proclaimeth my name, that he may *trample* upon governors as upon mortar, and as the potter that treadeth clay. [26] Who announced this from the beginning, that we might know it, and from aforetime, that we might say, Right ? Yea, there was none that announced it, yea, there was none that declared it, yea, there was none that heard your words. [27] Unto Zion †the first one† (announced) saying, Behold, behold them, and unto Jerusalem I (Yahwè) gave a bringer of good tidings ; [28] but when I *looked round* there was no one, and among these (vain gods) there was no counsellor, so that I might ask them, and they might give an answer. [29] Behold they are all vanity ; their performance is nothingness ; (as) wind and chaos are their molten images.

IV

Contrast between the Ideal and Actual Israel

CHAPTER XLII

I

vv. 1-4 (in italics) as the first of the Servant passages

[1] *Behold my servant whom I uphold, my chosen in whom my soul delighteth ; I have put my spirit upon him, he shall bring forth law to*

† *i.e.* Yahwè.

the nations. ² He will not clamour nor cry, nor cause his voice to be heard in the street; ³ a crushed reed he will not break, and a dimly burning wick he will not quench. Faithfully will he bring forth the law; he shall not burn dimly, neither shall his spirit be crushed till he have set the law in the earth, and for his direction do the coastlands wait.

⁵ Thus saith the (true) God, Yahwè, he that created the heavens, and stretched them forth, that spread forth the earth with its products, that giveth breath to the people upon it, and spirit to them that walk thereon. ⁶ I, Yahwè, have called thee in righteousness, and *taken hold of* thy hand, and *formed thee* and *set thee* for a covenant of the people, for a light of the nations; ⁷ to open blind eyes, and bring out captives from confinement, and those who sit in darkness from the prison-house. ⁸ I am Yahwè, that is my name, and my glory will I not give to another, nor my praise unto images.   ⁹ The former things——behold, they have come, and new things do I announce; before they shoot forth I tell you of them.

2

¹⁰ Sing unto Yahwè a new song, and his praise from the end of the earth; *let the sea roar,* and all that is therein, the coastlands and the inhabitants thereof.   ¹¹ Let the wilderness and the cities thereof lift up their voice, the villages which Kedar inhabiteth; let Sela's inhabitants shout for joy; from the top of the mountains let them cry aloud;   ¹² let them render glory to Yahwè, and declare his praise in the coastlands. ¹³ Yahwè goeth forth as a hero, as a man of war he stirreth up (his) jealousy; he giveth a shout, yea, a shrill battle-cry, upon his foes he showeth himself a hero.   ¹⁴ I have long time been silent; I have been still and restrained myself; (now) like a woman in travail will I groan, I will pant and gasp at once.   ¹⁵ I will lay waste mountains and hills, and all their herbage will I dry up, I will turn rivers into islands, and lakes will I dry up; ¹⁶ and I will lead the blind in a way that they know not, in paths they know not will I guide them; I will turn darkness into light before them, and rough places into a tableland.   These are the things I will surely do, and I will not omit them.   ¹⁷ (But) they shall surely draw backward; they shall be utterly ashamed, that trust in graven images, that say to molten images, Ye are our Gods.

3

¹⁸ Hear, ye deaf; and ye blind, look up that ye may see.   ¹⁹ Who is blind but my servant, and deaf as my messenger whom I send? Who is blind as he who hath been received into friendship, and *deaf* as the Servant of Yahwè?   ²⁰ Many things hast thou seen without observing them; one who openeth the ears and heareth not!   ²¹ It was Yahwè's pleasure for his righteousness' sake to make the direction great and glorious, ²² and yet it is (still) a people robbed and plundered; they are all snared in holes and hidden in prison-houses; they have become a prey, and there is none to rescue; a spoil, and there is none that

saith, Restore. ²³ Who among you will give ear to this, will attend and hear for the after time? ²⁴ᵃ Who gave up Jacob for a spoil, and Israel unto robbers [*v.* 24*b* a later insertion], ²⁵ and poured upon him in fury his anger and the violence of war, and it scorched him round about, but he heeded it not, and it burned him, yet he laid it not to heart?

CHAPTER XLIII

¹ And now, thus saith Yahwè thy creator, O Jacob, and he that formed thee, O Israel : Fear not, for I redeem thee ; I call thee by name, mine art thou. ² When thou passest through the waters I will be with thee, and through the rivers they shall not overflow thee ; when thou goest through the fire thou shalt not be scorched, neither shall the flame burn thee. ³ For I Yahwè am thy God ; (I) Israel's Holy One thy deliverer ; I give for thy ransom Egypt, Ethiopia, and Seba in thy stead. ⁴ Since thou art precious in my sight ; art honoured, and I love thee ; therefore will I give (other) men in thy stead, and peoples for thy life. ⁵ Fear not, for I am with thee ; from the sunrising do I bring thy seed, and from the sunsetting I gather thee ; ⁶ I say to the north, Give up ; and to the south, Keep not back ; bring my sons from far, and my daughters from the ends of the earth, ⁷ every one who is called by my name, and whom for my glory I have created, have formed, yea, have made.

V

Even blind Israel must bear witness for Yahwè against the idol-gods; the argument from prophecy repeated

⁸ Bring forth a blind people which hath eyes, and deaf who have ears. ⁹ All ye nations assemble yourselves, and let the peoples gather together. Who among them can announce such a thing ? Yea, former things let them declare unto us ; let them produce their witnesses that they may be proved in the right, and that * we may hear and say,* It is truth. ¹⁰ Ye are my witnesses, saith Yahwè, and my *servants* whom I have chosen that ye may acknowledge and believe me, and discern that I am He (that worketh) ; before me was no god formed, neither shall there be after me. ¹¹ I, (even) I am Yahwè, and beside me there is no deliverer. ¹² I myself have announced and delivered, and no strange (god) was among you ; and ye are my witnesses, and I am God, ¹³ even from this day forth I am He, and there is none that rescueth out of my hand ; when I work who shall let it ?

VI

The Fall of Babylon, and the new Exodus

¹⁴ Thus saith Yahwè, your redeemer, the Holy One of Israel : For your sakes have I sent to Babylon, and will bring down †as fugitives all of them,† and the Chaldeans †into the ships of their shouting,† ¹⁵ I

† Text here probably corrupt.

Yahwè, your Holy One, the creator of Israel, your King. ¹⁶ Thus saith Yahwè, who giveth a road in the sea, and a path in mighty waters, ¹⁷ who bringeth forth chariot and horse, a *large* force and powerful; together they lie down, they cannot arise, they are quenched, they have gone out as a wick: ¹⁸ Remember not former things, and things of old time consider not; ¹⁹ behold I accomplish a new thing—already it is shooting forth—do ye not perceive it? Yea, I will set a road in the wilderness (and) rivers in the desert. ²⁰ᵃ The beasts of the field shall honour me, the jackals and the ostriches. †

VII

Yahwè pleadeth with careless Israel

²² But it is not I upon whom thou hast called, O Jacob, much less hast thou wearied thyself about me, O Israel. ²³ Thou hast not brought me the sheep of thy burnt-offerings, nor with thy sacrifices hast thou honoured me. (Truly,) I have not made a slave of thee with offerings, nor wearied thee with incense. ²⁴ (Yet) thou hast not bought me sweet cane with money, nor with the fat of thy sacrifices hast thou sated me; thou hast altogether made a slave of me with thy sins, and wearied me with thine iniquities. ²⁵ Yet I, even I, am he that blotteth out thy rebellions for mine own sake, and thy sins I remember not. ²⁶ Put me in remembrance, let us plead together; recount, that thou mayst be justified. ²⁷ Thy first father sinned, and thy mediators rebelled against me; ²⁸ so *I profaned* consecrated princes, and *gave up* Jacob to the ban, and Israel to reproaches.

CHAPTER XLIV

¹ And now hear, O Jacob my servant, and Israel whom I have chosen; ² thus saith Yahwè thy creator, and he that formed thee from the womb, who helpeth thee: Fear not, my servant Jacob, and thou Jeshurun, whom I have chosen; ³ for I will pour water upon him that is thirsty, and streams upon the dry ground. I will pour my spirit upon thy seed, and my blessing upon thine offspring, ⁴ so that they shall shoot up *as grass amidst the waters,* as willows by watercourses. ⁵ This one shall say, I am Yahwè's, and that one *shall call himself* by the name of Jacob, and that one shall write *on* his hand, Yahwè's, and *be titled by* the name of Israel.

VIII

The sole Divinity of Yahwè proved by his Prophecies

⁶ Thus saith Yahwè, Israel's king, even his redeemer Yahwè Sebáoth: I am the first, and I am the last, and beside me there is no god. ⁷ And who is wont to call as I, since I established the people of antiquity?

† *vv.* 20*b* and 21 insertions.

Let him announce it and set it over against me! Yea, the future and things to come let them announce *to us.* ⁸ Shudder not, neither be terrified; have I not long since declared and announced it? And ye are my witnesses. Is there a god *or* a Rock besides me? [*vv.* 9-20 (21*b* and 22*b*) a later insertion on idolatry.] ²¹ᵃ Remember these things, O Jacob; and Israel, for thou art (indeed) my servant.† . . . ²²ᵃ I have blotted out as a mist thy rebellions, and as a cloud thy sins. . . . . ²³ Ring out joyfully, O heavens, for Yahwè hath accomplished his (work); shout, O depths of the earth, break forth, O mountains, into ringing joy, O forest, and every tree therein, for Yahwè hath redeemed Jacob, and glorifieth himself in Israel.

IX

Cyrus conquereth for the sake of Yahwè and of Israel

1

²⁴ Thus saith Yahwè, thy redeemer and he that formed thee from the womb: I am Yahwè, that maketh everything, that stretcheth forth the heavens alone, that spread forth the earth—*who was with me?*— ²⁵ that bringeth to nought the signs of the liars, and maketh the diviners mad, that turneth the wise backward, and maketh their knowledge folly, ²⁶ that maketh the word of his ‡*servants* to stand, and accomplisheth the counsel of his messengers, that saith of Jerusalem, Let it be inhabited, and *of* the temple, Be thy foundations laid, and of the cities of Judah, Let them be built, and its ruins will I raise up; ²⁷ that saith of the flood, Dry up, and all thy rivers will I parch; ²⁸ that saith of Cyrus, My shepherd (is he), and all my purpose shall he accomplish. [*v.* 28*b* a variant to 26*b*.]

CHAPTER XLV

¹ Thus saith Yahwè to his anointed, to Cyrus, whose right hand I have grasped, *to lay low* before him nations, and to ungird the loins of kings, to open doors before him, and that gates may not keep shut; ² I myself will go before thee, and will level §*the mountains;* doors of brass will I break in pieces, and bars of iron will I cut in sunder; ³ and I will give thee the treasures of darkness, and the hoards of secret places, that thou mayest acknowledge that it is I, Yahwè, who call thee by thy name, Israel's God. ⁴ For the sake of Jacob my servant, and of Israel my chosen, I called thee by thy name; I gave thee a title, though thou didst not know me. ⁵ I am Yahwè, and there is none else; beside me there is no God; I girded thee, though thou knewest me not, ⁶ that men might acknowledge from the sun-rising and from the setting thereof that there is none beside me—I am Yahwè, and there

---

† This line had become illegible.
‡ Read וַעֲבָדָי. See p. 249, note 1. Cf. also p. 281 (for *vv.* 26-28).
§ See p. 347 (הֲדוּרִים, corrupt).

is none else—⁷ that form light and create darkness, and make welfare and create calamity, I Yahwè am the doer of all this. ⁸ Shower, ye heavens, from above, and let the skies rain righteousness; let the earth open *and salvation blossom,* and let it cause victory to spring up together: I Yahwè have created it.

2

For *v.* 9 see p. 351

⁹ Ha! one that striveth with his fashioner—a potsherd like (other) potsherds of earth! Doth the clay say to its fashioner, What canst thou make? and *his* work, *Thou hast* no hands! ¹⁰ Ha! one that saith to a father, What canst thou beget! and to a woman, What canst thou bring forth! ¹¹ Thus saith Yahwè, the Holy One of Israel, and his fashioner: Concerning the things to come *will ye question* me? [concerning my sons] and concerning the work of my hands will ye lay commands upon me? ¹² It was I who made the earth and created the men upon it, mine the hands that stretched out the heavens, and upon all their host have I laid commands. ¹³ (So) it was I who stirred him up in righteousness, and all his ways will I make level; he shall build my city, and mine exiled ones shall he set free, not for price, and not for reward, saith Yahwè Sebáoth.

3

¹⁴ Thus saith Yahwè: The labour of Egypt and the earnings of Ethiopia, and the Sabæans, men of stature, before thee shall pass, and become thine: after thee shall they go, and in chains pass over; and unto thee shall they bow down, and unto thee shall they pray (saying), "Only in thee is God, and there is none beside—no Godhead at all. ¹⁵ Truly thou art a God that hideth himself, O God of Israel, deliverer!" ¹⁶ Ashamed, yea confounded are they all; together they are gone into confusion—even the idol-artificers: ¹⁷ (but) Israel is delivered by Yahwè with an everlasting deliverance; ye shall not be put to shame nor confounded unto all eternity.

4

¹⁸ For thus saith Yahwè, the creator of the heavens—he is the (true) God; the former of the earth and its maker—established it, not as a chaos did he create it, for inhabiting he formed it,—I am Yahwè, and there is none else. ¹⁹ Not in secret have I spoken, in [a place of] the land of darkness; I have not said unto the seed of Jacob, Seek me as chaos; I Yahwè speak truly, announce rightly. ²⁰ Assemble and come; draw near together, ye escaped of the nations: they are without knowledge who bear about their idol-logs, and pray to a god who cannot deliver. ²¹ Announce ye and produce (it); let them also take counsel together! who hath declared this from ancient times (and) long since announced it? Have not I, Yahwè? And there is no God beside me; a truth-speaking and delivering God there is not beside me. ²² Turn

APPENDIX

unto me and let yourselves be delivered, all ye ends of the earth; for I am God, and there is none else. ²³ By myself have I sworn, *a true word hath gone out of my mouth, a word that shall not be revoked,* that † *unto me every knee shall bow, every tongue shall swear.* ²⁴ Only through Yahwè hath ‡ *Jacob* victories and strength; unto him shall *they come* and be put to shame—all that were incensed against him.

X

The gods of Babylon and the God of Israel contrasted

CHAPTER XLVI

¹ Bel hath bowed down, Nebo hath crouched; their images have been given up to the beasts and to the cattle; that which ye carried about is borne as a load—a burden to the weary (beast). ² They have crouched, they have bowed down together; they could not rescue the burden, but themselves have gone into captivity. ³ Hearken unto me, O house of Jacob, and all the remnant of the house of Israel, who have been borne as a load from the womb, who have been carried from the (mother's) lap,—⁴ and even up to old age, I am the same, and even up to gray hairs *I* will support; it is I that have made, and I that will carry, it is I that will support and rescue. ⁵ To whom will ye liken and equal me, and compare me that we may be like? [*vv.* 6-8 a later insertion on idolatry; cf. xliv. 9-20.] ⁹ Remember the former things of old time, that I am God, and there is none else—¹⁰ one that announceth the issue from the beginning, and from ancient times things not yet done; one that hath said, My purpose shall stand, and all my pleasure will I perform; ¹¹ who calleth from the sun-rising a bird of prey, the man of his purpose from a far country;— I have spoken, I will also bring it to pass; (as) I have formed, (so) will I accomplish it. ¹² Hearken unto me, ye obdurate, who are far (in faithlessness) from (Israel's) victory; ¹³ I have brought near my (gift of) victory, it is not far off, and my deliverance shall not tarry; and I appoint in Zion deliverance, (and) to Israel my glory.

XI

A prophetic taunt-song upon Babylon

CHAPTER XLVII

I

¹ Come down and sit in the dust, O virgin-daughter of Babylon, sit throneless on the ground, O daughter of Chaldæa, for no more shalt thou be called, Tender and Dainty. ² Take the millstones and grind meal, lift off thy veil, take up the train, bare the leg, wade through

---

† Italics here simply conventional.
‡ Reading לְיַעֲקֹב. See p. 249, note 1.

rivers. ³ Bared be thy nakedness; yea, let thy shame be seen. Vengeance will I take and spare no man. ⁴ As for our redeemer—Yahwè Sebáoth is his name, the Holy One of Israel.

2

⁵ Sit silent, and enter into darkness, O daughter of Chaldæa, for they shall no more call thee, Mistress of Kingdoms. ⁶ I was wroth with my people, I profaned mine inheritance, and gave them into thine hand : thou didst show them no compassion, upon the aged thou madest thy yoke very heavy. ⁷ And thou saidst, I shall be *for ever, (yea) mistress perpetually* : thou didst not lay this to heart, neither didst thou mind the issue thereof.

3

⁸ And now hear this, Voluptuous, that sittest securely, that sayest in thine heart, I am, and none beside ; I shall not sit a widow, nor know the loss of children ; ⁹ and so there shall come to thee both these things in a moment, in a single day, loss of children and widowhood—in full measure shall they come upon thee, despite the multitude of thine enchantments, despite the vast number of thy spells, ¹⁰ᵃ and (though) thou wast secure in thy wickedness, and saidst, None seeth me.

4

¹⁰ᵇ Thy wisdom and knowledge—this hath perverted thee, so that thou saidst in thine heart, I am, and none beside ; ¹¹ and so there cometh upon thee a misfortune which thou hast not skill to charm away, and there shall fall upon thee a mischief, which thou shalt not be able to appease, and there shall come upon thee suddenly a crashing storm which thou hast not skill to . . . . ¹²ᵃ Persist, pray, in thy spells, and in the multitude of thine enchantments [wherein thou hast laboured from thy youth].

5

¹²ᵇ Perchance thou wilt be able to help, perchance thou wilt strike terror ! ¹³ Thou hast wearied thyself with the multitude of thy counsellors ; pray let them stand forth and deliver thee, who map out the heavens, who gaze at the stars, who make known, every new moon, whence (any troubles) are coming upon thee ! ¹⁴ Behold, they are become as stubble, the fire hath burned them ; they cannot rescue their life from the clutch of the flame [it is not a coal for giving warmth, nor a fire to sit before]. ¹⁵ Such are they become to thee about whom thou hast wearied thyself ; they, which have trafficked with thee from thy youth up, flee staggering, every one straight before him : There is none to deliver thee.

APPENDIX

XII

The New and the Old Prophecies

CHAPTER XLVIII

1

[*Note :* the greater part of *vv.* 1-11 consists of inserted matter; see p. 301.]

¹ᵃ Hear ye this, O house of Jacob; ³ᵃ the former things I announced long ago; ⁵ᵃ Yea, I announced it to thee long ago, before it came to pass I showed it to thee. ⁶ *Thou* hast heard it; †see it fulfilled†; and ye, will ye not *testify* it? I declare unto thee new things henceforth, yea, ‡ *difficult* things which thou hast not known. ⁷ᵃ Now have they been created, and not heretofore, and before (their) day thou heardest them not; ⁸ᵃ thou hast neither heard nor known them, neither did thine ear open heretofore. ¹¹ For mine own sake, mine own sake will I do it, and my glory will I not give to another.

2

¹² Hearken unto me, O Jacob and Israel, my called one; I am he, I am the first, I am also the last. ¹³ Yea, it was my hand that laid the foundation of the earth, and my right hand that spread out the heavens; when I call unto them they stand forth together. ¹⁴ Assemble yourselves, all of you, and hear; who among them hath announced this? He whom Yahwè hath loved shall accomplish his pleasure on Babylon, and (shall cause) his arm (to light down) *on Chaldæa.* ¹⁵ I myself have spoken, and also called him, have brought him, and prosperous shall his way be. [*vv.* 16-19 an insertion.]

²⁰ Go ye out from Babylon, flee ye from Chaldæa; with joyful cry announce and declare it: cause it to go forth even to the end of the earth; say, "Yahwè hath redeemed his servant Jacob; ²¹ and they thirsted not, though he led them through deserts, water from the rock he caused to flow for them, he clave the rock and water gushed out." [*v.* 22 a later insertion.] §

XIII

The Servant's Experiences and Hopes; Israel's Restoration

CHAPTER XLIX

1

vv. 1-6 (in italics), as the second of the Servant passages.

¹ *Hearken, ye coast-lands, unto me, and listen, ye far-off peoples: Yahwè hath called me from the womb, from my mother's lap hath he made mention of my name;* ² *and he made my mouth as a sharp sword,*

---

† The text here probably corrupt.
‡ For this reading see p. 372, note 3.
§ *v.* 22. This refrain due to the editor. See *Prologue,* p. xxx.

in the shadow of his hand he hid me; and he made me a polished shaft, ⁸ *in his quiver he covered me; and he said unto me, Thou art my servant in whom I will glorify myself;* ⁵ᵇ *and I was honoured in Yahwè's sight, and my God became my strength.* ⁴ *And as for me, I said, I have laboured in vain; for nought and for a breath have I spent my strength; nevertheless my right is with Yahwè, and my recompense with my God.* ⁵ᵃ *And now Yahwè saith, he who formed me from the womb to be a servant unto him, that I might bring back Jacob unto him, and that *unto him* Israel might be gathered,* ⁶ [*he saith*], *It is too light a thing that thou art unto me a servant, to raise up the tribes of Jacob, and to restore the preserved of Israel; so I set thee for a light of the nations, that my deliverance may be unto the end of the earth.*

2

⁷ Thus saith Yahwè, the redeemer of Israel, and his Holy One, unto him who is all-*despised, abhorred* of the people, a servant of tyrants : Kings shall see (it) and arise ; princes, and shall bow down, because of Yahwè who is faithful, and of the Holy One of Israel, who chose thee. ⁸ Thus saith Yahwè : In a time of favour do I answer thee, and in a day of deliverance do I help thee; and I form thee and set thee for a covenant of the people, to raise up the land, to assign the desolate heritages, ⁹ Saying to the bondsmen, Go forth, and to them that are in darkness, Show yourselves. They shall pasture on *all* ways, and (even) on all bare hills shall be their pasture. ¹⁰ They shall not hunger nor thirst, neither shall the †scorching wind† or the sun smite them, for he that hath compassion upon them shall lead them, and unto brimming fountains shall he guide them. ¹¹ And I will make all my mountains a road, and my highways shall be exalted. . . . ‡¹² Behold these —from afar do they come (and these from the ends of the earth), and behold, these from the sea, and these from the land of the Syenites. ¹³ Ring with joy, O heavens, and exult, O earth, and let the mountains break forth in ringing joy ; for Yahwè comforteth his people, and compassionateth his afflicted ones.

XIV

Consolation for Zion and her Children

1

¹⁴ And Zion said, Yahwè hath forsaken me ! ¹⁵ Can a woman forget her suckling so as not to compassionate the son of her womb? Should even these forget, yet will I not forget thee ! ¹⁶ Behold, on the palms of the hands have I graven thee ; thy walls are continually before me. ¹⁷ *They that build thee* make haste ; they that destroyed thee and laid thee waste go forth from thee. ¹⁸ Lift up thine eyes round about and see ; they are all assembled, they come to thee. As I live,

† For this rendering see p. 269 (שָׁרָב).
‡ For *v.* 12 see p. 275, note 2.

saith Yahwè, thou shalt surely clothe thee with them all as with an ornament, and bind them on thee as a bride doeth. [19] For thy ruined and desolate places, and thy land that is destroyed . . . for then thou wilt be too narrow for the inhabitants, and they who swallowed thee up shall be far away. [20] The children of thy bereavement shall yet say in thine ears, The place is too narrow for me, make room for me that I may dwell. [21] And thou shalt say in thine heart, Who hath borne me these, seeing I am bereaved and unfruitful †[an exile and banished]? And these, who hath brought them up? Behold, I was left alone; these—where have they been?

2

[22] Thus saith the Lord Yahwè : Behold, I lift up mine hand towards the nations, and set up my banner towards the peoples, and they shall bring thy sons in the lap, and thy daughters shall be carried on the shoulder. [23] And kings shall be thy foster-fathers, and their queens thy nursing-mothers ; with face to the earth shall they do obeisance to thee, and lick the dust of thy feet ; and thou shalt know that I am Yahwè, those that hope in whom shall not be put to shame. [24] Can the prey be taken from a hero, or the captives of * the tyrant * escape? [25] For thus saith Yahwè : Even the captives of a hero shall be taken, and the prey of the tyrant shall escape, and with him that contendeth with thee *I* will contend, and thy children *I* will deliver. [26] And I will cause thine oppressors to eat their own flesh, and with their own blood, as with new wine, shall they be drunken ; and all flesh shall know that I Yahwè am thy deliverer, and that thy redeemer is the Hero of Jacob.

3

CHAPTER L

[1] Thus saith Yahwè : Where is your mother's bill of divorce with which I put her away? Or which of my creditors is it to whom I sold you? Behold, for your iniquities were ye sold, and for your rebellions was your mother put away. [2] Wherefore, when I came, was there no man—when I called, was there none to answer? Is my hand too short to deliver? Or have I no power to rescue? Behold, with my rebuke I dry up the sea, I make rivers a desert, (so that) their fish stink for lack of water, and die for thirst ; [3] I clothe the heavens in mourning, and make sackcloth their covering. . . .

XV

The Servant as Martyr (the Servant speaks)

vv. 4-9 (in italics), as the third of the Servant passages

[4] *The Lord Yahwè hath given me the tongue of disciples that I may*

† A gloss, see LXX. and cf. p. 259 (סוּרָה).

edify the weary one with a word; morning by morning he wakeneth mine ear that I may hearken as disciples, ⁵[The Lord Yahwè hath opened mine ear], and I have not been rebellious, I have not turned back. ⁶ My back I gave to smiters, and my cheeks to them that pluck out the hair; my face I hid not from shame and spitting. ⁷ But the Lord Yahwè will help me; therefore am I not confounded; therefore have I made my face as flint, and I knew that I should not be put to shame. ⁸ Near is he that righteth me; who will contend with me?—Let us stand forth together. Who is mine adversary?—Let him come near unto me. ⁹ Behold the Lord Yahwè will help me; who is he that shall put me in the wrong? Behold they shall all fall to pieces as a garment; the moth shall eat them.

(vv. 10-11 a later insertion.)

XVI

Exhortation and Comfort: midway the Prophet encourages himself by Prayer.

CHAPTER LI

1

¹ Hearken unto me, ye that pursue righteousness, that seek Yahwè; look unto the rock whence ye have been hewn, and to the hole of the pit whence ye have been dug. ² Look unto Abraham your father, and unto Sarah that bare you, for as but one man I called him, and I blessed him, and increased him. ³ For Yahwè doth comfort Zion, doth comfort all her ruins, and maketh her desert as Eden, and her wilderness as Yahwè's garden; joy and gladness shall be found in her, thanksgiving and the voice of song. ⁴ Listen unto me, my people, and give ear unto me, O my nation; for direction from me shall go forth, and my law for a light of the peoples. † ⁵ *Suddenly* my redress draweth nigh, my deliverance is gone forth: and mine arms shall judge the peoples—for me the coastlands wait. ⁶ Lift up your eyes to heaven, and look upon the earth beneath; for the heavens shall vanish like smoke, and the earth fall to pieces like a garment, and the dwellers therein—like gnats shall they die; but my deliverance shall be for ever, and my righteousness shall not be annulled. ⁷ Hearken unto me, ye that know righteousness, the people in whose heart is my direction. Fear ye not frail man's reproach, and at their revilings be not dismayed! ⁸ For as a garment shall the moth eat them, yea, as wool shall the worm devour them; but my redress shall be for ever, and my deliverance from generation to generation.

2

⁹ Awake, awake, put on strength, O arm of Yahwè, awake as in the ancient days, the generations of old time. Art thou not it that didst

† For this reading see p. 268 (under רגע).

APPENDIX

dash Rahab to pieces, and put shame on the Dragon? ¹⁰ Art thou not it that dried up the sea, the waters of the great flood, that made the sea-deeps a way for the redeemed to pass over? [*v.* 11 inserted from xxxv. 10.]

3

¹² I, even I, am he that comforteth you; who, then, art thou that thou art afraid of frail man that dieth, and of the son of the earthly that is given up as grass; ¹³ᵃ and forgettest Yahwè thy maker, who stretched out the heavens, and laid the foundations of the earth, and tremblest continually all the day for the fury of the oppressor?

[In *v.* 13*b* and 14 the text is evidently corrupt; *vv.* 15-16 an inserted passage.]

XVII

Words of cheer to prostrate Zion

1

¹⁷ Arouse thee, arouse thee, stand up, O Jerusalem, who hast drunken at Yahwè's hand the cup of his fury; the goblet-cup of bewilderment thou hast drunken and drained. ¹⁸ There is none to guide her of all the sons whom she hath borne, and not one to take hold of her hand of all the sons that she hath brought up. ¹⁹ Twofold is (the woe) which befell thee: who can condole with thee?—devastation and havoc, famine and sword—who *can comfort* thee? ²⁰ Thy sons lay fainting at the corners of all the streets, like an antelope in a net, so full are they of the fury of Yahwè, of the rebuke of thy God. ²¹ Therefore hear now this, thou afflicted one, and drunken, but not with wine, ²² thus saith thy Lord Yahwè, and thy God that pleadeth for his people: Behold, I take out of thine hand the cup of bewilderment, the goblet-cup of my fury—thou shalt not drink it again; ²³ and I put it into the hand of thy tormentors, who have said to thy soul, Bow down that we may pass over; so thou madest thy back as the ground, and as the street for wayfarers.

2

CHAPTER LII

¹ Awake, awake, put on thy strength, O Zion, put on thy glorious garments, O Jerusalem, holy city! For no more shall there enter thee the uncircumcised and the unclean. ² Shake thyself from the dust, arise, O captive band of Jerusalem; loose thyself from the bonds of thy neck, O captive daughter of Zion. [*vv.* 3-6 a later insertion.]

3

⁷ How lovely upon the mountains are the feet of the messenger that bringeth good tidings, of him that proclaimeth peace, of the messenger of joyful tidings, of him that proclaimeth deliverance, who saith unto Zion, Thy God hath become king! ⁸ Hark, thy watchmen! they cry

aloud, they ring out joyfully together, for they behold eye to eye the return of Yahwè to Zion. ⁹ Break forth into ringing joy together, ye ruins of Jerusalem, for Yahwè hath comforted his people, he hath redeemed Jerusalem. ¹⁰ Yahwè hath made bare his holy arm in the sight of all nations, and all the ends of the earth shall see the deliverance of our God. ¹¹ Away, away, go out thence ! touch not an unclean thing ! Go out of the midst of her, purify yourselves, ye that bear the vessels of Yahwè ! ¹² For not in haste shall ye go out, and not in flight shall ye depart ; for before you goeth Yahwè, and your rear-guard is the God of Israel.

XVIII

lii. 13-liii. 12 (in italics), as the fourth of the Servant passages

The Servant's Martyrdom and its Rewards (lii. 13-liii. 12)

¹³ *Behold, my servant shall prosper, he shall rise, be exalted, and be very high.* ¹⁴ *According as many were appalled at *him,* so shall * . . . . ;* marred from a man's was his aspect, and his form from the children's of men,* ¹⁵ *so shall he* † *. . . many nations, before him kings shall shut their mouths ; for that which had not been told them they shall have seen, and that which they had not heard they shall have perceived.*

CHAPTER LIII

¹ *Who* (*indeed*) *can believe our revelation, and the arm of Yahwè— to whom can it disclose itself?* ² *He grew up as a sapling before *us,* and as a root out of a dry ground ; he had no form nor majesty that we should regard him, nor such an aspect that we should delight in him.* ³ *Despised* (*was he*) *and forsaken of men, a man of pains and acquainted with sickness, and as one from whom men hide the face—despised, and we esteemed him not.* ⁴ *But surely it was he who bare our sickness, and our pains—he carried them, while we—we esteemed him as stricken, as smitten of God, and afflicted.* ⁵ *But he was* ‡ **dishonoured* because of our rebellions, crushed because of our iniquities ; the chastisement of our peace was upon him, and through his stripes healing came unto us.* ⁶ *All of us like sheep had gone astray, we had turned every one to his own way, while Yahwè made to light upon him the guilt of us all.* ⁷ *He was cruelly entreated, but let himself be humbled, and opened not his mouth, as a lamb that is led to the slaughter, and as a sheep that before her shearers is dumb ; and opened not his mouth.* ⁸ *Through distressful doom was he taken away, and as for* § **his fate,* who thought thereon,—that he had been cut off out of the land of the living, that for my people's rebellion *he had been stricken* ‖ *unto death* ?* ⁹ *And his grave was appointed with the wicked, and*

† Hebrew text corrupt. ‡ Pointing מָחֳלָל, with Gunkel.
§ Reading דָּרְכּוֹ. ‖ Reading לָמוֹ נֻגַּע ; cf. p. 257.

APPENDIX

† with the *defrauders his mound*; although he had done no injustice, neither was there deceit in his mouth. [vv. 10-11 have probably been recast by an editor: note especially "an offering for guilt" (אָשָׁם). See p. 305, n. 1.] ¹⁰ But it pleased Yahwè to crush him ‡ . . . . If he were to make himself an offering for guilt, he would see a seed, he would prolong (his) days, and the pleasure of Yahwè would prosper in his hand ¹¹ § . . . . my servant would make the many righteous, and of their iniquities he would take up the load. ¹² *Therefore will I give him a portion among the great, and he shall divide spoil with the strong, because he poured out his life unto death, and let himself be numbered with the rebellious, while it was he who had borne the sin of many, and for the rebellious made intercession.*

XIX

Further Consolations for Zion, the restored Bride of Yahwè, under the new and everlasting Covenant

CHAPTER LIV

I

¹ Ring out joyfully, O barren, thou that hast not borne; burst forth into ringing joy, and cry aloud, thou that hast not travailed; for more are the children of the desolate than the children of the married one, saith Yahwè. ² Widen the place of thy tent, and thy habitation's curtains, let them stretch forth unhindered; lengthen thy cords, and fasten strongly thy tent-pegs. ³ For right and left shalt thou spread forth, and thy seed shall take possession of nations, and people desolate cities. ⁴ Fear not, for thou shalt not be put to shame; neither be confounded, for thou shalt not be put to the blush: nay, thou shalt forget the shame of thy youth, and the reproach of thy widowhood thou shalt remember no more. ⁵ For thy husband is thy maker—Yahwè Sebáoth is his name; and thy redeemer is Israel's Holy One, God of the whole earth is he called. ⁶ For as a wife forsaken and grieved in spirit Yahwè hath called thee, and a wife of youth—can she be rejected? saith thy God. ⁷ For a little moment did I forsake thee, but with great compassion will I gather thee; ⁸ in a gush of wrath I hid my face from thee for a moment, but with everlasting kindness will I compassionate thee, saith thy redeemer, Yahwè. ⁹ *Like the days of Noah* is this (crisis) unto me; as I sware that Noah's waters should no more pass over the earth, so do I swear that I will not be wroth with thee or rebuke thee. ¹⁰ For though the mountains should remove, and the hills should totter, yet my kindness from thee shall not remove, neither shall my covenant of peace totter, saith he who compassionateth thee, Yahwè.

† Reading וְאֶת־עֲשִׁיקִים בְּרָשָׁיו. Cf. Mal. iii. 5; Job xxi. 32.
‡ The untranslated word (הֶחֱלִי) here probably corrupt. See p. 259.
§ Original text here probably faulty.

2

¹¹ Thou afflicted one, storm-tossed, disconsolate ! Behold, I will set thy stones in antimony, and will found thee with sapphires ; ¹² and I will make thy battlements rubies, and thy gates carbuncles, and all thy border precious stones ; ¹³ and all *thy builders* shall be disciples of Yahwè, and great shall be the welfare of thy children ; ¹⁴ᵃ through righteousness shalt thou be established.

3

¹⁴ᵇ Put afar the thought of oppression, for thou hast nought to fear, and the thought of destruction, for that shall not come nigh thee.
[*v.* 15 a later insertion.]
¹⁶ Behold, it was I that created the smith, who bloweth upon the fire of coals, and produceth a weapon according to his craft ; and I it was that created the destroyer to do havoc : ¹⁷ no weapon formed against thee shall prosper, and every tongue that assaileth thee thou shalt put to the worse. This is the inheritance of the servants of Yahwè, and their justification that is of me, saith Yahwè.

XX

Invitation to the blessings of the new Covenant, followed by renewed prophecies of deliverance

CHAPTER LV.

1

¹ Ho ! all ye thirsty ones, come ye to the waters ; and he that hath no money, come ye, buy and eat, yea come, buy wine and milk without money and without price. ² Why should ye spend money for that which is not bread, and your earnings for that which cannot satisfy ? Hearken, hearken unto me, and ye shall eat that which is good, and your soul shall delight itself in fatness. ³ Incline your ear and come unto me ; hear, and your soul shall revive, and I will make with you an everlasting covenant, even the sure loving-kindnesses promised to David. ⁵ Behold, thou shalt call people whom thou knowest not, and people who know not thee shall run unto thee, because of Yahwè thy God, and for Israel's Holy One, inasmuch as he hath glorified thee. ⁴ Behold, for a witness *to the peoples* I gave him, a ruler and commander of the nations.

2

⁶ Seek ye Yahwè, while he may be found ; call ye upon him, while he is near.
[*v.* 7 a later insertion.]
⁸ For my thoughts are not your thoughts, neither are your ways my ways, saith Yahwè ; ⁹ but (as) the heavens are higher than the earth, so are my ways higher than your ways, and my thoughts than your

thoughts. ¹⁰ For as the rain cometh down, and the snow from heaven, and thither returneth not, except it have watered the earth, and have made it bring forth and sprout, and given seed to the sower, and bread to the eater ; ¹¹ so shall my word be that goeth forth out of my mouth ; it shall not return unto me void, except it have accomplished that which I pleased, and made to prosper that for which I sent it. ¹² For with joy shall ye go forth and in peace shall ye be led ; the mountains and hills shall burst out before you into ringing joy, and all the trees of the field shall clap the hand. ¹³ Instead of the thorn-bush shall come up the fir-tree, and instead of the nettle shall come up the myrtle tree : and it shall be unto Yahwè for a monument, for an everlasting sign which shall not be cut off.

END OF PART II.

INDICES

I. NAMES AND SUBJECTS

The numbers refer to pages throughout

ABRAHAM, not referred to by earlier prophets, 195 f., 273
——, Jacob (Israel), as semi-divine beings, 246, 352 note 2, 353
Adma, identified with Moab, 91
Agriculture, prophetic interest in, 187, 197, 224
Alexander the Great, 157 f., etc.
Alexander Jannæus, 161
Alexander Balas, 108
"All nations and languages" (late phrase), 378
Altaku, battle of, 230
Altar of sacrifice, 101
Aluka (a vampire-like demon), 210
"Amen, God of the" (phrase), 371
Anadiplosis, figure of (in Isaiah II.), 251, 255
Angels, 151, 342
Angel = prophetic spirit, 125
—— worship, 353
Ansan, 123
Antigonus, 105
Antiochus Sidetes, 161
Apocalyptic imagery, 150
(See also *eschatological features*)
Appendices, Isaianic and other, 38, 95, etc., 163 note, 172, 310
—— Messianic, xxiv.

Aquila, quoted, xxv. note 2, 34 note 2
Aramaisms and Aramaic words, 64, 100, 111, 126 note, 129, 168, *256*, 258, 261, 262, 263, 267, 299, etc.
Aramaic and Assyrian, 111 note
Archaising plural form, 259, cf. 340
Ariel, 167 note, 190, cf. 204
Arpad, 50
Artaxerxes II. (Mnemon), 156
Artaxerxes Ochus, 104, 118, 145, 156, 161, 172, 358 f., 362
Asharu = Syria,⎫
Asshur,   ⎬ 107 note
Ashdod, 120 f.
Ashdudimmu (= אַשְׁדּוֹד יָם the port of Ashdod), 121
Ashéra, 93 note, 160
Asmodeus, 210
Assurbanipal, 113, 114, 115, cf. 222
Assyria, a symbolic term, 62, 160, 202, cf. 223
—— overthrow of, typical meaning of, 53
Azazel, 70, 210

BABYLON, siege of, 124, 127, 154, etc.

ISAIAH

Babylon, allusions to the life of, in Isaiah II., 275 f.
Ben Sira, xviii. f., 187, 239
Berosus, 69 note
Biographies (prophetic), 213, 218, cf. xxviii.
Bozra (conventional expression), 211
Bredenkamp (ref. to), 25, 75 note 2, 247 f., 335, etc.
Briggs, Prof. (ref. to), 9 note 1, 155, 309, etc.
Brown, Prof. Francis (ref. to), 2, 6, 7, 16, 42 note 3, 63 note 2, etc.

CALNO, identification of, 50
Cambyses, 117
Canoes of reed, 96
Canon, growth of the, 383, note 3, cf. xvii. f.
Captivity, *see* Exile
Captives, Jewish, in Egypt, 105
Carchemish, 50
"City of desolation," 156, etc.
Collection of prophetic writings, 310, cf. xvii. f.
Colonies, Jewish, in Egypt, 106
Community, formation of the religious (? 432 B.C.), 345, 336, cf. xxxvi. f.
—— speech in the name of the, 178
Confessions of sin (in later writings), 354, 357
Cosmogony of Genesis, 65
Countries, conventional grouping of the names of, 62
Criteria of late date, 171, etc.
Criticism and the Church, viii. f.
Critical analysis a necessity, 1, 160, 161, etc.
—— of Second part of Isaiah, sketch of the history of, 284 f.
—— and Ewald, 285 f.
—— Geiger, 287 f.
—— Kuenen, 289 f.
—— Dillmann, 290 f., cf. xiii.
—— Prof. G. A. Smith, 291 f.
—— Budde, 292 f.
—— Cornill, 293

Critical Analysis of Second part of Isaiah, and Duhm, 293 f.
—— Wellhausen, 295
—— Isidore Loeb, 295
Cush, population of, 96 note
Cyprus, Phœnician colony in, (Citium), 140
Cyrus, 277 f.
—— cylinder inscription of, xxxvii.
—— edict of, 281
—— and the building of the Temple, 281

DAMASCUS, 50
Dates of the prophecies, xxvi. f. *et ad loc.* See also Appendix
Day of Atonement (law of), 328
Dead, awakening of the, 151, cf. 308
Death, abolition of, 152, cf. 371
Delitzsch, Franz (ref. to), 241, 286, etc.
Dew, prayer for the, (synagogic), 151
Diodorus Siculus quoted, 211
Dispersion, Jewish, 60, 61, 105, 271
Doctrinal developments, foreign influence on, 152 note 2, cf. 370 note 1
Doubling of words, emphatic, 150
Driver, Prof. (ref. to), xi. f., xxxv., 13, 17, 59 note 3, 79, 81 note 2, 128, 160, 249, 255, 276, 291, etc.
Dumah, 128
Dûr-ilu, battle of, 81, 227
Duff, Dr. (ref. to), 80 note 1, 86, 101 note, etc.

ECCLESIASTES, 156, 292
Editors as supplementers, 45, 93, 139, 181, 193
—— activity of later, 57, 298, 310, xx., and Prologue *passim*
—— combination of Isaiah I. and II. by, xviii. f., 238
—— pre-Exilic, 88
Edom, symbolic name, 202, 206, 211, cf. 348

INDICES

Edom and Assyrian and Babylonish Kings, 130
—— incursions of, 131
—— encroachments of, 210 f., cf. 349
Egypt, 96, 100, 105, 191, 282
—— Jewish colonists in, 105 f.
Ekron, 231
Elam, 133
Elijah narrative, legendary character of, 230, cf. 165
Emendations of the text, 202 note 2, 301, 321, 322 note, 326, 333 note 2, 336 note 2, 337 note 1, 338 note 1, 339 note 1, 343, 351 note 2, 355 note 1, 356 note 1, 368 note 1, 372, 376 note 1, 377 note 1, cf. 259, etc.
—— Lagarde's (on lxiii. 1), criticised, 348
Enigmatical designation of world empires, 151
—— titles of prophecies, xxv. note 3
Epanaphora, figure of (in Isaiah II.), 251, 255
Esarhaddon, stele of, 114, 115, cf. 223 and note 1
Eschatological features, xxvi. f., 150, 247, 370, etc.
—— terms :—
    "Sword of God," 151, cf. 204, 381
    "The trumpet" } 151
    "The dew"
    "New heavens and a new earth," 370, cf. 246
Ethical terminology, 175
Ethiopian dynasty in Egypt, 96
Ewald characterised, 57
—— on Isaiah xii., 57, cf. 285 f.
Exile equivalent to death, 24, 67, 135
—— Assyria and Egypt as lands of, 146
—— Babylonian, its effect, 53 note
—— return from, 68, 205 f., cf. also xxxiv. f.
Exodus, story of the, 22, 55

Ezekiel, the prophet of the Spirit 178
—— his prophecy of restoration, 280
Ezra, Book of, xxxv. f., 281
Ezra's arrival at Jerusalem (date of), xxxiv. f., 345
Ezra and Nehemiah, compositions of the age of, 381, etc.

FAST-DAYS, 327
Fasting, spiritual view of, 246
Festival processions, religious, songs for, 200
Field-mice, Herodotean legend of, 233
Foreigners, enslavement of, 69

GAD ("Fortune"), 365 f.
Gehenna, 303
Geographical names, 62
—— various meanings of, 97
—— ideas of Isaiah II., 274 f.
Giesebrecht (ref. to), 24, 38 note 3, 171
Gnomic words in Isaiah, 175
God and man, gulf between, 242
—— names of (common to Isaiah I. and II.), 254, cf. 270
Guilt, consciousness of *national*, 362
Gunkel (ref. to), 428 note
Guthe (ref. to), 36, 50 note 2, 63 note 2, 86 note 3, 185 note, etc.

HACKMANN, xiii., xxiii. note 3, xxv. note 1, 6 note 1, 28 note 2, 44 f., 63 f., 182 note 2, 186 note 1
Hallewi, R. Jehuda, quoted, 107
Hamath, 50
Ḥammânîm ("sun-pillars"), 160, cf. 93 note
Hanun of Gaza, 81
Hatred, Jewish, of the nations, 110 note
"Heavens, new, and a new earth," promise of, 246, cf. 370
Heliopolis, temple at, 103
Herodotus, 69 note, 116, 127

436   ISAIAH

Hezekiah, reforms of, 165 note
——— psalm of, xxiii. note 1, 224
Holiness of Israel (a late idea), 22, 27, 53
Holy Spirit, *see* Spirit
"Holy mountain, My, Thy, His," 67, 311 note, 365 note
——— city (cities), Thy," 355
——— applied to worshippers, 368, see further under קדש in Index II.
Hoonacker, van (ref. to), xxxiv. note 3
Howorth, Sir Henry (ref. to), xxxiv. note 2
Hyrcanus, John, 161

IBN Ezra quoted, 239, 353 note 2, etc.
Ideals, non-political, national, 153
Ideas, late, 69, 126, 169, 177, 312, 334, 352, 370, etc.
Idolatry, 197, 242
——— post-Exilic, 299, 300 note, 316 note 3, cf. 353
Idumæa (conventional expression), 211
Illegible passages, editorial substitutions for, 90, 93, 99, 141, 203, etc.
Insertions, late, in prophecy, of a comforting tendency, 93, 172, 182, 186, 189, 190, etc.
——— late, 192, 216, etc.
——— in Isaiah II. (chaps. xl.-lv.), 296 f.
——— supplementary, 202, etc.
Interpolations, 93 note, etc.
Invasions of Judah by Assyria, 38
Irregularities, religious, in Persian age, 157 f., 160
Isaiah, Book of, place of in Hebrew Canon, xv. f.
——— twofold consciousness in, 126
——— his hopes and fears for the future, 68
——— and foreign nations, 128
——— his gloomy message, 189
——— no fatalist, 164
——— later imitation of, 171

Isaiah as editor, 183
——— as psalmist, 57
——— "sympathetic emotion" in, 85
——— some characteristics of the style of, 86, 189, etc.; cf. 52
——— as historian of Uzziah, 214
——— as prophet, 248
——— as author, xxix.
——— traces of a work on the prophetic ministry of, xxx.
Isaiah II. characterised, 248
——— marks of style of, 255
——— syntactical features of, 255 f.
——— characteristic linguistic features of (list), 260 f.
——— as poet, 249 note
——— his prophecy orally delivered or written? 249 f., cf. 292
——— date and place of composition of his prophecies, 277 f., 282 f.
——— parallels between, and Isaiah I., 251 f.
Isaiah I. and II., stylistic and linguistic points of difference between, 254 f.
"Trito-Isaiah," the supposed, xxxi.
Isaiah II. and his school of followers, 341
——— parallelism in, with other writings, 271 f.
Israel as a missionary people, 244
——— faithlessness of, 54

JACOB, as synonym for Israel, 10, 252
Jeremiah, a prophet of the decadence, 89
——— a type of suffering Israel, 246, 305
Jerusalem, latter day glory of, 60
——— latter day siege of, 375
——— blockade of, *see under* Sennacherib
——— destruction of under Ochus (?) 156
Jinn (demons of the desert), 70
Job, non-prophetic ideas in, 70
——— speeches in, date of, 111

Job, parallels to, in "Hezekiah's Song," 225
—— Book of, a monument of the revival of mythology, 276
—— influence and history of the Book of, 308 f.
Jonah, story of, explained by the revival of mythology, 276
Josephus, 105, 156, etc.
Judah, name never mentioned by the true Isaiah II., 302
Judgment, a final on Yahwè's enemies (late idea), 53, 246
—— idea of, foreign to Isaiah, 54, 205
—— of Babylonian exile, 53 note

KAHANA, Rabbi Abba bar, 126 note
Kidrai (= "Sons of Kedar") in Assyrian inscriptions, 131
King, Israel's, visible enthronement of, 152
Kings, Deuteronomic author of, date of, 212, 215 note, 229
Kirkpatrick, Prof. (ref. to), xxxv. note 2, 160
Kosters, xxxv. f., 312 note 1, 336 note 1, 345, 382
Klostermann (ref. to), 247 f., 281, 321, 335 note 1, 356 note 1, 370, etc.
Kuenen as a critic, 298, cf. ix. f.

LACHISH, events at, in 701 B.C., 232, 235, 236
Law, divine, broken by mankind at large, 151
"Lebanon," 194 note
—— trees, figure of, 339 note 2
Legalists and prophets, 101
Leontopolis, temple at, 102 note, 103
Lilith (non-Jewish myth), 206, 207, 210 and note 2
Lion (= Assyrian invader), 91 note
Liturgical passages in Isaiah, 59, 166
—— songs, late collections of, 224

Local colouring of chaps. xl.-lxvi., 273 f.
Luli, king of Sidon, 144
Luzzatto (ref. to), 315 note 3, 339 note 1

MACCABÆUS, Judas, 108, 357
Maççeba, 101, 160
Magee, Archbishop, quoted, 128
Malachi, Book of, xvi. note 2
Medes (= Persians), 78
Men and animals, failure to distinguish between, 65
Menander quoted, 144
Meni ("Destiny"), 365 f.
Merodach Baladan, 81, 97, 122, 227
Mesha, inscription of, (Moabite Stone), 88
Messianic age, 6, 21, 90, 150, 170, 181
Messiah, as teacher, 60
Metre (Hebrew), see Rhythm
Moab, 159
—— conquest of, 88
—— a typical name, 160
Monotheism, conscious, 228
Mountain, the holy of the north, 70
—— the holy, 311 note
—— my holy, etc., see under Holy
Murder, prevalence of, after the exile, 331
Mythology, revival of after the exile, 276
——, designations of empires derived from, 151

NABATÆANS, invasion of Idumæa by, 211 note
—— occupation of Moab by, 161
Nabu-na-'id, 277 f.
Nahum, date of, 116
Name (= worship, etc.), 98, 313
Nature, transformation of, 197, 280 note 1
Necho, 115
Nectanebo II. (the last of the Pharaohs), 118
Nehemiah, 311 f.
—— his arrival at Jerusalem, xxxii. f.

Nehemiah, Book of, xxxv. f.
Nineveh, siege of, 69 note
Noah, not referred to in earlier prophets, 273
Noph (Memphis), 116
North Kingdom, origin of the, 35

On (Heliopolis), 102, 103
Onias, 103, 108
Oppression of poor by rich (after the Exile), 325
Overthrow of Assyria, typical meaning of, 53

Parallelism, artificial, 198
Parallelisms, linguistic, between Isaiah I. and II., 251 f.
Paronomasia, 86, 150 note, 166, 174, cf. 55
Particles, late uses of, 148, cf. 256 f.
"Paths" (= forms of morality or religion), 11
Patriarch-worship, 353
Patriarchal longevity, promise of restoration of, 246
Peoples, admission of to religious privileges, 152 f.
Peræa, 159
Period, the, preceding that of the early apocalyptic writing, 65
Persecution of poor, after the Exile, 317 f., cf. 323, etc.
Persian influence on Jewish beliefs, 152 note 2, 370
Peshitto quoted, xxv. note 2, 207
Pessimism in Isaiah, 26 f.
Peters, Dr. J. P. (ref. to), 19
Petrie, Flinders (ref. to), 102 note 1, 232, cf. 96 note 1, xxvi.
Phraseological data, 58, 60, etc.
Pianchi, 113 note
Plays on names of towns, 55
Poems (composite), 89
Prayer, precedence of to ritual sacrifices, 314
—— House of, 314, cf. 325
Prediction, ideas concerning the prophetic power of, 228, cf. 241
Priestly code (P), allusions to, 154

Priests, later prominence of, 153
—— and Levites, later distinction between, 377, cf. 381, 382
Proper name, conversion of simple epithet into, 56
Prophecy, imperfect fulfilment of, 209
—— later imitations of, 172, 174
—— later Jewish attitude towards, 190
Prophetic writing, tendency in, to become lyric, 127
—— writings, collection of, xxiv. f., 310
—— biographies, 213, cf. xxv.
Prophet and people identified, 246
Proselytes, foreign, among Yahwè's worshippers, 69
Proverbs, Book of, 175
Proverbial writers, imitation of, in Isaiah, 186
Psalm parallels, 38 note 2, 53 note 2, 168 f., 198, 224, etc.
—— headings, date of, 171
Psalter, date of, 171
Psamtik (= Psammetichus), 115

Quotations in the Book of Isaiah, 87, 305, 372

Rahlfs (ref. to), 200 note 1, 344 note, etc.
Reclining at meals, 126 note
Reformation, earlier and later conceptions of, 177
Regeneration, moral, idea of, 338
Register, heavenly (late idea), 371
Religion (organised) reaction against, 195
Religious ideas of the prophets, expansion of, 38, cf. 244
"Remnant," Isaiah's doctrine of the, 28, 52, 180, 182 note, 185
—— technical use of the term, 228
Renan, 87, 88 note, 127
Resurrection (of individual Israelites), 152 note, 158
Return, date of the, xxxiv. f., 279, cf. 374

Return, history of the, xxxvi. f.
—— prophecies concerning the, by Jeremiah and Ezekiel, 280
—— omission of reference to the, in later writers, 356
Revelation, prophetic, 100
Rhythm, in Isaiah, 2 note 4, 7, 23, 26, 62, 74 note, 82, 133, 134, 138, 152, *158*, 163, *225* f., 337
—— kîna, 349, 350 note, 365 note
"Righteousness" (divine), in Isaiah II., 245
—— meanings of, in chaps. xl.-lxvi. 326, etc.
"Righteous one, the" (= Israel), 148
—— (= Alexander), 161
Rutamen (= Urdamani of Assyrian inscriptions), 97
Ryle, Prof. (ref. to), xxxv. note 2, 160

SABBATH, silence of Jeremiah concerning, 312
—— reverence for (in chaps. xl.-lxvi.), 246, cf. 324
Sacrifices, spiritual, 106
—— prophetic view of, 383 note 3
—— old religious, 368, etc.
Samaria, 50, 81, 182
Samaritan temple, 383, 385
Samaritans, 316 f., 322
—— in the fifth cent. B.C., 367 f., 272 f.
—— and the prophets, 385
Sanday, Prof. (ref. to), 288
Sarah, not referred to in earlier prophets, 273
Sargon, 3 f., 81, 120 f., 124, 134, 135, 191, 217
—— defeat of by the Babylonians, 81, 227
Sayce, Prof., 3, 114, 134
"Seir, Mount" (conventional expression), 211
Senjirli inscription, and stele, 115, 223 note 2
Sennacherib, inscription of, 4, 231, cf. 236

Sennacherib, his blockade of Jerusalem (701 B.C.), 132, 135, 164 note, 165 note, 236
—— movements of, in 701 B.C., 235 f.
—— Did he invade Palestine a second time? 234, cf. 217
—— siege of Babylon by, 124
—— chronology of the reign of, 216 f.
—— overthrow of (typical significance), 172 note
Septuagint quoted, xxviii. note 2, 21, 59 note 2, 91, 102 note, 107, 195, 329 and note 2, 330 note 1, 346 note 2, 348 note 1, 384, etc.
—— Egyptian - Jewish element in, 103 note
—— insertions in, 329
"Servant of Yahwè," 244 f., 255, 279, 305 (ch. liii.), etc.
—— songs of, 293, cf. 305 f., 346 ("Servant" passages a cycle), 305 f.
—— varying conceptions of, xxxi.
—— later conceptions of, 346, 352
Services, religious, 169
Sethos (? Shabataka), 233 note 1
Shabaka (= Sib'e of Assyrians), 96
Shabataka, 96, 192, *see also under* Sethos
Sharon, the, 372
Shaddai, 70, 72
Shear-yashub, 27, 52
Shebna, 230 note 1
Sheól, popular idea of, 70, cf. 380
Signs, divine, different kinds of, 34
—— later Jewish craving for, 220
Simeon, Rabbi, 42
"Sinim," land of, 275 note
Sins, forgiveness of, 164
Sky-dragon myth, 303
Smend (ref. to), 21 note, 161, 309 note 1
Smith, Prof. G. A. (ref. to), 173, 291, *307*, etc.
Smith, Prof. Robertson, xiii. 23

note 1, 70 note, 80 note 1, 81 note 2, 88 note 1, 111 note 4, 163 note 2, 165 note 2, 202 note, 361, 367 notes, 368, 370, etc.
Sodom and Gomorrah (in comparison), 70, cf. 182
Soferim, as editors and redactors, 294
Song of Moses (date of), 59
Songs, late collections of, 219, 224
"Spirit," the, 242 f., cf. 336
—— Ezekiel, prophet of the, 178
—— Holy, personal indwelling of, 246, cf. xx. note 1, 302, 351 f., 354
Stade (ref. to), 165 note 3, 212 note 3, 214, 288, etc.
Star-deities, belief in the earthly jurisdiction of, 70
Stones, precious (in Isaiah II.), 276
Superstitions, heathen, alluded to in chaps. lxv.-lxvi., 276 f., 315 f., cf. 353, 364 f.
Swine, sacrificial use of, 366 f.
Symmachus quoted, 352 note 3
"Sympathetic emotion" in Isaiah, 85
Syncretism, religious (in Judah), 368 f.

TAHARQA (Assyrian Tarqu, Hebrew Tirhaqah), 96, 113, 114, 192 note, 234, etc.
Tammuz, Phœnician cultus of, 282
Tell el-Amarna tablets (ref. to), 4, 256
Tell el-Yahûdîyeh, 103
Temple, date of the foundation of, xxxiv. f.
—— rebuilding of the, 357
—— defilement of the, 156 .
—— destruction of (under Ochus), 358 f.
—— psalmody, 355
Temple, Samaritan, 383
Theophanies, effect upon universal nature, 25
—— frequent in late writers, 348

Time, later Jewish conception of, 149 note
"Towers" (= proud enemies without), 197
Totemism, Semitic, 368
Tree-worship, 7
Trees, hewn-down (figure of), 56
—— myrtle, etc., 273 f.
Tribal justice, 5
Tyre destruction of, 141 note 2, etc.
—— sieges of, 143 f., 158
Tyrians, Jewish hatred of, 139

UNIVERSE, renovation of the (late idea), 370
Universalism, Jewish, 105, 109, cf. 152 f.

VITRINGA (ref. to), xxii., 109 note, etc.

WÂDY EL-AḤSA, 84
"Watchers" (= interceding angels ?), 342, 344
"Ways" (= forms of morality or religion), 11
—— of Yahwè, 279 note
Wellhausen (ref. to), 66 note, 182 196 note 1, 211 note 1, etc.
Wright, Dr. C. H. H. (ref. to), 335, 356, 382 note 3

YAHWÈ, the divine name, 241 note
—— worship of, by the exiles at Babylon, 352
—— teachership of (late idea), 198, 222
—— knowledge of, 243
—— kingdom of, 244
—— name of, 199, 335
—— " the glory of" (phrase), 199, 298, 335, 339
—— attributes of (in Isaiah II.), 242
—— sword of, 204
—— book of, xxviii., 211
—— arm of, 243, 251, 255, 335
—— causing people "to err from his ways," 246
—— "our King" (late phrase), 170, 251

Yahwè " Father " of his people and Creator, 246
—— " work of (Yahwè's) hands," (phrase), 340 note 1
Yatnan (Assyrian name of Cyprus), 121

" ZION of Israel's Holy One," 340
" Zion " (= " fearers of Yahwè "), 345
Zoan (Tanis), 116, 192 note
Zoroastrianism, see " Persian influence."

II. WORDS AND PHRASES (HEBREW AND ARAMAIC) ILLUSTRATED OR EXPLAINED

[NOTE.—*It has only been found possible here to make a selection of the words cited in the book. The following should be supplemented by the lists on pp. 251 f., 260 f.*]

אָב (official title), 137
אָבְרִים (pathetic epithet), 146
אֶבְיוֹן (of the Jewish people), 147, 194 note
אֶבְיוֹנֵי אָדָם, 193
אָבַל and אָמְלַל, 166 note, 167
אֲבֵלִים, 321
אֲנַס (Aram. "to be troubled"), 111
אִנְמוֹן, 251
אֲדָּה (late), 225
אֲהִי, 148
אַדִּיר, 166 note, 167
אֲדָמָה (= "earth," non-Isaianic), 139
אַדְמַת יְהוּדָה, 100
אֱוִיל (plural), 208
אוֹנִים ("full strength"), 258
אוּר, "fire," הֵאִיר "to set on fire," etc., 146, *204*, 251, 303
אוֹרוֹת, "lights," 149
אֲשֶׁר־אוּר לוֹ (popular post-Exilic derivation of Ariel), 204
אוֹת for אֶת with suffix (late), 257, 304
אִי, "coastland" (Isaianic), 142
אִיִּים, "coastlands" (Isaiah II.), 242 note
אַיֵּה (אַיָּם) . . . וְיָדָיו (Is. xix. 12), construction, 112
אִיִּים, "jackals," 207
אֵילִים, "terebinths," 251
אֵימָה, 168

אֵינֶנּוּ (idiomatic use of), 111
אִישׁ coupled with אָדָם, 204
אִישִׁים (for אֲנָשִׁים), 258
אִטִּים, "mutterers of spells," 112
אָכֵן, 258
אֶל (for עַל), 384
(עָשָׂה, פָּעַל, יָצַר) אֵל, 300
אֱלֹהֵי יַעֲקֹב, 14
אֱלִילִים, "idol-gods," 255
אֱלִילִים (= אֵילִים), 319
אֱמוּנָה, "stability," 167
אַמִּיץ, 251
אֹמֶץ, 300
אנח (common in Aramaic), 149, 208
אֲנָחָה, 127
אָנוּ וְאָבְלוּ, 20, 111
אֲנִי, 168
אֲנִי, metrical and unemphatic use of, 225 note
אָנֹכִי and אֲנִי, 256 f., 314 note 2
אֹסֶף, 167
אַף, 148, 167, 207, *257*
אֶפְרָה, 199
אֶפֶס, 207, 251
בְּאֶפֶס, 303
אֶפְעֶה, "a viper," 252
אֶרְאֵלָם, "their heroes (?)," 166 note, 167
אֲרוּכָה, 328
אֲרוֹמֵם, 167
אֲרָצוֹת, 228

INDICES

אֲשֶׁר (omitted in relative clauses in Isaiah II.), 256
אָתָא, 129, 319
אֶתְמוּל, 202

BETH *essentiæ*, 256
בְּאַחֲרִית הַיָּמִים, 11 note 2
בְּאוּר יהוה (= בְּאוּרִיָא), 15
בְּאֵין מֵבִין (idiom), 319
בַּדִּים, "prating," 85, 261
בְּדִל, 261, 313, 333
בֶּהָלָה, 126, 372
בּוּס, 347
בחון, 141
בְּחִזָּיוֹן, 272
בָּחֻר (= בָּחָן), late, 302
בָּחַר בְּ (in a religious sense), 313
בָּטַח בְּי״י, 303, 321
בְּיַד (= בְּ), 222
בַּיּוֹם הַהוּא (in chaps. xl.-lxvi.), interpolator's formula, 304
בִּינוֹת (abstract plural of the gnomic style), 146
בֵּית יְהוּדָה, 137
בֵּית יַעֲקֹב (Isaianic), 14, 193, 223, 252, 325
בֵּית נְכוֹתוֹ, "treasure house" (chap. xxxix. 2), 229
בַּל, 74, 148, 167, *257*, 300
בָּלָה, "enjoy the full use of," 372
בְּלִי, before a finite verb, 178
בלע (= בלל), 112, cf. also 146
בלעדי, 258
בְּמוֹ, 148, 257
בָּמֳתֵי, 74
בֶּן־הַגֶּבֶר, 312, cf. 340
בְּעָה, 129
בְּצַע, 49
בֶּצַע, 319
בָּרָא, 21 note 1, 252, 372
בְּרִית, 261, 313
בֵּשַׂר, 261, 340, 344

גִּבְעָה נִשָּׂאָה, 198
גֵּוֶף (not used by Isaiah), 261
גָּרַשׁ, "heap up" (late), 322
גּוּר, "to be a guest," 168
גּוּר (= גָּרָה), "stir up strife," 259, 304
גָּוַע, 63, 64, 252

גֵּו, various meanings of, 73, 75 note, 312

דָּאַג, with accus. (Jeremianic), 320
דִּבֶּר בְּיַד, 119
דִּבְרֵי־סָרָה, 333
דִּבְרֵי סֵפֶר, 193
דָּנַר (also Targ. and Rabb. Hebrew), 207
דּוֹר, "generation," combinations with, 73, 260
דּוֹר וָדוֹר, 341
מִדּוֹר לָדוֹר, 207
דּוּר, "dwelling" (late), cf. דִּיר (Aramaic), 225, 262
דַּכָּא (in an ethical sense), 321
הֵלֵג (Piel), 208
דְּמוּת (used prepositionally), 72
דְּרָאוֹן, 377
דָּרַשׁ מֵעַל, 207
דָּרַשׁ י״י, 325
רָשֶׁן, 199, cf. 207

הָאָרֶץ, "the earth," 154
הַבָּאִים (with ellipsis of הַיָּמִים), 149
הָנָה, "to separate," 149
—— "to utter," 262, 333
הָגָה
= סוד } 64
הָדוּר
הֲדוּרִים } 347
הוֹד, 200
הָיָה for (הָיָה) הֵוֵא, 85
הוֹי, 94 note 3, 162
הוֹלִיד (for יָלַד), 259, 333
הוֹעִיל with negative (of false religious practices) [late], 320
הַחֳרִים, 206
הַטָּהֵר, 384
הָיוּ מַבְדִּילִים (idiom), 198 f., 256, 272
הֵכְעִים, 372
הָלוּךְ *after* בְּדַרְכֵי (Aramaism), 299
הָלַךְ (with accus.), 168, 303
הָלַךְ נְכֹחוֹת, 319
הִלֵּל, Hif. "to shine," 73, cf. 262
הִלֵּל, "to praise (God)," 262, 344
הָמוֹן, "riches," 340
הִנֵּה, הֵן, "behold," 141, 167, 174, 258, 313

ISAIAH

הֵן, "if," 258, 304
הֵנִיחַ לְפ׳, 71
הֵנִיף יָד, "wave the hand," 70
הֶעֱרִיץ, 193
הִתְפַּכֵּם (impatient exclamation, colloquial), 194
הֵקִיץ (of a rising again), 149
הָרַי, "my mountains," 79 note, 252, 372
הֲרִיסָה (and ending יח־), 259, 262, cf. 267
הֶרֶם, 102 note
הֵשִׁיב עַל־לֵב, 300
הִתְאַפֵּק, 272, 353
הִתְפָּרֲדוּ בְּ, 371
הִתְיַמֵּר, 344

ן (stat. constr. before), 207
ו (defining use of), 335
וְהָיָה with asyndetic impf., 188 notes 1 and 2
────── once only in Isa. xl.-lxvi., 372
וְהָיוּ (foll. by part.), construction, 198 f.
יח־ (ending), see הֲרִיסָה

וְבָל, 355 note 2
זֵר, זֵרִים, 73, 195
זֶה (as relat. pron.), 148
זוּ (as relat. pron.), 257, 299
זוּלַת (with suffix), 148, 258
זִיו, "udder," 381
זֵלִים, 300
זָרָיִךְ, "thy foreign enemies," 188 note

חוֹבֵי לוֹ, 198
חָזוּת, "vision," 126
חָח, "nose-ring," 222
חָסַם (late), 302
חַיְתוֹ, 319
חֵל, 149
חֶלֶד (late), 225
חֵלֶל (legal term), 312
חֵלֶק } in a religious sense, 319
גּוֹרָל }
חלשׁ (transitively), 74
חֵמָה (of Yahwè's anger), 206, 263
חֲמוּדִים, 300

חֶסֶד, 319
חָסָה בְּ, 252, 320 f.
חֹסֶן, 167
חֵפֶץ, "business" (late), 325
חָצִיר, 207
חֹרֶב, "wasteness," 263, 344
חֹרִים, 207
חרס, 106 note
חַרְצֻבּוֹת, 259, 263
חֲשֻׁכִּים, 258, 303
חָשַׁשׁ, 167
חתת (in Nif.), 32

מֵאמֵא, 74

יֹאמַר יְיָ, 7 note, 167, 250
יְאֹרִים, 166 note, 167
יִבְּבָיוֹן, 129, 166, for ending, cf. 259
יָגוֹן, 208
יָד, "stele," 313
יָרַע בִּינָה, 196
יְהוּדִית, 228
יוֹם יְיָ, "Day of Yahwè" (= world judgment), 69
יָם (= Nile), 98, 110
יָנָשׁוּף, 207
יַעֲקֹב (as syn. for יִשְׂרָאֵל), 252
יַעֲרוּ, 84
יַעַר, "forest" (= proud warriors or princes), 179
יצע, 74, 263
יֵצֶר, "mind" (new Hebrew sense), 149
יקד (Aram.) = Biblical שׂרף, 52, 168
יָרַד, "to be hewn down" (of animals), 207, (of forest trees), 178
יֶרֶק דֶּשֶׁא, 222
יְשׁוּעוֹת, 141, 167, cf. 263
יִשְׁתּוֹמֵם, 335
יִשְׂרָאֵל (בְּנֵי), of the people of Judah, 203
יֶתֶר, adv., 319

כְּאֶחָד (= יַחְדָּו), Aramaism, 258, 371
כְּבוֹד יְיָ (only in late insertions), 313, 381
כָּחַשׁ בְּיְיָ, 332, 333
כִּי אִם, 167

INDICES

בִּי פִי יי׳ דִּבֶּר, 7 note, cf. 298
כֹּל אֲשֶׁר (with impf.), 100
כֵּן, "the foot of the mast," 168
כְּנַעַן, "Phœnicia," 100, 141, 142 note, 143
בִּגְעָנֶיהָ, 142
כנף (Nif.), 198
כָּנָף, "an end (of the earth)," 61, 149
כָּסַח (Aramaism), 168
כְּעַל (ch. xl.-lxvi.), 258, 335, 355
כִּי, 198
בַּרְמֶל, 222

לֹא הָיָה, 84
לְאַחַד אֶחָד, 146
לְדוֹר וָדוֹר, 207
לוּא (לוּ), 258, 302
לְוִיתָן, 149
לֶחֶם צָר וגו׳, 198
לְחָרְבָּה, 356
לַחַשׁ, "charm-formula," 17
לַיִל, 84, 85
לִילִית ἅπ. λεγ. (of Babylonian origin), 207, cf. 206
לָכֵן, "this being the case," 36, cf. 197 note
לָמוֹ (non-Isaianic), 142, 148, 208, 257
לָנֶצַח נְצָחִים, 207
לָעַג (not earlier than Jeremiah), 222
לְעָבְרוֹ, "straightforward," 257
לִפְתֵּחַ פִּתְאֹם, 188
לֵץ, 193, 195
לֶקַח, 186, 196
לְרָחוֹק וְלַקָּרוֹב, "the far off and the near" (viz. with regard to the Temple), late, 322
לְרָצוֹן } 314, 340
עַל־רָצוֹן
לְשֵׁם, "to the place of the name," 340

מֵאָז, 89
מֵאֶרֶץ מֶרְחָק (= Isaiah's מִמֶּרְחָק), 72
מַבּוּעַ, 208, 264
מִבְטָחִים, 178
מִגֵּן, 355
מִדְבָּר, "wild pasture country," 194 note

מוֹעֵר, 167 note
מוֹקֵד, 168
מֹשְׁלִים, 195
מְזֶה, "dike" (perhaps an Egyptian loan-word), 143
מַזְפִּיר } 384
לְהַזְפִּיר
מַחְמַדִּים, 356
מַחֲשָׁה (of Yahwè's long-suffering), 320
מַטֶּה מוּסָדָה, "rod of destiny," 201
מִי (as an indef. pron.), 257
מִי־זֶה } 347
מִי־אֵלֶּה
מֵימֵי, 168
מִישׁוֹר, 64
מָלֵא, 142, 166 note, 167
מְלוּכָה } 207, 344
מַמְלָכָה
מִלְחֲמוֹת תְּנוּפָה, 201
מָלַט, "lay eggs," 207
הִמְלִיט, "bring forth (a son)," 381, cf. 264
מָנוֹחַ, 207
מְנוּחָה, 61, 384
מִנִּי (for מִן), 252
מְמֻשָּׁלָה (late), 137 note, 229
מַסֵּכָה, "a molten image," 199
מָעוֹז (late), 302
מַעֲשֶׂה, 344
מַעֲשֵׂה, "fruit," 178
מַעֲשֵׂה (of the divine judgment), 193
מַעֲשִׂים (of false religious practices), 320
מִפְּנֵי, 85
מָצֹר (late), 111, 335 note 1
מִקְוָה, 133 note
מָקוֹם, "instead of," 167
מִקְצֵה הַשָּׁמַיִם, 72
מקק, 207
מַר (adv. as מָרָה), 167
מרה and עצב combined, 354
מָרוֹם (of high social positions, etc.), 149
—— (of the divine dwelling-place), 166, 222, 264
מְרוֹמִים, "heaven," 168, 179
מֵרַחֲקִים, 167
מִשְׁכָּב (= the grave), 319

446 ISAIAH

מָשָׁל
מֶשֶׁל } 73
מְשֻׁלָּח, "driven away" (of the city), 146
מְשֻׁלָּם, 381
מִשְׁפָּט, 264
—— and צֶדֶק, 85, cf. 312
דֹּרֵשׁ מִשְׁפָּט, 85
מִשְׁפָּטִים, 325
מַשָּׂא, "oracle" (non-Isaianic), 67
מְעֻצָּב, 168
מָשׂוֹשׂ, 341
מִשְׂרְפוֹת, 167

נְאֻם יי׳, 251, 314
נְאַץ, 303
נָבָל (ethical use of), 174, 175 f.
נגה, "loathe," 384
נִדְחֵי יִשְׂרָאֵל, 61, 252, 314
נָדִיב, "a noble," 174
נָהַר, "to be radiant (with joy)," 340
נהר, confluere, 11
נוֹאָשׁ (Jeremianic), 320
נָוֶה, 146, 168, 207, 372
נוֹרָאוֹת, 354
נַחַל הָעֲרָבָה, 84 note
נְחֻמִים, 321
נפל
נשא } 355
נִכְחֹדוּחַ, 384
נִלְחָם עַל, 30 note
נִמְהָר, "headlong," 174, cf. 207
נְנַשֵּׁשָׁה, "we must grope" (form), 256, cf. 333
נֵס, "sail," 168
נִסְפָּה, 335
נֶסַע, 168
נוּן, (original form of), 112
נָפַל, "to be felled," 56
—— "to be born," 149
נָצָה (Nif. part.), "wasting," 222
נְצוּרִים, "secret places," 372
נֵצֶר, 64, 252, 341
נָקָם (for divine vengeance), 206, 265
נִרְצָה, 272
נִשְׁעַן, 54, 303
נִשְּׁתוּ (Nif. of נשת), 111, 265

סָגַר (late), 300
סוּר (in a moral or religious sense) 333
סוּגָה, 259
ספר = ספק, "strike," 178
סְפָרִים, חֵפֶר (= prophetic Scriptures), 210
סֵפֶר (used technically), 168

עָבַד (in ritual sense), 100
עָבַר בְּ, 73
עֲבוֹרָה, "fruit," 178
עַד, "booty," 167
עַד, "perpetuity," 253, 321
עֲדֵי־עַד (late), 257
עוֹד מְעַט מִזְעָר, 194
עוה, pervertere, conturbare, 149
עוֹל, 372
עוֹלָמִים, 149, 258
עֲוֹנִים, 259, 355
עוּר (Hif.), 73, 264
עָטָה (Hif.), 335
עֶלְיוֹן, 74
עַמֵּי הָאָרֶץ, 345 note 3
עָנָה, "to address (some one)," 73
עֻנָּה נֶפֶשׁ, 272, 325
עָנִי, 64, 65, 194 note, 266
עֲנִי, 64, 384
עֶצֶם, 167
עַרְבִי, 73, 129 note
עֲרָבִים, "poplars" (or "steppes"), 84, 266
עָרוֹת, LXX. ἄχι, 111
עֶרֶץ, 72, 195
עָשָׂה and הֵבִיא combined, 222
עֲשִׁירֻ, 259
עשׁק (late; cf. Aram. and Talm. עסק, "to busy oneself with"), 225
עֵת (with suffix), 340
עִתִּים, 167 note

פָּנָּה, 207
רָפָה, 7, 195, 208, 266
פֶּה, "brim" (of a river), 111
פָּחַד, "tremble (for joy)," 340
פֶּחָה, Assyrian pahat, "governor," 229
פְּלִינִים, 199
פְּלֵיטָה, 52

INDICES

פָּנִים (of Yahwè), 333
פֶּסַח, 203
פַּעַם, "foot," 149, 222
פָּקַר, 188
פְּקֻדָּה, "magistracy," 266
—— "store" (a collective), 341
פָּקַח (Nif.), 208, 229, 266
פָּרִיץ, 208
פֶּשַׁע, 266
פְּשָׁעִים, 300
פָּתַח (intrans.), 259

צֶאֱצָאִים, 137, 206, 253, 372
צָב, "litter," 381
עַל צָבָא, 203 note
צְבָא מִלְחָמָה, 72, 206
צְבִי, תִּפְאֶרֶת, נָאוֹן combined, 73
צִבְיָה, 188 note
צֶדֶק, צְדָקָה (in Isaiah II.), 267, 312, 318, cf. 343
צְדָקוֹת, "righteous acts (of men)," 168, 267, 355
צִוָּה (cf. Aram. צְוַח), 149, cf. 267
צוּר, of God (צוּר יִשְׂרָאֵל), 200, 254
צַח, 174
צִחְצָחוֹת, "dry places" (cp. Targ. צַחְצָחָן), 258, 326
צִי, 168
צִיִּים, "wild cats," 73, 141, 207
צַלְמוּת, 46 note
צִפָּה הַצָּפִית, 126 note
צֹפִים, 319, cf. 126
עֲפִירָה, "crown," 182
צִפְעוֹנִי, 64, 253
צָרִים (of Yahwè's or Israel's foes) in Isaiah II., 355

קָאַת, 207
קרש and derivatives, 267, cf. 193, 314 note
—— Hithp., 200
—— Hif., 71, 193
הַר הַקֹּדֶשׁ, 67, 146, 314, 321
קָדוֹשׁ (as proper name in Isaiah II.), 321
מִקְדָּשׁ (in chaps. xl.-lxvi.), 340
See also under "Holy," Index I.
קוֹל (interjectional use of), 72, 258, 381
קָלַל, 372

קָמֵל, 111, 166 note, 167
קִנְאָה, 355
קָנֶה, "balance beam," 300
קִצּוּן, 207
קְפוֹד, 207
קֵץ עָם, 19
קְצִינִים, 5
קֶצֶף (of Yahwè's anger), 206
קִצְרֵי יָד, 222
קְרָא (Pual), 259, 326
קָרָה = קָרָא, 207
קרב
קִרְבַת אֱלֹהִים } 325 note
קֶשֶׁר, 40

רָאַם, 207
רֻבָץ, 208
רָהַב, 253
רוֹנְבִים, 196
רָוָה, Piel (intensive), 207
רוּחַ וְכֵהָא, 384
רוּם, "lift oneself up," 198
רָם וְנִשָּׂא, 253
רֹמַח, 167
רָנָּה, 73, 260, 268
רְעָדָה, 168
רָעֵנָן, 319
רָפַשׁ (late), 322
רָצָה, 268
רחק and derivatives, 320
רְשָׁעִים (of non-Israelites), 73, 149
Cf. however 323

שַׁאֲנָן, 166 note, 167, 222
שְׁאָר (Isaianic, = late פְּלֵיטָה), 52, 72, 224
שְׁאֵרִית (non-Isaianic), 224
שְׁאֵרִי עַמִּי, 181, 255
שַׁבְּתוֹתַי, "my (i.e. Yahwè's) Sabbaths," 312
שָׁגַל, 73
שֹׁד וָשֶׁבֶר, 339, 381
שַׁדַּי, 72
שְׂרֵמוֹת, 84
שׁוֹפֵט (choice word for king), 90 note 4
שׁוּר, "journey," 320
שָׁחוֹר, 142
שָׁחַט (of human sacrifices), 384
שִׁי, 98

ISAIAH

שַׂיִט, 168
שָׁכוּל = שַׁכּוּל, 259
שָׁכוּר = שִׁכּוֹר, 259
שְׁלוּמִים, 207
שְׁלֵם אֶל־חֵיק, 371
שֵׁם יי׳, 303, 313
שָׂמְחָה (*nomen actionis*), 198
שָׁמַר (in a religious sense), 312
שָׁעָה, 269
שִׁעֲשַׁע (Pulpal), 381
שָׁפַט, 269
שֶׁפַח, 149
שִׁקְרֵי אָוֶן, 195
שִׁקּוּצִים, 384
שֶׁקֶל (used technically), 168
שֶׁקֶץ, 384
שֶׁקֶר, *perfide egit*, 354
שָׁרָב, "glowing heat" (*not* "mirage"), 208, *269*, cf. 274 note
שֵׁרֵת, 269, 340, 342 note
שָׁתֹת, 111

שֵׂבֶר (late, cf. Aram. סְבַר), 225
שָׂרַי, 319
שִׁיר, 167
שֵׁם עַל־לֵב, 260
שָׂעִיר, "satyr," 207
שְׁפַח פִּנֵּן, 106 note
תְּבוּנוֹת, 258, 270
תָּה (pathetic ending), 127
תֹּהוּ, 195, 253, 333
תְּהִלָּה, 340, cf. 262, 270
תּוֹעָה, "error," 175 note
תֹּעֵי רוּחַ, "the erring in spirit," 196
תְּעוּרָה, תּוֹרָה, 42, *253*
תּוּשִׁיָה, 186
תָּמִיד, 258
תַּנּוּר, "furnace," 204
תַּעֲלוּלִים, 384
תַּעֲנִית, 327
תִּפְתֶּה, 202
תֹּרֶן (parallel to נֵס), 167

III. PASSAGES FROM THE SCRIPTURES (CANONICAL AND APOCRYPHAL)

A Selection only of the more important references has been made

(A) OLD TESTAMENT

Genesis, iv. 23, p. 186
Judges, v. 13 (Targum), p. 152
2 Samuel, xvii. 25, p. 80
2 Kings, xviii.-xix. 37 (Exilic), p. 165
2 Chronicles, xxix. 30, p. 224 note
Ezra, i.-vi. p. 281 (see also Prologue, pt. iv.); iii. 8-13, p. 358; iv. 1-5, p. 373
Nehemiah, xi. 25, p. 210 note 3
Job, xiv. 11, p. 111
Psalms, xii. 6, p. 127; xxii. xxxv. lxix., p. 374; xxiv. 7-10, p. 349; xxx. vi., p. 226; xliv. p. 361 note 2; xlv. p. 105 note 4; xlvi. p. 38; xlvi. xlviii., p. 223; lxxiv. lxxix., p. 361 f.; lxxxvii. 4, pp. 139, 105; lxxxviii. 226, cxxvii. p. 311 note 3

Proverbs, i. 16, p. 329; xi. 7, p. 258
Jeremiah, iii. 17, p. 11; xvii. 19-27, p. 312; xxv. 31, p. 375; xxxiii. 26, p. 196; xliii. 13, p. 102 note; l. li., pp. 71 note, 205, 209; cf. p. xxiii. note 1
Ezekiel, xxxviii. 9-12, p. 170
Hosea, viii. 1, p. 39
Amos, v. 8, p. 46; ix. 8-15, p. 326 note
Obadiah, p. 211
Micah, iv. 9, p. 6; iv. 1-4, p. 10 f.; vi. 1-vii. 6 (date of), p. 116; vii. 20, p. 196
Habakkuk, ii. 13, p. 67 note; iii. p. 199
Zechariah, ix. 2-4, p. 159
Malachi, i. 1-5, p. 211

(B) NEW TESTAMENT

Mark, xiv. 25, p. 150
John, ii. 7 (Pesh.), p. 207

Romans, xi. 26, p. 330 note
Revelation, i. 16, ii. 12, etc. p. 151

(C) APOCRYPHA

Ecclesiasticus, xvii. 7, p. 151; l. 26, p. 211

THE END

www.ingramcontent.com/pod-product-compliance
Lightning Source LLC
Chambersburg PA
CBHW071221290426
44108CB00013B/1250